P9-DNB-850

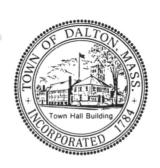

Free Public Library
Dalton, Massachusetts

First opened, May 1861   **Accepted by Town, March 1885**

★

MANY ARE THE CRIMES

BOOKS BY ELLEN SCHRECKER

*No Ivory Tower: McCarthyism and the
Universities*

The Hired Money

Mrs. Chiang's Szechwan Cookbook (with John Schrecker)

EDITED BY ELLEN SCHRECKER

The Age of McCarthyism

*Regulating the Intellectuals: Perspectives on
Academic Freedom in the 1980s* (with Craig Kaplan)

MANY ARE THE CRIMES

★

McCARTHYISM
IN
AMERICA

ELLEN SCHRECKER

LITTLE, BROWN AND COMPANY
BOSTON   NEW YORK   TORONTO   LONDON

FIRST EDITION

Cataloging-in-Publication Data

Library of Congress Cataloging-in-Publication Data
Schrecker, Ellen.
    Many are the crimes : McCarthyism in America / Ellen Schrecker.
      p. cm.
   Includes bibliographical references and index.
   ISBN 0-316-77470-7
    1. Anti-communist movements—United States—History. 2. McCarthy,
Joseph, 1908–1957. 3. Internal security—United States—
History—20th century. 4. Communism—United States—History.
5. Subversive activities—United States—History—20th century.
I. Title.
E743.5.S37 1998
973.9—dc21   97-42269
M V - N Y

10 9 8 7 6 5 4 3 2 1

Designed by Barbara Werden

Published simultaneously in Canada by Little, Brown & Company
(Canada) Limited

PRINTED IN THE UNITED STATES OF AMERICA

★

Security is like liberty in that many are the crimes committed in its name.

JUSTICE ROBERT JACKSON, dissenting in *U.S. ex rel. Knauff v. Shaughnessy* (1950)

★

*For my brother and sister, Tony Wolf
and Mary Hurtig*

★

CONTENTS

CONTENTS

★

INTRODUCTION

IT TOOK forty-three years to find out what happened to my sixth-grade teacher at the Oak Lane Country Day School. A large, shaggy man with the gift of transforming daily life into a learning experience, he got a class of self-involved preadolescent girls interested in chemistry by having us make lipstick and we worshipped him for taking us seriously, as few adults did. Suddenly, one day in 1953, he was gone. Since he still lived nearby, I and my friends visited him often and knew that he was having trouble finding a job. But none of the adults talked about why he was no longer teaching at Oak Lane, at least not to us.

We heard rumors that he wasn't really a teacher, that he'd changed his name, that he'd worked with a labor union — nothing that made sense at the time to an apolitical teenage girl. Only when I started to write a book about McCarthyism did the connections become clear. With a little research, I discovered that my sixth-grade teacher had lost his job for political reasons and everyone who knew about it had tried to hush it up. He hadn't been fired, exactly, just forced to resign. In a sense, he may well have been the most typical of McCarthy era victims — someone eased out of a job quietly, with no publicity, no fuss. The fifties were like that, less a world of fear than of silence.[1]

Forty years of silence have not, however, erased the stigma that both the victims and the perpetrators of the anticommunist political repression of the 1940s and the 1950s bear. Though the Cold War is over and Communism has all but vanished from the scene, the measures designed to eliminate its influence within the United States continue to provoke acrimony, mystification, and fear. Like a scab that will not heal, the McCarthy period remains so sensitive that some of its surviving actors still will not talk about what they did and the federal government will not release all its records. The statute of limitations expired years ago and no jobs are at stake, but the political account books remain open. It is time to settle them, reach some kind of closure, and come to terms with the meaning of that troubling chapter of the not-so-recent past.

Some parts of the story, it is true, stir little debate. There is a near-universal consensus that much of what happened during the late 1940s and 1950s was misguided or worse. In the name of protecting the internal security of the United States against the threat of Communism, thousands of people lost their jobs, went to prison, or were punished in other ways. Whether viewed as an unfortunate overreaction to a genuine danger or the product of a conscious campaign to wipe out dissent, the anticommunist crusade — incorrectly, though indelibly, identified with the gratuitous smears and unfounded accusations of Senator Joseph McCarthy — has few defenders today. The term *McCarthyism* is invariably pejorative.

It is also misunderstood. For McCarthyism (at least in the sense in which I use it in this book) encompassed much more than the career of the Wisconsin senator who gave it a name. It was the most widespread and longest lasting wave of political repression in American history. In order to eliminate the alleged threat of domestic Communism, a broad coalition of politicians, bureaucrats, and other anticommunist activists hounded an entire generation of radicals and their associates, destroying lives, careers, and all the institutions that offered a left-wing alternative to mainstream politics and culture. That anticommunist crusade — McCarthyism — dominated American politics during the late 1940s and 1950s. It used all the power of the state to turn dissent into disloyalty and, in the process, drastically narrowed the spectrum of acceptable political debate.[2]

When Joe McCarthy came onto the scene in 1950, brandishing his inaccurate and ever-changing lists of supposed communist agents within the federal government, the "ism" with which he was identified was already in full swing. Other politicians (including Richard Nixon, who built his career on the issue) had been making the same charges for years, differing from McCarthy more in style than in substance. Like him, they were trying to rid Washington of reds. But so, too, were many people who claimed to deplore what McCarthy was doing, as well as most of the federal officials the Wisconsin senator and his allies attacked as "soft" on Communism. Thus, to identify McCarthyism only with the outrageous charges and bizarre behavior of a single politician overlooks how much McCarthy shared with the rest of the political world. It also trivializes what happened by treating the anticommunist crusade as a passing aberration instead of the mainstream movement that it was.

McCarthyism got its power from the willingness of the men (few women here) who ran the nation's main public and private institutions to condone serious violations of civil liberties in order to eradicate what they believed was the far more serious danger of Communism. Whatever threat the dwindling band of American Communists may once have posed (and I will examine that threat in a later chapter) had been largely contained by the time the anticommunist furor escalated in the late 1940s. At no point did the nation's security require the dismissal of my sixth-grade teacher or the similar sanctions imposed on thousands of other law-abiding teachers, automobile workers, screenwriters, housewives, longshoremen, lawyers, public officials, and private citizens around the country.

The injustice of these proceedings was recognized at the time and may, in fact, explain why the issue remains so sensitive. A nation that prides itself on its commitment to democratic values has trouble confronting deviations from its ideals. The matter is more complicated, however, for the victims of the McCarthy era purges were not political innocents either. A few had passed information to the Russians; others had not told the truth about their relationship to the Communist party (CP). Since it is always hard to admit being wrong or having lied, many of the protagonists and their political supporters have never abandoned their original positions. As a result, these actors seem stuck in a time warp, still defending a worldview formulated more than forty years before. Moreover, the issues that once seemed so starkly black and white now yield a broad spectrum of grays. Instead of heroes or villains, the Communists, anti-Communists, and ordinary Americans involved with the events of the McCarthy period are complicated, fallible human beings who did not always recognize the implications of their actions. This book will investigate, not judge, their deeds.

To begin with, there was not one, but many McCarthyisms, each with its own agenda and modus operandi. There was the ultraconservative version peddled by patriotic groups and right-wing activists that manifested itself in campaigns to purge textbooks of favorable references to the United Nations. There was also a liberal version that supported sanctions against Communists, but not against non-Communists, and there was even a left-wing version composed of anti-Stalinist radicals who attacked Communists as traitors to the socialist ideal. In addition, there was a partisan brand of McCarthyism, purveyed by ambitious politicians like Richard Nixon and Joe McCarthy who hoped to further their own careers and boost the Republican party. All, however, sought in one way or another to protect the nation against the threat of domestic Communism. And all contributed in one way or another to the overall success of the anticommunist crusade.

Since each version of McCarthyism defined the communist menace in its own way, it is easy to emphasize the often striking differences between them. Nonetheless, though liberals and conservatives adopted different tactics and aimed at different targets, they also shared a consensus about the nature of Communism that made it possible for them to collaborate in repressing political dissent. The consensus was persuasive because it was plausible. Many of its underlying assumptions were grounded in what real Communists said and did. After all, neither Joseph McCarthy nor J. Edgar Hoover had invented American Communism. And, though the Communist party did not cause the repression it faced, many of its policies and procedures — like its connection to the Soviet Union or the secrecy that its members practiced — rendered it peculiarly vulnerable to that repression and helped shape the measures that were adopted to destroy it.

Certainly, if nothing else, Communism supplied the bodies. Despite the widespread contention that McCarthy and his colleagues picked on innocent liberals, most of the men and women who lost their jobs or were otherwise victimized were not apolitical folks who had somehow gotten on the wrong mailing lists or signed the wrong petitions. Rather, like my sixth-grade teacher, they had once been in or near the American Communist party. Whether or not they *should* have been victimized, they certainly were not misidentified.

But they were stigmatized, portrayed as members of an illegal con-spiracy that somehow threatened America's very existence. Stereotypes pre-vailed, turning individual Communists into alien beings whose destruction was, therefore, easy to justify. Because these stereotypes were not totally divorced from reality, they were widely accepted. But they failed to convey the complicated and contradictory nature of a political movement that was *both* subservient to the Kremlin *and* genuinely dedicated to a wide range of social reforms, a movement whose adherents sometimes toed the party line and sometimes did not even receive it. On the contrary, the officials who ran most of the machinery of McCarthyism overlooked such distinctions, adopt-ing a worst-case scenario that implicated all suspected Communists in ev-erything bad the party had ever done.

That scenario had not emerged spontaneously from an American popu-lation rendered panicky by the tensions of the early Cold War. Nor was it constructed by a reincarnated populist movement that welled up from be-low to express the insecurities and resentments of ordinary people over-whelmed by the confusing changes of the mid-twentieth century. On the contrary, as recent research in FBI files and other archives reveals, much of what happened during the McCarthy era was the result of a concerted cam-paign by a loosely structured, but surprisingly self-conscious, network of political activists who had been working for years to drive Communism out of American life. With the onset of the Cold War, these professional anti-Communists were able to sell their program to the nation's governing elites, who then put it into practice. Though most ordinary people supported what was going on, McCarthyism was primarily a top-down phenomenon.[3]

It was also quite effective. Obviously, compared to what happened in places like the Third Reich or Stalin's Russia, the political repression of the McCarthy period seems tame indeed. Only two people — Julius and Ethel Rosenberg — were killed; only a few hundred went to prison or were de-ported; and only about ten or twelve thousand lost their jobs. Nonetheless, the leniency of the sanctions did not lessen their efficacy. The fear of un-employment sufficed to squelch dissent for almost a decade. The political chill that settled over the United States during the late 1940s and 1950s made many Americans hesitate to criticize the government or join any or-ganization to the left of the Democratic party. By the mid-fifties, for ex-ample, graduate students at the University of Chicago were so fearful of having their names on a list that they would not sign a petition calling for a Coke machine in the physics laboratory.[4]

It took teamwork to create such timidity. The anticommunist crusade was, above all, a collaborative project. The economic sanctions that made it so effective followed a two-stage procedure. First, the politically tainted individuals were identified, usually by an arm of the state like the FBI or a congressional investigating committee. Then they were punished, usually by their employers. By identifying McCarthyism only with the first stage of the process, the men and women administering the second stage could insist that they had nothing to do with it. Such a diffusion of responsibility (and the mystification that it engendered) increased the effectiveness of the political repression by making it possible for people to distance themselves from — and thus participate in — something they claimed to oppose. From Harvard to Hollywood, employers in every sector of American society fired the men and women fingered during the first stage of McCarthyism.

Why did they do it? Why did so many otherwise well-meaning, intelligent, even liberal, Americans collaborate with the political repression of the late 1940s and 1950s? The question is crucial not only for reckoning with McCarthyism, but also for coming to terms with the way political repression operates in a democratic society and understanding how even today so many American citizens can condone similar injustices carried out in the name of the state. For, above all, it was the adoption of an anticommunist agenda by the federal government that brought the rest of the nation into the crusade. Patriotism, it seems, expedited the injustices of McCarthyism.

A major ideological shift facilitated the process. Only a few years before, the educators, labor leaders, and businessmen who later scrambled to oust alleged Communists would have been outraged at the idea that outside investigators could induce them to punish their employees and associates for political reasons. But by 1949, most of these people subscribed to a set of assumptions that placed national security above the Constitution and Communism below it. These assumptions — about the critical nature of the world situation and the alien nature of Communism — enabled most Americans to view the repressive measures taken against alleged Communists as necessary for the survival of the United States.

The Cold War was crucial here, though exactly how it contributed to the growth of McCarthyism is not as self-evident as it may superficially appear. After all, other nations also took part in the struggle against the Soviet Union without experiencing the same kind of domestic furor. The key transformation took place in Washington, D.C., where anticommunist activists like J. Edgar Hoover seized the opportunity presented by the deepening antagonism to the Soviet Union to sell their supposed expertise about Communism to the rest of the political establishment, whose members, it must be noted, knew little about the enemy they claimed to oppose. Once important sectors of the federal government endorsed the anti-Communists' agenda, it became possible to use the power of the state to disseminate and legitimize that agenda. Congressional hearings, criminal prosecutions, loyalty screenings, FBI investigations, Supreme Court decisions, and similar proceedings not only punished individual Communists, but, more important, alerted the rest of the nation to the alleged threat those Communists posed and thus cleared the way for the other sanctions against them and their associates.[5]

The multistranded nature of McCarthyism, the thousands of institutions and actors involved, made the process through which it operated both complex and convoluted. I will not, because I cannot, cover everything that happened. To do that would consume several lifetimes, since it would be easy to write a book about almost every big case — as many authors have already done. Those cases and many others are discussed in David Caute's encyclopedic 1978 survey, *The Great Fear,* a comprehensive work that I have no intention of replicating.[6]

Instead, I will focus on a handful of events and institutions that show not only how McCarthyism operated, but also how its different components interacted with each other. The cases I selected are representative; I could easily have taken others. Thus, for example, in chapter 8, where I deal with McCarthyism in the private sector, I examine its effect on lawyers. I could also have looked at doctors, social workers, or movie stars. And I could have written an entire book on the relationship between McCarthyism and the legal profession.[7]

I could also write a book about the overall impact of the anticommunist crusade on the United States; for, despite the widespread conviction that McCarthyism had profound repercussions, no one has systematically looked at them or tried to assess the damage — both direct and indirect —

that the institutions and individuals targeted during the McCarthy era sustained. Nor has anyone explored how that damage affects America today. But the accounting needs to be done; and I am going to try. In assessing the impact of McCarthyism, I am going to focus primarily on those sectors of American society that took the main hits: organized labor, the civil rights movement, the federal government, and the cultural world. But McCarthyism touched a much broader range of groups and individuals than one might suspect; and I will look at them as well.

I will also look at the patterns of repression that characterized the McCarthy era. In almost every venue, whether it was a criminal trial, congressional investigation, or loyalty-security board hearing, the same institutions, actors, and assumptions recur. Some, like the Communist party and the FBI, are so important to the story that I devote whole chapters to them. Others, like the House Un-American Activities Committee (HUAC), the Supreme Court, or the ex-communist professional witnesses, weave in and out of the entire narrative. Their multiple appearances elucidate the interconnections that made the campaign against American Communism work.

McCarthyism flourished for nearly ten years, roughly from 1946 until 1956. Though it had antecedents that reached back into the nineteenth century and before, the main features of the anticommunist crusade developed during the 1930s. It was then, at a time when American Communists had gained attention by organizing labor unions and fighting fascism, that most of the institutions and procedures that characterized the anticommunist political repression of the following decade came into being. Had World War II not diverted the nation's leaders from the issue of Communism, it is likely that some form of McCarthyism might well have entered American politics a full ten years before it finally did. From congressional committees to the FBI, all the machinery was in place.

That machinery went into operation during the late 1940s. Perhaps because of the notoriety that Senator McCarthy attracted, the movement that got his name has usually been identified with his four-year career in the early 1950s. Though these years certainly witnessed the most extreme manifestations of the anticommunist crusade, the crucial developments that brought McCarthyism to the center of American politics occurred between 1946 and 1949, when the nation's political elites, preoccupied with the issue of communism, took up the tools that the anticommunist network had so conveniently forged. Nor did McCarthyism end with the censure of the Wisconsin senator in November 1954, though it had begun to peter out. The sporadic harassment of Communists and supposed Communists continued for another decade, but the repression had definitely eased up in the late 1950s. Even my sixth-grade teacher, after four years of unemployment, found another job and, ironically, ended up in the mid-sixties teaching at the same school he had so quietly left more than ten years before.

Because McCarthyism reached so many corners of American society, studying it requires looking at sources that range from the personal papers of Supreme Court justices and FBI files to science fiction movies and the memoirs of former Communists. Obviously, I have had to be selective. Had I tried to look at all the materials relevant to McCarthyism, I would never have gotten out of the archives. Instead, I have tried to use as many different kinds of sources as possible rather than investigate each topic exhaustively. That broader approach has yielded the unexpected benefit of revealing much more strikingly than a more narrowly focused investigation might have the interconnections between superficially unrelated elements of the anticommunist crusade. When one finds references to exactly the same set of labor troubles in Supreme Court decisions, FBI reports, HUAC hearings, and the memoirs and correspondence of presidential aides, important patterns become clear.

FBI files, as well as the recently released KGB messages that the FBI and National Security Agency deciphered during the Cold War, require special mention. The Russian documents are the partially decoded texts of telegrams that the KGB's residents sent back to Moscow from the United States during World War II. The FBI intercepted these messages at the time but was unable to decipher them until the late 1940s, when a group of cryptographers assigned to what was called the Venona Project began to break the Soviet encryption. The highly secret process took years and not all the texts have been fully recovered. Nor, because the KGB used cover names, have all the people mentioned in these documents been identified. The FBI material is also fragmentary. The Bureau still withholds documents and those it has released are often full of deletions. Because they offer insights into the world of the secret police on both sides of the Iron Curtain, it is tempting to treat the FBI and Venona materials less critically than documents from more accessible sources. But there are too many gaps in the record to use these materials with complete confidence. Even so, the FBI's files were invaluable, especially for showing how the Bureau operated. Here again, I have looked at as many different files as I could.[8]

This book is about a set of events that I deplore. Yet, unlike much of the literature about McCarthyism, I have not taken a victim-centered approach. I do not think that I conceal my sympathy for many of the men and women who suffered during the McCarthy era nor my agreement with much (though not all*) of their political agenda. To focus solely on McCarthyism's evils, however, will not reveal enough about the way it operated, any more than simply cataloguing the sufferings of its victims will. I want to learn why my sixth-grade teacher lost his job, not just what happened to him. McCarthyism is about the use of power to repress a politically unpopular minority and, in order to understand it, we must look at the individuals and institutions that had that power. Perhaps by discovering how political repression once took hold within our democratic system, we can avoid a replay.

*And, yes, of course, Joseph Stalin was far more repressive than Joseph McCarthy and J. Edgar Hoover. And I do not now and never have believed that the Soviet Union offered any kind of model for the American left. Still, this book is about the United States and not about Russia and, while what happened in the Soviet Union was much worse than anything in this country, within the American context McCarthyism was a disgrace. It may well be a kind of final relic of the McCarthy era that requires this kind of statement on the part of someone writing about Communism even after the Cold War has ended.

★

PART ONE

ANTECEDENTS

★

CHAPTER 1

"WE WERE SITTING DUCKS"

THE WORLD OF AMERICAN COMMUNISM

WHEN STEVE NELSON became a Communist in 1923, he had just arrived in Philadelphia from his Croatian homeland. He was working as a carpenter and trying to understand "why I worked so hard while the boss did not," when a fellow worker slipped him some left-wing litera- ture. It gave him the answers he sought. Socialism, with its vision of eco- nomic equality, offered an explanation for, as well as an alternative to, the hardships and inequities that had troubled him. Communism, with its com- mitment to an ongoing revolutionary struggle, offered the means for trans- forming that alternative into reality. Nelson had toyed with a few other socialist organizations before he joined the Communist party. Those other groups, he recalled, "seemed to be *talking* about socialism; the CP seemed to be actively pursuing it." Nelson became a member because he was im- pressed by the party's dynamism and the commitment of its members.[1]

Nelson was not a typical recruit. His leadership abilities and political dedication soon propelled him into the CP's highest echelons. Nonetheless, in his desire for radical social and economic change as well as his willing- ness to throw himself into a movement that promised such a change, he was not unlike the thousands of men and women who came within the orbit of American Communism during the first half of the twentieth century — and

3

thus exposed themselves to the political repression of the McCarthy period.

In order to understand that repression, it is necessary to understand the movement Nelson and his comrades joined. For there could have been no McCarthyism without the American Communist party. The anticommunist crusade of the 1940s and 1950s was, after all, directed against the CP and it was usually right on target. Most of the men and women who were called before the committees or lost their jobs during the McCarthy era had once been in or near the Communist party. They had gotten into trouble because of their political affiliations and because most Americans then assumed that Communism was so dreadful in and of itself that anyone connected with it had to be guilty of something bad.

At the time, it seemed important to know if someone was a party member. Now it does not. Instead, what matters is what that membership actually entailed. After all, only by knowing what American Communists did is it possible to tell whether the repression directed against them was a realistic response to a genuine threat or the irrational scapegoating of an unpopular minority. Furthermore, although the Communist party did not cause McCarthyism, it did influence the way in which it operated and the specific methods that it adopted. In addition, the CP's policies and practices made the task of eradicating it easier. Not only did those policies and practices alienate many of the party's allies and increase the hostility that it faced, but they also made the CP peculiarly vulnerable to persecution.

Paradoxically, many of the elements that exposed American Communism to repression were also, at one time or another, either sources of strength for the party or measures of self-protection. In a sense the CP's history presents the old chicken-and-egg conundrum, for many of these damaging characteristics had themselves developed in response to earlier bouts of repression. Thus, for example, the party's secrecy was the understandable — though deleterious — response to the official and unofficial harassment that it often faced. Its rigid discipline kept the organization united in the face of repression and of the frequent changes in its line. Even its tie to the Soviet Union, the fatal flaw of American Communism, could be, in certain circumstances, genuinely advantageous from the CP's perspective.

These contradictions have not gone away. Was the party a progressive political reform movement or a revolutionary Soviet-led conspiracy? In fact, of course, it was both — and more. American Communism came in many flavors and changed significantly over time. On the one hand, the CP was a highly disciplined, undemocratic outfit that tried to apply Soviet prescriptions to American ills. On the other hand, it was also a genuinely forward-looking organization that stimulated many of the most dynamic political and social movements of the 1930s and 1940s. And it was often both at once.

No doubt because these contradictions seem so irreconcilable, those of us who study American Communism have trouble keeping our own political biases out of the story. It is hard to avoid taking sides or passing judgments, hard, in other words, to treat the CP as just history. Those on the left tend to view its record as one of heroic exploits or lost opportunities, while those on the right see it as a series of crimes. Perhaps all historical narrative is a "moral drama" as the historian Hayden White would have us believe. Certainly, if any history qualifies for such a treatment, it would be that of American Communism. Nonetheless, to the extent that it is possible, I would like to bypass the conventional moralistic approach to the CP's history. Thus, instead of focusing on the party's sins and virtues, I will examine the way it shaped the repression that was directed against it. I will not look at everything the CP did, but only at those actions that in one way or another contributed to Cold War anticommunism. Such a perspective renders traditional judgments irrelevant, but it may well offer more insight into the party's role in American life.[2]

To begin with, there is an important distinction to be made here between the Communist party and the communist movement. The two were closely linked, but not quite the same. The movement was a political subculture, a loosely structured constellation of left-wing individuals, ideas, and organizations of which the party was the institutional core. Members of that broader movement, "small c" Communists or "fellow travelers" as they were often called, participated in many of the same activities and shared many of the same values as their "capital-letter C" comrades. Many of them had, in fact, once belonged to the party. But, except for people who for some reason were not formally in the CP but were nonetheless under its control, these lowercase Communists had more autonomy than their dues-paying colleagues and were not directly subject to the party's discipline.[3]

That discipline was central to the CP's identity. True Communists followed the party line — but not everywhere, not all the time, and not in everything they did. Still, the discipline that characterized the CP distinguished its members from the other radicals in its orbit. In their political work (and for many activists in their daily lives as well) Communists were

5

expected to comply with party directives. Even during its more reformist phases, when there was little difference between the aims and actions of the "big C" and "small c" Communists, the American Communist party never abandoned its demand for conformity. It was — in theory and in ways that shaped the behavior of its members — a tightly organized, highly disciplined, international revolutionary socialist organization. It characterized itself as, and during the McCarthy years became caricatured as, a Marxist-Leninist party.

Marxism-Leninism was a term with many meanings. To a certain extent it defined the ideology and organizational structure that distinguished Communist parties throughout the world from all other political groups. But that ideology and organization could change considerably in response to changing conditions. And, ultimately, the concept of Marxism-Leninism simply became a shorthand way to refer to the international communist movement controlled by the Soviet party. That movement's original theory came, of course, from Karl Marx, who predicted the inevitable decay of capitalism and the triumph of a working-class revolution. Since it was never clear exactly how that revolution would occur and what the dictatorship of the proletariat, as the new regime was called, would look like, the socialist parties that developed in Europe and elsewhere in the late nineteenth century soon splintered as different factions advocated different methods for achieving power. Some groups urged a gradual approach and a reliance on parliamentary procedures; others attacked the presumably "revisionist" nature of that approach and called for immediate revolution. The Communist parties that emerged after the Russian revolution, though ostensibly devoted to the violent overthrow of capitalism, never resolved the dilemma either. They, too, struggled to maintain the proper balance between gradualism and outright revolution.

Lenin's legacy was to create a highly centralized and disciplined party of professional revolutionaries. Lenin had devised this organizational structure in response to the specific conditions facing Russian Socialists in the early twentieth century. Most Marxists believed that a socialist revolution would take place in a country like Germany with a large industrial working class; Russia, with its backward peasant economy and tiny working class, was hardly a candidate. In addition, Tsarist repression forced Lenin and his followers to operate underground, where they could not organize the kind of mass working-class political movement that existed in Western Europe. In order to compensate for these disadvantages, Lenin developed a vanguard party, the Bolsheviks, a tightly organized secret band of professional revolutionaries who would supply the necessary political leadership for the underdeveloped Russian working class.[4]

Even after Lenin and his followers took advantage of the collapse of Tsarism during World War I to create the world's first socialist state, the communist regime that emerged in the aftermath of the Russian revolution never quite shed the conspiratorial quality that the Bolsheviks' years of prison and exile had created. Moreover, because the acquisition of state power enabled the Soviet Communist party to dominate the international revolutionary movement, it imposed its organizational model on all the other parties under its aegis. As a result, Communists all over the world tried to apply Lenin's recipe for revolution to very different situations. The American party, which, like Communist parties everywhere, developed out of the left wing of the Socialist party, thus organized itself as a vanguard revolutionary organization that would ultimately capture power and impose a working-class regime. That such a conspiratorial style and unrealistic game plan was wildly unsuited to American conditions was only one of the CP's many disadvantages.

In the United States, the party's problems were exacerbated by the traditional failure of Socialism to gain much support. The American Socialist party (SP), even at its heyday in the early years of the twentieth century, never won the mass political following that Western European Socialists enjoyed. American Communists shared that unpropitious heritage. Their appeals for class solidarity had little impact on an ethnically diverse, racially divided working class that bought into the American dream of upward mobility and individual success. The party's secular emphasis and disregard for traditional religion further distanced it from the workers it was trying to convert.[5]

Understandably, the unpopularity of its cause tempted the CP to downplay its demand for a socialist revolution and seek adherents by advocating less-drastic measures in the hope that the American masses would somehow discover the futility of reforming the system and embrace the party's ultimate agenda. But that "somehow" had no real meaning and attempts to make the party's actions conform to Marxist theory simply led to confusion. As a result, the CP's leaders often seemed to be engaged in a constant struggle to find and apply the correct line. Ultraleftism and excessive revolutionary zeal would discourage potential supporters and transform the party into a tiny, isolated sect. A more moderate posture risked abandoning the party's commitment to Socialism and revolution. Accordingly, the CP often seemed to lurch from one extreme to another. Though many of these zigs and zags were charted in response to directions from Moscow, a more independent organization would still have experienced similar shifts between revolution and reform.[6]

Although the CP's Leninist structure and revolutionary goals were seriously out of touch with American realities, the party was, at least during the 1930s and 1940s, far more influential than its small size and chimerical objectives might suggest. Its discipline was, in part, responsible. Like Steve Nelson, who had been so attracted by the CP's energy in the 1920s, most American Communists tried to accommodate themselves to the general directives they received from above, because they believed that, despite its disadvantages, the party's discipline made their political work more effective.

For the American Communist party was, above all, an organization of activists. Even its rank-and-file members did much more than pay their dues. Though the party's slogan, "Every Evening to Party Work," may have been an exaggeration, ordinary Communists were expected to make a major commitment to the CP. They were supposed to attend meetings, read party literature, and become active in labor unions and other so-called "mass organizations" or "front groups." * Most of them complied. One New York City ex-Communist recalled that he had once gone to twenty-seven meetings in a single week, though the more common figure, at least as reported in a study of some Philadelphia rank and filers, was somewhere between six and twelve. Whatever the project, Communists were usually the most active and dedicated workers, "the ones," an ex-communist teacher remembered, "who would sweat it out all kinds of hours and come in on Saturdays."[7]

It was not an easy commitment to maintain; many people dropped out of the party after a few months or years, usually because of boredom or burnout or because they decided that the pluses of party membership no longer

---

*There is controversy about the name of the organizations within the party's orbit. The CP's euphemism was "mass organizations"; its opponents called them "front groups." I will use the latter term because it seems more historically specific.

outweighed its minuses. Many of these people, however, remained in the movement and, though unwilling to submit to party discipline, still signed the same petitions and showed up on the same picket lines as their card-carrying comrades.[8]

Other Communists made an even larger commitment. They worked full-time for the party or for the many front groups and labor unions associated with it. The CP was unique here. A high percentage of its members became professional activists, or cadres, as they were called. These people had made a full-time, often lifetime, political commitment. The party actively developed its cadres. It sent promising candidates to special training schools and placed them either in paid party positions or within the network of left-wing unions and organizations it controlled. Thus, for example, of the 766 delegates to the New York State Communist party's convention in 1938, 106 were full-time CP functionaries, 208 were labor union officials, and 253 held positions in the front groups.[9]

Of course, not all the people associated with American Communism were equally dedicated and individuals' experiences with the party differed. Besides the obvious distinctions between cadres and rank-and-file Communists, it is important to realize that where and when people joined the CP also shaped their experiences. A black sharecropper in Alabama belonged to a very different kind of organization than did a Jewish housewife in the Bronx, a Polish autoworker in Detroit, a Finnish farmer in Minnesota, or an Ivy League–educated screenwriter in Hollywood. Timing was as important as place. Especially during the Popular Front period of the 1930s and 1940s, when the party moderated its revolutionary stance and sought to join the mainstream, the activities of American Communists — both capital letter and lowercase — were often indistinguishable from those of the non-Communists with whom they worked. Before and after the Popular Front, the party was a more militant and sectarian organization that was largely isolated from American life.

Most members of the first generation of American Communists had been Socialists of one kind or another or else Wobblies, members of a radical labor organization, the Industrial Workers of the World (IWW). Like Communist parties the world over, the American CP originated in the disintegration of the international socialist movement during World War I. The preexisting conflicts between reformers and revolutionaries finally broke up each European Socialist party when it had to decide whether or not to support its country's war effort. Because of their distance from the trenches, American Socialists were more united than their Old World comrades in their opposition to the war, though no less divided in their attitude toward revolution. When the revolution finally came, far away in Russia though it was, the left-wing Socialists flocked to its support, splitting the American Socialist party in the process. By the middle of 1919, the SP's more radical elements, as well as most of its foreign-language contingents, had climbed aboard the Bolshevik bandwagon. For them, the Russian revolution was but the first phase of the imminent worldwide upheaval and they did not want to miss the show.[10]

From the start, American Communists defined themselves in terms of the mother revolution. During the Cold War, of course, the Moscow connection was to prove lethal, but during the early years of American Communism, the Soviet franchise gave the splintered and beleaguered party much of whatever credibility it had within the left — as well as much of its funding. After all, as the proprietors of the first socialist state with all the resources of a major nation behind them, the Bolsheviks had enormous prestige within the revolutionary world. To gain the Soviet imprimatur as the official American representatives of the Russian revolution was no small prize for the fledgling American Communists. Though their own party was tiny and fractured, it was still part of an international movement whose Soviet center was a world power indeed.[11]

Like every other Communist party, the American CP followed the line that emerged from Moscow. It was a member of the Comintern, the international organization established by Lenin in 1919 to coordinate the worldwide revolution that most Communists believed would soon break out. During the party's early years, a two-way flow of emissaries between the United States and the Soviet Union kept the Americans in touch with the Comintern's directives. Though these directives often reflected Soviet priorities, the American CP never hesitated to obey them. Even when the party grew during the 1930s and 1940s and took on the trappings of a much more Americanized reform movement, it never wavered in its internationalism and its support for the Soviet Union as the world's main socialist regime.

Especially during its early years, the CP relied heavily on the Comintern. It did so in part because it was so weak, but also because it was so divided. American Communism had begun its existence as two separate parties, each one competing for the official franchise. Even after the two parties merged, sectarian disputes and power struggles continued to plague the CP. Rival factions with such exotic names as "Geese" and "Liquidators" would ask Moscow to settle their quarrels only to find that the Kremlin's own internal divisions exacerbated the American party's proclivities for sectarianism and hairsplitting.[12]

Its illegal status further intensified the CP's early problems. Especially during the red scare of 1919–1920, when the federal government rounded up thousands of foreign-born radicals for deportation, official repression forced the fledgling party underground. In order to evade the authorities, communist leaders adopted aliases, wrote to each other in code, and held secret meetings. These precautions did not work. With the help of undercover informers, the FBI and local law enforcement officials raided the party's 1922 national convention and arrested twenty leaders on charges of criminal syndicalism.[13]

Even after the repression eased up in the mid-1920s, the party retained its conspiratorial aura. It also retained its penchant for sectarianism. With so little support beyond its ten thousand to twelve thousand, mostly foreign-born, members, the CP was under continual pressure from the Comintern to broaden its appeal, mend its schisms, and become more like the Soviet party. There was considerable irony here, for soon after the death of Lenin, the Kremlin was itself consumed by the far more deadly infighting that continued for over a decade. As a result, by the late 1920s the directives that came out of Moscow increasingly came to reflect the ideological maneuvers Stalin adopted to overcome his internal rivals. First he took a moderate position in order to isolate the more radical Leon Trotsky. Then he turned against his moderate allies and adopted the revolutionary line that Trotsky had previously advocated. Ultimately, Stalin abandoned ideology for murder. The show trials and executions that killed off Stalin's rivals began in 1936, but these earlier ideological shifts had prepared the way.

Thus it was that in 1928, just at the moment when the American CP was finally about to resolve its own factional struggles and adapt its policies to the realities of American life, Moscow imposed a more sectarian line. In the summer of 1928, the Sixth World Congress of the Comintern promoted an analysis of the world situation that predicted the imminent collapse of capitalism and claimed that the main obstacle to the success of the revolution was the Socialist parties of the West. This analysis, which became known as "Third Period Communism," encouraged the communist movement to devote itself to the struggle against "Social Fascism" — just when real fascism was about to become a threat.[14]

For the American party, the problems associated with the adoption of the new, more-radical "Third Period" line were exacerbated by the Comintern's repudiation of the CP's leading cadres. Though a majority of the party's top brass had supported the more moderate Jay Lovestone against his militant rival William Z. Foster, Stalin's turn to the left in 1929 forced Lovestone out. Lovestone's fall came not from his policy stance, but rather from his failure to adjust quickly enough to the fact that his previous mentor, the moderate Soviet leader Nicolai Bukharin, was no longer on the winning side. Once it was clear that Lovestone was out of favor, his former colleagues scurried to align themselves with the Comintern's new analysis. Success as a communist leader, Lovestone's ouster revealed, required adherence to whatever Stalin wanted.[15]

It was, of course, a narrow kind of success; for outside of the far left, Communism had little impact on American society during the 1920s. The political repression directed against the party, as well as the overall conservatism and relative prosperity of the era, did not encourage the growth of any kind of radical movement. Moreover, despite the drive and dedication of its adherents, the CP was too isolated and sectarian to appeal to many of the workers it claimed to represent. Membership still stood in the four-figure range by the end of the decade and the turnover within the rank and file was high. Like the future party leader Steve Nelson, probably 90 percent of the party's members were foreign-born, but so, too, was the majority of the working class. Moreover, despite pressure from the Comintern, the party had yet to Americanize itself, recruit more native English-speakers, make an impact on the labor movement, or pay attention to the problems of American blacks.[16]

Things changed in the thirties. The onset of the Depression suddenly gave communist organizers an audience. With capitalism in disarray, Socialism no longer seemed so threatening. The testimony of the men and women who joined the CP in the 1930s invariably notes their relief at finding an organization that, as it had done for Steve Nelson when he was a young Croatian immigrant in Philadelphia ten years before, seemed to provide answers to the problems they faced. The party's explanations made sense to this second generation of American Communists, who were coming of age in a world of economic hardship and rising fascism. There was, it was alleged, no unemployment in the Soviet Union and it seemed possible that Communism might well offer a solution to the devastation the Depression had wrought.

An even stronger draw than either the Soviet example or the party's ideology was the fact that Communists were responding to the Depression with actions as well as words. At a time of widespread hopelessness and despair, the party's cadres were doing something. They mobilized unemployed workers and marched them to local city halls to demand relief. They organized neighborhood groups to prevent homelessness by carrying the furniture of evicted tenants back into their apartments. They rallied college students to oppose compulsory military training. They formed militant unions of migrant laborers, miners, longshoremen, and textile workers. They saved nine black teenagers in Scottsboro, Alabama, from execution on trumped-up charges of rape. They sent delegations of intellectuals to help striking Kentucky miners. Communists, it seemed, were everywhere — or, at least, in most of the big social struggles of the early 1930s.[17]

No doubt this burst of energy was facilitated by the end of the open factionalism that had plagued the CP's top leadership for so long. Despite the serious personal and ideological friction between William Z. Foster and the CP's new boss, Earl Browder, the conflict did not disrupt the party. Browder had been abroad working for the Comintern during the 1920s and so had had no ties to either side during the CP's earlier internecine struggles. He was obviously Moscow's man; and, though he was later to be vilified as a revisionist, in the 1930s he was completely orthodox and subservient to Stalin's demands.[18]

Then, too, the party's hard line began to soften. The change did not occur overnight. "Third Period" Communism remained in place during the early part of the decade and the party continued its sectarian baiting of "Social Fascists." The sometimes violent repression that its demonstrations and other organizational efforts encountered certainly did not encourage party activists to moderate their attacks on the capitalist system. Nor did the advent of the Roosevelt administration in 1933 temper the Communists' opposition to bourgeois politics. At first, the CP claimed to see little difference between Franklin Roosevelt and his Republican opponents. FDR's program was, Browder announced in 1933, "the forerunner of American fascism."[19]

Yet, rhetoric aside, it was soon clear that the New Deal was making a difference. The Roosevelt administration had, after all, recognized the Soviet Union. More important, it shifted American politics to the left and opened up more space for radicalism. For the first time, the federal government actually condoned labor unions; and Communists, for whom labor organizing was a primary activity, threw themselves into the great surge of unionization that occurred in the mid-1930s. Within a few years, the party's official view of Roosevelt had changed so radically that the CP was acting in many respects as a junior partner within the New Deal coalition.

The rise of Hitler, as well as the realization that the hard times brought on by the Depression had not led to the inevitable revolution the Comintern had predicted, prompted the turnaround. Communists had not initially distinguished between fascists and other bourgeois political parties. That mistake soon became tragically obvious and by mid-1934 the party line began to change. The Führer was a menace to the Soviet Union as well as an enemy of the working class. The official transformation occurred in Moscow in August 1935 when the Seventh Comintern Congress formally adopted the Popular Front. The protection of the Soviet Union was still the dominant concern; now, however, it was to be accomplished through an antifascist coalition, first with other socialist and left-wing organizations, and then, as the Popular Front expanded, with bourgeois democrats as well. In order to allay the fears of such prospective allies, Stalin muffled the Comintern's revolutionary line. By the late 1930s, Communists outside the USSR had all but dropped their demands for Socialism.[20]

The new line brought new recruits to the party and reinvigorated the old ones. By taking the lead in antifascist activities in the United States, the party made a strong appeal to what was to become its most important constituency: urban, upwardly mobile, second-generation American Jews. The outbreak of the Spanish Civil War in the summer of 1936 reinforced the CP's antifascist credentials, especially since the Soviet Union was the only major power backing the legal Republican government against the German and Italian-supported rebels led by General Francisco Franco. The party took advantage of its international connections to send volunteers to Spain, where some 2,800 Americans fought in the CP-led Abraham Lincoln brigade. Three-quarters of them were Communists. Like Steve Nelson, the Lincoln Brigade's political commissar then working as a party organizer in the coalfields of eastern Pennsylvania, they saw the Spanish Civil War as "the front line of the struggle against international fascism."[21]

On the home front, the party threw itself into the newly formed CIO's campaign to unionize the nation's heavy industries. Participating in the broader democratic movements during the Popular Front years in the late 1930s changed the CP's culture. The party downplayed its revolutionary character and adopted an all-American image, placing Jefferson, Jackson, and Lincoln in its pantheon alongside Marx, Engels, and Lenin. "Communism," declared Earl Browder, "is twentieth-century Americanism." Energized by its new line and new respectability, the CP grew — from about 40,000 in 1936 to 82,000 by the end of 1938.[22]

The party now had a real role within the American polity. It served as the unofficial left wing of the New Deal, its cadres and rank and file supplying manpower and leadership for a wide array of social reform movements and progressive political groups. Though still small and marginal, the CP was no longer isolated. Especially in New York City, which accounted for about 40 percent of its membership, the party could mobilize sizable forces. It turned out large crowds for May Day parades and rallies in Madison Square Garden. National networks carried Browder's speeches. The Sunday edition of the *Daily Worker* had a circulation of 100,000 copies in 1938. "As long as we did not make too much noise about it," Browder later explained, "we became almost respectable. Never quite respectable. Almost."[23]

And then, overnight, it all disappeared.

Disillusioned by the Western democracies' failure to stand up to Hitler at Munich in 1938, Stalin abandoned his opposition to the Third Reich and signed a nonaggression pact with the Führer on August 23, 1939. It was a stunning blow to the American CP and one that would set it up for much of the later repression it faced. The party's leaders had no more advance warning than anyone else and initially announced that the treaty would bolster the drive against war and fascism. Within a few days, the word came from Moscow that the war between Hitler and the Western democracies was an imperialist struggle in which good Communists did not have to take sides. The party responded by toning down its antifascism and rediscovering its commitment to peace. It also turned against "Franklin Demagogue Roosevelt," now portrayed as a warmonger whose support for Great Britain was an attempt to drag the United States into "the imperialist war."[24]

The CP's different constituencies responded in different ways to the new line. Though there were a few highly public defections (mainly of intellectuals), the bulk of the party stayed put. But even its most dedicated cadres found the rapid switch hard to take. Throughout these people's memoirs and oral histories the same words appear. The pact was "a complete shock," "a megaton shock," "a thunderclap," an "utter shock," "a shocking thing and quite hard to take." It threw the party "into utter confusion," "left us limp and confused." "We were confused," "very confused," "in conflict." But they were loyal Communists and they stuck with the CP, rationalizing the pact as having prevented a deal between Hitler and the West and giving the Soviets time to prepare for the expected Nazi onslaught.[25]

What party veterans found more difficult to justify was the CP's own response to the pact and the aggressive way in which American Communists were expected to defend it by attacking FDR's foreign policy. "At the time of the pact," one former Harlem party leader reminisced, "we should have said: 'That's the Soviet Union's business, they have a country to run.' But we had to come down and defend it, to make it the number one priority in the Party. Well this piece left, and that piece left, and we were beginning to lose our base." Another leader made the same observation. "We declared war on both sides, which was the Soviet position but did not necessarily have to be ours.[26]

Some elements of the party were less affected than others. Within the CP's African American constituency, concerned above all with racial issues, the pact made little difference. For some black activists, intellectuals in particular, the new line with its stress on anti-imperialism was actually congenial. Similarly, in the all-important trade union circles, Stalin's deal with Hitler did not completely damage the CP's standing. The CIO's leader,

John L. Lewis, was a staunch isolationist and, at least at first, welcomed the party's support for his opposition to FDR's interventionism. Within other parts of the labor movement where Communists were active, like the largely Irish Transport Workers Union, the party's new anti-British policy may well have have been more popular than its earlier antifascist stance.[27]

Nonetheless, it would be incorrect to underestimate the negative consequences of the pact. Party membership did decline, but mainly because the CP could not recruit new members to counteract its normally high attrition rate. In addition, the pact placed considerable strain on the loyalty of the thousands of men and women who had joined the party to fight fascism during the Popular Front. They accepted the new line, but the psychological toll that the shift demanded began the subtle process of undermining their allegiance to the CP. It destroyed, as many of them were later to admit, the moral authority of the party.[28]

More important, it also destroyed the CP's coalition with American liberals. Though the coalition was restored after Hitler invaded the Soviet Union in June 1941, the memories of the about-face of 1939 lingered. The underlying distrust emerged a few years later to reinforce the anticommunist foundations of Cold War liberalism. More immediately, the party's loss of its liberal allies and its open attacks on the Roosevelt administration exposed it to serious repression.

In many respects, therefore, it was a great relief to American Communists when the German invasion of the Soviet Union brought them back into the antifascist camp. After the United States officially entered the conflict, patriotism became the order of the day. Naturally, the party also urged all-out aid to Moscow. The survival of the Soviet Union really was at stake, and the CP clamored for the opening of a second front in Western Europe to take the pressure off the Red Army. Rank-and-file Communists threw themselves into the American war effort as well. By January 1943, one-fifth of the men in the CP were serving in the military. Local party units were running blood drives, collecting tin cans, and selling war bonds.[29]

In fact, as the CP's literature pointed out, it was hard to tell the difference between a Communist and a member of the middle-class Order of Kiwanis. The revivified Popular Front, like the original one, abandoned the language of class conflict and urged blacks and industrial workers to postpone their legitimate social and economic demands until after the war. This new moderation mirrored that emanating from the Kremlin. Stalin, for example, courted the favor of his British and American allies by dissolving the Comintern in the spring of 1943. The American CP followed suit; and in 1944 its leaders decided to dissolve the party. A supposedly less threatening Communist Political Association replaced it. And Browder, who predicted that the wartime unity between Communists and capitalists would extend into the postwar world, was, he claimed, even willing to extend a hand of conciliation to Wall Street banker J. P. Morgan. There was little open opposition within the party to the new line; it seemed to fit both American conditions and Soviet foreign policy.[30]

Within a year, however, the party's embrace of the bourgeoisie had been ruptured. Again the word came from Moscow, this time by way of Paris in what later became known as the "Duclos Letter," an article by the French communist leader Jacques Duclos that appeared in the French CP's theoretical journal in April 1945. It castigated Browder's abandonment of the notion of class struggle as "a notorious revision of Marxism." Duclos's words, the Americans realized, must have been inspired by Moscow. Not only was it unusual for a party leader in one country to criticize another party, but the article contained passages from an unpublished letter by William Z. Foster that could have reached Duclos only by way of the Kremlin. The CP's leaders interpreted the piece as an indication that Moscow disapproved of Browder's policy.[31]

Although that policy had been popular and had made the party more politically acceptable, it was unthinkable for American Communists to defy what they interpreted as a directive from the Soviet Union. In a series of intensive meetings in May and June, the CP's top leaders reversed course, dissolving the Communist Political Association and formally reestablishing the party. More important, they disavowed the presumably revisionist policies that they had been following and reoriented the CP strongly to the left. Since Browder refused to recant, he was removed from his post and replaced by Foster. The other party leaders, who until then had enthusiastically supported Browder's supposed revisionism, quickly embraced the new militancy. Many of them had doubts about Foster's emphasis on the imminent danger of war and the impending economic collapse of capitalism, but they dared not challenge his position openly for fear of being accused of Browderism.[32]

The party's new hard line did not necessarily coincide with reality right after the war. Although the United States was soon to enter a forty-year struggle against the Soviet Union, it was by no means obvious in mid-1945 that such would be the outcome of its foreign policy. While becoming increasingly upset by Soviet behavior in Eastern Europe, the Truman administration had not yet abandoned all attempts to reach some kind of accommodation with the Kremlin. Nor was a domestic anticommunist crusade necessarily in the offing. In many areas of American life, the wartime Popular Front remained intact. Party membership climbed from fifty thousand in 1946 to seventy-five thousand in 1947; even after the Cold War had begun in earnest by the middle of 1948, the CP still contained sixty thousand members. Communist rallies could draw twenty thousand people to Madison Square Garden; the CP could raise $250,000 in twenty days. And Communists still controlled dozens of vibrant front groups and retained considerable power within the labor movement.[33]

Within a few years, all that influence was gone. Though most of its cadres remained in the party until the mid-fifties, it had dwindled into a sect. The repression it faced was crucial here; but so, too, was its more sectarian line. The CP's support for the Soviet Union would have made it unpopular; its other policies, like its disastrous embrace of the third-party presidential campaign of former vice president Henry Wallace in 1948, only worsened the situation, alienating its allies and increasing its isolation from American life. Nonetheless, though the CP's misguided policies may have aggravated the political repression of the McCarthy period, they certainly did not cause it. The anticommunist crusade of the 1940s and 1950s would have occurred even if the party had adopted a milder stance. Its political errors simply increased the effectiveness of that crusade.[34]

Understandably, but deplorably, the repression that the CP faced reinforced its extremism. It lent credibility to Foster's pronouncements that war and fascism were just around the corner. Anticipating that it might soon become illegal, the party began to prepare for sending some of its leaders and lower-level cadres underground. Especially after FBI informers began to surface at political trials during the late forties, security became an obsession. People who saw psychotherapists were automatically dropped from the CP. In a bizarre replication of the federal government's own fixations, homosexuals were also expelled on the grounds that their vulnerability to blackmail in the repressive sexual climate of the period would endanger their comrades. At the same time, a highly sectarian campaign against "white chauvinism" claimed additional victims.[35]

The Kremlin dealt the final blow. Early in 1956, the Soviet leader Nikita Khrushchev delivered a speech to the Soviet Union's Twentieth Party Congress in which he described Stalin's crimes. Demoralized to find out that they had been justifying a monstrous regime and unable to reform the CP from within, the party's most talented cadres, the Spanish Civil War hero Steve Nelson among them, finally quit. The bulk of the membership had long since done so. By 1958, the CP was down to three thousand members and was again the same kind of inbred, isolated sect it had been in the 1920s.[36]

Besides its flips and flops, the CP had other institutional characteristics that were to increase its vulnerability to McCarthyism — characteristics that made the party easy to demonize as a dangerous conspiracy against the United States. It was, to begin with, a secretive organization that operated in a highly authoritarian manner. And, of course, it was totally committed to defending the Soviet Union. When the Cold War turned the CP into a political pariah, these structural and ideological flaws compromised its moral authority and made it hard for the liberals and others who claimed to oppose McCarthyism to defend the political and civil rights of Communists.

After all, it was commonly argued, party members would no doubt violate the rights of their enemies if they could. Their acceptance of the Soviet purges seemingly proved that contention. Though it is unclear to what extent the willingness of American Communists to endorse what was going on in Moscow indicated a propensity for the same kind of viciousness within the United States, it was, nonetheless, inexcusable. The terror that the Soviet government unleashed against its own people during the 1930s and 1940s was a genuine atrocity. An entire generation of communist leaders was put on trial, falsely accused of collaborating with the enemies of the regime, forced to confess, and then shot. And millions of other people were executed or died in the slave labor camps of the Soviet gulags.[37]

At the time, the American Communist party seemed to condone it all. Now, most former party members realize how indefensible their complicity with the Soviet regime was. The literature of ex-communist confessions is replete with mea culpas. Even in the thirties, it was possible to have recognized the travesty of Stalin's show trials of the 1930s, but surprisingly few Communists did. The trumped-up charges that surfaced during the Moscow trials were so unbelievable that most contemporary observers — communist and non-communist alike — simply could not believe they were *not* true. "I found no reason to question the public confessions of top Bolshevik leaders like Bukharin and Radek," former *Daily Worker* editor John Gates recalled.

> It seemed incredible to me that men of their stature could confess to these grave crimes unless they had committed them; I could not conceive of myself ever confessing to crimes of which I was not guilty. The possibility of Stalin coercing them into false confessions we refused even to consider. Could such vileness be perpetrated by the man who was doing more than anyone else in the whole world to help democracy in Spain?

Peggy Dennis, the wife of the party's future general secretary, was actually in Moscow during the purges and saw several friends disappear. She knew what was happening, but accepted it "as part of the brutal realities of making a revolution, of building an oasis of socialism in a sea of enemies."[38]

The tough-mindedness that could lead someone like Dennis to condone Stalin's purges also deformed the CP's internal operations. The party's reliance on the Soviet Union led it to embrace a Bolshevik-style command structure. It adopted an undemocratic decision-making procedure, euphemistically called "democratic centralism," in which directives came down from national headquarters to be discussed by the rank and file, but not altered. A top-down authoritarianism, with its rigid, self-righteous Stalinist mentality, became the norm among the CP's leaders. Often the higher the position, the more serious the lapses. Earl Browder seems to have been in the words of one historian "an arrogant and uncompromising party dictator." Party functionaries in lower ranks could often be equally arrogant, claiming that the nobility of their cause justified their insensitive behavior.[39]

Especially debilitating in this regard was these leaders' "gradual loss of independent judgment." The rapidity and unanimity of the party's flips and flops indicates, as if such proof were necessary, how little self-government the American party had. Its quasi-military culture precluded real debate. Members of a vanguard party, lower-level cadres actually prided themselves on their discipline. As one labor organizer recalled, "edicts were handed down and we didn't examine them." Rationalizations for that kind of unthinking behavior were invariably deferential: "Our leaders know best." Of course, not every party leader was a rigid, bureaucratic ideologue. Like Steve Nelson, many were (or at least later claimed to have been) unhappy with the lack of internal democracy. They acquiesced because not to do so would have shattered the CP's unity and rendered it even more vulnerable to its outside enemies.[40]

In fact, some party units did exercise a certain amount of initiative. In many instances, poor communications and local exigencies, rather than a conscious desire for autonomy, seem to have granted them considerable independence. As historian Robin Kelley has noted with regard to Alabama Communists during the 1930s,

> because neither Joe Stalin, Earl Browder, nor William Z. Foster spoke directly to them or to their daily problems, Alabama Communists developed strategies and tactics in response to local circumstances that, in most cases, had nothing to do with international crises. Besides, if Alabamians had waited patiently for orders from Moscow, they might still be waiting today. Not only were lines of communication between New York and Birmingham hazy throughout the 1930s and 1940s, but Birmingham Communists had enough difficulty maintaining contact with comrades as close as Tallapoosa County.

Local organizers who were being harassed by the authorities couldn't always follow central directives. One former cadre from the Midwest recalls how her unit responded to orders from party headquarters. There would be "big discussions. And we would listen, and we would pay respects to everyone. And then we'd go back and do our own work."[41]

Some cadres and rank-and-file members were allowed more autonomy than others. The so-called "influentials" who exercised leadership within the labor movement operated with considerable independence. So, too, did intellectuals and professionals like lawyers. They were often given a looser

22

rein, in part because they might have rebelled had it been otherwise and also because the secrecy that sometimes surrounded their affiliation made it hard for the CP's functionaries to discipline them.[42]

The party's lack of democracy lessened its effectiveness. Communications from below rarely penetrated the ears of party officials for whom "democratic centralism" meant having rank-and-file Communists discuss and then accede to the line from above. The party's leaders became a separate sect, concerned more with one another's views than those of their constituents and increasingly unable to respond creatively to their members' needs. A former Brooklyn activist was still bitter about the way in which the hierarchy's directives to emphasize foreign policy issues aborted her successful tenant organizing campaign. Moreover, as the CP became increasingly self-absorbed, it lost the ability to communicate with outsiders. Party language was sectarian, loaded with jargon and the kind of invective that made publications like the *Daily Worker* unable to reach those beyond the fold.[43]

The Communist party's secrecy may have been even more damaging. There had always been a conspiratorial cast to the CP's activities, the legacy of its early days when the threat of deportation and criminal prosecution made legal operations impossible. But even during the Popular Front of the 1930s, the party never quite abandoned its revolutionary identity and, thus, retained many of its furtive practices. Party schools taught cadres how to operate underground and new members routinely took party names. While such measures might have been necessary to avoid repression in the rural South or among the migrant farmworkers of California's Imperial Valley, where communist organizers really were risking their lives, party members elsewhere did not need so much concealment. In no other democratic nation did Communists practice that kind of secrecy.[44]

The CP also harbored an underground offshoot that seems to have been at the service of the Kremlin. References to it have surfaced in the memoirs of both friendly and unfriendly ex-Communists. Recently released documents from the former Soviet archives and the intercepted KGB telegrams deciphered by U.S. intelligence agencies during the Cold War also allude to this apparatus and offer a few glimpses into its operations. Some of its members seem to have been federal civil servants or people in other sensitive positions who could not operate openly as Communists. Others may well have been spies. Still others worked directly for the Comintern as couriers and organizers in Europe and the Third World. While Steve Nelson was at the Lenin School in Moscow during the early thirties, both he and his wife, Margaret, carried money and messages to underground party members in Eastern Europe and China. Like the American volunteers for the Spanish Civil War, who traveled illegally in order to avoid the American government's ban on serving with the loyalist forces, the men and women who worked for the Comintern often used false passports and identities.[45]

There were also moments, especially when international tensions mounted and the CP found itself isolated and under attack, when the party would order some of its cadres and high-level leaders to drop their ordinary activities and go into hiding. Thus, if the government were to crack down and declare the CP illegal, an experienced nucleus would survive that could mobilize underground resistance movements as European Communists had done during World War II. The Nazi-Soviet pact stimulated one such burst of clandestinity. Steve Nelson stashed mimeograph machines in the California woods and then went underground near San Francisco; Eugene Dennis, an even more important party leader, spent seventeen months hiding out in a series of summer cottages in upstate New York.[46]

The Cold War spurred the CP's most self-destructive descent into the underground. In the summer of 1951, after the Supreme Court affirmed the criminal convictions of Dennis and ten other party leaders on the charge of "teaching and advocating" the overthrow of the government, the CP succumbed to William Z. Foster's apocalyptic vision of the imminence of fascism. It was "five minutes to midnight," time for the party to begin to go underground. Four of the convicted leaders jumped bail and went into hiding. Two were soon caught, but the other two, Gil Green and Henry Winston, continued to make policy as they shifted from one hiding place to another. Other indicted Communists also began to make themselves "unavailable," as did many of the party's top cadres and most reliable rank and filers. They were ordered to leave their families, take new identities, and keep themselves in readiness for whatever secret work the party might demand. Some even went behind the Iron Curtain. For a time, in the early fifties, roughly one-third of the CP's cadres had gone underground.[47]

In retrospect, this furtive operation was a stupid mistake. McCarthyism was not fascism and the Communist party's overreaction indicates how far from reality its leaders had strayed. For the cadres who made themselves unavailable at the party's command, going underground was a personal and political disaster. Lonely and isolated, few of them were to remain in the CP after the late 1950s. At the same time, their devious behavior reinforced the stereotype of the party as an alien and conspiratorial sect. And, of course, the FBI knew where most of these "unavailables" were.[48]

Even more deleterious than the CP's descent into the underground was the secrecy individual Communists practiced on a daily basis. Though some people revealed that they were in the party, many others did not. The militance or moderation of the CP's current line seemed to make little difference. There was almost as much secrecy during the Popular Front and World War II as there had been when the party took a more openly revolutionary stance. These clandestine practices generated controversy and ambivalence throughout the CP. Its labor cadres were especially uncomfortable. Concealing the party's role in organizing unions, the single most important activity Communists participated in, not only deprived the CP of credit for its contribution to the labor movement, but also made it look bad. In 1937, the party's chief labor organizer argued for more openness. "Concealing our identity deliberately breeds distrust among workers. They cannot understand why we are ashamed; why we hide the fact that we are Communists." Ordinary party members were also troubled by the deception they practiced. Many of them did not like to lie and they knew that their dishonest behavior reinforced the CP's negative image within the rest of society.[49]

On the other hand, revealing themselves as Communists created problems. People could lose their jobs. This was especially the case for the party's middle-class and professional members and the CP usually discouraged these people from disclosing their affiliation. Open party members who were schoolteachers or civil servants would have been automatically dismissed. Even during the Popular Front period and World War II, when, as one rank-and-file member explained, "it was more so-called kosher to come out into the open . . . no one really came out and said, 'I'm a Communist,' because they would lose their jobs the next day."[50]

Union officials and activists might not lose their jobs if they admitted they were in the party, but they might lose their effectiveness. American workers, so the reasoning went, were so innately prejudiced against Communism that it would be impossible for any open Communist to organize them successfully. It "would have been ridiculous to go up to the average worker and start talking socialism to him," a former union organizer explained; "you're ruining your chances of building a union." Union work was

25

political work, so these labor cadres claimed; they could build Communism later. In retrospect, many of them realized that they had deceived themselves about the militance of the workers they organized and had assumed that these people's willingness to accept (albeit unacknowledged) Communists as union leaders was the first indication of a class-consciousness that would ultimately bring them into the party's fold.[51]

In fact, of course, the secrecy wasn't particularly effective. Some labor leaders admitted their political affiliation, but they were usually either already known as Communists or else were so entrenched within their unions that they ran few risks. Others were only slightly less open. "I do everything now except call myself a Communist," one union president admitted. Another Communist recalled, "We didn't go out and shout from the rooftops whether we was party members or not. But on the other hand — in the shop there was nobody that paid any attention to the union had any doubt in their mind who was Communist and who wasn't."[52]

People often refused to discuss their party membership on civil libertarian grounds or because doing so would contribute to red-baiting. "I'd tell 'em it's immaterial," a former Communist explained, "if I'm a Catholic, if I'm a communist, if I'm a Lutheran, if I'm a Republican or Democrat, well, what's the difference? This is the work that I'm doing, I ain't hiding anything." Other people simply denied that they were in the CP. Whether justified or not, they were lying.[53]

More important, the party's secrecy gave its enemies perhaps their strongest weapon: exposure. American Communists would no doubt have suffered anyhow during the early years of the Cold War, but more openness might have lessened the impact of the so-called $64 question: "Are you now or have you ever been?" In addition, while someone's formal affiliation may have remained a secret, his or her activities in the wider communist movement were not. As a result, it was not hard for anticommunist investigators in the 1940s and 1950s to uncover a pattern of behavior that all but labeled an individual a Communist. The duck test became prevalent: "If someone looks like a duck, waddles like a duck, and quacks like a duck. . . . "[54]

The ducks had not waddled randomly across American society. When the witch-hunters of the McCarthy era looked for witches, they knew exactly where to go. They sought out left-wing labor leaders, civil rights activists, and all the men and women who had collected money for the Spanish Republic, circulated petitions against nuclear war, or engaged in activities the Communist party promoted. Labor, civil rights, international affairs — if an issue was important to the CP, Communists were sure to be around. As a result, the individuals and organizations involved with causes backed by the party became, along with the CP itself, the main targets of the McCarthy era political repression.

All Communists were expected to reach beyond the party, engage in some kind of "mass" political work, and become active in other organizations. Theoretically, these organizations were supposed to serve as so-called "transmission belts" for the party's program and ideology as well as to bring in recruits. From the start, Communists threw themselves into organizing unions, their single most important activity. As the self-appointed vanguard of the American working class, the party could hardly ignore the workers' main institutions. Until the mid-1930s, however, the infighting, flip-flops, and sectarianism that plagued the CP kept it from having much of an impact on the labor movement. It could never decide whether to organize separate unions or "bore from within" already existing ones. But it did begin to assemble a corps of experienced cadres who in the 1930s would go on to build the United Automobile Workers (UAW) and the nation's other big industrial unions.[55]

Committed and competent, communist organizers led some of the most important labor struggles of the early thirties. From the coalfields of Kentucky to the San Francisco waterfront, they plotted strategy, recruited members, and organized picket lines. And they even won some strikes. The New Deal was the catalyst here. Unlike his Republican predecessors, Franklin Roosevelt seemed to encourage rather than oppose unions. New laws — especially the 1933 National Recovery Act and the Wagner Act, as the 1935 National Labor Relations Act was called — energized the entire labor movement. With the federal government's apparent blessing, previously unorganized workers in every field began to form new unions or join preexisting ones. Because the CP was already on the ground, with hundreds of experienced labor cadres, it was able to play a key role in what was to become the most important unionization drive in American history.[56]

Communists were especially influential within the new CIO, the organization of industrial unions that the powerful United Mine Workers president John L. Lewis formed in the mid-thirties when he broke with the older American Federation of Labor (AFL) over its refusal to organize unskilled workers. Since party members were already active within the very industries Lewis wanted to reach, he wasted little time recruiting them. Sixty of the two hundred full-time organizers the CIO threw into the steel industry were reputedly Communists. Lewis had no intention of handing control of his new venture over to the party, but he recognized that it could provide him with the experienced personnel he needed if his organizing drive was to succeed. "Who gets the bird," Lewis reputedly quipped, "the hunter or the dog?" And, in fact, once the temporary Steel Workers Organizing Committee evolved into a more established union in the early 1940s, its communist organizers were gone. But, for a few years, they had played a key role in mobilizing local support for the union and bringing steelworkers into it.[57]

Communists also helped organize the automobile industry, where they gave crucial leadership to what was arguably the single most important strike in American history: the 1937 sit-down at the Fisher Body plants in Flint, Michigan, that forced General Motors to recognize the United Auto Workers. Besides helping to coordinate the actual sit-down, the CP's cadres within the fledgling union drew on all the party's resources within the Detroit area to bolster picket lines, mimeograph leaflets, and provide the support services that enabled the striking autoworkers to hold out. Though its Communists were indispensable to building the UAW and remained an undeniable presence within it for years, they never dominated it and were ousted when the Cold War began.[58]

The CP retained more power on the waterfront. Sailors and dockworkers had a long tradition of radicalism; and the left-wing maritime unions that the party helped organize may well have had a higher proportion of Communists within their ranks than any other outfits within the CIO. On the West Coast, the International Longshoremen's and Warehousemen's Union (ILWU) led by Harry Bridges dominated the labor scene. Though he denied it for years, the Australian-born Bridges was probably a party member. An articulate labor leader, he came to power during a bloody 1934 maritime strike that brought San Francisco to the verge of class warfare. When the fighting stopped and the negotiations began, the ILWU was in control of the hiring system on the docks and was soon able to extend its influence beyond the Bay Area to the entire West Coast. By the end of World War II,

Bridges and his men had even organized the workers in the sugar-cane and pineapple plantations of Hawaii. Other waterfront unions, especially the National Maritime Union that dominated shipping on the East Coast and the small, heavily black West Coast Union of Marine Cooks and Stewards, also came within the party's orbit.[59]

The CP's flagship union was in the electrical industry. The United Electrical, Radio, and Machine Workers of America (UE) was the largest and most powerful organization run by Communists and their allies. Organized during the spurt of CIO activity in the late thirties, the UE grew along with its industry during World War II. It had important locals in the big Westinghouse and General Electric plants in Pennsylvania, New York State, and New England as well as units in dozens of smaller factories throughout the industrialized Northeast and Midwest. By the end of the war, it was the third-largest affiliate in the CIO and had a higher proportion of female members than any other big union. As in many of the other communist-controlled unions, the UE's president was not a party man, though its two other top officers and many of its staff members were. They ran their union in an effective and egalitarian manner, making a major point of the fact that no union official earned a higher salary than any of its members.[60]

Though communist labor leaders would no doubt have preferred to gain influence by organizing workers at the rank-and-file level, it sometimes happened that a particular union would come within the CP's orbit because its leaders recruited Communists as staff members and organizers. This was the case, for example, within the Denver-based International Union of Mine, Mill and Smelter Workers (Mine-Mill), whose increasingly erratic president came to depend on the party members he brought onto his staff. Mine-Mill represented a mixture of Anglo and Hispanic hard-rock miners in the West and Southwest, zinc and lead miners in the Midwest, black and white iron-ore miners in Birmingham, Alabama, and predominantly Irish and Italian metalworkers in Connecticut's Brass Valley. It was an unstable coalition; and as the CP's presence within Mine-Mill grew, so, too, did its factional infighting. Even before the end of World War II, the union was on the verge of flying apart.[61]

Mine-Mill's factionalism was typical of that which plagued most of the unions in which Communists were active. Typical, too, was its recruitment of minority workers. The ideology behind the party's brand of labor organizing emphasized the enfranchisement of the most oppressed members of the working class and accounted for the left-led unions' special efforts to reach blacks, Mexican Americans, women, and other workers whom the more mainstream labor organizations had overlooked. During the 1930s, these efforts led Communists into extraordinarily dangerous and unpromising organizing campaigns among such marginalized groups as migrant farmworkers in California's central valleys and sharecroppers in the Deep South. These ventures were not particularly successful, though the small unions that emerged from them usually remained close to the party.[62]

Ironically, Communists were also active in the white-collar unions at the other end of the labor spectrum. In part, this stemmed from the CP's appeal to middle-class intellectuals and professionals during the 1930s. Like their fellow Communists, these men and women believed that labor organizing was the most important work a party member could do. Accordingly, they enthusiastically applied their class consciousness and organizational skills to the task of building unions within their own fields. By the end of the decade, Communists and their allies had considerable influence within the guilds and unions that represented screenwriters, teachers, journalists, social workers, and architects, to name a few. Party members were also active in trying to unionize clerical workers and public employees. Though some of these organizing drives were just symbolic gestures, others did lift wages and improve working conditions.[63]

Along with the rest of the labor movement, the communist-influenced unions grew during World War II. By the end of the war, party members and their allies had control over unions representing perhaps 20 percent of the CIO's membership, including the 900,000-member UE, the ILWU, Mine-Mill, the National Maritime Union, the New York City–based Transit Workers Union, the Food, Tobacco, and Agricultural Workers Union, the openly communist Fur and Leather Workers Union, and a few white-collar unions. There were pockets of CP influence within the UAW and the Packinghouse Workers, as well as in several AFL unions. Party members were also active within the state and municipal industrial union councils and held important positions on the CIO's central staff.[64]

Communists and their allies had achieved power within the labor movement not because they had recruited large numbers of workers into the party, but because, on the whole, they were hard-working, honest, and effective union leaders. Until the Cold War rendered their positions untenable, they were able to retain the support of the noncommunist rank and file because they delivered the economic goods. Although their political convictions may have initially led them into the labor movement, some of them soon came to see themselves as unionists first and Communists second. They were, in short, dedicated labor leaders who, though better educated, more articulate, and more class-conscious than most, were primarily concerned with the institutional well-being of their organizations.[65]

A few of these people, like William Sentner, the UE's main leader in St. Louis, were open Communists. Most were not. Still, their political affiliations were usually known, or at least suspected. Until 1938 and again after World War II, most of the unions in which the CP was active had party "fractions" that met separately to discuss union issues and hammer out collective strategies.[66]

Most of the political, as opposed to economic, activities of the communist-led unions involved what one former party member called "the resolution bit," offering messages of solidarity and resolutions about political issues at annual conventions and local meetings. Depending on the party line of the moment, left-led unions supported the Scottsboro Boys, recognition of the Soviet Union, the Spanish Republic, the Second Front. Rarely did these unions' support for party causes go beyond passing resolutions, marching in May Day parades, contributing money, or publishing editorials in their newspapers. The only job-related actions that had to do with international affairs by a communist-controlled union that I have been able to find were the refusals of West Coast longshoremen to load scrap metal for Japan before the Second World War.[67]

Still, the public posturing of the CP-led unions did differentiate them from the rest of the labor movement. In retrospect, many ex-Communists believed that taking stands on matters that had nothing to do with labor had been a mistake. "We should have limited activity on [the] Marshall Plan and concentrated more on economic issues." When Cold War pressures built up, it was all too easy to cite the resolutions as evidence that the unions and their leaders were following the party line. "We were sitting ducks," a former UE organizer recalled. "We paid too much attention to Russia."[68]

There was, however, one vitally important area where the CP's directives transcended symbolism and pushed the unions it influenced to embark on substantive action — and that was race relations. The American workplace had long been segregated. Most traditional craft unions were lily white and many American workers were antiblack. Because of its commitment to racial equality, the party pressed its labor activists to fight discrimination in employment. This was not necessarily a popular position and in some unions, like New York City's largely Irish Transport Workers Union, communist leaders initially hesitated to confront their members on the matter. But the issue was too central to American Communism to be avoided and ultimately even the TWU began to press for the hiring of black motormen and bus drivers. During World War II, when African Americans broke the color line in previously closed industries, some left-wing unions even pioneered an early form of affirmative action to help these newly hired workers keep their jobs after the war.[69]

The Communists' support for racial equality did not endear them to white workers. But it did appeal to minority ones and gave some left-led unions like the NMU, Food and Tobacco, United Furniture Workers, and Mine-Mill a foothold in the South and in such racially diverse areas as Hawaii and the Southwest. As a result, once the anticommunist purges began, these unions were often more able to retain the loyalty of their African American and Hispanic members than their white ones. After all, as one black Mine-Mill worker explained, "I've never known a Communist in the labor movement to mob a man outside city hall, lynch him, castrate him, and everything else, even shoot him on sight. . . . It's the good white man who does that, you see. So, why am I going to go out and fight somebody who doesn't do the things that the good white folks have done?"[70]

The CP's commitment to African Americans was unique on the left and was, paradoxically, partly the result of pressure from Moscow. At its Sixth World Congress in 1928, the Comintern adopted a policy calling for a separate nation in the heavily black sections of the American South. Though clearly out of touch with American realities and the desires of African Americans for an end to poverty and discrimination, the "black belt" program, as it was called, did force American Communists to confront what was after all the worst social problem in the United States. As a result, the CP was for years the only primarily white organization not specifically devoted to civil rights to pay serious attention to African Americans.[71]

Though the party never attracted large numbers of blacks, it did have considerable appeal to certain groups within the African American community. Intellectuals, for example, were among its earliest recruits, drawn by the vision of the Soviet Union's supposedly interracial society as well as by the CP's anti-imperialism and later opposition to Mussolini's invasion of Ethiopia. Once the Depression hit, the party's economic programs and its street-level campaigns to obtain relief and prevent evictions brought visibility within the nation's major black ghettos. So, too, did its support for the judicial victims of Southern racism. The 1931 Scottsboro case of nine black teenagers arrested in Alabama for a rape they did not commit was crucial. The CP's legal arm, the International Labor Defense (ILD), organized the young men's defense and stirred up enough international outrage to save their lives. Throughout the next two decades, the party, first through the ILD and then through its successor organization, the Civil Rights Congress (CRC), was to take up the cases of the black victims of a biased legal system — both in the South and in the North.[72]

Especially during the 1940s and early 1950s, before the North had been fully desegregated, rank-and-file Communists threw themselves into the struggle against racial discrimination. They picketed segregated restaurants, amusement parks, and barber shops whose proprietors refused to cut African Americans' hair. They hired black secretaries at a time when white-collar jobs went only to whites. They tried to desegregate housing and even campaigned for the integration of professional baseball. The party's promotion of black culture was also ahead of the times. The CP supported the work of African American writers and artists and, decades before multiculturalism became prevalent, communist teachers were offering black history to students in Harlem and bringing African American culture into the curriculum.[73]

The CP was also sensitive to racial issues on a more personal level. The party struggled to create an oasis of genuine interracialism by helping its members overcome their own prejudice. Black and white Communists were expected to work and socialize together; and they often did. Even when it spun out of control, as it did during the campaign against "white chauvinism" in the 1950s that became so extreme people were allegedly expelled from the party for serving watermelon to their guests, the CP's attempt to create a multiracial community was, at the time, exceptional.[74]

Because Communism offered more than tokenism to its black members, it also gave them opportunities for leadership that did not exist in the outside world. Thus disproportionately large numbers of black cadres went to Moscow for training.[75] Nowhere was the party's emphasis on black leadership as evident as in the realm of electoral politics. In 1932 the CP ran James Ford for vice president, the first time any black had run for national office. Obviously, Ford's candidacy was more symbolic than real, but that was not the case with his successor as head of the Harlem branch of the CP, the lawyer Benjamin Davis, Jr., who was elected to the New York City Council on the Communist ticket in 1943. Davis's candidacy benefited from a coalition between the party and local activists who wanted Harlem to be represented by a black councilman and recognized that only the CP could deliver enough white votes to elect a black. By 1945, Davis was so entrenched in his post that he got the Democratic party's endorsement.[76]

Outside of New York, however, open communist participation in electoral activities rarely produced victories. And, in fact, there was something mildly absurd about the whole enterprise of communist presidential, gubernatorial, and school board candidates. Still, the party usually went through the motions, largely because, given the American context, using the electoral system was seen as a way to get the CP's message across. It was not a particularly rewarding activity — at its peak the party was able to garner only 102,991 votes for Foster and Ford in 1932. Steve Nelson was probably not alone in welcoming what he thought would be the end of the CP's electoral campaigns with the formation of the Communist Political Association. "By 1944 I had already gone through the Party's electoral efforts of 1928, 1932, 1936, and 1940, and I thought we weren't really doing anything effective in those elections. It was a formality, a hell of a lot of work gathering signatures, and no results." [77]

Communist participation in the electoral process, however, encompassed more than running candidates on the party's line. Both as individuals and as members of organized coalitions, Communists — both capital *C* and lowercase *c* ones — worked within major party and third-party campaigns. Their skill and dedication gave them more influence than their mere numbers might suggest. Though candidates may have welcomed individual

Communists as campaign workers, the party's outright support was another matter. As a result, much of the CP's electoral activity was under the table. In 1936, for example, though the party strongly backed the reelection of Franklin Roosevelt, it recognized that its open embrace might actually give substance to those of FDR's critics who claimed that he was a Communist in disguise. So it ran Earl Browder, while urging its members and sympathizers to work for FDR.

In most cases, during the 1930s and 1940s, Communists simply entered mainstream politics without openly identifying themselves. They were especially active in the political action committee that the CIO organized to bring out the vote for FDR in 1944. In California, the CP was an important — though unacknowledged — element in the Democratic party itself. "Nearly everyone in the local Democratic Party," a Los Angeles CP member complained about a meeting of precinct workers, "was a Communist." [78]

Besides their support for Franklin Roosevelt and the New Deal, Communists also participated in third parties. As in the labor movement, the issue of separatism arose: should the CP work within the regular two-party system or should it back other parties as well? In most cases, local conditions as well as the CP's line of the moment determined such decisions. Its main successes seem to have been in those states where a third party was able to establish itself as the local vehicle for the New Deal. This happened in New York City, where the largely Jewish labor movement organized the American Labor party (ALP) as a way to avoid the machine politics of the regular Democratic party and support both FDR and the Republican reform mayor Fiorello La Guardia. Communists quickly became central to the new party. Mike Quill, the communist leader of the Transport Workers Union, was able to win election to the New York City Council on the ALP line. Similarly, in Minnesota, party members were active in the Farmer-Labor party during the 1930s; and in Washington State, they worked within the Washington Commonwealth Federation, a left-wing pro–New Deal coalition that elected fourteen state legislators. [79]

The most important, as well as the most ill-fated, third-party venture was the CP's participation in the 1948 Progressive party presidential campaign of former vice president Henry Wallace. Given Wallace's stature as the main political heir to FDR's old left-liberal coalition, his opposition to Truman's involvement in the Cold War, and his courageous support of racial equality, it is hard to imagine the American communist movement *not* supporting him. But that support was counterproductive. Though Wallace wanted to distance his campaign from the CP, he could not do so. And the party, seemingly oblivious to the disastrous impact it was having on the Progressive party's chances, only worsened the situation. Fearful of being seen as Browderists, the CP's leaders refused to replicate Browder's 1936 strategy of mounting a separate campaign, even though Wallace himself admitted publicly that "if the Communists would run a ticket of their own this year, we might lose 100,000 votes but we would gain three million." Even worse, the party made the campaign seem subservient to Moscow by blocking a resolution at the Progressive party's convention that would deny a "blanket endorsement to the foreign policy of any nation." [80]

Besides hurting their candidate, the CP's participation in the Wallace campaign damaged the rest of the communist movement. Its demand that its labor cadres back the Progressive party destroyed whatever influence the party had within the mainstream of the labor movement. The left-wing union leaders realized that support for Wallace would bring them into direct conflict with CIO president Philip Murray, but the CP ordered them to back the third-party campaign, "even if," as the party's New York State chairman admitted, "it splits the C.I.O. right down the middle." A few labor leaders, including the TWU's Mike Quill, balked and left the CP; others followed the party line, defied Murray, and were forced out of the CIO a year later. [81]

As the presidential campaign wound down in the fall of 1948, many of Wallace's noncommunist supporters began to jump ship. Truman's liberalism, the fear of a Republican victory, and the communist domination of the Progressive party were decisive. As a result, instead of the four to five million votes Wallace's supporters expected, he got a million and a half. His defeat was particularly crushing to the CP, for it destroyed the mystique that had developed about the party's political prowess. American Communism, for all the continuing dedication of its adherents, was revealed as a marginal force within the United States. Its obvious political isolation was to make it increasingly vulnerable to attack. At the time, however, nobody on the left or elsewhere realized that the Progressive party campaign was going to be the last significant activity the CP would participate in. From then on, American Communism would turn inward, defending the core of party-affiliated organizations and clinging to the organizational gains of an earlier era.[82]

Those gains had been significant. During its more vibrant periods, the Communist party had been at the center of a dynamic left-wing world composed of dozens of organizations. Labor unions were the most important, but there were also the party's many front groups, the main vehicles through which the CP reached out into the rest of American society. Every Communist was expected to join one or more of these organizations. There were all kinds of them: dance groups, professional societies, refugee relief organizations, adult education centers, summer camps, legal defense groups, choral societies, tenants committees, bookstores, theatrical troupes, peace groups, folk music clubs, ethnic and fraternal societies, literary magazines. The list seems endless, though, in fact, most of the groups dealt with international solidarity, political defense, culture, education, and professional or ethnic concerns.

By offering its supporters so many outlets, the CP had created a separate society, a self-contained subculture that reinforced its adherents' political commitment. It was possible for Communists to find a front group or other party-linked activity that would satisfy just about every social, political, and personal need they might have. There were even singles resorts that helped lonely left-wingers find partners. Especially in those cities with a political density that supported it, party members could live in an entirely communist world where even their dentists and dry cleaners were in the movement. The informal ties that bound these people together were even more important. Friends and family all belonged to the same left-wing world. Its value for maintaining the cohesion and commitment of the communist movement and its members cannot be overestimated.[83]

Because Lenin and his colleagues described the front groups as "transmission belts" for the party, there has been a tendency on the part of later commentators, both friendly and hostile, to discuss these groups mainly in terms of their autonomy or lack thereof from the CP itself. Such an approach loses sight of the actual functions of these organizations and of the different ways in which they contributed to shaping American Communism's unique subculture. Still, the relationship of these adjunct outfits to the party is certainly crucial to understanding how they operated. Whether they were membership or letterhead organizations, all or nearly all of them were staffed by party cadres; their officers, however, were usually eminent non-Communists whose presence was supposed to lend prestige and respectability to the venture. Sometimes, especially during the more sectarian phases of the CP's history, these groups appealed mainly to party members; at other times they reached a much broader constituency.[84]

Few of these groups were explicitly communist; their letterheads did not read "The Civil Rights Congress: A Communist Front." Still, the secrecy that was so deleterious to the CP's union and electoral work was not quite so problematical for these outfits. In most cases, it was pretty obvious that the organizations were close to the party. They would pass resolutions on the issues of the day, send contingents to May Day parades, and do whatever they could to advance the communist cause. Thus, for example, in 1932, during a protest meeting in Washington, a CP-influenced farmers organization demanded the recognition of the Soviet Union as well as a moratorium on mortgage payments. In 1934, the first issue of the *Partisan Review,* then the literary outlet of New York City's communist writers club, announced that it had enlisted "in the struggle of the workers and sincere intellectuals against imperialist war, fascism, national and racial oppression" and added that the "defense of the Soviet Union is one of our principal tasks."[85]

These groups served and serviced the CP and their members in many ways. The largest, and the one which may have reached the least politicized clientele, was the International Workers Order (IWO), a fraternal benefit society established in 1930 by the communist faction within the main left-wing Jewish fraternal group in New York City. In many respects the most successful of the front groups, the IWO enrolled nearly 190,000 members at its peak in 1947. From the start, the group's political stance was obvious. "The International Workers Order is more than an insurance organization," its founders announced. "It is part of the fighting front of the working class." Its main leaders were high-level cadres and it routinely supported all the CP's causes, raising money and passing resolutions on everything from the Scottsboro boys to the Second Front. During the early 1930s, the IWO even endorsed communist political candidates.[86]

But it was not politics that built the organization. One scholar estimates that only 7.3 percent of the IWO's members were actually in the CP in the mid-1930s; the rest joined to obtain its low-cost insurance and take part in its cultural activities. Licensed as an insurance carrier in eighteen states and the District of Columbia, the IWO operated just like any other insurance company except that, unlike most commercial insurers, it did not charge higher rates to blacks or people in risky occupations like coal mining. By the late 1940s, it had also set up medical plans in New York, Chicago, Detroit, and Los Angeles that offered a full range of services from doctors' house calls to dental work, all for $4.30 a month. The IWO also covered funeral expenses and ran cemeteries in fourteen cities for its "departed policy holders." [87]

Organized along ethnic lines, the IWO was a federation of some thirteen nationality groups, with the bulk of its membership in its Jewish and Slavic units. There were Russian groups and Ukrainian, Slovak, Hungarian, Croat, Serb, Polish, and Czech sections, even a separate Carpatho-Russian section, as well as smaller Greek, Finnish, Hispanic, and Italian groups. African American members presented a problem; the IWO welcomed them, but because of the CP's opposition to segregation, never let them organize a separate section. Each group sponsored a wide variety of cultural and recreational activities. Many of these programs had a strong political component. The Jewish section's Yiddish schools taught the works of Lenin and celebrated the October Revolution. But there were also IWO drum and bugle corps that marched in local Labor Day parades in the Midwest as well as choral societies, athletic teams, and dance groups. [88]

The IWO offered the communist movement perhaps its most important entree into the ethnic working-class community. Active members could be recruited into the party, and fraternal lodges could be mobilized in support of left-wing causes. When the CIO began its organizing drive in the steel industry, it relied heavily on the IWO's lodges, leaders, and members as its institutional core of support within the largely Slavic workforce. [89]

The IWO's fortunes fluctuated with those of the CP. The Nazi-Soviet pact, for example, cost it several thousand Jewish members, though the decline in its overall membership, from 161,000 to 155,000, was not enormous. It recouped during the war, when it became particularly active within the Slavic community by taking advantage of its connections with the Soviet Union and the anti-Nazi partisans in Eastern Europe. By 1946, the organization had become so respectable that its Jewish component was accepted as a constituent organization by the mainstream American Jewish Congress. Three years later, it was expelled. Despite the nonpolitical nature of its main operation, the IWO's ties to the communist movement rendered it vulnerable to all the pressures that erupted during the McCarthy years.[90]

While a group like the IWO might sponsor a wide range of activities, other front groups had narrower missions, typically focused on a single cause or project. The Joint Anti-Fascist Refugee Committee (JAFRC), for example, was organized in 1941 to help refugees from Spain who had fled to France after the end of the Spanish Civil War. The American Committee for Protection of the Foreign Born (ACPFB) defended party-linked immigrants against deportation. The Council on African Affairs supported the left-wing Pan-African movement's struggle against imperialism. Most of these groups came into existence in the late thirties and early forties and lasted until they were destroyed by the political repression of the McCarthy period. Some groups were even more ephemeral — ad hoc organizations formed to support a single defendant or mount a one-time event.

Most of these front groups were organized by Communists and were clearly within the CP's orbit. But there were a few other organizations that, like the left-wing labor unions, were not really front groups, but rather genuine coalitions in which party members and nonmembers worked together. One of the most important of these groups was the National Lawyers Guild. A product of the same drive toward collective action that resulted in the founding of white-collar unions like the Screenwriters Guild and American Newspaper Guild, the NLG became the main institutional expression of the Popular Front within the legal profession.[91]

At its founding toward the end of 1936, the Guild brought together a group of liberal and left-wing lawyers who were alienated by the business-oriented, anti-Semitic, lily-white legal establishment represented by the American Bar Association. All the NLG's members supported labor and the New Deal, but they came from very different sectors of the legal profession. Many, perhaps most, were small practitioners who were barely making a living during the Depression. Catholics, Jews, and blacks, they had been barred from the major law firms and were attracted by the Guild's interest in raising the economic status of the poorer members of the bar. The organization also appealed to the legal profession's intellectual elites — the best and the brightest of the New Deal lawyers, as well as law school professors, a few judges, and some civil libertarians.[92]

Politically, the Guild's leaders ranged from liberals like the ACLU's co-counsel Morris Ernst and future Supreme Court justices Robert Jackson and Abe Fortas to Communists like the labor lawyers Lee Pressman, Maurice Sugar, and Nathan Witt. The Guild's executive secretary was a party member as well. But there was also an important contingent of independent radicals and civil libertarians whose presence ensured that the NLG did not disintegrate when the Popular Front fell apart nor disappear entirely during the McCarthy era. Because it was a coalition and allied with, but not actually run by, the Communist party, the Guild, like the left-wing labor unions, was wracked by internal conflicts that ultimately led its more conservative members to resign.[93]

During the Cold War, all of these groups, from the IWO to the NLG, came under fire and most of them disappeared. They and their members were, along with the party and the left-led unions, the witch-hunters' main targets. Even the genuinely apolitical individual who was occasionally affected usually turned out to be someone who had an, albeit innocuous, connection to the broader world of American Communism: perhaps she had once sent a check to the Spanish refugees or his father had owned an IWO insurance policy.

Thus, even when it seemed most capricious, there was nothing random about the Cold War crusade against American Communism. The targets it chose, the weapons it wielded, had been, in a sense, preselected by the movement it opposed. Though the CP itself was to survive the repression unleashed against it, the larger universe within which the party operated did not. The front groups and labor unions that were so central to the communist movement's dynamism and to whatever broader influence it had were all destroyed. McCarthyism had set out to eradicate Communism from American society; and it did. The party, through both its own failings and its successes, facilitated the process.

★

CHAPTER 2

"RED-BAITERS, INC."

THE DEVELOPMENT OF AN ANTICOMMUNIST NETWORK

THE FBI was stymied. For over two years, the Bureau had been engaged in the exhaustive task of compiling a compendium of legally admissible evidence that would prove the unlawful status of the Communist party. From every field office, agents had sent in massive reports on the party's activities in their areas. In Washington, the Bureau's top experts on Communism sorted through this material, eventually amalgamating it into a 1,700-page brief that they hoped would provide the basis for taking the party to court. But there were gaps in its historical record. At a strategy session toward the end of 1947, the Bureau's executives suggested that in order to get the necessary information, "we consider approaching discreetly trusted representatives of the AF of L and the DAR and that we consider contacting Monsignor Fulton J. Sheen, Walter Steele, Ray Murphy, Ben Mandel, Karl Baarslag and Father Walsh." [1]

This was not a random list. With perhaps the exception of Monsignor Sheen, whose weekly radio broadcasts had made him the most well known Catholic priest in the United States, the other figures mentioned by the FBI were hardly household names, but they were key members of a surprisingly self-conscious and effective network that helped shape the anticommunist crusade of the 1940s and 1950s. Labor leaders, journalists, priests, bureaucrats, ex-Communists, and ordinary private citizens — the members of this network came from many backgrounds but were all committed to the task of eradicating Communism from American life. They had devoted their lives to the project and because of their alleged "expertise" about the CP were to have an inordinate amount of influence over the anticommunist crusade of the early Cold War. The FBI's list contained the names of some, though not all, of the network's main members.

No one, for example, was as indispensable to the network as the former New York City typing teacher Benjamin Mandel. An ex-Communist repeatedly described as "the best-informed person in this country who is doing such work," and "a fountain of knowledge regarding persons and details in connection with the Communist Party," Mandel had been an activist in the New York City Teachers Union in the 1920s before becoming a full-time party organizer in Boston and New York and briefly serving as the business manager of the *Daily Worker*. But he had allied himself with Jay Lovestone's faction within the CP and when Lovestone was expelled in 1929, Mandel's party career came to an abrupt end. After flirting with a variety of smaller radical sects, Mandel finally broke with the left and found a new home within the anticommunist world. By the end of the 1930s, he was on the staff of the newly formed House Un-American Activities Committee (HUAC). In 1951 he became the research director of Senator Pat McCarran's Senate Internal Security Subcommittee (SISS), a position that allowed him to design many of the most important congressional investigations of the entire McCarthy era.[2]

Mandel's trajectory, from the CP to the Senate, was typical of that of the former party cadres who metamorphosed into professional anti-Communists. Other members of the network developed their expertise on Communism in other ways. Often, they simply collected names from left-wing publications and the letterheads of front groups. Walter Steele, another figure on the FBI's list and a professional patriot who published his own anticommunist newsletter, was one such pack rat. He had been accumulating material and indexing names for decades; by the late 1940s, he had compiled information on some forty thousand people, which he willingly shared with congressional committees and such organizations as the FBI, the Civil Service Commission, and the American Legion. Raymond Murphy was the same kind of anticommunist professional; as the State Department's in-house countersubversive, he had been tracking Soviet agents in the United States since the 1920s.[3]

Karl Baarslag was yet another network stalwart who, as he put it in his unpublished autobiography, "avidly collected stamps and former Communist and Soviet defectors." He had gotten into the anticommunist business by way of the labor movement, where he had been active in a small maritime radio-telegraphers union. After his faction lost out to the union's Communists, Baarslag became a naval intelligence officer specializing in communist affairs. In 1947, he landed a position in the American Legion where he published a monthly bulletin and oversaw what he claimed was "a sort of national clearing house for dedicated and intelligent anti-Communists from all over the country."[4]

An even more important member of the anticommunist network was J. B. Matthews, a former Methodist minister who had initially recruited Benjamin Mandel to HUAC's staff in 1939. During the 1930s, Matthews had been (at least by his own account) one of the nation's leading fellow travelers, the head of the largest left-wing peace group in America. After he split with the movement, Matthews parlayed his massive collection of left-wing letterheads and memorabilia into a lucrative career as a consultant for clients ranging from Joe McCarthy to the Hearst Corporation. A host whose dinner party invitations conferred status to all anticommunist wannabes, Matthews was at the very center of the network, the unofficial éminence grise of American anticommunism. He and Mandel collaborated for years, sharing information and doing whatever they could to further their mutual cause.[5]

And then there was Alfred Kohlberg, a New York City lace importer with extensive business connections in prerevolutionary China. A key network supporter, Kohlberg funded a wide variety of Republican politicians, anticommunist organizations, and right-wing publications. With the help of Father John F. Cronin, one of the Catholic Church's main countersubversives, Kohlberg backed a group of former FBI agents whose newsletter, *Counterattack,* specialized in exposing Communists in the entertainment industry and elsewhere. Kohlberg's chief claim to fame, however, was his role in the so-called China Lobby, an informal group of politicians and opinion makers who disseminated the charge that Communists within the State Department had somehow "lost" China to Mao Zedong.[6]

What gave the network its effectiveness were the personal and institutional contacts among its members. In addition to his work with the

SISS, Benjamin Mandel corresponded regularly with Matthews and Kohlberg, helped Baarslag edit a short-lived anticommunist newsletter, gave information to the FBI, and screened entertainers for the Hollywood
blacklist. Besides pooling their information, Mandel and the other members of the anticommunist network got each other jobs and found financial
backing for one another's projects. Not counting FBI agents and military intelligence officers, there may have been several hundred of these "real hard-
core antis," as Baarslag called his network colleagues. His papers contain a
list of some 130 names; the guest list for a 1954 testimonial dinner for the
chief counsel of the McCarran Committee has about 240. The core group
was probably smaller. The State Department's Ray Murphy estimated it at
about sixty to seventy-five real experts, most of whom knew and worked
with each other.[7]

Though rather shadowy figures to the American public, Mandel and
his colleagues were indispensable to the anticommunist crusade. In the
late 1930s and again after World War II, when the nation's political leaders became concerned about Communism, these dedicated activists were
already in place, with an elaborately developed set of explanations and
remedies that mainstream politicians — who actually knew very little about
the CP — could employ. As a result, the professional anti-Communists became disproportionately influential in shaping the political repression of
the McCarthy period. They selected its targets and developed the mechanisms through which that repression operated. Even more important, because they were considered the nation's leading experts on the subject, they
came to dominate the national debate about domestic Communism, shaping
the ideas that most ordinary Americans, as well as politicians, held about
Communists. They had, in short, a lot of power.[8]

The network was more than a collection of individuals. The Baarslags, Man-
dels, and Matthewses had institutional connections with specific interest
groups and organizations that had their own reasons for promoting anticommunism. As the cause attracted new supporters, the network became
increasingly diverse and influential. By the late 1940s just about every important sector of American society had representatives within its ranks.
These anti-Communists came in all political flavors. Eventually most of

them drifted to the right, but when they first joined the crusade, many of them, like Matthews and Mandel, thought of themselves as radicals. The network did not expand in a single direction, whether from right to left or the reverse. If anything, it could be described as a movement from the margins to the center.[9]

But it was a turbulent center. During its heyday in the 1940s and 1950s, American anticommunism reverberated with anxiety. Even today, the subject evokes such an emotional response that it is clear it must have touched some deeper recesses within the national psyche. At the time, liberal critics treated the phenomenon (or at least that part of it they called McCarthyism) as a mental aberration, a moment of national madness that deviated sharply from the otherwise commonsensical trajectory of American history. Such explanations came easily to the social scientists of the day, who, more than anyone else, structured the way that the anticommunist crusade is still conceptualized. The fifties were, after all, the heyday of American Freudianism, when almost all human problems were interpreted as the products of individual psychopathology. Though social science has long since abandoned the promiscuous psychologizing of that era, its intellectual residue remains in the medicalized metaphors that come to mind when McCarthyism is described: paranoia, delirium, frenzy, hysteria.[10]

Such language is disturbing. If there are less-complicated explanations for the anticommunist crusade, is it necessary to resort to the psychiatrist's couch? And yet to deny the irrationality at the heart of McCarthyism is to misinterpret that phenomenon just as surely as reducing it to only a neurotic symptom would be. For the fervid anticommunism of the early Cold War did tap into something dark and nasty in the human soul. What happened during these years was not just politics as usual. There was a strong element of irrationality, and though that irrationality cannot explain everything that happened, it cannot be overlooked. If nothing else, it "helps explain the structure of the countersubversive imagination," as Michael Rogin, the most insightful interpreter of this strain of American political demonology, so thoughtfully noted.[11]

That countersubversive imagination or tradition, as Rogin also calls it, was at the emotional center of the anticommunist crusade, the source of that movement's special intensity. In its most basic form, the countersubversive tradition embraced the notion that some kind of alien external force had entered the body politic and threatened to destroy it from within. During the 1940s and 1950s, that alien force was Communism and the countersubversive tradition expressed itself by demonizing the American CP, making Communism into an evil caricature of itself, and transforming its adherents into abnormal beings.[12]

The countersubversive tradition can be traced back to the Mayflower and may, in fact, be endemic to all human societies that seek to ostracize the "other" and deny the humanity of whatever groups or individuals those societies repress or otherwise refuse to accept. Contemporary scholars offer profuse and often convincing explanations for this impulse. There is, for example, considerable validity to the view that the process of demonization makes it easier for people in power to retain their control. By picturing subordinate groups or nations as peculiarly barbaric and dangerous, the countersubversive tradition enables the powers that be to present themselves as potential victims. Demonizing and, thus, dehumanizing the people they actually oppress not only offers the dominant groups a way to reaffirm their own sense of superiority, but also makes it psychologically possible to deprive their victims of their basic human rights. Even today that process may be at work, transforming poor women into "welfare mothers."[13]

Whatever combination of guilt, sexuality, aggression, or other impulses produce the countersubversive mind-set, Americans have never suffered from a shortage of scapegoated aliens. In its early years, native Americans and African slaves supposedly threatened the nation from within. In the nineteenth century, the demonization had spread to Catholics and immigrants. By the mid-twentieth century, Communists, a political minority, had supplanted the earlier racial, religious, and ethnic subgroups as the most common version of this subversive "other."

Significantly, the language of demonization remains constant. The upholders of the countersubversive tradition use the same figures of speech whether defending the values of Puritanism against the subversive Iroquois, maintaining the Anglo-Saxon establishment against a wave of Irish and later East European immigrants, or protecting the American way of life against the threat of Communism. The enemy within is rarely human. Earlier generations of Americans called Indians "monsters," "infuriated hell-hounds" with a "native thirst for human blood." They viewed nineteenth-century immigrants as "venomous reptiles," "the very scum and offal of Europe."

And in the mid-twentieth century, Communists were, among other things, "poisonous germs," "snakes," "tigers," "rats," "termites," and "slime."[14]

And always the situation is critical. Eighteenth-century slaves in revolt would "possess themselves of the whole Country" and proceed to the "utter Extirpation" of white inhabitants. In the 1840s, Catholic immigrants put "our very institutions . . . at the mercy of a body of foreigners." A few decades later, it was radicals who, in the words of a late-nineteenth-century newspaper editor, threatened "our National existence, and, as well, our National and social institutions." By 1948, when a former FBI agent surveyed the problem for the National Security Council, Communism had become "a far greater threat to our existence than any other threat," so dangerous that if the United States "does not successfully cope with the Communist threat, then it need not worry about any other threat to the internal security of this nation, because it is not impossible that there will be no nation."[15]

The same language, the same patterns of thought, pervade all these conceptualizations. The dehumanizing of the supposed threat as well as the quasi-hysterical tone in which it is addressed are too similar not to have come from some common source. It is easy to find traces of the earlier waves of countersubversion in the political repression of the McCarthy era. After all, a strong current of hostility to the left had always been a staple of American political life. It existed long before the Cold War brought the anticommunist network to power, long before the Communist party itself came into being. Just as the first generation of American Communists had emerged from the preexisting socialist and syndicalist movements, so, too, the earliest members of the anticommunist network came from previously established centers of antiradical activity that had been in operation for nearly half a century.[16]

Anticommunism in its modern form as a consciously organized campaign against the left began in the 1870s. The Paris Commune of 1870–71 and the great railroad strikes of 1877 had turned vague fears of working-class revolution into reality. As industrial capitalism developed within the United States, the greater visibility of urban poverty exacerbated by periodic crises of unemployment made the possibility of social unrest a real source of concern for both the business community and the respectable middle classes. That so many of the new industrial workers were foreign-born only intensified this concern, enabling it to feed off the emotions associated with the countersubversive tradition's long-standing demonization of immigrants. An equally powerful element here was the hostility of important segments of the business community to organized labor.[17]

Anticommunism gave employers an effective way to fight labor unions. If there is any one element that, along with the targeting of foreigners, remains constant throughout the history of American political repression, it is the way in which those business groups that were most hostile to organized labor tapped into the countersubversive tradition to gain support for suppressing unions. Until the issue of national security became paramount during and after World War II, most major red scares occurred in response to labor unrest. Red-baiting offered anti-union employers a way to legitimize opposition to organized labor without having to refer to economic issues.

Routinely employed, this technique first appeared in response to the industrial unrest and working-class movements of the 1870s and 1880s. As was to become common in such situations, businessmen and their allies in the press and government circulated charges of foreign subversion. They mounted the usual appeals to the anti-immigrant sentiments of the American public. In addition, they played upon the violence that sometimes accompanied the repression of strikes and demonstrations as well as the radical rhetoric of such revolutionary groups as anarchists to drive a wedge between the organized workers and the rest of the nation.

The most ferocious of these early red scares occurred in response to the Haymarket tragedy of 1886, when a bomb exploded in the midst of a group of policemen at a Chicago labor demonstration. In the wave of what one observer called "police terrorism" that followed the bombing, hundreds of foreigners, radicals, and union leaders were arrested. Anarchists, who were presumably behind the violence, were the main victims; after a rigged show trial, four of the movement's leaders were executed. Just as McCarthyism was to do sixty years later, the Haymarket red scare destroyed the entire left. When the furor finally subsided, not only were the anarchists crushed, but the main working-class organization of the 1880s, the Knights of Labor, had also disappeared. For the leaders of what would become the nation's dominant labor organization, the newly formed American Federation of Labor, the lesson was clear. From then on they would distance themselves from anything that even hinted of radicalism.[18]

Significantly, that first wave of antiradical repression also sparked the development of a countersubversive infrastructure within the nation's law-enforcement community. Until the federal government intervened during World War I, local police forces and their allies in the private sector handled most of the actual work of political repression. They were among the earliest recruits to the anticommunist network and the techniques they developed to harass the left were to be deployed for years to come. In the nation's major cities, as well as in the steel and coal towns of Pennsylvania, West Virginia, Ohio, and Alabama, state and municipal authorities put radicals and union organizers under surveillance. They also clamped down on these people's activities by selectively enforcing local ordinances against public meetings, littering, vagrancy, and disturbing the peace. In three hundred scheduled public appearances between 1908 and 1911, the anarchist leader Emma Goldman was arrested over a hundred times.[19]

Police departments had close ties with some segments of the business community. Often, they were directly on the corporate payroll. Chicago businessmen paid that city's finest a $100,000 annual subsidy in the five years after the Haymarket bombing. Similar arrangements existed in Los Angeles, New York, Detroit, and elsewhere. There was a thin line here between the subsidized antisubversive activities of local and state police and those of private security agencies like the Pinkertons. And, in fact, there was considerable overlap between the two. Not only were they sometimes paid by the same employers, but they often did the same kind of work — breaking strikes and infiltrating unions and left-wing organizations. They also shared an interest in exaggerating the danger of radicalism in order to drum up the lucrative business that red-squad work provided.[20]

Containing radicals was also, at least within the law enforcement community, a source of prestige. Though used by business interests to put down unions, police officials were not just hired hands. The nation's red squads were elite outfits that attracted ambitious lawmen who prized the professional status of the assignment as well as its patriotic value and intrinsic interest. These officials shared a common mind-set, one that came to dominate the law enforcement community at every level. Its members had an ideological and occupational stake in countersubversion and the suppression of dissent; and they brought to the anticommunist network both a propensity for repression and the technical means for achieving it. The hierarchical, quasi-military structure of the nation's police forces reinforced the inherent authoritarianism of their work. They were also predisposed to countersubversion, perceiving themselves as a beleaguered minority, a "thin blue line," maintaining order in a hostile world.[21]

J. Edgar Hoover is perhaps the most well known personification of this law-and-order mentality; certainly he was its most important representative within the anticommunist network. And his views may well be typical of those of his professional colleagues. Even though he was a native of Washington, D.C., and had grown up on Seward Square just a few blocks from the Capitol, Hoover represented an essentially provincial middle-class culture that, as his biographer Richard Gid Powers puts it, shared "the values of the old Seward Square itself, those of Southern, white, Christian, small-town, turn-of-the-century Washington." Hoover taught Sunday school, joined the Masons, and, throughout his career, pushed the traditional values of family, flag, and church.[22]

The director led an emotionally constricted life. Except for his mother, with whom he lived until he was forty-three, Hoover had few personal attachments and spent most of his time in the almost entirely male world of the FBI, usually in the company of his number two man, Clyde Tolson. It is possible that there was a connection between the nearly pathological rigidity of Hoover's personal habits and his lifetime obsession with Communism. To the extent that the CP stood for the forces that menaced the FBI director's orderly world, it could be seen as a direct challenge to his very being. Certainly, Hoover's rhetoric, with its panicky jeremiads about the decline in moral values and the need for reinforcing the family, is suffused with excess emotion. But that kind of language was standard at the time. Hoover was hardly the only member of the anticommunist network who used such overblown rhetoric or described Communism as a threat to Christianity and Western civilization.[23]

The FBI director's bureaucratic politicking was as crucial to the development of the law enforcement component of the anticommunist network as his cultural concerns. Hoover was an empire builder and it is hard to ignore the opportunistic elements that pervaded his and his agency's handling of the communist threat. But again, though the FBI's operations were so central to the anticommunist crusade that I am devoting all of chapter 6 to a discussion of them, they were not unique. Officials in other agencies — military intelligence officers and immigration inspectors, for example — shared the same agenda and had the same hostility toward the alleged unruliness of the left. And, as we shall see, they often collaborated with the FBI in putting it down.

The distinctions between the official forces of law and order and the unofficial ones were not always clear. Vigilantism was common; voluntary outfits like patriotic and veterans groups had close ties to local red squads. When they doffed their uniforms, many policemen put on their American Legion caps and helped break strikes. In the South, local red squads worked with the Ku Klux Klan. In Detroit, the Black Legion, a KKK-type organization that specialized in bombing radical meeting halls and bookstores, had a hundred recruits within the police department. These vigilante groups flourished throughout the early part of the twentieth century but became especially important during and after the First World War, just at that moment when American anticommunism officially came into being.[24]

World War I gave the fledgling forces of anticommunism their initial opportunity to influence national politics when, for the first time, national security became central to the repression of left-wing dissent. The wartime and postwar crises not only enabled the traditional opponents of radicalism to wrap themselves in the flag, but also brought the vastly greater resources of the federal government onto the scene. Washington could deport foreign-born radicals; it could also prosecute them under the wartime espionage and sedition laws; it could even call out the army. Though much of the impetus for such activities came, as before, from those sectors of the business community that were hostile to organized labor, an additional incentive came from the government's desire to eliminate all opposition to the war. In 1917, for example, a successful organizing drive in the West by the radical Industrial Workers of the World (IWW) ran into federal as well as employer opposition. President Woodrow Wilson invoked national security and sent the army to crush strikes in the lumber camps of Washington State and the copper mines of Montana. Not only did the government want to maintain production, but, more important, it also wanted to punish the Wobblies (as the IWW's members were called) for opposing the war.[25]

Had the rest of the American public been wholeheartedly enthusiastic about the conflict, the administration might not have been so repressive. But the nation was seriously divided. After all, American voters had reelected Wilson in 1916 in large part because he ran as a peace candidate; he had, so his campaign slogan went, "kept us out of war." As the United States edged toward belligerency, large sectors of the population remained reluctant to intervene. Midwesterners were particularly hostile to a conflict that they saw as benefiting the international bankers of Wall Street. But so, too, were the millions of foreign-born workers who had little enthusiasm for a war against their former homelands or in alliance with their previous oppressors. The main left-wing organizations, the IWW and the Socialist party, also opposed the war. Though that opposition expressed itself more in rhetoric than in action, the possibility that a class-conscious antiwar movement might reach the largely immigrant working class worried the Wilson administration. It sought to head off this prospect by wooing the nation's mainstream labor unions and carrying out a massive propaganda campaign while at the same time stifling dissent. The patriotic firestorm that erupted victimized both radicals and foreigners; and it set precedents for future political repression as well.[26]

Journalists and politicians demonized Germans, creating stereotypes that were later transferred from the dreaded Huns to the equally dreaded Bolsheviks. Some of the frenzy that this propaganda encouraged was vented symbolically: schools no longer taught German, symphony orchestras stopped playing Wagner, and sauerkraut was renamed "liberty cabbage." Some was more vicious. Mobs beat up, tarred and feathered, or, in a few cases, even lynched Germans, Wobblies, and lukewarm patriots. Across the country, antiwar teachers and civil servants lost their jobs. The Department of Justice encouraged the activities of the American Protective League, a business-supported quasi-vigilante group of 250,000 private citizens who rounded up draft dodgers and looked for spies with more enthusiasm than due process.[27]

The federal government also cracked down on opponents of the war. The Espionage Act of 1917 made it illegal to interfere with the draft. A year later, the Sedition Act criminalized "disloyal, profane, scurrilous or abusive language" about the government, Constitution, flag, or "uniform of the Army or Navy." Wilson and his Attorney General, Thomas W. Gregory, pushed the measure in order to head off an even more repressive bill that threatened to turn miscreants over to the army. These laws were rigorously enforced. Postmaster General Albert Burleson, for example, interpreted the Espionage Act's provisions against the mailing of treasonous literature so broadly that he destroyed or crippled dozens of left-wing and foreign-language publications.[28]

Nor did the Justice Department shrink from prosecuting the Socialists, anarchists, and Wobblies who opposed the war. In September 1917, federal agents raided sixty-four IWW offices around the nation to gain evidence for cases against the organization. The government then staged mass trials of Wobblies all over the country, including one in Chicago with 166 defendants. The Socialist party got hit as well. The Justice Department prosecuted many of its top leaders, among them its 1912 presidential candidate, Eugene Debs, and the Milwaukee politician Victor Berger, indicted while he was campaigning for the Senate. Before the furor ended, the Wilson administration had brought 2,168 people to trial under the Espionage and Sedition Acts.[29]

These trials foreshadowed the anticommunist prosecutions of the Cold War in both their procedures and their outcomes. In the IWW cases, for example, the government, as it was later to do when prosecuting the CP, based its case almost entirely on the organization's literature, rather than on its activities. The trials also featured professional informers and ex-Wobblies who were coerced into testifying. Technically, the government's case against many of these radicals was not very strong, forcing the Justice Department to drop many prosecutions before they came to trial. Nonetheless, given the hysteria of the times, convictions were easy to obtain; and the federal judiciary, including the Supreme Court, rarely overruled them. The situation was considered to be so critical that ordinary free speech had to be waived. Similar justifications would resurface in the 1940s and 1950s.

Whether or not they resulted in convictions, the prosecutions in and of themselves were as devastating to the Socialists and Wobblies as the Cold War ones would be to the Communists. There was considerable personal suffering. A few IWWs, for example, languished in jail for years before their cases were dropped. Though the Supreme Court ultimately reversed Berger's conviction, it upheld Debs's and he remained in the Atlanta Federal Penitentiary until late 1921. On an institutional level, the Socialist party was seriously hurt by the wartime crackdown and the IWW essentially destroyed. It had to devote all of its dwindling resources to self-defense, an effort that was crippled by the Post Office Department's refusal to let the organization send any material through the mail. Even without such blatant harassment, the IWW's defense was hampered by its increasing isolation. The liberal reformers who before the war had supported the Wobblies' civil liberties, if not their political program, dropped by the wayside. The wartime frenzy had so poisoned matters that even the well-known social reformer and peace activist Jane Addams would not endorse the defense of antiwar radicals. "I am," she explained, "obliged to walk very softly in regard to all things suspect."[30]

Meanwhile, in Russia, a new world was being born. For the beleaguered American left, the Bolshevik revolution promised a new beginning. Socialists and Wobblies alike welcomed Lenin's victory as but the prelude to a worldwide revolution. "Here is what we have been dreaming about," crowed Wobbly leader Big Bill Haywood, "here is the IWW all feathered out." But if the Bolshevik revolution reenergized American radicals, it terrified the rest of the nation. Not only did the events in Russia seem to threaten the stability of the capitalist world, but they also directly affected the Allied war effort. The new Soviet regime quickly made peace with the Germans and withdrew from the fighting. The Wilson administration, already antagonistic to Bolshevism on ideological grounds, circulated charges that the revolution was a German plot and sent U.S. troops to Russia ostensibly to reestablish an Eastern front. Anti-Bolshevism, thus, became an integral part of the war effort and the Russian revolutionaries inherited all the hostility that the government and private patriots had been directing against the Germans. Thus it was that even before the armistice, the ideological groundwork had been laid for the postwar red scare.[31]

Peace brought further unrest. Europe seemed on the verge of a revolution; and respectable Americans feared the contagion might spread. Scare stories about Soviet atrocities circulated widely, bolstered early in 1919 by several weeks of lurid testimony before a special Senate investigating committee. In the United States, inflation, unemployment, and a workforce that had postponed demands for wage increases and unionization during the war augured a new wave of labor unrest, if not outright revolution.[32]

By the end of 1919, one-fifth of the nation's workers had gone out on strike. From Boston to Seattle, policemen, coal miners, shipbuilders, meat packers, all walked off the job. The most important work stoppage took place in the steel industry, where a quarter of a million workers struck under the leadership of the former Wobbly and future Communist William Z. Foster. In response, the business community and its allies in the press and elsewhere mounted a massive publicity campaign that exaggerated, if it didn't sometimes invent, the violence that accompanied these walkouts and claimed, in the words of the head of U.S. Steel, that the strikers were seeking "the closed shop, Soviets, and the forcible distribution of property."[33]

A sense of panic spread throughout the nation, fed by the strike wave and the sporadic acts of violence indulged in by anarchist bombers and right-wing vigilantes. By the time an Italian anarchist blew himself up while planting an explosive device in front of Attorney General A. Mitchell Palmer's house in the beginning of June 1919, the stage was more than set for a massive crackdown on the left. Yet when it came, the red scare of 1919–1920 was not a coordinated campaign, but rather a number of public and private initiatives undertaken to punish radicals and blunt labor organizing. The businessmen, newspaper editors, professional patriots, and law enforcement officers who engineered the red scare were neither marginal nor powerless Americans, but very much a part of the establishment. Many were also liberal and progressive. Attorney General Palmer, who more than anyone else had responsibility for the red scare, was, in the words of his biographer, a "champion of the underprivileged." As was to be the case during the McCarthy era, the federal government was central. Its wartime successes in mobilizing public opinion and prosecuting political undesirables set useful precedents. In addition, it possessed in its ability to deport politically undesirable aliens what seemed to be the most efficacious weapon then available.[34]

Both legal procedure and public relations determined that the federal government would rely heavily on immigration proceedings in its dealings with the red menace. The Espionage and Sedition Acts were due to expire when the war ended; and without a peacetime sedition act, the Department of Justice had no legal basis for prosecuting political undesirables. Moreover, because a series of late-nineteenth-century Supreme Court rulings had effectively deprived aliens facing deportation of most constitutional protections, immigration proceedings presented fewer legal obstacles than criminal prosecutions.[35]

Xenophobia converged with law here. Recent immigrants, especially the much maligned Slavs, Italians, and Jews who had arrived in the United States in the late nineteenth and early twentieth centuries, were already demonized and thus ripe for repression. The long-standing countersubversive belief that foreigners and their radical ideas caused most social unrest made such aliens convenient targets. Moreover, since so many of the nation's radicals were, in fact, foreign-born, shipping them out of the country seemed to be a good way to eliminate the alleged menace. Attorney General Palmer claimed that his department's investigations "into the ultraradical movement during the course of the last year has clearly indicated that fully 90 per cent of the communist and anarchist agitation is traceable to aliens." Similar allegations were common throughout the law enforcement community. They were to reappear, in almost identical language, during the McCarthy period as well.[36]

Political opportunism also entered the picture. Bolshevik-bashing was popular and Palmer was planning to run for president in 1920. Jolted by his own close brush with violence, he was also, Palmer later recalled, under considerable pressure from Congress "to do something and do it now and do it quickly, and do it in a way that would bring results to stop this sort of thing."[37]

There was, thus, an aura of inevitability to the Palmer raids, the notorious roundup of foreign-born radicals in November 1919 and January 1920 that became the symbolic culmination of all the wartime and postwar political repression. The raids were important, as well, because they were J. Edgar Hoover's first big assignment. Once Palmer decided in the summer of 1919 to carry out mass deportations of alien radicals, he put Hoover, then an ambitious twenty-four-year-old graduate of the George Washington Law School who had just taken over the future FBI's Radical Division, in charge of the details.[38]

Though it is hard to tell just when Hoover's obsession with Communism began, his preparatory work for the Palmer raids must have certainly contributed to it. As part of those preparations, he immersed himself in the left-wing press. The literature that he encountered was to remain at the core of the FBI's case against the CP for the next fifty years. It represented American Communism at its most revolutionary moment, when in the afterglow of the Russian revolution the newly formed Communist parties were openly calling for "proletarian revolution, the overthrow of capitalism and the establishment of the dictatorship of the proletariat." Though the CP's later activities certainly contributed to the future FBI director's antagonism, the ideological nature of Hoover's anticommunism — which was to have so much influence over the way in which the rest of the nation viewed Communism during the Cold War — was in many respects an artifact of that first exposure to the flaming rhetoric of America's early Communists.[39]

There were parallels as well between the outrages that accompanied the Palmer raids and those that took place during the McCarthy period. These similarities were no accident; they occurred because it was not possible either in 1919 or in 1949 to clamp down on political agitation without seriously compromising freedom of speech and the rights of individuals. It was, after all, not against the law to call for a proletarian revolution or, later, to be a Communist. This lack of a clear statutory prohibition against what they wanted to suppress tempted officials like Hoover to operate in the murky area at the margins of legality. Understandably, they sometimes went over the edge, either because they exceeded their own authority or because the laws they were trying to enforce did not forbid the activities they considered illegal.

During the 1919 red scare, for example, the government relied on the Immigration Act of October 1918 in large part because it contained wording that allowed for what would later become known as "guilt by association," making it possible to deport people simply because they belonged to a revolutionary organization. The authorities did not, in other words, have to prove that the radicals they were trying to punish had actually done anything. Still, there were limits to the government's power. It had to follow legal procedures and it had to produce some kind of evidence linking the deportable aliens to the proscribed organizations. Moreover, federal judges and higher officials within the Labor Department, the agency then in charge of immigration, did not always support the way in which lower-level authorities applied the rules. As a result, evidence that seemed convincing to the near-hysterical immigration officials in the Pacific Northwest was considered insufficient grounds for deportation on the calmer East Coast or when the prospective deportees got adequate legal advice.[40]

Antiradical officials faced other problems as well. The main information about the activities and membership of specific individuals came from government informers, but once they surfaced in a deportation hearing, their value as informers was gone. Thus, in order to preserve their agents' identities, Hoover and his colleagues hoped that organizational records and individual confessions would yield the evidence they needed. Accordingly, they planned to raid the radicals' headquarters, seize their papers, and detain them without bail or access to lawyers. Not only would such roundups supply the literature and confessions the government required, but they would also, both Hoover and Palmer hoped, be dramatic enough to convince the nation of the need for a peacetime sedition law.[41]

The first raids took place on November 7, 1919, the second anniversary of the Bolshevik revolution. The main target was a left-wing immigrant group, the Union of Russian Workers, but Hoover and his men also picked up Emma Goldman and a few other top anarchists. Neither the violence that accompanied the raids nor such violations of civil liberties as beatings and warrantless arrests diminished the apparent popularity of the measures. Six weeks later, a converted troopship carrying Goldman and 248 other allegedly dangerous radicals sailed out of New York harbor to the cheers of politicians and the press. The *Cleveland Plain Dealer* saluted the departure of the so-called "Soviet Ark" with the expectation "that other vessels, larger, more commodious, carrying similar cargoes will follow in her wake."[42]

The newly formed Communist parties were the targets of the second roundup. Undercover agents got orders to call meetings for the night of January 2, 1920, to facilitate the raids. Again, there were massive violations of human rights and due process. Somewhere between six thousand and ten thousand people were arrested in New York, Boston, Detroit, and thirty other cities, often without a warrant. As a result, although the raids netted most of the nation's leading communist aliens, they also picked up nondeportable citizens and such innocent bystanders as the curiosity seeker in Newark who was arrested because he "looked like a radical." Some of the detainees were beaten and others were held without hearings for weeks and even months, often in dangerously overcrowded facilities.[43]

Ultimately, the blatant violations of civil liberties, as well as the obvious lack of a revolutionary danger, ended the red scare. A group of prominent attorneys publicly condemned the raids. A few federal judges balked at the process. And Assistant Secretary of Labor Louis Post, who had long been critical of his subordinates' antiradical fervor, began to question the legitimacy of their actions and refused to deport anybody on the basis of illegally seized evidence, ultimately releasing over half the detained aliens. Right-wingers and professional patriots squawked; the newly formed American Legion called for his scalp; and Congress began impeachment proceedings. But Post defended himself ably and convinced most of his hearers of the need for due process. Finally, when Justice Department predictions of radical violence on May Day turned out to be groundless, public opinion calmed down. The revival of elite opposition to the red scare had been crucial. Once respectable public figures jumped off the bandwagon, the worst excesses of the period came to an end.[44]

The furor left its mark, nonetheless. Though it subsided before Attorney General Palmer and his supporters could get a peacetime sedition law through Congress, most states adopted such measures. By 1921, thirty-five of the forty-eight plus Hawaii and Alaska had some kind of antiradical statute on the books. Over thirty states and cities also had "red flag" laws that criminalized the display of revolutionary banners. The frenzy was most visible in New York. A state investigating committee raided socialist schools and offices as well as communist ones; and the state legislature refused to seat five legally elected socialist members. Elsewhere the repression varied. Overall, local authorities arrested at least fourteen hundred people and sent about three hundred of them to prison, including many leaders of the new Communist parties. Prosecutions dwindled by the early 1920s; but the new state laws were rarely repealed, to be disinterred in future years to punish labor organizers during the 1930s and alleged subversives in the fifties.[45]

The nation's judiciary placed few limitations on such proceedings, at either the state or the federal level. And, in fact, the constitutional legacy of the red scare turned out to be quite far-reaching. For the first time, the Supreme Court had to deal with the issues of free speech and political dissent. The decisions that the justices rendered in these wartime and postwar prosecutions — *Schenck v. United States* (1919), *Abrams v. United States* (1919), and *Gitlow v. New York* (1925) — established the parameters for all future First Amendment cases. As happened again during the McCarthy era, the Court generally backed the government and erected few constitutional barriers to the suppression of unpopular views. The main one emerged in Justice Oliver Wendell Holmes's celebrated opinion in the *Schenck* case. After noting that "the most stringent protection of free speech would not protect a man in falsely shouting fire in a theatre," Holmes articulated what became known as the "clear and present danger" test:

The question in every case is whether the words used are used in such circumstances and are of such a nature as to create a clear and present danger that they will bring about the substantive evils that Congress has a right to prevent.

The test seemed to protect those radicals who produced leaflets rather than bombs. But, in reality, that protection turned out to be limited. Few justices, either in the immediate aftermath of World War I or later during the early Cold War, would ever question the government's broad assessment of "the clear and present danger" political dissidents posed.[46]

The red scare was devastating to the left in other ways as well. Instead of starting a revolution, the leaders of the two fledgling Communist parties took their organizations underground, in the process adopting the clandestine and conspiratorial style of operations that would heighten the isolation and vulnerability of the American CP. The labor movement also suffered. The red-scare tactics of the business community during the postwar strike wave not only checked the drive to organize the nation's mass production industries but also began to nibble away at already established unions. There was considerable irony here, for the AFL's own enthusiastic red-baiting did not protect it from the business community's assault on organized labor.

The red scare left a different legacy on the right, an ideological and institutional one. Besides launching the career of J. Edgar Hoover, the immediate aftermath of World War I also spawned the American Legion. As the largest mass-based organization within the countersubversive world and the one that most single-mindedly and continuously pushed an anticommunist agenda, the Legion typified the various patriotic organizations that were so crucial to the network of anticommunist professionals. Along with their counterparts in such groups as the Daughters of the American Revolution and the Veterans of Foreign Wars, the right-wing patriots of the Legion were among the most steadfast carriers of the traditional countersubversive ideology, their activities often giving Cold War anticommunism the extremist spin that accounted for the more notorious incidents of the McCarthy era.

Because there has not been much scholarly work on the organizations of the patriotic right, it is hard to tell how widespread the Legion's influence was or how accurately its leaders represented their constituents. After all, not every Legionnaire was an anticommunist zealot. For many veterans, joining the local Legion post was a way to make business or professional contacts or just have a good time on Saturday nights. To what extent ordinary members subscribed to the nationalistic, xenophobic brand of countersubversion proffered by the professional patriots on the organization's staff is hard to tell. Karl Baarslag estimated that even during the height of the McCarthy era, only about two or three hundred of the Legion's seventeen thousand posts actively fought Communism. But the zeal of the top Legionnaires and the fact that they claimed to speak for millions of veterans certainly bolstered their clout.[47]

The Legion had been anticommunist from birth. Fearful that the American soldiers who remained in Europe after the armistice might be infected by the revolutionary unrest that was sweeping the Old World, the leaders of the American Expeditionary Force in France encouraged the efforts of a band of officers to form a new patriotic veterans group. The Legion's founders were all wealthy establishment types who were clearly determined to protect the status quo. The organization's initial funding came from Wall Street, including a $100,000 loan from J. P. Morgan and Company. But the early Legionnaires quickly concealed their upper-class origins and adopted an essentially middle-class, theoretically egalitarian stance. In order to attract as many veterans as possible, they also avoided taking controversial positions on any issues that might offend large numbers of members. Accordingly, the Legion quickly narrowed its agenda down to four items: veterans' benefits, good works, Americanism, and fun.[48]

Americanism, or as the preamble to the new organization's constitution expressed it, "one hundred per cent Americanism," turned out to be anticommunism. The concept seems to have originated with Teddy Roosevelt, the organization's ideological godfather as well as the biological father of one of its founders, Theodore Roosevelt, Jr. The Legion mirrored TR's militaristic version of muscular patriotism and his hostility to aliens and reds. Though the group expanded its activities in the following years, its commitment to countersubversion was so pervasive that even its community service projects had an anticommunist tinge. "American Legion Junior Baseball," a high-level Legionnaire explained, "is a medium through which we can combat Communism."[49]

Initially, however, that combat took a much more violent form than essay contests and boys' baseball teams. The Legion threw itself into the 1919–1920 red scare. It had, as one of its Los Angeles leaders put it, declared "a war of extermination against members of the IWW and against Bolshevism." Legionnaires waged that war with fists, stones, and firearms, often providing personnel for the mobs that attacked striking workers and broke up radical meetings. The most notorious incident took place on Armistice Day, 1919, when the shoot-out that accompanied a march to the local IWW hall in Centralia, Washington, left four Legionnaires dead and precipitated the grisly lynching of a Wobbly official. The American Civil Liberties Union, which was tracking the veterans' accomplishments, recorded at least fifty illegal instances of Legion violence in 1919.[50]

The Legion's official Americanism program was in part a public relations move to control its members and distance the organization from its rowdy image. By the 1920s, it was lobbying for anticommunist legislation at the state and national level. The organization also sought to instill appropriately patriotic values within the rest of the population. It was eager to Americanize immigrants and increase the veneration of the flag and other national symbols. Legionnaires also busied themselves with trying to bar radicals from speaking in public. Even more important was the Legion's campaign to eliminate subversives from educational institutions and ensure that public schools inculcated one hundred percent Americanism. By the late 1940s, the Americanism Commission had an ex-teacher on its staff who did nothing but check out textbooks.[51]

The Legion's anticommunism was typical of that of a broader group of right-wing and even near-fascist organizations, as well as of the small but growing network of self-appointed experts on Communism. Walter Steele was one of these professional anti-Communists; even more influential for a time was Elizabeth Dilling, a Chicago housewife whose 1934 privately printed exposé of the subversive threat, *The Red Network,* went through four printings in nine months. Quite a few of these countersubversive activists had military backgrounds of one sort or another; others came up through the Legion or other patriotic groups. They constituted what most contemporary and later observers considered a kind of lunatic fringe of the anticommunist movement, though some of their formulations were to gain considerable influence during the McCarthy era.[52]

Like the Legion, these early countersubversives shared a tendency to be expansive about the nature of the threat. In the mid-twenties, when the CP was barely functioning, they became concerned about "dupes," "super-intellectuals," and organizations that were "sincere in purpose, but of radical thought." What these ideologues considered radical, however, was often pretty tame; one Legion official actually claimed that the Young Men's Christian Association was a communist front. And among the nearly eighteen hundred allegedly dangerous groups and individuals Elizabeth Dilling listed in her book were Albert Einstein, future Supreme Court justice Felix Frankfurter, Eleanor Roosevelt, Jane Addams, the YWCA, and the president of the University of Wisconsin. The ACLU, which had been so critical of the Legion during the red scare, was a major target, as was the peace movement, whose female leadership and challenge to militarism made it repugnant to the Legion and its allies.[53]

It is easy to poke fun at this wing of the anticommunist network. Historians and contemporary observers alike tended to view its members as marginal, in large part because their accusations were often so erratic and wide of the mark. But such an assessment ignores the persistence of these patriots and the contacts they established (not to mention the files they shared) with other, more presumably respectable anticommunist professionals like congressional investigators and FBI agents. Though the Legion and its allies were responsible for some of the sillier episodes in the history of American anticommunism, their main achievement may well have been to keep the countersubversive ideology alive throughout the late 1920s and early 1930s.

By the mid-thirties, the professional anti-Communists were back in business, their activities stimulated by the revival of the left during the early New Deal. Again, as earlier, labor struggles were crucial. The revitalization of the labor movement, in particular the surge of union organizing that accompanied the formation of the CIO, reinvigorated the countersubversives. Professional patriots, antiunion businessmen, and law-and-order traditionalists all sprang into action. The parallels to earlier episodes of red-baiting were striking. Though the CIO replaced the IWW as the locus of hostility, the old themes of foreign conspiracies and outside agents were heard again.

At the same time, the anticommunist network expanded beyond its traditional right-wing constituency. New groups and individuals, many of them much farther to the left, joined the cause. Some of these recruits, like Benjamin Mandel, had once been in or near the Communist party; others were its rivals within the labor movement or the left. They brought a much more sophisticated brand of anticommunism to the movement, for they knew what the CP was and how it functioned. As a result, they were able to help the old countersubversives refine their techniques, focus more accurately on real Communists, and reach a much broader segment of American society.

The renewed vigor of the anticommunist network mirrored that of the CP. The end of the internal squabbling that had so plagued the party during the 1920s allowed it to take advantage of the opportunities that the Depression was to offer. As the party stepped up its activities, it gained members and attention. Ironically, its seemingly phoenix-like resuscitation after its near demise in the 1920s made an indelible mark on J. Edgar Hoover. When the combined forces of government repression and internal dissatisfaction again seemed to have destroyed the communist movement in the mid-fifties, the FBI director refused to accept his own success and continued to believe that the CP might yet rise again.[54]

The party's revival during the Depression had, after all, also occurred in the face of massive resistance. All the traditional forces of law and order had tried to stop the upsurge of radicalism that seemed to threaten the status quo during the early 1930s, even if, as so often happened, they had to use violence to do so. Rarely did a communist-led unemployment demonstration occur without a police crackdown. Beatings and arrests were commonplace. Steve Nelson recalled that when he was organizing unemployed councils in the anthracite region of Pennsylvania, the local police chief would throw the key cadres in jail every Friday night to keep them from speaking at demonstrations on the weekend. Strikes, whether party-run or not, as well as student antiwar and, later, antifascist protests, also encountered police resistance. Local officials often reinforced private vigilantism (if they didn't participate in it themselves) by prosecuting the victims. In one instance, after the American Legion raided a communist children's camp in California, local authorities took the campers to juvenile court and charged the counselors and maintenance staff with "conspiracy to teach the tenets of Communism." [55]

Of course, most of the targets of this type of political repression were communist union organizers, not communist children. And, since many of the party's most energetic cadres had gone into the labor movement in the early thirties, there was no scarcity of Communists for state and local officials to harass. Even without the CP's participation, the union struggles of the 1930s would still have encountered enormous resistance: antilabor repression was a long-standing American tradition. One scholar claims that eighteen thousand striking workers were arrested between 1934 and 1936. Still, Communists were especially vulnerable. State and local officials resuscitated the antiradical statutes that had been passed during the post–World War I red scare. By the mid-thirties, there were sedition cases in Ohio, New Jersey, Pennsylvania, California, Kentucky, Oregon, Michigan, Utah, Iowa, Georgia, Washington, Illinois, and Virginia, many of them directed against party activists. [56]

In the South, the CP's challenge to the racial as well as the economic status quo unleashed a veritable reign of terror. Again, the local forces of law and order condoned, if they did not actually instigate, the shootings, beatings, and violence that accompanied the party's attempts to organize sharecroppers and unemployed black workers. Life for Communists was so precarious that one woman cadre in Alabama had to send her daughter to live with her sister in another state. The city of Birmingham actually made it illegal to possess "radical" literature, a prohibition that covered left-liberal magazines like *The Nation* and the *New Republic* as well as party tracts. In rural areas, the repression was worse, with murders and Latin American–style "disappearances" not uncommon. To be an active Communist in the early thirties — North or South — was to expect to be beaten up and jailed. [57]

Congress got into the act as well. Early in 1930, stimulated by the CP's unemployment demonstrations and by charges that the Soviet Union was directly subsidizing party activities, the House of Representatives voted 210–18 to investigate. The New York Republican and American Legion founder Hamilton Fish headed the probe; he took several months of testimony from a wide variety of civil servants, policemen, labor leaders, Soviet officials, American Communists, and professional patriots. Most of these witnesses — or at least the friendly ones — supplied Fish with reams of documents that presumably showed how the CP threatened the American way of life. These witnesses also called for new laws and more deportations. Not surprisingly, the committee's final report made the same recommendations, urging, as A. Mitchell Palmer had also done, a federal peacetime sedition act and the deportation of alien reds. Only the call for deportations had reverberations outside the countersubversive community. Taking action against immigrants, who allegedly took jobs that citizens could fill, was a popular response to the Depression; and the Hoover administration did, in fact, step up deportations of political radicals. But it ignored the rest of Fish's suggestions.[58]

There was more action at the state level, where politicians were more responsive to pressures from business groups, Legionnaires, and the press. Most of the initiatives dealt with education, a long-term Legion preoccupation and one of the few areas in which state legislatures did indeed wield power. Loyalty oaths for teachers were a popular device. They were cheap and symbolically satisfying. By 1936 twenty-one states and the District of Columbia had adopted them. Several legislative committees looked for alleged communist influence in their state's universities and public school systems but found little.[59]

Ineffectual as these investigations were, they demonstrated the crucial role of the press in the anticommunist crusade. The Hearst papers were particularly influential. For the following twenty years, until the demise of Senator McCarthy, the Hearst empire and its stable of right-wing columnists could always be counted on to play up charges of communist subversion. The Hearst corporate culture, with its hostility to radicals and emphasis on sensationalism, readily embraced the countersubversive scenario. Not only was the professional anti-Communist J. B. Matthews on the payroll, but both of Hearst's chief lieutenants at the time, John F. Neylan and Richard Berlin, were themselves key figures in the anticommunist network, Neylan as Hearst's main representative on the West Coast and the lesser-known Berlin as a behind-the-scenes operator who had important contacts at the highest levels of business and government.[60]

Most of the efforts of the Hearst apparatus, as well as those of the rest of the anticommunist network, were directed against organized labor. As in the 1919–1920 red scare, all of labor's traditional enemies collaborated in the project of trying to crush unions. And, as in that earlier period, anticommunism supplied much of the ammunition. This time, however, real Communists were involved.[61]

The furor was fiercest in California. The state's well-organized business community had been fighting unions for years, especially within the maritime industry and among the big-time growers in the rich central valleys. In 1934, when the farmworkers in the Imperial Valley began to organize under the auspices of a CP-led union, the growers responded by forming first the Imperial Valley Anti-Communist Association and then the Associated Farmers of California. The latter organization hired Harper Knowles, the head of the California American Legion's Subversive Activities Committee, to help it "protect agriculture from subversive groups." He was successful. In collaboration with local authorities, the growers' campaign of red-baiting, vigilante raids, arrests, and the long-term imprisonment of the farmworkers' main communist organizers on charges of criminal syndicalism utterly destroyed the organizing drive.[62]

On the San Francisco waterfront, longshoremen and their seafaring allies faced a similar onslaught, but in this case they triumphed. Again, Communists supplied much of the leadership, but the waterfront workers themselves had a strong syndicalist tradition that contributed to their solidarity. They needed it, for the three-month maritime strike in the spring and summer of 1934 plunged the West Coast into a state of virtual class warfare. There was the usual police harassment and American Legion vigilantism; early in July when the employers and police tried to open the docks, a full-scale battle took place. Under the direction of Hearst lieutenant John F. Neylan, the waterfront employers and their allies red-baited ferociously, invoking the specter of Communism and begging for federal troops. "The strike is not a conflict between employers and employees," the Chamber of Commerce declared, "it is a conflict which is rapidly spreading between American principles and un-American radicalism."[63]

The references to un-American elements were intentional. The leader of the strike was the Australian-born Harry Bridges. With his rank-and-file perspective and articulate class consciousness, Bridges personified everything that traditional countersubversives and antilabor businessmen feared: he was a foreigner, a Communist, and a militant union leader. From the moment he emerged as the main spokesman for the waterfront workers early in 1934, Legionnaires and business leaders clamored for his deportation. The issue became a national crusade. For the next two decades, it would be possible to gauge the strength of American anticommunism by the intensity of the campaign to deport Harry Bridges.[64]

When the passage of the Wagner Act in 1935 stimulated a massive drive to unionize the nation's basic industries, the antilabor red-baiting intensified. Though the real target of this campaign was the recently organized CIO and the new industrial unions associated with it, the conservative businessmen and their allies in Congress and the press relied heavily on red-baiting. They inflated the significance of the communist presence in the labor movement both to disguise their underlying hostility to unions and to gain support for their opposition to the New Deal, which they believed sided with labor. The countersubversive scenario that this campaign disseminated, one that accused the CIO and the Roosevelt administration of colluding with Communists, was to have a long life and was to reemerge in a barely altered form during the Cold War.

Much of that red-baiting was effective. The CIO's sit-down strikes alienated respectable citizens and made it possible to arouse them against the new labor movement and its communist organizers. At the height of the countersubversive offensive, companies organized anti-union citizens groups and mobilized public opinion in the steel towns of Pennsylvania and Ohio to push the notion that the CIO was, in the words of a local minister, "the advance guard of Communism." In many respects, it seemed like 1919 all over again. The American Legion was out in force, local police were beating up strikers, red-baiting was virulent, and union organizing came to a halt.[65]

★

But it was not 1919. Neither unions nor anticommunism disappeared. Within a few years, World War II made it possible for the rest of the nation's mass production industries to be unionized. At the same time, however, the anticommunist network expanded. Ironically, an important branch of that network was to develop within the labor movement itself.

There had always been anti-Communists within the nation's unions, especially among the conservative leaders of the AFL. Their hostility to radicalism reflected in part the relatively secure position of the skilled white male workers they represented and their own desire for respectability and acceptance by the nation's political and economic elites. But it was also a conscious maneuver to deflect opposition by distancing their organization from anything that smacked of Socialism or class conflict. Actually, even if the AFL's leaders had been less concerned about appearances, they still might have turned against the CP. The party was not easy to love. Its often devious tactics alienated its potential labor allies and its atheism offended the federation's largely Irish-Catholic rank and file.[66]

The expansion of the labor movement in the late 1930s threw the AFL's old-line leaders on the defensive and increased their hostility to Communism. Unwilling to seek new members by organizing broad-based industrial unions instead of narrowly focused craft ones, the federation's conservatives energetically red-baited the industrial unionists within their own ranks — especially those who were Communists. The formation of the CIO merely exacerbated the situation. Those AFL leaders whose jurisdictions were most threatened by the new industrial unions squawked the loudest. Like John Frey, the head of the federation's Metal Trades Department, they had few qualms about working with businessmen, professional patriots, and right-wing politicians to denounce the CIO as a communist front. Often, in fact, it was hard to differentiate between the AFL's brand of anticommunism and that of the American Legion.[67]

Within those unions, like the UE, where the party had, in fact, been active, the anticommunism that developed was much more concrete and narrowly focused than that of the traditional conservatives of the AFL. It was also much more effective. Many of its practitioners had worked closely with Communists and, unlike the AFL's old guard, did not ordinarily oppose the party's labor agenda. They turned against their former allies for any number of both sincere and opportunistic reasons. But, because Communism was involved, even ordinary power struggles took on an ideological coloration that often enabled the Communists' opponents to gain outside support. In some unions the conflict over Communism raged throughout the 1930s, in others it developed later. By the late 1940s, there was usually some kind of anticommunist faction within almost every union where the CP had power.[68]

In New York City, with its relatively large concentration of party members, the infighting was fierce and sometimes bloody. Battles between Socialists and Communists wracked the garment industry for years and occasionally spilled over into the city's white collar unions as well. At one point in the mid-1930s, for example, the civil war inside the New York City Teachers Union, the organization that gave the anticommunist stalwart Benjamin Mandel his political start, was so intense that an outside tribunal under the philosopher John Dewey put the union's Communists on trial.[69]

Similar skirmishes broke out within the CIO's big industrial unions as well. In the UAW, which was more an uneasy amalgam of independent locals than a strongly centralized organization, factions had contended from the start. The importance of the automobile industry had drawn organizers from every political group and grouplet. Though the Communists probably had the strongest contingent, there were Socialists, Trotskyists, Lovestoneites, Musteites, Wobblies, and Coughlinites. The conflicts between these groups added to the new union's instability and ensured that its internal politics would become a stew of factionalism. The union's shop floor struggles exacerbated the dissension. At one point, the infighting was so intense that the CIO stepped in and brokered an arrangement that essentially put the UAW into a CIO-run receivership.[70]

Walter Reuther, the union's most dynamic and ambitious socialist leader, had once worked so closely with the Communists that he had been red-baited himself. But he turned against his former allies after the CP double-crossed his brother in a state CIO election. It took years for Reuther to build a centrist coalition that could oust the Communists and their allies. And it was not until the Cold War, when foreign policy issues enabled him to isolate the party, that Reuther could finally eliminate all CP influence from the union.[71]

The UAW was the most faction-ridden as well as the most important CIO union in which Communists and anti-Communists contended, but it was hardly unique. Most of the other unions that harbored important communist contingents experienced the same kind of internal warfare. In many of these organizations, anticommunism often provided a cover for the power struggles and religious, ethnic, or racial conflicts that also plagued these unions. As in the UAW, the Communists usually retained their influence until the Nazi-Soviet pact and the Cold War injected outside political issues into the struggle.

Within the electrical industry, the conflict began in 1940 after the UE denied reelection to its first president, James B. Carey, because of his incompetence and failure to support the union's interests. Carey cried "red" and, assisted by a strong cohort of Catholic anticommunists, began what was to become a ten-year campaign to oust his UE rivals. The communist-led New York City Transport Workers Union encountered similar problems. The CP had been the union's midwife and many of its top leaders, including its charismatic president, Mike Quill, were in the party. But although most of the TWU's members were Irish-Catholic and at least nominally anticommunist, Quill's popularity enabled him to deflect the red-baiting that antiunion priests and internal dissidents had launched. He and his colleagues denied their political affiliation, eschewed radicalism, and concentrated on union business.[72]

The struggles within the Mine, Mill and Smelter Workers Union were more destructive. Regional as well as ethnic, religious, and bureaucratic differences exacerbated the infighting. An unstable coalition of Midwestern die-casters, Eastern brass workers, and Southern and Western hard-rock miners, the union was presided over by a mercurial character named Reid Robinson. Though Robinson had initially come to power as the candidate of Mine-Mill's right-wing faction, by the early 1940s he was aligned with the union's communist organizers and staff members. The Irish-Catholic workers in Connecticut's Brass Valley rebelled. They lacked the power to oust Robinson, but their challenge to his leadership was so disruptive that the CIO had to intervene. In the South, racial issues split the union. By 1945 secession movements were endemic throughout Mine-Mill and a vigorous anticommunist cadre was already in place. And the Cold War had not yet begun.[73]

The Catholic Church helped build that cadre — and not just in Mine-Mill. In almost every union where Communists had a presence, Catholic activists, both clergy and lay, fought long and often effectively against the party. The labor movement may well have been the most important battleground for the Church's struggle against the CP, but the crusade extended throughout the rest of society, throughout the rest of the world actually, for the

Catholic hierarchy considered Communism — "godless, atheistic Communism" — as perhaps its most dangerous enemy.

The contest involved both turf and ideology. After all, both Church and CP were international organizations that made major demands on the lives of their adherents. The party's Socialism, with its openly materialistic goals, clashed directly with Catholicism's spiritual mission. Moreover, by claiming to speak for the working class, most of whose members were Catholic, Communists directly threatened the Church's hold over its followers.[74]

They also threatened its very existence. As far as the Catholic hierarchy was concerned, Bolshevism and Christianity were locked in mortal combat. Father Edmund A. Walsh, one of the anticommunist experts Hoover's aides wanted to consult, had represented the papacy in Russia during the 1920s and had witnessed the Soviet regime's crackdown on organized religion. He returned to the United States determined to alert the rest of the nation to the communist menace. His colleagues within the Catholic hierarchy needed little convincing. Early Cold Warriors, they viewed the Kremlin as the epitome of all the secular evils they had been battling for years. Throughout the 1920s, they spearheaded the struggle against official recognition of the Soviet Union and were outraged when Roosevelt opened diplomatic relations in 1933.[75]

The Spanish Civil War intensified the Catholics' anticommunism. Already mobilized by an earlier campaign against the anticlericalism of the Mexican revolution, the Church's leaders uniformly condemned the Spanish Loyalist regime. Not only was it, so they claimed, communist, but it had committed unspeakable atrocities against the Spanish Church. The brutality of Francisco Franco's German and Italian allies they overlooked. The Pope, Pius XI, vigorously backed Franco and, in a 1937 encyclical, essentially called for a holy war against Communism. Even fascism was considered better.[76]

While many American Catholics — both clergy and lay — sought to combat the communist danger by denunciation, more sophisticated ones realized that if the Church was to retain the loyalty of its flock, especially its male members, it would have to become involved with the problems of the industrial working class. Catholic social thinkers criticized the injustices of the capitalist system, calling instead for what one activist termed "economic democracy." The Depression forced the issue, making many influential Catholics realize that combating Communism required a commitment to organized labor. The Church was not monolithic here. Some conservative clergymen opposed unions altogether and others supported only the traditional AFL ones. Still others, like Monsignor Charles Owen Rice of Pittsburgh, perhaps the most influential American labor priest, backed the CIO, viewing it, in Rice's words, as "a bulwark against Communism." [77]

To strengthen that bulwark, the Church sought to create a vibrant Catholic presence within the labor movement. It established labor schools to train Catholic workers for union leadership by giving them the same kind of intellectual and organizational tools that the party supplied to its cadres. Students at these schools studied papal encyclicals instead of Marxist classics, but they also learned labor history, public speaking, and how to run a mimeograph machine. And, in a few unions, most notably the New York City transit workers, they began to organize anticommunist factions. [78]

In 1937, a group of activists from the left-wing Catholic Worker movement formed the Association of Catholic Trade Unionists (ACTU), the main lay organization devoted to the anticommunist struggle within the labor movement. By 1941, the ACTU had chapters in Detroit, Pittsburgh, New York, Chicago, and a few other industrial centers. It sponsored labor schools and organized opposition movements within the UAW, UE, Transit Workers Union, Newspaper Guild, Mine-Mill, and other unions with a party presence. Though unsuccessful at first, the ACTU later became a key component of the coalition that drove the CP out of the labor movement after World War II. In the process, as many historians have noted, the organization abandoned its demand for social reform and became narrowly anticommunist. [79]

The Church, with its vast institutional resources, also provided another service to the anticommunist network. It operated an economic and institutional safety net for repentant former Communists. In some instances, it even facilitated their rupture with the CP and rewarded their contrition with teaching positions in Catholic colleges. Monsignor Fulton J. Sheen specialized in the conversion of high-profile ex-Communists, bringing some of the nation's top professional witnesses back to the religion that they had left years before. Louis Budenz, perhaps the most important ex-Communist witness reconverted by Sheen, taught at both Notre Dame and Fordham and, when he became too ill to work, got $600 a month from the archbishop of Boston.[80]

Ironically, just as Communism helped left-wing immigrants and their children become assimilated into American society during the 1930s, anti-commmunism fostered the Americanization of the Catholic Church. "It is not in defense of my faith that I condemn atheistic Communism," New York's Cardinal Francis Spellman told the readers of *Cosmopolitan* in 1946, "but as an American in defense of my country." The anticommunism he and other Church leaders espoused gave Catholic organizations — the Knights of Columbus as well as the ACTU — a cause that the rest of the nation could endorse. Since the party's traditional materialism and hostility to organized religion antagonized God-fearing citizens of every faith, combatting Communism helped Catholic activists overcome the sectarianism that, until then, had kept the Church outside the American mainstream. It took a while for the Catholic brand of anticommunism to blend with that of the rest of the nation. But by the mid-1950s, Father John F. Cronin, one of the leading clerical members of the anticommunist network, who had begun his struggle against the CP in a wartime Baltimore shipbuilding union, would be writing speeches for the vice president of the United States.[81]

Anticommunism made strange bedfellows. Although the Catholic anti-Communists should presumably have been as hostile to the materialistic Socialists, Trotskyists, and all the other left-wing sectarians as they were to the Communists, they were not. As Father Rice noted in a retrospective assessment of his own activities,

> the Socialists . . . set out to influence me, and they succeeded. Due to their indoctrination, I was not a routine Red baiter, but an informed one. . . . With their store of information and their hoard of bitterness, [they] were the great source of ammunition for Catholic anti-Communists.

And for non-Catholic ones as well. The Socialists and other left-wing anti-Communists functioned as a kind of intelligence service for the rest of the network. Their familiarity with the Communist party and its personnel meant that they could distinguish between card-carrying Communists and other radicals. Such precision gave anticommunism greater legitimacy, especially among liberals and others dismayed by the inaccurate red-baiting of the traditional countersubversives.[82]

These left-wing anti-Communists came in many varieties. There were Socialists, Trotskyists, Lovestoneites, Musteites, and a wide array of unaffiliated radical intellectuals and activists, many of whom had once been party members. The ex-Communists were, of course, crucial. Some, like Benjamin Mandel, worked behind the scenes, while others, like the former Harlem leader Manning Johnson, the Southern organizer Paul Crouch, or the labor activist Joseph Zack Kornfeder, became professional witnesses who testified regularly at political trials and congressional hearings. It later turned out that many of them lied — and, in fact, Manning Johnson admitted as much when he testified against Steve Nelson in the early 1950s. But during the late 1930s and 1940s, when the structure of McCarthyism was being erected, the former Communists had considerable authority. Only they could identify someone as a party member and only they could discuss the inner workings of the CP. "When civilization is in mortal danger," the chief counsel of the Senate Internal Security Subcommittee explained, "the ex-Communist is one of the most valuable members of society."[83]

Though less dramatically, the rest of the old left also contributed to the anticommunist cause. Socialists were the first on the scene. Ever since their party's 1919 convention, when the SP's right wing called in the Chicago police for crowd control against the future Communists in the party's left wing, American Socialists had battled Communism. But it was a complex struggle — part sibling rivalry and part total war — that did as much to shape the SP's political identity as anything written by Karl Marx. The two parties did, after all, share a common history; they also had the same goals even if they differed on the means for attaining them. And, at least in the early period, many Socialists still supported the Bolshevik revolution. "From the crown of my head to the soles of my feet," the party's imprisoned leader Eugene Debs announced in 1919, "I am a Bolshevist and proud of it." A year later, the SP even tried to join the Comintern. But disillusionment soon followed. There was to be no reconciliation with the Communists, though the exact nature of the SP's anticommunism became a matter of ferocious internal debate that ultimately tore the party apart.[84]

Members of the SP's right-wing Old Guard faction and their influential journal *The New Leader* articulated a nominally socialist worldview that promoted a sophisticated but nonetheless intense brand of anticommunism. By the mid-thirties the Old Guard had drifted so far to the right that it lost control of the party. The more moderate and left-wing Socialists who took over were hardly soft on Communism. The position of Norman Thomas, the party's perennial presidential candidate, reflected the SP's characteristic wariness. Like many of the middle-class intellectuals he appealed to during the thirties, Thomas was ambivalent about the Soviet Union — repelled by the regime's political repression, but attracted by its economic program. He was also ambivalent about American Communists. He was sometimes willing to work with them, but rarely willing to trust them.[85]

Thomas's caution, common to most of his constituents, was the product of many disappointments and bad experiences. Communists were not good allies. They were secretive, authoritarian, opportunistic, and insulting. Socialists and many independent intellectuals as well could never forgive the CP for having broken up a 1934 rally for Austrian Socialists at Madison Square Garden. Nor could they condone what they believed was the Communists' practice of trying to infiltrate and control every group they worked with. The Socialists' sensitivity, perhaps even hypersensitivity, to communist tactics made it hard for them to cooperate effectively with the CP. They were often so concerned about keeping Communists out of the groups they worked with that they sometimes inadvertently sabotaged those organizations' original purpose. Thus, for example, one reason why the attempt to build a movement for the rural poor foundered was that the socialist organizers of the Southern Tenant Farmers Union would not cooperate with their counterparts in a communist-led agricultural union.[86]

Unlike the Old Guard, Norman Thomas and the more radical members of the Socialist party did not turn to the right. Still, by the end of the decade, they were just as hostile to the CP. But they subscribed to a different, more nuanced type of anticommunism, one infused with a sense of personal betrayal as well as a distaste for what they saw as the CP's unprincipled opportunism. This emphasis on the manipulative nature of American Communism may well have been the most important contribution that the Socialists made to the development of American anticommunism.

As the Popular Front began to fall apart in the early 1940s, it became hard to distinguish the Socialists' critique of Communism from that of the liberal left. The similarities were no coincidence, for by then many of the nation's leading liberals, like the UAW's Walter Reuther and the theologian Reinhold Niebuhr, were former Socialists. Some of these people left the SP because of its impotence, sectarianism, and isolation; others because it opposed World War II. But whatever the reasons for their defections, they never completely abandoned their hostility to Communism or their commitment to social reform; and they were to transmit at least those aspects of their once socialist concerns to the rest of the nation through the Americans for Democratic Action (ADA), the anticommunist liberal organization they helped to found in the forties.[87]

There were similar defections among the other organizations in the noncommunist left in the 1930s. Though much smaller even than the Socialist party, these sects — the Trotskyists, Musteites, Lovestoneites, and all the other Leagues, Unions, Parties, and factions that they spawned — were just as influential in the formation of the anticommunist network. Most of their prominent cadres had once been in the CP or else had been among its intellectual hangers-on and, along with those ex-Communists who later joined the anticommunist network, they were to become the network's main experts: the professional witnesses, writers, and committee staffers whose testimony and advice would do so much to define the contours of American anticommunism. These people popularized the notion that only ex-Communists could understand real Communists. Their allies among the traditional anti-Communists, grateful for the legitimacy that the old leftists' expertise conveyed, reinforced that perception and welcomed them with open arms. Soon many of them were, like Mandel and Matthews, on the Hearst or HUAC payrolls, where they were to become indistinguishable in their political views from the rest of their countersubversive colleagues.

The Trotskyists were the first on the scene. A group of about one hundred leading Communists and their followers, they were expelled from the party early in 1929 when they sided with Trotsky against Stalin. A few months later, about three hundred allies and followers of the CP's then executive secretary, Jay Lovestone, were also kicked out of the party for backing the wrong horse in Moscow. Both groups considered themselves true Bolsheviks. But over the course of the 1930s, many of their adherents, along with many of the other ex-Communists, Socialists, and independent radicals within the world of the left-wing sects, began to lose their revolutionary ardor as they meandered from one tiny fringe group to another.[88]

The Nazi-Soviet pact and the beginning of World War II forced the sects to reassess their basic positions. And, as was common among such powerless groups, confronting the problems they had tried to ignore simply created new schisms. The Trotskyists split into two groups and the Lovestoneites solved their internal dissension by dissolving themselves altogether. There were few mourners; institutionally, the sects left a meager legacy.[89]

And yet, in the long run, the left-wing sectarians were not marginal at all. For within ten years, most of their ideas about Communism, if not about much else, had become part of the American political mainstream. The sects and their graduates, in particular that group of largely Jewish first- and second-generation writers and thinkers known as the New York intellectuals, were largely responsible for teaching American liberals how to think about Communism. Not only did they legitimize anticommunism in the eyes of the educated elites, but the formulations that they crafted helped to structure the way in which the anticommunist political repression of the McCarthy years functioned. Since they were among the best minds of their generation, many of these people might well have developed their interpretation of Communism without having passed through the sects of the thirties. Still, there is an immediacy to their formulations and a sense of urgency that only direct participation could have produced.[90]

Though some of the New York intellectuals had been in or near the CP in the early 1930s and a few of them later joined one or another of the sects and even on occasion led them, they had an ambivalent relationship with the actual organizations of the old left, more commonly identifying themselves with the literary circles they traveled in and the journals they wrote for than with any party or political group. The trajectory of their most important magazine, *Partisan Review,* is emblematic. Begun in 1934 as the literary outlet of the New York City branch of the CP's John Reed Club, its main editors, Philip Rahv and William Phillips, broke with Communism in 1936, then flirted with Trotskyism, and finally became Cold War liberals in the late 1940s. Throughout, the magazine defined its political identity in terms of its relationship with Communism.[91]

The distinctive feature of the anticommunism that Phillips, Rahv, and their colleagues embraced was its emphasis on the malignant nature of the Soviet regime. As intellectuals, they had gravitated toward Communism in the early thirties because, in large part, its ideas attracted them. Accordingly, the Soviet Union, or rather the *idea* of the Soviet Union, the world's first workers' state, was an important element in their relationship with the CP, more important, perhaps, than it was to their less cerebral comrades who were more involved with the routine party work of leafletting, demonstrating, and organizing unions. Moreover, precisely because ideas mattered so much to them, the New York intellectuals had a greater investment in the political correctness of their undertaking. After all, their professional concern with intellectual independence and critical thinking had already kept some of them from formal affiliation with the party and brought others into edgy conflict with it. As a result, when they became aware of how vicious the Soviet regime was, they felt compelled to expose it.

The Moscow purge trials of the late 1930s were crucial. The shock of seeing the most illustrious old Bolsheviks not only stand accused of conspiring with Trotsky, Hitler, and the other enemies of the Soviet Union but then admitting it was shattering. Whether they were guilty or innocent — and at first even the New York intellectuals were unsure about what was going on — the moral implications were clear. Something was rotten in Moscow. The show trials coincided with the New York intellectuals' own political evolution away from the Communist party. Trotskyism was at first an attractive alternative. It seemed to offer them the theoretical rigor and flexibility that the CP's, to them, intellectually flabby Popular Front could not. At the same time, it was still radical enough for the most alienated intellectuals. And, finally, there was Trotsky himself, the perfect role model of the intellectual (and a Jewish intellectual no less) as revolutionary hero.[92]

As the New York intellectuals became increasingly involved with Trotskyism and especially with the campaign to see that Trotsky's version of the Moscow trials got a fair hearing, they came under vicious attack from communist circles. The CP's "if you're not with us, you're against us" mentality had a self-fulfilling quality. The New York intellectuals, who, after all, were not known to shrink from polemic themselves, responded in kind. "It was in the fight against the Moscow trials," Trotskyist leader Max Shachtman later noted, "that so many American radical intellectuals learned to understand the modern Communist state and movement."[93]

And what they learned was that, at least on the issue of Trotsky, Stalin demanded and largely received the unquestioning obedience of his American supporters. From that lesson they were to make the obvious — though by no means entirely accurate — generalization that there was a complete identification between the Soviet regime and the American CP. The term "Stalinist," which became a common epithet in left-wing anticommunist circles, expresses that particular understanding of the nature of American Communism. At the same time, the New York intellectuals developed a new interpretation of Soviet Communism. Again a single word, "totalitarian," encapsulates that understanding. It underscored the New York intellectuals' moral revulsion against Moscow by making few distinctions between Stalin's crimes and Hitler's and stressing the similarities rather than the differences between Communism and fascism.[94]

Many of the charges that the New York intellectuals made about both Soviet and American Communism were true. In fact, what was happening in Russia was even more horrible than these people made it out to be. Nonetheless, within the domestic political context their anticommunism lacked perspective. The American Communist party, for all its flaws, was neither strong nor dangerous. It may well be, therefore, that for some of the New York intellectuals, their justifiable revulsion against Stalin's crimes, which they were helpless to prevent, allowed them to overcome their hesitations about collaborating with their traditional enemies on the right and making their own, albeit limited and indirect, contribution to the postwar wave of political repression. In October 1939, Trotsky apparently accepted an invitation to testify before HUAC, but had to postpone his appearance because of the State Department's refusal to give him a visa. He was about to give a deposition to a member of the HUAC staff when he was assassinated. One wonders what the old revolutionary would have said; it is even more interesting to speculate about what would have been done with his statement.[95]

By the end of the 1930s, the political diversity of the groups and individuals that opposed the American Communist party was quite remarkable. One group, however, had not yet fully endorsed the anticommunist campaign: the liberals. Since they dominated the executive branch of the American government, their lack of interest in that campaign protected the CP from serious reprisals. With the Nazi-Soviet pact, the liberals' neutrality toward Communism came to an end and they, too, joined the anticommunist network.

Actually, some liberals had turned against the party even before Stalin and Hitler made their deal. They were political activists who, like the Socialists, had been collaborating with Communists in the Popular Front and had soured on their former allies. The ACLU's cocounsel Morris Ernst, an energetic New York attorney who helped found the National Lawyers Guild, was typical of the breed. Though he never held an important federal position, Ernst was an able, if mildly self-important, activist who prided himself on his high-level connections and his talent as a behind-the-scenes political operative. Among the top officials to whom he gave "tidbits" of information and assisted with "off-the-record chores" were Franklin Delano Roosevelt, Harry S. Truman, and J. Edgar Hoover. His reputation as a civil libertarian made him particularly useful to Hoover, who often turned to him for help in dealing with the liberal community.[96]

During the 1930s Ernst had encountered Communists in many of the organizations he worked with — the ACLU, American Newspaper Guild, National Lawyers Guild, and American Labor Party. By the end of the decade, he had come to feel that the CP presence not only rendered these groups vulnerable to right-wing attacks, but also destroyed their effectiveness by making it impossible for them to command respect or influence outside the left. For these organizations to regain their acceptability within the American mainstream, the Communists had to go. Exposure, Ernst believed, was the key; once the party's secret affiliations and machinations were publicly revealed, its influence among liberals would disappear. Ernst was especially enamored of measures that would force all political organizations to disclose their main financial sources of support; and he spent years trying to convince the Roosevelt and Truman administrations that such a tactic should be used against undesirable outfits of all political persuasions.[97]

In the late 1930s, Ernst tried to purge the National Lawyers Guild. Dissension had broken out at the end of 1937, when the Guild's official bulletin published a controversial committee report on the Spanish Civil War. The NLG's more conservative members, who were already upset about what one Chicago judge called the "shysters . . . disreputable ambulance chasers" and "incompetents" drifting into the organization, became even more distressed and insisted that the Guild should not take stands on foreign policy issues. They feared that the controversial report would, another NLG attorney explained, only confirm "the opinion entertained by many, that the Guild is a small body of left-wing lawyers, not representative even of the liberal part of the American bar." Ernst agreed and circulated a statement signed by thirteen NLG eminences to counteract the unfavorable publicity the report on Spain had supposedly engendered. "It would be inimical to the future usefulness of the Guild," Ernst's statement said, "if a pseudo-legal report — one purporting to be dealing with legal issues but in fact based on considerations of policy — were to be sponsored or endorsed by the Guild." [98]

The conflict escalated the following year at the NLG's annual convention in February 1939, when Ernst proposed an amendment to the Guild's constitution announcing its opposition "to dictatorship of any kind, whether Left or Right, whether Fascist, Nazi, or Communistic." In making this recommendation, Ernst was deploying what was to become a standard technique for distancing liberal organizations from Communism. Labor unions were especially partial to such "Communazi" resolutions, as these allegedly evenhanded denunciations of both Communists and Nazis were called. In 1939 and again in 1940, for example, the CIO unanimously came out against "totalitarianism, dictatorships and foreign ideologies such as Nazism, Communism and Fascism." So, too, did many of its constituent unions, including many that had important CP contingents. The National Lawyers Guild did not. Perhaps because Ernst had jumped the gun and introduced his resolution before the Nazi-Soviet pact, the NLG board balked at adopting it and tried instead to paper over the conflict. [99]

But the damage had been done. Reports about the struggle reached the press and precipitated an exodus of liberals from the organization. At the same time, factional warfare broke out inside the Guild's local chapters. Within a year, Ernst and many of the NLG's most prominent liberals were gone. Unsuccessful in their attempt to oust party members and their allies from the Guild's National Executive Board, they resigned instead. [100]

Ernst had more success in eliminating Communists from the American Civil Liberties Union. He had been trying to purge the organization since 1938, but had only managed to polarize it. Meetings degenerated into what the former board secretary described as "dog-fights" as Ernst and his allies, including the socialist leader Norman Thomas, struggled to have the ACLU take a public stand against the Soviet Union. Rebuffed in April 1939, when the board reaffirmed its traditional commitment to defending the rights of all unpopular groups and its lack of concern "with movements abroad or foreign governments," the ACLU's anti-Communists persisted.

Less than a year later, under the impact of the "increasing tension" produced by the Nazi-Soviet pact, the organization reversed its position and at its annual meeting in February 1940, adopted a variant on the "Communazi" resolution that declared it "inappropriate" for officers of the ACLU to belong to "any political organization which supports totalitarian dictatorship in any country." Ironically, in their professed desire to defend the organization against "anti-democratic objects or practices," Ernst and his allies had gotten their measure onto the agenda by a devious subterfuge that flouted the ACLU's own rules.[101]

The resolution they obtained was more than theoretical. It was aimed directly at one of their fellow board members, Elizabeth Gurley Flynn, a feisty former Wobbly who had been one of the ACLU's founders. When she joined the Communist party in 1937, she told her colleagues on the board about it, but they raised no objections and in 1939 unanimously reelected her to another three-year term. Since Flynn refused to resign after the anticommunist measure went into effect, Ernst and his allies pressed charges and forced the board to hold a formal hearing. The trial, which took place at a New York City men's club on the night of May 7 and lasted until 2:30 in the morning, was a harbinger of the McCarthy era's reliance on guilt by association. Charging that Flynn's affiliation with the party, in and of itself, disqualified her as a civil libertarian, her accusers refused to acknowledge that individual Communists could operate independently of party orders or that they could really care about civil liberties. "If this trial occurred elsewhere," Flynn noted, "it would be a case for the A.C.L.U. to defend!" The final tally revealed the liberal community's underlying ambivalence about Communism. By a bare one-vote margin, the ACLU's board decided to oust Elizabeth Gurley Flynn.[102] The nation's most important liberal organization had officially signed on to the anticommunist crusade.

The denouement was delayed, however. Hitler's invasion of the Soviet Union and the wartime alliance between Washington and Moscow aborted what would otherwise have become a full-fledged red scare. But much of the institutional structure of that repression was in place and many of its key operatives were ready to move. Less than ten years later, they did. As the following chapter reveals, the concurrence of the federal government was crucial in bringing anticommunism into the center of the political arena. But it is clear that the existence of an already mobilized anticommunist cadre was just as important.

Because they differed in so many other ways, it is hard to conceive of such disparate political actors as Norman Thomas and J. Edgar Hoover collaborating in the same effort. But it was the very diversity of the anticommunist network that made it so powerful. The political repression that occurred during the McCarthy era was a collective enterprise. Each of its components reinforced the others, even when, as was sometimes the case, it looked as if they were operating independently.

The interconnections are crucial. The men and women who comprised the anticommunist network's main cadres worked together regularly during the 1940s and 1950s. The congressional committee hearings, political trials, blacklists, and loyalty programs that formed the core of the McCarthy era political repression all relied on the same cast of characters: J. Edgar Hoover, Louis Budenz, Benjamin Mandel, J. B. Matthews, Morris Ernst, and the dozens of other men and women who dedicated themselves to the eradication of Communism from American life.

What is particularly striking about these people's collaboration was how self-conscious it was. In November 1948, Eugene Lyons, one of the nation's leading anticommunist writers, wrote to Matthews suggesting, not completely in jest, that they organize themselves as "Red-Baiters, Inc." The ex-communist witness Paul Crouch actually tried to incorporate a group called the Federation of Former Communists. Neither organization ever came into being. As Joseph Zack Kornfeder, another professional witness, noted, such formations already existed — "resistance centers" he called them — and were, he added, quite "effective . . . in the fight against infiltration in government, etc." He knew whereof he spoke.[103]

★

CHAPTER 3

"IN THE INTEREST OF NATIONAL SECURITY"

ANTICOMMUNISM AND THE ROOSEVELT ADMINISTRATION

THE ACCESSION of the federal government to the anticommunist network transformed the struggle against Communism from a minor concern to a major one. Not only did Washington's participation bring the power of the state to the anticommunist campaign, but it also gave that campaign legitimacy, especially after the outbreak of World War II made it an issue of national security. The government's embrace of anticommunism was not an overnight affair; federal officials did not wake up on the morning after the Nazi-Soviet pact to decide "Today we will take care of the Commies." Rather the process occurred slowly, as precedents and pressures built up during the late 1930s and early 1940s that were to provide the underpinning for the more extensive and better-known purges of the following decade. In a sense, then, the Roosevelt years were a rehearsal for McCarthyism, a period when the nation's anti-Communists developed the machinery of the later political repression and perfected its operations.

Washington signed on to the anticommunist crusade in a fitful, meandering way. The government was not monolithic; its different parts worked separately and often in opposition. Not only did Congress, the Roosevelt administration, and the federal judiciary follow different trajectories, but even within each branch there were debates and disagreements. J. Edgar

Hoover, whose FBI was the single most important bureaucratic component of the process, operated with considerable independence, often ignoring the orders of his ostensible superiors in the Justice Department. Such contradictions made Washington's treatment of domestic Communism during the Roosevelt administration look like a mess. But that confusion did not produce a random result. Rather, it allowed those individuals and interest groups that did have a well-defined mission — like Hoover and the professional anti-Communists on the staff of the House Un-American Activities Committee — to take advantage of the mushiness at the center of the government and implement their own agendas.

Because the more virulent stages of the anticommunist crusade erupted after his death, Franklin Delano Roosevelt has come to be viewed — especially within the remnants of the old Popular Front constituency — as a greater defender of civil liberties than, in fact, he was. Neither particularly sympathetic nor particularly hostile to Communism, Roosevelt certainly cared about improving people's lives, but he was above all a pragmatic political operator who had little interest in abstract ideology. To the extent that the communist issue affected other political struggles, he dealt with it, but on an ad hoc basis, not from any coherently articulated ideological position. Accordingly, the few instances in the late 1930s and 1940s in which FDR took some kind of initiative reveal little consistency or planning, for the president usually had other things on his mind.[1]

Roosevelt's nonideological approach makes it hard to figure out exactly what he thought about Communism. If he devoted attention to the party, he probably shared the view of many liberals at the time that American Communists were noisy pests. He might well have agreed with his secretary of labor Frances Perkins that they were "crackpots and a nuisance" or seconded the opinion of his wartime vice president, Henry Wallace, a man who was himself later red-baited, that "a typical American communist is the contentious sort of individual that would probably be shot in Russia without any ceremony." In short, they were a bother, not a threat.[2]

Nonetheless, at those moments when Communists and their allies created problems for his administration, Roosevelt had few reservations about repressing them, especially if they interfered with national security or his own political career. He was not a civil libertarian. He was more than willing to spy on, harass, or prosecute any group or individual that opposed his policies. Though he had refused to send the army into San Francisco to put down the maritime strike of 1934, he was quite prepared to throw its leader Harry Bridges out of the country a year later. At times, especially when the CP turned against his foreign policy, the president could be quite ferocious. FDR's wrath, however, was short-lived and once the party line shifted, he was often more willing than other members of his administration to relax the government's pressure. In any event, the far right attracted much more of his attention than the far left; and in the early months of World War II, he was continually hounding his Attorney General to crack down on the native fascists and their antiwar propaganda.[3]

Given his basically humanitarian worldview, Roosevelt's casual regard for constitutional niceties would probably have caused little damage had he not also encouraged J. Edgar Hoover to put American Communists under surveillance. The FBI flourished during the 1930s. Hoover manipulated his agency's crime-fighting exploits to fashion an image of the Bureau and its incorruptible chief as the incarnation of most red-blooded American values. Roosevelt supported Hoover's campaign, for the president realized that boosting the FBI would help the New Deal as well as the Bureau. In addition, Hoover provided a more direct service to Roosevelt by supplying him with reports on his political enemies. FDR appreciated the information the Director provided and seemed unconcerned about the less than constitutional methods through which the Bureau obtained it. Once, when an FBI agent was caught red-handed in the act of bugging Harry Bridges's hotel room, Roosevelt viewed it more as a joke than an outrage. "By God, Edgar," Attorney General Francis Biddle recalled the president chortling, "that's the first time you've been caught with your pants down!"[4]

There was no law or official regulation that allowed the FBI to spy on the party. The widespread surveillance of political radicals that the Bureau had mounted during and immediately after World War I officially ended in 1924 when the Attorney General limited the FBI's investigations to violations of federal laws and prevented it from collecting intelligence in the political field. Roosevelt changed all that — but in secret. By 1934, he had become concerned about Nazi sympathizers in America and ordered the Bureau to look into their activities. Two years later he broadened that request to include Communists as well. From the start, both Hoover and Roosevelt wanted to keep the FBI's new mission a secret. At the August 24 meeting at which he authorized the FBI's surveillance of "the general [communist] movement and its activities," the president insisted that there be no written record of that request. Hoover, who was just as obsessed with concealing his agency's activities as he was with combating Communism, was glad to comply.[5]

Though ultimate responsibility for the Bureau's expanded operations clearly belongs to Roosevelt, it is equally clear that Hoover carried out his new mandate in accordance with his own deeply conservative view of the communist threat. Except for one fleeting reference to the activities of the right-wing priest Father Charles Coughlin, Hoover's account of his 1936 discussion with Roosevelt dealt entirely with Communism. The party, he warned the president, controlled or planned to control such unions as John L. Lewis's United Mine Workers, the Newspaper Guild, and Harry Bridges's longshoremen so that it could "paralyze the country" by stopping shipping, halting industry, and shutting down the press. Hoover also told Roosevelt about the CP's machinations within the executive branch. This presentation contained the basic agenda for McCarthyism. For the next twenty-five years, American countersubversives would focus on the same issues Hoover had raised — the threat posed by Communists in labor unions and the federal government.[6]

Though the American CP proved to be far less powerful and far more law-abiding than the FBI director had predicted, Roosevelt and his advisers took action against it nonetheless. Ironically, this was not because left-wing revolutionaries threatened the nation, but because right-wing politicians threatened the administration. Allegations of communist influence similar to those that Hoover made were to become the substance of an increasingly powerful congressional assault on the New Deal. The Roosevelt administration fended off that attack in its usual fitful manner, but ultimately felt compelled to do something to prove that it was not soft on Communism.

Roosevelt had long had enemies on the right. Demoralized at first, conservatives within the Republican party and among some of FDR's original supporters were attacking the president by 1934. Opposition to the labor movement and to the administration's perceived support for it inspired much of this hostility. So, too, did the realization that the New Deal was contesting the business community's previously undisputed control over the nation's economy. Such concerns, expressed often in the notion that the president was becoming a "dictator," were also rendered in the traditional language of anticommunism. By 1936, the Hearst press called Roosevelt "the unofficial candidate of the Comintern" and Frank Knox, the GOP's vice presidential candidate, announced that FDR was "leading us towards Moscow."[7]

At the same time, a group of powerful congressional leaders also turned against the New Deal. Like the business community with which many of them had close ties, they resented the administration's rhetoric as well as its welfare spending, fiscal impositions, and support for organized labor. Many of these politicians came from rural areas and reflected their constituents' suspicions of the apparent urban bias of the New Deal. The Southern Democrats among them feared that the administration might attack the system of white supremacy upon which their power was based. However, because Roosevelt still retained popular support, his congressional critics could do little more than grumble. But, beginning in 1937, a series of events damaged the administration's prestige and strengthened its opponents.[8]

In the first place, the serious recession that began in 1937 threw into question the efficacy of all the earlier New Deal measures. There was also the growing public hostility to the sit-down strikes, orchestrated in large part by a massive propaganda campaign which sought to link the New Deal, the CIO, and the Communist party together in the public mind. And, finally, there was Roosevelt's ill-advised court-packing plan, which alienated moderates as well as conservatives. As a result, when FDR's attempt to purge his senatorial enemies in the 1938 elections backfired, he had already lost control of Congress, at least with regard to domestic issues. Moreover, by the late 1930s the international situation had become so volatile that the president stopped seeking new social reforms for fear of antagonizing the congressional conservatives whose support he needed for his equally controversial foreign policy.[9]

In 1938, the creation of the Special House Committee on Un-American Activities (or HUAC, as it later came to be known) gave the administration's political enemies an institutional vehicle for their campaign against the

New Deal. By a lopsided 191–41 vote, the House of Representatives authorized Texas Democrat Martin Dies to mount a seven-month investigation of un-American propaganda. From the start, it was clear that the Dies committee, as HUAC then was called, had embarked on a thoroughly partisan venture that was designed to embarrass the administration. Chairman Dies, a glad-handing Texan who had long advocated the deportation of foreign radicals, had turned against the New Deal after the sit-down strikes. With the exception of a few token liberals, the other committee members, whether Democrats or Republicans, were equally hostile to the administration. Though it did take some testimony about the nation's leading Nazi sympathizers, the committee devoted most of its efforts to exposing alleged communist influence in CIO unions and New Deal agencies.[10]

The anticommunist scenario that Dies and his colleagues purveyed was a remarkably effective weapon for attacking the Roosevelt administration. Anticommunism, it turned out, made headlines and the committee's investigations invariably received enormous publicity. Even Dies, who was hardly a shrinking violet, was initially surprised by the front-page attention the hearings attracted. Moreover, because the Gallup poll recorded consistently high public approval ratings for the committee's investigations, few congressmen dared to oppose Dies, whether they approved of his activities or not. Every year, from 1938 until HUAC became a permanent committee in 1945, the committee's reauthorization passed by overwhelming margins. The House had little choice, as a liberal Democrat from Pennsylvania observed when he voted for the committee's continuation in 1941. "On the one hand, to adopt this resolution is to seemingly approve the un-American procedures of the Special Committee to Investigate Un-American Activities. On the other hand, to defeat the resolution is to seemingly approve of a continuation of subversive activities."[11]

Naturally, within the committee's own conservative constituency, the support for its activities was even stronger. Dies's attacks on the CIO ensured the backing of businessmen and AFL leaders alike. Henry Ford even offered to supply automobiles to HUAC and its staff. Though the FBI initially remained aloof, most other sectors of the anticommunist network collaborated with the new committee. Local red squads, for example, facilitated the committee's raids on party offices and front groups. The HUAC staff itself, a collection of former FBI agents, industrial spies, ex-Communists, and patronage appointees, represented a good cross section of the anticommunist world. J. B. Matthews and Benjamin Mandel handled much of the committee's research and choreographed its hearings, prepping witnesses and selecting targets.[12]

Though some of the committee's charges, like Matthews's allegation that the child film star Shirley Temple had been duped by the party, backfired, others often seriously embarrassed the Roosevelt administration and its allies. They drew real blood, effectively casting suspicions of communist influence on several New Deal agencies and politicians. After a HUAC hearing in Michigan helped defeat that state's liberal governor, Roosevelt tried to curb the committee's power, but to no avail. Dies was unstoppable and HUAC could not be killed.[13]

Unable to destroy the committee, Roosevelt tried to appease it and his other conservative opponents. He took steps designed to show the public that the administration was fully as alert to the menace of Communism as Dies and his colleagues, while at the same time quietly moving to eliminate potential sources of embarrassment. These efforts, however, simply legitimized the committee's charges and set important precedents for the future. But — and it is important to keep this qualification in mind — the administration was not always responding only to Dies, nor was it invariably reluctant to crack down on alleged reds. When his administration had to confront similarly partisan attacks in the late 1940s and 1950s, Harry Truman responded in exactly the same way. He appeased his enemies by attacking Communists he did not want to protect.[14]

The case of the National Labor Relations Board is instructive here. Both the most vulnerable and the most controversial of the New Deal agencies, the Board had been set up to oversee the collective bargaining process that the 1935 Wagner Act put under federal protection. For obvious reasons, it was not popular with employers, nor did the AFL appreciate its seeming partiality toward the CIO. Even Roosevelt and his secretary of labor Frances Perkins were unhappy about what they felt was its "improperly" prolabor bias. Dies had targeted the agency from the start, but so, too, had the FBI and Representative Howard Smith of Virginia, the powerful chairman of the House Rules Committee, who launched a special investigation of the board in the summer of 1939. Because there were Communists within the NLRB, including its energetic secretary Nathan Witt, the agency was particularly vulnerable to right-wing attack.[15]

Given the political weakness of the Roosevelt administration and the strength of the coalition that opposed the NLRB, a full-scale assault on the board by congressional conservatives might also have gutted the Wagner Act. Just as bad was the prospect of the damage to Roosevelt's third-term campaign that might be caused by the Republican party's exploitation of the charges of communist influence within the embattled agency. Since neither Perkins nor Roosevelt had much sympathy for the NLRB anyhow, they sought to head off such an eventuality by purging the board. They managed to kill Congressman Smith's attempt to revise the Wagner Act, though not before he had publicized allegations of communist influence within the NLRB. But they did succeed in defanging the NLRB; by the mid-1940s, its decisions were decidedly less friendly to labor.[16]

Even more threatening to the administration was the campaign against it for failing to deport Harry Bridges. This was a highly cynical maneuver on the part of the Dies Committee and FDR's other political opponents, who used the issue to disseminate the charge that the administration was "soft" on Communism. Ever since Bridges's emergence in the 1934 maritime strike as the West Coast's scrappiest and most effective labor leader, a coalition of Legionnaires, employers, and union rivals had been trying to deport the Australian-born longshoreman. The president and his advisers, though hardly sharing the paranoia of West Coast conservatives, did not oppose the measure as long as it could be legally done. But the 1918 immigration statute then in force required the government to prove that Bridges had either sought to overthrow the government by "force and violence" or joined an organization that did. Though the Department of Labor, which was then in charge of the Immigration and Naturalization Service, had been investigating Bridges since 1934, it did not have enough evidence to begin proceedings against him.[17]

The situation changed in 1938. With the help of the anticommunist network, the district director of the Seattle INS had unearthed witnesses willing to testify that Bridges was in the party. And the administration was under so much pressure that Secretary Perkins decided to act. The Labor Department brought charges against the ILWU leader on March 2, 1938, and prepared to make its case at a scheduled hearing in April on the West Coast. Then it postponed the hearing. A federal appeals court in New Orleans had just ruled against the government in a similar deportation case and Perkins had to put the Bridges case on hold until after the Supreme Court settled the law. The postponement unleashed a storm of protest. Dies was particularly vituperative, attacking the government for delaying the deportation proceedings and charging that the secretary of labor was trying "to protect, rather than deport" Bridges.[18]

The conflict escalated in January 1939, when the future chairman of HUAC, New Jersey Republican Parnell Thomas, called for the impeachment of Perkins and her chief subordinates. The spectacle of a high federal official having to defend her department's actions before the House of Representatives illustrated how embarrassing the issue had become. Though the Judiciary Committee soon exonerated Perkins, the administration's failure to deport the longshoremen's leader was taking a political toll. Some of Roosevelt's more conservative advisers believed that the American public was so determined to deport Bridges that, as Postmaster General James Farley suggested, "whether he [was] deportable or not, Bridges ought to be sent out of the country for the sake of the Democratic Party."[19]

But he was not. When the proceedings resumed after the Supreme Court's decision, the eminent outside examiner whom Perkins had appointed to handle the case ruled against deporting the longshoremen's leader. Two months of hearings had produced such contradictory testimony that the special examiner, Harvard Law School's Dean James M. Landis, felt compelled to throw out the case. The evidence against Bridges was just too tainted. The 152-page decision that Landis delivered at the end of December 1939 described the government's witnesses as, among other epithets, "a problem in contumacy," "a self-confessed liar," "pathological," and someone whose "evasions are truly labyrinthine in nature."[20]

By the time Landis rendered his decision, the Nazi-Soviet pact had been signed, Hitler had invaded Poland, Great Britain and France had declared war on Germany, and the American Communist party had abandoned its support for collective security and was opposing the war in Europe. The CP's dramatic policy shift destroyed the Popular Front against fascism, antagonizing liberals and further legitimizing the growing anticommunist campaign. Actually, the party's volte-face only accelerated a process that was already under way. By 1939, the CP had become so unpopular that, even if Stalin had not made his deal with Hitler, many of the politically repressive measures that were taken during the two-year period between the Nazi-Soviet pact and Hitler's June 1941 invasion of the Soviet Union would still have been adopted.

Congress, for example, was in such a state of frenzy about Communists, fascists, Nazis, and foreigners of all persuasions that it had passed several pieces of countersubversive legislation even before the fighting began. "If you brought in the Ten Commandments today," a California congressman noted in mid-July 1939, "and asked for their repeal and attached to that request an anti-alien law, you could get it." By then the Foreign Agents Registration Act had already become law and Congress was about to pass the Hatch Act. Though primarily designed to curb the Roosevelt administration's electoral activities, the measure also contained provisions for dismissing government workers who belonged to "any political party or organization which advocates the overthrow of our constitutional form of government in the United States."[21]

Nonetheless, despite the already high level of political intolerance that existed before August 1939, the Nazi-Soviet pact did mark a qualitative shift in the campaign against the party. Once World War II transformed Communism from a political issue into a matter of national security, the Roosevelt administration, hitherto an often reluctant and fitful participant in the anticommunist crusade, definitively turned against the CP. It now viewed the party's noisy opposition to its rearmament efforts and its nearly unconditional support for the British as a genuine problem.[22]

Within a few months of the Nazi-Soviet pact, the Roosevelt administration was openly repressing the CP. Earl Browder, the party's general secretary, was the first and most prominent victim. Hauled before HUAC on September 5, only a few days after the war had begun, Browder, who mistakenly assumed that the statute of limitations had run out, exposed himself to prosecution by admitting that he had made a false statement on a passport application. It is unclear whether the Roosevelt administration, which had long known of Browder's infraction, would have prosecuted him had there been no political pressure. But there was. On October 22, the Republican National Committee released a statement by HUAC member Parnell Thomas attacking the Justice Department for its "strangely indifferent and listless" behavior in the face of Browder's transgression. The next day, the government began the prosecution. Browder was indicted in November and tried in January. Convicted after less than an hour's deliberation by the jury, the communist leader received an unprecedentedly stiff four-year sentence and a $2,000 fine. On February 17, 1941, the Supreme Court upheld his conviction; he entered the Atlanta Federal Penitentiary the next month.[23]

Ordinary people did not go to prison for four years for failing to reveal that they had once held passports under a different name. And, as the government launched criminal and deportation proceedings against dozens of other high-level Communists and left-wing union leaders, it was clear that the administration had embarked on a campaign of selective prosecution against the party similar to the one that would take place during the McCarthy years. In December 1939, Interior Secretary Harold Ickes noted in his diary that the Attorney General had proudly boasted to the cabinet that "every possible effort is being made to indict any Communist who has violated the criminal laws in any respect."[24]

The Dies committee got into the act as well. In September 1939, HUAC raided the Washington, D.C., office of the party's main antifascist front group and seized its membership and mailing lists. In April 1940, the committee made more raids on party headquarters in Pittsburgh and Baltimore. In Philadelphia, the city's red squad helped Dies and his men load two trucks full of files, mailing lists, and other materials from the local offices of the CP and the International Workers Order. Though a federal judge condemned the raids as a "conspiracy to violate the Bill of Rights" and ordered the committee to return its booty, Dies had carefully arranged to photograph the documents before he gave them back.[25]

The FBI, which got access to the materials Dies had seized, made similar forays — though usually with greater stealth. On February 6, 1940, however, the Bureau launched a series of predawn raids in Detroit and Milwaukee to arrest a dozen people for having recruited volunteers for the Abraham Lincoln Brigade. This time, however, the FBI had gone too far. The sight of the Spanish Civil War vets and their supporters handcuffed and in chains aroused such a furor among liberals that Attorney General Robert Jackson quickly dropped the case.[26]

State and local officials followed Washington's lead. Eager prosecutors filed charges against rank-and-file Communists as well as party leaders. The CP's preparations for the 1940 presidential elections came under special attack. Fifteen states, including New York, Illinois, and Ohio, simply ruled it off the ballot. Elsewhere local vigilantes and police harassed the men and women who were circulating the party's nominating petitions. Over three hundred canvassers were arrested in a dozen states and charged with everything from criminal syndicalism in Illinois and Oklahoma to robbery, assault, housebreaking, and disturbing the peace in Kalamazoo, Michigan. Bail was high, as much as $30,000 for some Pennsylvania canvassers; and most of the defendants were convicted and spent time in prison.[27]

Besides throwing them in jail, state and local officials found other ways to harass Communists during this period. The Massachusetts Insurance Commission refused to renew the IWO's license to sell insurance. Other states tried to weed out subversive employees. In California and New York, the legislatures set up what came to be known as little Dies committees. The California committee, headed by the future Los Angeles mayor Sam Yorty, was supposed to investigate welfare abuse, but it was soon converted into a HUAC clone under state senator Jack Tenney. New York's Rapp-Coudert committee, initially formed to look at school finances, instead investigated Communists in education. It called up dozens of New York City high school and college teachers and forced the Board of Higher Education to fire more than fifty of them.[28]

Meanwhile, dozens of bills directed against aliens, Communists, Nazis, and the like were speeding through Congress. As of early April 1940, Roosevelt and his advisers still retained enough confidence in their ability to protect civil liberties to veto the first alien and sedition measure that reached the Oval Office. But the bills kept coming, including a prohibition against employing Communists in the Works Progress Administration and a proposal specifically designed to deport Harry Bridges that the House passed 330–42 on June 13. By then, with Hitler rampaging through Western Europe, even such previously committed civil libertarians as Attorney General Jackson started to waver. As a result, Roosevelt did not veto the Alien Registration Act that the Senate passed with a voice vote on June 15th and the House by a 382–4 margin on the 22nd.[29]

Besides requiring that all aliens be registered and fingerprinted, the Smith Act, as the measure came to be called after its powerful sponsor Virginia's Howard Smith, gave the United States the peacetime sedition law that J. Edgar Hoover and his allies had been seeking since 1919. Under its provisions, it was no longer necessary to prove that someone was actually building bombs or collecting dynamite; simply talking about overthrowing the government by "force and violence" was enough. The act also contained provisions that, by allowing for the deportation of aliens who had once belonged to an organization that advocated force and violence would, in the words of a jubilant Alabama congressman, change "the law so that the Department of Justice should now have little trouble in deporting Harry Bridges and all others of similar ilk." [30]

The Roosevelt administration got the message, especially after the House of Representatives passed yet another bill specifically calling for Bridges's deportation. On August 24, 1940, the attorney general reopened the case with the announcement that he was authorizing the FBI to investigate the West Coast labor leader. Responsibility for immigration matters had just been transferred from the Labor to the Justice Department in an administrative reorganization that, though rejected in the spring of 1939, had suddenly seemed "a pressing need" a year later with the wartime emergency and FDR's controversial bid for a third term. [31]

The transfer of the INS from the Labor to the Justice Department clearly owed much to the firestorm of right-wing criticism that blazed up after Landis had ruled against Bridges's deportation. But it also reflected a more profound transformation within the administration that occurred in response to the German conquest of Western Europe. When Roosevelt referred to "the startling sequence of international events" in justifying his decision to give the Attorney General jurisdiction over immigration, he was not just concealing the obviously partisan considerations behind his action. By the spring of 1940, the president had come to believe that America's own security depended on the survival of Great Britain and the ultimate defeat of Germany. The CP's opposition to FDR's program of rearmament and aid to the Allies was, thus, a threat to the nation. [32]

Though the party's public agitation, which included a daily picket line in front of the White House, hardly endangered Roosevelt's attempt to mobilize the American people, the possibility that Communists might use their positions within the labor movement to cripple the nation's defense effort was taken more seriously. Hoover had been warning about such sabotage for years, sending the White House increasingly graphic descriptions of how party members in the National Maritime Union and UAW might scuttle the nation's shipping or bring assembly lines to a halt. Hoover's warnings fell on receptive ears. In a handwritten memo on the bottom of one of the Director's descriptions of possible sabotage within the munitions and automobile industries, Roosevelt instructed his aide "Pa" Watson to "tell J.E.H. to go after this." Other New Deal officials were equally concerned.[33]

Even though none of the physical mischief that Hoover predicted ever took place, the fear that Communists might sabotage ships, utilities, and defense plants lingered for years and was to justify a wide range of loyalty-security measures throughout the 1940s and 1950s. The Roosevelt administration was actually much more concerned about the possibility that Communists within the labor movement would cripple the defense effort by calling political strikes. Such fears were, or at least seemed to be, more realistic. After all, communist theorists in their more apocalyptic moments had talked about seizing power through general strikes; and there had been a few instances in which communist-led unions had walked off the job for political reasons. As a result, it was not hard to envision a situation in which the party might order its adherents within the labor movement to impede war production by calling strikes.[34]

The strike wave that broke out in 1940 when the CIO resumed the unionization drive that had been stalled by the 1937–38 recession gave substance to these fears. The walkouts were called to demand union recognition and higher wages, not to hamper the rearmament effort. Communists participated, but so, too, did non-Communists. There is no credible evidence that any of the communist-led strikes occurred for other than economic reasons, nor did left-wing unions walk off the job with any greater frequency than mainstream ones. In fact, many communist-led unions did not stop work at all during this period. Harry Bridges's longshoremen signed a no-strike agreement in November 1940, and the electrical workers union did not strike against any company with a defense contract between January and June 1941. In one instance, a prominent communist official within the UE actually begged the workers at a torpedo factory to delay a walkout because of the importance of their work to the defense effort.[35]

But not all left-wing labor leaders showed such patriotic restraint and the undeniable communist presence in a few major strikes gave substance to widespread concern both within the administration and the broader public that the party was trying to sabotage America's defense. Because many of the military officers and businessmen who were running the nation's rearmament effort were traditionally hostile to unions, they readily embraced the scenario of communist defeatism; it reinforced their already strong desire to clamp down on restive workers and roll back the labor movement's recent gains. But even liberal New Dealers worried about communist-led defense strikes. Alienated by the CP's opposition to American foreign policy and alarmed by rumors that job actions by communist unions in France and Belgium had hastened the German advance in 1940, these liberals also came to believe that the party threatened the nation's security.[36]

Three strikes in particular bolstered that perception. Two took place in southern California at the Vultee and North American Aircraft Company plants and the third occurred in the Allis-Chalmers Manufacturing Company's facilities outside Milwaukee. Because they took place in plants that had large defense contracts, all three strikes attracted considerable attention. Moreover, because many of the strike leaders were in or near the Communist party, the issue of Communism came to overshadow the specific workplace disputes and internal union struggles that had, in fact, precipitated the walkouts.[37]

The California strikes grew out of the chaotic labor relations within the aircraft industry, where thousands of new workers flooded into the booming factories only to be confronted by low wages and turf warfare between rival AFL and CIO unions. The UAW sent some of its best organizers into the area, including its most prominent Communist, Wyndham Mortimer. In November 1940, the Vultee workers walked off the job because the company would not negotiate with their newly formed local. The work stoppage lasted twelve days, long enough for politicians and the media to charge that it was a communist attempt to sabotage the war effort. Bombarded by reports from the FBI and military intelligence agencies about communist troublemakers in the labor movement, many members of the Roosevelt administration expressed similar concerns.[38]

Torn between the desire to consolidate the organizational breakthroughs obtained by the defense strikes and the fear that the backlash against those strikes might provoke new antilabor legislation, the CIO's top leaders began to court the Roosevelt administration. As a result, when the same UAW organizers who had led the Vultee strike became involved in a work stoppage at the North American Aircraft Company in the late spring of 1941, the CIO and UAW's high command did not oppose the government's decision to intervene. The strike seems to have been the result of the local union's need for some kind of militant action in order to fend off an AFL rival and win over the inexperienced workers pouring into the plant. But Roosevelt was furious. On June 10, five days after the strike began, he sent in the army to reopen the factory. As the then Attorney General Robert Jackson recalled, "We prepared to seize the company as an example, among other things, that war production could not be stopped by a Communist led strike." [39]

Though the North American work stoppage was the most dramatic of the communist-led defense-period strikes, the seventy-six-day walkout by UAW Local 248 at the Allis-Chalmers Company in the spring of 1941 had the most serious repercussions. Labor relations at the Wisconsin company had long been stormy, for the Allis-Chalmers management was notoriously antiunion. Its refusal to recognize the UAW as the exclusive bargaining agent for its workers generated enormous unrest. Work stoppages were endemic long before the big strike. So, too, was red-baiting, for many of Local 248's leaders were in or near the Communist party and the company played up their affiliations in an attempt to weaken support for the union. [40]

Because of Allis-Chalmers's antilabor record, its red-baiting did not get much attention until the United States geared up for the war that had already begun in Europe. Then the company became a major military contractor; and its anticommunism took on a patriotic cast. It mounted a massive campaign to convince the federal government and broader public that its labor troubles originated in Moscow. And it succeeded. When the local finally called its long-awaited strike in January 1941, the company's charge that the Communists who controlled Local 248 were sabotaging the nation's defense gained wide currency within the media. The detailed reports about the strike leaders' party connections that the FBI and military intelligence had been disseminating within the administration convinced Roosevelt and his advisers of the same thing. The walkout was a nasty one; negotiations got nowhere; and an attempt to restart production led to so much violence that the governor of Wisconsin had to intervene. Ultimately federal mediators pressured the company to come to terms, but not before Roosevelt had become so upset about the strike's impact on defense production that he was about to seize the plant.[41]

Because it had seemingly translated the threat of communist sub-version into reality, the Allis-Chalmers strike continued to affect official thinking about left-wing labor throughout the war and for many years there-after. Repeatedly evoked to justify continued surveillance of communist-led unions, the administration worried that the party might again endanger the nation. "If it [the CP] becomes anti-war," warned the liberal Justice Department official James Rowe, Jr., early in 1942,

> American war industry may well be paralyzed. I say this advisedly but I do not believe it is an exaggeration. Sabotage will be rampant. The entire country will have its hands full in handling the problem. The Allis-Chalmers strike was merely a token payment.[42]

Rowe recognized that the danger he was describing was "not a probability at the moment." Hitler's invasion of the Soviet Union on June 22, 1941, had led to another flip-flop by the party. It dropped its opposition to inter-vention and advocated resistance to fascism and all-out aid to the Allies. Though the CP's renewed support for Roosevelt's foreign policy could not erase all memories of its earlier isolationism, the anticommunist crusade did abate — at least within the political mainstream. It was, after all, hard to insist that Communists threatened national security when Roosevelt em-braced Stalin as a valued ally and the party was the nation's most fervent champion of organized labor's "No Strike Pledge." Moreover, official mis-treatment of Communists might send the wrong signal to the Soviet Union, whose efforts were so central to the defeat of Hitler.[43]

The honeymoon was not long-lived, nor did it bring about more than a superficial relaxation of the earlier antagonism to the party. Even among liberals, suspicions lingered. But, at least for the moment, cabinet members spoke at front-group rallies and the national radio networks broadcast the speeches of party leader Earl Browder.[44]

Browder's situation symbolized the CP's new status. Though he was still in the Atlanta Federal Penitentiary at the time of Pearl Harbor, the campaign for his release had begun to attract many eminent citizens, including the 1940 Republican presidential candidate Wendell Willkie. Recognizing that there was nothing to be gained by forcing the party's leader to serve out the remainder of his patently unfair sentence, Roosevelt released him from prison on May 16, 1942, on the grounds that it "will have a tendency to promote national unity."[45]

Even more indicative of the new attitude toward the former communist menace was the abatement of the demand for deporting Harry Bridges. Once the Germans invaded the Soviet Union, the longshoremen's leader collaborated so enthusiastically with the West Coast maritime industry in support of the war effort that many of the politicians and businessmen who had clamored so vehemently for Bridges's deportation only a few years before now petitioned the government to drop the case. It did not. Despite his reputation as a civil libertarian, Attorney General Francis Biddle had been convinced by the FBI reports that came across his desk that Communists endangered the nation. In addition, he was concerned about the prospect of a congressional backlash if the government dropped the case yet again.[46]

The Supreme Court would decide Bridges's fate and it seemed increasingly likely that it might do so in his favor. On June 21, 1943, by a 5–3 majority, the Court ruled in the similar deportation case of the California party leader William Schneiderman that the Justice Department had failed to show that the Communist party was trying to overthrow the American government. The decision was momentous, for it went to the heart of the government's basic case against the CP — the assertion that the party and its adherents were part of an illegal conspiracy to destroy the American government by force and violence. Nonetheless, when the Court overturned Bridges's deportation two years later, it did so on the much narrower grounds that the government had not proved that Bridges belonged to the CP.[47]

Though the *Schneiderman* decision seemed to presage a greater toleration for civil liberties within official Washington, on other issues both the Court and the Roosevelt administration revealed a disturbing willingness to violate individual rights in the name of national security. The CP was no longer the main target of these incursions against civil liberties, but precedents were set that could be and were used against the party when its wartime acceptability waned and the Cold War turned it into a threat to national security. Ironically, many Communists applauded these measures at the time.

They did not, for example, seriously oppose the federal government's decision to evacuate Japanese Americans from the West Coast and send them to detention camps. Though the CP recognized "the malicious racism" behind the relocations, it did not want to do anything that might hamper the war effort. The Roosevelt administration defended these relocations in the language of national security. And the Supreme Court, just as it was to rule when it deprived Communists of their political rights in the late 1940s, invoked a similar justification when it condoned the wartime roundup of the Japanese.[48]

An equally ominous precedent was set by the government's initial prosecutions under the 1940 Smith Act. The first case was that of the Trotskyists in the Socialist Workers Party (SWP) who had been active in an important Teamsters Union local in Minneapolis. The prosecution, a political favor to the Teamsters president who had long wanted to purge his radical subordinates, resulted in the June 1941 indictment of twenty-nine Trotskyist leaders on two counts of trying to interfere with the military and teaching and advocating the forcible overthrow of the U.S. government.[49]

The five-week trial later in the year prefigured the later Smith Act case against the Communist party both in the type of evidence that was produced and in the final outcome. Besides relying on the testimony of former SWP members, the government introduced dozens of documents, including the *Communist Manifesto,* as evidence for the Trotskyists' advocacy of force and violence. The jury returned a mixed verdict, acquitting some of the defendants outright and recommending lenient sentences for the rest. Significantly, the Supreme Court refused to review the case, thus upholding, at least for the time being, the constitutionality of the Smith Act. Though the CP's leaders realized that the law might someday be used against their own party, their wartime loyalty to FDR and hostility to Trotskyism kept them from speaking out against the Minneapolis prosecution.[50]

The second Smith Act trial was also a battle of the books. This time, however, the defendants came from the other end of the political spectrum, a motley collection of native fascists and German propagandists that FDR had long been pestering his Attorney General to indict. The main case, a Smith Act prosecution of more than thirty assorted defendants, was a raucous proceeding that ended in a mistrial when the judge died of a heart attack in November 1944. But the Smith Act survived.[51]

Though Roosevelt and his advisers may well have been relatively more solicitous of civil liberties than earlier wartime regimes, the administration's overall record was hardly reassuring and set unfortunate precedents. It had seriously eroded the constitutional barriers to a future attack on the CP by obtaining rulings that enshrined national security as a justification for political repression. And, below the surface, in the less public realm of bureaucratic politics, the administrative structure of the coming assault on Communism was being erected.

The reprieve from official repression that the Communist party experienced during World War II should not be exaggerated. The mellower image of the Soviet Union that accompanied the wartime alliance did not extend to native Communists. Nor did the party's growing moderation and all-out support for the war effort lessen popular hostility. The anticommunist network was still in operation and at least in certain sectors of the government wielded some clout.[52]

The treatment of the veterans of the Spanish Civil War reveals that influence. Though the Office of Strategic Services (OSS), the forerunner of the CIA, actually recruited some Lincoln Brigade veterans for undercover operations in Europe, the rest of the military treated them with hostility. For several years, the War Department had an unofficial policy of segregating the men who had fought in Spain and other known Communists and keeping them out of combat. These people would often go through basic training and then, at the last moment, when the other members of their units were shipped overseas, they would be held behind and put through yet another training program. They were, in the Army's bizarre terminology, "premature antifascists," subject to harassment by military intelligence officers and, in many cases, sent to special camps where they were treated almost like prisoners of war.[53]

Of more importance than the sporadic harassment of communist soldiers and other party members was the way in which wartime measures stimulated the growth of those aspects of the federal government's internal security system that became so important during the McCarthy era. Many of these developments reflected the empire building of J. Edgar Hoover. Roosevelt's hostility toward the critics of his foreign policy led him to enlarge Hoover's mandate during the 1930s; World War II accelerated that process. Even before the Nazi-Soviet pact, the FBI had shoved aside its civilian competitors and, along with the intelligence branches of the army and navy, won exclusive jurisdiction over all cases of espionage, counterespionage, and sabotage. As the FBI's responsibilities grew, so, too, did its size; it went from 851 agents in 1939 to 4,600 in 1943. National security obviously demanded more personnel than chasing bank robbers and car thieves.[54]

Besides widening their Bureau's jurisdiction, Hoover and his men took advantage of the wartime situation to eliminate many of the legal restrictions on what they could do. National security was the standard excuse. It was, for example, the justification that President Roosevelt gave in May 1940 when he explicitly overrode the Supreme Court's 1937 decision to outlaw wiretapping and authorized the FBI to use electronic surveillance against "persons suspected of subversive activities against the Government of the United States." The Supreme Court, Roosevelt insisted, "never intended" to have its decision against wiretapping "apply to grave matters involving the defense of the nation."[55]

Once unleashed, the FBI quickly expanded its operations, often without explicit authorization. When, for example, the Justice Department refused to let the Bureau investigate the National Lawyers Guild, the FBI did so anyhow. Another of Hoover's independent projects was the creation of the Security Index, a list of politically suspect individuals to be rounded up for detention during an emergency. The Director began the program a few days after the Nazi-Soviet pact, but for almost a year he did not tell his superiors about it. Hoover's reticence was warranted, for the index and the authoritarian values it enshrined quickly became a source of contention between the FBI and the Attorney General. On July 16, 1943, Attorney General Biddle officially ended the program. Not only was there "no statutory authorization or other present justification for keeping a 'custodial detention' list of citizens," he told Hoover, but "the notion that it is possible to make a valid determination as to how dangerous a person is in the abstract and without reference to time, environment, and other relevant circumstances is impractical, unwise, and dangerous." The FBI director ignored the order. Instead of abandoning the program, he changed its name. The "Custodial

Detention List" became the "Security Index." And, of course, the Justice Department was not told about the transformation.[56]

The wartime emergency also let the FBI expand into the area of industrial security, where it helped the military intelligence agencies screen workers in defense plants. Operating in a more authoritarian environment than the civilian-controlled FBI, the army's G-2 and the Office of Naval Intelligence seem to have had even fewer scruples about wiretaps, break-ins, and other illegal activities. All three agencies relied heavily on the undercover informants whom they had recruited within the nation's war industries. The army had 250,000 informants, the FBI over 80,000. They were not very productive. Though millions of people were investigated, Hoover's top advisers noted that "the number of worthwhile cases reported to the Bureau through those informants was practically negligible."[57]

Since there were few Nazi saboteurs to be found, the FBI and the military intelligence agencies looked to the left. Drawing on the supposed lessons of the Nazi-Soviet pact period, they operated on the common assumption that, despite the wartime patriotism of the Communist party, its members remained a potential threat. "They cannot be trusted," a high-ranking army officer told the UAW in Detroit in July 1942, "since their attitude is likely to be guided by whether Russia remains in the war on the side of the United States or not. . . . Russia deserted the Allies in the last war and may do it again in this war."[58]

Understandably, militant left-wing unions that tried to organize workers in defense industries received special attention. Military officers, HUAC staff members, and FBI agents treated communist-led unions with enormous hostility, often viewing them as little more than adjuncts of the Soviet secret police and breeding grounds for saboteurs. The Federation of Architects, Engineers, Chemists and Technicians (FAECT), a small left-wing union of technical workers that had been trying to organize locals in navy yards and army bases, was particularly suspect. After all, as one army intelligence officer reported to his superior a few months before Pearl Harbor, the union had been "started by JEWISH RADICALS [sic] and at present are so controlled." It was, he explained, "a typical Communist front organization" whose operations "are subversive in intent and definitely interfere with military efficiency and National Defense effort."[59]

The attempt of some young physicists who were involved with the atomic bomb project to organize a FAECT local at the University of California's Berkeley Radiation Laboratory further reinforced the intelligence community's assessment of the subversive nature of the union. Secretary of War Henry Stimson was so alarmed by the Berkeley FAECT that he warned FDR in a September 1943 memorandum that "it is unquestionable that the union organization will be used to further espionage activity of agents of a foreign power."[60]

Other left-wing unions, like Bridges's longshoremen and the UE, seemed to pose similar threats. Their leaders were in or near the Communist party and they operated in areas like the maritime and electrical industries that were crucial to the nation's defense. Even liberals expressed concern about some of these unions. For the military intelligence agencies and the FBI, with their authoritarian, law-and-order mind-set and their underlying hostility to militant labor, almost any type of industrial conflict involving a left-wing union seemed to have a hidden agenda. None of these agencies made careful distinctions between suspected subversion and legitimate trade union activities. Thus, for example, when a group of UE workers at the Sperry Gyroscope Company on Long Island staged a half-hour sit-down strike for higher wages, the Bureau classified the action as "sabotage."[61]

Although the prospect of labor unrest kept the FBI and its military associates from acting on all their suspicions, from the perspective of the defense plant workers who ran afoul of the Bureau and military intelligence, the industrial security program seemed thoroughly inquisitorial. It is hard to tell exactly how many people in private industry were, as a New York City FBI agent put it, "discharged in the interest of National Security." One we know of was Julius Rosenberg and there may have been several thousand more. The army, for example, forced more than two thousand people from their jobs. Whatever its direct impact may have been, this wartime program created precedents for the similar industrial security measures that were established during the Cold War. It also created a paper legacy; and there is evidence that information from the individual files generated during the war resurfaced in the loyalty-security proceedings of the late 1940s and 1950s.[62]

Of even greater consequence was the intensification of the campaign to eliminate Communists from the federal government. Ostensibly a matter of ensuring the loyalty of federal employees, the Communists-in-government issue, as it emerged during the Roosevelt administration, was in reality a partisan stratagem by the New Deal's conservative opponents. They used charges that there were reds in Washington to bolster their allegations that FDR was "hand in glove with the Communist Party." The Dies committee specialized in making these accusations. The committee's first target was the Federal Theatre project, which it pilloried and essentially destroyed in a set of hearings in August and November 1938. Dies then went after the rest of the New Deal. His standard strategy was to take testimony from professional ex-Communists and disgruntled civil servants and then challenge the administration to dismiss the alleged subversives his witnesses had named.[63]

The committee's definition of what constituted potential subversion was somewhat fuzzy. Since Communists usually kept their political affiliation secret and it was hard to prove that someone actually belonged to the party, HUAC came to rely on indirect evidence — support for left-wing causes and affiliation with front groups and other organizations close to the CP. Using this kind of evidence could and did lead to widespread abuse, but compiling it was easy. The committee's staff, under J. B. Matthews and Benjamin Mandel, harvested names from left-wing letterheads and the communist press as well as from the membership and mailing lists of Washington, D. C., front groups that had been seized during raids and break-ins. All went into the committee's files and fed its allegations that the New Deal harbored subversives.[64]

Dies named names and gave numbers, pioneering the technique later associated with Joe McCarthy by punctuating his charges against the Roosevelt administration with lists of allegedly disloyal employees. Since his campaign masked a domestic political agenda, such world events as the Nazi-Soviet pact or Pearl Harbor had little impact on it. And, in fact, the turnaround occasioned by the entry of the Soviet Union into World War II brought no diminution in the Texas congressman's demands for a purge. On the contrary, as he explained in October 1941,

> there is a new influx of subversive elements into official Washington. It must, of course, be apparent to all that our present foreign policy of all-out aid to Russia is one that makes it very easy for communists and their sympathizers to pose as the most ardent patriots. The very grave

danger exists that our Government, by its aid to Russia on the Eastern Front, has opened up for Stalin a new Western Front right here in the capital of America.

And he vociferously defended that front throughout the war. In September 1941, Dies attacked five people in the Office of Price Administration, including its director; in October he sent the Attorney General a list of 1,121 suspect civil servants; in February 1942, it was thirty-five alleged subversives in the Bureau of Economic Warfare; the following year, there were another thirty-nine names. The charges were far from random and were almost always aimed at those New Deal and wartime agencies whose liberal policies most offended Dies and his conservative allies.[65]

Much as Roosevelt and his advisers would have liked to ignore Dies, they could not. The noisy Texan's call for eliminating Communists from the federal payroll had enormous congressional and popular support. In June 1941, Congress, which had presumably disqualified such disloyal employees under the Hatch Act two years before, attached provisions to the annual appropriations for the Department of Justice specifically allocating $100,000 to the FBI to investigate all federal workers "who are members of subversive organizations or advocate the overthrow of the Federal Government" and requiring the Bureau to "report its findings to Congress." Thus, when Dies sent the Justice Department his list of 1,121 names in October 1941, it was clear that the administration would have to check them all out. And that was only a start. In 1942 Congress doubled the FBI's appropriation for these Hatch Act investigations.[66]

The Dies list, as it came to be called, was to become a lethal time bomb for the Democratic administration. It read like a Who's Who of Popular Front Washington and contained the names of many of the New Deal's best and brightest lawyers and bureaucrats — and most of its Communists. Some of the names, like those of Alger Hiss and Harry Dexter White, were to become all too familiar in the early Cold War years. Because they were on the list, both Hiss and White were interviewed by FBI agents early in 1942. Both men denied that they were Communists and kept their jobs.[67]

So did most of the other people on the Dies list. The Roosevelt administration never carried out the widespread purges that Dies and his colleagues had called for. Out of the 1,121 names on the original Dies list, only two people had been fired for disloyalty as of September 1942. Other investigations produced equally meager yields; only thirty-four of the 2,910 civil servants that the FBI was also investigating for loyalty lost their jobs. In his letter transmitting the FBI's 1942 report to Congress, Attorney General Biddle noted that "a large proportion of the complaints . . . were clearly unfounded and . . . should never have been submitted for investigation in the first instance." Obviously, such results were not what Congress had in mind. As a result, despite a belated attempt by Roosevelt to defuse the issue by appointing a high-level Interdepartmental Committee on Employee Investigations, the furor escalated.[68]

The struggle went all the way to the Supreme Court. It was triggered by Dies's allegations on February 1, 1943, that he had found thirty-nine more Communists, "fellow-travellers," and "irresponsible, crackpot, radical bureaucrats" on the federal payroll. At first, the House of Representatives wanted to fire everybody Dies had fingered; then it created a special subcommittee to investigate them. After questioning nine of these people, the subcommittee recommended the removal of three noncommunist but left-leaning employees of the Federal Communications Commission and Interior Department. When their superiors refused to fire them, the House attached a rider to an emergency appropriations bill that specifically refused to pay the three men's salaries. As expected, the Supreme Court ultimately overturned the measure, ruling in 1946 that it was a bill of attainder that illegally punished people without a trial. The episode was a portent. The fact that even in the middle of World War II such a clearly unconstitutional measure had managed to slip through Congress indicated how politically explosive the Communists-in-government issue could become.[69]

Not only did the issue set Congress against the White House, but it also created friction within the executive branch. As the Roosevelt administration struggled to create an employee loyalty program that would contain the damage Dies and his allies were trying to inflict, it became enmeshed in its own internal disputes. To begin with, there was considerable disagreement among FDR's advisers over how to deal with the problem. Some of the more liberal New Dealers wanted to resist. They believed, in the words of Interior Secretary Ickes, that "this is a dog-eat-dog political fight" and urged the administration to "strike hard against Dies." Others were more conciliatory and hoped that a pro forma attempt to purge the bureaucracy would appease the critics. Still others, J. Edgar Hoover and many military officials among them, were in ideological accord with the Dies committee and were anxious to weed presumed subversives out of the government. The bureaucratic skirmishes that these differences engendered were never as noisy nor as contentious as the ones between the administration and its congressional critics, but they prevented the executive branch from taking a strong or coherent position on the issue. They also contributed to Hoover's growing alienation from the Democratic regime.[70]

From the first, it was clear that the FBI had its own agenda for handling the investigations. Ever alert to expanding his empire, Hoover continually pressed to get a monopoly over the operation and exclude other agencies like the Civil Service Commission. He also worried about the Bureau's reputation, fearing that a less than energetic administration of the loyalty program might make the FBI as vulnerable as the rest of the executive branch to charges of coddling Communists. And, of course, he wanted to drive the reds out of Washington. As a result, he became increasingly distressed about the seemingly lackadaisical way in which other federal officials were responding to his Bureau's disclosures.[71]

At the heart of the conflict was the Director's long-standing belief that people who associated with left-wing groups or causes were just as dangerous as Communists. He wanted to oust such people from the government; the rest of the administration did not. The FBI had devoted considerable resources to its Dies list investigation and had uncovered substantial evidence of the left-wing connections of many federal employees. By the summer of 1942, it had compiled a massive five-volume report full of names and details for submission to Congress. But the administration rejected those findings. It wanted the Bureau's investigations to discredit the Dies committee, not reveal the extent of alleged subversion within the government. To Hoover's dismay, the Attorney General forced the FBI to condense its report into a cursory twenty pages and to remove all the names of individuals and organizations. Even worse, at least from the Director's perspective, was the failure of the Justice Department and most other federal agencies to follow up on the Bureau's investigations and fire the people whose supposedly subversive connections the G-men had unearthed.[72]

The administration's inaction revealed the underlying contradictions of the Communists-in-government issue. Hoover's reds were Biddle's liberals. In addition, though the Justice Department had jurisdiction over the loyalty investigations within the civilian branches of the government (the army and navy handled their own employees), it could only forward FBI reports to individual departments and did not control the final disposition of cases. Some of the bureaucrats who handled these cases distrusted the information they received from the Bureau. They were reluctant to fire people on the basis of anonymous allegations that sometimes contained little more than hearsay and hunches. To cite but one example, the only substantiation that the FBI gave the Treasury Department to back up anonymous informant "T-4"'s allegation that one of the department's employees was "in fact a member of the Communist Party of the District of Columbia" was "because his wife is known to be a Communist; because [the employee] is Jewish; and because he is very active in union affairs."[73]

Since the most useful evidence the Bureau had was the presence of someone's name on the membership list of a front group or other left-wing organization, the FBI worked to develop procedures for ensuring that belonging to such a group would be considered an automatic indication of disloyalty. The result of these efforts was what later came to be known as the Attorney General's list, a bureaucratic device designed to routinize the process of identifying undesirable employees by designating certain organizations as "subversive." Dies had already named thirteen such groups and Hoover was eager to expand the list and send information about the organizations to the rest of the government.[74]

The procedure caused problems from the start. Though Attorney General Biddle agreed to designate both the German-American Bund and the Communist party as subversive organizations and to send out descriptions of other groups supposedly under subversive control, it was hard to develop satisfactory criteria both for identifying a specific organization and for assessing an individual's relationship to it. Even at the time, Justice Department officials recognized that the obvious influence the Communist party exerted over a group like the International Workers Order did not necessarily mean that all its rank-and-file members toed the party line. Nor was it always the case that the people whose names appeared on an organization's mailing list actively supported the group. They could be fund-raising prospects who had once given money to a similar outfit in the past. Even more problematic were the FBI's citations of labor unions and organizations like the National Lawyers Guild and American Civil Liberties Union that Communists joined but did not necessarily control.[75]

The loyalty investigations quickly became a source of contention within the administration.[76] The New Deal's liberals were upset about the political biases which suffused the FBI reports that turned up on their desks. As early as the spring of 1942, the poet Archibald MacLeish, who headed the Office of Facts and Figures, complained to Hoover and Biddle about the Bureau's apparent inability to differentiate between liberals and Communists:

> I notice the recurrence of the phrase that the applicant is said to be "associated with various liberal and Communistic groups." This suggests that investigators have been told to consider liberalism as suspicious. . . . For the sake of our reputation in the history books, don't you think it would be a good thing if all investigators could be made to understand that liberalism is not only not a crime but actually the attitude of the president of the United States and the greater part of his administration.

MacLeish was also upset that "any association with Loyalist Spain is given as a basis of suspicion of loyalty to the United States." He was not alone; many other New Dealers were equally concerned about the Bureau's illiberal predilections. They did not, however, publicize their misgivings. And it was not until the summer of 1943 that another public official, a pseudonymous Mr. "XXX," voiced the same concerns in a two-part article in *The Nation*. Entitled "Washington Gestapo," XXX's piece described the kinds of improper political questions FBI and Civil Service investigators were asking and accused them of trying "to strain anti-fascists and liberals out of the government."[77]

In retrospect, XXX seems both prescient and hysterical. He had clearly identified the right-wing political bias that animated the federal investigators; but the widespread purges of liberals that he warned against did not take place. Even Communists did not always lose their jobs, unless they were particularly blatant about their political activities. Since many people in or near the Communist party lied about their political affiliations — often, as in the case of Carl Marzani, an OSS employee who was to figure in one of the most important early Cold War loyalty cases, with the implicit knowledge of their superiors — they slipped through the net. In addition, the FBI was overextended and its agents did not necessarily follow up on all the leads they had. Thus, for example, when the Bureau investigated William Remington, the future protagonist of another big Cold War loyalty and espionage case, it only queried the most obvious sources and so did not find out about his activities in the Tennessee communist movement.[78]

It is unclear how many federal employees lost their jobs during the Roosevelt administration. One authority claims that about a thousand government workers were dismissed for political reasons between 1939 and 1944. But members of the Roosevelt administration had much more important things to do than try to eliminate their left-wing employees. A few years later, priorities changed and the Communists-in-government issue heated up. This time the charges took a greater toll, for the Truman administration was less tolerant of Communism than its predecessor and even more vulnerable to partisan attacks.[79]

★

PART TWO

REPRESENTATIONS

★

CHAPTER 4

"THEY ARE EVERYWHERE"

THE COMMUNIST IMAGE

ON JULY 29, 1942, FBI Special Agent Robert Ryan was carrying out one of the Hatch Act investigations mandated by Congress when he asked Carl Marzani if he had been in the Communist party. Though Marzani was under oath, he felt confident enough in the support of his superiors within the Office of Strategic Services to lie. The men he worked with knew he had been a Communist, but they prized his services as a graphic designer and so did not concern themselves about his politics. Four years later, Marzani was asked the same questions by a security official in the State Department, where he was then working. But this time his denials did not suffice. Marzani was obviously within the communist orbit; he had been working on a film for UE; and by the middle of 1946, it was clear that someone with Marzani's left-wing affiliations was no longer welcome in the federal government. Within a year, Marzani had not only lost his State Department job, but had been convicted of perjury and faced a three-year prison term.[1]

What had happened? What had taken place within the American polity that transformed Carl Marzani from a valued federal employee into a felon?

Much of that transformation was perceptual. With the advent of the Cold War, Communists, once viewed as a political problem, now became a threat to the United States. A new, more demonized image of Communism took hold along with a heightened sense of the danger that it posed. Most treatments of McCarthyism overlook this transformation; they operate on the assumption that the Cold War automatically led to the repression of American Communists. But that was not the case. The nation's policymakers and the public had to be convinced that Communism was so bad and dangerous that it had to be driven out of American life.

It was a complex process, involving partisan politics, bureaucratic infighting, intellectual conversions, legal proceedings, congressional investigations, and the not always well coordinated activities of the various elements of the anticommunist network. Criminal prosecutions were crucial. More than any other element of the anticommunist crusade, political trials transformed the vague and largely ideological threat of Communism into something much more concrete: real people taking real actions that seemed to be part of a Moscow-led conspiracy. By changing Communism from a matter of politics into one of law enforcement, these cases simplified the task of mobilizing public opinion against the CP. The aura of criminality that suffused the entire process helped dehumanize individual Communists. It turned them into crooks.[2]

By the late 1940s, almost anything a Communist did could be the pretext for a criminal prosecution. The specific crime was irrelevant; Communism in and of itself was or, many prosecutors believed, should have been against the law. And in the most important of all Cold War political trials, the Smith Act case against the CP's highest leaders, the government tried to do just that: set the judicial precedent that, in the words of the FBI's assistant director D. M. Ladd, "the Communist Party as an organization is illegal." But every case did its part.[3]

The government fashioned its arguments, chose its exhibits, and prepped its witnesses to bolster its contention that the CP was a criminal conspiracy under Soviet control. Because the communist trials had an educational as well as a legal function, much of the evidence produced in them bore little relation to the alleged offense. Instead, prosecutors presented specific scenarios that gave credibility to the notion that the party threatened America's security. In Carl Marzani's 1947 perjury trial, for example, all the government had to do was prove that Marzani had once been in the CP. But it also embellished the case with hours of testimony to show not only that

Marzani had lied about being a Communist, but that being a Communist entailed disloyal and even dangerous behavior. By the late 1940s, such testimony, recycled in congressional hearings, official reports, and media accounts, as well as in the courtrooms where political trials were under way, had convinced most Americans that Communism deserved to be repressed.[4]

The CP's demonized image was persuasive in large part because it was based on reality. The distinctive traits that came to be associated with Communism, though often similar to those of a generically traditional "other," did, in fact, bear some relationship to what American Communists actually did. The stereotypes that emerged during the early Cold War were not, therefore, composed of random elements. They reflected, albeit in an often highly distorted manner, real party practices and policies. And real people. It was common to personalize the communist image by linking it to a specific individual who presumably typified one or another aspect of American Communism.

Similarly, the threat that domestic Communism allegedly posed, distorted and exaggerated though it was, also had a basis in what Communists (or at least some Communists) said and did. The very plausibility of the scenarios that showed how the CP endangered the nation's security was one reason why it was possible for so many Americans to adopt anticommunism so quickly — and close their eyes to the injustices propagated in its name.

Though plausible, the stereotyped portrayal of American Communism was also inaccurate, not so much because it was untrue, but because it oversimplified the communist movement by ignoring its diversity and its changes over time. A more nuanced and realistic picture of the world of American Communism would get little attention during the early years of the Cold War, for the demonized images that suffused McCarthyism were easy to sell. By the late 1940s those images were everywhere. They pervaded the news and every sector of the mass media. Columnists and radio commentators used them. So, too, did public officials and politicians of both major parties. And so, too, did all the ex-Communists and other experts who wrote and testified about Communism in venues that ranged from congressional hearings to scholarly publications. These images even made it to Hollywood.

★

In the very first scene of the classic Cold War film *I Was a Communist for the FBI,* the camera pans from an airplane taking off to an FBI agent at a phone booth. "He's on board, all right." A teletyped message appears on screen: "Attention, Washington Office. Gerhardt Eisler left La Guardia aboard Flight. . . ." The scene shifts to Pittsburgh, where the film's hero, FBI informer Matt Cvetic, is called out of his mother's birthday party to meet Eisler. The encounter takes place in a fancy hotel suite. The actor who plays Eisler, a generic Nazi-type villain with the requisite German accent and heavy glasses, serves our hero champagne and caviar and offers a toast "to Comrade Stalin" before getting down to business — arranging to paralyze the Pittsburgh steel industry.[5]

Though the film bears little relation to reality, both Eisler and Cvetic were real people, a coincidence that no doubt accounted for the film's 1951 Academy Award nomination as a documentary. Aside from Cvetic himself, an undercover informant who became one of the most notorious professional witnesses of the 1950s, Eisler is the only other "nonfictional" character in the film. Everyone else, including the film's main villain, a thuggish party boss ostensibly modeled on Steve Nelson, the Pittsburgh CP's leader at the time, received a pseudonym. Why did Gerhart Eisler get special treatment? The reasons may well have been legal. In 1951 Eisler was in East Germany, where it was unlikely that he would initiate a lawsuit to clear his name. A more plausible explanation for Eisler's cameo appearance has to do with his symbolic value as the personification of the foreign elements that allegedly controlled the American Communist party.[6]

Though long since forgotten, Gerhart Eisler's name would have been well known to movie audiences of the early fifties as that of the Kremlin's main man in America. His had been one of the first big "cases" of the Cold War. It began in late 1946 and by the time Eisler left the country in the spring of 1949, he had been repeatedly subpoenaed, arrested, prosecuted, and jailed. Newspapers and popular magazines followed the action, routinely characterizing this rather cerebral refugee as the ruthless overlord of all American Communists, the man who transmitted Stalin's orders to the party faithful. Though Eisler had, it is true, worked for the Comintern in the 1930s, by the end of 1946, when his case broke, he no longer held any position of power and was, in fact, anxious to get back to Europe. Much of the attention that he received had actually been manufactured by the FBI and other members of the anticommunist network to show that the Communist party was under Soviet control and thus endangered American security.

The hyping of Gerhart Eisler was part of that larger campaign to mobilize public opinion against the CP by creating a demonized image of American Communism. The most important component of that image was the notion that the party was run by Moscow. This concept provided the ideological bridge to the growing preoccupation with the Soviet threat abroad. It explained how party members could endanger America's internal security and so justified the repressive measures invoked against them. The identification of Eisler as the Kremlin's chief emissary to the CP gave a human form to the Soviet connection and made it easier to demonize the party.[7]

Actually, if Gerhart Eisler hadn't existed, the Cold War would have had to invent him. He was the quintessential embodiment of the specter of international Communism, invariably portrayed as a sinister Central European whose shadowy power was all the more terrifying because it was so intangible. That Eisler was a foreigner, and a German foreigner at that, merely increased his value as a symbol. The connection between immigrants and radicalism pervades the history of American political repression. Eisler simply updated the image of the bomb-wielding, foreign-born anarchist of the late nineteenth century. His German nationality was a major boon. It was hard to come up with a convincing personification of the Russian enemy, but Eisler's antagonists could tap into two world wars' worth of evil Huns and Nazis.[8]

A German intellectual who had been an important communist functionary since the early 1920s, Eisler first came to the United States in the early thirties as the official representative of the Comintern, the Moscow-based organization that ran the world's Communist parties. Though he later admitted his membership in the German party, Eisler never publicly let on that he had worked for the Comintern, claiming instead that his mission was to raise money and support for the anti-Nazi cause. After leaving the United States in 1936, he was in Spain during that country's civil war and then spent the first two years of World War II in a Vichy French concentration camp before he was granted political asylum in Mexico. But he never got there.[9]

Instead, he ended up on Ellis Island, where the Immigration and Naturalization Service detained him and his fiancée for two months in the summer of 1941. Because Eisler's German nationality technically made him an enemy alien, he was not allowed to continue on to Mexico and had to remain in the United States for the duration of the war. Once the fighting stopped, he tried to return to Europe, but the State Department would not grant him the necessary exit permit. Eisler had been under investigation by the FBI from the end of 1941. By the middle of 1943, the Bureau, though originally viewing him as just another German Jewish political refugee, had come to believe that he was an important Comintern agent and a "key figure in Communist activities in the United States."[10]

Whether or not Eisler was then "the top Comintern representative in the United States," the FBI was increasingly convinced that he was. The evidence that its agents accumulated from overhearing his conversations, breaking into his apartment, reading his mail, and keeping him and his associates under surveillance revealed a seemingly suspicious character. So, too, did the testimony of the professional anti-Communists the Bureau interviewed about him. Eisler's sister, Ruth Fischer, an ex-Communist who had broken with him politically in the 1920s, gave a bitter account of his career. Whittaker Chambers, the future protagonist in the Alger Hiss case, was another source who, along with Manning Johnson, Joseph Zack Kornfeder, and some of the FBI's other ex-communist informants, recalled Eisler from the 1930s as a shadowy, but apparently important, figure who went by the name "Edwards." Eisler's activities in the 1940s, his use of another pseudonym, "Hans Berger," in articles about Germany for communist publications, his false statements to the INS and State Department about his political activities, and his almost daily visits to the party-connected Joint Anti-Fascist Refugee Committee (JAFRC) seemed equally shady. Bureau suspicions were confirmed when it turned out that Eisler was receiving $150 every month from the JAFRC in the form of checks made out to "Julius Eisman."[11]

By the end of the war, the FBI believed it had a big fish on the line. Eisler's apparently furtive behavior (or at least behavior that from the Bureau's perspective seemed furtive) gave plausibility to that characterization. For Hoover and his men, who were convinced that the Communist party was by definition an illegal conspiracy, Eisler's actions strengthened that belief. By the spring of 1945, they were already planning to prosecute him.[12]

It is easy to put a conspiratorial spin on Eisler's activities; some were technically illegal and they did take place within the context of a secret, ostensibly revolutionary, operation. But they were hardly dangerous. Many of the ruses Eisler employed were standard practices within a movement that often faced serious repression. While an affectation in the United States, a false passport and an assumed name were indispensable for someone who, like Eisler, was trying to organize a communist-led resistance movement within Nazi-controlled Europe. Moreover, by the time Eisler reached the United States in 1941, he was literally fleeing for his life. He lied to the immigration authorities about being a Communist because, as he later confessed, he was afraid that otherwise he might not be admitted into the country and, having just escaped from a concentration camp, he was terrified of being returned to Europe.[13]

Though he had been a Comintern representative in the 1930s, he was probably not one in the 1940s. A refugee, involuntarily detained in the United States, he spent the war years in Queens, hanging out with his fellow *fluchtlings,* writing and lecturing about the future of Germany. He seems to have had no official connection to the party, which apparently viewed him as "a ghost from the past." Though his exploits in the Spanish Civil War and the aura of Berlin cabarets and Viennese coffeehouses that clung to him made him a romantic figure among party members and non-Communists alike, he had trouble supporting himself. The communist publications that carried his articles paid little if anything and he was forced to rely upon his wife's earnings as a bookkeeper, the generosity of his composer brother, Hanns, and his share of the "Julius Eisman" stipend that the JAFRC gave to a group of European refugees in the name of a dead German Communist.[14]

As the Bureau was accumulating evidence in the hopes of convincing the Justice Department to prosecute, Eisler and his wife were preparing to return to Germany. For some reason (and here the deleted passages in Eisler's FBI files may conceal the full story), the Bureau slipped up and allowed the Eislers to receive an exit permit in the summer of 1946. But that oversight was soon corrected. On October 13, five days before Eisler was due to sail, the former *Daily Worker* editor Louis Budenz gave a radio talk in Detroit about the Comintern's mysterious agent in America. "This man never shows his face. Communist leaders never see him, but they follow his orders or suggestions implicitly."[15]

Why Budenz made these allegations is unclear. He had been asked about Eisler during the extensive interviews he granted the FBI soon after his defection from the party in the fall of 1945 but had little information to offer. He recalled him as a "Dutch Jew" who wrote articles in the *Worker* under the name "Hans Berger," though he did add, tipped off perhaps by his interlocutors' evident interest in the man, that "Berger must have been an important person." But Budenz, who was to become the most important of all the ex-communist witnesses, was adept at embroidering his testimony and may well have fingered Eisler in order to promote his forthcoming book. In any event, Budenz's revelations revived the Bureau's interest in the German Communist. Two days later, the FBI convinced the State Department that they should rescind Eisler's exit permit and the Bureau put him under twenty-four-hour surveillance to ensure that he didn't sneak out of the country. Though the extraordinarily visible surveillance was meant, at least in part, to show how dangerous Eisler was, Hoover would have preferred to make that point by incarceration.[16]

Ever since the FBI became convinced that Eisler was the top Soviet agent in America, Hoover and his men had wanted to prosecute him. The Bureau realized that, as the FBI official who handled the case later admitted, a trial would show "the public just how closely the CPUSA was tied to Moscow." But it took several years before the Bureau could get Eisler indicted. Its legal advisers could not figure out exactly what law he had broken.[17]

As the FBI was to discover, it was not easy to use the criminal justice system for political purposes. Unpopular as American Communism was, it was not illegal and the ordinary political activities of its adherents did not violate any laws. As a result, because it was so hard to find legitimate grounds for taking Communists to court, prosecutors often resorted to what the political theorist Otto Kirchheimer has so aptly termed "offense artifacts." They turned ordinary infractions into political crimes. Perjury was invaluable here. It became the indictment of choice against suspected Communists when evidence for their other misdeeds was unavailable or the statute of limitations had run out. Contempt of Congress was also useful, as were, in the case of foreign-born undesirables, deportation and denaturalization proceedings. To emphasize Communism's special threat, the government often launched multiple prosecutions against a single defendant. Steve Nelson, who headed the CP in Pittsburgh during the late 1940s and 1950s, may have held the record. Not only did he face denaturalization, contempt of Congress, and Smith Act charges, but he was also accused of sedition under a 1919 Pennsylvania law.[18]

Eisler faced several prosecutions as well. Though Budenz had not mentioned his name in his initial revelations, he was soon identifying Eisler in public as "the agent of the Kremlin who directs all Communist activities in the United States." By the time Budenz repeated these allegations before the House Un-American Activities Committee on November 22, the German Communist was front-page news. The Hearst press ran a series of five articles by Ruth Fischer about her brother, including one entitled, "Gerhart Eisler: The Career of a Terrorist." Other writers embellished Fischer's charges and added some of their own, the most sensational being allegations of atomic espionage. *Time* and *Life* ran major articles and Eisler even appeared on "Meet the Press." Meanwhile, the FBI was trying to drum up indictments by sending detailed reports to the Attorney General, INS, and the Internal Revenue Service.[19]

HUAC demanded Eisler's presence and urged the FBI to put him under surveillance. By that point, the Justice Department could no longer resist the appeals for his incarceration. On February 4, 1947, two days before Eisler's scheduled session with the committee, the Attorney General finally issued a warrant for his arrest as an undesirable alien. Denied bail, Eisler showed up at his hearing a federal prisoner under guard. He refused to testify until he was allowed to read a prepared statement. The committee wanted to swear him in first and jousted with him for a minute or so before deciding that he was in contempt. Two weeks later, on February 17, the full House, at the request of Richard Nixon, a young congressman from California making his maiden speech about Eisler, voted 370–1 to cite him for contempt.[20]

HUAC was also responsible for Eisler's second indictment. As they were collecting information to present at the February hearings, committee investigators were tipped off by the State Department that Eisler had gotten an American passport under another name in the 1930s. The committee aired the charges and then urged the Attorney General to initiate criminal proceedings. At the very least, Eisler could be indicted for perjury, if not for some more serious offense.[21]

Eisler's notoriety finally forced the wavering Justice Department to act. By the spring of 1947, he was facing two separate criminal proceedings: one for contempt of Congress and the other for perjury. His contempt trial began in June and lasted four days. The jury found him guilty and the judge sentenced him to a year in prison. A month later, Eisler was on trial again. Another conviction resulted, with the judge imposing a one-to-three-year sentence for perjury. Eisler appealed both decisions. His battle against HUAC's contempt citation quickly blossomed into the most important early test case of the committee's power to force reluctant witnesses to talk about their political beliefs. On November 8, 1948, the Supreme Court granted his petition for certiorari and agreed to hear the case.[22]

The INS took action as well; on February 2, 1948, its agents arrested Eisler in connection with deportation proceedings. He was held without bail on Ellis Island for over three months until, along with four other foreign-born Communists, he went on a hunger strike and won his release. Eisler's predicament was Kafkaesque. The government wanted him deported but would not let him go. Eisler's detention by the INS at a time when he was trying to leave the country makes little sense unless we view that incarceration as a public relations gimmick, designed to bolster Eisler's image as a threat.[23]

By that point, Eisler's situation was truly pathetic. He was desperate to get to Europe and had, in fact, tried to strike a bargain with the Justice Department, offering to plead guilty if he could be deported after sentencing. The government turned down his proposition and, in the beginning of 1949, initiated yet another action against him, this one a civil suit for $1,400 worth of back taxes on the "Julius Eisman" money. He must have felt like a trapped animal. The FBI was constantly at his side and had, in fact, secretly helped him get a phone so that, in the Bureau's peculiar phraseology, "an appropriate technical surveillance can be installed."[24]

At the same time that his legal problems were multiplying, Eisler was becoming increasingly isolated. The JAFRC, which had once regularly supported him, severed its ties. The organization was itself under attack. It had been the first communist front group to be investigated by HUAC after the war; and the refusal of its executive secretary and board of directors to comply with a subpoena to hand over the group's records brought them a contempt citation. The JAFRC's connection to Eisler simply increased the organization's vulnerability and it responded by publicly distancing itself from its controversial client. The Communist party's leaders also kept their distance and the only substantial assistance Eisler got came from two legal defense front groups, the Civil Rights Congress and the American Committee for Protection of Foreign Born.[25]

As his cases wound through the federal courts, Eisler tried to raise money and public support by taking to the left-wing lecture circuit, but even that expedient failed. Meeting halls were denied, hecklers interrupted his speeches, and, by the beginning of 1949, college administrators were routinely banning him from their campuses. Nor could he earn a living; as he explained to one of his attorneys, "I am penniless." He was homeless as well. He and his wife had been forced out of their apartment in Queens by their neighbors' harassment and were living out of suitcases in other people's houses. And, if the FBI's suspicions were correct, his wife had begun an affair with her Russian teacher.[26]

Vilified and desperate, Eisler finally took matters into his own hands. On May 6, 1949, while the Supreme Court was deliberating on his contempt of Congress case, Eisler bought a twenty-five-cent visitor's ticket for the Polish liner *Batory* and remained on board as it sailed out of New York Harbor. He was briefly detained and then released by the British government. He ended up, as he had long wanted to, in East Germany, where, after being greeted by government leaders, brass bands, and a troop of flower-bearing children, he became a high official in the communist government.[27]

Though Hoover and his men were initially chagrined that they had let Eisler slip away,* it was soon clear that his escape was more useful to the anticommunist cause than a long prison term would have been. It seemed to show that the Kremlin's American boss was a thoroughly unscrupulous character who, like all Communists, believed himself beyond the law. The image of Gerhart Eisler as a devious, conspiratorial figure was thus complete. The legal proceedings against him were central to creating that image. Had Eisler been allowed to leave the United States in 1945 as he had wanted, there would have been no "Eisler" around to gain notoriety as the mysterious Soviet agent who controlled the American Communist party.[28]

Even before his escape presumably demonstrated how dangerous a character he was, references to Eisler pervade the anticommunist discourse of the late 1940s. Since he had been established in the popular imagination as the man who transmitted Moscow's orders to the American CP, it could

---

*There is an ironic twist to the FBI's role in Eisler's escape, for there were Bureau agents watching the *Batory*. But they were looking out for Valentin Gubitchev, the Russian principal in the Judith Coplon spy case, and so were not on the alert for Eisler.

be (and was) argued that any contact with him showed that the group or individual in question belonged to the Soviet conspiracy. Thus, for example, he figured prominently in the government's 1949 Smith Act prosecution of the party. Several key witnesses, including Louis Budenz, mentioned their dealings with him, presumably as evidence for the Communist party's links to the Soviet Union and its propensity for force and violence. HUAC also used references to Eisler to probe for the Moscow connections of its witnesses. During its 1948 investigation of a purported Soviet spy ring within the federal government, HUAC asked most of the people who had been named by the self-confessed Russian agent Elizabeth Bentley if they knew Eisler. In the early 1950s, when Joe McCarthy's charges dominated the headlines, there was even an attempt to find a connection between Eisler and the so-called "loss" of China that McCarthy and others blamed upon the State Department.[29]

A sampling of lesser-known proceedings indicates a similar reliance on Eisler. In the autumn of 1946, for example, when the notion of destroying the CP by forcing it to register with the government first surfaced in Congress, Eisler's activities were cited as evidence for the need of such a measure. When the registration provisions were finally incorporated into the McCarran Act (as the Internal Security Act of 1950 was usually called), he was mentioned again — this time in the Subversive Activities Control Board (SACB) hearings where Kornfeder, Manning Johnson, and some of the other professional witnesses repeated their earlier stories about Eisler's conspiratorial doings to bolster the Justice Department's attempt to force the party to register. The government actually based its case on the evidence that federal attorneys had assembled for Eisler's perjury trial.[30]

Eisler also figured in the campaign against the so-called "front groups." He had, after all, worked with or been supported by the JAFRC, the American Committee to Protect Foreign Born, and the Civil Rights Congress. Since linking Eisler to these organizations helped identify them as part of the international communist conspiracy, congressional investigators, journalists, and Justice Department attorneys pushed the connections for all they were worth. Eisler was, in fact, so contagious that any contact with him could be politically lethal. Merely placing him in the same city as a suspect organization or individual was enough to prove Soviet influence. And having the same lawyer was grounds for suspicion.[31]

Not even the Truman administration, despite its vigorous pursuit of the beleaguered refugee, was immune. Richard Nixon was only one of several politicians and journalists who claimed that Eisler's ability to remain at large while he was being prosecuted showed that the government was soft on Communists; his flight confirmed the charge.[32]

The political discourse and criminal docket of the McCarthy era were rich in icons like Eisler. Alger Hiss personified the Communists-in-government issue; the Rosenbergs represented the threat of atomic espionage; lesser-known figures contributed in smaller ways to shaping the anticommunist ideological scenarios. There was also a generic Communist, a monolithic stereotype embodying all the supposedly vicious traits that distinguished party members from ordinary law-abiding, God-fearing Americans. This characterization accentuated those aspects of the CP's beliefs and practices — like its connection to Moscow or reliance on secrecy — that made the party so easy to demonize.

Central to the stereotype was the assumption that all Communists were the same. They presumably subscribed to the same beliefs, mouthed the same slogans, and followed the same orders. The notion of a monolithic Moscow-run party was utterly crucial to the political repression of the McCarthy era; it made it possible to treat each suspected Communist as the embodiment of every sinister practice in the Kremlin's repertory. Distorted though it was, the image of a lockstep party and the automatons within its ranks contained enough plausibility to make it thoroughly believable to anyone who had been watching the fluctuations in the CP line since the 1930s.[33]

Paradoxically, despite the near-universal assumption that all party members were under Stalin's control, the anticommunist experts offered little concrete proof that they were. For obvious reasons, neither the American CP nor the Soviet government openly acknowledged the relationship between them. And, although the American intelligence community had intercepted and decoded some wartime telegrams from Moscow that revealed the party's contacts with the KGB, those materials, the product of the so-called Venona Project, were too highly classified to be produced in a courtroom or similar forum. Whatever other documentation the FBI might have possessed may well have been obtained illegally and was equally unavailable. As a result, during the 1940s and 1950s, the prosecutors, investigators, and others who needed to make a case against the Communist party and its members tended to rely on indirect, often literary, evidence to prove that Stalin ran the show.[34]

The so-called Duclos letter was a common item. The letter — a supposedly Moscow-inspired criticism of the American party that the French Communist Jacques Duclos published in his party's theoretical journal in April 1945 — prompted the CP's leaders to change their line and drop Earl Browder. The speed of the about-face that the article inspired seemed to demonstrate Moscow's control. FBI reports routinely refer to the document, as do federal prosecutors and their witnesses. HUAC was so interested in the Duclos letter that the index to the first fifteen years of the committee's hearings contains more references to the French Communist leader than to the American party's own general secretary Eugene Dennis. Private investigators referred to Duclos as well. And, of course, it was none other than Gerhart Eisler who, according to his sister, recognized the import of the Duclos letter and took charge of "whipping the Party into subservience to the new line."[35]

Another artifact that presumably illustrated the CP's control over its adherents was an oath that new members had supposedly taken in the 1930s, pledging themselves "to remain at all times a vigilant and firm defender of the Leninist line of the Party." This text and a similar statement on the application form for membership in the party came from the same document, a 1935 manual for organizers. Since the manual's author was a shadowy Hungarian Communist named J. Peters, who was reputed to be one of Eisler's close associates as well as the main handler of Whittaker Chambers, the oaths seemed sinister indeed. But, as even the FBI's own informants admitted, the oaths were rarely, if ever, taken; moreover, the Peters manual had been withdrawn from the party's bookstores soon after publication.[36]

Still, the belief that Communists were under total Soviet control was too compelling to discard for lack of proof. Perhaps the most ubiquitous image was that of a puppet, with Stalin in the Kremlin pulling the strings. "The average Communist, no matter how much his desire for integrity," Louis Budenz explained on the day he first fingered Gerhart Eisler, "tends to become a puppet." J. Edgar Hoover agreed. "Communist members," he told the Grand Lodge of the Masons in 1950, "body and soul, are the property of the party." Elizabeth Bentley, the unstable Vassar graduate whose revelations about her activities as a courier in the communist underground were to make her one of the McCarthy era's key professional witnesses, used the same kind of language in her 1951 memoir. Her former colleagues "had become in the hands of the Communist movement, no longer individuals but robots; they were chained in an intellectual and moral slavery that was far worse than any prison." [37]

And the sentence was for life. A recurrent theme in the discourse of anticommunism was the notion that once someone joined the CP, it was impossible to leave. It was a point that many former party members like the writer Richard Wright often made. "No one can resign from the Communist Party." Bentley gave a more dramatic spin to the proposition, describing a conversation with a disillusioned comrade during which she asked him,

"Why don't you get into something else?"

He took his eyes off the road and stared at me savagely. "You don't know what you're saying! No one ever leaves the organization; it's not like the Catholic Church, where you only lose your soul."

Even academics subscribed to this interpretation. "The C.P.," philosopher Sidney Hook announced in 1949, "no more accepts resignations than an army does." [38]

Nor was the credibility of these assertions affected by the fact that the people making the most lurid claims about how the party enslaved its members had themselves somehow broken the chains. After all, the notion that Communism held its adherents for life was extremely useful to anticommunist investigators and prosecutors. Once it was known that someone had previously been in the CP, then it could be assumed that he or she was still in its clutches. "I have always gone on the theory," a member of the federal government's Loyalty Review Board explained in 1951,

that if a person was shown to be a Communist or there was serious evidence to that effect at any time in the past, there was a presumption that that condition continued up to, and including, the present time, unless there was positive evidence of some rejection of the previous philosophy.

This notion was at the heart of many federal prosecutions. Since most perjury cases relied on proving that the defendant was a Communist, expert witnesses like Louis Budenz were in constant demand to explain that no one could ever resign from the CP. At one perjury trial, no fewer than seven former Communists testified that it was impossible for people to leave the party.[39]

But not totally impossible. Truly penitent "sinners" could be redeemed. Naturally, such apostates had to give the FBI or their loyalty boards "positive evidence" that they had repudiated their former beliefs and associates. Because of the common assumption that Communists lied, a mere disclaimer of membership would not suffice. Congressional committees demanded that former party members name names. It was, as one HUAC member explained, "the final test of credibility of a witness purporting to be a former Communist." In other venues, acceptable evidence for a break could be anything from denouncing Stalin to becoming an informer. The common wisdom held that belonging to the party was such a totalizing experience that one could free oneself from the Kremlin's clutches only by a painful and public rupture.[40]

The rupture would have to be linguistic as well. Communism supposedly exercised such absolute control over its members' minds that it even dictated the very words they used. The jargon in the party's publications and the official statements of its leaders proved it — or so it was believed. The CP's often heavy-handed language — which even its more literate adherents disliked — supposedly made its members more amenable to discipline. This type of "Marxist conditioning," as ex-Communists described it, supposedly allowed the party to establish "such authority over its members that it can swing their emotions now for and now against the same person or issue." Such notions often conflated the well-known literary portrayals of "think-speak" and "double-talk" found in novels like George Orwell's *1984* with the more mundane reality of the party's pedestrian prose.[41]

They also reflected the fifties' obsession with "brainwashing," the fiendishly powerful process through which communist authorities supposedly kept their subjects in line. The false confessions that Stalin had coerced from his rivals in the Moscow show trials of the late 1930s seemingly revealed how easily men's minds could be controlled. So, too, did the "thought reform" that occurred during the Chinese Revolution and the Korean War when prisoners of war and other detainees underwent intensive interrogations and apparently absorbed the political values of their captors. The confessions that were extorted from the American POWs seemed particularly disturbing, for they indicated how vulnerable ordinary people were to the technique. Robots themselves, Communists could also turn other people into robots.[42]

Portraying party members as mindless automatons transformed them into strange beings who were, it seemed, something other than human or, as *Life* magazine characterized Gerhart Eisler, "almost a separate species of mankind." Communists endangered American society in much the same ways as the mutants and space invaders of the contemporaneous science fiction films threatened the planet. Like party members, the aliens of the sci-fi films of the fifties often hid their powers behind a mild, even benevolent, exterior. In *The Invasion of the Body Snatchers,* outer-space invaders took control of ordinary people just as concealed party members presumably subverted labor unions and liberal causes. Such contradictory images pervade the countersubversive tradition. Like the Japanese during World War II, Communists during the Cold War were both subhuman and superhuman. They were inferior beings who were at the same time uniquely powerful. They certainly weren't just folks.[43]

What made them so dangerous was that they were believed to belong to a worldwide conspiracy. They were individual cogs in a far-reaching Soviet network that sought to overthrow the American government and, in the words of Supreme Court Justice Robert Jackson, "forcibly . . . recast our whole social and political structure after the Muscovite model of police-state dictatorship." Especially prevalent was the notion that everything the party and its members did was part of the Kremlin's plot to take over the United States. Though that was certainly not the case, there was enough plausibility in such a characterization of the CP to make it possible to view the party's behavior, albeit in a considerably exaggerated and distorted way, as that of a highly conspiratorial organization.[44]

There was, for example, the idea that Communists had been rigorously

135

trained to carry out their seditious work. This notion put a sinister spin on the party's educational activities and the schools it ran for its members. Its practice during the 1930s of sending its most promising cadres to the International Lenin School in Moscow seemed especially ominous. In the 1940s and 1950s, it was common for Lenin School alumni who became professional witnesses to offer explicit testimony about how Gerhart Eisler and their other instructors trained them in espionage, sabotage, and other revolutionary techniques. The villainous Steve Nelson character in *I Was a Communist for the FBI* had, the movie made clear, been schooled in Moscow. Labeling such a party leader as "Soviet trained" automatically transformed him into a sinister figure. The epithet appeared frequently in the litany of anticommunism. Similar instruction could be gotten at home. The memoirs and public testimony of ex-Communists invariably describe the many secret meetings and classes that were, the FBI's undercover informant Herbert Philbrick explained, "devoted almost exclusively to the study of the fundamental techniques of violent revolution against capitalism."[45]

Violence was central to the curriculum — or so the ex-Communists said. In part because the main laws used against the CP contained language about "force and violence," most of the legal proceedings against the party tended to stress its willingness to use bloodshed to achieve its ends. Individual Communists would, it was widely asserted, commit any kind of crime, including murder, if the CP ordered them to do so. They had "no scruples against sabotage, terrorism, assassination, or mob disorder." So common was that assumption that when a delegation of clergymen visited the White House to plead for clemency for Ethel and Julius Rosenberg, one of Eisenhower's advisers confided to his diary that, because he had been told that the group's rabbi was a Communist,

> I watched his hands intently during the interview. I was concerned about the President and sat as closely as I could to him because it seemed to me if I were a dyed-in-the-wool Communist, the one thing I would want to do would be to shoot the President of the United States.[46]

The rabbi had not been packing a pistol; nor was there any hard evidence that Communists, at least within the United States and outside of the movies, had actually assassinated anyone. Professional informers like Matt Cvetic spoke darkly of suicides that might not have been "suicide," but these references were never specific. Still, there were a few unsolved cases that might conceivably have been the work of communist hit squads. One incident that regularly turned up in the stories of anticommunist professionals was the mysterious disappearance of Juliet Stuart Poyntz. A Barnard graduate who had been prominent in the party during the late twenties and early thirties, Poyntz had, according to the testimony of several ex-Communists, worked in the underground for several years before losing faith in the cause. Then one day in the summer of 1937 she vanished. Soon rumors began to circulate within the anti-Stalinist left that she had been either murdered or abducted by the KGB.[47]

Though neither the FBI nor the New York City Police Department ever found out what happened to her, by the late 1940s professional witnesses were offering vivid (and obviously fictionalized) accounts of her demise. Whittaker Chambers gave several versions, including one in which Poyntz was lured into Central Park, where two men pushed her into an automobile, and another that had her entombed in a Greenwich Village wall. Benjamin Gitlow supplied even more graphic details, replete with descriptions of her anguished pleas for life. Paul Crouch, the professional witness who had tried to form an association of ex-Communists, gave a different version, claiming that Poyntz had been originally buried in Yonkers and then disinterred and thrown into the Hudson River. Crouch also named names. He brought Eisler into the story, hinting that the German Communist may have set Poyntz up for the kill. Ruth Fischer implicated her brother as well.[48]

Most important, Crouch identified (or at least claimed to) the actual murderer. He was George Mink, a former taxi driver from Philadelphia who had organized maritime workers in the 1930s. Just as Eisler symbolized the CP's Kremlin ties, Mink came to epitomize its propensity for bloodshed. His exploits after the party's leaders relieved him of his waterfront responsibilities and apparently detailed him to the Comintern remain obscure. In 1935 he was arrested in Copenhagen with several false U.S. passports in his possession. He spent some time in a Danish prison and was then released into Soviet custody. Later he surfaced in Spain, where he reportedly served as the Comintern's hatchet man during the civil war. Afterward, he may have returned to the United States. Then he, too, disappeared.[49]

The FBI had been tracking Mink for years without much success. He seems to have been quite a mysterious character, endowed by his waterfront activities with an aura of toughness as well as the kind of mobility and international connections that easily fueled suspicions. His FBI file is full of lurid stories passed on to the Bureau by its informants. One set of reports identified him as a high-level Soviet agent who ran all the Comintern's communications networks. Other accounts described him as a "close friend" of Harry Bridges's and "the power behind the scenes" in the American party. Still other informants recalled Mink as the "Bloody Butcher" of Barcelona, where, as the head of the Soviet secret police, he had supposedly "introduced American gangster methods" to the KGB during the Spanish Civil War. There were even rumors that he had taken part in the assassination of Leon Trotsky. The Bureau discounted that one, though it did note that "such activity is by no means beyond Mink's possibility." And, of course, he reputedly had connections to Gerhart Eisler.[50]

Mink never got the publicity Eisler received. He was, after all, no longer around in the 1940s. Sightings were reported until the early fifties, often in connection with one or another labor dispute that Mink was supposedly masterminding. But the FBI had lost track of him in the late 1930s and assumed that he had been purged or killed during the war. Still, there were no other candidates for the role of party hit man, an indication, no doubt, of how mild American Communism really was.[51]

While the Communists instigated little, if any, violence in the United States, there was plenty of it in the Soviet Union. Stalin's purges, therefore, figured prominently in the case against the American CP. Only their lack of power kept the party and its members from indulging in the same kind of bloodthirsty behavior that Stalin and his henchmen exhibited — or so it was believed. Whether or not this was the case (and there was, of course, no way to test such a hypothesis), in the eyes of most Americans the evils of the Soviet regime tainted everything the CP and its sympathizers did. And in any event, even if the party didn't actually endorse violence, its theory called for the dictatorship of the proletariat, which was, at least as practiced in Russia, a very brutal system indeed.[52]

Moreover, the CP's obvious devotion to a regime that perpetrated such crimes against its own citizens rendered it difficult for party members and their allies to make a believable claim that they were (as many of them, in fact, were) genuinely committed to human rights. On the contrary, it became common to insist that because there were no civil liberties in the Soviet Union, Communists should not get them in the United States. Such a formulation had serious consequences, for it enabled many otherwise tolerant men and women to justify political repression. "Those who deny freedom to others," Attorney General Tom Clark declared in 1947, "cannot long retain it for themselves — and under a just God they do not deserve it." Similar arguments were invoked for firing professors whose adherence to Communism presumably nullified their devotion to academic freedom. Ironically, the advocates of this position were often liberals who claimed that they were protecting the Bill of Rights by denying its extension to those who would rescind it in the inconceivable event that they should come to power.[53]

There was, of course, more than enough hypocrisy to go around. Demonized though they were, Communists did not have clean hands. Besides supporting Russia, their most egregious sin — and the one that it turned out would be the easiest to punish them for — was that they lied. Probably no other aspect of the CP's organizational behavior did so much to reinforce its image as a conspiracy. The party did, after all, operate in a clandestine manner; its members concealed their affiliation and denied that they were Communists. Whether they did this because the nature of Communism required it or because they were trying to protect themselves and their movement from repression, the inherent dishonesty of their behavior proved damaging in the extreme.

If nothing else, it gave the movement's enemies a strong ideological weapon. The CP's duplicity, it was claimed, was the essence of Communism, the inevitable product of the underlying evil of Marxism-Leninism. Significantly, much of the evidence invoked to show that Communism required its adherents to lie was literary. It is hard to understand why anti-Communists relied so heavily on the works of Lenin and Stalin when there was no dearth of stronger confirmation for the party's attempt to cover its tracks. Perhaps they realized that such an approach would indirectly reinforce the authority of that type of evidence in instances where it was harder to prove CP wrongdoing. Or perhaps they sincerely believed that the communist classics clinched their case.

One quotation was particularly ubiquitous. In the passage, an excerpt from Lenin's 1920 tract *Left-Wing Communism, an Infantile Disorder,* the father of the Bolshevik revolution gave his disciples the following guidelines for infiltrating labor unions: "It is necessary to agree to any and every sacrifice and even — if need be — resort to all sorts of stratagems, maneuvers, and illegal methods, to evasions and subterfuges . . . in order to carry on Communist work." Professional anti-Communists had been calling attention to those words for years. The passage appeared everywhere, from academic treatises and magazine articles to the 1959 report of a special presidential committee investigating the federal loyalty programs. Prosecutors and professional witnesses cited it routinely in criminal proceedings and hearings before the SACB. And when the CIO expelled the communist-led unions in 1950, Lenin's magic words graced the report of every single trial committee.[54]

No doubt the passage got so much usage because it expressed what by the 1950s had become a solid consensus. Even people who opposed other aspects of the anticommunist crusade assumed that Communists did not tell the truth. Communists are "such liars and cheats," Eisenhower explained to his attorney general in 1953, "that even when they apparently recant and later testify against someone else for his Communist convictions, my first reaction is to believe that the accused person must be a patriot."[55]

The CP's attempts at secrecy — its underground organizations, secret conclaves, forged passports, and false names — were self-defeating. They fooled no one and just reinforced the party's image as a conspiracy, especially since its adversaries ensured that these practices would not go unnoticed. Rarely, for example, was Eisler mentioned without some reference to his many aliases. Eisler, "Eisman," "Edwards," "Berger" — his multiple identities made the alleged Soviet agent seem even more devious and alien. Similarly, at Carl Marzani's trial, the prosecution and its witnesses constantly referred to Marzani's party name, "Tony Whales."[56]

Though most of the CP's clandestine practices had been adopted as defensive measures, the party's opponents put a far more malevolent spin on them. Communists hid their political affiliations, pretending to be ordinary liberals or concerned citizens so that they could worm themselves into other organizations and take them over. Whatever the CP and its adherents did to reach beyond the confines of the party, thus, got a sinister twist. Hoover claimed to be especially worried that Communists might succeed in recruiting the well-meaning but unsuspecting men and women who became involved with the ostensibly "liberal progressive causes" that the CP espoused.[57]

The solution, the FBI director and his allies believed, was exposure. Revealing the party's hand behind the seemingly innocuous activities that it sponsored might well eliminate the subversive threat these activities posed to the rest of the nation. Such disclosures were educational, they claimed, not punitive. Once Communists and the organizations they controlled were publicly identified, ordinary citizens would then steer clear of them. This line of reasoning was especially attractive to Congress. Not only did it vindicate the work of HUAC and the other investigating committees, but it also shaped the McCarthy era's only important piece of legislation, the 1950 Internal Security Act, or McCarran Act, as it was called, with its provisions for official registration of the CP, its members, and its front groups.[58]

Communists must be forced into the open, the proponents of exposure explained, because they were so hard to find. It was, Eisenhower's Attorney General Herbert Brownell announced, "almost impossible to 'spot' them since they no longer use membership cards or other written documents which will identify them for what they are." Their invisibility increased their menace. "They are everywhere," one of Brownell's predecessors told a group of advertising men in 1950, "in factories, offices, butcher stores, on street corners, in private businesses." Worse yet, as the undercover informer Herbert Philbrick explained,

> Where Communism is concerned, there is no one who can be trusted. Anyone can be a Communist. Anyone can suddenly appear in a meeting as a Communist party member — close friend, brother, employee or even employer, leading citizen, trusted public servant.

Though the CP drew most of its recruits from only a few sectors of American society, the notion that "anyone" could be a Communist was widespread. Since most Americans had never encountered an actual party member, fantasies were rife. Only 10 percent of the respondents in a 1954 poll said they knew someone who might be a Communist. When asked to explain why that individual had aroused their suspicions, these people's answers were vague. "He was not like us." "Would not attend church and talked against God." "He brought a lot of foreign-looking people into his home." "I just knew. But I wouldn't know how to say I knew."[59]

Communists supposedly differed from ordinary citizens in their cleverness; they were as smart as they were devious. They had "fancy ideas" and, as Roosevelt's secretary of labor Frances Perkins recalled, were able to manipulate the people they worked with because they "were brighter than they were" and "could think quicker." Eisler was a man of "brilliance and charm." The communist protagonist in Hollywood's 1952 melodrama *My Son John* was an intellectual, seduced into the CP by "superior minds" and "daring thoughts." These characterizations, like Joe McCarthy's attack on "twisted-thinking intellectuals," introduced an element of anti-intellectualism into the stew, as if intelligence were somehow subversive in itself. Certainly, if nothing else, their supposed shrewdness made the Communists all the more dangerous.[60]

So, too, did their diligence and attention to detail. The legendary devotion of its members to the party was no myth. As both their enemies and supporters admitted, Communists "work like hell" at their political tasks. Their hard work and careful planning made it possible for small numbers of Communists to take control of the organizations that they had infiltrated. "While another trade union leader will naturally expect to see his family from time to time, to have a night off with the boys, to relax every now and then with his feet up on a desk," the influential columnists Joseph and Stewart Alsop explained in 1947, "a communist will devote every minute of his working hours and every ounce of energy to a mission given him by the party."[61]

Such efforts paid off, especially at meetings where their vaunted mastery of parliamentary procedures and ability to "pack the meetings with stooges" enabled Communists to "strong-arm the motions that they want to put over. They can get away with it," one observer noted, "because the right-wing unionists either do not attend the meetings or do not take as active a part as the Commies." Party members were notorious for outstaying their rivals and passing resolutions or electing officers after everyone else had left a meeting. To combat this tactic, the anticommunist labor priest

Charles Owen Rice advised the readers of his widely circulated pamphlet on "How to De-Control Your Union of Communists": "Stay for the Whole Meeting."[62]

Though unions were recognized to be the party's main targets, almost any kind of organization could be infiltrated and subverted by the CP. Churches, civic groups, even the Boy Scouts were at risk. Communists, so it was believed, were endowed with such skill and dedication that they threatened every sector of American society. That there were only a few of them made them no less dangerous. In fact, as Hoover and the other anticommunist professionals warned, the party's apparent lack of success was deceptive. It might mislead the American people into prematurely lowering their guard.[63]

History corroborated this concern. When they wanted to buttress their case that the small size of the CP bore no relation to the threat it posed, anti-Communists pointed to the fact that Lenin had overthrown the entire Russian empire with a mere handful of supporters. This notion, that it might be possible for the tiny American party to replicate the Bolsheviks' success, had been current since the 1920s. "There are more Communists in the United States today than there were in Russia when the government was overthrown," the head of the American Legion's Americanism commission noted in 1936. Ten years later, Hoover made the same observation to the Legion's annual convention; in 1947 he gave HUAC the scary statistics.

> In 1917 when the Communists overthrew the Russian Government there was one Communist for every 2,277 persons in Russia. In the United States today there is one Communist for every 1,814 persons in the country.

This contention, which Hoover reiterated in most of his major public statements of the period, was also a standard component of the government's arguments in the main anticommunist trials of the early Cold War. Prosecutors, witnesses, even judges cited the Russian precedent to bolster their assertion that the American party was more dangerous than mere numbers might suggest.[64]

What made the tiny CP such a threat, as Hoover and others repeatedly pointed out, was that "for every party member there are ten others ready to do the party's work." The party was "like an iceberg," Attorney General Brownell explained. "Only a small part can be seen, but the bulk is beneath the surface." This image of the CP with its hard core of disciplined Stalinists enhanced by legions of secret supporters served the professional anti-Communists well, giving them an argument that would sustain their mission no matter how insignificant the party became. Hoover had been tracking American Communism long enough to have seen it nearly disappear in the 1920s and then revive a few years later. The party's obvious decline by the late 1950s could thus be equally transitory and might, in fact, be a cause for alarm. Most of the committed anti-Communists agreed. "Today, the Communist Party, though reduced in size as a formal entity," HUAC's chairman announced in 1958,

> is a greater menace than ever before. It has long since divested itself of unreliable elements. Those who remain are the hard-core disciplined agents of the Kremlin on American soil.[65]

The apocalyptic tone of such pronouncements was typical. Whether or not they believed their own rhetoric, the nation's political leaders routinely used highly charged language to describe the threat that Communism posed to the nation. America's very existence was at stake. Disease metaphors were common. Communism was like a plague, the Attorney General noted in 1950; each party member "carries in himself the germ of death for our society." For the Minnesota liberal Hubert Humphrey, the CP was "a political cancer in our society." For Adlai Stevenson, the perennial Democratic presidential contender, it was worse "than cancer, tuberculosis, and heart disease combined." These "poisonous germs," a former FBI official warned the National Security Council in 1948, infected "every phase of American life."[66]

Though such a formulation implied that no one was safe, mainstream politicians and Cold War liberals like Humphrey focused on the dangers that Communism posed to the government or to those institutions like unions and civil rights groups whose agenda the party shared, while conservatives stressed its spiritual and cultural threat. Hoover claimed to be particularly worried about the CP's challenge to Christianity. "The danger of Communism in America," he told a group of Methodist ministers in 1947,

> lies . . . in the awesome fact that it is a materialistic religion inflaming in its adherents a destructive fanaticism. Communism is secularism on the march. It is a moral foe of Christianity.

The Catholic Church had been making the same argument for years. Probably no other idea was as widely held about the party. It was the most common answer given by respondents in a 1954 national survey that asked what Communists believed.[67]

Within more secular circles, a different perception of the party's relation to religion reigned. Here, the emphasis was not so much on the CP's atheism as on the religious quality of Communism itself. The party was like a church, its ideology, in the words of New York intellectual Daniel Bell, "a secular religion." Many of its members, Judge Learned Hand explained in his influential 1950 opinion upholding the Smith Act conviction of the CP's top leaders,

> are infused with a passionate Utopian faith that is to redeem mankind. It has its Founder, its apostles, its sacred texts — perhaps even its martyrs. It seeks converts far and wide by an extensive system of schooling, demanding of all an inflexible doctrinal orthodoxy.

Moreover, as the Alsop brothers explained, the unquestioning faith that the CP demanded of its adherents made "every party member . . . as much a fanatic participant in a holy war as every whirling dervish."[68]

"Fanatic" — the word reverberates throughout the anticommunist literature of the Cold War. Like the notion that they were robots, the depiction of Communists as fanatics distanced them from ordinary people. Fanaticism implied irrationality and even madness, taking Communism out of the political realm and into a world of abnormal psychology where the specific causes and ideas embraced by its members were easy to ignore. Especially among moderates and liberals, the notion that Communism was some kind of psychological disorder came to be quite common.[69]

Not all anti-Communists, however, viewed party members as mental cases. Conservatives like Hoover did not share the therapeutic culture of the 1950s. As a result, when the discussion about Communism touched upon personal issues, there was an obvious difference between the psychologizing of the secular liberals and the moralizing of their more traditional compatriots. Hoover and his cohorts called Communists "godless atheists"; Ernst and his called them "emotionally unstable." The pejorative intent was the same.[70]

Both sides, for example, believed that Communism subverted marriage and the family. From Hoover's perspective, the atheism that party militants inculcated in their children "illustrates the depths of their degradation as parents." Liberals emphasized the emotional toll that Communism took on its adherents and their families. But all observers, whether working from a psychological or a moralistic perspective, viewed the party through the family-oriented lenses of the 1950s, a decade when divorce was still a rarity, premarital sex taboo, and women were expected to stay home with their kids and bake brownies. Since the reality was different, the contradictions that dominated the discourse about Communists and their families may well have been projections of the underlying confusion about gender roles that characterized the era.[71]

The main victims of the party's assault on family values were its own members, their spouses, and children. Both scholarly and popular writers claimed that the CP expected its cadres to subordinate all personal relationships to the cause. To be a good party member," a Yale political scientist quoted a former Communist as saying, "you have to give up the niceties of life. You have to forget you have a family — you have no time for them." Elizabeth Bentley made the same point in her fictionalized memoir. "We are forbidden to form close friendships and, especially, to fall in love." Not the least of Gerhart Eisler's crimes, as *Life* magazine pointed out, was that he abandoned his second wife and daughter.[72]

There was a touch of reality to these formulations. The party did make enormous demands on its members' time. Some of its most active cadres did sacrifice their families to their politics. We can only imagine what the professional anti-Communists would have made of the fact, had they known it, that Eugene Dennis and his wife Peggy had left a five-year-old son in the Soviet Union because the child spoke only Russian and his existence was a "liability" that the CP, already vulnerable to charges of Moscow control, could ill afford. But such extreme cases were rare; and political activists were not the only absent dads of the 1950s.[73]

Bad mothers were also a menace. The anticommunist literature contained a strong strand of misogyny that blamed domineering and overprotective moms for turning their sons (rarely daughters) into Communists, while at the same time, it also accused communist mothers of neglect. Ethel Rosenberg's allegedly cold and unemotional behavior was presumably a sign of her political indoctrination and showed that she deserved the penalty she received. J. Edgar Hoover, who had originally opposed the death sentence because she was a mother, claimed that he changed his mind after she rejected her own mother's plea that she confess for the sake of her children. Sometimes simply belonging to the party could be a sign of poor parenting. During the early fifties, there were actually cases in which judges refused custody to women accused of "Communist leanings."[74]

Just as their political affiliation branded communist women bad mothers, it also made them poor marital partners. "The tendency seems to be that in Communist marriages the wife is the more dominant partner," Morris Ernst explained, adding the widely circulated tidbit that "it was generally assumed among Communists that Earl Browder was henpecked." Among ex-Communists, a more sinister interpretation prevailed. Raïssa Browder had once worked for the Soviet secret police and Elizabeth Bentley was not the only person who believed that "she still worked for it. One of her duties was to keep her husband in line and make reports on him. Browder had evidently no choice in his marriage; the powers-that-be in Moscow had issued the orders and he had to follow them."[75]

Ethel Rosenberg was also reputed to have bossed her husband. Besides convincing himself that she was a bad mother, Hoover relied on a psychological profile written by an attorney who had never met the couple. The study, which concluded that "Julius is the slave and his wife, Ethel, the master," circulated widely throughout the federal government and seems to have convinced President Eisenhower that he should deny clemency in the case. As he explained to his son three days before the couple's execution, one of the reasons why he was willing to allow a woman "to receive capital punishment . . . is that in this instance it is the woman who is the strong and recalcitrant character, the man is the weak one. She has obviously been the leader in everything they did in the spy ring." The author of the study that Eisenhower found so compelling was J. Edgar Hoover's good friend Morris Ernst.[76]

But Ernst did not have the last word. Ethel Rosenberg's was an image full of contradictions. For she was also viewed as an ordinary housewife who was not involved with any serious political matters. Federal investigators knew that she had been a Communist, but the only espionage activity that she was ever charged with was the traditionally female one: typing. And the government was not sure she had done even that. On the list of questions that the FBI had prepared to ask Julius at Sing Sing on the night of the couple's execution in the event that he had a final change of heart was the utterly devastating one: "Was your wife cognizant of your activities?"[77]

Since politics was usually considered a man's business during the 1940s and 1950s, most opponents of the CP tended to ignore its women. When the Justice Department prosecuted the party's top leaders under the Smith Act in 1948, for example, it indicted every member of the politburo except Elizabeth Gurley Flynn. The way in which an anticommunist investigating committee in Ohio treated its female witnesses reveals a similarly dismissive view of women. Though it charged some of them with contempt and heard witnesses testify about their active role in the party, it operated on the assumption that these women knew little about politics and cared only about their homes and families. It questioned them as much about their husbands' activities as their own and even asked one woman if she had baked a cake for the cause.[78]

Fewer contradictions plagued the public discussion of the party's attitudes toward sexuality. Here the traditional stereotypes of free love and promiscuity held sway despite the evidence that Communists were not particularly randy. Ever since 1919, when Senate investigators gave currency to lurid tales about the nationalization of women after the Russian revolution, depictions of sexual misconduct and immoral behavior had suffused the rhetoric of anticommunism.[79]

Homosexuality was so far beyond the realm of acceptability that it rarely figured in any discussion of the CP's sexual practices. There were, it is true, intimations that Communism was somehow effeminate. Joe McCarthy led the charge with his diatribes against the "Communists and queers" in the State Department and his macho disdain for its leader, "the Red Dean [Acheson] of Fashion." But class antagonisms shaped McCarthy's language as much as homophobia did. Nonetheless, the two groups received the same treatment. In 1950, the Senate responded to rumors that there was something "queer" within the government by authorizing a special investigation. The language of the committee's preliminary report could have been written by HUAC. The images are almost identical. Like Communists, "sexual perverts" concealed their activities presumably in order to seduce unsuspecting prospects. Their influence over "young and impressionable people" was so powerful that even "one homosexual can pollute a Government office." And, because their sexual practices made them vulnerable to blackmail by Soviet agents, they were a threat to security. Ironically, the CP purged its gay members for exactly the same reason. Still, we should not impose our contemporary sensibilities on those of the early Cold War years and conflate the two outcast groups in ways that people at the time did not. Though considered aberrant, most Communists were depicted as thoroughly straight.[80]

High party leaders were, for example, reputed to get "special sexual privileges." Supplying such services was supposedly just another political chore for a female Communist. And, if she got impregnated by "a regular Party guy" (the CP's slang, so one former FBI plant claimed, for a man who "doesn't want to get caught in marriage"), there would be an illegal abortion, often funded by passing the hat among the comrades. The party's girls were also assigned the task of luring new prospects into the movement. The communist seductress, identified as "the Bad Blonde" by cultural historian Nora Sayre, was a stock figure in the movies of the Cold War, as she was in some of the more lurid confessional literature and testimony by ex-Communists. The Soviet secret police, so Benjamin Gitlow claimed, routinely used good-looking women as political call girls. The party even set up an organization, the so-called Sweethearts of Servicemen, whose members, a former FBI informant told the Senate, "had no morals or moral standards whatsoever" and "would go to any extreme to 'entertain' service men" whom they picked up on the streets, plied with liquor and sex, and then did "the indoctrination job" on.[81]

Nonetheless, for all their charms, it was clear that the CP's femmes fatales had not recruited all the people who entered the party's orbit. Nor was it believed that ordinary political considerations had attracted many converts. Communism was assumed to be so obviously repugnant that no rational person would join the CP or work with it. Yet people did; and, if the menace of Communism was to be countered, it was considered necessary to understand the reasons for its appeal. The standard explanations relied on two suppositions: either party members and sympathizers were deceived or they were abnormal.

There was one exception here. It was acknowledged, especially among liberals, that the party did, in fact, appeal to people with legitimate grievances. As a result, it was common to argue that righting these wrongs was the best way to fight Communism. "Making democracy work," labor leader Walter Reuther told the readers of *Collier's* magazine in 1948, was the answer to the CP challenge. Such an argument provided a good cover for liberals like Reuther who did not want to be seen as advocating the same causes as Communists. Thus, for example, civil libertarians who opposed the worst excesses of McCarthyism commonly argued — as the socialist leader Norman Thomas did in criticizing a particularly egregious prosecution — that "there is no better aid to Communism than denial of justice in a land which boasts of the devotion to justice." Poverty was also, liberals agreed, a "wonderful breeding ground for Communism." Many of the party's top cadres had signed on during the Depression, attracted, so it was believed, by the economic panaceas the CP was peddling. If that kind of appeal was to be blunted, it would be necessary to alleviate economic hardship both in the United States and abroad.[82]

Discrimination also played into the party's hands. The disproportionate numbers of Jews in the party obviously required explanation. And it was widely assumed that the CP had a special appeal to second-generation Americans who rebelled against the old-country ways of their immigrant parents, yet felt "rejected by the dominant American culture." That explanation, rather than, for example, the party's opposition to Hitler in the thirties, supposedly accounted for Communism's attractiveness to so many Jews (because of the era's squeamishness about ethnicity, though, the specific identity of these socially alienated recruits to the CP was rarely mentioned).[83]

Racism was another big recruiter. Mainstream civil rights groups had been questioning the sincerity of the party's commitment to civil rights ever since the Scottsboro case in the early thirties, but they recognized the challenge it posed. When liberals embraced the cause of racial equality during the early years of the Cold War, they often did so on the grounds that, at least in part, eliminating segregation was a vital component of the world-wide anticommunist crusade. The existence of Jim Crow in the South, many policymakers believed, made it hard for them to convince people in Third World countries that the American way of life was better than the Soviet one. And, of course, they did not want American blacks to turn red.[84]

Conservatives who had less sympathy for, if they did not actually oppose, integration also recognized the party's appeal to African Americans. But like Hoover, whose racism is well known, they viewed the Communists' advocacy of equality as a divisive tactic, "the cause of much of the racial trouble in the United States at the present time." The CP's valiant effort to encourage interracial socializing at a time when even the North was largely segregated evoked the traditional stereotypes of troublemaking outsiders pandering to the depraved instincts of the supposedly contented blacks. These stereotypes contained sexual overtones as well, hints that the party's pandering to African Americans was literal as well as figurative and that it did, in fact, encourage the miscegenation that segregationists most claimed to fear.[85]

Implicit in all the worried rhetoric about Communism's appeal for the downtrodden and discriminated against was the assumption that the men and women who fell prey to the CP's chicanery had failed to see through its propaganda. They were, in short, "dupes" who had been lured into the party and its front groups or had let the Communists take over their organizations. Long concerned about the CP's "innocent, gullible, or willful allies," Hoover devoted his Bureau's considerable public relations apparatus to warning the nation about the party's seemingly harmless activities, though his formulations, like those of many conservatives, often conflated Communism with almost every left-wing cause. Liberals also fretted about the credulity of America's do-gooders. In *The Vital Center,* his influential 1949 appeal for a tough-minded moderation, Arthur Schlesinger, Jr., castigated what he calls the "Doughface progressive," the fellow traveler whose "sentimentality has softened [him] up . . . for Communist permeation and conquest."[86]

Obviously not all the people who supported Communism did so

because they were duped or discriminated against. Many party members not only knew what kind of organization they were joining, but had consciously sought it out. Since it was assumed that no sane person would become a Communist, the CP had to be attracting the unbalanced. According to the survey research of contemporary social scientists, as well as the testimony of former Communists, many of the men and women who gravitated to the party were misfits or neurotics who sought to deal with their own inadequacies by embracing the CP. So thoroughly had the 1950s transformed political dissent into psychological distress that almost any kind of left-wing activism could be considered a sign of mental illness. In 1955 a New York City judge sent an actress to the psychiatric ward of Bellevue Hospital for having defied an air raid drill.[87]

Lonely people were particularly drawn to the party. It offered community and "'belongingness,' a feeling of comradeship." The psycholiterature of anticommunism is replete with descriptions of the pathetic creatures who joined the CP because, as Arthur Schlesinger, Jr., explained, it gave them the "social, intellectual and even sexual fulfillment they cannot obtain in existing society." They were typically portrayed as homely, scruffy, and badly dressed. Cvetic describes his "commie uniform" as "a shirt with a wrinkled collar and a dirty front" and "a few ties that had got soupy."[88]

Joe McCarthy was not alone in his contention that "practically every active Communist is twisted mentally or physically in some way." It was commonly believed — and by the mid-fifties there were academic studies to back it up — that the party contained "a large proportion of emotionally maladjusted individuals who were seeking to solve their emotional problems by attacking society, rather than face up to their personal inadequacies and conflicts." Significantly, the most common clinical symptom these disturbed individuals displayed, and the one that seemed to have brought them into the party, was hostility. Most of them, at least according to the studies that purported to analyze the appeals of Communism, were simply seething with rage. They turned to the CP because it preached class warfare and, thus, offered them a way "to control their hostility, by giving them an opportunity to express it under 'socially acceptable' terms." There was a literary dimension to this analysis: the strident language of the CP's publications was taken to indicate a similar emotional state within its members.[89]

But, of course, the party was not just a threat to the mental health of a few pathetic individuals. Though such people might be drawn to the CP because of their own personal inadequacies, once they enlisted in the communist cause they menaced their fellow citizens as well. They had become Communists, endowed with all the scary characteristics that the anticommunist discourse of the late 1940s and 1950s had attached to that identity. With the advent of the Cold War, those characteristics, in particular the Communists' discipline and servility to Moscow, now endangered the entire nation.

★

CHAPTER 5

"A GREAT AND TOTAL DANGER"

THE NATURE OF THE COMMUNIST THREAT

DURING THE mid-50s, everybody who applied for a permit to fish in the New York City reservoirs had to sign a loyalty oath. In 1957, nearly three years after the United States Senate censured Joe McCarthy, the state's commissioner of water supply, gas and electricity refused to grant fishing permits to two Communists. Absurd as such provisions may seem today, at the time they had considerable logic. The commissioner was simply protecting the city's drinking water from possible saboteurs who might poison it while pretending to troll for trout.[1]

It is all too easy to dismiss such seemingly irrational behavior as the symptom of a mass emotional aberration, the political by-product of the nation's underlying psychic insecurities. But such measures as the banning of communist fishermen from the New York City reservoirs also reflected an, albeit unsophisticated, attempt to deal with what was then perceived as a serious threat. Americans at every level of society genuinely believed that Communism endangered the nation. The perceived threat was quite specific: subversion, espionage, and sabotage. Communists would try to overthrow the government or at least undermine its policies on behalf of their Soviet masters. They would spy for the Kremlin. And if war came, they would try to sabotage the nation's defense industries and other vital facilities.

154

Whatever the reality of the communist threat may have been — and in the light of the new evidence that has emerged from Moscow's and Washington's formerly closed archives it turns out that the Kremlin's undercover operations may well have been more extensive than many historians had previously assumed — what is important for understanding the political repression of the McCarthy period is the way in which that threat was perceived. At that moment in the late 1940s when the superstructure of anticommunism was being erected, there were enough instances of supposed subversion, espionage, and sabotage to convince political leaders and ordinary citizens alike that Communists endangered the United States and required a drastic response. It was the plausibility of the threat — based on the connection between the commonly exaggerated image of Communism and an equally exaggerated notion of the nation's vulnerability to it — that spurred American policymakers to protect internal security by cracking down on domestic Communists.

The main danger, of course, came from abroad. In the crucial early years of the Cold War, as the struggle with the Soviet Union came to dominate American foreign policy, federal officials increasingly came to view domestic Communism as part of a worldwide Soviet conspiracy. Accordingly, communist activities that had previously been opposed for political and ideological reasons now became matters of national security. The perception that domestic Communism was a threat evolved in tandem with the growing confrontation with the Soviet Union. The two, in fact, fed each other, their preexisting antagonism to Communism intensifying the hostility and suspicion with which some American policymakers regarded the Russians.[2]

Thus, in order to understand the sense of crisis that permeated the perception of a communist threat in the late 1940s, it is crucial to examine the growth and intensification of the Cold War. Relations between the United States and the Soviet Union had never been good and the alliance against Nazi Germany did not eliminate the underlying tensions between the two nations during World War II. Besides their ideological opposition to Communism, American policymakers disliked the secretiveness of the Soviet regime and its hostility toward outsiders. The Kremlin was equally suspicious, apparently fearing that its capitalist allies were purposefully delaying the second front in order to let the Soviet army exhaust itself in its single-handed struggle against the Third Reich. The invasion of Normandy in 1944 and the two summit conferences at Teheran in late 1943 and Yalta in February 1945 temporarily defused some of the conflicts — mainly by ignoring them.[3]

By the beginning of 1945 the Red Army's imminent victory over the Reichswehr had opened Eastern Europe to the Soviet Union, making it likely that the USSR would control the area in order to ensure it would never again face a hostile power on its Western border. None of the Allies wanted a confrontation while the war was still on, so the most controversial issues were swept under the rug. At Yalta, for example, Roosevelt, Churchill, and Stalin postponed a possibly acrimonious discussion of Germany's future and agreed to a high-sounding "Declaration on the Future of Liberated Europe" that promised democracy to Eastern Europe despite the Western Allies' already obvious inability to prevent a Soviet takeover of the region. In East Asia, where the Americans were eager for Moscow to enter the war against Japan, a secret protocol gave the Russians major concessions at China's expense.

Because Roosevelt had played his cards so close to his chest and had misleadingly portrayed Yalta as the harbinger of democracy in Europe, his death a few months later left his successor unprepared for the complex realities of the postwar world. The fluctuations in Truman's policy toward the Soviet Union during his early months in office reflected the uncertainties he inherited. At first he took a hard line, apparently on the assumption that the Kremlin's imposition of a communist regime on Poland violated the Yalta accord. Then he began to relent. Perhaps Stalin could be handled after all. But the Potsdam summit conference on the future of Germany that summer resolved few major questions and again postponed the most sensitive ones for future deliberation.

Truman was at Potsdam when he heard about the successful detonation of the first American atomic bomb at Alamogordo, New Mexico. He was elated but soon discovered that the possession of nuclear weapons brought no diplomatic benefit to the United States. Both Roosevelt and Truman had kept the Manhattan Project a secret from their Russian ally and the American policymakers initially assumed that their atomic monopoly would give them, in Secretary of War Stimson's words, "all of the cards" in negotiating with the Russians. But atomic diplomacy was not a poker game. Stalin, who was already speeding work on his own nuclear device, did not make the concessions in Poland, Germany, and elsewhere that the Americans wanted. Instead, the bomb and the issue of its international control became an additional source of contention in the intensifying Cold War.[4]

Stalin's obvious determination to control Eastern Europe as well as what the Americans viewed as his expansionist moves toward the Middle East convinced most of the important military and civilian policymakers within the Truman administration that the Soviet Union endangered international stability. The Kremlin's rhetorical embrace of a worldwide revolution was another source of concern. American policymakers worried that Moscow was encouraging European communist parties to block the restoration of the capitalist economic system that most U.S. officials considered vital to their nation's, as well as the world's, well-being. Since Truman and his advisers viewed all of postwar Europe (not to mention the Third World) as peculiarly vulnerable to a communist takeover, the situation seemed dire indeed. The Soviets were challenging the United States on every front: ideological, economic, and strategic. Or so it seemed.

As a result, by the beginning of 1946, confrontation rather than negotiation had come to characterize American foreign policy. Containment, as this policy was soon to be called, required the United States to stop the Soviet Union's supposedly insatiable drive for expansion by the concerted application of counterpressure. But containment would be costly and it was by no means clear that the American people, who had after all just elected an economy-minded Republican Congress in November 1946, realized the extent of the supposed danger or were willing to make the necessary sacrifices to avert it. Thus, although the administration had clearly opted for a policy of containment, Truman hesitated to make that decision publicly known.

By the beginning of 1947, however, because Western Europe seemed on the verge of economic collapse, the administration felt compelled to act. In order to persuade the American people to bail out Europe, Truman and his advisers painted an exaggerated picture of Soviet expansion. In the so-called Truman Doctrine, a speech delivered to a joint session of Congress on March 12, the president called for economic and military aid to Greece and Turkey (neither of which was directly threatened by Soviet forces) and publicly committed the United States to a worldwide policy of containing the USSR. He presented that policy in ideological terms, enlisting the nation in a struggle to "support free peoples who are resisting attempted subjugation by armed minorities or by outside pressures."

Over the next few years, the Cold War escalated as both the United States and the Soviet Union took ostensibly defensive actions that looked ever more threatening to the other side. The USSR solidified its hold over Eastern Europe, imposing communist governments throughout the region largely in order to ensure its own security. Truman and his advisers, however, assumed that the Kremlin's desire for expansion had no limits; and they came to view all American foreign policy within the context of a world-wide struggle against Communism. Containment shaped every program, whether it was the economic aid to Western Europe envisioned under the Marshall Plan or military assistance to the French in Southeast Asia.

Moreover, as the antagonism intensified, containment took on an increasingly military cast — and an increasingly global one. Washington exaggerated the Kremlin's power and assumed that Stalin was orchestrating every anti-imperialist or revolutionary struggle from Vietnam to South Africa. Outside of Eastern Europe, this was not the case; most of the insurgencies that Washington claimed were run by Moscow had indigenous roots, even if, as in Vietnam, they were led by Communists. In 1949, the communist victory in China and the detonation of a Soviet atomic device heightened the sense of crisis. Could the United States be losing the Cold War? Truman ordered the development of the hydrogen bomb and requested a major reassessment of American foreign policy. That reassessment, enshrined in the National Security Council report of April 1950, known as NSC-68, viewed the Kremlin as a threat to all of Western civilization and called for a massive military buildup to save the world.[5]

By the time the North Korean army crossed the 38th parallel on June 25, the United States had become so ideologically mobilized that there was no debate about the Soviet Union's responsibility. Though the invasion was actually the culmination of a festering civil war, most American policymakers and ordinary citizens assumed that Stalin was testing the nation's resolve. Determined to avoid a replay of the West's prewar appeasement of Hitler at Munich, they would not capitulate to an aggressor. This time, Washington would resist the supposed Soviet advances even if it required direct intervention in Korea or increased aid to the French in Indochina, where another struggle was looming. Of course, both conflicts were far more complicated than that and were to involve the United States in years of bloody, fruitless warfare. But in the face of all the stereotypes and oversimplifications that had developed with regard to the Soviet Union, a more realistic assessment of the situation in Korea and Southeast Asia was out of the question. Moreover, the growing anticommunist repression within the United States that accompanied the intensification of the Cold War ruled out any serious debate about foreign policy.[6]

The linkage is obvious. In a crude but not incorrect way, McCarthyism can be seen as the home front of the Cold War. As the confrontation with Soviet Communism escalated, so, too, did the campaign against domestic Communism. The intensification of the Cold War made it increasingly easier for Hoover and the other members of the anticommunist network to convince the rest of the Washington political establishment that the internal threat had also grown. Not only was there evidence that made the existence of the threat seem plausible, but the deepening sense of crisis engendered by the conflict with Moscow made it possible to put a damaging spin on activities that had once been considered harmless.

By 1950, American policymakers tended to view American Communism as just another weapon in Stalin's arsenal. They assumed that the Soviets, who were implacably committed to the destruction of the capitalist world, would do whatever they could to weaken the United States. The openness of American society made the nation peculiarly vulnerable to the Kremlin's advances. As the authors of the influential NSC-68 described it, the threat, though dire, was quite specific; it was "serious espionage, subversion and sabotage, particularly by concerted and well-directed communist activity."[7]

The most obvious Soviet agents were, of course, Russians. And, in fact, even before the Cold War escalated, there was considerable concern about the activities of Russian nationals in the United States. The FBI, which seems to have kept Soviet diplomats under routine surveillance, assumed that they and their compatriots in other Russian agencies were involved in espionage. Late in 1946, Hoover became upset about a group of Soviet engineers who were supposedly looking at air compressors in Ohio but were actually "taking copious notes, obtaining blueprints, diagrams and photographs of electrical, sewage, gas and water systems, power plants, transportation terminals, bridges and other strategic points in such cities as Washington, New York, Chicago and Philadelphia." The FBI director was sure they were up to no good and he communicated his concern to the

White House, where it was also taken seriously. In a provocative report on the nature of the Soviet threat that he prepared for the president in September 1946, Truman's aide Clark Clifford quotes verbatim from the FBI's complaint about these Soviet engineers. Two years later, the Soviet engineers reappear in a National Security Council report on internal security. Congressional anti-Communists were also upset; HUAC's Karl E. Mundt complained publicly about the easy access the Russian visitors had to major factories, railroad yards, power plants, and the TVA.[8]

Whether or not there was a nefarious component to the Soviet engineers' interest in the sewer systems of America's big cities, J. Edgar Hoover's worries were not without foundation. After all, Soviet emissaries in the United States were engaged in espionage. When the Russian code clerk Igor Gouzenko defected from his country's mission in Ottawa in 1945, he produced documentary evidence to show that Soviet diplomats and military officials had run spy rings inside Canada. There were Russians as well in the stories that the self-confessed American spies told about their undercover activities. Identified as "Peter," "Al," and "John" by Elizabeth Bentley, Whittaker Chambers, and the other Cold War witnesses, many of these individuals, albeit with different names, also appear in the Venona documents, the recently declassified translations of the telegraphic correspondence between the KGB and its representatives in New York and Washington during World War II. Though fragmentary and incomplete, the documents reveal that members of the Soviet intelligence agencies were busily engaged in spying on the American government.[9]

None of these Russians were ever apprehended. They figured in the memoirs of the ex-communist witnesses and in the popular imagination as shadowy figures like Gerhart Eisler, powerful, menacing, and foreign. The only Soviet citizen ever caught in the act at the height of the McCarthy era was Valentin Gubitchev, a Russian engineer in the UN Secretariat arrested in March 1949 during a New York City rendezvous with a Justice Department employee named Judith Coplon, whose case will be examined later.[10]

The activities of Soviet diplomats and other Russians were, of course, only a subsidiary aspect of the internal security problem and one that could be handled mainly as a matter of routine counterintelligence. The main danger, and the one that was to transform the concern about Soviet operations in the United States into the pretext for a wave of domestic political repression, was the fear that thousands of American citizens might also be working for the Kremlin.

Several key assumptions undergirded that fear and shaped the government's approach to internal security. One was that the Soviet Union exercised complete control over Communist parties throughout the world and used them as instruments in its struggle for international hegemony. Another dehumanized individual Communists and posited that their robotlike obedience to party discipline made them all potential Soviet agents, "requiring," as Clark Clifford put it in 1946, "only the direct instruction of a Soviet superior to make the potentiality a reality." This formulation appears with astonishing regularity in the official correspondence of the period. FBI reports routinely recycle it either as a direct warning from Hoover or else as the testimony of one or another of the major ex-Communist informers: "Every American Communist should be considered a potential agent for Soviet Russia."[11]

As a result, once the Cold War transformed the Soviet Union into an enemy, it took little imagination to see American Communism as a threat to national security. It became commonplace to view all the CP's activities if not as actual efforts to undermine the United States at least as preparations for doing so. Moreover, since party members were active in so many areas, alarmists could detect the Kremlin's hand everywhere.[12]

One alleged threat was political subversion. While no one in a position of authority seriously worried that the CP would overthrow the government, communist propaganda directed against the nation's defense and foreign policies was another matter. The party's supposed attempts to subvert the military seemed particularly menacing. The danger came from the Leninist doctrine of "revolutionary defeatism" that urged Communists to take advantage of the opportunity presented by an unpopular war to turn the army against the government and mount a revolution. Though obviously useful to the Bolsheviks in the war-torn Russia of 1917, such a program was absurd with regard to the stable American political system of the 1940s and 1950s. Nonetheless, concern about subversion of the military surfaced whenever the CP opposed United States foreign policy, first during the Nazi-Soviet pact period and then during the Cold War.[13]

References to revolutionary defeatism grace the big communist trials of the 1940s and 1950s. In the 1947 perjury trial of Carl Marzani, a New York City undercover policeman testified that Marzani had urged young Communists to join the army during the Nazi-Soviet pact period "so that we can disintegrate the morale of the men." Similar charges surfaced during the 1949 Smith Act trial of the CP's leading officials. Not only did the prosecutors read into the transcript the most damaging passages on revolutionary defeatism in the works of Lenin and Stalin, but they also had FBI informers testify about meetings at which party leaders discussed "the possibility, feasibility, and so forth . . . of turning a war into a civil war through the medium of civil disobedience."[14]

Communists, it seemed, did more than just talk about subverting the military. As the Soviet Union tightened its grip on Eastern Europe in the aftermath of World War II, Truman and his advisers began to worry that the rapid demobilization of the United States's armed forces was weakening the nation's ability to oppose the Kremlin's advance. Because of the widespread clamor for the return of American soldiers, it would have been politically suicidal in 1945 and 1946 for the government to have urged the retention of large numbers of troops overseas. But, for some policymakers, the demand for rapid demobilization concealed something more ominous than mere homesickness. Early in 1946, American GIs in Europe, the Philippines, and Hawaii mounted demonstrations to dramatize their desire to go home. The presence of alleged Communists among the organizers of these protests convinced both military intelligence and the FBI that Moscow was involved.[15]

Another activity that seemingly indicated subversion within the armed forces was what the Joint Chiefs of Staff called "anti-caste" agitation, i.e., protests against racial discrimination. Such charges surfaced in Marzani's trial; he was reputed to have been working "to sow resentment and discontent among Negroes." These allegations were not new; the CP had long been accused of taking advantage of the grievances of African Americans and using them for its own purposes. The Cold War transformed such accusations into a matter of national security. Again, there seemed to be evidence, especially after Paul Robeson, perhaps the most well known African American in the party's orbit, made the widely reported remark at a communist-sponsored peace conference in Paris in 1949 that if war broke out between the United States and the Soviet Union, American blacks did not have to fight for their country.[16]

Few public officials or politicians expressed much concern about the CP's open opposition to American foreign policy. Its covert impact, however, was assumed to be more dangerous. Secret party members might gain influence within the government and use their positions to further Soviet objectives. Such a scenario aligned the new Cold War concern about communist subversion with the highly partisan Communists-in-government issue and gave credibility to the damaging allegations of Joe McCarthy and his allies that Communists and fellow travelers had penetrated the New Deal and were still directly influencing policy.[17]

There was little, if any, evidence for such allegations. The Truman administration certainly never took such charges seriously. But its opponents did — or at least claimed to. The FBI and the rest of the anticommunist network assembled enough pieces of circumstantial evidence for the administration's conservative enemies to construct a number of ostensibly plausible scenarios that purported to show how highly placed communist agents had subverted American foreign policy. Most of these scenarios either identified particular individuals as party members or else cited specific incidents in which officials had come into contact with alleged Communists and then implemented policies that supposedly hurt American interests. Since the contacts had existed and since Communism was assumed to be peculiarly virulent and contagious, it is possible to understand why even the most outrageous charges of someone like Senator McCarthy could have a certain patina of plausibility.[18]

In 1946, several years before he was to accuse the former State Department official Alger Hiss of espionage, Whittaker Chambers told Raymond Murphy, the department's security officer, that the main job of his underground party unit "was to mess up policy." Chambers repeated these allegations before HUAC in August 1948, claiming that the Communists he worked with had entered the government not "for the purpose of espionage, but for the purpose of infiltrating the government and influencing government policy by getting Communists in key places." When pressed by the FBI to give examples of how the members of his underground unit had influenced policy, he mentioned NLRB decisions, farm mortgages in Oklahoma, and an attempt "to influence a decision regarding sugar beet workers."[19]

Chambers did not offer any substantive evidence that Hiss or the other alleged Soviet agents had subverted American foreign policy. But for Republican critics of the Roosevelt and Truman administrations, Hiss's presence within the American delegation at the Yalta conference in 1945 was proof enough. After all, Yalta had been the place where, so these critics claimed, Eastern Europe and China had been sold out to the Russians. Hiss had never made policy, however. The highest official linked to the supposed ring of communist agents was Harry Dexter White, an assistant secretary of the Treasury during and immediately after World War II. White was responsible for much of the Treasury Department's postwar international financial planning. He played an important role in establishing the International Monetary Fund and was its first American director. He was, so the FBI charged, "in a position to secure favorable consideration for the U.S.S.R. in financial matters" and "would have the power to influence to a great degree deliberations on all international financial arrangements." [20]

Later on White was also charged with having helped the Communists take over China. For those members of the anticommunist network who believed that the CP had infiltrated the policy-making levels of the Roosevelt and Truman adminstrations, the "loss" of China in 1949 definitively confirmed their suspicions. According to the scenario, which Alfred Kohlberg, Joe McCarthy, and the other professional anti-Communists pushed during the early fifties, the State Department had let Mao Zedong take over China because the officials who dealt with East Asian affairs were under the CP's influence. Though it was true that many of the nation's China hands were critical of Chiang Kai-shek, they neither favored the Chinese Communists, nor, more important, had anything to do with their eventual triumph. Chiang's Nationalist regime was perfectly capable of losing China on its own. But, as we shall see, there was enough circumstantial evidence for Kohlberg and his allies to construct a plausible case that communist influence within the State Department had caused the loss of China. [21]

The other sensitive area of American politics in the 1950s was nuclear weapons. Naturally espionage was a concern; but there were policy considerations as well. Again, the allegation that there had been communist influence at the highest levels was used by people with other agendas. The main target here was J. Robert Oppenheimer, the nation's most famous atomic scientist. Oppenheimer was completely loyal, but he did question both the development of the hydogen bomb and the air force's enthusiasm for strategic bombing. Moreover, Oppenheimer's past had been suspicious enough to raise some eyebrows.

He had come out of Berkeley, which even in the 1930s was a hotbed of radical politics. Oppenheimer had not been in the party, but many of his friends and students, as well as his ex-girlfriend, brother, and sister-in-law, were. And his wife (whose first husband had been killed in the Spanish Civil War) was a friend of Steve Nelson's, the party's local organizer during the late thirties and early forties. Though he abandoned his left-wing politics in 1942 when he became the Manhattan Project's scientific director, Oppenheimer remained an object of suspicion. Worse yet was an incident in which a Berkeley friend named Haakon Chevalier had conveyed a request to spy for the Russians. Oppenheimer had rejected the proposition out of hand but when he informed the Manhattan Project security people about the incident, he initially tried to shield Chevalier and said that three unnamed individuals had made the approach. He soon told the truth but the original lie continued to hurt him.[22]

The FBI had been on Oppenheimer's trail for years. In 1941 it put him on its list of potential subversives to be picked up for custodial detention. In the years that followed, Hoover repeatedly warned the military authorities and the Truman administration about the distinguished physicist's "Communist affiliations." Nonetheless, it was not until 1953 that his enemies within the defense establishment finally got his security clearance revoked. In the November 1953 letter to J. Edgar Hoover that officially triggered Oppenheimer's fall, William L. Borden, the former executive director of the Joint Congressional Committee on Atomic Energy, claimed that "more probably than not," the physicist "acted under a Soviet directive in influencing United States military, atomic energy, intelligence, and diplomatic policy."[23]

Borden also charged Oppenheimer with espionage. But that charge, unlike the one that Oppenheimer had delayed the development of the hydrogen bomb, was based on little besides the common assumption that "every American Communist is potentially an espionage agent of the Soviet Government." The most dramatic component of the communist threat, allegations of espionage figured prominently in many of the key political trials of the early Cold War. Interestingly, the nation's top policymakers were less concerned about spying than about such other elements of the communist threat as sabotage and propaganda. But espionage was easier to dramatize and, as a result, became central to the popular perception that Communists endangered the United States. The anticommunist network was eager to spread the charge. And, of course, some of it was true.[24]

Naturally, the FBI had a strong investment in proving that such spying took place and in exaggerating its importance. Counterespionage had always been the Bureau's main mission in the field of internal security and its activities in that area had expanded enormously during World War II. Peace, therefore, posed a problem; the FBI would have to reduce its operations unless there was a new enemy to protect the nation against. Soviet spies certainly fit the bill. Given J. Edgar Hoover's ideological predilections as well as his agency's institutional needs, it is easy to see why the Director and his men emphasized the threat of espionage and stressed that all party members would spy for the Russians if given the chance. The message got through, largely because the big spy cases of the early Cold War amplified and legitimized the FBI's contentions, convincing most Americans — public officials and ordinary citizens alike — that the Communist party was breeding spies.

These cases have yet to be completely resolved. The end of the Cold War has opened many previously sealed Soviet and American records. As the evidence accumulates, it does seem as if many of the alleged spies had, indeed, helped the Russians. Though the FBI and its informers may have embroidered the details a bit in order to get publicity, preserve a witness's credibility, or — most important — get a conviction, it is clear that some kind of espionage took place during the 1930s and 1940s. However, because the data is so incomplete, it is hard to assess how extensive that spying was. The U.S. intelligence agencies that released the Venona translations claim that they mention two hundred Americans. But not all the individuals can be identified. In addition, most of the names are aliases and we have to rely on the intelligence agencies' assertion that the cover name "Liberal," for example, actually refers to Julius Rosenberg. It took years to decode the KGB's telegrams and the agencies involved have not indicated when the documents were first deciphered nor how the identifications were made.[25]

Though the FBI seems to have operated on the assumption that anybody who had been in or near the Communist party and then associated with people who associated with Russians was involved with espionage, many of the records that have been released do not reveal whether the transmission of secrets actually occurred or whether American intelligence agents just assumed that it had. In a sense, it makes little difference. Because Communism had been so thoroughly demonized, it did not take much evidence to convince most Americans that Communists spied for Russia. As a result, whether true or not, the espionage scenarios were believable. They amplified the perceived threat of American Communism, thus allowing many moderates and liberals to acquiesce in and justify forms of political repression that under other circumstances they would never condone.

Even cases that did not go to trial built up the perception that Communists spied. One such case, for which the evidence remains unclear, occurred at the Berkeley Radiation Laboratory, where a group of Oppenheimer's former students — David Bohm, David Fox, Max Friedman, Giovanni Rossi Lomanitz, and Joseph Weinberg — worked for the Manhattan Project during the war. Some of these young scientists had been in or near the Communist party and when they tried to organize a union at their laboratory, the project's security officers saw red. The union, the left-wing Federation of Architects, Engineers, Chemists and Technicians (FAECT), was already an object of suspicion within the military and intelligence community. The FBI viewed the new Berkeley local as "a very definite menace to the internal security of this country and one which provides a well-nigh perfect avenue for either Russian-inspired or voluntary espionage for Russian benefit by the Communist Party of the United States." The military also worried, as did Secretary of War Henry Stimson, who alerted Roosevelt to the threat posed by the union and urged him to have the CIO disband the local.[26]

Actually, as far as the intelligence community was concerned, the espionage that it feared FAECT would encourage had already taken place. Besides organizing a union, the left-wing Berkeley scientists had been in touch with Steve Nelson, who had been in touch with members of the Soviet consulate. According to the later testimony of several Manhattan Project security officers, the lab's scientists had passed secrets several times. One incident that led these officials to assume that espionage had occurred was a late-night visit that Joseph Weinberg paid to Steve Nelson at which, according to the security men who watched the transaction from their perch in a tree outside Nelson's house, Weinberg dictated a secret formula to the communist leader. Another incident took place in a San Francisco fish restaurant, where some government agents eavesdropped on a conversation between the Manhattan Project scientist Martin Kamen and some Soviet officials. Though the intelligence officers did not specify what kind of information had been passed at these assignations, they obviously believed atomic espionage had taken place. Nelson, Weinberg, and Kamen insisted that they had done nothing wrong and denied the charges. It is still not clear what happened, though it may well be that, at least in Kamen's case, the security agencies simply assumed that anyone on the Manhattan Project who was at all sympathetic to the left and then associated with Russians or with people who associated with Russians had to be an atom spy.[27]

In any event, whatever their evidence was, the Manhattan Project's security officers did not hesitate to act on it and force the main offenders from the project. Lomanitz's draft deferment was canceled; Kamen lost his security clearance and had to work in a shipyard. Naturally, the FAECT local disappeared. The case, however, did not. The FBI got jurisdiction over the matter after the war and throughout the late 1940s continued to press the investigation.[28]

By that point, the issue of spies within the Manhattan Project had become entangled with the controversy about the peacetime uses of atomic energy. Should the United States try to avoid an arms race by offering to share the results of its scientific research? Or should it retain its monopoly over the development of atomic energy and guard the secret of the bomb as vigilantly as it had during the war? Most of the scientists involved realized that the so-called "secret" of the bomb did not exist and that it would be only a matter of time before the other major powers, in particular the Soviet Union, would be able to build their own atomic weapons. The military establishment disagreed. Its members and their supporters could not believe that any other nation — especially one as allegedly backward and barbaric as the Soviet Union — could replicate the American feat. To share scientific knowledge was to weaken the United States and lessen, not increase, the chances of world peace.[29]

The battle was joined over the issue of civilian control of atomic energy. When they discovered that Congress was about to pass a measure putting nuclear matters entirely in the hands of the armed forces, the Manhattan Project scientists organized a massive lobbying effort. The military and its allies fought back. One of their main weapons was an attempt to discredit the scientific community by portraying its members as softheaded and even disloyal. The FBI supported these efforts. As early as the fall of 1945, just as the Senate was debating the matter, Hoover began sending the White House reports on some of the scientists and others who were trying to ensure civilian control over atomic energy.[30]

HUAC also entered the battle. It subpoenaed the Berkeley scientists in 1948, along with Robert Oppenheimer and his physicist brother Frank. The committee's efforts to uncover the alleged communist infiltration of the atomic bomb project proved no more successful than the FBI's. Some of the scientists admitted they had been in the CP, others denied the committee's charges, and a few, Lomanitz, Bohm, and Fox among them, took the Fifth Amendment and refused to answer any questions about their politics.[31]

HUAC's failure to prove that the Berkeley scientists had spied was irrelevant. The inquiry served other functions. The committee was just coming into its own as a vehicle for publicizing the threat of communist espionage. It collaborated with the FBI and offered Hoover and his men an invaluable forum for airing charges in cases that the Justice Department could not or would not prosecute. The Berkeley Radiation Laboratory hearings also helped the military regain control of the atomic energy program by reinforcing the unfavorable image of scientists; and they gave conservatives an opportunity to attack the Truman administration as unconcerned about national security.[32]

Just as it had when Gerhart Eisler refused to testify, HUAC amplified the charges against its uncooperative witnesses by trying to prosecute them — though not, it should be noted, for espionage. The men who had taken the Fifth were indicted for contempt of Congress. And Joseph Weinberg, whom the committee had sensationally labeled in its reports as "Scientist X," was charged with perjury. Not only had he denied giving atomic secrets to Steve Nelson, he denied even knowing Nelson. Ultimately all the former Berkeley scientists were acquitted. But the damage had been done. Most of them lost their jobs and were blacklisted. More important, the publicity that accompanied their cases reinforced the connection between Communism and atomic espionage in the public mind.[33]

★

The earlier Gouzenko case had established that connection. Though it took place in Canada and involved only one atomic scientist, it convinced many American policymakers that the threat of communist espionage was real. The case began on the evening of September 5, 1945, when Igor Gouzenko, a code clerk in the Soviet embassy in Ottawa, defected from his post, taking with him a sheaf of documents indicating that over twenty pseudonymously identified individuals had been transmitting secret information to the Soviet military intelligence. One, the British physicist Alan Nunn May, had been involved in the Manhattan Project and had given a few samples of enriched uranium to his Russian contacts. The other agents were Canadian scientists and bureaucrats who supplied technical and political data of varying value. Most of them belonged to a secret Communist party unit of middle-class intellectuals and had been recruited as spies by party officials at Moscow's request.[34]

At first, the Canadian government hesitated to act. The war had just ended and neither Prime Minister Mackenzie King nor his American and British counterparts, whom he immediately notified, wanted a public furor that might compromise their ongoing negotiations with the Soviet Union. King was not, however, planning to bury the case and had made arrangements to round up the suspects once the diplomatic situation changed.[35] He was finally forced to act when Washington columnist Drew Pearson mentioned Gouzenko in a radio broadcast on the evening of February 3, 1946. There has been considerable speculation about who leaked the story to Pearson and why. King believed it was hard-liners in the American State Department. The FBI was a likely prospect, as was Major General Leslie Groves, the head of the Manhattan Project. Groves did not want to cede control over nuclear energy to civilians or negotiate about the bomb with Russia; he may have assumed that revelations about atomic espionage would abort both initiatives.[36]

In any event, once the news got out, King put his prearranged machinery into operation by appointing a special two-man Royal Commission to take charge of the investigation. The government arrested thirteen people, including the Canadian Communist party's first and only elected member of Parliament. They were all incarcerated under a wartime regulation that allowed the government to hold people indefinitely without charges. The evidence against them was not strong and the Canadian authorities interrogated them for several weeks in the hope that they would confess if they were kept incommunicado and not allowed to see their lawyers or families. Though four of the purported spies refused to cooperate with the commission and had to be acquitted for lack of evidence, most of the others confessed and went to prison. In England, Alan Nunn May, the only principal in the case who had been involved with the atomic bomb, also confessed and received a ten-year sentence.[37]

The report of the Royal Commission makes it clear that the commissioners considered the suspects' radicalism as incriminating as Gouzenko's revelations. Belonging to the Communist party, the Commission implied, was an almost surefire indication of guilt. The report even noted, presumably as incriminating, that one man had a library full of Communist books, "including Marx, Engels, and Lenin." The significance of such associations, the commissioners explained, was obvious: "The Communist movement was the principal base within which the espionage network was recruited." As a result, Communism could no longer be viewed as merely a repellent ideology; as of early 1946 it had become a threat to national security.[38]

And not just in Canada. The case had serious repercussions south of the border as well. Until Gouzenko's revelations became public, the Truman administration had not been concerned about communist spies. It had not, for example, pressed hard for the prosecution of a group of public officials and journalists arrested in June 1945 in connection with the leaking of government documents to the left-wing magazine *Amerasia*. Though Hoover and his aides believed that espionage had been involved, the administration did not pursue the case. Nor, at first, did Truman and his aides seem particularly interested in the Gouzenko affair. Even after Hoover informed the White House that Gouzenko claimed that "an assistant to an Assistant Secretary of State under Mr. Stettinius was a paid Soviet spy," the president did not seem worried. Perhaps Gouzenko's failure to supply the name of the official involved kept the Truman administration from taking any immediate action on the Russian defector's charges. Moreover, many top policymakers were still ambivalent about the Soviet Union and did not want to further poison relations with Moscow by publicizing Gouzenko's allegations. Still, once the case broke, it could not be ignored and it began to reinforce the growing assumption on the part of public officials and ordinary citizens alike that Communists spied for the Kremlin.[39]

★

Gouzenko, it turned out, was not the only Soviet agent to defect. On the evening of November 7, 1945, a thirty-seven-year-old Vassar graduate named Elizabeth Bentley walked into the FBI's New York City field office and began to tell a convoluted story about working as a courier for an espionage ring of federal employees. She had contacted the Bureau earlier, but had been ignored until Gouzenko's revelations gave credibility to her account. In her November statement to the FBI, she explained that she had joined the CP in the mid-thirties and had become involved in Soviet espionage through her late lover, Jacob Golos, a high-ranking American Communist who operated the Soviet Union's official tourist agency in New York. For three years, from the summer of 1941 to the end of 1944, she had shuttled between New York and Washington, D.C., where, she claimed, she collected information and party dues from a number of government officials to whom she gave communist literature and Christmas presents.[40]

Bentley named names. Her most important contacts were in "the Silvermaster ring," a group of government economists headed, so Bentley claimed, by Nathan Gregory Silvermaster and his wife, Helen. Silvermaster and his agents, among them Harry Dexter White and a White House aide named Lauchlin Currie, purloined all kinds of documents that were then photographed by ring member Ludwig Ullman in the basement of the Silvermaster home. At first, her contacts gave her political data, but then, Bentley explained, they branched out into "everything under the sun. . . . They'd go in for production figures of all varieties," though not, she was careful to state, "information about the atomic bomb." Another ring of her agents was led by economist Victor Perlo and included some of the people Whittaker Chambers had mentioned. There were also some individual contacts like William Remington. Over the next few months, Bentley was to add new names to her list and new details to her story.[41]

She was not a reliable informant. Even filtered through the bureaucratic prose of the FBI agents who debriefed her, the early statements of this melodramatic, unstable, and alcoholic woman seem slightly hysterical, filled with references — later edited out — to alleged advances from various men. She also fabricated parts of her original account and, like Louis Budenz, had a propensity for coming up with fresh information that would keep her services in demand. By 1953, even the Bureau, which sometimes had to baby-sit her through her drinking binges, had become exasperated with Bentley's tendency to embellish her testimony with new and important details.[42]

But the FBI was not so sceptical in 1945. Even before Bentley was fully debriefed, the Bureau swung into action. On the day after her first interview, Hoover informed Truman that "a number of persons employed by the Government" were giving information to "persons outside the Federal Government" who were handing it over "to espionage agents of the Soviet Government." By the end of November, Bentley had given the FBI over eighty names, including those of thirty-seven federal employees. Meanwhile, recognizing that her charges had become, in the words of one harassed G-man, "the most important case confronting the Bureau at the present time," the FBI put 250 agents on it. They tapped the phones of the people Bentley had fingered and placed them under surveillance in the hope of finding evidence to corroborate Bentley's story.[43]

They did not come up with much. True, there was considerable contact among the people Bentley named. They were friends and professional colleagues; and the Bureau had no trouble finding evidence that they saw each other often. In addition, the agents who had gained entry into the Silvermaster home by pretending to work for the gas company discovered a darkroom in the basement. And the testimony of Whittaker Chambers and other informers provided details that substantiated parts of Bentley's story. But until the Venona documents were deciphered in the late 1940s or early 1950s, the government could not find any corroborating evidence of espionage. The FBI interviewed all the principals intensively, but to no avail. Later attempts to obtain testimony before congressional committees and a grand jury were equally unsuccessful. Though several of the alleged conspirators were Communists, the government could not prove that they had been spies.[44]

Still, it was clear that something had been going on. In his 1954 application for parole, William Remington, who had been convicted of perjury, admitted that he had given information to "unauthorized persons" knowing that one of them "was a dedicated Communist party member." Comintern archives in the former Soviet Union have also corroborated parts of Bentley's story. Though her name does not appear in any of them, American researchers have found documents that refer to some of Bentley's purported agents. There is further substantiation in the recently published memoirs of

John Abt, a communist lawyer Chambers had fingered, who admitted that his secret group of federal officials had sometimes sent information to the CP's New York headquarters.[45]

The most important corroboration comes from the Venona documents, which identify Bentley by the covername "Good Girl" and discuss the information transmitted by Silvermaster, White, and other people in her ring. Even in the garbled form of these intercepted KGB telegrams, Bentley's most readily identifiable trait comes through. In evaluating the information he got from "Good Girl," the Soviet intelligence agent handling it noted: "Possibly she is making this up and exaggerating." What is important, however, is the fact that little of this corroboration was available *at the time.* The Soviet archives were closed, the Venona documents remained undeciphered, and the people whom she fingered denied Bentley's story.[46]

The corroborating evidence that the FBI had been unable to find for Bentley's charges was, however, available in what was to become the most important case of alleged espionage within the federal government, that of Alger Hiss. Hiss had been under suspicion for years. The FBI believed that he was the Russian agent in the State Department Gouzenko had mentioned. Bentley had also referred to Hiss, explaining that he "innocently" gave information to the Silvermaster ring. His main accuser was Whittaker Chambers, who claimed that he had worked with Hiss in Washington's communist underground during the 1930s. From 1939 on, Chambers had been trying to alert the State Department and FBI to the secret party cells that he claimed were operating within the government. Hiss was one of the people he named, as were John Abt, Victor Perlo, the NRLB's executive secretary Nathan Witt, and the CIO's chief counsel Lee Pressman, all of whom had been more closely identified with the CP than Hiss.[47]

At first the FBI considered Chambers's allegations mainly "history, hypothesis, or deduction," but the overlap with Bentley's story renewed the Bureau's interest and prompted Hoover to circulate the charges against Hiss throughout the government and elsewhere. These accusations darkened Hiss's once glowing diplomatic career. In 1947 he left the State Department to take a job as head of the Carnegie Corporation.[48]

When Chambers publicly identified Hiss as a Communist at a HUAC hearing in August 1948, Hiss denied it and soon after sued for libel. Until then Chambers had not mentioned espionage; instead, he had been insisting that the Communists in his network had infiltrated the government in order to influence policy. But during the course of the pretrial depositions in the libel case, Chambers changed his story and gave his attorneys sixty-five typewritten documents and four small handwritten memos allegedly transmitted by Hiss in 1938, as well as four sheets of yellow lined paper in Harry Dexter White's handwriting. Two weeks later Chambers melodramatically delved into a hollowed-out pumpkin on his Maryland farm to hand two strips of developed film and three undeveloped rolls of film to a team from HUAC. These materials, Chambers claimed, had been handed to him for transmission to the Soviets by Hiss, White, and others. When he broke with the CP, he had given these items to his wife's nephew as a "life preserver" in case something were to happen to him.[49]

The case remains problematic in many ways. No further corroboration has surfaced for Chambers's allegations that Hiss gave him information for the Russians. Neither the former Soviet archives (so far) nor the Venona decrypts, with the exception of one somewhat puzzling document that the U.S. authorities claim "probably" refers to Hiss, contain Hiss's name. But since he may have been involved with the Soviet military rather than the KGB, it is possible that there are references to him in some as yet unopened Russian files. Hiss went to his grave denying everything, without, however, satisfactorily explaining his political activities in the 1930s. Chambers was hardly more convincing. He contradicted himself repeatedly during the course of his multiple public and private confessions. In addition, his belated revelation of espionage, after having explicitly denied that the people he was servicing were spies, does create questions. Still, the man was so strange that he could well have withheld information out of his stated desire "to preserve the human elements involved." The case, in short, is not fully resolved and may never be, though the documents that had apparently been typed on the Hiss family's old Woodstock machine provided enough physical evidence to convince a jury to convict Hiss of perjury (the statute of limitations for espionage having run out).[50]

There were documents, too, in the next big espionage case, that of Judith Coplon. A political analyst in the Foreign Agents Registration section of the Justice Department, Coplon had access to FBI files. Her political past as a student radical may have aroused suspicion, though, according to former FBI official Robert J. Lamphere, it was the Venona project's deciphering of a KGB cable about a Soviet agent in the Justice Department that alerted the Bureau to her late in 1948. At that point, her phone was tapped and she was put under surveillance. Soon after, the FBI followed her to New York and observed two separate rendezvous with Valentin Gubitchev, a Russian engineer who worked for the UN. Both times the two acted as if they were trying to avoid being followed. They wandered around the streets of Washington Heights, jumped in and out of subway cars, and once simply passed each other while walking in different directions on the sidewalk. When the FBI finally arrested them on a New York City street early in March 1949, Coplon's pocketbook contained a handwritten copy of an allegedly top-secret memorandum and a sealed package that held about thirty so-called "data slips," little pieces of paper with information from the FBI reports that came across her desk in the Justice Department.[51]

The government charged Coplon with espionage and put her on trial twice: once in Washington for taking the documents and then in New York for trying to pass them to the Russians. Her defense was unconvincing. Her trial lawyer had apparently persuaded her to say that she and Gubitchev were lovers and had behaved furtively in order to evade his wife. Given the strength of the evidence against her, the story did not convince a jury. Nonetheless, Coplon did not go to prison. Because she had been illegally arrested and wiretapped by the FBI, her convictions were overturned on appeal. Still, it is hard to avoid the conclusion that she had been planning to transfer the documents in her purse to Gubitchev. The Venona decrypts seem to confirm her guilt and indicate that she had been working for the KGB since 1944. One document discusses her value as a source of information and notes that she "gives the impression of being a serious person who is politically well developed and there is no doubt of her sincere desire to help us."[52]

The Venona releases also show that the KGB was equally pleased with Julius Rosenberg and his work. According to these documents, Rosenberg, a mechanical engineer, was an active agent who recruited about ten of his friends, CCNY classmates, and fellow FAECT members into an espionage ring that provided the Soviet Union with a wide array of technical information. The documents do not identify all of Rosenberg's people, but the ones they do, like Joel Barr, Alfred Sarant, Max Elitcher, Michael Sidorovitch, and William Perl, have long been connected to the case. During the war these scientists and engineers gave Rosenberg information about the weapons they were working on that he then photographed and handed to the KGB. Rosenberg's involvement with the atomic bomb seems to have been a genuine fluke, made possible by the army's assignment of his wife's brother, David Greenglass, to the Manhattan Project's Los Alamos site. A machinist in the shop that assembled the bomb, Greenglass had no access to high-level scientific information, but whatever he picked up, no doubt, went straight to Moscow once his brother-in-law recruited him for the cause.[53]

Though the FBI had long known of Rosenberg's communist connections, it may not have realized that he was a Soviet agent until Greenglass implicated him in the summer of 1950.* The chain of evidence that led to that moment developed after the detonation of the Soviet bomb the year before. Since it was assumed that only a major espionage operation could explain the Russians' achievement, a massive spy hunt ensued. Its main trophy was Klaus Fuchs, an émigré German physicist who had belonged to the British contingent at Los Alamos and had been giving the Soviets atomic secrets since 1942. By the end of 1949, the Venona decrypts had yielded enough information for the FBI to identify Fuchs. Arrested by Scotland Yard, he soon confessed. Fuchs then helped the FBI identify his American courier, a Philadelphia chemist named Harry Gold. Gold confessed and led the Bureau to Greenglass, who then fingered his brother-in-law.[54]

At that point, the confessions stopped. Rosenberg denied everything and would not even admit that he and his wife had been in the party. Because the Venona documents were too highly classified to be produced at a trial, the government had to build its case against Rosenberg on other evidence — of which there was little. The most important was the testimony of his brother-in-law David Greenglass, who appears to have doctored his story a bit in order to make a case against his own sister, whom the government had indicted in the hopes of forcing her husband to talk.[55]

The prosecutors clearly expected Rosenberg to confess. His failure to do so led to his execution and that of his wife. Myles Lane, one of the Justice

* Since the Venona documents that I have seen do not indicate when they were deciphered, I cannot tell if they led the FBI to Rosenberg before Greenglass named him.

Department attorneys handling the case, told a secret session of the Joint Committee on Atomic Energy just before the trial that

> the only thing that will break this man Rosenberg is the prospect of a death penalty or getting the chair, plus that if we can convict his wife, too, and give her a stiff sentence of 25 or 30 years, that combination may serve to make this fellow disgorge.

Ethel, in other words, was only a lever. "The case is not too strong against Mrs. Rosenberg," Lane explained. "But for the purpose of acting as a deterrent, I think it is very important that she be convicted too, and given a strong sentence." The government did not even know whether she had been aware of her husband's activities. She probably was; but her real crime was to stand by her man.[56]

His crimes were more extensive, though they did not include delivering the secret of the bomb to Moscow or, as Judge Irving Kaufman claimed when he sentenced the couple to death, causing the Korean War. The government's evidence against the Rosenbergs was not overwhelming, but given the political atmosphere in the spring of 1951 the guilty verdict was probably inevitable. Nonetheless, the prosecution left little to chance and it fixed the case. Not only did it encourage its witnesses to embellish their testimony, but it also colluded directly (and illegally) with Judge Kaufman to ensure that he would impose the death penalty.[57]

The Rosenbergs' conviction bolstered the contention that Communists spied. The executions reinforced that message. Just as the logic of the Cold War demanded a demonized and stereotyped enemy, so, too, it required an idealized American state, one that by definition could not possibly kill innocent people. Thus, psychologically, if not legally, the death of the Rosenbergs confirmed their guilt. It also emphasized the supposedly heinous nature of what they (and presumably all the other Soviet spies as well) had done.

But were these activities so awful? Was the espionage, which unquestionably occurred, such a serious threat to the nation's security that it required the development of a politically repressive internal security system? It may be useful to take a more nuanced position and go beyond the question of guilt or innocence to ascertain not only how dangerous the transmission of unauthorized information was, but also why it occurred. Because espionage is an issue that carries such heavy emotional freight, it is usually treated in a monolithic way that overlooks distinctions between different types of spying and different types of spies. This was especially the case during the early years of the Cold War, when an exaggerated notion of the damage caused by Soviet espionage bolstered, and was bolstered by, the contention of the FBI and the rest of the anticommunist network that Communism endangered the United States and had to be wiped out.

It is clear that some genuinely damaging espionage did take place. Klaus Fuchs and a young Harvard-trained physicist named Theodore Hall did give information to the Soviet Union that enabled it to produce an atomic bomb a year or two sooner than it otherwise would have. Other military secrets also reached the Russians. The Venona decrypts, for example, reveal that some of the people recruited by Julius Rosenberg transmitted what the KGB considered to be "highly valuable" information about radar, jet planes, and other advanced weapons systems. Some of Bentley's people sent material on arms production, naval deployments, and other subjects that certainly seemed to be of military interest; the Canadian spies gave the same kind of technical data as well. Some of these people, it is true, claimed that they were careful not to deliver any really sensitive material; and, significantly, the Royal Commission agreed that the technical data that had been transmitted was of little importance.[58]

The Soviet Union also got political and economic information. The Venona decrypts, for example, deal with lend-lease allocations, trade missions, and diplomatic negotiations between the United States and its allies. The somewhat earlier documents that surfaced in the Hiss case are a similar melange, as are the materials that came from the people Gouzenko fingered. The Comintern archives held similar items. Judith Coplon's contributions were different; she was handing over information from the FBI. While the snippets from its files that were found in Coplon's purse certainly embarrassed the Bureau, unless one shares J. Edgar Hoover's own vision of his agency and its mission, it is hard to claim that the revelations of the FBI's political snooping seriously damaged American security. Nor did the information on the Trotskyist movement and the various Soviet defectors that appears in the Venona documents and elsewhere. Still, the political materials these spies passed to the USSR may not have been completely innocuous, even if there is no indication that their transmission caused any actual harm.[59]

It seems useful to make a distinction here between the more or less routine collection of political intelligence and the kind of espionage that involved the transmission of sensitive military secrets. It may well be that many of the alleged Soviet agents did not consider their activities spying, but merely the common practice of leaking inside information to sympathetic diplomats, political colleagues, and friendly journalists. This was, for example, what John Stewart Service, the key State Department employee involved in the *Amerasia* case claimed he was doing.[60]

A careful reading of the Venona decrypts leaves the impression not only that the Soviet intelligence agencies were dealing with many types of sources, but that the KGB officers stationed in the United States may have been trying to make themselves look good to their Moscow superiors by portraying some of their casual contacts as having been more deeply involved with the Soviet cause than they actually were. These documents do not tell us, for example, whether some of the New Deal officials Bentley worked with were consciously spying for the Russians or just sharing confidences with political allies and friends. A case in point is a cryptic Venona message reporting that Harry Dexter White believed the Soviets could get better terms on a loan than the American government had offered them. Was he betraying his country or merely making small talk? The document doesn't tell.[61]

The communist lawyer John Abt offers an insider's perspective on this kind of activity. For a few years in the mid-1930s, Abt belonged to the secret party unit that Whittaker Chambers later serviced. He and his comrades, Abt recalled,

> mainly talked about our work in the various agencies where we were employed, what this indicated about the drift and policies of the Roosevelt administration. If there were developments we thought were particularly interesting or important, someone would be asked to draft a report to be given to Hal [Ware, the unit's party contact], who presumably passed it on to the national leadership in New York for its consideration in estimating the direction of the New Deal and what might be done to influence it.

Abt denied that this was espionage. "We were simply providing political analyses of New Deal policy, based on our positions as insiders in various government agencies." He admitted that their information could have reached the Kremlin, but doubted that it was of much use. He was probably right; it is hard to see how the hot tips about the federal government's agricultural policies that Abt and his colleagues dispatched to CP headquarters could have done much damage.[62]

Unlike Soviet agents later in the Cold War, the men and women who gave information to Moscow in the 1930s and 1940s did so for political, not pecuniary, reasons. They were already committed to Communism and they viewed what they were doing as their contribution to the cause. Klaus Fuchs, for example, had been in the communist underground in Nazi Germany before he fled to England. Once he realized the significance of his work on the bomb, he contacted the Soviet embassy. While some espionage agents, like Fuchs, approached the Russians directly, others were recruited by the CP or, more commonly, by their own political associates who were already working with the Soviets. It is important to realize that as Communists these people did not subscribe to traditional forms of patriotism; they were internationalists whose political allegiances transcended national boundaries. They thought they were "building . . . a better world for the masses," not betraying their country.[63]

Moreover, most of their espionage took place during World War II, when the United States and the Soviet Union were on the same side. These people were not, therefore, spying for an enemy. Especially for Communists, who knew better than anyone else how central the Soviet Union was to the struggle against Hitler, assisting the Russians could be — and often was — rationalized as furthering the war effort. "There was no choice for a communist," a Canadian party member recalled.

> It was a situation where the Soviet Union was bleeding to death, and the government was refusing to give them information that would help in the development of their own defenses. We just felt that anybody in a position to help, would help and should help. It was as straightforward as that.

Everybody involved offered the same rationale. "After all," William Remington's ex-wife told the grand jury that indicted her former husband for perjury in 1951, "we were allies with the Russians at that time, and it wasn't so dreadful, perhaps, in trying to give them secrets over the heads of the

Governments." As late as 1949, the Truman administration's Loyalty Review Board agreed with that assessment when it decided to clear Remington on the grounds that "Our government's attitude toward Russia in 1942 was such that giving the Russians information with respect to the progress of our war effort wouldn't necessarily spell disloyalty."[64]

By the early 1950s, as Remington himself noted, "what was black is now white, and vice versa." Sending secret information to the Soviet Union once the Cold War had heated up would have raised far more serious issues of loyalty. But by then there were few, if any, Communists left on the federal payroll. And if any of them engaged in espionage, we know nothing about it.[65]

Ironically, it is possible that the most damaging assault on the nation's security during the McCarthy era was self-inflicted. The anticommunist activities of the American government helped China develop its nuclear weapons and guided missiles. Several thousand Chinese citizens had been studying in the United States in the years after World War II; many were gifted scientists who were working in defense-related fields. The communist victory in their homeland created serious problems for these people. Though they wanted to remain in the United States, Beijing was pressing them to return. When China intervened in the Korean War, the Justice Department decided to deport them. But other U.S. authorities invoked national security and refused to let the Chinese scientists go. Eventually, some of them left voluntarily, some managed to stay, and some, like the eminent rocket scientist Tsien Hsue-shen (Qian Xuesen), remained in limbo.[66]

One of the world's leading experts on jet propulsion and missile design, Tsien had been in on the development of space flight from the start. In 1950, when his problems began, he was at the top of his field, a professor at the California Institute of Technology and an important consultant to the Pentagon. Tsien was no political activist; he was much too absorbed in his research. But during the late 1930s, while a graduate student at Cal Tech, he had hung out with a group of left-wing scientists who gathered at the home of physicist Sidney Weinbaum to play music and talk politics. Tsien sympathized with such aspects of the Popular Front as its support for China against Japan but had probably not been a Communist. An undercover agent from the Los Angeles Police Department, however, claimed that he was and said that he had seen a party registration form with Tsien's name on it. These allegations had been known to the military for years, but Tsien, like Oppenheimer, was too valuable to the government for his left-wing past to keep him from being cleared — until the Cold War changed the rules.[67]

Sidney Weinbaum's troubles precipitated Tsien's. Accused of concealing his party membership during a security hearing, Weinbaum was convicted of perjury and given a four-year prison sentence in the summer of 1950. Tsien came under suspicion as well and lost his security clearance. At that point, he decided to return to China. He had booked a flight to Hong Kong and started to ship his belongings overseas when he was stopped. The Defense Department felt he was too important a scientist to be allowed out of the country. Meanwhile, customs officials had intercepted the scientific materials he was sending to China and announced that they were top-secret military documents. Then the INS arrested him for deportation and held him in its Terminal Island detention center for two weeks.

Like Gerhart Eisler, Tsien could neither leave the United States nor stay here permanently. He continued to teach at Cal Tech, though he could no longer pursue his former research. For nearly five years, Tsien remained under near house arrest until he was finally deported in an apparent swap for a group of American airmen downed in Korea. Once in China, he resumed his scientific work and, along with a group of other involuntarily repatriated American-trained scientists, developed his native country's bombs and missiles.[68]

Though communist espionage seems not to have been a major concern within the Truman administration, communist sabotage was. The nature of the threat is obvious: Communists, loyal above all to Moscow, insinuated into vital sectors of the economy, could during a time of war sabotage the nation's ability to defend itself and render it helpless in the face of the enemy. Reality had little to do with the perception of this threat. Communists did not blow up factories, derail trains, or dynamite bridges. Nor did the FBI ever find credible evidence that the CP planned to attack the nation's physical infrastructure. But the implausibility of such an eventuality did not keep the Bureau from insisting, as a Washington field office report put it, that all Communists "unquestionably would sabotage this country's effort in resisting Russia and that this . . . is a great and total danger to the security of this Nation." Remote as that danger might be, its theoretical existence would be invoked to justify a wide-ranging security program designed to keep alleged subversives out of sensitive jobs — as well as to prevent Communists from fishing in New York City reservoirs.[69]

The main danger came from communist unions, or so it seemed. In his 1946 report on the Soviet menace, presidential aide Clark Clifford had been quite explicit, pointing out that the CP would practice revolutionary defeatism on the home front by trying "to capture the labor movement. This would cripple the industrial potential of the United States by calling strikes at those times and places which would be advantageous to the Soviet Union." Hoover, as usual, had been concerned about the problem for years. "The Communists," he noted in a 1944 memo, "will only be a menace to U.S. if they can seize labor control & this they are gradually doing." The threat was not totally illusory. After all, party members and their sympathizers did have influence within the labor movement.[70]

Moreover, the prospect of a communist-led political strike against the American defense industry was not just a theoretical possibility; such strikes had already occurred. During the Nazi-Soviet pact period in 1940 and 1941, when the CP was pushing an antiwar program, communist-run unions at the Allis-Chalmers, Vultee, and North American Aircraft Company plants walked off the job. Just as the Hiss and Rosenberg cases made the threat of espionage plausible, these strikes gave credibility to the notion that Communists might sabotage American industry. Allegations that the walkouts had been inspired by Soviet orders to halt American defense production were unfounded. But the assumption that communist-led labor unions were uniquely disloyal, though partially submerged by the CP's hyperpatriotism during World War II, resurfaced soon after the fighting stopped.

A massive strike wave that began in late 1945 provided the setting for a renewed concern about the threat of militant labor. The business community, which had long wanted to roll back the gains that unions had made since the late 1930s, took advantage of the strikes to mount a broad public relations campaign to convince the American people that the labor movement had too much power. Red-baiting was an effective part of that campaign. By 1946, it was possible to link Soviet intransigence in Eastern Europe with labor troubles in the United States and claim that they were all part of a single conspiracy against the American way of life. The invocation of the earlier defense strikes gave such charges a salience that they might not otherwise have had and contributed to the process of delegitimizing union militancy. Within a year, the business community's well-orchestrated attack on the labor movement resulted in the passage of the Taft-Hartley Act over Truman's veto. That the measure contained provisions against communist union officials was no coincidence.[71]

Communists actually had little to do with most of the big post-war strikes — in the coal, steel, railroad, and automobile industries. Still, in those areas of the economy where communist-led unions were active, charges that they were carrying out Kremlin orders began to circulate. In his exasperation, Truman, who at one point had publicly threatened to draft strikers, privately noted with regard to a threatened maritime strike in September 1946 that "The Reds, the phonies and the 'parlor pinks' seem to have banded together and are becoming a national danger. I am afraid that they are a sabotage front for Uncle Joe Stalin." Hoover, of course, was supplying the president with juicy items about the CP's role in the strike wave.[72]

It is possible that the mere juxtaposition of the growing Cold War and the CP's presence within the labor movement would have been sufficient to generate the idea that communist-inspired political strikes threatened the nation. An eleven-month walkout at Allis-Chalmers, already notorious as the site of a bitter confrontation before Pearl Harbor, seemed to prove it. The work stoppage, which began in April 1946, focused on the same issues as all the other postwar strikes: wages, grievances, and union security. But the company, long antagonistic to organized labor, mounted a massive publicity campaign that featured a deluge of red-baiting. For fifty-nine days, the Hearst chain's *Milwaukee Sentinel* published a series of articles supplied by a company writer under the name "John Sentinel," describing in detail the communist connections of UAW Local 248 and its leaders.[73]

The strike had national significance. It became the showpiece in a set of congressional investigations in the spring of 1947 when, during the course of the hearings that were to culminate in the Taft-Hartley Act, both the House and Senate labor committees let the Allis-Chalmers management present its case against the union. The House Labor and Education Committee then called in Local 248's former president Harold Christoffel and his successor, Robert Buse, and badgered them about the 1941 strike and their party ties. HUAC got into the act as well and mounted a similar inquiry.

The crucial witness was Louis Budenz, who charged that the party had ordered both the 1941 and 1946 Allis-Chalmers strikes. In his mid-March testimony before the Education and Labor Committee, Budenz described a secret meeting in Milwaukee in late 1940 at which party leader Eugene Dennis ordered Christoffel to "pull a strike at Allis-Chalmers." Budenz was to repeat these charges at future hearings and trials, including the 1949 Smith Act proceeding against Dennis and the rest of the party's top leadership. The story was probably a fabrication. In their report on the intensive debriefing sessions they held with Budenz soon after he defected from the party, FBI agents J. Patrick Coyne and J. J. Winterrowd do not mention the Allis-Chalmers walkout. Since they had specifically asked the former *Daily Worker* editor about political strikes during the Nazi-Soviet pact period, it is hard to believe that he could have forgotten or his FBI interlocutors could have overlooked a reference to something as important as Allis-Chalmers.[74]

After Budenz finished his testimony, a young first-term congressman from Massachusetts noted the discrepancies between it and that of the two union leaders. "I suggest," John F. Kennedy said, "that this committee indict Mr. Christoffel and Mr. Buse for perjury." This was exactly what the Allis-Chalmers management was looking for. A criminal prosecution coming on top of the highly publicized congressional investigations strengthened the company's hand against its striking local. A week after a special subcommittee of the House Education and Labor Committee came to Milwaukee to nail down the case, the walkout was over. Six months later, Local 248's membership had fallen from over 8,000 to 184. Within a year, Harold Christoffel was on trial for perjury. Though the Supreme Court initially acquitted him on the technical grounds that the House committee had lacked a quorum, Christoffel was retried, reconvicted, and ultimately served three years in a federal penitentiary.[75]

The company had orchestrated the entire case. In collaboration with Louis Budenz, two congressional committees, the Justice Department, the

FBI, the press, the Milwaukee police department, and a motley assortment of hired investigators and CIO dissidents, it had transformed its own labor troubles into a symbol of the communist threat to the nation's economy. At the very moment when the Truman administration's appeal for aid to Greece and Turkey was transforming anticommunism into an international crusade, the evocation of Allis-Chalmers seemed to provide concrete evidence for the perception that domestic Communists were as dangerous as foreign ones.[76]

References to Allis-Chalmers became commonplace whenever there were attempts to place legislative and other restrictions on communist unions. In September 1948, for example, when he decided to bar two left-led unions from representing workers at facilities that were under contract to the Atomic Energy Commission, AEC chairman David Lilienthal specifically invoked the example of the 1941 Allis-Chalmers strike. So, too, did the Supreme Court. In the majority opinion in *American Communications Association v. Douds,* the 1950 decision that upheld the constitutionality of the anticommunist provisions in Section 9(h) of the Taft-Hartley Act, Chief Justice Fred Vinson discussed the danger of political strikes and implicitly referred to Allis-Chalmers. "Section 9(h)," Vinson asserted, "is designed to protect the public not against what Communists and others identified therein advocate or believe, but against what Congress has concluded *they have done and are likely to do again* [emphasis mine]."[77]

One of the main reasons why the labor unrest at Allis-Chalmers received so much attention was that the company had been involved in defense production, had even, so one witness told HUAC, done work for the Manhattan Project. It would have been harder to mobilize public outrage had a communist-led union halted production in a toy factory. Still, once the Cold War escalated, it became possible to offer a national-security rationale for taking action in almost every industry that harbored a communist-controlled union.[78]

In the electronics field, that was hardly a problem. The communist connections of the main union in the industry, the United Electrical, Radio, and Machine Workers of America, were well known. Still, there had never been any evidence that the UE or its leaders had ever acted against the nation's interest. Despite its opposition to American foreign policy during the Nazi-Soviet pact period, the union had not authorized any walkouts. Nor were there any indications that the union had changed its position during the Cold War. Nonetheless, because so many of the UE's top leaders and staff members were Communists, the union's mere presence within the defense industry was seen as a threat — "a dagger at the heart of our industrial system," so the Senate Internal Security Subcommittee claimed in 1953. Rumors circulated that the government would withdraw contracts from plants where the union represented the workforce. In September 1948, concerned about the possibility of "a political strike or other organized sabotage," the Atomic Energy Commission ordered the General Electric Company not to accept UE as a bargaining agent at its new Knolls Atomic Power Laboratory near Schenectady. The AEC soon extended that ban to every GE plant in the area involved with atomic energy.[79]

Another left-wing union that supposedly menaced the nation's defense was the American Communications Association. Branching out from its original base among marine telegraphers, the ACA had expanded throughout the communications industry. Though still a relatively small union, its position, many observers noted, was particularly strategic. "In addition to being able to tie up America's vital telegraph service at a moment's notice through a Kremlin inspired strike," a Republican senator complained in September 1953, "members of this union are in a position to intercept Government messages, including secret wires on defense matters." Nor was the ACA the only small union to cause alarm. FAECT had aroused suspicions long before its most famous member, Julius Rosenberg, hit the headlines.[80]

Still another threat to national defense supposedly came from the International Union of Mine, Mill and Smelter Workers, which dominated the copper industry. Copper was, labor journalist Victor Riesel explained in 1951, "the very gut of our defense operation. . . . Yet that field seethes with agents of the Communist party." At a 1952 SISS hearing and again at the 1954 perjury trial of Mine-Mill organizer Clinton Jencks, the professional witness Harvey Matusow claimed that the union was planning to call a strike in the copper industry "under the guise of wage increases, etc., and better working conditions for the guys in the shops . . . in an effort to cut down production of copper for the Korean war effort." Though Matusow subsequently recanted, his charges that the Communists in Mine-Mill would sabotage the nation's defense received wide currency.[81]

Just as threatening to the nation's security were the maritime unions, which could, it was alleged, completely tie up the nation's ports in time of war. Though neither of the main left-led unions, Harry Bridges's ILWU and Joseph Curran's NMU, had gone on strike during the Nazi-Soviet pact period, sailors and longshoremen were highly politicized and, especially in Europe, had a tradition of work stoppages for political reasons. The ILWU's expansion into Hawaii and Alaska was an additional cause for alarm. As one anticommunist journalist noted, the union's Alaska locals would put "a Communist machine in America's nearest approach to Russia." So vulnerable was the waterfront assumed to be that when the Korean War began, the government imposed a stringent port security program to keep potential saboteurs away from the docks.[82]

The national security implications that surrounded federal employment were equally obvious, though by the mid-fifties some judges did begin to question the firing of workers in such sensitive places as cafeterias. Concern about the opportunities for espionage, sabotage, and subversion that presented themselves to civil servants, as well as the partisan pressures that it faced, encouraged the Truman administration to impose a widespread loyalty-security program. However, because the main union within the field, the United Public Workers (UPW), had left-wing leaders, the government's screening procedures, as we shall see, often ended up targeting union militants.[83]

It was more of a stretch to purge people from private jobs unrelated to defense; but at the height of the McCarthy period, creative anti-Communists could find a security rationale in almost every field. "There could be subversive activities even in mathematics," one Illinois legislator insisted. "For an example, when the boys entered the Army it was found that most of them had a deplorable lack of training in mathematics. . . . Inadequate and improper teaching of any subject could be considered as subversive." Even communist hotel employees and waiters could threaten security, so the ex-Communist Benjamin Gitlow explained, because they might overhear conversations among prominent people and let Moscow in on the secrets.[84]

Communist infiltration of the mass media could also have security implications. Professional blacklisters in the broadcast industry claimed that entertainers could "transmit pro-Sovietism to the American public." The chief counsel of the NLRB worried about the "influence exercised over

189

the minds and thinking of the American people" by members of the Author's League of America. And the FBI compiled dossiers on the nation's leading literary figures. Still, not every kind of writer was a security threat. As the *New York Times* explained when it fired a copy editor in the news department, if only the man had been on the sports desk he could have kept his job.[85]

The readiness of so many politicians and employers to invoke the nation's security whenever they confronted the issue of Communism during the 1940s and 1950s makes it clear that *any* communist presence *anywhere* in American society could be seen as a threat. Wildly exaggerated though that perception was, it was plausible enough to convince important people in both the public and the private sector to implement a wide-ranging program of political repression. The specific cases — Gouzenko, Hiss, Bentley, Allis-Chalmers — had seemingly proved that Kremlin agents had tried to subvert, sabotage, and spy on the United States. Little wonder, then, that so many Americans went along with measures to ensure against a recurrence.

By the mid-1950s, American Communists had few rights that any official body had to respect. The apocalyptic vision of the dangers of domestic Communism had been so successfully disseminated that it was hard for anyone openly associated with the communist movement to lead a normal life. Though the party itself was theoretically legal, the criminal cases of the late 1940s, in particular the 1949 Smith Act prosecution of the CP's top leaders, had removed so many restraints on what could be done to it and its members that they were fair game for whatever politically repressive measures ambitious politicians or right-wing ideologues might devise.

The federal government's victory in what came to be known as the *Dennis* case and the Supreme Court's willingness to uphold it virtually outlawed the party as well as legitimized the rest of the anticommunist crusade. This case is so important that it deserves special attention. It also shows how valuable the demonized image of Communism was in Washington's campaign to destroy the Communist party. In addition, by effectively placing Communism outside the Constitution and making the day-to-day activities of the CP's leaders against the law, the successful invocation of the

Smith Act made all the other forms of repression against Communists, ex-Communists, and alleged Communists that much easier to justify.

Such was, of course, its purpose. Even before World War II ended, Hoover had decided to take the Communist party to court. On July 7, 1945, the Director ordered all his field offices to gather material about "the illegal status and activities" of "the Communist Movement in the United States" that could be used as the basis for a legal brief that would establish the CP's illegitimate nature. "The importance of this project cannot be over-emphasized," Hoover insisted as he prodded his agents to step up their collection of party documents and pump their informers about the CP's illicit activities.[86]

A successful prosecution would, the FBI's leaders believed, make it possible to get new laws that would plug the loopholes in the existing anti-subversive legislation, as well as make it easier for the Bureau to keep Communists and other political undesirables under surveillance. Above all, it would, Assistant Director D. M. Ladd explained in a 1948 memo to Hoover, "result in a judicial precedent being set that the Communist Party as an organization is illegal" and thus make it possible for the government to prosecute its "individual members and close adherents or sympathizers."[87]

The brief took years to compile and Hoover did not tell his superiors in the Justice Department about it until February 1948. By then the Justice Department, which had not been able to get indictments against the men and women Elizabeth Bentley had identified, was eager to take some Communists to court. Under pressure from congressional Republicans, Attorney General Tom Clark asked the FBI to help construct a case against the CP. Hoover sent the brief the next day. It was a bulky document and it took time for the Justice Department attorneys to digest the 1,850 pages of party documents and testimony from ex-Communists and informers that Hoover's men had assembled to prove that the CP advocated force and violence. Though the Smith Act defendants, their supporters, and many later historians assumed that the decision to try the party's top leaders had been made at the highest echelons of the Truman administration, there is no evidence that the president was ever consulted about the pending action. Even the Attorney General and his top aide, who had apparently authorized the prosecution in April, were surprised and upset to discover that their subordinates were about to present it to a grand jury in June. But the case was too far advanced to be halted; on July 20, the grand jury handed down the indictments and the FBI began to round up the party leaders.[88]

Despite the importance of the case, there was an oddly fortuitous quality to its implementation. Until just before the arrest warrants went out, for example, the Justice Department had not decided whom to indict. Though it ultimately prosecuted all the members of the party's national board except Elizabeth Gurley Flynn and William Z. Foster (who was severed from the case because of his health),* it had also considered the heads of the CP's schools and publications. The chief prosecutor, John F. X. McGohey, and his colleagues were also unsure about what law to use. A prosecution under the Foreign Agents Registration Act or the similar Voorhis Act of 1940 would highlight the CP's connections to Moscow, but the government had no evidence that any individual party leaders were acting as Russian agents. The best bet seemed to be a conspiracy charge based on the Smith Act. Conspiracy was a useful prosecutorial device because it required less evidence than having to prove that the defendants had actually committed the crime. But the Smith Act, with its language about force and violence, raised serious constitutional and evidentiary problems.[89]

Even J. Edgar Hoover recognized, as he noted in a memo to Ladd, "It is going to be a tough case at its best." The difficulty, of course, was having to prove that the CP's leaders called for "force and violence." Though the Smith Act's criminalization of "teaching" and "advocating" freed the prosecution from having to prove that the nation's top Communists were building bombs, it still created a serious evidentiary burden. For the party's leaders weren't preaching revolutionary violence either; and the FBI knew it. The Supreme Court had intensified those difficulties in two wartime deportation cases that, while not specifically ruling on the key issue of whether the Communist party wanted to overthrow the American government, nonetheless raised the possibility that it might be "a tenable conclusion" that the CP "desired to achieve its purpose by peaceful and democratic means." The decision made the government's attorneys understandably nervous about how the court would treat their case. They might well have to prove that the party advocated force and violence.[90]

---

*Besides Dennis, the defendants were Benjamin Davis, Jr., John Gates, Gil Green, Gus Hall, Irving Potash, Jacob Stachel, Robert Thompson, John Williamson, Henry Winston, and Carl Winter.

The FBI, whose strategy in this regard essentially shaped the prosecution, had been trying to find such evidence for years. Though the Bureau had collected reams of information, none of it showed party leaders talking about force and violence. Ultimately, the FBI (and the Justice Department later on) was to rely on a semantic trick. It would claim that a commitment to force and violence was inherent in what the CP's constitution called its "historic mission." In particular, so this line of reasoning went, the party's adherence to the doctrines of Marxism-Leninism automatically obligated it to seek the overthrow of the government by force and violence. The brief reiterated this proposition.[91]

Besides stipulating that Marxism-Leninism was "broadly the doctrine of the necessity of the violent overthrow of capitalist governments," the Bureau's casuists also insisted that such important elements of the CP's program as its opposition to imperialism, its support for other Communist parties, and its defense of the Soviet Union further indicated "the illegal aims and purposes of the Communist Party." The CP's domination by Russia was the central motif. It was also the easiest to prove. The 1945 Duclos letter that led to the ouster of party leader Earl Browder was the smoking gun, at least as far as the FBI and Justice Department were concerned. Not only did the abrupt about-face that followed the receipt of the French article seem indisputable proof that the CP was obeying orders from Moscow, but the harder line that emerged showed the party's reinvigorated dedication to Marxism-Leninism, a.k.a. force and violence. Even better, that reversal fell within the statute of limitations.[92]

The party's clandestine operations were also relevant. As they prepared to bring the case to court, FBI agents and federal prosecutors seized on whatever evidence they could find about the CP's underground activities, the use of false names and passports, and its members' penetration of labor unions and other groups. But even the party's public activities, like its leaders' speeches and articles opposing American foreign policy, were given a conspiratorial cast. This was "propaganda," a 1946 FBI report noted, designed to create "internal discord and dissatisfaction in an effort to disrupt the operation of our established form of government." Citing Lenin's appeal to the Russian soldiers of World War I to turn their guns against their officers and join the revolution, the government treated the party's rejection of the official American line on the Cold War as an example of its adherence to the Leninist doctrine of "revolutionary defeatism" and another indication of its support for force and violence.[93]

In a similar vein, the party's activities in the labor movement were labeled "infiltration." The CP's "industrial concentration" policy, its drive to become a more proletarian organization by recruiting more working-class members and assigning middle-class ones to blue-collar jobs, was treated as a prelude to sabotage. The party, so one FBI document explained, "has constantly endeavored to place people in key positions in vital industries, such as the automobile, steel and oil industries, so that at an opportune time when the Communist Party desired these individuals could ferment strikes and disorders within the industries." The prewar Allis-Chalmers strike was Exhibit A. At the trial the government's key witness, Louis Budenz, repeated his damaging story about the secret meeting in Milwaukee in 1940, at which Dennis allegedly ordered Harold Christoffel to pull his local off the job.[94]

The FBI's files reveal that the officials who prepared the Bureau's brief realized that much of the evidence about the party's ostensibly illegitimate activities that was so convincing to committed anti-Communists like themselves might well seem inconclusive at a trial or before an appellate court. They were particularly troubled by the fact that the prospective defendants not only did not call for the overthrow of the American government by force and violence, but explicitly denied that they wanted to do so. Even worse were the inconvenient passages in the party's constitution that specifically abjured revolutionary violence and provided for the expulsion of people who advocated it.[95]

Enter "Aesopian language." The phrase refers to a statement by Lenin in the preface to a later edition of one of his early works in which he discussed how, in order to avoid Tsarist censorship, he had to make political observations "with extreme caution by hints in that Aesopian language — in that cursed Aesopian language to which Czarism compelled all revolutionaries to have recourse whenever they took up their pens to write a 'legal' work." Could it be that the troublesome phraseology in the CP's constitution was just an "Aesopian" subterfuge, designed like Lenin's language to protect the party from the hand of the law? Such a formulation would solve the government's problems; it would let future prosecutors claim that whenever the CP's leaders denied that they advocated force and violence they were simply using "Aesopian language."

On March 12, 1947, a teletype went out to all the FBI's field offices asking them to investigate the party's use of the term. From Boston, Detroit, Chicago, Philadelphia, San Francisco, and elsewhere, the responses were all the same. Informants were "not aware of the existence of the Aesopian language," "unable to offer any explanation, definition, or interpretation of the Aesopian language." One New York informant did get a definition of the term from a longtime party member, but noted, "When I asked if the term was used today, Sam seemed very surprised and said 'Of course not. We are a legal organization, and it isn't necessary for us to hide what we want to tell the people.'" There was, in short, no evidence that American Communists practiced double-talk to evade censorship. Nonetheless, the notion of "Aesopian language" was so useful for the prosecution that it did not disappear. It became central to the testimony of Louis Budenz and was to become a staple of later communist cases as well.[96]

Still, the government did have to come up with some more positive evidence that Communists espoused the violent overthrow of the state. It found it in the party's bookstores. Political trials, because they often deal more with words than deeds, can sometimes be literary affairs. And the Smith Act case, because it involved "teaching" as well as "advocating," was especially dense with texts. They included the most incendiary passages in the works of Marx, Lenin, Stalin, and other communist heavies, excerpted in order to show that the "basic doctrines of Marxism-Leninism" required revolutionary violence. The final brief that the Bureau compiled and sent to the Justice Department contained over six hundred such snippets from the communist classics and the party's pamphlets and periodicals.[97]

Since many of these selections were, to put it mildly, rather dated, the government needed to link the words of long-dead authors to real live defendants. The prosecution, as one of McGohey's aides noted, would have to find witnesses to "testify that such literature is not mere rhetoric but rather that it completely expresses the present-day objectives of the Communist Party." Because of the Smith Act's language about "teaching," the FBI and Justice Department zeroed in on the party's schools. Field offices pressed their informants for syllabi and descriptions of the classes they attended. Special agents checked out the assigned readings for passages advocating force and violence.[98]

The prosecution was planning to use the Bureau's undercover informers as its main witnesses. They alone could recount recent conversations with party leaders and describe what had been taught in party schools.

Though some FBI field agents grumbled about losing coverage of the CP by letting their best informants surface at the forthcoming trial, headquarters was adamant. "The present prosecution of the National Board members is a showdown with the Communist Party," one of Hoover's top aides noted. "We can always develop informants against the Party in the future, but it may not be possible to bring about another trial of the Communist Party should this one be unsuccessful." [99]

The FBI's files reveal that the federal attorneys who were handling the case interviewed about sixty Bureau informants. Not all were selected for the big "showdown." Because the prosecutors wanted to focus on the party's educational work, they did not want any witnesses who had not been to a party school. Nor did they want ones with possible skeletons in their closets or who were too eager "to say just what was wanted." Potential witnesses had to be both presentable and well versed in the party's advocacy of force and violence. Informants who had never heard anyone in the CP talk about overthrowing the government were, the prosecutors implied, simply uninformed. Some of the people who did pass muster refused to testify. They feared the consequences of public exposure — the vilification as "stool pigeons," the possible loss of their jobs, and the threat of retaliation against them and their families. As a result, the government ended up depending rather heavily on a handful of informers and a few ex-Communists who were willing to testify and whose testimony wasn't "too remote." [100]

The trial, which ran from January 17 to October 14, 1949, was one of the longest and noisiest in American history. Despite the literary nature of the case, the courtroom proceedings were anything but sedate. Lawyers, defendants, and Judge Harold Medina sparred, shouted, and insulted each other. The party's five attorneys had few illusions about their chances for a victory at the trial stage. They assumed the case would go to the Supreme Court and, in many instances, their ostensibly disruptive courtroom tactics were designed to lay a groundwork for the appeal. The CP had decided to offer what it called a "labor defense." Instead of relying on such artifacts of the bourgeois legal system as the First Amendment, the Communist leaders would take their case to the people. They would mobilize their followers, organize demonstrations, and circulate petitions in the hopes that the pressure of the aroused "masses" would force the government to drop the prosecution. Similar tactics had worked in the 1930s to save the Scottsboro boys from execution on trumped-up rape charges. But the Cold War was not the Popular Front and a federal courtroom in New York City had more legitimacy than one in the Jim Crow black belt of Alabama. Moreover, by 1949 Communism was so unpopular that even a decorous appeal to civil liberties would have been futile.[101]

The communist leaders made matters even worse by overriding their attorneys' strong objections and using the trial to present the party line. Eugene Dennis, the party's general secretary, decided to serve as his own attorney so that he could make the CP's case directly to the jury. It was a misguided decision, for the communist leaders sacrificed their only chance to win liberal support. Unable to free themselves from the party's sectarian vocabulary, they came across as wooden, doctrinaire ideologues instead of as the victims of government repression that they also were. Worse yet, the decision to use the courtroom as a bully pulpit for preaching Marxism to the American people played into the prosecution's hands. The defendants inadvertently collaborated with the Justice Department's strategy of making the case a test of the legitimacy of the CP's policies rather than a struggle about free speech and the First Amendment.[102]

Budenz was the government's first and most important witness. As the former managing editor of the *Daily Worker* and the most prominent Communist to defect after World War II, he had enormous credibility both as an expert on Marxism-Leninism and as someone who had supposedly participated in the party's highest decision-making circles. In addition, Budenz was willing to tailor his testimony to the government's needs. During the trial, he developed the key argument that the CP's dedication to Marxism-Leninism meant "that the Communist Party of the United States is basically committed to the overthrow of the Government of the United States." He was also the main vehicle for inserting the most lurid passages from the party's literature into the record and explaining that the concept of "Aesopian language" meant that only those texts which called for revolutionary violence were authentic expressions of Marxism-Leninism. Any more conciliatory statements, he maintained, were "merely window dressing asserted for protective purposes."[103]

The FBI informers who followed Budenz to the stand testified about the more mundane details of party life. The first double agent to surface was

Herbert Philbrick, a clean-cut Boston advertising executive who had been reporting to the Bureau since 1940. Though he had not risen very high within the CP, Philbrick's appearance as a prosecution witness stunned the defendants, who until then had not realized how deeply the FBI had penetrated their organization. Philbrick talked mainly about the party's schools and their instruction in force and violence. The five other informers who took the stand gave similar testimony that bolstered the prosecution's main themes — the party's reorganization after the Duclos letter, its clandestine activities, its attempt to penetrate strategic defense industries, and its advocacy of revolutionary defeatism.[104]

The defense attorneys challenged the government's entire case. Time and again they questioned the admissibility of the books and articles that Budenz, Philbrick, and the other government witnesses were introducing. Most of these works had been written long before the passage of the Smith Act and were hardly representative of the party's current thinking. Nor were the selections an accurate sampling of the CP's basic philosophy. But Judge Harold Medina overruled each objection. "This book is, as I understand it," Medina explained as he allowed the government to introduce Lenin's 1917 tract *State and Revolution*, "part of the paraphernalia, one of the implements that are alleged to have been used by the defendants in forming the conspiracy that is alleged in the complaint."[105]

Medina was hardly an unbiased arbiter. Recently appointed to the bench, the communist trial was his first big case. He was haunted by the spectacle of the previous Smith Act trial, in which the judge died in the middle of the proceedings, seemingly sent to his early grave by the raucous behavior of the pro-Nazi defendants and their attorneys. Medina believed that the CP was preparing a similar fate for him and he viewed the communist leaders and their attorneys as potential assassins who were trying to provoke a mistrial by harassing him to death.* Not surprisingly, he handled the party's lawyers and their clients with overt hostility, treating their objections as delaying tactics and openly baiting both attorneys and witnesses. The party's lawyers responded in kind. It was not a decorous proceeding.[106]

---

*I once met Judge Medina, at a dinner party in the 1960s, long before I had begun any research on McCarthyism. Medina spent most of the evening in a monologue about the communist trial in which he explained that whenever he looked at the spectators during the trial, he consciously forced himself to keep his eyes moving so that he wouldn't let himself be placed in a trance by the hypnotists that the party might have placed in the courtroom.

Nor was it a fair one. Whether through bugs or informers, the FBI got inside information about defense strategy that it passed to the prosecutors. In the courtroom, Medina cut off cross-examinations when they appeared to be damaging the government's witnesses and he refused to let the CP present the same kind of evidence that the prosecution had. The government used the judge's bias to good advantage by forcing the party's witnesses into contempt by asking them about other people in the communist movement. When, as expected, they refused to name names, Medina ruled them in contempt and refused to let their testimony continue. At the end of the trial, Medina took the unprecedented step of charging all the defense attorneys with contempt as well. They had, he claimed, conspired to obstruct the trial and destroy his health.[107]

On October 14, 1949, the jury returned the expected guilty verdict. Just as predictably, the party appealed. It lost at both the appellate and the Supreme Court level. But even if the CP had won in the higher courts, the trial had already destroyed the party's legitimacy. The press coverage of the proceedings reinforced the government's case. Most of the media treated the communist defendants as thugs or traitors and were so sympathetic to Medina that he became a popular hero, the recipient of thousands of fan letters lauding him for defending American liberty. By the time the Supreme Court began its deliberations on the case at the end of 1950, the consensus that the party was outside the law was so widely accepted that the justices barely talked about the issue. Their discussion of the case, Justice William O. Douglas noted with dismay, "was largely *pro forma.*"[108]

The majority opinion that Chief Justice Fred Vinson delivered on June 4, 1951, relied heavily on the ruling of Learned Hand, the widely respected jurist who had decided the case at the appellate level the previous year. There was a kind of circularity in the process. Though Hand had obviously been affected by the outbreak of the Korean War only a few weeks before, he was also influenced by a recent Supreme Court decision on the Taft-Hartley Act that indicated that the justices were no longer solicitous about protecting the political freedom of Communists. Both Hand and Vinson emphasized national security. In adopting Hand's reformulation of the "clear and present danger" doctrine to allow the government to override the First Amendment if "the gravity of the 'evil,' discounted by its improbability, justifies such an invasion of free speech as is necessary to avoid the danger," the chief justice cited "the inflammable nature of world conditions, similar uprisings in other countries, and the touch-and-go nature of our relations with countries with whom petitioners were in the very least ideologically attuned." [109]

One of the most striking aspects of the *Dennis* decision was its incorporation of the entire case against the party that the FBI and Justice Department had constructed. In doing so, it confirmed all the stereotypes about the CP's conspiratorial goals and activities. Because of the importance of the case and the prestige of the high court, the case shaped the way in which people like intellectuals and educators came to view Communism. When the nation's opinion makers discussed the issue, they tended to do so within the parameters of the *Dennis* case, often using exactly the same arguments and examples that the prosecution used. [110]

Just as Hoover and his lieutenants had hoped, the Court's findings not only ratified the FBI's contention that the party was a criminal conspiracy, but also opened it up to additional sanctions. At the same time, the CP's self-destructive response to the *Dennis* decision confirmed the negative image that emerged from the trial. A few days after the ruling came down, the party's leaders issued a public statement claiming that the Supreme Court had accelerated "the process of creeping fascism" and then prepared to send their best cadres underground. Four of the defendants went into hiding as well, their flight from justice additional corroboration, or so it seemed, of the underlying illegitimacy of American Communism. [111]

★

PART THREE

INSTRUMENTS

★

CHAPTER 6

"A JOB FOR PROFESSIONALS"

THE FBI AND ANTICOMMUNISM

THE *Dennis* case was J. Edgar Hoover's triumph. The Bureau
had conceived of it, shaped it, and brought it to a successful conclusion. As
the centerpiece in the educational campaign to alert the rest of the nation to
the dangers of Communism, *Dennis* legitimized the countersubversive mission that Hoover and his men had embarked on in the late 1940s. Since they
had been preoccupied with the CP for years, the decision to intensify their
anticommunist operations did not change the FBI's orientation so much as
enhance one of its already crucial components. The Director's ideological
proclivities and professional ambitions fed into each other. By exaggerating
the threat of Communism and then making the Bureau indispensable to
eradicating that threat, Hoover not only increased the power of his agency,
but also advanced the anticommunist cause.[1]

Had observers known in the 1950s what they have learned since the
1970s, when the Freedom of Information Act opened the Bureau's files,
"McCarthyism" would probably be called "Hooverism." For the FBI was the
bureaucratic heart of the McCarthy era. It designed and ran much of the
machinery of political repression, shaping the loyalty programs, criminal
prosecutions, and undercover operations that pushed the communist issue
to the center of American politics during the early years of the Cold War.

The FBI director's strategic position within the Washington bureaucracy enabled him to control the government's internal security apparatus, ensuring that his own deeply reactionary vision of American Communism, as well as his agency's essentially preemptive approach to its eradication, would gain widespread acceptance.[2]

It is customary — and not really wrong — to make few distinctions between Hoover and the organization he ran. As Joe McCarthy put it, "The FBI is J. Edgar Hoover." He formed it, led it from 1924 until his death in 1972, and imbued it with his own patriarchal values and beliefs. It was an authoritarian, hierarchical world in which the Director's word was law. Every agent was expected to be "a personal representative of Mr. Hoover," conforming in his behavior as well as his dark socks and short hair to the rigid regulations that the Director had imposed. Often ridiculed as the personal fetish of an aging control freak, the carefully crafted image of respectability and professionalism that these regulations reinforced contributed mightily to the FBI's success — as Hoover well knew.[3]

Long before the spin masters took over the District of Columbia, the Director understood the value of public relations for expanding his agency's power. Besides courting editors and journalists, he established a highly sophisticated publicity department to manipulate the Bureau's image by puffing its exploits. Thus, when the FBI decided to go all out against Communism, it also embarked on an ambitious educational campaign to create "an informed public opinion." Much of that campaign took place in courtrooms and congressional hearings, but it also involved the work of the FBI's misleadingly named Crime Records Division and the hundreds of speeches, books, articles, movies, radio, and (later) television shows that it produced or inspired. Designed to warn the nation about Communism, these PR efforts also reinforced the Bureau's reputation for professionalism, expertise, and political neutrality.[4]

Besides boosting their own agency, Hoover and his aides worked to keep other players out of the game. They sought an exclusive franchise over the official task of protecting the United States against the threat of internal Communism and they fought hard to keep outside agencies — both public and private — from infringing on their turf. The Bureau's main rival was the CIA. During World War II, Hoover openly competed with its predecessor, the Office of Strategic Service, and its ambitious director Colonel William J. "Wild Bill" Donovan, whose empire-building he resisted and whose willingness to work with Communists he abhorred. When the CIA was estab-lished in 1947, Hoover treated the new agency as an enemy, feeding critical stories about it to the press and discouraging his subordinates from cooper-ating with it. It was not until the end of 1952, for example, that the FBI even informed the agency about the existence of the Venona decrypts.[5]

Actually, Hoover had trouble cooperating with almost every other di-vision of the federal government. He even squabbled with his Bureau's clos-est allies, the military intelligence agencies, though these conflicts usually subsided without undue acrimony. After all, the FBI and the armed services shared the same conservative mind-set and political constituency and the Director was not going to risk his Bureau's influence by taking on the army. This was not the case with less powerful or more liberal agencies. But, what-ever their politics, Hoover was continually maneuvering to shove other in-vestigators aside.[6]

While the Director could be vituperative in his attacks on his competi-tors and even more blistering toward his subordinates, he was far more dip-lomatic in dealing with his superiors. His job, of course, depended on it and he devoted considerable attention to currying favor with the White House by feeding its residents tidbits of political intelligence that he hoped they would enjoy. He was also eager to convert the chief executives to the Bu-reau's view of the world and he peppered them with frequent bulletins on the communist menace. Their effectiveness is unclear. Most of them prob-ably never reached the presidents' desk. Still, it is hard to imagine that over the years even the most casual perusal of these missives — warning as they did about such things as the communist presence in specific labor unions or the party's opposition to American foreign policy — did not have *some* kind of impact on the men in the White House and at least in part shape the way they and their aides conceptualized the problem of domestic Communism.[7]

Hoover was also, as former Attorney General Tom Clark noted with considerable understatement, "rather meticulous about his relationships with Congress." The FBI director worked hard at developing good con-nections on the Hill, often going behind the backs of his ostensible superi-ors in the Justice Department to forge close ties with a bipartisan coterie of conservatives who shared his political outlook. The Director knew who his friends were and courted them assiduously by leaking useful informa-tion or detailing FBI agents to chauffeur them around and perform personal chores.[8]

He also used his files. Capitol Hill folklore had it that the Bureau had dossiers on every senator and representative and would deploy them to keep recalcitrant congressmen in line. As one of Hoover's top aides described it, there was nothing subtle about the process. "The other night we picked up a situation where this senator was seen drunk, in a hit-and-run accident, and some good-looking broad was with him. By noon of the next day the good senator was aware that we had the information and we never had any trouble with him on appropriations since."[9]

Even without blackmail, it is hard to imagine many congressmen taking a tough line on the FBI or cutting its appropriations. The Bureau was simply too popular. Congressional oversight did not exist and, at least until the mid-1960s, Hoover had little to fear on Capitol Hill. "I have never cut his budget," explained John J. Rooney, who chaired the House Appropriations subcommittee that dealt with the FBI from 1949 until after Hoover's death, "and I never expect to." Not only did nineteen of Hoover's last twenty-one budget proposals go through without changes, but in the only two times the lawmakers tampered with the Bureau's annual requests, they gave the Director more money than he had asked for.[10]

In its unquestioning approval of the FBI's funding, Congress was quite literally writing a blank check. No statutory regulations governed the Bureau's operations, for Congress had never passed any law defining the FBI's responsibilities or authorizing it to undertake political investigations. Though Hoover could have easily gotten such a piece of legislation, he never requested it. Even the broadest set of guidelines would have been more restrictive than the near-total freedom from oversight that the Bureau's informal mandate offered.

Instead, the FBI relied for its authority on a series of executive orders dating from the late 1930s. The first two, issued by Roosevelt in 1939 and 1943, had been designed to centralize intelligence gathering and prevent the kind of vigilante hysteria that had occurred during World War I. Hoover, however, interpreted these orders pretty much as he pleased and manipulated later presidents and Attorneys General into expanding the Bureau's mandate by convincing them that FDR had granted it almost unrestricted investigative power. When Truman and Eisenhower issued their own executive orders in July 1950 and December 1953, they believed that they were merely reproducing Roosevelt's original directive. In fact, however, because

Hoover had inserted the crucial and essentially open-ended phrase "subversive activities and related matters" into the new orders, the Director was able to expand his agency's official jurisdiction so that it could investigate almost any form of political dissent. Its unofficial jurisdiction, of course, stretched even further.[11]

Because Hoover often ignored the formal limitations on his agency's activities, it is tempting to treat the FBI as a thoroughly rogue operation that functioned outside the law. However, it was only a *partially* rogue operation. Much of the Bureau's work was completely legal, routine, and nonpolitical. As the investigative arm of the Justice Department, its primary responsibility was to collect information that would enable United States Attorneys to prosecute violations of federal laws. The demands of the criminal justice system structured much of this work and required it to be within the law. The evidence, exhibits, and potential witnesses that the FBI gathered had to be acceptable in court and stand up under appeal.

Many of the Bureau's investigations had nothing to do with politics. Bank robberies, kidnappings, mail fraud, and car theft were as much within its bailiwick as spying or sabotage. Still, its political jurisdiction was vast, for the anticommunist umbrella covered so many different "crimes" that the FBI was able to embark on a wide range of officially sanctioned investigations. Though it was not illegal to be a Communist, there were enough laws proscribing what Communists allegedly did to allow the Bureau to prepare cases against thousands of men and women. The investigative activity involved in preparing these prosecutions gave the Bureau and its agents ample opportunities for gathering information and keeping Communists under surveillance.[12]

Even so, Hoover and his aides worried. They did not feel that law enforcement alone enabled them to fulfill their self-imposed mission of protecting the nation's internal security against the threat of Communism. They wanted to prevent subversion, not just punish it. Accordingly, the Bureau unilaterally decided to prepare for the emergency detention of American Communists, an undertaking that would also give them a pretext for putting most party members under surveillance. The FBI's inflated estimate of the CP's mischief-making potential seemed to justify such a program. "Any members of the Party occupied in any industry," Assistant Director D. Milton Ladd explained in an important memorandum to his boss in

February 1946, "would be in a position to hamper the efforts of the United States by individual action and undoubtedly the great majority of them would do so."[13]

Though it had begun to compile lists of allegedly dangerous people in 1939, the FBI had no mandate for creating such lists. In fact, the Director had been specifically ordered to drop the project in 1943 by Attorney General Francis Biddle. But Hoover ignored his superior's directive, renamed the program, and continued to add names to the now-retitled Security Index. The list grew during the early years of the Cold War. With the passage of the McCarran Act after the outbreak of the Korean War, Congress finally authorized the custodial detention plan the FBI had been unofficially implementing for years. By July 1950, there were nearly 12,000 people on the Security Index; by the end of 1954 there were over 26,000, most of them Communist party functionaries and other activists, the "most potentially dangerous" of whom "were scheduled to be arrested within one hour after the order is given."[14]

The Bureau had also compiled separate lists of slightly less dangerous individuals, mostly intellectuals, professionals, and labor leaders who, it believed, "in a time of national emergency, are in a position to influence others against the national interests or are likely to furnish financial or other material aid to subversive elements." The operation was a bureaucratic windfall. By emphasizing the need to prepare for a national emergency, the FBI was able to parlay its lists of people slated for detention into a program of widespread political surveillance. By 1960, it had opened over 430,000 files on allegedly subversive groups and individuals.[15]

There was no realistic need for this kind of surveillance. Whatever influence the American Communist party had once wielded had so dissipated by the mid-fifties that even the Justice Department had come to treat the Security Index as something of a joke. But the FBI continued to accumulate information. As a bureaucratic maneuver that prolonged the life of the Bureau's anticommunist mission, the detention program had considerable value. And Hoover, at least, still believed that the CP might rise again.[16]

The FBI's empire extended far beyond the realm of law enforcement and preventive surveillance. The Bureau also became involved with clearing people for both public and private employers. It had gotten into the business during World War II, when it collaborated with the military in checking out workers in defense plants and investigated federal employees charged with disloyalty. Both of these activities continued after the war and were to expand enormously once the Cold War got under way.

The Bureau's surveillance of defense industries was a good way to protect its turf, attract attention, and show that the G-men were on the job. The program relied primarily on the informants that the FBI had recruited in the various plants it was protecting. Though these sources provided little useful intelligence during World War II, the FBI did not completely abandon the program once the war ended. And, in fact, Hoover's aides recommended its expansion when the Korean War broke out, as much for its public relations value as for the intelligence that it would produce. At the program's peak in June 1953, the FBI had 109,119 informants at over 10,745 defense plants, research centers, and the other installations like bridges and telephone exchanges that the Defense Department had identified as "vital facilities." [17]

Even more important to the growth of the Bureau's anticommunist empire was the inauguration of a new loyalty-security program within the executive branch. The FBI had been officially screening federal employees ever since the passage of the Hatch Act in 1939 prohibited Communists, Nazis, and other political undesirables from working for the government. When the partisan Communists-in-government issue heated up after the war, the Truman administration, eager for the political protection the FBI's popularity provided, essentially let the Bureau shape its loyalty-security program. [18]

Truman did this mainly to preempt Congress. HUAC had begun to look into the administration's loyalty procedures. So, too, had a subcommittee of the House Civil Service Committee, which held two weeks of hearings in July 1946 and recommended the appointment of a presidential commission to design a program "to protect the Government from disloyal employees." But until the Republicans won control of Congress in the November 1946 election, rooting out subversive civil servants was not a high priority at the White House. After the elections, however, Truman decided to appoint a Temporary Commission on Employee Loyalty rather than risk the possibility that a hostile Congress might launch its own investigation. [19]

Hoover had anticipated the moment. On July 25, 1946, less than a week after the House subcommittee had recommended such a commission, the Director sent a memo to Attorney General Tom Clark suggesting that the

Justice Department appoint as its representative to the body someone "who has a broad, overall picture of the problems and policies of the various units of the Department of Justice." He even proposed a candidate.[20]

Sure enough, when the commission was established, Hoover's nominee, A. Devitt Vanech, was on it — as its chair. He knew why he was there and what his obligations were. "I want you to know how much I appreciate the confidence you have evidenced in me," Vanech wrote the FBI director on the day his appointment was announced, "and assure you that I will do everything within my power to make a success of this assignment." The commission began its work in December 1946 and submitted its report two and a half months later. From the start, it was clear that Hoover and his men exercised considerable control over the proceedings. They worked—mainly behind the scenes — to ensure that the commission would accept the FBI's reading of the situation and most of its recommendations for action.[21]

The commission's members disagreed about how dangerous a threat communist infiltration actually was. The FBI's assistant director, D. Milton Ladd, insisted that it was "a very serious problem," but to the disgust of Stephen J. Spingarn, a Treasury Department representative on the panel, Ladd "presented almost no factual information to support this statement." Vanech refused to press him for more evidence, leading Spingarn to complain, "It is now obvious that Justice and FBI have thrown up (and will continue to throw up) a smoke screen to attempt to create the impression that anything *significantly* bearing on the scope of our problem . . . is too secret to be revealed." Actually, the Attorney General had assured the commission that the "disloyalty problem was not as serious as it once was" and that there were, in fact, few Communists in government, but the group still adopted the more alarmist view pushed by the FBI.[22]

The Bureau was almost as successful in taking over the administration of the new program. Though it was unable to persuade the commission to recommend that all federal employees and applicants be fully investigated by the FBI, it did get provisions for the Bureau to do name checks and mount a full field investigation if any "derogatory information" turned up in someone's file. And it was able to scuttle the commission's proposal that the departments be given access to the FBI's dossiers on their employees. Allowing outsiders to see the files, Hoover complained to the Attorney General, would not only reveal the tightly held identities of Bureau informants, thus de-

stroying their effectiveness and making it impossible to recruit new informers, but it would also expose "our techniques, including among others,
technical surveillances which are authorized by you." Tom Clark understood the Director's not so thinly veiled warning and the offending recommendations were removed.[23]

Hoover also got the commission to create a central Loyalty Review
Board. Disappointed by the Roosevelt and Truman administrations' failure
to dismiss the federal employees his agents had fingered, Hoover wanted a
body that would have the power to make individual departments and agencies fire people. He did not get his wish; the board could only review cases.
Still, the FBI got most of what it wanted. The few provisions that the Director objected to — mainly ones that gave power to rival agencies — were
never fully implemented and the Bureau emerged from the process with a
near monopoly over the investigation of federal employees, even if it could
not always get them fired.[24]

The FBI grew to meet its new responsibilities. By the beginning of
1952 it had checked out two million federal employees and conducted
20,000 full-field investigations. Its roster of agents increased from 3,559 in
1946 to 7,029. The Bureau's influence also expanded. Its reputation was so
high that only a few Americans recognized the ominous implications of
the FBI's dominant role in designing Truman's loyalty-security program. By
basing their program on Hoover's inflated assessment of the communist
threat, its authors heightened the public's concern with Communism and
contributed to the growth of McCarthyism. Moreover, the Bureau's procedures led to widespread injustice. Its politically conservative standards of
evidence and fetish for self-protection cost thousands of government workers their jobs.[25]

And not just federal employees. Hundreds, maybe thousands, of other
workers also lost their jobs and were blacklisted because of the FBI. At the
time, many of these men and women suspected the Bureau's hand, but because the FBI kept its involvement a secret, they could never be sure.
Norman Cazden, an assistant professor of music at the University of Illinois,
was one of them. In the beginning of 1953, he was, he recalled, summoned
into the president's office and shown "an anonymous typewritten document
purporting to present unverified allegations as to my past associations."
Though Cazden was a good teacher and a productive scholar who was

clearly destined for tenure, Illinois did not renew his contract when it expired two months later. The sheet of paper that the university's president told Cazden "somebody just dropped" on his desk was obviously a "blind memorandum" from the FBI. Created so that they could not be traced to their source, these documents were compendiums of material from the Bureau's files that were typed on plain unwatermarked paper and hand-delivered to selected university presidents, congressmen, journalists, or whomever the FBI wanted to secretly feed information to.[26]

Cazden's dismissal was part of the Bureau's secret "Responsibilities Program," established in February 1951, to alert governors and other "appropriate authorities" to the alleged subversives in their employ. Before the Responsibilities Program was discontinued in March 1955, the FBI had fingered over eight hundred people, more than half of them public school and college teachers. Most, of course, lost their jobs. The Bureau also gave information to such other quasi-public organizations as bar associations, the Boy Scouts, and the American Red Cross, and to some private individuals as well. Since these disseminations were clearly unauthorized, the Bureau made obsessive efforts to cover its tracks. Because the victims of these leaks must also have tried to conceal why they had been dismissed, it is hard to tell how many people lost their jobs because of the FBI's "blind memoranda." My sixth-grade teacher may well have been one of them.[27]

Hoover's power, though formidable, was not unlimited. He and his Bureau required collaborators. Under the Responsibilities Program, for example, the FBI could identify political undesirables, but it needed agency heads or school superintendants to fire them. No single organization, not even the FBI, could create and operate a nationwide system for identifying and eliminating the alleged threat of communist subversion in the expansive way that the Director and his allies had defined it. At the same time, however, Hoover's obsession about protecting his turf complicated the situation, for the Bureau's partners were also its rivals.

Relationships with local governments and law enforcement agencies were usually good. Turf warfare was muted in large part because most big city red squads generally welcomed the Bureau's assistance, recognizing the

G-men's hegemony in the field of national security. The FBI had spent years cultivating state and local authorities and had been exchanging information on an informal basis even before the Responsibilities Program regularized some of those transactions. A few conflicts broke out, especially when ambitious governors and other politicians sought to beef up their state's anti-subversive machinery and encroach upon the Bureau's jurisdiction. Such efforts invariably provoked Hoover's fury. "If these people," he grumbled, "got any idea that they could go out on their own in forty-eight states looking for reds there would be chaos in this country and violation of civil rights, et cetera." [28]

Of course, civil rights were hardly the Director's main concern. He wanted to defend his bailiwick and ensure that other agencies within the federal government and elsewhere would not make the Bureau look bad by finding material that the G-men had overlooked. This had happened when State Department investigators had discovered enough evidence against the former OSS and State Department employee Carl Marzani to enable the government to indict him for perjury. Hoover was furious at the "State Dept's usurpation." He instructed his aides not only to emphasize the FBI's jurisdiction over loyalty investigations, but also to refuse to cooperate in any case brought by another agency. "It is rather humiliating," he complained, "that a case like this was made by the State Dept & *not* the FBI." [29]

A similar "usurpation" occurred during the House Un-American Activities Committee's investigation of Alger Hiss. Though the Bureau had been investigating Hiss for years and leaking information about him as well, Hoover was annoyed that HUAC and Richard Nixon took credit for breaking the case. "We have missed the boat in many ways," he grumbled to his aides. "*We* . . . didn't bring out the Hiss-Chambers connection." The grievance rankled for years, resurrected whenever it appeared that the Bureau had somehow failed to find material that surfaced elsewhere. When the FBI's longtime informant Louis Budenz supported the charges of Senator McCarthy by telling a congressional committee about the supposed communist connections of the East Asia scholar Owen Lattimore, Hoover was outraged that the Bureau, which had been interviewing Budenz since the fall of 1945, had apparently fumbled again. "It begins to look like another Chambers case where we didn't press for information." [30]

Still, for all of Hoover's territorial ferocity, the Director nonetheless

213

recognized that his agency needed to share information with other organizations and individuals. The most extensive exchanges were with the military intelligence agencies, since the late 1930s regular recipients of Bureau information. When agents in the field reported back to Washington, they often sent carbon copies to the army, navy, and air force. The FBI also shared information with other agencies in the executive branch, sometimes on an ad hoc basis and sometimes by maintaining regular liaison officers, as it grudgingly did at the CIA. There was nothing unusual or illegitimate about these exchanges. The Bureau was, after all, the federal government's main investigatory agency and it is important not to overlook the fact that much of its workload was entirely legitimate.[31]

The FBI's collaboration with Congress during the McCarthy period was, however, less appropriate. Though theoretically prohibited from disseminating information from its files beyond the executive branch, the Bureau regularly leaked materials to its friends on the Hill. Some of these transactions were relatively innocuous, like the background checks on staff members that the FBI performed for some of the House and Senate's most influential committees or the speeches that the Crime Records Division wrote for Hoover's favorite lawmakers. Others, like the publication of FBI documents disguised as committee reports and the direct leaks of information from Bureau files, were more questionable. The FBI indulged in these practices in order to obtain results that its more legitimate activities could not otherwise achieve — the dismissal of federal employees, for example, or the publicizing of cases that could not be prosecuted.[32]

The FBI's use of Congress to hound Alger Hiss was typical. Despite Hoover's later chagrin at being upstaged by HUAC, the Bureau's leaks were probably crucial in bringing the case to the public in the first place. The initial disclosures seem to have taken place in 1946 when Hoover decided to force Hiss's ouster from the State Department by sending information about him to conservative congressmen. One of Hoover's top lieutenants apparently hand-delivered a Bureau report on Hiss to Mississippi Senator James Eastland. Later on, when the FBI was trying to use the Hiss case to draw attention to the Communists-in-government issue, it funneled information to HUAC's Richard Nixon through a variety of direct and indirect intermediaries, including the Catholic priest Father John F. Cronin.[33]

HUAC may well have been the most frequent recipient of the FBI's largesse. During the early years of the Cold War, the committee received all kinds of materials from the Bureau, from copies of the party cards of Hollywood's main Communists to the financial records of Gerhart Eisler. But the relationship had its rocky moments; Hoover's willingness to cooperate with HUAC tended to fluctuate in accordance with his assessment of the trustworthiness of the committee's members and staff. Ironically, since the FBI used leaks expressly to publicize cases it couldn't prosecute, HUAC's most common sin — at least in Bureau eyes — was its desire for the limelight. Hoover and his men continually expressed contempt for the committee's publicity-hungry members and staffers and their propensity for leaking information that might embarrass the FBI. "Headlines," the Director scrawled on the bottom of a report by one of his top aides about an unproductive meeting with HUAC's counsel, "mean more to them than ultimate security." [34]

During the 1950s, the Senate Judiciary Committee's Internal Security Subcommittee (SISS) replaced HUAC as the FBI's main congressional conduit. Hoover worked well with both of the Judiciary Committee's powerful Democratic chairs, Nevada's Pat McCarran and Mississippi's Eastland. As SISS staff director Jay Sourwine noted, McCarran was eager to "do just about everything the director asked him to." Soon after SISS was established in March 1951, it met secretly with Hoover and Attorney General J. Howard McGrath and hammered out an "arrangement" whereby the Bureau would assist the committee by running name checks and sending it blind memoranda with "appropriate leads and suggested clues" for the committee's "confidential use and guidance." The collaboration was a high priority for the FBI; ten senior supervisors were detailed to a "Special Squad" to handle SISS requests. Bureau relations with research director Benjamin Mandel and the rest of the subcommittee's staff were good. Robert Morris, the SISS counsel, was, Assistant Director Louis Nichols noted, "thoroughly trustworthy and thoroughly reasonable." He was discreet, did not seek publicity, and was willing to help out "whenever the Bureau needed a forum for a matter it could not handle." [35]

Relations with Joseph McCarthy were more strained. Initially, Hoover helped out. He liked McCarthy personally and supported his efforts to expose Communists in the Truman administration. The Director gave the senator political advice and helped recruit former FBI agent Don Surine for his staff. He also had his subordinates pass information to McCarthy, usually by way of Surine. By the middle of 1953, however, Hoover had begun to worry that the senator's growing recklessness might somehow compromise the Bureau and so he cut off the flow.[36]

The Bureau's relations with Congress, though often concealed, have gotten some attention from historians. Its contacts with the business community have not. As recently released FBI files reveal, they seem to have been considerable but were not apparently formalized. Many of these contacts developed during and after World War II when the Bureau became involved with the security of defense plants. FBI agents got in touch with management at many of these facilities and often received access to personnel records and other corporate files. In return, the Bureau supplied these companies with information about the left-wing unions operating in their plants and the political activities of their employees. Corporate officials were usually glad to cooperate with the FBI by transferring or firing workers. As one agent noted after a conversation with the vice president of the Anaconda Copper Company, "Mr. McGlore said that he would move any employee of the company into a less vulnerable spot or discharge any such persons from the service, if the writer wished to suggest it and that no questions would be asked."[37]

The FBI also leaked information to the press. Most of the leaks went to what an internal FBI memo called the "anti-Communist writers who have proved themselves to us." Among this elect were George Sokolsky, Drew Pearson, Westbrook Pegler, Walter Winchell, Frederick Woltman, Fulton Lewis, Jr., and the Washington bureau chiefs of the United Press and *Chicago Tribune.* Some of the information that the FBI sent to these people got published; some, like the blind memos that the Bureau sent to Hollywood gossip columnist Hedda Hopper, fed blacklists or served other functions. In addition, many of these journalists supplied the FBI with information. The Hearst columnist George Sokolsky, for example, sent Hoover so much material about the Communists in Hollywood that the Bureau created a "special procedure" for handling it.[38]

In many respects, the contacts between the Bureau and journalists like Sokolsky were part of that larger web of information and power that bound the anticommunist network together and made it so effective. Catholic trade union activists, American Legion officials, and professional ex-Communists were all among the Bureau's regular collaborators, to be consulted, stroked, and fed information. In many instances, the FBI's routine information-gathering procedures were designed as much to enhance its political alliances and strengthen that network as they were to accumulate material for its files.[39]

The FBI's relations with the American Legion are illustrative here. In 1940 the FBI created a formal American Legion Contact Program, which recruited approximately sixty thousand Legionnaires as informants within defense plants and ethnic communities. The program, which was reactivated at the outbreak of the Korean War, yielded little information. Its main function was to prevent unauthorized vigilantism and, in the Director's words, to give the Legion "an opportunity to assist in the protection of the internal security of the United States." In short, some networking and public relations. There were personal as well as programmatic ties between the Bureau and the Legion. Lee Pennington, who had handled the FBI's liaison with the organization, became the head of its Americanism Commission one week after he resigned from the Bureau. In the late 1950s, Cartha DeLoach, the head of the Bureau's Crime Records Division, handled the Legion's public relations at the same time.[40]

Pennington's career illustrates another way in which the Bureau amplified its influence. It placed former agents in strategic positions throughout a wide range of public and private institutions. Some of these people had special assignments, like J. Patrick Coyne, who served as the National Security Council's resident expert on internal security matters; other Bureau alumni went into the Justice Department, where they were especially well represented in the Internal Security Division. Elsewhere in the executive branch, former special agents often ran the various departmental loyalty programs. The FBI was equally well represented on the staffs of congressional committees. In 1943, Hoover loaned one of his top aides to the powerful House Appropriations Committee and the arrangement continued for decades. Former FBI men also served as investigators for the main anticommunist committees and even, in the person of Illinois congressman Harold Velde, as HUAC's chair. Because of their professional training and experience, as well as their Bureau connections, ex-agents were also in demand at the state and local level, where they were hired by investigating committees and police departments.[41]

Former G-men were equally ubiquitous in the private sector, where they often handled security matters and labor relations. Assistant Director Louis Nichols was probably the highest-ranking official to go into the corporate world when he resigned from the FBI to become an executive vice president for Schenley Industries. Ford Motor Company vice president John Bugas had been Detroit's Special Agent in Charge before he took over the company's previously notorious union-busting Service Department. Former agents may well have looked particularly attractive to companies like Allis-Chalmers that used red-baiting tactics to fight labor. In February 1947, a few days after he had submitted a report to the Bureau on the connections between Allis-Chalmers's UAW local and the Communist party, Special Agent Jack Lee went on the company's payroll.[42]

Other former FBI men went into industrial security firms and private detective agencies, where they often came to specialize in anticommunist activities. Some became professional blacklisters, like the three ex-agents who got funding in 1946 from Alfred Kohlberg and Father John F. Cronin to set up an outfit called American Business Consultants. Capitalizing on their Bureau experience and connections, they proposed to collect and disseminate the kind of information that the FBI was prohibited from revealing. They checked out employees for a variety of corporate clients and published a newsletter, *Counterattack,* that highlighted the alleged communist connections of entertainers, union leaders, and other subversive folk. Their 1950 oeuvre *Red Channels,* with its compilation of the presumably questionable connections of some 151 show business people, soon became the main reference tool for blacklisters within the broadcasting industry.[43]

It would be hard to exaggerate the importance Hoover and his men placed on maintaining the FBI's reputation as a professional, nonpartisan investigating agency.[44] That perception was the key to its power. By insisting that it was above political considerations, the Bureau ensured that it would receive support from all constituencies and that few restrictions would be placed on its activities. That image, of course, was a myth. Far from being an impartial agency that simply looked for facts, the Bureau had a very definite political agenda that it sought to implement in any way it could. And many of the FBI's activities went far beyond what it was authorized to do.[45]

In order to maintain its reputation, therefore, the Bureau had to devote considerable resources to concealing what it was doing. Much of that effort was designed to win liberal support. Though the FBI's natural constituency was on the right, Hoover realized that by manipulating his agency's image to present it as a progressive, professionalized law enforcement organization he could also win the support of liberals who might otherwise be unresponsive to traditional appeals to law and order. Hoover's task was not as difficult as, in retrospect, it might appear. To begin with, the Bureau was a typical New Deal agency in that it shared the Roosevelt administration's commitment to big government. When he dealt with liberals, the Director made much of his ties with FDR and even pointed out that the FBI was accused of "being too liberal, and in fact of being inclined toward at least a 'pinkish' tinge if not a radical tinge."[46]

Hoover courted liberals and sought, whenever possible, to deflect criticism of the Bureau by espousing his solicitude for individual rights. His clandestine alliance with the ACLU's Morris Ernst was particularly useful. Ernst, who shared Hoover's almost visceral antagonism toward the CP, ran interference for the FBI with the liberal community. Throughout the 1940s and 1950s, Ernst helped Hoover fend off complaints about the Bureau's undemocratic practices and wrote articles and letters to the editor praising the FBI and its Director. The relationship seems a bit smarmy; Ernst liked to feel he had access to power and enjoyed his position as intermediary. "A lot of people," Ernst wrote Hoover, "think I am just a stooge for you which I take as a high compliment. There are few people I would rather publicly support."[47]

Hoover paid serious lip service to civil liberties, rarely losing an opportunity to denounce "hysteria, witch-hunts and vigilantes" and affirm the need for "protecting the innocent as well as . . . identifying the enemies within our midst." The professionalism of its agents was an important theme in Bureau propaganda. Hoover never forgot the criticism directed against the excesses of the post–World War I red scare. He tried to conceal his own role in the Palmer raids and he made sure that his agents would be perceived as under firm control. Other agencies with less-well-trained personnel might be guilty of improprieties or violations of civil liberties, but the FBI had higher standards. On paper, at least, the Bureau was meticulous about ensuring that its agents protected the civil rights of the people they investigated.[48]

Since the Bureau's investigatory practices did not always accord with its liberal rhetoric, rumors that FBI agents harrassed innocent liberals or interfered with union organizers were a constant source of concern. By the late 1940s, Hoover and his men were sophisticated enough to know that their agency could only be damaged by allegations that the G-men obstructed labor organizing or asked people if they subscribed to *The New Republic*. The Bureau's standard response to such charges was to describe the special training its agents received, as well as their instructions that, in the words of Assistant Director Ladd, "they are not supposed to inquire as to reading matter, political affiliations, other than Communism, etc."[49]

Hoover's campaign to present his agency as a champion of civil liberties was a huge success. With only a few demurrals, most Americans, even most liberals, trusted the FBI. In part, the Bureau's reputation for competence and discretion had as much to do with the failings of other agencies as it did with its alleged professionalism. The perception that the FBI was a bulwark against irresponsible politicians, cops, and vigilantes was widespread. When the Truman administration was trying to defend itself against what Attorney General Tom Clark called HUAC's "political activity," it contrasted the strident congressmen with "the continuous but quiet watchfulness of the Federal Bureau of Investigation." Democrats picked up the theme during the 1948 election campaign. "As you read and hear the hysterical outbursts of wishful-thinking Republican politicians, just remember the record of the FBI."[50]

Liberals in the 1940s and 1950s wanted to believe the FBI's line. By championing the Bureau as a responsible as well as efficient anticommunist agency, they could clear themselves of charges that they were soft on Communism while at the same time encouraging effective action against the red menace. Adlai Stevenson, the two-time Democratic candidate for president, was a case in point. As governor of Illinois he had twice vetoed a state loyalty oath bill, but he had also been instrumental in prodding the FBI to inaugurate the Responsibilities Program. For him, as for so many liberal politicians, the Bureau was a counterweight to the unenlightened anticommunism of the right. "I do not believe that oaths and affidavits are much good, for a real communist never hesitates to lie," Stevenson explained in 1952.

I think generally that close screening of government employees and the quiet professional work of the FBI is the best way to turn over every stone in this country to see what lies beneath it. This is a job for professionals, and I think it can be done without slandering innocent people.

Like Stevenson, an entire generation of Democratic politicians sought political cover in the arms of J. Edgar Hoover.[51]

Obviously, if the Bureau was to maintain its cozy relationship with liberals, it had to ensure that it did not reveal its conservative bias or allow evidence of its illegal activities to reach the public. Such an effort required much more than propaganda. During the 1940s and 1950s the FBI engaged in a massive cover-up that ranged from simple lies to a formidable campaign to smear and ultimately destroy the political legitimacy of its few remaining critics.

Agents were constantly warned not to do anything that would hurt the FBI's image. The Bureau was ready to limit or even abort an investigation rather than risk an embarrassment. In 1946, for example, the FBI agents who had been maintaining a highly public round-the-clock vigil on the German Communist Gerhart Eisler were pulled off the job when Eisler and his attorney complained about the surveillance. Hoover's aides feared that Eisler's supporters might be able "to photograph Bureau Agents on the surveillance or otherwise to pull some stunt which might be very embarrassing to the Bureau." Even more embarrassing was the "stunt" actually pulled by some Honolulu radicals when they recorded and then broadcast the tape of a conversation in which two FBI agents tried to convince a Smith Act defendant to become an informer. The Bureau was sure that the CP had planned the episode and it warned its men never again to interview a Communist on his own turf.[52]

Even more damaging to the Bureau's reputation than the overzealousness of its agents were implications that the confidentiality of its files had been breached. The FBI's reputation required that its records remain inviolate. Bureau rhetoric is revealing here; Hoover and his allies constantly refer to the "sanctity" of the FBI's files. They were even willing to forfeit a conviction rather than produce those records in court. Naturally, the Bureau was adamant about ensuring that the recipients of FBI leaks did not reveal their source. Thus, for example, it rigorously monitored all disseminations under the Responsibilities Program. Every leak had to be approved by headquarters and agents had to ascertain in advance the reliability of the individual to whom they gave the information. Most transmissions were made orally or else in the form of blind memoranda and were to be accompanied by explicit warnings not to let on where the information came from.[53]

Leaks about Bureau leaks invariably threw the Director into a rage. Whenever an institution or individual hinted that the FBI had been supplying information, Hoover moved to cut off the flow. Governors who let on that they had been privy to material from the Bureau were stricken from the Responsibilities Program; newsmen who intimated that they got stuff from the Bureau were taken off its "Special Correspondents" list.[54]

In public, the FBI's leaders justified their obsession with the confidentiality of their files in terms of national security and civil liberties. The identities of secret informants might be revealed, thus drying up the supposedly vital information they were supplying as well as making it harder to recruit new informants. FBI spokesmen also claimed that because the Bureau files often contained raw information and unevaluated rumors, releasing them would hurt innocent people. "I would not want to be a party to any action," Hoover told a Senate committee in 1950, "which would 'smear' innocent individuals for the rest of their lives." Within the executive branch, the Bureau offered additional rationalizations. Not only would access to FBI files violate executive privilege, it would also embarrass the administration by revealing what Hoover euphemistically called "confidential techniques" — his agency's buggings, wiretaps, and illegal break-ins.[55]

The public occasionally caught glimpses of these activities. In 1945, just as the government was preparing its case against the journalists and officials involved in the leaking of classified documents to the left-wing magazine *Amerasia,* one of the defendants discovered that FBI agents had illegally entered his apartment. Even more damaging revelations came out during the first trial of Judith Coplon in the summer of 1949. Since the FBI documents that were in her purse at the time she was arrested were central to the government's claim that Coplon had compromised the nation's security, the judge ordered that they be produced. Hoover was horrified and urged the Attorney General to drop the case rather than release the material. But the Justice Department wanted a conviction and so surrendered the documents.[56]

The materials, which described contacts between Americans and Russians, contained nothing that endangered the United States but quite a lot that embarrassed the FBI. They showed that the Bureau was improperly concerned about people's political activities and had investigated and wiretapped a wide range of private citizens, including the film star Frederic March. Then, at Coplon's second trial in New York City later the same year, the FBI admitted that it had tapped Coplon's phone and so had presumably listened in to her conversations with her lawyers. As a result of these disclosures, Coplon's conviction was overturned on appeal. Losing the case was bad enough, but from the FBI's perspective, the damage to the Bureau's reputation was the real disaster.[57]

Never again. The FBI immediately took steps to prevent a recurrence. It intensified its efforts both to protect its files and to ensure that they would no longer reveal evidence of its agents' misdeeds. Actually, the Bureau had long been doctoring its records to conceal unauthorized investigations and unlawful practices. Some files were intentionally written to be opaque, others were altered or destroyed. In still other cases, agents simply did not report illegal activities like break-ins to their superiors or, when they did, used complicated filing procedures to hide that information. In response to the Coplon trial, Hoover created even more misleading filing procedures and developed ways to ensure that information about his agency's more questionable activities would not come out in court.[58]

The FBI's damage containment was not limited to falsifying its records, however. It also went on the offensive against its critics. The FBI routinely opened files on the writers and journalists who criticized the Bureau and its Director and, when possible, sought to disrupt the careers of these, in Hoover's words, "coyotes of the press." After all, even with the Bureau's attention to public relations, there had always been some questions about what he and his men were doing.[59]

The Coplon trial brought these questions to the fore and led to demands for an investigation. The main organization pressing for the probe was the National Lawyers Guild, a longtime critic of the Bureau's political activities. In June 1949, when the Coplon materials became public, Clifford Durr, the Alabama attorney who then headed the Guild, wrote to Truman asking him to appoint a high-level committee to study "the operations and methods of the Federal Bureau of Investigation." When it became clear that the administration was not going to act, the NLG mounted its own investigation. It analyzed the FBI materials that had been released at the Coplon trial and issued a report in January 1950 noting the illegalities of the Bureau's operations and again calling on Truman to investigate. "On a strictly numerical basis," the NLG report concluded, "the FBI may commit more federal crimes than it ever detects." [60]

Many of those crimes had been committed against the National Lawyers Guild. The Bureau had a protracted vendetta against the guild. From 1940 on, FBI agents routinely burglarized its offices and planted illegal wiretaps on its phones and on those of its leading members. Hoover had also tried to persuade several Attorneys General to cite the NLG as a subversive organization. The absence of any evidence linking the guild to the CP, as well as Tom Clark's reluctance to target an organization in which he had friends, kept it from being officially listed. Unofficially, however, Hoover did what he could to undermine the group and sabotage its campaign against the Bureau. This was not too difficult, for the FBI's buggings and burglaries ensured that it had full information about the guild's strategy. [61]

Hoover and his aides used that information to head off the NLG's demand for an investigation of the FBI. They peppered the Attorney General and the White House with so much derogatory material on the guild that Truman came to view its leaders as "crackpots . . . who like very much to stir up trouble." The Bureau also ensured that timely red-baiting by its friends in Congress and the press would distract public attention from the content of the NLG's charges. On the day before the organization was to hold a press conference on its about-to-be-released report on the FBI, HUAC member Richard Nixon called for an investigation of the guild "to determine the truth or falsity of charges that it is being used as a Communist front organization." The smears were effective; the NLG's report — the most serious attempt to investigate the Bureau until the Watergate years — had no impact. And the guild, put on the defensive by constant FBI-inspired harassment throughout the 1950s, lost all access to an audience outside the tiny remnants of the American left. [62]

From the Bureau's perspective, the kind of damage control that it employed against the NLG was necessary if it was to protect the real heart of its operations, the collection of information for its files. Because of the extent of the FBI's illegal activities, it is easy to overlook how much of the material it accumulated, though obviously constituting a serious invasion of individual rights, had been acquired in perfectly legal ways. When, for example, the Bureau decided to investigate the United Electrical, Radio and Machine Workers of America in May 1941, it began by subscribing to the union's newspaper. It collected literally tons of press clippings, pamphlets, congressional reports, and other published items. Hoover's men also went to public meetings and demonstrations, mainly to take notes on the speeches and collect handouts. They even did research in libraries.[63]

FBI agents also carried out the more classic gumshoe operations that are normally associated with them. They put people under surveillance, though usually on a sporadic basis. Bureau resources were hardly inexhaustible and mounting a full-time reconnaissance was, to put it mildly, extremely labor intensive. Among their other legal, though hardly unobjectionable, practices were such activities as checking out the license plates of cars parked outside political meetings and soliciting information from professional anti-Communists like J. B. Matthews and Alfred Kohlberg.[64]

The Bureau used more intrusive and often illegal methods to keep track of what the people it was investigating did outside the public eye. It rifled through their trash, intercepted their mail, broke into their homes and offices, and planted illegal microphones and wiretaps. These procedures seem to have been routine. Almost every FBI file I saw contained some evidence of an illegal break-in, trash cover, or electronic surveillance. The Bureau usually did not, though it probably could have, obtain search warrants or other legal permits for these operations. It preferred secrecy, since it did not want to risk its reputation by revealing the extent of its political investigations. This type of illegally obtained evidence did have one major shortcoming: it could not be used in court. But since much of the Bureau's anticommunist intelligence gathering was not intended to produce criminal indictments, the formal inadmissibility of its results was irrelevant.[65]

Illegal entries were common. Between 1947 and 1951 the FBI burglarized the National Lawyers Guild's Washington offices at least fourteen times. The Communist party's New York headquarters was broken into so routinely that, as one agent later noted, it had been "burgled more than a fur company in the Bronx." These "black bag jobs," as they were known, also targeted regional party headquarters as well as the offices of front groups, left-wing unions, dissenting journalists, and attorneys. They yielded such otherwise unobtainable materials as membership lists and internal corre- spondence and enabled the Bureau to plant or service microphones. Major operations, often requiring nearly two dozen agents, break-ins were presti- gious assignments within the Bureau. "We picked only the top people for bag jobs," explained a former assistant director, "men with nerves of steel. We didn't send lunkheads off on those jobs."[66]

The FBI also engaged in the illegal wiretapping and electronic bug- ging of the subjects of its investigations. Roosevelt had allowed the Bureau to use wiretaps if national security was involved; and Hoover, as was his wont, stretched his mandate far beyond the limited authority he had re- ceived. Theoretically all the FBI's wiretaps and microphone installations were supposed to be approved by the Attorney General, but many were not. Even so, the Justice Department's records reveal that during the late 1940s and 1950s, the Bureau had several hundred authorized bugs and wiretaps.[67] G-men listened in to all the usual suspects — the CP, the NLG, the left-wing unions, front groups, and individuals ranging from party functionaries, la- bor leaders, and journalists to the physicist J. Robert Oppenheimer.[68]

Identified in Bureau files as coming from "an anonymous source" or "a confidential source who had furnished reliable information in the past," the material obtained from break-ins and wiretaps was often used in coun- terintelligence operations against the people and organizations from whom it had been collected. Thus, for example, Hoover and his men exploited the information they got from breaking into the National Lawyers Guild's office to neutralize the impact of that organization's campaign against the Bureau. While it is unclear whether the FBI gave plant managers the information about their local union's negotiating strategies that it had picked up from its wiretaps and bugs, it certainly passed on illegally obtained intelligence to the Justice Department.[69]

The most egregious such leaks came from the Bureau's illegal surveil- lance of the NLG and the left-wing lawyers who were its leading members. Because they were among the few attorneys willing to handle communist- related cases, guild lawyers were involved in many of the key legal battles of the early Cold War and the FBI's illegal activities may well have seriously tainted those cases. The Bureau, for example, had a bug on the phone of one of the Hollywood Ten's lawyers and passed on details about the defense team's legal strategies to the Justice Department attorney in charge of the case. It did the same with the material it got from a "confidential source" (possibly a bug or break-in) that provided information about the CP's defense in the first Smith Act trial. Between 1948 and 1951, when the FBI was tapping their office phone, the Washington attorneys Joseph Forer and David Rein dealt with over twenty cases that reached the Supreme Court. Had the justices known of these bugs, who knows what the legal history of the period might have been.[70]

In the mid-fifties the FBI began to use its undercover operations for harassment as well as information gathering. To a large extent, this switch, which was formalized by the August 1956 creation of the Counterintelligence Program, or COINTELPRO, as it was called, was just a codification and intensification of what the Bureau was already doing. Prompted by a series of recent Supreme Court decisions that had thrown out many of the government's cases against the CP, Hoover and his men decided to use dirty tricks instead of criminal prosecutions to neutralize the party. Informers were to become agents provocateurs, to spread rumors and promote dissension within the ranks. "Snitch jackets," falsified documents that created the suspicion that someone was an FBI informer, were planted on party stalwarts. There were also leaks to the media, anonymous letters, IRS audits, attempts to get people fired, and disruptions of public activities by encouraging building owners to cancel meetings. All told, the Bureau mounted over 1,330 anticommunist COINTELPRO actions. But it did not advertise them. As with so many of the FBI's other countersubversive activities, COINTELPRO was secret and unauthorized. When Hoover eventually informed his superiors in the Eisenhower and Kennedy administrations about the program's existence, he did so in a misleading way that concealed the extent of its illegality.[71]

The Bureau was proud of its surreptitious activities. In a 1947 memo to Assistant Director Ladd, J. Patrick Coyne, the FBI agent who would become Hoover's man at the National Security Council, boasted about the material the Bureau got from the "repeated black bag jobs performed by our Agents in Los Angeles." But he then admitted that valuable as that material was, he needed more live informants. Informers were central to the FBI's anticommunist operations. Like all police forces, the Bureau relied on information that only insiders could give. Accordingly, the FBI was always looking to recruit new people to spy on the party and other left-wing groups. The special agents who developed such informers, like the men who handled the "black bag jobs," got rewarded with raises and commendations.[72]

The FBI used all kinds of informants, not just the stereotypical double agent who had penetrated the CP and its front groups to reveal their secrets to the feds. There were paid informers — in Bureau terminology "informants," a euphemism no doubt designed to avoid the negative connotations of the word "informer." There were also "confidential sources," a varied assortment of men and women who volunteered information to the Bureau. Some were ex-Communists; others were individuals whose occupations made them useful, like taxi drivers, bank employees, and university registrars. The FBI also got information from people in organizations like the Association of Catholic Trade Unionists who reported on their communist rivals as well as from someone like Ronald Reagan, no doubt the Bureau's most illustrious "confidential source," who briefed the FBI on the political activities of his colleagues in the Screen Actors Guild during the 1940s and 1950s.[73]

The Bureau recruited its sources in different ways. Its defense plant informants, for example, often belonged to patriotic groups like the American Legion or else were friends and relatives of the FBI's own employees. A few informants, like Herbert Philbrick, the Boston advertising man who seems to have been one of the Bureau's favorite informers, apparently volunteered for the job out of patriotism — or at least were willing to do so once the FBI approached them. Others may have been coerced into becoming informers. When desperate for information, the Bureau was ready "to adopt shock tactics" and use what Hoover called "the utmost moral persuasion" of a subpoena with its "background" threat of perjury. The FBI also used economic pressure, as the following memo from the Baltimore field office in 1953 reveals: "Office advised that they are going to attempt to develop [name deleted] as an informant by pointing out to her that if she did not cooperate with them, she would undoubtedly lose her employment."[74]

Though the numbers fluctuated, the FBI seems to have had about a thousand informers within the CP and its front groups during the late 1940s and 1950s. Many of them were African Americans. It had put an enormous effort into recruiting its informants and had, in fact, managed to insinuate some of them, like the brothers Morris and Jack Childs, into the highest levels of the party. Roughly half of these informers were unpaid volunteers, taking occasional Bureau money for their party dues or *Daily Worker* subscriptions. The others were on some kind of retainer that would, a 1953 memorandum by one of Hoover's top aides noted, "enable them to devote their time to the service." The stipends varied from the token payments of up to ten dollars a month that defense plant informants got during World War II to the one to two hundred dollars a month paid the men and women who surfaced at the first Smith Act trial.[75]

Informers got other rewards as well. The FBI sometimes helped them find jobs and it eased their way through security clearance procedures. During the Korean War, it intervened with the Selective Service system to get draft deferments for those "whose work is vital to our internal security program." It also arranged for some of the informants who surfaced at major trials to make "contact with a reliable publisher."[76]

One of the main reasons why the Bureau was willing to do such favors for its informers was that it needed to keep their loyalty and ensure that they didn't embarrass the FBI. Controlling these people was, Assistant Director Ladd explained, "a major problem." To begin with, some informers began to have second thoughts about what they were doing. As Communists, they were pariahs in Cold War America and suffered accordingly. Not only did his neighbors harass Robert Dunham, an Ohio informant who had been in the party for thirteen years, but they would not let their children play with his six kids. Moreover, once an informant surfaced in a trial or congressional committee hearing, he or she would be excoriated as a "stool pigeon" by former comrades and their attorneys. It was not a pleasant experience and Hoover and his aides recognized that some informers were unhappy with their lot.[77]

An even greater headache was the unstable characters on the Bureau's payroll. Matt Cvetic, the undercover "hero" of the film *I Was a Communist for the FBI,* was a real embarrassment. The FBI had terminated his services early in 1950 "due to the excessive financial demands that he was continually making on the Bureau and the fact that he had revealed his confidential relationship with the Bureau on several occasions despite repeated warnings to the contrary." But the FBI could not keep Cvetic from talking with the press nor from giving HUAC the names of other informers. Harvey Matusow was another self-promoter. Even before he recanted and confessed that he had fabricated much of his testimony, Matusow sought to exploit his past as a Communist for the FBI. He wrote articles, gave speeches, and testified before any forum he could find.[78]

Hoover and his aides were furious and fretted about the possibility that other informers might also be tempted to cash in on their experiences and do something that would damage their credibility and that of the Bureau. They cautioned their subordinates not to recruit anybody who was "mentally or emotionally unbalanced" or had a "tendency . . . to brag or emphasize his own importance, which tendency might later result in his approaching the newspapers." But the FBI had little leverage. Because its ex-informants were independent contractors rather than employees, the Bureau had, Assistant Director Ladd noted, "no legal right to compel them to maintain their information in confidence." It could only use moral suasion, appeals to their patriotism, and hints about the "derogatory information" in their files. It did try to buy some of them off, making lump-sum payments to Budenz and its other key witnesses as a form of "insurance" to keep them from embarrassing the FBI or saying something that might destroy the value of their future testimony.[79]

Maintaining the credibility of its informants was crucial. If it became known that, like Harvey Matusow, the Bureau's undercover informers had been lying about their experiences in the party, the elaborate ideological edifice that Hoover and the rest of the anticommunist network had so painstakingly constructed would fall apart. That edifice had, in fact, been built on perjury. Witnesses shaded the truth because it enabled them to give the kind of testimony that the government needed in order to get a conviction. This was especially the case in Smith Act trials and other anticommunist proceedings where it was necessary to show that the CP was teaching or advocating "force and violence."[80]

The FBI recognized that some of its star informers were embroidering their original stories to reveal "startling facts which . . . had not been previously reported to the Bureau." Budenz was a serious problem. "It should be borne in mind," Ladd warned the Director in May 1948, after the former *Daily Worker* editor had just made some explosive allegations about the CP's inroads into the American government, "that Budenz apparently is inclined to make sensational charges which the press interprets as startling new information when, in fact, the information is old and not completely substantiated by actual facts." The FBI catalogued the discrepancies in its informants' statements but did not make them public. As one of Hoover's aides explained in 1955, "It is to the Bureau's best interest that Louis Budenz be kept in high esteem by the public since he has testified on so many occasions for the Government."[81]

To what extent did the FBI encourage or at least wink at such prevarications? Agents could apparently be quite persuasive. Ethel Rosenberg's sister-in-law, Ruth Greenglass, recalled that during her interrogations "at a certain point the agents become friends, they can elicit whatever they want from you." The Bureau's files also contain many references to interviews in which the agents reported that they helped someone "refresh his recollection." They asked specific questions about specific groups or individuals, thus making it possible for a cagey operator to figure out what kind of information the FBI was seeking.[82]

The Bureau also supplied its informants with a framework into which they could fit their stories. Ten days of "detailed questioning" during his initial FBI debriefing helped Budenz understand the "conspiratorial activities" of Gerhart Eisler. "If it were not for our detailed questioning of Budenz," J. Patrick Coyne explained in a 1946 memo about Budenz's forthcoming memoir,

> I strongly suspect that his book would not be anywhere near as effective as it is in its present form because until our interviews with him took place he was unaware of the true nature of his association with various individuals named in the book who are unquestionably Soviet agents.

Unquestionably. Coyne's remarks indicate that the FBI had a ready-made scenario into which it plugged the information about American Communism that it accumulated. Hoover and his agents shared a worldview that made it possible for them to process the material they were collecting in such a way that it bolstered their own exaggerated perception of a communist threat. They regarded defense plant strikes as sabotage, conversations with Soviet diplomats as spying. The Bureau's educational campaigns ensured that these interpretations got wide dissemination, especially when they became part of the record in highly publicized criminal trials.[83]

★

Still, the FBI did not succeed in all its missions. It never, for example, managed to round up all the party leaders who went underground when the CP sent them into hiding in 1951. Though powerful, Hoover wasn't all-powerful, nor did his agency have unlimited resources. Its files record a litany of complaints about investigations that could not be pursued for lack of manpower. And its agents were not always as competent as the Bureau's publicity alleged. Outsiders were sometimes dismayed when they encountered the narrow-mindedness and provincialism of some of Hoover's men. In July 1953, the president of the Bar Association of the City of New York complained to President Eisenhower about the FBI's loyalty check on the well-known public official John J. McCloy. "I was asked if he could be trusted with classified documents and information." [84]

Nonetheless, though the FBI's investigations may have been more inept than was recognized at the time, its bureaucratic politicking was world-class. If it would further his double mission of destroying American Communism and building the FBI, Hoover was even willing to take on his own superiors in the Justice Department and the White House. And he usually won.

Of all the presidents Hoover served, Harry Truman may well have been the least sympathetic to the Director's operations. He did not share Hoover's fears about "the Communist 'bugaboo.'" Moreover, though he mouthed the standard liberal line about the Bureau's professionalism, in private Truman distrusted the FBI. In a 1947 memo, written during the height of a battle between Hoover and the Civil Service Commission over the loyalty-security program, one of Truman's aides noted: "Pres. feels very strongly anti-FBI and sides positively with [Civil Service Commissioners] Mitchell and Perkins. Wants to be sure and hold F.B.I. down, afraid of 'Gestapo.'" Nonetheless, the president was too experienced a politician to risk a confrontation and he kept his reservations from the public. [85]

Despite Truman's circumspect behavior, Hoover viewed the administration as an adversary. He did not openly let his superiors know that he opposed them. Still, the lukewarm quality of his allegiance must have been obvious. In the summer of 1950, for example, when the White House was futilely trying to keep Congress from passing the anticommunist law that became known as the McCarran Act, it asked the Director to issue a statement against the measure. Hoover refused. He would do nothing to help the administration and, in fact, covertly maneuvered to hurt it. Though ostensibly nonpartisan, he had aligned himself with the GOP by the late 1940s and supported the Republican presidential candidates in 1948 and 1952.[86]

The Director's hostility had been building for years as he fretted about the administration's seeming indifference to the problem of Communists in government and its failure to act on the FBI's information about them. Not only was he upset that the government had not fired all the alleged subversives his agents had uncovered, but he was terrified that the negative reaction to the administration's supposed inertia might rub off on his beloved Bureau and damage its reputation.[87]

As the early Cold War cases unfolded, Hoover and his aides began to take precautions. While they continued to press for the removal of suspected subversives from federal jobs, they also began to defend the Bureau's record by complaining to friendly journalists and congressmen. In every case — Carl Marzani, Alger Hiss, or Elizabeth Bentley's spy ring — Hoover's grievance was always the same: the Bureau had been on the job, the rest of the administration had not. In an early 1947 letter to HUAC member Karl Mundt, the Director gave his version of the Marzani case:

> It will thus be seen that the FBI had established Marzani's Communist Party affiliations and activities as early as the spring of 1942 and had brought them to the attention of the proper officials of the government but that these officials declined to take action upon the case.

The Treasury Department, where many members of Bentley's "Silvermaster Ring" were employed, was especially delinquent. Despite the FBI's warnings, it did not rush to dismiss all the people Bentley had fingered.[88]

The main target of the Director's wrath during the late 1940s, however, was much closer to home, his own associates in the Justice Department. As with so many of Hoover's vendettas, the conflicts involved both turf and ideology. Like Truman, Tom Clark, Hoover's immediate superior, did not share the FBI's alarmist view of the communist menace. When he took over the Justice Department in 1945, he later recalled, "there was a large increase, a phenomenal increase in reports that I would get from him with reference to alleged Communist infiltration." Most of these reports "were very general," others, he remembered, "were just fantastic." He soon had an assistant screen them for him.[89] Hoover, for his part, felt that the department was not adequately protecting the FBI's reputation. He did not keep these feelings to himself. "It is an outrage to submit the Bureau to such unjustified criticism of its operation," Hoover protested to the Attorney General after a Justice Department handout made it seem as if the FBI had not warned the OSS and the State Department about Carl Marzani. "This is by no means the first time in which the Bureau's operations have been improperly portrayed in Departmental press releases." The Director was equally infuriated when "the gabby Dept. crowd" ruined his Bureau's cases and threatened its reputation by leaking unauthorized materials from the files.[90]

Ever since Hoover had subverted Attorney General Biddle's order to end the Custodial Detention List by renaming it and keeping its existence a secret, he had been hiding his agency's most sensitive operations from his superiors. Though Hoover was able to persuade Tom Clark to authorize the Security Index in 1946, he did not tell him that the program had never stopped functioning. Nor did he tell Clark or his successors about the "Communist Index" and other lists of potential subversives that the FBI had compiled as adjuncts to the Security Index.[91]

Hoover and his aides also concealed many of their break-ins and wiretaps from the department. The Bureau simply stopped reporting its surreptitious entries after Attorney General Howard McGrath decided that he could no longer consent to them for the purpose of planting bugging devices. Even after the administration changed and Eisenhower's Attorney General Herbert Brownell reauthorized such operations, the FBI still kept most of them secret. It also lied about the targets of its taps. Since Hoover knew that Truman's Justice Department opposed an investigation of the National Lawyers Guild, he did not tell his superiors that he had tapped its office phone. Instead he sought authorization to listen in to the phone of a man named Robert Silverstein (coincidentally the NLG's executive director) in order "to follow the activities of the Communist Party in Washington, D.C." Sometimes the Bureau even concealed its legitimate operations. When Hoover ordered his men to draw up a brief for prosecuting the Communist party in 1945, he kept the document's existence a secret and did not send a copy to the Justice Department until 1948. Nor did he tell either the Attorney General or Truman about the Venona decrypts.[92]

Hoover struggled with his superiors about other matters as well. He was, for example, annoyed at the department's unwillingness to add more groups like the NLG and the left-wing labor unions to the Attorney General's list. The FBI and the Justice Department also disagreed about the need for new legislation. His superiors repeatedly rejected the Director's appeal for a law to authorize the FBI's custodial detention program. Taking such a request to Congress would, they claimed, "only bring on a loud and acrimonious discussion" and provide an opening for the administration's congressional opponents to exploit its political vulnerabilities or enact a deeply repressive anticommunist measure. Hoover, whose popularity insulated his agency from such concerns, naturally had no such fears.[93]

The most serious conflicts were about prosecuting Communists, especially about the advisability of initiating specific cases. Sometimes the Bureau was eager to go to court and the department hung back, sometimes it was the reverse. Some of these conflicts seem trivial, but they rankled, nonetheless, and may have encouraged Hoover and his men to look for alternative ways to punish Communists. In 1947, for example, after the department finally gave in to Bureau pressure to take some kind of action against Gerhart Eisler, the Director was annoyed that it had arrested the alleged Comintern agent as an enemy alien instead of seeking a criminal indictment or trying to deport him. The Bureau had also apparently hoped that the Justice Department would make a criminal case out of the Soviet attempt to contact J. Robert Oppenheimer during World War II. "The facts," Assistant Director Ladd reminded Hoover in November 1947, "were presented to the Department and prosecution was declined." The disappointed Director fired off another memo to the Attorney General about the case.[94]

Naturally, the most serious clashes occurred in those cases where the FBI's reputation was on the line. One of the earliest and most damaging of these conflicts involved *Amerasia*. Ever since OSS and FBI investigators, alerted by the publication of a secret OSS report in the January 1945 issue, discovered piles of classified documents in the magazine's offices, Hoover had been eager for a prosecution. Truman also wanted to prosecute "as an example to other persons in the Government Service who may be divulging confidential information." During the course of its investigations, the Bureau tapped the phones of the leading suspects and surreptitiously entered their homes and offices. Despite the fears of the FBI's own legal counsel that the Bureau's illegitimate activities might scuttle the case, Hoover felt there would be enough legally obtained evidence for a conviction. And the Justice Department, expecting that at least one of the culprits would confess, agreed to risk a prosecution.[95]

On June 6, 1945, the government arrested six people — *Amerasia's* editor, Philip Jaffe, and his coeditor, Kate Mitchell, Andrew Roth, a lieutenant in the Office of Naval Intelligence, journalist Mark Gayn, and State Department employees Emanuel Larsen and John Stewart Service. None of them confessed and the Justice Department did not press them very hard. Harvey Klehr and Ronald Radosh imply that a political deal had been made to abort the prosecution. It is also possible that the department realized the potential weakness of its case and wanted to cut its losses. In any event, when the United States Attorneys went before a grand jury, they could only get indictments against Jaffe, Roth, and Larsen. Larsen then learned that the FBI had been in his apartment. At that point, the Justice Department agreed to a plea bargain with Larsen and Jaffe and dropped the charges against Roth.[96]

J. Edgar Hoover was furious. He had become suspicious about the department's lack of enthusiasm for the case, noting on a memo from an aide that "certain aspects of this matter 'smell.'" The deal with Larsen was the last straw. "Of all the wishy washy vacillations this takes the prize." The publicity about the case did not reflect well on the Bureau and Hoover felt betrayed by the administration. He was particularly upset about the Justice Department's failure to indict Service, a foreign service officer whose "political sympathies," the Director told the Attorney General, "are with the Chinese Communists." During the course of a wiretap on Thomas Corcoran, a former Roosevelt adviser whom Truman had asked the Bureau to check out, the FBI inadvertently learned of the behind-the-scenes effort to have the Justice Department exonerate Service. For someone with the countersubversive mind-set of J. Edgar Hoover, the evidence was clear: the failure to push the prosecution was part of a liberal plot to cover up a major espionage case.[97]

Though Hoover could not openly challenge his superiors' actions in the *Amerasia* case, he worked covertly to keep the charges alive. He leaked information to a right-wing congressman whose allegations led to a 1946 investigation by a House Judiciary subcommittee. The probe got scant attention at the time; the committee report said little about *Amerasia*, calling instead for a better employee loyalty program. The case resurfaced in 1950, when Joe McCarthy raised the issue. By then, Alfred Kohlberg and his cohorts in the anticommunist network had blended the charges about the administration's mishandling of the *Amerasia* case into their broader assault on the State Department's "loss of China." Within the FBI the case was a constant irritant, contributing significantly to Hoover's growing antagonism toward the Truman administration.[98]

Another serious and long-lived dispute between Hoover and his superiors involved Elizabeth Bentley's alleged spy ring. This time, the department wanted to go to court and the Bureau did not. The FBI had been unable to find evidence to corroborate Bentley's story and Hoover warned the Attorney General that he "was very reluctant to see this case prosecuted." Tom Clark, however, was eager to stage a major spy trial and so sent the case to a grand jury. As Hoover predicted, the venture failed. For nearly ten months, the grand jury sat in New York City's federal courthouse listening to federal prosecutors interrogate suspected spies and ex-communist informers. But because most of the people Bentley named either denied the charges against them or took the Fifth Amendment, it was impossible to substantiate her allegations. By April 1948, it had become clear that there would be no espionage indictment. Hoover was right — and furious. He had known all along that the evidence was too weak to sustain a prosecution and had been urging the Justice Department to get the protagonists fired instead.[99]

The failed prosecution of Judith Coplon may have been the final blow. By that point, in the spring of 1949, the relationship between Hoover and the Truman administration was probably already beyond repair and the Justice Department's decision to produce the FBI materials that Coplon had purloined rather than forgo her prosecution only reinforced the Director's antagonism. From the Bureau's perspective, the outcome was catastrophic. Not only did the government lose the case on appeal, but the FBI had been seriously embarrassed by the release of its records and revelations of its illegal wiretaps. The case rankled for years. As Hoover complained to Morris Ernst late in 1953, "We have not yet recovered from the set backs we suffered when 26 reports were ordered produced in the record in the first Coplon case as a result of a decision made by the then Attorney General."[100]

By then, however, Hoover had gotten his revenge on Harry Truman. The new Republican regime under Eisenhower was eager to show that it could handle internal security matters more competently than its predecessor. It resuscitated the Bentley case after a routine reorganization of the Justice Department's files revealed that Truman had appointed Treasury official Harry Dexter White to head the International Monetary Fund *after* having received FBI reports about White's alleged espionage activities. Attorney General Brownell broke the story on November 6, 1953. The revelation was dynamite. It reopened the earlier Communists-in-government issue with a vengeance. Brownell was accusing Truman of deliberately ignoring the FBI's warnings about White and permitting an alleged Soviet agent to take a high-level position in an important international agency. Truman immediately countered Brownell's charges, claiming that Hoover had not tried to block White's appointment.[101]

But he hadn't tried to push it through, either. In February 1946, at the time White's IMF nomination was pending, the Director had sent a summary of the charges against White to the State and Treasury Departments as well as to the White House. When Bureau officials discussed the situation with the cabinet members involved, they explained that since the FBI still had White under surveillance and had not found any evidence to corroborate Bentley's account, it "would be undesirable" to air the case in public. Because the Senate had already confirmed the nomination, it was decided that unless White would resign voluntarily, Truman would have to let the appointment go through. To do otherwise would provoke a major uproar. The FBI director had presented the administration with a no-win situation.[102]

In 1953, however, Hoover wanted to ensure that a more favorable account of his agency's role reached the public. At the same time, Brownell was anxious to have the popular Director rescue him from the charge that he had made a purely partisan attack on the previous administration. Accordingly, Hoover went before the Senate Internal Security Subcommittee, where he countered Truman's story and exonerated the Bureau. The FBI had, the Director claimed, repeatedly warned members of the Truman administration that there were subversives in the government only to have its warnings repeatedly ignored. Given Hoover's reputation for being above politics, his testimony provided stunning reinforcement for the partisan accusation that the Truman administration had been soft on Communism.[103]

As he leafed through the hundreds of congratulatory letters and telegrams he received after his Senate appearance, the Director must have been

1 Steve Nelson after refusing to testify before HUAC in 1948. He was soon to be indicted for contempt of Congress, as well as for sedition, by both the federal government and that of Pennsylvania.

2 A Russian War Relief rally at Madison Square Garden during World War II. The 20,000 spectators and the eminence of the speakers, who included Roosevelt's alter ego, Harry Hopkins, and New York mayor Fiorello La Guardia, testify to the respectability of Communism during World War II.

3 The professional anti-Communist Benjamin Mandel before HUAC in 1949.

4 J. B. Matthews, whose letterhead collection and hospitality made him the hub of the anti-communist network, at the time he was appointed staff director of Senator Joseph McCarthy's Senate Investigations Subcommittee in 1953.

5 "When civilization is in mortal danger," the chief counsel of the Senate Internal Security Subcommittee explained, "the ex-Communist is one of the most valuable members of society." And no one was more valuable than the voluble former editor of the *Daily Worker* Louis Budenz, here displaying his expert knowledge of CP propaganda as he testifies at a deportation hearing in 1948.

6 Elizabeth Bentley was an equally ubiquitous professional witness, shown here in one of her earliest congressional appearances, in July 1948.

7 Liberals could be anti-Communists, too. The ACLU's cocounsel, New York attorney Morris Ernst, admired J. Edgar Hoover and urged the exposure of party members in every organization they belonged to.

8 The so-called China Lobby man, New York businessman Alfred Kohlberg, displaying some of the documents he provided to back up McCarthy's 1950 charges that communist agents in the State Department had betrayed China to Mao Zedong.

9 Gerhart Eisler at his home in Queens, soon after he was identified as Stalin's top American agent by Louis Budenz in October 1946.

10 Igor Gouzenko, the former code clerk from the Soviet embassy in Ottawa, whose defection in September 1945 provided the first concrete evidence that Communists spied for the Soviet Union during World War II, shown here (*with hood*) in an interview with columnist Drew Pearson in 1954.

11 Alger Hiss, soon to be convicted of perjury in conjunction with Whittaker Chambers's allegations that he had spied for the Soviet Union, tries to identify Chambers's picture as he testifies before HUAC in August 1948.

12 Some HUAC members in March 1948 are (*left to right*): Richard B. Vail, committee chair Parnell Thomas, John McDowell, committee counsel Robert Stripling, and Richard Nixon.

13 J. Edgar Hoover's finest hour as he testifies before the Senate Internal Security Subcommittee on November 17, 1953, that the Truman administration had not taken his advice about Harry Dexter White in 1946. Clyde Tolson, his longtime sidekick, is on his left. Louis Nichols, the FBI's chief public relations man, is on his right.

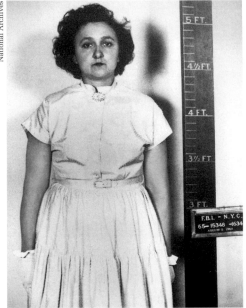

15 Ethel Rosenberg in the official FBI mug shot of her after she was arrested in August 1950, in order to put pressure on her husband to confess.

14 Julius Rosenberg, emerging from a federal van after his conviction for espionage in 1951.

16 Judith Coplon, the Justice Department employee arrested in the company of a Soviet engineer on a New York City street with a package of government documents in her purse, shown here as she appeals her conviction for espionage in 1949.

17 Carl Marzani, the former State Department employee whose 1947 conviction made him the first person to go to prison for perjury during the Cold War.

18 Harold Christoffel, the former president of UAW Local 248 at the Allis-Chalmers plant in Milwaukee, Wisconsin, appearing before the House Labor Committee in March 1947 to deny Louis Budenz's charge that he had organized a strike in 1940 at the CP's behest.

19 The Communist Party's top leaders arrive for their Smith Act trial in 1949. Emerging from the paddy wagon are (*from back to front*) Benjamin Davis, Eugene Dennis, and Henry Winston.

20 Judge Harold Medina, though hardly an unbiased adjudicator, became something of a folk hero for his courtroom sparring with the Smith Act defendants and their attorneys.

21 Senator Joseph McCarthy (*left*) and his committee's chief counsel Roy Cohn (*right*) at the Army-McCarthy hearings in the spring of 1954.

22 A more powerful, if less notorious, anticommunist politician than Joe McCarthy, Senator Patrick McCarran chaired the Senate Internal Security Subcommittee whose hearings into the so-called loss of China in the early 1950s had a disastrous impact on American foreign policy.

23 Johns Hopkins professor Owen Lattimore, initially identified as the main Soviet agent in the United States by Joe McCarthy, testifies before McCarran in July 1951.

24 The most eminent individual to lose a security clearance during the 1950s, the former Manhattan Project scientific director J. Robert Oppenheimer in his office at the Institute for Advanced Studies in June 1954.

25 Lawyer and union activist Doris Brin Walker at the time she was fired by the Cutter Laboratories because she was a Communist. Her 1949 dismissal was upheld by the Supreme Court in 1956.

26 For years, businessmen, politicians, and federal officials tried to deport the Australian-born labor leader Harry Bridges. Here he protests the expulsion of the left-wing unions from the CIO at its convention in 1949. To his left, the Mine-Mill secretary-treasurer Maurice Travis (*with eyepatch*) and its attorney Nathan Witt.

27 The San Cristobal Valley Ranch in the 1940s or 1950s.

28 Soon after the publication of his memoir, *False Witness,* early in 1955, the ever-inventive Harvey Matusow tells the Senate Internal Security Subcommittee that much of his earlier testimony about the Communist party was untrue.

29 Clinton Jencks is the tall, blond man on the left in this still from *Salt of the Earth*. Rosaura Revueltas, the actress holding the young child in the foreground, was deported before the film was completed. Juan Chacon, president of Mine-Mill Local 890, stands behind her.

30 The Hollywood Ten and their attorneys at the time of their arraignment for contempt of Congress early in 1948. They are (*left to right*): *first row, Salt of the Earth* director Herbert Biberman, attorney Martin Popper, former California attorney general Robert Kenny, Albert Maltz, Lester Cole; *second row,* Dalton Trumbo, John Howard Lawson, Alvah Bessie, Samuel Ornitz; *third row,* Ring Lardner, Jr., Edward Dmytryk, and Adrian Scott.

31 Paul Robeson *(left)* and W. E. B. DuBois in Paris at the Communist-sponsored peace conference, April 1949, at which Robeson claimed that American blacks would never go to war against the Soviet Union. Robeson was soon to be blacklisted and lose his passport, and DuBois would be indicted as an unregistered foreign agent.

proud of his Bureau's achievements.[104] Together Hoover and his men had alerted the rest of the nation to the alleged dangers of domestic Communism and then had created and operated much of the machinery that was used to combat that menace. Though the Bureau often tried to hide its tracks, the evidence that remains makes it clear that the FBI was the single most important component of the anticommunist crusade and the institution most responsible for its successes — and its inequities. The legacy of the Bureau's McCarthy era activities — both in the actual damage they inflicted as well as in the precedents that were set for expanding the government's illegal operations — still haunts us today.

★

CHAPTER 7

"IN THE GUTTER"

THE ANTICOMMUNISM OF JOE McCARTHY

ON NOVEMBER 24, 1953, a week after J. Edgar Hoover testified before the Senate Internal Security Subcommittee that former President Truman had ignored the FBI's warnings about Harry Dexter White, Joe McCarthy charged that the Eisenhower administration was also soft on Communism. The Wisconsin senator had gotten free air time to respond to Truman's denunciation of McCarthyism and, as often happened, McCarthy overstated his case. Though most of his speech contained the standard Republican charges that the Truman administration had been "crawling with Communists," he attacked his own party as well. He objected to Eisenhower's recent announcement that his administration had handled internal security so effectively that Communism would not be an issue in the 1954 elections. "The raw, harsh, unpleasant fact," McCarthy contended, "is that Communism is an issue and it will be an issue in 1954." Not only had the State Department still not fired John Paton Davies, a foreign service officer tainted by the so-called loss of China, but it had yet to get tough with the Chinese Communists and was still sending them "perfumed notes, following the style of the Truman-Acheson regime."[1]

McCarthy, as usual, had gotten his facts wrong. John Paton Davies had been fired three weeks before. And John Foster Dulles was hardly flirting with China. Like a little wind-up toy that bumps into objects but cannot stop until it runs down, the Wisconsin senator could not keep from attacking the nation's top officials. By directly taking on the Eisenhower administration, he had started on the self-destructive path that would lead to censure and his expulsion from the American political mainstream within a year. Because McCarthy was such an outrageous individual, observers both at the time and later have tended to view his career as equally aberrant, a temporary blip that may have roiled American politics during the early 1950s but was too anomalous to have much impact. Such an interpretation, however, places McCarthy in a vacuum, ignoring his connections to the broader anti-communist crusade and to the professional anti-Communists who flocked to his side.[2]

McCarthy gave their movement its name and, in return, they gave him his agenda and ammunition. As the point man of the anticommunist network, he brought to the cause enormous energy, a genius for publicity, and a refusal to play by the rules. He had always been a renegade. After entering politics as a local judge, he switched parties, lied about his military record, and then won election to the Senate in the Republican sweep of 1946 as a traditional Midwestern conservative. Since red-baiting was a common GOP campaign practice that year, McCarthy's use of the tactic against his Democratic opponent was unexceptional. Nor, except for his sleaziness, did he distinguish himself during his first few years in Washington. Under attack in Wisconsin for illegal campaign practices, he also took money from companies whose interests he furthered and he defended the German SS men responsible for the 1944 massacre of unarmed civilians and American POWs in Malmédy, Belgium. Throughout, he displayed the same crudeness, dishonesty, and lack of principles that later got labeled as McCarthyism. But until he latched onto the Communist issue, he remained largely unknown.[3]

All that changed on February 9, 1950, when he announced to the annual Lincoln Day Dinner of the Ohio County Women's Republican Club in Wheeling, West Virginia, that he held in his hand a list of 205 Communists in the State Department. He continued to allude to his lists over the next few days as he traveled through the Rocky Mountain states on a speaking tour for the Republican party. Pressed for specifics, he began to change the numbers and the charges. Perhaps it was only fifty-seven Communists, as he told reporters in Salt Lake City on February 10, or eighty-one, as he explained to the Senate ten days later. Maybe they weren't really "card-carrying" Communists, but "loyalty risks" or "people with Communist connections." His allegations would probably have been dismissed as just so much Republican hot air had Truman and the State Department not scrambled to rebut them, demanding that he supply them with every name he had. As a result, by the time McCarthy returned to Washington, he had thrown the administration onto the defensive and reinvigorated the GOP's charge that the Democrats were soft on Communism.[4]

Because he was such a flagrant self-promoter, the sincerity of McCarthy's commitment to anticommunism has long been open to doubt. He certainly came to it late — identifying himself with the Communists-in-government issue several years after other politicians had taken it up. At times, he even told his friends that he had embraced the issue to enhance his career. But he had never shied away from red-baiting and, if he was not at first a true believer, he soon became one. Long after expediency would have dictated greater moderation, he clung to the cause, determined to root out the Communist conspiracy that, he claimed, threatened the United States.[5]

If misrepresentations, threats, or outright lies were needed, he had no qualms about employing them. "I don't enjoy this task," he announced. "It is a dirty, disagreeable job, but a job which must be done." And he would liken it to his boyhood chore of killing the skunks that menaced his mother's chickens, "a dirty, foul, unpleasant, smelly job. And sometimes after it was done, people did not like to have us sit next to them in church." He gloried in his toughness, his image as an Irish barroom brawler who "deals with Commies via the fist" and "fights like a truck driver." Because of his notoriety, it became common to equate him with the use of unfair tactics against Communists. But, as we have seen, J. Edgar Hoover and many of the other professional anti-Communists also bent the rules where Communism was concerned.[6]

Even so, Joe McCarthy was noisier, more impulsive, and more skillful in gaining publicity than the rest of the anticommunist network. Newspapers were still the nation's leading source of information and McCarthy knew how to get his message on the front pages. He played for headlines, recognizing the importance of feeding reporters with the 1950s version of sound bites. He knew how to time his public statements to meet the wire services' constant demand for updated stories and how to provide the concrete details, names, and numbers that made his charges seem fresh. The more sensational his allegations, the better. "McCarthy was a dream story," the head of the *Chicago Tribune*'s Washington bureau recalled. "I wasn't off page one for four years."[7]

In many respects, the press was the Wisconsin senator's chief collaborator. It created the monster it then chronicled. The prevailing journalistic ethos of objectivity meant that most newspapers simply recorded McCarthy's charges without commenting on them or telling their readers how little substance those charges usually contained. McCarthy was, after all, a member of the United States Senate and few journalists during that simpler epoch would question the veracity of such a highly placed politician. As one early editorial writer noted, "It is unbelievable that a United States Senator would publicly and repeatedly make such charges if he did not have any evidence to support them." Eventually the press grew more skeptical but during the crucial early months of McCarthy's ascent, it was as credulous with regard to his allegations as the American Communist party had been about the Moscow trials of the 1930s. Even his enemies found it hard to believe that he actually lied. "Where there was so much smoke," the publisher of the anti-McCarthy *St. Louis Post-Dispatch* explained, "there must have been some fire."[8]

There certainly was plenty of *chutzpah.* McCarthy often had no idea what he was talking about. He had, for example, brought no list to Wheeling nor did he then know anything about the State Department's loyalty cases. For all his claims about presenting new information, his allegations of communist penetration of the government were identical to those made by other Republicans. In fact, his Wheeling speech actually contained several paragraphs lifted almost verbatim from one that Richard Nixon had delivered a few days before. The novelty was in the numbers. McCarthy's charges seemed too concrete and specific to be ignored. They were not, however, new. The names and numbers came from some lists compiled by loyalty investigators in the late 1940s. The lists had been circulating within the anticommunist community for years and were readily available to the right-wing journalists who wrote McCarthy's speeches. The individuals he identified, like John Stewart Service, the State Department official implicated in the *Amerasia* affair, or Gustavo Duran, an anti-Franco Spanish émigré who worked for the UN, had all been named before.[9]

But, because his charges were gaining attention, McCarthy began to

243

attract support. Once the GOP's leaders realized that he was hurting the Democrats, they embraced his campaign. Even the cerebral Robert Taft encouraged the Wisconsin brawler. "If one case doesn't work out," the Ohio Republican suggested, "bring up another." And, it appears, he secretly fed information to his noisy colleague.[10]

The anticommunist network was more open in its support. Even before Wheeling, McCarthy had been close to many of the nation's most powerful anti-Communists. Hoover, for example, had socialized with the Wisconsin senator since 1947; the two men dined out and went to the races together. Richard Berlin, the Hearst company's influential president, was a drinking companion. It was, therefore, quite understandable that McCarthy would solicit — and receive — a little help from his friends. The Hearst chain fixed him up with "a few good reporters" and provided the services of its in-house anticommunist expert J. B. Matthews. The collaboration ran in both directions, with columnists like George Sokolsky supplying information and then publicizing McCarthy's use of it. Hoover assisted as well, not only by leaking materials, but also by recruiting ex-FBI agents for the senator's staff. McCarthy also got information from what he called his "Loyal American Underground," disgruntled civil servants who illegally sent him personnel records on the federal employees he wanted to expose.[11]

One of McCarthy's most useful contacts was the New York lace importer Alfred Kohlberg. Obsessed with the notion that the nation's China policy had been subverted by Communists, Kohlberg had long been compiling information about the CP connections of the writers and public officials responsible for that policy. Ever since 1945, he and Benjamin Mandel, then still working for HUAC, had been looking for a way to publicize his charges. They were especially eager to expose the allegedly procommunist machinations of the Institute of Pacific Relations, an independent research organization that Kohlberg believed was running the State Department. Though he got some nibbles from the likes of Richard Nixon and the powerful Senate Republican Styles Bridges, nobody mounted a full-scale investigation until McCarthy came along.[12]

The loss of China was just what the Wisconsin senator needed. For years, GOP conservatives had criticized the Truman administration's East Asian policy. The bipartisanship that had enabled Truman to fight the Cold War in Europe did not extend past Hawaii. Most Republican right-wingers were Asia-Firsters. During World War II, they had wanted the United States to concentrate on the Pacific. After the war, they continued to call for a stronger American commitment to Nationalist China and to condemn what they correctly saw as the State Department's bias toward Europe. In addition, of course, the administration's East Asian policy was easy to criticize, for, from the GOP's perspective, it had obviously failed. By the end of 1949, the Chinese mainland had fallen to the Communists.[13]

There was little that Washington could have done to prevent such an outcome. China had been convulsed by civil war for years. Chiang Kai-shek, whose corrupt and dictatorial Kuomintang (KMT) regime nominally controlled the country, had been fighting Mao Zedong and the Communists since 1927. When the Japanese invaded China ten years later at the start of World War II, Chiang offered little resistance. He wanted to save his army for a postwar showdown with the Communists. Mao, on the other hand, was deep in the interior of northwest China mobilizing peasants to fight the Japanese.[14]

Even before Pearl Harbor brought the United States officially into the war, Washington had been encouraging the Nationalists to stand up against Japan. Roosevelt and his advisers sent as much aid as they could to Chiang, while at the same time urging him to reform his government, eliminate corruption, make peace with the Communists, and fight the Japanese. It was a hopeless venture. Washington dispatched one special mission after another, but nothing worked. Chiang would not come to terms with Mao, nor would he let his army seriously engage the Japanese. Worse yet, although all the American diplomats on the scene warned that the KMT was heading for disaster, the Roosevelt administration created future problems by publicly denying reality and pretending that China was strong and Chiang was democratic.[15]

Once World War II ended, the civil war resumed. Nobody connected with the making of America's China policy wanted the Communists to win; nor did any of these people question Washington's basic commitment to the Nationalist regime. They wanted a strong, united China under a liberal government headed by the moderate elements of the KMT, but they were not optimistic that it could be achieved. China was so huge, Chiang Kai-shek's administration was so corrupt and his army so demoralized that there was little Washington could do to save him — especially since neither the government nor the American people were willing to commit the enormous resources of manpower and money required to influence the outcome of the civil war. The Soviet Union was not a factor. In return for major concessions in Manchuria, Stalin was willing to recognize Chiang's control of the rest of China. Until the final moments of the civil war, he conspicuously refrained from sending aid to Mao Zedong.

The only, albeit remote, hope for avoiding a total debacle was to induce the two sides to form some kind of coalition. At the end of 1945, Truman sent General George C. Marshall, the World War II Chief of Staff, to China to try to broker such a settlement. After a year of trying, Marshall admitted failure and brought his mission home. The civil war intensified. Though the United States sent hundreds of millions of dollars of aid to the Nationalists, it did little good. By the beginning of 1949, Chiang Kai-shek and his armies were in flight and the Communists were in Beijing.[16]

This was not what the American government wanted. Though its experienced China hands had few illusions about the nature of Chinese Communism, they were not convinced that Mao was Stalin's puppet. The State Department's initial response to the revolution was, therefore, to wait until the dust settled and then see if the new regime could be encouraged to act independently of Moscow. However, even before the Korean War rendered such a cautious policy unthinkable, the Truman administration had lost political control over its options in East Asia. Because none of the American policymakers had leveled with the public about the true situation of Chiang Kai-shek until it was too late, the GOP was able to take advantage of the perceived "loss" of China to mount a devastating attack on Truman and his advisers.[17]

What made this onslaught so effective was that the January 1950 perjury conviction of Alger Hiss enabled the Republicans to link their critique of the administration's foreign policy to the even more damaging Communists-in-government issue. The scenario, developed by Kohlberg and his allies, claimed that subversion within the State Department had precipitated the debacle. The supposed betrayal touched the highest levels of the Truman administration and included not only Secretary of State Dean Acheson and his predecessor, George Marshall, but just about every foreign service officer who had been in China. By downplaying the threat of Chinese Communism and withholding aid from the Nationalist regime, so Kohlberg and the others argued, these people had undermined Chiang Kai-shek and delivered Beijing to Moscow.[18]

McCarthy bought the package. From the start, many of his charges involved China. There was, for example, the Yalta Conference, where, the Wisconsin senator insisted, Hiss and the State Department's other subversives had supposedly betrayed the Chinese to Stalin. There was the *Amerasia* case, resuscitated by McCarthy to show how the retention of John Stewart Service, the China hand who had leaked documents to the magazine's editor, revealed the State Department's refusal to clean house. Instead of ignoring these allegations, the Truman administration and its congressional allies amplified them by appointing a special Senate committee under Maryland conservative Millard Tydings to investigate. Though the Democrats assumed that the panel would deflate McCarthy's charges, the Wisconsin senator and his fellow anti-Communists were thrilled. "You must be tickled pink at this chance to unload," Mandel wrote Kohlberg in the beginning of March 1950. "I told you the opportunity would come sooner or later."[19]

Much of the stuff Kohlberg was unloading as he helped McCarthy prepare for the Tydings hearings concerned the Institute of Pacific Relations. It was, therefore, no surprise that when the Wisconsin senator needed some new names to update his allegations, he would produce that of Owen Lattimore, the former editor of the IPR's journal, then teaching at the Johns Hopkins University. Kohlberg had been attacking the eminent sinologist for years. A brilliant linguist and prolific writer, Lattimore was one of the nation's leading commentators on East Asian affairs. Though he had no college or graduate degrees, he had grown up in Shanghai and had been one of the few Westerners to travel widely throughout China in the 1920s. Fascinated by the peoples and cultures of Central Asia, he had written several books about his adventures in Mongolia before joining the IPR staff in 1933. During the war, he served as the American government's liaison with Chiang Kai-shek and then headed the Office of War Information's Pacific operations. But he had never worked for the State Department.[20]

Nor had Lattimore been a Communist. If he harbored any attachment to a foreign regime, it was probably to the Mongols of Ulan Bator, not the Bolsheviks of Moscow. But he was a feisty, outspoken liberal who, like most of his fellow China experts, had few illusions about Chiang Kai-shek's corrupt and undemocratic regime. In 1941 Lattimore's left-of-center politics attracted the FBI's attention; though it later tapped his phone, read his books, and accumulated a massive file on him, it never found anything incriminating. McCarthy, however, needed someone to personify the so far unconvincing subversion narrative he was constructing and, no doubt encouraged by all the material he was receiving from Kohlberg and his allies, decided to make Lattimore his pièce de résistance.[21]

In his typical fashion, McCarthy milked his supposed revelation for all it was worth. He dropped hints that he was about to give Tydings the name of "the top espionage agent in the United States, the boss of Alger Hiss"; then he announced that he was "willing to stand or fall on this one." On March 26, columnist Drew Pearson revealed Lattimore's identity. Typically, McCarthy soon changed his story. The Johns Hopkins sinologist was no longer a spy. His role was far more important than mere espionage: he had been "the main architect of America's China policy." Lattimore, who was on a UN mission to Afghanistan at the time, quickly returned to deny McCarthy's charges. His indignant testimony before the Tydings committee seemed to deflate McCarthy's balloon.[22]

Enter Louis Budenz. In the spring of 1950, a few months after the first Smith Act trial had come to its successful conclusion, the former *Daily Worker* editor's reputation as the nation's leading expert on Communism had never been higher. If he could connect Lattimore to the party, McCarthy's charges might yet be believed. Both J. B. Matthews and Kohlberg contacted Budenz and found him willing to cooperate. Though his FBI files make it quite clear that he knew nothing about Lattimore, Budenz had soon tagged the Johns Hopkins professor as the CP's main conduit for influencing the nation's China policy. In his testimony before the Tydings committee, he claimed that his party superior Jack Stachel told him that the CP considered Lattimore to be a Communist and that he was identified as "L" or "XL" in the top-secret onionskin reports that circulated within the party's highest echelons. Budenz's testimony saved the day. He had so much prestige that even the Democrats on the Tydings committee deferred to him, treating his totally unsubstantiated charges as if they might in fact be true and thus giving plausibility to McCarthy's loss-of-China scenario.[23]

Even so, the Tydings committee's Democrats did not buy the Wisconsin senator's allegations. In his final report, Tydings denounced those charges as "a fraud and a hoax." But the committee's Republicans refused to sign the report, thus diluting its impact by making it seem a partisan white-wash of the administration rather than a serious investigation of the State Department's security problems. Tydings had failed; instead of muzzling McCarthy, his committee had publicized his charges.[24]

The outbreak of the Korean War just as Tydings was writing up his report strengthened McCarthy's position. With the United States on the verge of "losing" yet another East Asian nation to Communism, the Wisconsin senator's allegations of treason in high places no longer seemed quite so far-fetched. Liberals, who had never bought into the loss-of-China scenario, nonetheless found it hard to resist the surge of anticommunism that accompanied the conflict. In the summer of 1950, for example, as Congress debated a bill to force Communists and their front groups to register with the Attorney General, some of the Senate's leading liberals complained that the measure was not tough enough and sought to replace it with one that would round up subversives during an emergency. Though the liberals were obviously trying to protect themselves from appearing soft on Communism, their support for such a repressive piece of legislation gave additional legitimacy to Joe McCarthy and his cause.[25]

Further vindication came in November when Millard Tydings and a few other Democrats were defeated for reelection. McCarthy had a hand in the campaign against Tydings, channeling funds and consultants into the race and helping to coordinate a rather sleazy attempt to smear the Maryland senator by means of a doctored photograph that showed Tydings in a tête-à-tête with former CP head Earl Browder. Even without McCarthy's intervention, the incumbent senator might well have lost. Maryland's Democratic party was split and the conservative Tydings had alienated many of its traditional voters within the black community and labor movement. Still, McCarthy's efforts probably did have some impact, especially among Catholics, the Wisconsin senator's strongest supporters. In any event, whether or not McCarthy caused Tydings's downfall, most Senate Democrats believed that he had. And they were terrified.[26]

By the end of 1950, Joe McCarthy was riding high, bolstered by the aura of political invincibility that the fears of his opponents served to enhance. But it was more than cowardice that kept Senate moderates from curbing their unprincipled colleague. They also agreed with much of what he was doing. That consensus, expressed in the often-repeated statement "I agree with his goals, but not his methods," doomed all the early efforts to restrain McCarthy. Even people who questioned his "reckless" behavior, like Vermont's Senator Ralph Flanders, who a few years later would initiate the upper house's censure resolution against him, agreed that he had "drawn attention to a serious problem." This consensus about the underlying value of McCarthy's campaign legitimized his otherwise illegitimate activities. In the eyes of many of the nation's political elites, the Wisconsin senator was *bad,* but he wasn't *wrong,* a conviction that has exonerated a wide range of political malefactors from Joe McCarthy to Oliver North.[27]

McCarthy's allegations got additional reinforcement in mid-1951 when Senator Pat McCarran resumed the investigation of the Institute of Pacific Relations that his junior colleague from Wisconsin had begun. As the chair of the Senate Judiciary Committee, the Nevada Democrat was a much more powerful figure than Joseph McCarthy, but his worldview was the same. The investigation that McCarran's newly formed Senate Internal Security Subcommittee carried out not only made the same case against the IPR, but relied on the same people to make it. Benjamin Mandel became the SISS's research director and Robert Morris, a long-time anticommunist activist who had been the Tydings committee's minority counsel, was appointed special counsel. Kohlberg, Hoover, and Matthews supplied the SISS with materials from their files and the same friendly and unfriendly witnesses appeared.[28]

This time, however, the China lobby's allegations took hold. Not only did the relative sobriety of McCarran's sessions contrast favorably with McCarthy's patent irresponsibility, but the SISS had the documentation that the Wisconsin senator could never produce. McCarran's investigators had seized the IPR's records from a barn in Massachusetts and brought them under armed escort to Washington. Having these files enabled the committee to feed selected documents into the record during the hearings to underscore the connections between the IPR, the nation's policymakers, and their treatment of Chiang Kai-shek.[29]

There was just enough truth behind the committee's charges to make a plausible case. After all, some of the IPR's associates and staff members, including Frederick Vanderbilt Field, the head of its American section, were Communists. Moreover, almost everybody who had a hand in making America's China policy had belonged to the organization or been in touch with it. And some, like Philip Jessup, one of Secretary of State Dean Acheson's closest associates, helped lead it. In addition, most of these people had supported the American government's unsuccessful attempt to broker a negotiated settlement that would avert a civil war in China after World War II. The failure of that venture, though followed by the Communists' takeover, certainly did not cause it. But McCarran and his committee set out to prove that it had and that it had done so as the result of Communist influence.[30]

Whatever testimony friendly witnesses gave, whether it was about the CP connections of IPR people or the misguided policies of State Department officials, could fit somewhere into the broader story. All the big-time professional witnesses showed up: Louis Budenz, Elizabeth Bentley, Joseph Zack Kornfeder; even the normally reticent Whittaker Chambers put in an appearance. Before the hearings ended, Budenz had identified forty-three people connected with the IPR as Communists. Few were. Anticommunist icons like Alger Hiss and Harry Dexter White were repeatedly invoked, their connections to the supposed conspiracy established by the letters from IPR files that Morris or Mandel read into the record. Gerhart Eisler got mentioned when his former wife, Hede Massing, testified about her activities in the communist underground and named a few names.[31]

Most of the IPR people who had been identified as Communists refused to talk about their politics, their invocation of the Fifth Amendment, in Joe McCarthy's words, "the most positive proof obtainable that the witness is a communist." Other witnesses were put on the defensive by nitpicking questions about what they had done ten or fifteen years before. The committee was especially tough on the State Department's China hands like John Stewart Service, John Carter Vincent, and John Paton Davies. Lattimore got the roughest treatment. He spent twelve acrimonious days on the stand jousting with McCarran while trying to defend his ideas and his reputation.

He did not succeed. Even before the hearings ended, the once widely respected Lattimore had become a pariah, his public appearances canceled and his academic position in jeopardy. Worse yet, he was soon facing criminal charges. In its final report in July 1952, the SISS called on the Justice Department to indict Lattimore for perjury. McCarran wanted a political trial to reinforce his committee's findings just as the proceedings against Hiss and Christoffel had bolstered earlier anticommunist investigations. There were, however, no legitimate grounds for prosecuting Lattimore. Though the FBI had been watching him for years, no one familiar with his file believed that it contained enough evidence for a prosecution; and neither the Bureau nor the Justice Department wanted to begin a case that would not hold up. "To charge technical perjury to minor questions," the former FBI agent the Justice Department assigned to the case warned his superiors, "is to invite a full acquittal and thus place Lattimore on a pedestal and make him a martyr, a role he would relish but does not deserve."[32]

But McCarran, as head of the Senate Judiciary Committee, had the power to get his way. By threatening to veto the nomination of James McGranery as Attorney General, the Nevada senator was able to make him indict Lattimore. On December 16, 1952, Roy Cohn, the aggressive young prosecutor McGranery was forced to put on the case, obtained a seven-count indictment; its main charge accused the Johns Hopkins sinologist of having perjured himself when he denied "that he had been a promoter of Communism or Communist interests." The other six counts were embarrassingly petty — allegations that Lattimore had lied about the date of a luncheon engagement and that he had falsely denied knowing that several individuals were Communists.[33]

These charges were so vague and frivolous that the trial judge, Luther W. Youngdahl, the former Republican governor of Minnesota, threw most of them out. The Justice Department, as it often did when it lost a big anticommunist case, got a second indictment; this one, on the grounds that Lattimore was a "follower of the Communist line," fared no better than the first. Youngdahl again rejected the charges. "The Government seeks to establish that at some time, in some way, in some places, in all his vast writings, over a fifteen-year period, Lattimore agreed with something it calls and personally defines as following the Communist line and promoting Communist interests." Not only were such allegations impossible to prove, but many of the policies that supposedly showed Lattimore's espousal of the Soviet line were those of the American government as well.[34]

By the middle of 1955, when the Justice Department finally dropped the case, many of its other anticommunist prosecutions had also begun to unravel. The crisis atmosphere of the late 1940s and early 1950s was dissipating. Moreover, revelations that some of the leading ex-communist witnesses had perjured themselves raised serious questions about the government's evidence. The professional informer Harvey Matusow, who had told the SISS that the party's bookstore pushed Lattimore's works, openly recanted. And both the Justice Department and the FBI began to distance themselves from Budenz and the other ex-Communists.[35]

Perhaps if Lattimore had actually been a Communist or former Communist, the government might not have abandoned his case. The Justice Department did, after all, pursue other anticommunist prosecutions well into the 1960s. But Lattimore was just a liberal and had more establishment support than most other McCarthy era targets. Even President Truman believed that the Johns Hopkins scholar had been "shamefully persecuted." The partisan nature of the harassment directed against him ensured that, at least among liberals and academics, he had defenders.

Even so, his career had been shattered. His brush with the criminal justice system took a heavy toll. Though his attorney, the future Supreme Court justice Abe Fortas, defended him on a pro bono basis, the case was financially draining. It was humiliating as well. For someone like Lattimore, a brilliant scholar who had never been modest about his intellectual accomplishments, to be arrested, handcuffed, and fingerprinted like a common criminal was demeaning to say the least. The years of litigation and uncertainty were equally devastating. "Until a decision is reached," Lattimore complained to Fortas, "my life . . . is at a standstill." Johns Hopkins, it is true, kept him on, but the university closed the Walter Hines Page School that Lattimore headed and essentially ended his teaching career. Shunned by everybody outside of East Asian studies, his speaking engagements dried up, as did his access to outlets in the mass media. The damage extended to his associates. His students were blacklisted and his former secretaries lost their jobs. His legal victory did not end the marginalization. In 1963, Lattimore left the United States to become the head of Chinese studies at the University of Leeds in England. Even today, his reputation remains in limbo. Some scholars still claim that he brought his troubles upon himself by his failure to criticize the Soviets in the thirties and his contentiousness in the fifties.[36]

The process that had transformed the nation's leading China expert into a nonperson illustrates an important aspect of McCarthyism. Though McCarthy could never prove that Lattimore was a Communist, he had made him controversial. And by the early 1950s, controversy was almost as damaging to the men and women tainted by it as Communism. For many observers, then and now, the extension of the anticommunist crusade to Lattimore and other non-Communists was the most deleterious aspect of the McCarthy era and was what McCarthy and McCarthyism was all about. The Wisconsin senator and his right-wing allies used the techniques that had been successfully employed against the far left to attack the liberal mainstream. By embedding their charges in a broader partisan political agenda, they drew widespread support from other conservatives and made it hard for moderates and liberals to defuse those charges without themselves being accused of a cover-up. As a result, by the early 1950s, it was possible for people with no connections to the communist movement to suffer at the hands of McCarthy and his followers. Being controversial was enough.

Moreover, as the case of Philip Jessup reveals, not even the most eminent individuals could escape the damage. In the fall of 1951, a Senate Foreign Relations subcommittee voted 3–2 not to confirm Jessup as a delegate to the UN General Assembly. A professor of international law at Columbia and a long-time State Department adviser, Jessup had easily been cleared by the Senate five times before. But as chair of the IPR board, he had long been under attack by the China Lobby and was one of the first people McCarthy named. The Wisconsin senator showed up at the confirmation hearings, brandishing his usual documents and claiming that Jessup had belonged to a few front groups. His charges were unconvincing. Some of the organizations McCarthy cited had no connection to the CP; others had no connection to the nominee. All Jessup had done was let his name be used as a sponsor of some fund-raisers during the war. Actually, the most damaging charges came from the former Republican governor of Minnesota and perennial presidential candidate Harold Stassen, who claimed, incorrectly, that Jessup had supported the recognition of Communist China. Innocence, however, was no protection. Though Jessup was, in the words of the New Jersey senator who voted against him, "one of the most honorable men I know," he was nonetheless "too controversial" to be cleared.[37]

The timidity that doomed Jessup's nomination was thoroughly bipartisan. The Democrats, of course, had been shell-shocked by the defeat of Tydings. For Republicans, the political dilemma was more complex. They could hardly be accused of softness toward Communism, but few of them were willing to stand up against McCarthy. For years, the party had been split between the moderates in its Eastern wing and the conservatives in its Midwestern one. The conflict pitted Wall Street against Main Street, internationalists against isolationists, NATO supporters against Asia Firsters, big businessmen against local druggists, and, in the campaign for the 1952 presidential nomination, Eisenhower against Taft. McCarthy exacerbated the schism. Though many moderate Republicans were repelled by his hard-line tactics, most of them kept their peace, unwilling to risk anything that might exacerbate the party's internal split.[38]

Once the Republicans won the 1952 election, the Wisconsin senator became a problem the GOP could no longer ignore. His vigorous campaign-ing for other candidates and the defeat of some of his most outspoken sena-torial critics made him seem invincible, though, in reality, he had not done so well. Eisenhower, not McCarthy, had swept the Republicans to victory. In those states where McCarthy appeared, GOP candidates did worse than they had before. In Wisconsin, he trailed the ticket and might well have lost had he not had Ike's coattails to ride on.[39]

Eisenhower, whose ties were to the moderate Eastern wing of the party, disliked McCarthy. But he also shrank from confronting him. The de-fining moment occurred during the election campaign when Ike's political advisers forced him to delete a favorable reference to George Marshall from a speech he was to give in Milwaukee. McCarthy had attacked Marshall in June 1951, when he delivered a sixty thousand–word speech accusing the distinguished military leader of participating in the Democratic administra-tion's conspiracy to betray both Eastern Europe and China to the Commu-nists. Though McCarthy's diatribe was part of a broader GOP campaign against Truman's handling of the unpopular Korean War, it was one thing to criticize the president, it was another to blast someone as eminent and widely respected as Marshall. And many Republicans, as well as Demo-crats, felt McCarthy had gone too far.[40]

Eisenhower was among them. The Republican presidential candidate despised the Wisconsin senator, but he did not want to divide the party by taking him on. So he limited his campaign statements to generalities about decency and fair play. When his handlers added an unwanted appearance in Wisconsin to his schedule, Ike decided to use the opportunity to praise Marshall and condemn the way McCarthy attacked him. At the very last minute, however, he pulled the passage from his Milwaukee speech. The professional politicians in his entourage had convinced him that such a di-rect rebuke to McCarthy might split the Wisconsin GOP and lose the state in November. Ike's reluctance to confront McCarthy was to continue after the election.⁴¹

There was, of course, always the possibility that once his own party was in power, the Wisconsin Republican might abandon the Communists-in-government issue. He did not. In addition, since he had received the chair of the Senate's Government Operations Committee with its Permanent Subcommittee on Investigations, he now had his own institutional base from which to root out subversion in high places.

He staffed the committee with true believers: former FBI agents, professional ex-Communists, and other stalwarts from the anticommunist network. For a brief moment in 1953, both J. B. Matthews and Karl Baarslag were on the payroll. McCarthy's key aide was Roy Cohn, a twenty-six-year-old former U.S. Attorney who had been recommended to the senator by George Sokolsky and his Hearst allies. By the time he became the McCarthy committee's chief counsel, Cohn had already worked on some of the biggest anticommunist cases of the Cold War — the Rosenbergs, Remington, Lattimore, and the main second-string Smith Act trial. Smart, ambitious, and thoroughly devoted to the cause, the young New York lawyer was also Jewish and so would protect McCarthy from charges of antisemitism. He was arrogant as well and as impetuous and irresponsible as his boss. Nonetheless, he soon became indispensable to the Wisconsin senator. "He's a brilliant fellow," McCarthy told a friend. "He works his butt off and he's loyal to me. I don't think I could make it without him." Likened by one writer to a pair of "hyperkinetic three-year-olds," the committee chairman and his chief counsel were ready to take on the world.⁴²

Or at least the State Department. Though it was now under Republican control, McCarthy itched to weed out the subversive elements that he suspected still remained from the tainted Truman-Acheson regime. His committee's first target was the Voice of America, the State Department's overseas broadcast operation. An unhappy amalgam of vociferously anticommunist East European émigrés and idealistic New Dealers left over from the Office of War Information, the organization was torn by a struggle over whether it should be an objective news outlet like the BBC or a more overtly propagandistic one. McCarthy had no problem taking sides and using the information supplied by disgruntled VOA right-wingers to insinuate that technical decisions about such things as siting the agency's transmitters or discontinuing its Hebrew-language broadcasts were really "sabotage" by officials whose actions "would have been the same had they been representing Joe Stalin." He found no subversives, but he did drive one VOA employee to suicide and push dozens of others from their jobs, including the organization's second-in-command, forced to resign because of something he had written as a college student more than twenty years before.[43]

Then McCarthy and Cohn set out to purge the State Department's overseas libraries, which harbored, so the senator claimed, thousands of subversive books by "Communists," "pro-Communists," "former Communists," and "anti-anti-Communists." There were few such volumes, for the new secretary of state, John Foster Dulles, had just tightened up the government's book selection policy to discourage the use of anything produced by "a person whose ideology or views are questionable or controversial." But McCarthy's interest in the process led the department to revise its guidelines yet again and impose an outright ban on books by "any controversial persons, Communists, fellow travelers, et cetera." Within a day someone had deleted the embarrassing phrase, "controversial persons," from the directive, but the "et cetera" remained. Terrified foreign service officers rushed to jettison books by Communists as well as by such offenders as Whittaker Chambers, NAACP head Walter White, and the secretary of state's own cousin, diplomatic historian Foster Rhea Dulles. For lack of storage space in a few installations, some of the discarded volumes were burned.[44]

As this "book burning" incident showed, Dulles was quite willing to collaborate with McCarthy. He was eager to distance himself from the previous administration and thus acquiesced in, if in fact he didn't actually agree with, most of the Wisconsin senator's demands. He had seen how seriously the charges of Communism damaged his predecessor and he was determined not to waste any political capital in tussles with congressional witch-hunters. The selection of Scott McLeod as the State Department's security chief symbolized the new regime. Though Dulles seems not to have been involved in McLeod's appointment, most contemporary observers assumed that he had hired the former FBI agent and aide to Senator Styles Bridges specifically to placate McCarthy and his congressional allies. Certainly, there was no question about McLeod's determination to purge the foreign service or his heavy-handed McCarthy-like methods for doing so. "Congress wanted heads to roll," he explained to a journalist, "and I let 'em roll. Blood in the streets and all that."[45]

The State Department's China experts were among the most prominent of those heads. Some, like John Stewart Service, had already been ousted by Acheson, though it had taken seven loyalty board reviews to do the job. Dulles soon got rid of the other people targeted by the China Lobby. He forced the courtly Southerner John Carter Vincent to resign. Perhaps the most highly respected of all the East Asian specialists, Vincent was destined for the highest reaches of the State Department when McCarthy and the IPR investigations derailed his career. But Dulles was determined not to have any holdovers from the previous regime in place to embarrass him. A few months later he fired John Paton Davies, whose fervent anticommunism did not outweigh his China connection.[46]

Not every head McCarthy demanded was to roll. When, for example, he tried to scuttle the appointment of Charles Bohlen as ambassador to the Soviet Union, Eisenhower, who strongly backed the nominee, held firm and managed to force the confirmation through. But most of the time, neither Dulles nor Eisenhower offered much support for those of their subordinates who tangled with the senator from Wisconsin. They did not even back up the foreign aid administrator Harold Stassen in March 1953 when he lashed out against McCarthy for having "undermined" the nation's foreign policy. The Wisconsin senator had personally negotiated an arrangement with a group of Greek shipowners not to trade with the Chinese Communist regime. But, instead of defending the State Department from McCarthy's unauthorized diplomacy, both Dulles and the president rushed to conciliate him and force Stassen to eat his words.[47]

Such incidents were particularly galling to the moderate Republicans who had come to believe that the Wisconsin senator was hurting the administration. Stassen, after all, had once been close to McCarthy and had helped him block the 1951 nomination of Philip Jessup to the UN. If Eisenhower would not back someone with such strong political credentials as his own foreign aid administrator, McCarthy might well become unstoppable. But, despite the pleas of his moderate friends and advisers to repudiate the Wisconsin senator, the president hung back. Because the GOP's conservative lawmakers still supported their colleague, Ike feared that a confrontation might split the party's congressional delegation and make it impossible to govern. Moreover, an open brawl with McCarthy would demean the presidency. "I will not," he repeatedly explained, "get in the gutter with that guy." Such a battle would also be counterproductive. Nothing had furthered the Wisconsin senator's career so much as the Truman administration's over-reaction to his charges. Instead, Eisenhower would exercise what one scholar called his "hidden-hand" style of leadership, deny McCarthy the publicity that he craved, and do what he could to help him self-destruct.[48]

McCarthy, of course, did not need the president's assistance to get attention from the media. Nor, it turned out, did his committee need much of a push to court trouble both at home and abroad. In April 1953, Cohn and G. David Schine, the wealthy young heir to a hotel-chain fortune whom Cohn had persuaded McCarthy to put on the committee's staff, careened through Western Europe on a two-and-a-half-week inspection tour of the State Department's overseas installations. The two made embarrassing headlines and demoralized American diplomats everywhere they went. They played silly cloak-and-dagger games, pulled books from library shelves, grilled foreign service officers, and chased each other around the lobby of a German hotel. McCarthy seemed unperturbed by the pair's bad press.[49]

For years, liberals had opposed the Wisconsin senator on the grounds that his activities hurt the cause of anticommunism. Now, even his supporters began to worry about his erratic behavior. "We live in terror," Whittaker Chambers wrote to a friend, "that Senator McCarthy will one day make some irreparable blunder which will play directly into the hands of our common enemy and discredit the whole anti-Communist effort for a long while to come."[50]

The appointment of J. B. Matthews as McCarthy's research director in June 1953 nearly turned out to be such a blunder. By then the liberal opposition to McCarthyism had coalesced under the auspices of the innocuous-sounding National Committee for an Effective Congress, which was looking for a way to check the Wisconsin senator. Matthews provided the group with ammunition when he published an article in the July issue of the right-wing American Mercury that called the Protestant clergy "the largest single group supporting the Communist apparatus in the United States." Within days, the NCEC had disseminated the piece to the press and was orchestrating a chorus of public outrage. Since ministers were easier to defend than bureaucrats, even Eisenhower was willing to speak out. It was, a White House staff member chortled, "the first real nail in the McCarthy coffin."[51]

J. Edgar Hoover hammered in another nail when he, too, turned against the Wisconsin senator. Though he disapproved of the Matthews appointment and had long worried about McCarthy's recklessness, it was the senator's recruitment of increasing numbers of FBI agents that caused the break. The presence of so many former G-men on McCarthy's staff might seriously compromise the Bureau by revealing embarrassing information about its activities. In addition, the turf-conscious director grumbled, Roy Cohn and the committee were "crossing wires in our current investigations" and "wrecking our internal security coverage." And, of course, Hoover would never have risked taking the wrong side in a showdown between the president and Joe McCarthy. In the summer of 1953, he stopped sending the senator materials from the FBI's files.[52]

By then McCarthy and his men were investigating a supposedly rich vein of subversion at the Army Signal Corps Laboratory at Fort Monmouth, New Jersey. Many of its civilian employees were Jewish engineers from New York who, like Julius Rosenberg (an employee there in the early 1940s), had been excluded from private-sector jobs by antisemitism in the 1930s and 1940s. Some of them had been on the fringes of the Popular Front; one, in fact, had been at CCNY with Rosenberg. Most had been repeatedly investigated and cleared. At the time McCarthy appeared on the scene, the army was reviewing their cases yet again in accordance with Eisenhower's new security program. It found no spies or even security risks. But it suspended a few people anyhow. "I wanted to reinstate all thirty-five of them," army counsel John Adams recalled, "but I knew that was out of the question. . . . If the secretary reinstated the whole batch at once, some 'patriot' would squeal, and McCarthy would come crashing down demanding blood, probably mine."[53]

Despite the army's rush to propitiate him, the Wisconsin senator stepped up his attack on Fort Monmouth. By the time he began public hearings in late November, he was out of control, drinking heavily and trying to bully Army Secretary Robert Stevens into producing the loyalty review board members who had cleared the suspected employees. He was also challenging the Eisenhower administration directly with his televised speech of November 24, attacking it for failing to reverse the "whining, whimpering appeasement" of the "Truman-Acheson regime" by not forcing America's allies to cut off trade with the Chinese Communists. This time, however, neither Eisenhower nor Dulles backed down. The normally reticent secretary of state answered McCarthy in a press conference at which he publicly defended his foreign policy and condemned the "blustering, domi-neering, or arrogant methods" that the senator (whom he did not name) wanted him to use. Eisenhower weighed in with a similar rebuke the follow-ing day, expressing his "full accord" with Dulles and reiterating his "previ-ously expressed conviction that fear of Communists' actively undermining our government will not be an issue in the 1954 elections." He didn't name McCarthy either; he didn't have to.[54]

Undaunted, the Wisconsin senator continued to harass the military. The Fort Monmouth hearings petered out in December, but McCarthy had not abandoned the investigation. He was planning to subpoena the loyalty board members who had cleared the Signal Corps engineers. Such a pro-ceeding could easily escalate into a direct conflict with the administration, since Eisenhower, like Truman, was determined to keep McCarthy from prying into personnel records and other confidential information. He reit-erated his predecessor's 1948 directive that ordered executive branch em-ployees not to comply with any outside demands for loyalty files. The issue transcended partisan politics; the power of the presidency was at stake.[55]

Under pressure from the White House and the other Republicans on his committee, McCarthy backed away from a confrontation, but he had not abandoned his quest for Communists inside the defense establishment. Early in 1954 he found a new security lapse within the military: the Army had promoted Irving Peress. A Brooklyn dentist who had invoked the Fifth Amendment when he filled out the military's standard loyalty question-naire, Peress had been automatically commissioned as a captain at the time he was drafted in October 1952. Though initially tagged for overseas duty in East Asia, he had gotten a humanitarian reassignment to Camp Kilmer in New Jersey to be near his sickly wife and daughter. He was soon under in-vestigation by military intelligence, which urged his dismissal as a security risk. Instead, he got promoted. The paperwork that should have ended his military career had been sent to the wrong place and then ignored. Eventu-ally, the army caught up with him and hustled him out of the service. But not before McCarthy found out about the snafu.

The case was too good to resist, especially since the army had not only promoted the politically undesirable dentist, but had also granted him an honorable rather than a dishonorable discharge. Clearly there was some-thing rotten in New Jersey — and perhaps in the Pentagon as well. "Who promoted Peress?" was a question that, at least in McCarthy's mind, might well reveal some soft spots in the nation's anticommunist defenses. On February 18, he interrogated General Ralph Zwicker, the commander of Camp Kilmer. Though Zwicker had been aghast at the army's failure to get rid of Peress, he would not defy the executive order that prevented him from revealing the names McCarthy sought. The senator was livid and berated the highly decorated World War II hero for defending his subordinates. "Any man who has been given the honor of being promoted to general and who says 'I will protect another general who protects Communists' is not fit to wear that uniform, general."[56]

The battle had been joined. The Pentagon was furious. If the morale of the armed services was to be maintained, McCarthy's abusive treatment of Zwicker could not be tolerated. The task of standing up for the military fell to Secretary of the Army Robert Stevens, an ineffectual New Jersey textile manufacturer who had spent most of the fall currying favor with the Wisconsin senator and his staff. But even Stevens had his limits and he issued a statement denouncing the senator's behavior and refusing to let Zwicker or any of his other subordinates appear before the committee unless McCarthy agreed to treat them with respect. That, McCarthy was unwilling to do and he forced the politically inept Stevens to back down. By then, however, Eisenhower and his advisers were ready for a confrontation. Though the White House continued to conceal its hand, it had decided to bring McCarthy down. On March 11, it began the process by releasing the army's record of McCarthy's efforts to obtain special treatment for Private First Class G. David Schine.

Schine was Roy Cohn's special friend — though exactly how "special" remains a mystery. Cohn's homosexuality is well known but, despite widespread rumors, the two men, though inseparable, were probably just friends. Schine had little expertise as an anticommunist investigator; his main talent seemed to have been flaunting his wealth in nightclubs. Nonetheless, Cohn had gotten him onto the McCarthy committee as an unpaid consultant. In the summer of 1953, when it appeared as if his sidekick might be drafted, Cohn began to pester the military to grant a commission. Schine's utter lack of qualifications made that impossible. In November, he went into the army as a private. He was, however, a highly privileged recruit. His wealth, Cohn's badgering, and McCarthy's clout got him passes every weekend and ensured that he would be excused from KP and other unpleasant duties.[57]

The senator actually cared little for Schine, but Cohn was his right arm. As a result, he reluctantly seconded his aide's efforts to put pressure on the army. Though the committee might have investigated Fort Monmouth and Peress anyhow, Cohn may also have pushed the inquiries in order to force concessions from the military. If so, it didn't work. The Korean War had so seriously damaged the morale of the armed services that the Pentagon could not afford to let it be known that political pressure would get special treatment for a well-connected draftee. For McCarthy, the ramifications of harassing the army at the same time he and his chief counsel were trying to extort favors from it turned out to be disastrous.[58]

Once the administration revealed the committee's string-pulling, an investigation was inevitable. The Army-McCarthy hearings became a public spectacle. The infant television industry carried the proceedings live. For two months, the nation's viewers watched the Wisconsin senator repeatedly disrupt the proceedings by calling for a "point of order" in order to bully witnesses, deliver lectures, and make crude and insulting remarks. The denouement came on June 9, the thirtieth day of the hearings. The army's counsel, a crafty Boston lawyer named Joseph Welch, had been needling Roy Cohn for several days. Toward the end of the afternoon he sarcastically begged Cohn to "tell somebody about them quick" whenever he learned about "a Communist or a spy anywhere." McCarthy intervened, as he often did. Since Welch was so eager to learn about subversion, the Wisconsin senator noted helpfully,

> I think we should tell him that he has in his law firm a young man named Fisher, whom he recommended, incidentally, to do work on this committee, who has been for a number of years a member of an organization which was named, oh years and years ago, as the legal bulwark of the Communist party.

McCarthy's charge was no news to Welch. When he had been putting his staff together in preparation for the hearings, he had wanted to bring Fred Fisher, a young associate from his law firm, to Washington with him. But Fisher informed him that he had once been active in the National Lawyers Guild and the army's advisers decided to drop him from the team. Welch knew that McCarthy knew about Fisher, but he had gotten an informal promise from Cohn that Fisher's NLG connection would not be raised at the hearings if he in turn did not mention Cohn's equally embarrassing draft status. Still, Welch knew how erratic the Wisconsin senator could be and he was not unprepared. His dramatic riposte to McCarthy's charges was, thus, not quite as spontaneous as it appeared. "Until this moment, Senator, I think I never really gauged your cruelty or your recklessness," Welch announced.

> Little did I dream that you could be so reckless and so cruel as to do an injury to that lad. It is true he is still with Hale and Dorr [Welch's law firm]. It is true that he will continue to be with Hale and Dorr. It is, I regret to say, equally true that I fear he shall always bear a scar needlessly inflicted by you. If it were in my power to forgive you for your reckless cruelty I would do so. I like to think that I am a gentle man, but your forgiveness will have to come from someone other than me.

McCarthy, however, seemed oblivious to what he had done and continued his assault on Fisher. Welch begged him to stop. "Let us not assassinate this lad further, Senator. You have done enough. Have you no sense of decency, sir, at long last? Have you left no sense of decency?" By then even Roy Cohn was signaling McCarthy to stop. Welch quickly wrapped up his cross-examination of Cohn and the session came to an end. Eight days later the hearings were over. The Wisconsin senator's reputation would never recover. From then on, until his death from alcoholism three years later, McCarthy was a marginal and increasingly pathetic figure.[59]

Actually, the Wisconsin senator's power had been disintegrating all spring. In early March, the respected journalist Edward R. Murrow aired a documentary that revealed the emptiness of McCarthy's charges and the unfairness of his tactics. The Army-McCarthy hearings further eroded his popular support; television viewers disliked the crude, insulting figure they saw on their screens. By June McCarthy's Gallup poll ratings had fallen to 34 percent from their 50 percent figure in January. The nation's political elites had finally turned against the senator. Eisenhower's, albeit indirect, opposition emboldened other politicians and opinion makers. It was now safe to take on McCarthy.[60]

On the day after the Fred Fisher incident, Vermont's Ralph Flanders proposed that the Senate deprive McCarthy of his committee chairmanships. Flanders soon changed his strategy and, instead of calling for a sanction that attacked the sacred principle of seniority, called for censure, a much milder action. Symbolically, however, it was quite a drastic measure and the Senate's leaders handled it with caution. Thus, for example, the special committee that investigated Flanders's charges dropped most of them, recommending merely that McCarthy be censured for his mistreatment of Zwicker and his contemptuous behavior toward the Senate. The final vote was postponed until after the election. When it came, the motion had been revised yet again to eliminate the charge about Zwicker and focus only on McCarthy's abuse of his colleagues. Then, on December 2, by a margin of sixty-seven to twenty-two, the Senate censured Joe McCarthy.[61]

Despite the lopsided vote against McCarthy, what was clear from the narrowness of the charges was that the Senate had merely disciplined him for his bad manners. "We have condemned the individual," New York's Herbert Lehman noted, "but we have not yet repudiated the 'ism.'" And it was true.[62]

McCarthyism outlasted McCarthy, just as it predated him. The official campaign against domestic Communism and all the individuals, institutions, and ideas associated with it would have effectively hounded its targets and ruined the lives and careers of thousands of people without the help of Joe McCarthy. It would also have been as damaging to the American political system. Because the senator from Wisconsin drew so much attention during his heyday, he has come to symbolize the entire anticommunist movement. Such an identification is not altogether wrong. McCarthy was more flamboyant than his fellow crusaders, but the dishonesty, opportunism, and disregard for civil liberties that he practiced were commonplace within the rest of the anticommunist network. Though he was, in many ways, its creature, not its creator, McCarthy did ratchet up the intensity of the anticommunist crusade. It may not have been totally misnamed.

★

CHAPTER 8

"A BADGE OF INFAMY"

ANTICOMMUNIST ECONOMIC SANCTIONS AND POLITICAL DISMISSALS

LAWRENCE PARKER was upset. A waiter on the SS *President Cleveland,* Parker had been screened off the waterfront as a "security risk" early in 1951 and could not find out why. The mimeographed form letter that he got from the Coast Guard contained no specific charges; it merely stated that his presence aboard ship was "inimical to the security of the United States." Parker's outbursts during his hearing before the Coast Guard's Security Appeals Board in March 1951 reveal his bewilderment. "Why I would be considered a poor security risk is something I just can't figure. I just can't understand it at all." Since being deprived of his livelihood, Parker had been unable to support his seven-year-old daughter or meet the payments on his car. "I would like to have some reason or something definite," he begged the hearing examiner. "I would like to know whether I will be able to work." [1]

Parker's plight was typical of that of the thousands of men and women who like my sixth-grade teacher lost their jobs for political reasons during the McCarthy era. The personal suffering that these dismissals caused was unwarranted, for these people had done nothing wrong, nor did they threaten national security. The injustices that characterized the rest of the anticommunist crusade deformed its economic sanctions as well. Here, too, people were unfairly punished, due process was violated, and proceedings were undertaken in the name of security that often had another purpose. Here, too, the FBI and the rest of the anticommunist network built the machinery and picked the targets. And, here, too, the process was collaborative. It involved almost every sector of American society, though Washington led the way. The government's loyalty and security programs provided models for dismissing workers that could be — and were — copied by public and private employers throughout the nation.

Moreover, because the economic sanctions of the McCarthy era rested on the same distorted view of the nature and dangerousness of American Communism as the period's criminal prosecutions and congressional investigations, they often produced the same kinds of abuses. Even at the time, many people recognized how unfair these political tests for employment were. Yet the partisan and ideological forces that made it possible for McCarthyism to violate individual freedoms and civil rights in so many other areas allowed it to do so in the economic realm as well. These injustices were no aberration; they were the product of all the assumptions and procedures that had been built into the structure of American anticommunism from the start.

Lawrence Parker's administrative hearing shows how unfair that system could be. Parker never did find out why he lost his job. The Coast Guard's trial examiner told the twenty-eight-year-old waiter that he was suspected of being a member of the Communist party and sympathetic to its doctrines but offered no evidence or specific information that might help Parker disprove those allegations. "Irrespective of his merits as a marksman," Parker's lawyer complained, "he was given no target at which to fire." It was simply not possible to offer a meaningful defense in such a situation and the best that Parker could do was tell his own life story in the hopes that the information he thus revealed might somehow rebut the unknown charges that unknown informers had made against him.[2]

Parker's dismissal came about under a port-security program that had been implemented soon after the start of the Korean War. Though it got little attention at the time, the program probably took a higher body count than any other Cold War measure. Every maritime worker had to be checked out before being allowed to sail on an American ship or load one. Nearly three thousand longshoremen and seamen failed to pass the screening. Invoking the traditional image of the communist saboteur, the Coast Guard's commandant explained that these workers had been denied clearance in order

267

to protect the nation's waterfronts from anyone who might "engage in acts of sabotage such as sinking vessels in harbors or channels or at sea, causing fires, explosions or other damage . . . inducing unrest, strikes and work slow-downs, or . . . espionage."[3]

From the start, however, it was clear that security was subsidiary to the program's real objective: destroying the communist-led maritime unions. Neither Harry Bridges's International Longshoremen's and Warehousemen's Union nor the left-wing Marine Cooks and Stewards Union (MC and S) that Lawrence Parker belonged to had been invited to the late July meeting in Washington, D.C., that devised the program. The employers and labor leaders who did attend (including representatives of three breakaway ILWU locals) quickly reached a consensus on barring from the waterfront all "Communist Party card carriers, subversives, or [men] who are notorious as consistently carrying out policies of the Communist Party." When Senator Warren Magnuson introduced the bill that incorporated the group's recommendations, he explained, "[S]ome of the last strongholds of the Communist [sic] in this country exist in some of the waterfront unions, despite the efforts of patriotic maritime labor leaders to clean out some of those unions." The federal government, Magnuson implied, would have to finish the task.[4]

The implementation of the waterfront program revealed just how incidental security concerns were to its mission. At first, the Coast Guard screened only the people who handled ships and cargoes bound for the Korean theater. A few weeks later, in response to pressure from employers and anticommunist unions, the clearance procedures spread to ships going to other ports. Passenger liners bound for Hawaii, coastal freighters, fishing vessels, even the ferries that sailed to Catalina Island, were now off limits to alleged subversives. By the end of 1956, long after the Korean War was over, the port security program had even reached the Mississippi River. But it did not include passengers. Thus several blacklisted seamen had no trouble obtaining passage on the very ships from which they had just been barred. Another worker ejected from the docks by the Coast Guard was a petty officer in the navy and had, according to his attorneys, "full and complete access to the very bases from which, as a longshoreman, he was screened."[5]

Though security was not at issue, union activism was. On his last voyage before he was prevented from sailing, Lawrence Parker had been the most outspoken opponent of the attempt of a rival union to raid the MC and S. He was the only crew member screened off the *President Cleveland*. A similar pattern characterized most of the union's other cases. In an informal survey of thirty-one blacklisted MC and S members, it turned out that eighteen had been ship's delegates and eleven had served on strike committees. Coast Guard examiners were quite explicit about the labor politics that drove the program. One longshoreman was actually told that he would be cleared if he could prove that he had supported the anticommunist faction within the ILWU. Other maritime workers got the message; activists and ordinary seamen alike, they kept a low profile and reduced their demands on employers.[6]

Race also mattered. Merchant ships, like most American workplaces at the time, were segregated, with the good jobs going to whites and the more menial kitchen and janitorial positions reserved for African Americans. The MC and S organized these people, winning their strong support as a result. Lawrence Parker was typical of the union's black members. He had come to San Francisco in the early forties seeking economic advancement only to find that discrimination by employers and other unions shut him out of everything but dead-end jobs. Then he made contact with MC and S; he "had heard that it was a union where there was no discrimination, where if you qualified for a job you could get it." Such, in fact, was the case. Not only did Parker get the opportunities he sought, but even when he was the only black waiter onboard a vessel, he encountered no prejudice among his mates and was soon elected to leadership positions within the union. But, like many of the other African Americans in the MC and S, Parker discovered that his loyalty to the union was to cost him his job. Estimates varied, but most observers calculated that somewhere between 50 and 70 percent of the sailors and longshoremen who were dismissed under the port-security program were either blacks or foreigners.[7]

The unions fought back, hiring lawyers to help their screened members return to work. Lawrence Parker's was the test case. His attorneys, Richard Gladstein, who had helped defend the CP's leaders in the *Dennis* case, and his partner Norman Leonard, argued that the government's refusal to give Parker and his fellow plaintiffs any information about the nature of the charges against them was such a violation of the Fifth Amendment's guarantee of due process that the entire program should be abolished. After several years of litigation in the lower courts, the union won its case. In October 1955, the Ninth Circuit Court of Appeals restored Parker's job. "Is this system of secret informers, whisperers and tale-bearers," the court's majority asked, "of such vital importance to the public welfare that it must be preserved at the cost of denying to the citizen even a modicum of the protection traditionally associated with due process?" To ask the question was to answer it.[8]

Parker v. Lester was a landmark decision, the first time that the federal judiciary had thrown out a loyalty-security program because it violated people's constitutional rights. But the Coast Guard's failure to let maritime workers know why they were being deprived of their jobs seemed unacceptably Kafkaesque — even in Cold War America.[9]

It would be comforting to relate that Lawrence Parker's courtroom triumph ended the ordeal that he and his fellow workers experienced, but that did not happen. Few of the screened sailors or longshoremen got their jobs back. In some jurisdictions, the Coast Guard continued to deny clearance. Instead of reissuing the ousted workers their papers, it sent them form letters stating that their "character and habits of life" made their presence on the waterfront "inimical to the security of the United States." Accompanying the letters were interrogatories, lists of questions about each person's past political activities and present views. Gladstein and Leonard went back to court and forced the Coast Guard to rescind these questionnaires.[10]

Nonetheless, the blacklisting continued. The anticommunist maritime unions took up the cause and refused to dispatch the previously screened seamen to any ships. The Coast Guard's practice of stamping the documents of these people with a statement indicating that the papers had been issued under a court order made the unions' task easier. "It just happens," an MC and S lawyer complained early in 1958, "that everyone with a stamp is denied registration and no one without a stamp is denied registration." Once again, the blacklisted sailors went to court. By 1960, when they finally won their case and officially regained their jobs, almost ten years had passed since the port-security program had gone into operation. The Marine Cooks and Stewards Union had long since disappeared, an institutional victim, like its most active members, of the economic sanctions imposed by the forces of McCarthyism.[11]

There were thousands of human victims as well. Samuel G. Whitney, a construction worker in Richland, Washington, dismissed by the Atomic Energy

Commission in 1947, because, the AEC's hearing panel told him, he had been "affiliated with the Communist Party," spoke for many of them. Like Lawrence Parker, he had received no specific charges and could not mount an effective defense. "I am being treated unjustly by my own country," he complained in a letter to President Truman. "I am being accused of being a criminal without having first had a fair trial according to our constitution. I am deprived of the right to earn a living for my family by my own government whose laws I have strictly obeyed." [12]

As Whitney's anguish reveals, the loyalty-security programs imposed serious penalties. Though ostensibly less punitive than a prison sentence, dismissal of a worker for alleged disloyalty was widely recognized to be a drastic matter. As Supreme Court justice Tom Clark noted in a 1952 decision invalidating an Oklahoma loyalty oath, to be "excluded from public employment on disloyalty grounds" was a serious penalty. "In the view of the community, the stain is a deep one; indeed it has become a badge of infamy." Nor was it just a matter of reputation. Once fired for political reasons, it became almost impossible for people to find another job. This, too, was well known at the time. "A man is ruined everywhere and forever," the chairman of the Truman administration's Loyalty Review Board admitted. "No reputable employer would be likely to take a chance in giving him a job." [16]

What made these sanctions so effective was their vast scope and the industriousness with which official and unofficial blacklisters applied them. During the late 1940s and 1950s there were few, very few, sectors of the economy, public or private, to which these political tests for employment did not extend. There were the various loyalty-security programs that covered federal civil servants as well as the similar ones that state and local governments imposed on their employees. There were loyalty oaths for teachers, lawyers, entertainers, and all sorts of public and private employees, as well as the many screening programs that federal agencies administered within the private sector. [14]

Like the port-security program, most of these measures had some ostensible connection to national security, though their real function was to destroy the power of the left. The Defense Department's industrial employment program, for example, denied security clearances to alleged subversives who worked in defense plants. The AEC did the same to the scientists and others who came into contact with nuclear weapons. American citizens

271

who worked for the UN and other international organizations were also screened by the federal government. So, too, was everyone who applied for a passport. Though the State Department's passport screening program might not be formally classed as an economic sanction, for a blacklisted entertainer like Paul Robeson, losing his passport meant that he could not earn a living overseas. The armed services' practice of denying honorable discharges to politically tainted draftees was similarly punitive. Many American industries would not hire someone who had not been honorably discharged from the military.[15]

Private employers had their own programs for screening political undesirables. Though some of these programs, especially those in the defense and entertainment industries, developed into elaborate security systems run by full-time personnel, most were ad hoc responses to some kind of outside pressure. These sanctions were the second stage in the two-step procedure that in most cases had initially been triggered by an arm of the state like HUAC or the FBI. The coercive power and legitimacy of these official agencies were crucial to the process. It is hard to imagine that universities or movie studios would have dismissed left-wing professors or screenwriters if those people had not been targeted under the FBI's Responsibilities Program or forced to take the Fifth Amendment before congressional committees.[16]

Because most dismissals that took place within the private sector seem to have occurred as the result of an employer's willingness to collaborate with an official agency, it is not necessary to make major distinctions between public and private efforts to eliminate allegedly subversive employees. There were differences, to be sure. No university would try to oust a tenured faculty member on the kind of vague charges and refusal to produce evidence that characterized the Coast Guard's proceedings against Lawrence Parker. Even so, faculty committees, Hollywood studios, and military hearing boards often asked exactly the same questions. They wanted to know about someone's associations with the CP and its front groups and what he or she thought about Socialism, the Marshall Plan, and race relations in the United States. After all, each of these institutions operated in accordance with the same assumptions and utilized roughly the same procedures.[17]

To begin with, few employers questioned the need for removing alleged Communists from their payrolls. Whether the stated rationale for dismissing such people involved national security, intellectual integrity, public relations, or the elimination of "agitators who create labor unrest," there was a broad consensus that politically tainted employees had to go. Card-carrying members of the Communist party were obviously beyond the pale. But since few party members carried their cards conspicuously upon their persons, identifying such undesirables became the main function of almost every loyalty-security program, as well as the source of most of those programs' injustices.[18]

The procedures that governed these programs were remarkably uniform. Unless someone was fired under a "pretext" and told (as many of the men and women targeted under the FBI's Responsibilities Program were) that his or her position was being phased out, most of the people who lost their jobs during the McCarthy era received some indication that they were in political trouble. Sometimes, as for example, when they took the Fifth Amendment or refused to sign a loyalty oath, the employees themselves ostensibly triggered their own dismissals; in other situations, charges might be preferred. Many employers allowed people to contest their dismissals and rebut the allegations against them. Often there was a hearing like the one Lawrence Parker had and even several layers of appeals. At the very least, people could file written rejoinders. And if all other avenues were closed off, there was always litigation. As a result, most loyalty-security proceedings took on a quasi-judicial tone and came to involve such artifacts of the legal process as formal charges, witnesses, evidence, testimony, and attorneys.[19]

But for all their juridical paraphernalia these proceedings were profoundly political operations. Calculations of power, not justice, determined their outcomes. They often came into being in response to specific political pressures. A congressional investigation or the threat of one would often be enough to trigger a wave of firings or the tightening up of an ostensibly lenient loyalty program. When Senator McCarthy began to probe the army's Signal Corps Laboratories at Fort Monmouth, New Jersey, the Pentagon rushed to suspend every civilian employee he fingered. Moreover, even when people like Lawrence Parker and the Fort Monmouth engineers managed to reverse their dismissals, the ordeal that they suffered deterred their coworkers from risking their jobs by taking part in left-wing political activities.

★

273

Union activists were among the most important targets of the McCarthy era's economic sanctions. Dorothy Bailey, whose dismissal became the main test case for the federal government's loyalty-security program, was the president of her United Public Workers local. She had worked for the Department of Labor since 1939, drawing up training manuals for the department's educational programs. She had not been involved with the Communist party and was, the former president of her union recalled, "as pure as the driven snow," but she was, he also noted, "a hell of a good union person." In the summer of 1948, Bailey was suspended from her job. There was, the Regional Loyalty Board of the Civil Service Commission explained, derogatory information in her file and it sent her a list of questions to answer. At her hearing in November, she was interrogated extensively about her political views and union activities. But at no point was she given any information about the specific charges against her or told who had made them. The union hired the well-connected law firm of Arnold, Fortas and Porter to represent Bailey and prepared to fight her dismissal all the way to the Supreme Court.[20]

As Bailey, her union, and her attorneys soon realized, her litigation would have far-reaching ramifications for all American workers. As was the case in so many other areas of the anticommunist crusade, the main impetus for the imposition of political tests for employment came from Washington, which legitimized their use and provided the models. Ever since the passage of the Hatch Act in 1940, the federal government had been off-limits to subversive employees. The loyalty-security program that cost Bailey her job was the most important prototype. Established by President Truman's Executive Order 9835 on March 21, 1947, it was large, well publicized, and early. With only minor variations, the procedures it developed became standard within other federal agencies, state and local governments, and private institutions. These uniformities reflect both the legitimating power of the federal government and the fundamental assumptions that all these programs shared.

They also reflect the enormous influence of the anticommunist investigators. Since the first stage of identifying the men and women to be subjected to the political tests for employment was usually performed by anticommunist professionals, it enabled Hoover, HUAC, and such people as the Hearst expert J. B. Matthews and the Senate Internal Security Subcommittee's Benjamin Mandel to shape the entire program. By selecting the individuals to be charged, they set the parameters of political acceptability. The FBI was especially important here. Though it theoretically had authority to investigate only defense plant workers and the federal government's civilian employees, Hoover had created such a prestigious and intrusive organization that its techniques for identifying so-called subversives were widely accepted and copied. In addition, of course, the Bureau surreptitiously sent information to all sorts of employers.

The information provided by the professional anti-Communists and their allies undergirded the entire process. The operations of the Truman administration's loyalty program, to take the most important example, began with a name check of every federal employee or applicant in the files of the FBI, HUAC, the Civil Service Commission, and a handful of other agencies. If the files revealed any "derogatory information," the Bureau then carried out a full field investigation. If that investigation did not clear the individual, the FBI sent a report to the employing agency. Investigators in other parts of the government and the private sector followed the same procedures. Television producers and advertising agencies would send lists of actors, writers, and technicians to professional blacklisters for similar vetting. J. B. Matthews used his personal files to check out lists of names for his clients in film studios, private corporations, and philanthropies.[21]

These procedures were hardly foolproof. Mistaken identities were common. Out of the first 7,667 full field investigations performed under Truman's Executive Order 9835, nearly five hundred had been based on information that related to another person. The character actor Everett Sloan found himself blacklisted in the early 1950s because he had been confused with an ex-communist entertainer named Allan Sloane. Probably the most egregious example occurred in 1950 when Senator McCarthy tried to prevent the appointment of Anna Rosenberg as assistant secretary of defense on the grounds that she had attended a meeting of the party's John Reed Club in the 1930s. Rosenberg denied the charge and the FBI confirmed her denial; another Anna Rosenberg had been involved.[22]

A far more serious problem, however, stemmed from the criteria that the investigators used to identify someone as a Communist. Because of the party's secrecy, the security officers and professional anti-Communists who ran those programs or triggered them usually relied on the well-known duck test: "If someone walks like a duck and swims like a duck and quacks like a duck, he is a duck." Many investigators, however, had trouble separating the communist ducks from other unconventional waterfowl, especially since their own political biases made them suspicious of anyone left of center. "A liberal," explained one military intelligence officer who helped formulate the Truman administration's loyalty program, "is only a hop, skip, and a jump from a Communist. A Communist starts as a liberal." [23] Such assumptions, if not always so blatantly expressed, became embedded in the operations of many employment security programs. [24]

Since the FBI and other security officials believed that so-called sympathizers were as dangerous as party members, their main "duck test" tended to treat participation in CP front groups as an indication of party membership. This not entirely unfounded assumption shaped the Truman administration's loyalty program. Executive Order 9835 was quite explicit: "membership in, affiliation with, or sympathetic association with" one of these organizations could be a sign of disloyalty. The order contained provisions for the Attorney General to designate specific groups as "totalitarian, fascist, communist, or subversive" or dedicated to "force or violence." This provision not only brought the well-known Attorney General's list into being, but also legitimized what came to be labeled as "guilt by association," a mechanistic method of tagging people by the groups and individuals they were connected to that, opponents of the loyalty program insisted, opened the way to considerable abuse. [25]

And so it did. Though most of the men and women identified in accordance with these criteria were probably left-wing activists, if not party members, the literature of the 1950s is full of horror stories about the political innocents whose jobs were lost and careers destroyed because they inadvertently associated with groups on the list. They bought insurance policies and cheap cemetery plots from the International Workers Order or else had sent a check to the Loyalists during the Spanish Civil War. Kendrick Cole, the protagonist in a key Supreme Court decision of the mid-fifties, lost his job because he liked mountain climbing. A lanky, balding New Englander who worked as an inspector for the Food and Drug Administration in New York City, Cole was an outdoorsy fellow who spent his free time hiking in the Catskills. His brush with subversion occurred when he befriended some members of the Nature Friends of America, an outfit on the Attorney General's list. Not only had Cole used a campsite maintained by

276

the Nature Friends, but he had paid the group $1.50 for firewood, helped clear a trail, and played the labor anthem "Joe Hill" on his harmonica at a beer party. Sometimes the damaging associations were even more far-fetched. One man almost lost his job because, as one of the charges against him noted, "you wrote a thesis which was based on material obtained from the Institute of Pacific Relations."[26]

More shocking, because more common, were all the people who got into trouble because the people they associated with had bad associations. Husbands and wives invariably tainted each other. One particularly ghoulish case involved a maritime worker who was screened under the port-security program because of the political associations of his wife's late husband, who had died before the man had even met his future spouse.[27] Mothers, fathers, and siblings could also compromise somebody's job. Milo Radulovich, a young meteorologist who was then a graduate student at the University of Michigan, was tagged as a security risk by the air force because he had, as he explained, "maintained a close and continuing relationship with my dad and my sister" whose activities were "questionable" and who once "read what are now called subversive newspapers." Sometimes people faced charges because of their connections to people who themselves faced loyalty proceedings.[28]

Francis Carpenter, for example, was tainted by his thesis advisers. A graduate student in Chinese history at Stanford, Carpenter went to work in the State Department before finishing his dissertation. Neither a forceful person nor a political activist, Carpenter was totally stunned when he was suspended from his State Department job in 1953. After a year in limbo and a harrowing two-day hearing that included a lie-detector test, he was reinstated. As he learned from his interrogators, his problem was that he had been working with the Stanford sinologists Arthur and Mary Wright, whose main sin had been to support their colleague Owen Lattimore. Carpenter had suspected that the Wrights were the cause of his troubles and at the time of his suspension, he decided to break with them. He did not answer their letters and, of course, never finished his thesis. Naturally, he kept a low profile once he returned to work. There were hundreds, maybe thousands, of people like Francis Carpenter who, though usually reinstated after appeals, suffered considerably from the mechanistic application of the prohibition on left-wing associations.[29]

At least someone like Carpenter who faced specific charges, however far-fetched, could defend himself. For many of the men and women caught up in the various loyalty programs of the period, the very nature of the charges against them was unknown. Lawrence Parker was not alone in his inability to find out why he lost his job. The same trial examiner who had ruled against Parker told another seaman that the only information he could give him about his case was that he was "supposed to be presently a member of the Communist Party and has been for some time and is believed to be sympathetic with the Communist Party." When pressed to give the specifics behind the government's charges, he refused. "The Coast Guard," he announced, "does not present any case." Similarly, the panel that was hearing her appeal refused to give Dorothy Bailey, the Labor Department employee who became the protagonist in the loyalty program's main test case, any details about the time, place, or content of the allegedly disloyal acts that precipitated her firing.[30]

Some tribunals even refused to let people learn what they had been charged with. "I was told that the hearing board had recommended that Miss Brown [a pseudonym] be discharged, but I was not told why," the attorney for a former employee complained.[31] The military was the main offender here. When the army suspended the civilian employees at the Fort Monmouth Signal Corps Engineering Laboratory after McCarthy began to investigate the facility, it drew up charges against them and even gave them a hearing. But the employees who were not cleared never learned which counts had precipitated their dismissals.[32] Enlisted men charged with disloyalty and threatened with less than honorable discharges did not always get hearings; and, if they did, were not always told what they were accused of. Sometimes they were not even notified of the outcome of their hearings. The army had gotten so much negative publicity when it reversed the favorable decisions of a few hearing panels that it simply stopped telling servicemen what those panels had decided. The individuals involved could appeal, but blindly, since they would not know until the moment of their discharge whether or not they had been cleared.[33]

Such practices came under considerable criticism. Even the people who administered these programs recognized the inequities, not to mention the terrible public relations, involved in refusing to tell people why they were in trouble. Until he was reprimanded by his superiors, for example, one coast guard examiner would unofficially let the screened seamen and their attorneys know the general nature of the charges they were facing. Eventually, as McCarthyism receded, the stonewalling that characterized so many of these proceedings began to disappear as agencies revised their own regulations or federal judges forced them to. As a result, by the mid-fifties most of the men and women facing loyalty-security hearings were able to find out what they were being charged with. And, if the allegations were specific enough, they could even sometimes rebut them.[34]

But they could rarely find out who made the charges. At the insistence of the FBI, which was, of course, hiding its dirty laundry as well as protecting its informants, the identities of informers were invariably withheld. Even the loyalty boards that handled these cases did not get this information. Often all they knew was that the material on which they based their judgments came from, in the Bureau's terminology, a "reliable" source. The chair of the panel that heard Dorothy Bailey's appeal admitted that he knew nothing about the people who had accused her. "I haven't the slightest knowledge as to who they were or how active they have been in anything." Lacking information about the backgrounds and motivations of the informers, loyalty boards had no effective way to evaluate their credibility and had to take the FBI's statements at face value.[35]

The injustices involved were obvious. Without knowing the source of the charges against them, employees who were trying to disprove them could not effectively counter those allegations and demonstrate their falsity. Usually the difficulty came from the way in which the FBI interpreted and processed the material it transmitted to other agencies. The Bureau, for example, did not tell the loyalty boards whether the information it submitted to them came from an undercover agent, a vindictive ex-husband, or a gossipy neighbor. Nor did it reveal when it had transformed casual observations into specific charges. FBI agents often put their own political and bureaucratic spin on the material they collected. Not only did they treat nonconformity as a sign of disloyalty, but they also presented their findings in the Bureau's traditional manner — as evidence for a prosecution.[36]

Hearing examiners who had been able to question witnesses or had conducted their own investigations after receiving an FBI report found out, as one of them remarked, "how misleading such an accumulation of information can actually be." One Interior Department loyalty board had managed to cross-examine the Bureau's informants. "It was interesting to see," a member of that panel recalled, "how the case against the employee pretty well evaporated as we went along, notwithstanding the fact that we had witnesses strongly against him." Little incidents had burgeoned into generalizations, the existence of an internal union dispute had been concealed, and a man who reputedly claimed that the employee had been pushing the *Daily Worker* recollected mentioning a different publication. "I am at a loss to see how the employee in this case could have defended himself," the official concluded, "if we had not opened up the evidence and afforded him a chance to confront the witnesses."[37]

Few loyalty panels gave employees that chance. Though they recognized that the failure to let people confront their accusers did, in the words of Seth Richardson, the first head of the Truman administration's Loyalty Review Board, "give rise to most serious questions in the minds of the general public," they refused to do so. In their eyes, national security overrode fair play. The 1956 report of the Defense Department's personnel security officials presents the argument in a typically apocalyptic fashion.

> No American welcomes the necessity for the non-disclosure of sources of information. But a necessity it is. The necessity is real because the conspiracy is real. The struggle is for the survival of a whole nation. Without the confidential informant that struggle could not be successful.

J. Edgar Hoover was, of course, adamant on the subject, insisting that his agency's ability to protect American security required concealing its informers. Such was the FBI's prestige during the 1940s and 1950s that few loyalty-security officials questioned the Bureau's refusal to identify its sources.[38]

Nor did the nation's judiciary. Despite the obvious injustices that the loyalty programs' reliance on so-called faceless informers entailed, federal judges avoided ruling against all but the most abusive elements of these programs. Some of this reluctance to intervene came from the policy of judicial restraint, a doctrine that prevented judges from interfering with the legitimate activities of other branches of government. As it did with regard to the actions of Congress and the Justice Department's prosecutors, the federal judiciary shrank from imposing constitutional limitations on the administration's loyalty-security programs.[39]

Usually, however, national security, not judicial restraint, was the justification for the judiciary's willingness to condone the loyalty program's violations of due process. Dorothy Bailey's case was decisive here. Her dismissal was a striking example of the program's reliance on anonymous informers. Charged with belonging to the party and having "long and consistently followed Communist policies" and "associated intimately" with local party leaders, Bailey testified freely at two hearings, brought in several character witnesses, and produced over seventy affidavits from eminent people all vouching for her loyalty. The government offered no evidence at all. In contesting her dismissal, Bailey's attorneys, Thurman Arnold and the future Supreme Court justice Abe Fortas, argued that she had been deprived of her constitutional right of due process because she could not confront her accusers. The use of secret informers seemed so patently unfair that Arnold and Fortas assumed they would win.[40]

But they did not. In its 2–1 decision early in 1950, the Washington, D.C., Court of Appeals ruled, as it and other tribunals were doing in similar employment cases (and in deportation cases as well), that because losing a job was not a criminal punishment, Bailey had no right to a fair hearing. "The question," Judge E. Barrett Prettyman explained, "is not whether she had a trial. The question is whether she should have had one." But the real issue was "the world situation in which not merely two ideologies but two potentially adverse forces presently exist, and certainly we cannot require that the President and the Congress ignore it." In short, even if Bailey had the right to a trial with all the constitutional trimmings, the "inexorable necessities of the Government" would still demand the protection of FBI informers.[41]

The Supreme Court agreed to take the case, but then dawdled over its decision. At their conference on *Bailey v. Richardson* in October 1950, five of the justices wanted to overrule the lower court's decision. The government's reliance on anonymous informers seemed too inequitable even for such cautious jurors as Felix Frankfurter. But over the next few months that majority began to erode; Sherman Minton, one of the Court's less distinguished members, had changed his mind. By the time the justices finally issued their ruling, in April 1951, the Court was split down the middle. Its 4–4 decision upheld the lower court's ruling. No opinions were issued on the case, thus leaving Judge Prettyman's decision the main word on the constitutionality of the loyalty program and its reliance on secret information. More important, by refusing to put any serious limitations on the government's power to fire its workers for their politics, the Court had legitimized the economic sanctions that were at the very heart of McCarthyism.[42]

Besides the anonymous accusations against her, there were other aspects of Bailey's ordeal that horrified the nation's liberals. During the course of her hearing, she had been grilled at length about her political views and union activities. Members of the Loyalty Review Board wanted to know about her connections to several left-wing groups both on and off the Attorney General's list. They also questioned her about her contacts with a number of alleged Communists, most of whom were officials in her union. They wanted to know her opinions on a wide range of contemporary political and international issues. And, in a line of inquiry that was to draw enormous public outrage, one of the loyalty board members asked, "Did you ever write a letter to the Red Cross about the segregation of blood? . . . What was your personal position about that?"[43]

The man who asked those questions later explained that he had done so because "objection to blood segregation is a recognized 'party line' tactic" and he had wanted to find out whether Bailey (who was herself an African American) had been following the party line when she wrote the letter. This official was not alone; many loyalty boards imposed racially discriminatory duck tests that were strongly biased against civil rights activists, especially in departments like the Post Office, which had large numbers of black employees. "Of course," the chairman of a departmental loyalty panel admitted, "the fact that a person believes in racial equality doesn't *prove* that he's a Communist, but it certainly makes you look twice, doesn't it? You can't get away from the fact that racial equality is part of the Communist line."[44]

These kinds of assumptions, about race and about people's political activities, suffused many of the loyalty-security proceedings. Hearing officers were seeking information that they believed was relevant to determining the loyalty of the men and women they were questioning. Thus, in addition to asking about the specific activities and associations that precipitated the inquiry, panels questioned people about their ideas as well as their actions. From professors to longshoremen, just about everybody who faced a loyalty-security investigation was interrogated about Cold War issues. Like Dorothy Bailey, they were asked what they thought about the Soviet

Union, the Marshall Plan, and NATO. During the Korean War these people would be asked their views on that conflict; a few years later Indochina was on the agenda. Panels often questioned people about hypothetical situations. Would they fight for the United States if it got involved in a war with the Soviet Union? Would they turn in fellow workers if they found them to be Communists? Other questions involved domestic politics: socialized medicine, public ownership of utilities, and, of course, race. African Americans were asked if they had white friends, whites if they had black ones. And people of all colors were asked if they owned Paul Robeson records. There were questions about art, literature, and religion. One federal employee was even asked, "What do you think of female chastity?"[45]

In retrospect, it is clear that these questions infringed upon some rather basic personal and political rights. But at the time, the men and women who posed them believed themselves justified in doing so because they assumed there was no other way to assess an individual's loyalty. Though many loyalty-security officials may well have been conservative ideologues who were trying to smoke out liberals as well as Communists, most of them were probably just following the bureaucratic imperatives of their mission. Francis Carpenter recalls that the State Department security officers who questioned him in 1954 seemed almost as scared as he was. Such people did not want to risk the nation's security or their own careers by clearing any potential subversives who might be concealing their communist connections.[46]

Scholars know very little about the types of people who ran the various loyalty-security programs. Clearly, there were no left-wingers among them. Truman had gone out of his way to appoint card-carrying Republicans to the main Loyalty Review Board; and people who had even the mildest whiff of controversy were subsequently dropped from the body. The ones who remained on the twenty-six-person panel were certainly well-meaning, though not, it seems, a particularly distinguished group. Nor were the roughly 2,200 people who sat on the various departmental and agency loyalty boards. The full-time bureaucrats who staffed the programs were similarly unimpressive. Contemporary assessments describe the government's "difficulty in attracting competent personnel." Many had no legal credentials; and, though they were sometimes given short training courses, few of these security officials knew much about the American left.[47]

Naturally, they took few chances. They heeded J. Edgar Hoover's warnings about the covert nature of the Communist party and they operated on the assumption that anybody with a questionable association in his or her past might well be a secret Communist. Security officers and loyalty boards thus needed to be convinced that these people had broken with their former associates and repudiated their earlier political views. Employees who did not seem to recognize the harmful nature of their own past activities or who claimed to oppose the CP but voiced opinions that hearing officers associated with Communism were "lacking in credibility" and could not be cleared.[48]

Besides espousing politically correct ideas at their hearings, employees also had to display an appropriately deferential attitude. People who tried to stand on their rights and refused to cooperate with the loyalty panels rarely got cleared. By the mid-1950s, taking the Fifth Amendment had become automatic grounds for dismissal within the federal government and some major corporations. Non-Communists and even anti-Communists could lose their jobs if they seemed too feisty and individualistic. That had happened to an automobile worker who, despite the strong support of the anticommunist leaders of his union, bungled his hearing "by making speeches instead of doing what [his lawyer] told him to do, which was answer questions." People had to be contrite, sincere, and, above all, unsympathetic to the left. "You had to hide what you believed in," an attorney who handled many loyalty cases recalled. "You wanted to win the case and you couldn't say 'I did these things because I thought they were right and I still think they're right.' Because if you did that you'd be dead."[49]

For workers who had never belonged to any questionable groups, disavowing their past affiliations could present serious problems. Among the MC and S people who were screened in the early days of the port-security program was a Spanish *sous*-chef whose employer wanted him cleared and had managed to see his file. Except for a brief flirtation with an anti-Franco organization during the Spanish Civil War, the man's record was clean. "Just because they don't have anything on you," his employer advised him, "you've got to prove that nothing has happened; because something may have happened or you may have done something that they don't know about, and they'll take no chances." Another employee had an even worse problem. She had never joined anything except the union and a motorcycle

club. Her employer begged her to make something up. "You must have belonged to some organization, and the only thing you can do, Miss Whitmore,
is to say that you belonged and to say you're sorry, and that you'll have nothing to do with it in the future, and that you've already repudiated it, etc." [50]

Naming names, though central to the public rituals staged by HUAC
and the other committees, was not always demanded by employers. Universities, for example, usually expected candor, but not names. Nonetheless,
informing was considered a useful sign of contrition; and in some situations, especially if someone had been in the CP or was vulnerable in some
other way, an employer might demand it. In the middle of 1953, Harvard's
Dean McGeorge Bundy ordered the ex-Communist Sigmund Diamond to
clear himself with the FBI. When Diamond discovered that such a clearance
required identifying other people, he refused — and lost his job. [51]

In many cases, the status of an individual determined how rigidly he
or she would be screened. It was only the eminence of J. Robert Oppenheimer, for example, that enabled the Manhattan Project leader to retain his
security clearance until late 1953. A more obscure scientist or technician
with the same record of compromising personal associations and political
affiliations would have been denied clearance years before. Such distinctions were rarely acknowledged, but a survey of the published collections
of security cases indicates that well-educated people with good connections
seem to have been more readily cleared. They could afford lawyers and,
if the abuses against them were sufficiently egregious, they could attract
enough publicity to gain reinstatement. The figures for dismissals within
the Truman administration reveal the same disparities. The Post Office, with
its unskilled workforce and large numbers of minority-group employees,
had the highest percentage of discharges. The more prestigious State Department had the lowest. [52]

Similarly, some industries or organizations were able to protect their
employees from outside pressures, while others were more sensitive to
those pressures and devised more demanding clearance procedures. The
CIA, for example, successfully invoked national security to shield its people
from the humiliating partisan attacks leveled against other federal agencies.
Private universities were more likely to retain Fifth Amendment witnesses
on their faculties than public ones. But the entertainment industry, which
felt particularly vulnerable, hired professional blacklisters like George

Sokolsky, J. B. Matthews, and the former FBI agents who published *Counterattack* to pass on every actor or technician the studios and networks wanted to hire. These institutional distinctions are obvious, but they do need to be made.[53]

★

Timing was also crucial. The relative severity or leniency of the various loyalty-security programs fluctuated in response to changes in the overall political atmosphere. The Korean War was the turning point. It intensified the overall sense of crisis and made it increasingly unlikely that loyalty review boards and other panels would overrule a dismissal. Thus, for example, though appropriately contrite ex-Communists might have been allowed to retain their positions in the late 1940s, by the 1950s such people were no longer acceptable. Moreover, as standards changed, men and women who had already been cleared found themselves again on trial.[54]

There were many reasons for reopening a case. New information in a file could lead to new charges. Often, however, it turned out that the "new information" was only the record of the earlier action; and it was not uncommon for people to be charged with having denied the previous charges against them. In one case, for example, a federal employee almost lost his job because of his association with a suspicious character — the union lawyer who had represented him at his first loyalty hearing. Moreover, each time the rules changed, loyalty boards reassessed their old cases. Thus, all the people who had been cleared by the Loyalty Review Board under the original 1947 loyalty program had to undergo new investigations when the Truman administration revised its standards in the spring of 1951. The same thing happened after Eisenhower took office and modified the program yet again.[55]

Invariably, the most controversial people, like nuclear physicists and the State Department's China hands, endured multiple trials. It became almost a reflex action on the part of the officials who handled these cases to reopen them each time politicians brought up the subject or new allegations reached the press. Oppenheimer was screened four times before he was finally denied clearance; John Stewart Service, the State Department employee involved in the *Amerasia* case, went through seven loyalty reviews before he was fired; his colleague John Paton Davies had eight. But even blue-collar workers and ordinary civil servants found themselves in repeated jeopardy. Lawrence Parker had already been screened off the waterfront and reinstated when the coast guard finally stopped him from sailing in February 1951. Several of the Fort Monmouth workers singled out for attack by Senator McCarthy had also been investigated before. And of the fifty people whose cases were studied by the Ford Foundation's Fund for the Republic, seventeen had undergone more than one interrogation.[56]

Since the communist threat, such as it was, diminished even as the security measures that were being taken to counter it increased in severity, it was obvious that politics, not security, drove the nation's loyalty programs. Such had been the case from the start. Truman and his advisers had never seriously worried about disloyal federal workers. "We did not believe," former White House aide Clark Clifford recalled, "there was a real problem. A problem was being manufactured." The solution was, as we have seen, to issue Executive Order 9835 and set up an elaborate loyalty-security apparatus. But because the Communists-in-government issue was too juicy for ambitious politicians to ignore, the loyalty program did not provide the political protection the White House wanted. By the middle of 1948, HUAC and several other congressional investigators were again on the attack, this time blaming the administration for its failure to dismiss such tainted employees as William Remington. With the covert assistance of the FBI and the public testimony of ex-Communists like Elizabeth Bentley and Whittaker Chambers, the committees were able to make the New Deal appear riddled with reds.[57]

The administration was in a bind. Its loyalty program satisfied no one. Republicans attacked the program as too lenient; liberals assailed it as too harsh. The presidential election campaign was under way and it seemed likely that the Communists-in-government issue would dominate the politicking. "There is paydirt here," a White House aide admitted, "and the Republicans have no intention of being diverted by appeals from anguished liberals who see the Bill of Rights transgressed." At the same time, it was becoming clear to those "anguished liberals," both within the administration and outside of it, that E. O. 9835 had sanctioned considerable injustice. Scientists, labor leaders, and civil libertarians were particularly upset about the program's reliance on anonymous accusers and the way in which apparently innocent people were being stigmatized by its unfair procedures. Truman's surprise electoral victory seemingly bought the administration some breathing space and by the middle of 1949 several White House aides were thinking about establishing an advisory committee of prominent citizens to revise the program.[58]

It was not to happen. The political reprieve that Truman's advisers hoped might lead to a reevaluation of the government's loyalty-security procedures disappeared when the Cold War escalated and Joe McCarthy entered the arena. Communists-in-government *was* McCarthy's issue. The president rushed to defuse it by encouraging Maryland senator Millard Tydings's investigation of McCarthy's allegations and by having the Loyalty Review Board reexamine the cases the Wisconsin senator had brought up. There were about forty of them, including that of John Stewart Service, who was on his way to a post in New Delhi when the State Department summoned him back to Washington for yet another hearing on the old *Amerasia* charges. But Truman and his aides were dissatisfied with this kind of slap-dash response to McCarthy. Thus, even before the Tydings committee submitted its report, they were again considering the possibility of appointing a special committee to study all of McCarthy's cases and perhaps even review the entire loyalty program.[59]

Instead, the Korean War broke out. In the bipartisan frenzy that swept over Capitol Hill in the summer of 1950, Congress overwhelmingly ratified a major revision of the loyalty-security program. Public Law 733, as the measure was called, was a Defense Department proposal that authorized eleven key departments and agencies to dismiss employees summarily if they constituted a threat to security.* Individual loyalty was no longer an issue. People could be fired if they were gay or drank too much or could not keep a secret or if they appeared to be vulnerable to some kind of pressure either through their own wrongdoings or their family connections. Under this formulation, a security risk could be a perfectly loyal, even rabidly anticommunist, employee with relatives behind the Iron Curtain or an apolitical individual who played around with women. Since the armed forces and the State Department already had such powers, the main impact of P.L. 733 was symbolic. It codified an ongoing practice and erased the distinction between security and loyalty.[60]

But it did not protect the administration from continuing criticism.

---

*The agencies involved were the Defense, State, Justice, and Commerce Departments, and the army, navy, air force, coast guard, Atomic Energy Commission, National Security Resources Board, and National Advisory Committee for Aeronautics.

Because congressional conservatives refused to drop the Communists-in-government issue, Truman and his advisers remained on the defensive, vulnerable to charges that the executive branch had still not completely cleaned house. And, at least from the perspective of the hard-core anti-Communists, such was indeed the case. The body count was surprisingly low; very few of the thousands of employees who were investigated were actually fired.

Unjust as the loyalty program may have seemed to liberals, it was not entirely arbitrary. Federal employees charged with disloyalty who appealed their dismissals usually won reinstatement; loyalty review boards cleared from 70 to 90 percent of the cases that reached them. These figures led to considerable controversy within the administration. Liberals viewed them as an indication that the threat of subversion had been greatly exaggerated; and they pressed for a revision of the loyalty program. Conservatives, on the other hand, worried that the standards for assessing employees were too lenient and exposed the executive to unnecessary congressional criticism; and they, too, wanted a change.[61]

Truman sympathized with the liberals. He was, he admitted, "very much disturbed with the action of some of these Boards" and he was eager "to find some way to put a stop to their un-American activities." In the fall of 1950, therefore, the White House resuscitated, yet again, the proposal for a nonpartisan commission to review its loyalty program. This time, the project almost got off the ground. Truman nominated a nine-person panel chaired by Admiral Chester Nimitz and containing the requisite mix of Wall Street bankers, lawyers, churchmen, and former politicians. It was not a particularly distinguished group and there is ample evidence that at least some of its members were more than willing to subordinate individual rights to national security. Nonetheless, the mere existence of the Nimitz commission was anathema to the anticommunist network. Columnist George Sokolsky led the attack and Senator Pat McCarran, who may well have been jealous of the panel's potential incursion onto his own turf, used his power as chair of the Senate Judiciary Committee to scuttle it.[62]

Meanwhile, the administration decided to toughen its loyalty program. Those departments like State and Commerce that housed such embarrassing employees as Service and Remington were under constant attack from congressional conservatives like McCarran and McCarthy. Accordingly, they pressed for new regulations that would make it easier to fire suspected subversives. Executive Order 10241, which Truman issued on April 28, 1951, did just that by adopting a new standard that replaced E.O. 9835's requirement of "reasonable grounds" for believing that someone was disloyal with the looser formulation of "reasonable doubt." Loyalty panels could then rule against an employee whenever they harbored any suspicion about his or her loyalty.[63]

Though the Loyalty Review Board immediately ordered the review of over a thousand cases that had been reversed on appeal under the earlier guidelines, the pressures on the administration did not abate. Senator McCarran's 1951–52 investigation of the Institute of Pacific Relations, for example, forced yet another round of loyalty board hearings for John Stewart Service, John Paton Davies, and the State Department's other China hands. At the same time, despite the collapse of the Nimitz commission, the White House continued to seek some way to alleviate the injustices the system imposed. In July 1951, Truman asked the National Security Council to study the loyalty program. Though the 1952 presidential campaign ensured that the NSC's investigation would be stillborn, its report did pinpoint the main problems the loyalty program would continue to confront.[64]

The primary one was that of distinguishing between security and loyalty. Since not every federal worker handled atomic secrets, there was a growing consensus among the loyalty program's administrators that the system might work better if it focused on eliminating the people who could actually endanger the country. The NSC study also recognized that different departments enforced the loyalty regulations in different ways. This had been a problem from the start. Security officials believed that one of the reasons that the State Department had been so vulnerable to congressional attacks was that its loyalty boards did not fire people, but instead pressed them to resign. Standardization of procedures might eliminate such problems in the future.[65]

The controversies about government employees continued even after the Republicans took office in 1953. Despite his campaign promise to overhaul the loyalty and security programs, Eisenhower was to find the issue no more amenable to an equitable and politically safe solution than Truman had. His more liberal advisers suggested that he appoint a high-level panel to review the program, but the new president demurred. Whatever measures his administration took would have to convince McCarthy and the other congressional conservatives that the government was cleaning house at last. Accordingly, it took some symbolic actions, like appointing the politically well connected former FBI agent Scott McLeod to head the State Department's security operations. And, of course, it revamped the loyalty-security program.[66]

Executive Order 10450, which Eisenhower issued on April 27, 1953, extended the application of P.L. 733 from the eleven agencies and departments that it originally covered to the entire government. Under the new program, security, not loyalty, was to determine the fate of federal employees. Individual workers could now be dismissed if their continued employment was not "clearly consistent with the interests of the national security." People with bad families or bad habits became suspect, especially if, like homosexuals or adulterers, they were supposedly vulnerable to blackmail. Under pressure to prove that the new regime had eliminated the problem, agency heads were ordered to reopen every case that had been investigated under the previous administration.[67]

The program was not a success. McCarthy could not be appeased; and the abuses that the new regulations encouraged upset even moderates. Ultimately, the Supreme Court was to render E.O. 10450 essentially unenforceable. In the beginning, however, Eisenhower and his advisers expected the new system to work. The administration's strategy was to release official figures that ostensibly showed how many security risks it had managed to eliminate and, thus, demonstrate both how lax the Democrats had been and how vigilant the Republicans now were. The problem, however, was that few of these dismissed employees had been charged with Communism; and once the nature of its statistical ploy became obvious, the administration was to face an embarrassing credibility gap. McCarthy, meanwhile, was tearing into the army, en route to his blazing finale in the spring of 1954. At the time, however, it was by no means clear what kind of impact McCarthy's downfall would produce; and the loyalty-security program continued to operate as before. In fact, at the very moment that millions of Americans were watching the Wisconsin senator's antics on television, the Atomic Energy Commission was about to decide that J. Robert Oppenheimer was a security risk.[68]

★

And yet the system was changing. The transformation was gradual; but by the end of 1954, the climate of opinion had certainly shifted. Traditional interpretations stress that year's Army-McCarthy hearings as a turning point. And to some extent they were, for they severed the alliance between the hard-line anti-Communists and the political mainstream. The election of a Democratic Congress in November also helped defuse the Communists-in-government issue. At the same time (and in part because McCarthy's outrageous behavior raised questions about the entire anticommunist crusade), the mass media began to expose what was going on. If nothing else, the abuses of the loyalty-security program produced great human interest stories.

On October 23, 1953, CBS newscaster Edward R. Murrow dramatized the case of Milo Radulovich in television's first-ever piece of investigative reporting. Radulovich, who was being forced out of the military because of his father's allegedly subversive activities, was a typical victim of the loyalty-security program's system of anonymous informers, vague charges, and guilt by relationship. The air force called no witnesses and presented its charges in a sealed manila envelope whose contents it would not reveal to Radulovich, his attorneys, or the television audience. Such was the power of the new medium in generating public outrage that five weeks later the secretary of the air force appeared on Murrow's show to announce Radulovich's reinstatement.[69]

Though publicity did not always bring a reprieve — the Fort Monmouth scientists were to regain their jobs only after a five-year court battle — Radulovich's success indicated that something had changed. A year later, the story about the similar injustices perpetrated against a civilian navy employee named Abraham Chasanow gained the future *New York Times* columnist Anthony Lewis a Pulitzer Prize and restored Chasanow to his job. By then, of course, there were probably no Communists or even ex-Communists left in the government and it was easier to enlist sympathy for the less politically tainted employees who were so obviously being hassled.[70]

The Oppenheimer case had a profound effect here. It involved sensitive issues of nuclear policy as well as charges of Communism. Oppenheimer's enemies had been trying to force him from power for years. His eminence, however, made both the Truman and Eisenhower administrations reluctant to take action. Ike finally lifted the physicist's security clearance in December 1953, after Hoover sent him and several cabinet members a letter from the former administrator of the Joint Congressional Committee on Atomic Energy that charged Oppenheimer with possible espionage as well as with trying to influence American "military, atomic energy, intelligence, and diplomatic policy."[71]

At his hearing in the spring of 1954, Oppenheimer confessed his earlier political sins and admitted that he "was an idiot" in the wartime incident in which he had tried to conceal the identity of the friend who transmitted a Soviet offer to spy. The most damaging testimony came from scientists like Edward Teller, who questioned Oppenheimer's motives in opposing the development of the hydrogen bomb. The Atomic Energy Commission ultimately cleared Oppenheimer of the charge that he was disloyal but it still found him a security risk. Though it is now clear that FBI and AEC officials bent the rules to punish Oppenheimer, at the time the proceedings did not seem as arbitrary as those that affected less-eminent individuals. Nonetheless, there was considerable outrage that someone as important as Oppenheimer could be deprived of his security clearance for a policy dissent and a lapse in judgment over ten years before. Scientists and scholars were particularly upset by the ruling. Eisenhower, though unwilling to reverse the AEC's decision, was sensitive to criticism about the case and even began to think about appointing yet another special panel to review the loyalty-security program.[72]

A few months later, the Wolf Ladejinsky case forced the White House to act. Ladejinsky was a State Department economist, responsible for implementing land reform policies in Japan and Korea. In the fall of 1954, he was slated to become agricultural attaché in the Tokyo embassy and was transferred to the Agriculture Department. Though he had been cleared several times before, the Agriculture Department, which disliked all kinds of land reform, decided that Ladejinsky was a security risk. He had emigrated from the Soviet Union in the 1920s and still had sisters behind the Iron Curtain, though he had long since lost touch with them. Since the foreign policy establishment considered his work vital to the struggle against Communism in East Asia, Ladejinsky was immediately reassigned to an even more sensitive position directing the land reform program in South Vietnam. But the revocation of his clearance had caused such a furor among the liberals in

Congress that it forced the administration to revise its employment security program.[73]

The reforms were minor — an administrative reorganization and some new guidelines. Nonetheless, for the first time the federal government had responded to criticism of its loyalty-security program by easing up rather than cracking down. While these reforms were largely a public relations gesture, the political climate had clearly changed. As Karl Baarslag complained to J. B. Matthews in February 1955,

> It's going to be a tough year there for the antis. I hear Scotty McLeod is on his way out. Same thing in Civil Service, the real hard core antis who booted out the commies are shaking in their boots. They frankly admit they felt safer under Truman and Acheson than they do under Eisenhower and [Attorney General] Bill Rogers.

Just as earlier crackdowns had not stopped right-wing attacks on earlier administrations, Eisenhower's reforms did not silence his liberal critics. By the summer of 1955, the revelations of FBI informer Harvey Matusow that government witnesses lied brought renewed attention to the abuses of the anticommunist crusade. Two Senate committees began investigations; and Eisenhower at last decided to appoint the special commission he had been considering for years.[74]

It was an anticlimactic gesture. The commission itself was a rather conservative body. Headed by Loyd Wright, a California attorney and former president of the American Bar Association, who had been selected by Richard Nixon, the panel contained, among others, the chairman of HUAC. With the FBI's D. Milton Ladd as its administrative director, it was obvious that the commission would not challenge the system. Nor did it rush its conclusions. Established in August 1955, it did not hold its first meeting until December. It conducted no public hearings and postponed its final report until June 1957.[75]

By then, the government's loyalty-security programs were in disarray. The Supreme Court had done them in. Like the rest of the nation, the Court had begun to rescind its earlier support for the anticommunist crusade. Its decisions restoring the rights of federal employees were part of a broader judicial rollback of McCarthyism that was as important in diminishing its power as the Court's earlier rulings had been in reinforcing it. Both the political atmosphere and the composition of the high court had changed. The Korean War was over, McCarthy was on the skids, and the Cold War seemed less terrifying. Moreover, between 1953 and 1957 four of the Court's more conservative members either died or resigned, to be replaced by a group of moderates and civil libertarians.[76]

Though President Eisenhower had not intended to create a more liberal tribunal, some of his appointments, especially those of Chief Justice Earl Warren and Justice William Brennan, did just that. As a result, beginning in 1955, the Court began to reverse its earlier position in cases involving Communism and civil liberties. However, because of the Court's own internal divisions, the justices shrank from openly confronting the sensitive political and constitutional issues these cases presented and sought whenever possible to base their decisions on the narrowest and most technical grounds they could find. Still, the tide had clearly turned; and by the late 1950s the Court was rendering decisions in a wide range of areas that made it increasingly more difficult for the anticommunist crusade to continue. It reversed Smith Act convictions, overturned deportations, and voided state sedition laws — though mainly on technicalities. In its employment security cases as well, the Court usually managed to find some kind of procedural ground for taking a more liberal stance.[77]

Its first opportunity to act came in the case of Dr. John P. Peters, a nutrition expert from the Yale Medical School who had been a consultant for the Public Health Service. Hardly involved in sensitive matters, Peters spent a few days a year in Washington reviewing grant proposals from other medical researchers. Though he was an active health-care reformer, he had never been a Communist or even belonged to a group on the Attorney General's list. At the time the secretary of health, education, and welfare asked the department's Loyalty Review Board to reopen his case, Peters had already survived two previous investigations. He cooperated fully with the examiners at his May 1953 hearing and produced the former president of Yale and four other eminences to vouch for his loyalty. The government, as usual, offered no witnesses at all; its case rested entirely on the allegations of some FBI informants whose identity even the board members did not know. Nonetheless, the panel decided that there was "a reasonable doubt" about Peters's loyalty.[78]

Peters sued and hired as his attorney Thurman Arnold, the same Washington lawyer who had represented Dorothy Bailey. Arnold hoped that Peters's case would test the constitutionality of the loyalty-security program and he made the appeal an attack on the government's reliance on anonymous informers. Though the Court reinstated Peters, Arnold was disappointed by the limited scope of its June 1955 decision. By ruling only that the review board had no authority to reopen a case that had already been settled, the justices set no useful precedent.[79]

The following year they did. The case was that of Kendrick Cole, who had been fired from his position with the Food and Drug Administration for hiking with the wrong people. In October 1953, he was called to Washington, accused of associating with Communists, and questioned about his friends and the books they read. When he was suspended a month later, he refused to answer the formal charges against him, claiming that "any request of me to make explanation regarding my personal choice of friends is an invasion of my personal rights." Though he changed his mind and asked to reopen the case so he could show how harmless his leisure-time activities had been, the secretary of health, education, and welfare fired him anyhow. Under Eisenhower's Executive Order 10450, Cole's employment was not "clearly consistent with the interests of national security."[80]

With the support of the ACLU, he sued and appealed his dismissal all the way to the Supreme Court. Unlike Bailey, Parker, and Peters, Cole was not challenging the vagueness of the charges against him or the use of anonymous informants. He and his attorneys were questioning the right of the government to fire people on security grounds who held nonsensitive jobs. It was, after all, hard to make a case that Cole, who spent his working hours tracking down harmful chemicals, insects, and mouse droppings, could really threaten the nation's security. The Supreme Court agreed. There was no way that the government could justify applying P.L. 733's specific security provisions to all federal employees, regardless of their relationship to the nation's internal or external defense.[81]

The *Cole v. Young* decision was lethal to the loyalty-security program. Within days of the ruling, the order went out reinstating all government workers in nonsensitive positions who had been suspended as security risks and blocking future actions. About a hundred people regained their jobs, over half of them Post Office employees. More important, the loyalty-security program hung in limbo as congressional leaders and administration officials tried to figure out what to do.[82]

At first it seemed as if Congress would override *Cole v. Young*. Like the other liberal Supreme Court rulings of the late 1950s, the decision encountered enormous opposition. Security-minded politicians and officials charged that it left the government dangerously open to subversive penetration. "One never knows," Justice Tom Clark insisted in his dissenting opinion, "just which job is sensitive. The janitor might prove to be in as important a spot security-wise as the top employee in the building." The obvious solution was to revise P.L. 733 and extend its provisions to all federal employees. Congress was receptive; and the measure to designate all government jobs as sensitive was soon speeding through the House.[83]

But the administration did not push it strongly. Though some officials were eager for a new law, the Justice Department, which was handling the matter, wanted to wait until the presidential commission under Loyd Wright finished its report. As a result, not much happened. One measure passed the House but never got to the Senate floor. Another almost passed, defeated only in the final hours of the 1958 session by the threat of a liberal filibuster. Meanwhile, the Wright Commission's report appeared and was quietly shoved under the rug. It proposed few major revisions and its main recommendation, for a central security office, was opposed by the Justice Department on the grounds that "the potential caseload, in the Federal personnel field at least, is too limited to justify the elaborate and expensive establishment" of such a body. In short, as Attorney General William P. Rogers explained to Eisenhower early in 1959, "the moment [had] long since passed" when the administration had to worry about the Communists-in-government issue.[84]

In the fall of 1962, when the Senate Internal Security Subcommittee began to think about a new investigation of the government's loyalty-security program, it asked all the departments and agencies for reports on what they were doing. The Post Office's response was typical: "This Department has not had a security hearing under Executive Order 10450 since *Cole v. Young*." By the early 1960s, Washington's loyalty-security program had become a dead letter. Even John Stewart Service returned to the State Department (though, it is true, he never received a decent posting). In response to bad publicity, adverse judicial decisions, and the officials' own sense of fair play, the most egregious violations of due process within the federal government came to an end. Though such a reversal can be celebrated as a victory for the underlying strength of American democracy, it can also be seen as the result of the program's almost total success.[85]

The witch-hunting stopped because there were no more witches. The actual number of employees driven out of their jobs by the federal government's loyalty-security programs is surprisingly low. In the first year of E.O. 9835's operation, for example, 80 people were dismissed and between 150 and 200 resigned. By the end of the Truman administration, there had been 518 loyalty dismissals and 2,636 resignations. The Eisenhower regime's figures were harder to disaggregate. Though 1,456 employees had been dismissed in the early months of E.O. 10450, it is impossible to tell how many lost their jobs because of their association with Communism. Since the administration resisted revealing those figures, they were probably low. Between 1956 and 1959, for example, one report notes that there were only eleven people who lost or were denied federal employment because of "reasonable doubt as to loyalty."[86]

Most of its politically vulnerable employees left the government voluntarily. As early as 1946, there was enormous pressure on people with questionable backgrounds, such as Alger Hiss and Carl Marzani, to quit their jobs. Resignations avoided difficult hearings and allowed these men and women to keep their records clean. Since thousands of civil servants quit their jobs every year, it is not possible to tell how many of them did so under duress. Still, there are some figures from the Eisenhower era indicating that ten times as many people with security problems in their files resigned as were fired. Thousands more never even tried to get a position that required them to be cleared. By 1958, for example, there were no members of the National Lawyers Guild on the federal payroll; and none applied for a government job again until 1970.[87]

1970 was also the year in which the NLG elected its first woman president. She was Doris Brin Walker, or Dobby, as she was called, a longtime guild activist and CP member from the San Francisco Bay area, whose 1949 dismissal from a pharmaceutical company became the main test case of the ability of a private employer to fire a Communist. Walker was hardly unique. Thousands of other workers also lost their jobs for the same reasons. But because she was both a clerical worker and a self-employed professional, as well as the subject of a key Supreme Court decision, her story is a useful way to look at how public and private agencies collaborated in administering the economic sanctions of the McCarthy era.

Walker's first job after she graduated from law school in 1942 was with the federal government, where she worked as an enforcement officer with the Office of Price Administration and headed the OPA's white collar union. In early 1944, she resigned from the government to join Richard Gladstein's law firm, but had to leave at the end of 1945 when a new partner refused to work with a woman. Walker treated her ouster with equanimity, for, as she recalled, "I had decided that I should become a worker." The Communist party was then pushing its "industrial concentration" line, urging members to get factory jobs and build unions.[88]

Accordingly, Walker hitched up with the CP-led Food, Tobacco, Agricultural and Allied Workers (FTA) and went to work in a cannery. Since she was not, she recalled, "very subtle," she soon lost her job. She worked at and was fired from two more canneries before ending up as a label clerk at the Cutter Laboratories Berkeley plant. Though the company had been organized in the early 1940s by the Federation of Architects, Engineers, Chemists and Technicians (FAECT), the local, by then an affiliate of the same left-wing United Office and Professional Workers of America (UOPWA) union that my former sixth-grade teacher had worked for, had lapsed into inactivity. The party suggested that Walker try to reenergize it. She did, becoming a shop steward, member of the executive board, chief steward, and, finally, president of the local. She led the union through a difficult strike in 1947 and was in the middle of tense contract negotiations when she was fired on the morning of October 6, 1949. She recalls Cutter's personnel director coming to her desk and making her gather up her things and then being "escorted out of the plant and told never to come back again."[89]

Cutter had been investigating Walker and the other UOPWA leaders since 1947. It hired private detectives, approached the FBI, and soon learned that Walker was a Communist. Nonetheless, despite the evidence in its possession (which included letters she had written to party headquarters in the early 1940s), Cutter waited two years before firing her. When it did so, it claimed that her political affiliation, not her union activities, had triggered her dismissal. Not only had she falsified her job application by concealing her legal training and her three earlier cannery jobs, but she had also refused to answer questions about her party activities at a 1948 NLRB hearing. "The nature of our company's business," Cutter officials explained, "requires more than the usual precaution against sabotage and subversion." It had a "responsibility" to fire a communist employee. The UOPWA filed a grievance, claiming that Walker's ouster was an anti-union measure, not an anticommunist one. Since Walker had never seriously tried to conceal her political affiliation, Cutter's willingness to retain her for several years made its pronouncements about national security less than convincing.[90]

At first, Walker's appeal was successful. The arbitration panel that initially dealt with the case ordered her reinstatement because an employer "should not be entitled to carry mutually known grounds for discharge in [his] hip pocket indefinitely for future convenient use." The panel did not question Cutter's right to fire a Communist, just its timing. The California supreme court overruled the arbitrators. Communists were so dangerous, it asserted, they could be fired at any time. By the time the appeal reached the U.S. Supreme Court, all the litigants recognized that it presented the key issue governing the economic sanctions of the McCarthy era: could a Communist hold a job? Yet, when the divided Court rendered its decision, exactly one week before it reinstated Kendrick Cole, it characteristically avoided ruling on the substance of the case. Instead of deciding whether private employers violated the First Amendment by firing party members, the majority opinion in *Black v. Cutter Laboratories,* as the case was called, stated that the issues involved did not concern the federal government. Whatever the wording, the import of the ruling was clear: Communists had no right to a job.[91]

In explaining why party members like Dobby Walker deserved to be fired, the company, its corporate allies, and the courts not only invoked national security but also relied on a demonized image of Communism. Their arguments are familiar. Though it had no evidence that Walker planned to adulterate the vaccines Cutter produced, the California supreme court noted the possibility and cited an "array of congressional and legislative findings" to establish that "a member of the Communist Party cannot be loyal to his private employer as against any directive of his Communist master." A company could legitimately dismiss such an employee, the Court explained, since "acts of sabotage by Communists are reasonably to be expected at any time such acts may be directed by the party leaders."[92]

By the middle of 1956, when the Supreme Court decided her case, Dobby Walker had long since abandoned her foray into the working class. She had returned to the practice of law that she had given up in 1945. And she was having a hard time. Because she was one of the few attorneys willing to take on political pariahs, she had, as she wanted, "a left-based practice." She worked with the California Smith Act defendants, represented unfriendly witnesses before HUAC, handled labor complaints, fought deportations, and even assisted in the only federal sedition case of the Cold War, the prosecution of a former American journalist in China who had published allegations that the U.S. military used germ warfare in Korea.[93]

Walker had her own legal problems as well, for the organized bar did not welcome communist attorneys. Though lawyers should presumably have been more sensitive than other Americans to the violations of individual rights that characterized the McCarthy era, they were not. Just like the federal government and other public and private employers, the legal profession tried to impose political tests on its members. As early as 1946, the Attorney General had hinted that the bar might have to crack down on communist attorneys and advised his fellow lawyers to take them "to the legal woodshed for a well-deserved admonition." Most bar associations were all too willing to comply.[94]

Much of the impetus for such admonitions came from conservative attorneys and prosecutors with close ties to the anticommunist network. Because of their dedication to the cause of eradicating Communism at a time when liberals offered little resistance to their efforts, these individuals had the same disproportionate influence within the nation's bar associations that other anticommunist activists had within other public and private institutions. In September 1950, a small group of these lawyers pushed an anticommunist resolution and a loyalty oath through the American Bar Association's annual meeting. Two months later the ABA set up a special committee "to study Communist tactics, strategy, and objects." The committee's main targets were left-wing attorneys and the National Lawyers Guild, to which most of those attorneys belonged. Since the FBI had long viewed the NLG as an enemy and was eager to expel alleged Communists from the legal profession, it readily cooperated with the new committee's request for information about the guild and its leaders. At the same time, local bar associations began proceedings to disbar their most visible radicals. There were about fifteen such cases.[95]

Walker's was one of them. A few months after the Supreme Court reached its decision in *Black v. Cutter Laboratories,* the state bar of California appointed a special committee to look into her fitness to practice law. Her 1947 failure to tell Cutter that she was an attorney might be, the committee implied, sufficent cause to oust her from the profession. Her November 1956 hearing, however, dealt mainly with her party membership, her activities in various front groups, and her legal practice; it also featured the same questions about her attendance at specific CP unit meetings in the 1940s that had been asked at both her 1948 NLRB hearings and the Cutter proceedings. This time, however, the case was dropped. The political climate had changed so much by 1957 that the anti-Communists who had been trying to oust radicals from the legal profession had become as marginalized as those radicals had been only a few years before.[96]

Like Walker, most of the lawyers who faced disbarment proceedings were also cleared, though sometimes it took more than a decade. Like Walker, these attorneys seem to have been singled out because they had represented notorious clients or else had themselves been involved in some kind of controversy. Thus, for example, had he not died suddenly of a heart attack, the Rosenbergs' lawyer might well have been ousted from the legal profession. The FBI, it turns out, was secretly slipping information about him to the New York City bar association. The *Dennis* case attorneys, already confronting Judge Medina's contempt charges, also faced disbarment proceedings, as did lawyers who relied on the Fifth Amendment. Candidates for the bar who were unwilling to answer questions about their political affiliations and beliefs ran similar risks. Such behavior, their examiners explained, revealed that they were lacking in the "good moral character" that membership in the legal profession required. Most of these people were ultimately reinstated, especially after the judiciary began to fear that punishing left-wing lawyers was making it hard for political defendants to find counsel.[97]

That concern was not misplaced. Except for a handful of left-wing labor lawyers, civil libertarians, and National Lawyers Guild activists, few noncommunist members of the bar were willing to represent political undesirables. Some attorneys had ideological qualms; they did not want to take on clients they claimed to abhor. Others recognized the bar's responsibility for unpopular defendants but nonetheless ducked the assignment. Many, if not most, of the bar's leading figures were, it is true, corporate lawyers who did not ordinarily handle criminal cases. But many prominent liberals were also reluctant to take on unpopular clients. "We have decided," Abe Fortas, Owen Lattimore's lawyer, explained as he justified his refusal to represent some of the Berkeley Radiation Laboratory physicists at their 1949 HUAC hearing, "that we don't think we can ever afford to represent anybody that has ever been a Communist."[98]

As Fortas himself was to discover when the ACLU dawdled interminably over whether it would support Lattimore, even the nation's preeminent civil liberties organization shrank from controversy. It refused, for example, to enter the Rosenberg case on the grounds that no civil liberties issues were involved. Moreover, when it did take on a case, it did so only at the appellate, not the trial, stage, invariably prefacing its briefs with a strong anticommunist disclaimer. Such wishy-washy behavior reflected the ACLU's internal divisions. Its more conservative members, like Morris Ernst, wanted to attack Communism and its more liberal ones wanted to defy McCarthyism. As a result, the organization was paralyzed, its inaction indirectly reinforcing the reluctance of liberal lawyers to defend politically unpopular clients.[99]

The bar's timidity made it almost impossible for Communists and alleged Communists to obtain counsel — especially if they did not want to be represented by someone who was already tainted. It took Hymen Schlesinger, a Pittsburgh lawyer who was threatened with disbarment for taking the Fifth Amendment, eight months before he found someone to handle his case. Steve Nelson had the same problem. He, too, could find no one to defend him in his 1951–52 Pittsburgh sedition trial and ended up acting as his own attorney. Elizabeth Gurley Flynn and the other second-string Smith Act defendants in New York City were turned down by more than two hundred lawyers. Similarly, when Dobby Walker's law partner Robert Treuhaft was called before HUAC in December 1953, none of the eminent attorneys he approached would represent him. Though they agreed with his decision to take the First and Fifth Amendments and admitted, Treuhaft told the committee, that political pariahs like himself should have good counsel, they did not think they could risk taking on such an unpopular client. "Why

don't you find some older lawyer, someone who is in a better financial position to take this risk?" one well-established attorney asked Treuhaft. "Try
to find a younger lawyer," suggested the even more well established attorney
Treuhaft next consulted. "The activities before this committee would be too
strenuous."[100]

The strain, of course, was economic, not physical. True, a few left-
wing lawyers did face contempt citations and other types of sanctions, but
such punitive measures were rare. What people most feared was the loss of
business and respectability that might occur if clients and colleagues identified them with the pariahs they represented. At times these fears verged
on paranoia. One Washington lawyer who refused to handle any loyalty
cases also refused to refer them to other attorneys. "I wouldn't be caught
dead sending them on to another lawyer — for fear he would think I think
he's a Communist, or something." Though exaggerated, these concerns did
have some basis in reality. The evidence, though largely anecdotal, does reveal that representing controversial clients did hurt people's practice. Washington attorney Joseph Forer recalls that taking on Gerhart Eisler as a client
"immediately cost us half of our business." Alger Hiss's lawyer lost a federal
judgeship. A survey in Pittsburgh found that though the few conservative
lawyers who handled unpopular clients reported no problems, 30 percent
of the liberal attorneys who took such cases suffered to some degree, and
over 50 percent of a national control group of lawyers who routinely represented leftists did.[101]

Perceptions are important here. Assumptions that communist defendants tainted their attorneys were so widespread that the attorneys who
were willing to take on such cases did, in fact, become tainted. One man
whose income declined by 20 percent after he defended someone in a state
sedition trial stopped getting new local clients. No one thought he was disloyal, he explained. "Their attitude is, rather, that I am rather peculiar and
that it may be better to put their affairs in the hands of a more normal sort of
person."[102]

Even radicals sought "respectable" attorneys. They believed — incorrectly as it turned out — that juries and judges might be more sympathetic
to an establishment lawyer than to someone identified with the left. The
party itself subscribed to that assumption and in some of its biggest cases
replaced its usual legal advisers with more mainstream ones. This attitude

was so pervasive that the lawyers who routinely handled unpopular cases lost their traditional left-wing clients. After New York attorney Victor Rabinowitz successfully argued Steve Nelson's sedition case before the Supreme Court, the communist-led labor union that constituted the core of his practice severed its ties with his law firm. That action, by an organization that was itself under attack during the 1940s and 1950s, shows how deeply the timidity bred by McCarthyism had penetrated.[103]

That timidity extended far beyond the legal community. The literature of the McCarthy era abounds with stories of former friends crossing the street to avoid having to greet unfriendly witnesses and insurance companies refusing to write policies for government officials who lost their jobs. Such manifestations of anxiety were extreme, but not entirely unrealistic. Given the effectiveness and broad scope of the era's economic sanctions, it was not irrational for people who had associated with the communist movement to fear some kind of economic repercussions. Though many more people lost their jobs than their freedom or their lives during the McCarthy era, the process that imposed the economic sanctions they faced was closely linked to the more overt system of political repression that kept Gerhart Eisler under surveillance and sent Carl Marzani to prison for perjury. The same mechanisms, assumptions, and institutions came into play. McCarthyism functioned along a spectrum that extended from such relatively minor damage as the withdrawal of a judgeship from Alger Hiss's lawyer to the judicial murder of Julius and Ethel Rosenberg. And neither one could have occurred without the other.

★

PART FOUR

INTERCONNECTIONS

★

CHAPTER 9

"HOW RED IS A VALLEY"

CLINTON JENCKS AND HIS UNION

DOBBY WALKER'S dismissal from Cutter Laboratories did not end the FBI's interest in her. For years the Bureau monitored her activities and kept tabs on the people she associated with. Among the names that appear in her FBI file are those of Craig and Jenny Vincent, the owners of a New Mexico resort, the San Cristobal Valley Ranch. During the early 1950s, the Bureau reported several contacts between Walker and the Vincents: a cocktail party in San Francisco, a trip by Walker and her husband to the ranch, phone calls, and visits. From the FBI's perspective, these associations must have seemed menacing. The Bureau viewed the Vincents' ranch as the "headquarters for and meeting place of CP members in northern New Mexico"; Walker, it noted, was "reported to have cooperated with the CP Underground and should be considered capable of potential espionage." [1]

From another perspective, however, the contacts between Walker and the Vincents reveal not a Moscow-led conspiracy, but the web of personal and institutional connections so crucial for sustaining the vitality of an ongoing social movement. The San Cristobal Valley Ranch was a small piece of that movement, a resort that catered to a multiracial, left-wing clientele from all over the United States. Here, in a former boarding school deep in the Sangre de Cristo mountains, not far from Taos, union officials,

309

blacklisted screenwriters, and other denizens of the left could vacation in a congenial political atmosphere. Besides the usual dude ranch activities, the Vincents offered their guests field trips to local pueblos and archeological sites, theatrical productions, lectures, and discussions. On Saturday nights, there would be dancing or a songfest at which the ranch's guests and people from the local community sang Spanish Civil War and Mexican folk songs to the accompaniment of Jenny Vincent's guitar and accordion.[2]

To a certain extent, the ranch was itself a product of the anticommunist crusade. Craig Vincent was a former New Deal official whose radical leanings ensured that he would be under a cloud had he stayed in the government. Instead, after running Henry Wallace's presidential campaign in Colorado, he moved to New Mexico, married Jenny, and in 1949 opened the ranch. Vincent, like so many other leftists forced out of public life in the late 1940s and 1950s, found a niche within the world of American Communism. But it was a shaky haven, indeed. Because the Vincents and their patrons were often under surveillance, it was clear that a sojourn at the San Cristobal Valley Ranch might well be politically lethal. Jenny Vincent recalls that her neighbors were told to keep track of the license plates of the cars that visited the resort. By the end of 1953, the ranch had attracted so much attention that, unwilling to subject their guests to the risk of a congressional subpoena or the loss of a job, the Vincents closed up shop and put their spread on the market.[3]

The notoriety that forced the San Cristobal Valley Ranch to fold came from its guests as well as its owners. Protagonists in the anticommunist proceedings of the McCarthy era found that their vacations at the so-called "communist dude ranch" sometimes figured as additional evidence for their allegedly conspiratorial doings. The case of Clinton Jencks did the most damage. Jencks, an organizer with the International Union of Mine, Mill and Smelter Workers in southern New Mexico, was a regular at the ranch. At one of his visits, he met Harvey Matusow, the FBI informer who later testified against him. At another, he met Paul Jarrico, the blacklisted screenwriter who produced a film about Jencks's Mine-Mill local. Like the Vincents, Jencks, Matusow, and Jarrico were all caught up in the political repression of the McCarthy era.

Though no single story can encompass every element of that repression, that of Clinton Jencks comes close. His experiences and those of the people who both worked with him and persecuted him reveal the dense web of personal and institutional relationships that constituted the inter-connected worlds of American Communism and anticommunism. They also show the machinery of McCarthyism in operation. What is striking about that machinery is its complexity, how many different components it contained and how interdependent they all were. Constructed in the late 1940s, it was a system that reached its peak during the 1950s when federal bureaucrats, labor leaders, businessmen, judges, law enforcement officials, politicians, journalists, and professional anti-Communists all cooperated in driving Communism and all the individuals, institutions, and ideas associated with it out of American life.

As Clinton Jencks's recently released FBI files reveal, he got caught up in this machinery in part because he belonged to the communist movement, but mainly because he was active in a left-wing union. His experiences, therefore, make it possible to examine the crucial, but all too often overlooked, relationship between organized labor and the anticommunist crusade.

They also make it possible to explore another key component of that crusade, its routine use of unfair and undemocratic methods. For, as Jencks's FBI files make clear, it took a lot of cheating and collaboration to destroy the left-labor milieu within which Clinton Jencks — as well as the Vincents and their guests — had made their lives.

Jencks's story begins at the San Cristobal Valley Ranch, for that is where he met Harvey Matusow. Matusow had come to the ranch because of his con-tacts with the left-wing folk music world that Jenny Vincent also inhab-ited. A professional musician who collected and performed the songs of the Spanish-speaking inhabitants of the American Southwest, Vincent sang regularly before front groups and unions. When she visited New York dur-ing the late 1940s and early 1950s, she would sing along with Pete Seeger and his musical colleagues and talk about the ranch. It must have been at one of those sessions sometime in the winter of 1949–50 that she first en-countered Harvey Matusow. A few months later, Matusow showed up in New Mexico.[4]

At that time, Matusow was a twenty-three-year-old informer for the FBI. The son of a cigar-store owner, he had grown up in the Bronx and joined the Army in October 1944, when he was only eighteen years old. He served in France and Germany before being mustered out in the summer of 1946. Though bright and energetic, Matusow was an unstable character who soon found himself at loose ends in civilian life. He took a course or two at CCNY, worked at a succession of low-level advertising and clerical jobs, and drifted into the Communist party because, as he later explained, it gave him "the feeling of belonging." Soon he was on the payroll, working at party-connected bookstores and summer camps and even for a while as a switchboard operator at the CP's New York headquarters. By the end of 1948, he had talked himself into a job selling books and records for Pete Seeger's left-wing folk music outfit, People's Songs.[5]

According to most people's recollections, Matusow was something of an operator, always hustling some kind of scheme. Jenny Vincent remembers him as "very pushy and very aggressive" and several other people who encountered him at the ranch recall him as simply "weird." He was not, to put it delicately, good at details. Even before he became an FBI informer, Matusow was congenitally dishonest. He seems to have been regularly fired from his various party-linked jobs for acts of petty thievery like stealing books or ringing up fraudulent sales. In 1948, he won a free trip to Puerto Rico for selling more subscriptions to the *Sunday Worker* than anybody else. Later it was discovered that many of Harvey's subscribers had fictitious names or else were receiving three and four copies of the paper.[6]

Matusow craved attention and soon grew disillusioned with the party's failure to give it to him. At the same time, he became apprehensive about the intensifying public hostility to Communism. In February 1950, he contacted the FBI and volunteered to become an informer. It was an offer the Bureau did not refuse and Matusow soon turned his formidable energies to snitching on his comrades. But his new career was no more satisfying than the old one and by the middle of 1950, he decided to leave New York for Los Angeles. He ended up in New Mexico, where, he claimed, the local FBI agent asked him to spy on the San Cristobal Valley Ranch. He stayed there for a week, calling square dances and trying to con the Vincents into making him the ranch's social director. He then moved to Taos, drove a cab, took a few art courses, and finally returned to New York. By then, his activities had aroused so much suspicion that he was formally expelled from the party "for being," in the *Daily Worker*'s words, "an enemy agent."[7]

While he was at the ranch, Matusow reported to the FBI about Clinton Jencks. He had, he said, talked about the party with Jencks and heard him lecture on "The Trade Union Fight for Peace in Relation to the Stockholm Peace Appeal." Though Jencks has never admitted to being a Communist, it is hard to imagine that he was not. A native of the Southwest, he had grown up in a conservative, rather religious working-class family in the mining town of Colorado Springs. Some of his relatives were missionaries and their zeal, if not their faith, rubbed off on Jencks, who even as a boy had a strong streak of idealism. He worked his way through the University of Colorado, where he led the campus branch of the radical American Student Union. Then he moved to St. Louis, worked in a tractor factory, and continued his political activities. In 1942, he went to war. Trained as a navigator, he served in the Pacific, winning the Distinguished Flying Cross and six Air Medals for combat service. After his discharge in 1945, he ended up in Denver, again becoming active in the local left. He held jobs at Continental Airlines and then at a smelting plant. In 1947, Mine-Mill sent him to the Silver City area of Grant County in southern New Mexico as an organizer.[8]

Rich in silver, zinc, lead, and copper, the corner of New Mexico that Clinton Jencks moved his family to had long been mining country. Most of the miners who lived in the small agricultural settlements and company towns scattered across the arid landscape were Mexican Americans. The discrimination they enountered was similar to that facing blacks in the Jim Crow South. There were segregated schools, segregated housing, segregated jobs. "In the Kennecott operation," a Mexican American union leader recalled, the dressing rooms, dining rooms, even the time clocks, were segregated; and, of course, the "pure Anglos [were] getting higher pay." Even after the union eliminated the worst abuses by the late 1940s and got rid of the separate Mexican and Anglo pay scales, Mexican Americans still held the dirtiest, most dangerous, and lowest-paying jobs. They also got the worst housing. The homes of the Mexican American miners in the Empire Zinc company town of Hanover, New Mexico, for example, were separated from those of the Anglo workers and lacked indoor plumbing.[9]

There were five Mine-Mill locals in Grant County when Jencks got there. Within a year, the energy and commitment of "El Palomino," as

313

the miners affectionately called their tall, blond organizer, transformed the union. The separate locals merged into a single unit, the Amalgamated Bayard District Union Local 890, with a new union hall, local newspaper, weekly radio program, and an active women's auxiliary. Like the other left-led unions, Mine-Mill promoted racial equality and concerned itself with minority groups. Jencks's activities in the Silver City area were part of that effort. He encouraged the local's Mexican American members to take leadership positions, become shop stewards, and settle grievances themselves rather than, as had been the tradition, letting the Anglo organizers handle the task.[10]

Over the course of the next few years, Local 890 struggled to get its members the same wages and working conditions that hard-rock miners in the rest of the country enjoyed. It was not always easy. Besides their traditional contempt for Mexican Americans, the mine owners did not want to give up any of their control over the workplace. Their resistance was part of a nationwide campaign by the business community to roll back the gains that unions had made since the New Deal. We have already seen the reflection of this campaign in the struggles at Allis-Chalmers. The conflict was equally intense within the hard-rock mining industry, where labor relations had long been bitter and where the economically unstable metallurgical industry careened from crisis to crisis. Mine-Mill's association with Communism only worsened the situation, since it gave mine owners a patriotic reason not to bargain. All too often, the union could respond to that intransigence only by going out on strike.[11]

Local 890's bitterest and most celebrated confrontation occurred in 1950–51 when it staged a fifteen-month walkout against the small mine operated by Empire Zinc in Hanover, New Mexico. Though technically about such issues as paid vacations, the strike soon turned into a struggle for survival; the company was determined to break the union's power and the union was equally determined to stand fast. The first few months were uneventful and most of the local community generally took a hands-off approach toward the walkout. But when the company attempted to reopen the mine in the middle of 1951, a brawl ensued. A few union officials were arrested and the next day Empire Zinc got an injunction from a Silver City magistrate forbidding the union to block access to the mine. The local was in a bind. It would lose the strike unless it could prevent the mine from reopening, but it could not afford the fines and jail sentences that defying the injunction would entail.[12]

At that point, Jencks and another Mine-Mill official suggested that the miners' wives take over the picket line. The women actively supported the strike and they were willing to take on the task. But their husbands demurred. They feared for their wives' safety and were reluctant to see such a major reversal of traditional gender roles. There was, however, no other alternative; and on the following day the women began to man the picket lines. The situation remained quiet for a few days until the local sheriff decided to act. He arrested a few women but others soon took their place. They held the picket line all day, fending off every effort by deputies and nonstrikers to break through. By evening, there were over sixty women and children in the overcrowded county jail, including a six-week-old baby. They got national attention and the embarrassed sheriff finally had to let them go.

The women's participation revitalized the union and ensured that the strike would continue despite the growing opposition of local authorities, the deepening antagonism between the Mexican American and Anglo communities, and an intensifying red-baiting campaign that stressed the archetypical image of the outside agitator. Jencks was the target here, responsible, so the union's opponents claimed, for stirring up the otherwise docile Mexican American miners. By the end of August, the tensions that built up at the picket line exploded into a full-scale riot. At that point, the other members of Local 890 joined the strike. Since the international union was planning an industry-wide walkout in September anyhow, the New Mexico miners were only jumping the gun by a few weeks.[13]

Though the international soon negotiated its settlement, the Empire Zinc strike continued. It was, however, unclear how much longer the miners could hold out. The local's resources were dwindling, the international's leaders were anxious to end the walkout, and the company was importing more and more strikebreakers. The anticommunist propaganda was also taking its toll. Mine-Mill had long been under attack and its nationwide walkout precipitated charges that the union was trying to sabotage the war in Korea. By the end of the year, the strike was all but lost. The overwhelming hostility of the local authorities and the company's continuing resort to injunctions and other legal harassments made it impossible for the increasingly isolated strikers to hold out. At that point, Empire Zinc, which may well have wanted to preserve a weakened local rather than see it replaced by a stronger rival, decided to negotiate. Both sides made genuine concessions and soon reached a settlement. On January 24, 1952, the handful of remaining strikers ratified the agreement and the strike was over.[14]

At one point, in the middle of the strike, Clinton Jencks took his wife and children to the San Cristobal Valley Ranch. The entire family had been involved in the action from the start. Jencks's wife, Virginia, was beaten up at a demonstration and then charged with assaulting her assailants. Their thirteen-year-old daughter, Linda, was arrested on the picket line and their nine-year-old son, Clinton Michael, was teargassed. The family needed the kind of respite and support that they knew they would find among the Vincents and their politically compatible guests. For the embattled Communists and others who patronized the ranch, the Jencks's stories about the Empire Zinc miners and their spunky wives must have seemed inspirational at a time when so much of the movement they belonged to was under assault.[15]

No one was more fascinated by Jencks's account of the strike than the blacklisted screenwriter Paul Jarrico. Along with a few other Hollywood outcasts, Jarrico had just formed an independent production company to make movies about subjects that the rest of the film industry would not touch. Though they had no trouble raising money, it was harder to find a story that would be both entertaining and politically correct. As he talked about the Empire Zinc strike with Jencks, Jarrico became excited about its cinematic possibilities and set off at once for Grant County. The strike was still on when he got there. Though his age and gender barred him from the picket line, both his wife and eleven-year-old son took part. A few days later, Jarrico was back in Los Angeles; he had found the story. The Empire Zinc strike was about to become the movie *Salt of the Earth.*[16]

The men who made *Salt of the Earth* — Jarrico, his brother-in-law screenwriter Michael Wilson, and director Herbert Biberman — were among the film industry's most energetic Communists, members of a vibrant radical community that flourished in southern California during the 1930s and early 1940s. Like Jarrico, most of these people joined the CP during its Popular Front period, attracted by its commitment to social justice and its strong stand against Hitler. Screenwriters predominated; Hollywood's intellectuals, they were, like many of the CP's middle-class recruits, a largely Jewish cohort. Their political activities differed little from those of other middle-class party members, though, it is true, few of them peddled the West Coast counterpart of the *Daily Worker* from door to door. Instead, they helped organize the Screen Writers Guild, taught at labor schools, and founded theater companies, little magazines, and writers groups. As the film colony's most ardent antifascists, they established its main interventionist and anti-Nazi groups in the 1930s and then threw themselves into FDR's 1944 reelection campaign. In the late 1940s, they worked for Henry Wallace.[17]

And, of course, they raised money. With salaries like Jarrico's $2,000 a week and Dalton Trumbo's $3,000, they were among the nation's wealthiest Communists and overall may have contributed millions of dollars to the CP and its causes. In addition, they provided access to the glamour of the film capital. Only in Hollywood could the party bring screenwriters, directors, and movie stars to the picket lines to support striking farmworkers or recruit celebrity signatures on petitions to abolish HUAC. The publicity was invaluable — and the CP knew it.[18]

Ironically, the one area in which Hollywood's Communists had very little impact was in the films they made. It was hard to insert proletarian class consciousness into such vehicles as *Sweetheart of the Campus, Charlie Chan's Greatest Case,* or *Our Blushing Brides.* As a result, many Communists simply ignored the trivia they worked on and threw themselves into fund-raising and other extracurricular activities. Others were more conflicted and tried to introduce some kind of political message into their pictures. Except for their involvement with the making of a few "social problem" films in the late 1940s, they had little success. The producers controlled the final product and, though happy to use the talents of their left-wing writers and directors, they were not going to let anything subversive onto the screen. At best, the Hollywood Communists could cast a few black actors or write war movies that stressed cooperation rather than individual heroics. But even here it is hard to see how a line in which a navy officer points to a Soviet plane and shouts, "It's one of ours all right!" could subvert many moviegoers.[19]

Nonetheless, the visibility of the Hollywood left and the obvious, though unacknowledged, presence of the CP within it drew strong opposition. Conservative ideologues feared that Communists were poisoning the American screen; anti-union producers and their allies abhorred their labor militancy. As a result, purging the movie industry became a high priority within the anticommunist network. Many of the confrontations involved organized labor. The Screen Writers Guild was an early battleground. As was so often the case in a union in which Communists were influential, the SWG faced both external red-baiting and internal factionalism. The struggles in the guild and elsewhere were particularly vicious during the Nazi-Soviet pact period, when the collapse of the Popular Front destroyed the CP's alliance with liberals. Though the war restored a temporary truce, the conflict was rekindled in 1945.[20]

By then the film colony's conservatives had mobilized and were ready for action. In 1944 they had founded the Motion Picture Alliance for the Preservation of American Ideals to combat "the growing impression that this industry is made up of, and dominated by, Communists, radicals and crackpots" and oppose all efforts "to divert the loyalty of the screen from the free America that gave it birth." The Alliance soon became the movie industry's unofficial link to the anticommunist network. Its key figure was Roy Brewer, a pudgy labor leader imported from Nebraska to help the conservative and corrupt technicians' union, the International Alliance of Theatrical Stage Employees (IATSE), fend off its left-wing challengers. By the late 1940s, Brewer had become one of the most powerful men in Hollywood. Whether he was a true believer or simply a man with an eye on the main chance, Brewer ingratiated himself with the producers and took upon himself the task of purging the film colony of reds. He had many allies.[21]

The most useful was HUAC. Just as it helped J. Edgar Hoover expose the men and women who could not be punished by more orthodox sanctions, the committee's intervention proved to be the catalyst that enabled Hollywood's anti-Communists to carry out their agenda. HUAC well knew the publicity value of the film world and had been looking for Communists in the motion picture business ever since the late 1930s. So, too, had California's own HUAC clone, state senator Jack B. Tenney's Fact Finding Committee on Un-American Activities. Both groups held hearings, as did a Los Angeles grand jury, but until the fall of 1947 these efforts had little impact.[22]

The left-liberalism of the New Deal still held sway within the film colony and the major producers, while hardly sympathetic to the CP, felt no need to purge its members from their payrolls. Money, as well as politics, determined their behavior. If he were to fire the well-known Communists in his employ, MGM head Louis B. Mayer explained to a disgusted FBI agent in July 1947, "these writers would be grabbed up by the other studios immediately and paid more than he [Mayer was] paying them at the present time." Moreover, Mayer and his colleagues viewed the outside pressure for a political purge as an attempt to interfere with the conduct of their business, as unwelcome in its way as the screenwriters' demands for more control over their own scripts — and as easy to ignore.[23]

HUAC's hearings in October 1947 changed that assessment. Most accounts cite economic factors as the reason, the producers' fear that retaining communist employees would hurt them at the box office. But other considerations were just as important, especially the growing legitimacy of anticommunism among top business and political leaders and the willingness of other branches of the federal government to assist HUAC by, for example, prosecuting its unfriendly witnesses. In turn, the Hollywood hearings were just as crucial for consolidating the committee's power. They were a major turning point in the consolidation of the machinery of McCarthyism. Not only did the contempt proceedings that emerged from them define permissible behavior for future witnesses and make it impossible for them to rely on the First Amendment, but by precipitating the blacklist, the hearings established the pattern of economic sanctions that was so central to the committee's success and that of the rest of the anticommunist crusade.

In the spring of 1947, when HUAC began its postwar investigation of the film industry, it was unclear exactly how influential the probe would be. The committee held a series of executive sessions in Los Angeles at which activists from the Motion Picture Alliance testified that the party had subverted the film industry and producers insisted that their movies were intact. Though names were named, the main thrust of this first phase of the investigation was ideological. The committee wanted to know how Hollywood's Communists got CP propaganda onto the screen. Naturally, HUAC hoped the producers would fire the party members in their employ, but it also wanted them to change the content of their pictures, embrace anticommunism, and renounce all favorable references to Russia.[24]

The committee, its friendly witnesses, and the FBI, which was engaged in a parallel investigation of the "alleged Communistic propaganda" seeping into the movies, all shared the same ideological agenda, one that, it should be noted, was also being pushed in an aggressive public relations campaign by the organized business community. Movies should celebrate traditional individualism and treat businessmen as heroes. It was a sure sign of "thoroughgoing Collectivism," a Hollywood informant told the FBI, if a film left the impression that "American industrialists were greedy monsters." Friendly witnesses at HUAC's October hearings made similar observations about the film industry's supposedly subversive and antibusiness orientation. Though the high drama of the committee's confrontation with its unfriendly witnesses would overshadow the ideological components of HUAC's attack on Hollywood, that attack was just as successful in eliminating left-wing ideas from American movies as it was in purging left-wing individuals.[25]

The committee's spring hearings were only preliminary, designed to gather information about the scope of the problem and test the film industry's willingness to take action. If HUAC was to be effective, it would have to produce something more than the unsubstantiated charges of communist propaganda purveyed by the Motion Picture Alliance. Accordingly, it sought and received the FBI's assistance. Hoover recognized how valuable HUAC might be in helping him educate the American people about Communism and he ordered the Los Angeles field office to "extend *every* assistance to this Committee." Since the Bureau was running informers within the film community as well as bugging the phones of Los Angeles leftists and pulling regular "black bag jobs" on the local CP headquarters, it could give HUAC a lot of help. FBI agents conferred regularly with committee staffers, supplying them with blind memoranda that detailed the supposedly subversive connections of the people they wanted to subpoena. The Bureau also sent photostatic copies of these people's party cards and even prepared questions for individual congressmen to use in interrogating witnesses.[26]

Hollywood knew that the committee was planning a major investigation. HUAC staff members told studio executives that the committee "meant business" and warned them that they might be called up in public. On September 21, the committee issued forty-three subpoenas. Most went to friendly witnesses — producers, Alliance members, and movie stars who, like Ronald Reagan and Gary Cooper, could be counted on to deplore the influence of Hollywood Communists and congratulate the committee on its work. Nineteen went to potentially unfriendly ones.* HUAC's principles of selection are unclear. FBI files show that, until the moment it issued the subpoenas, the committee kept changing its lists of possible witnesses. It called up some, but not all, of the film colony's most notorious reds. It also subpoenaed people who were barely active in the party, and at least three who had never been Communists at all.[27]

From the start, the Nineteen were determined to present a united front. *Salt of the Earth*'s future director, Herbert Biberman, was their main organizer. He called a meeting and brought in several attorneys to advise them. The prospective witnesses faced two separate, but related, perils. They could lose their jobs and they could go to prison. They wanted neither outcome. Nor did they want to cooperate with the committee. It is important to realize that constitutionally, politically, economically, and in terms of public relations these people were dealing with a largely unknown situation. As of September 1947, no one had gone to jail for defying the committee and no one had ever been blacklisted. "The Ten were virgins," Dalton Trumbo recalled. "We didn't know how hot the water was."[28]

It took considerable wrangling before the prospective witnesses agreed upon a strategy for confronting the committee. They knew that they would be asked what had come to be known as "the $64 question." "Are you now, or have you ever been, a member of the Communist Party?" Several people wanted to answer it. The non-Communists among them had already sent letters to their producers denying that they were in the CP and they wanted to do the same on the stand. A few party members, who had long chafed under its demands for secrecy, wanted to tell the committee, "Yes, I'm a Communist, and what do you want to make of it?" From a public relations perspective, such a forthright response was a good idea, but legally it had serious drawbacks. Not only would it make the witness vulnerable to

---

They were Alvah Bessie, Herbert Biberman,* Bertolt Brecht, Lester Cole,* Richard Collins, Edward Dmytryk,* Gordon Kahn, Howard Koch, Ring Lardner, Jr.,* John Howard Lawson,* Albert Maltz.* Lewis Milestone, Samuel Ornitz,* Larry Parks, Irvin Pichel, Robert Rossen, Waldo Salt, Adrian Scott,* and Dalton Trumbo.* (The people whose names are starred became the Hollywood Ten; the other nine, though subpoenaed, were not called to the stand in 1947.)

Though not a friendly witness, Brecht was not really part of the group and he left the country within days after his deliberately confusing appearance before the committee.

questions about other people's political affiliations, but it also created the possibility, especially for non-Communists, that the committee might find people who would rebut their testimony and expose them to charges of perjury. In addition, answering HUAC's questions had the disadvantage of seeming to recognize the committee's legitimacy. Finally, the party would not have agreed.[29]

The unfriendlies, thus, had to find a way to avoid cooperating with the committee and still not go to jail. They had six attorneys, all of them members of the National Lawyers Guild, and some of them, like Robert Kenny, the former attorney general of California, and Bartley Crum, a politically well connected former Republican, quite eminent. Since the constitutional issues that refusing to cooperate with HUAC involved had yet to be decided by the Supreme Court, the lawyers themselves were unsure about what to do, especially since the Nineteen also wanted to win public support and keep their jobs. The First Amendment seemed the best bet.[30]

The main test cases that were to determine whether or not HUAC could question witnesses about their political affiliations were still under litigation. The first was that of Edward Barsky and seventeen other officers and members of the executive board of the Joint Anti-Fascist Refugee Committee. At their hearings in April 1946, Barsky and his colleagues had refused to surrender their organization's records to the committee and were cited for contempt. At the time the Hollywood people were considering their options, Barsky and his codefendants were still fighting their conviction at the appellate level. So, too, was Gerhart Eisler, whose contempt case seemed destined to become the most important early legal test of the committee's power to compel testimony from its witnesses. There was, of course, no way that the Nineteen's lawyers could have known in the fall of 1947 that the Supreme Court would refuse to review Barsky's appeal or that Eisler would flee the country before his case was decided or that two of the Court's most liberal justices would die unexpectedly in 1949.[31]

In its most recent free-speech decision, a 1943 flag-salute case involving some Jehovah's Witnesses, the Supreme Court had seemed to be solicitous of unorthodox opinions. In addition, its 1943 decision to void the denaturalization of the California CP leader William Schneiderman had revealed a relatively tolerant view of American Communism. Thus, it was perfectly reasonable for their attorneys to advise the Nineteen to use the First

322

Amendment. As civil libertarians, who wanted to bolster the Bill of Rights, these lawyers also knew that a defense of free speech and association would appeal to liberals. And, of course, they thought it would win in the Supreme Court.[32]

They could have, it is true, advised their clients to take the Fifth Amendment, to invoke the Constitution's protection against having to testify against oneself. This was to become the strategy that later witnesses used when they did not want to cooperate with the anticommunist investigating committees. In the fall of 1947, however, it was by no means clear that witnesses who relied on the Fifth Amendment's privilege against self-incrimination would be able to escape a prison sentence. There were no precedents; for the Supreme Court had yet to decide whether membership in the Communist party exposed people to criminal sanctions and, thus, justified their refusal to talk. The Court ultimately ruled that men and women who belonged to the party were vulnerable to prosecution under the Smith Act and could thus invoke the Fifth Amendment with regard to that membership. But the Court did not render that decision until 1950 and, until it did, unfriendly witnesses who relied upon the Fifth, Steve Nelson and the former Berkeley Radiation Laboratory scientists among them, got cited for contempt.[33]

In short, the Fifth Amendment posed just as much of a risk as the First. And it looked worse. Witnesses who relied on their privilege against incriminating themselves seemed slightly disreputable, as if they had something to hide. "For the group to intimate [as they would by taking the Fifth] that their political beliefs could conceivably be criminal under our country's institutions and principles," one of the Nineteen's attorneys noted, "would in fact be tacitly to concede in the public eye what [former HUAC chair Martin] Dies . . . had long been trying to prove." Moreover, since the unfriendly Hollywood witnesses viewed their confrontation with the committee in political as well as legal terms, they knew that they had to win popular support.[34]

In much the same way the CP's leaders were to proceed the following year after they were indicted under the Smith Act, the Nineteen adopted a Hollywood version of what was known in party circles as a labor defense strategy. Even before their hearings began, they would take their case to the American people. Once the rest of the nation understood that HUAC was attacking basic constitutional rights, an outraged public would repudiate the committee and deprive it of all political power. Accordingly, the Hollywood people planned rallies, petition drives, and media blitzes, all designed to get their message to the widest possible audience.[35]

This strategy was not unrealistic. The unfriendly witnesses presented themselves as civil libertarians fighting for free speech. They argued that, in the words of Herbert Biberman, "we had not come to Washington to defend ourselves. We had come there to defend the First Amendment." And, at least in the weeks before the hearings, many people agreed. After all, liberals had long despised HUAC as a partisan outfit that wanted to demolish the New Deal; and they had little respect for its members or its operations.[36]

Because they feared that the forthcoming hearings might be an attempt to censor the movies and violate freedom of speech, the film colony's liberals formed an ad hoc group to fight the committee. Their organization, the Committee for the First Amendment, sparkled with stars; Humphrey Bogart, Lauren Bacall, Lucille Ball, Judy Garland, Danny Kaye, Gene Kelly, Burt Lancaster, and Frank Sinatra were just a few of the more than three hundred celebrities who lent their names. The group took out ads, paid for nationwide broadcasts, and chartered an airplane to send the biggest stars to Washington to flaunt their opposition to the hearings. From the start, the CFA's organizers made it clear that they had nothing to do with Communism. "No member of our group," its leader, director William Wyler, insisted, "is a Communist or sympathetic to the totalitarian form of government." He and his colleagues had mobilized to fend off HUAC's threat to the film industry, not to support the rights of individual Communists.[37]

Though few producers joined the Committee for the First Amendment, most of them were, at least at first, no less antagonistic to HUAC. Some were liberals who deplored the committee's incursions against political freedom; others were simply protecting their turf. "No half-ass Congressman is going to tell MGM how to run its business," producer Eddie Mannix assured the soon-to-be-blacklisted screenwriter Lester Cole. Nonetheless, the studios were nervous. They hired Eric Johnston, the former head of the national Chamber of Commerce, to deflect the committee's damage; and Johnston wanted them to purge their ranks. Though some of the producers were privately pressing their subpoenaed employees to break with the party, in public, at least, the studios held the line. As the hearings opened with the Motion Picture Alliance members and other friendly witnesses testi-fying about the CP's supposed subversion of the silver screen, Johnston quashed rumors that there would be a blacklist. "As long as I live, I will never be a party to anything as un-American as a blacklist." "Tell the boys not to worry," he assured one of the Nineteen's attorneys, "We're not going totalitarian to please this committee." [38]

But once the unfriendly witnesses actually confronted the committee, the film world's support evaporated. At Kenny's suggestion, the unfriendlies had decided that each of them would make a formal statement explaining why he was refusing to cooperate. Each witness would claim that he was willing to answer the committee's questions, but would do so "in my own way." This tactic, the Nineteen believed, would win liberal support and re-fute the charge that they were being obstructionist. It would also let them maintain, if they were indicted for contempt, that they would have cooper-ated with HUAC if only they had been allowed to. Unfortunately, the strata-gem backfired; committee chair Parnell Thomas refused to let the unfriendly witnesses read their statements, insisting instead that they answer the com-mittee's questions. [39]

As a result, from the moment screenwriter John Howard Lawson, the first of the unfriendlies, took the stand, the hearing degenerated into a shout-ing match. As Lawson and the others accused the committee of trying to muzzle them, Thomas tried to gavel them down and even summoned U.S. marshals to eject them from the room. Once each unfriendly witness fin-ished testifying, a HUAC staff member would read off a list of that person's communist affiliations and display a facsimile of his party card. After ten of these confrontations, the committee stopped the hearings.

Neither side won. The committee seemed unfair and authoritarian. But the unfriendly witnesses seemed just as culpable. Their membership in the party and their refusal to be open about it seemed reprehensible; so, too, did their behavior at the hearings. Instead of appearing as virtuous de-fenders of the First Amendment, they came across as disruptive ideologues. They insisted that they were just good Americans, defending the Bill of Rights, but they did so in a highly polemical way, calling the committee "fascist" and "reactionary." Moreover, they raised their voices. As a result, their conduct at the hearings, rather than their defense of free speech, be-came an issue. And their liberal and moderate support melted away.

"They should have quietly but firmly refused to cooperate with the Committee," producer Dore Schary explained,

> and then held a dignified press conference where they said eight of us are Communists, but all of us are Americans and patriots, and the public and the press would have backed them one hundred percent.

Schary was voicing the general consensus among liberals that the unfriend-lies had botched their public relations, that by yelling at the committee and evading its questions they had destroyed their claim to moral superiority. Such a position did not necessarily imply approval of HUAC; the committee was still disreputable in liberal eyes. But, Schary and others insisted, the witnesses were equally to blame; they should have been more open, if not with the committee, at least with the American people. As the FBI's files reveal, even one of the Hollywood Ten's own attorneys agreed and pressed his clients to "declare themselves" and publicly disclose their political affiliations.[40]

From the first there was an element of hypocrisy to such a demand. Despite their protestations that they did not care whether the unfriendly witnesses were Communists, many of the liberals who criticized the Hollywood Ten were, in fact, upset to learn that the men they had supported belonged to the party. As was the case throughout the McCarthy period, liberals and moderates generally refused to defend the civil liberties of Communists. Thus, HUAC's devastating documentation of the CP affiliations of the unfriendly witnesses seemed to have been just as responsible as those witnesses' rowdy behavior for the evaporation of liberal support. Certainly, the committee believed that was the case. Parnell Thomas thanked the FBI effusively for its contribution to the success of his hearings. Being able to produce the party card of an unfriendly witness, "giving the date and number on the card," Thomas explained, "was responsible for his Committee not being put out of business." An unidentified FBI informant within the film community reinforced that assessment. "They nailed Lawson," the informant reported. "The town is shocked. People didn't believe that Lawson was Communist. The only thing they will believe is the Party card." Though the FBI's files obviously reflect the Bureau's own version of events, the informant's observation certainly accords with the desire of the liberal community in Hollywood and elsewhere to distance itself from Communism.[41]

The studios shared that desire. Their spokesman Eric Johnston had followed Lawson to the stand. Though criticizing the committee for its unwarranted attacks on the movies, he stated that the film industry would not tolerate Communists and he thanked the committee for helping to expose them. The rest of the film colony got the message. Within weeks, the big-name stars who had so recently been attacking HUAC rushed to recant. Insisting that "I am not a Communist" and "I detest Communism just as any other decent American does," Humphrey Bogart distributed a statement admitting that his trip to Washington "was ill-advised, even foolish." Under pressure from their employers, other luminaries made similar efforts to distance themselves from the recalcitrant witnesses. And the studios made plans to fire the Ten.[42]

A few days after the hearings ended, a group of producers met in New York with Johnston and another of their outside advisers, the former American Legion head and high New Deal official Paul McNutt. At issue was not whether they would dismiss the unfriendly witnesses, but how. Presumably, the economic future of the entire industry was at stake, though, as a Gallup poll commissioned by the studios actually revealed, the hearings had little impact on the public's attitude toward the movies. Nonetheless, the studio heads were sensitive to anything that might offend their potential customers. Johnston was instructed to consult with the film industry's other big hired gun, former secretary of state James Byrnes, and write up a statement the moguls could adopt.[43]

By the time the producers met again, in late November at the Waldorf-Astoria Hotel in New York, RKO and Fox had already decided to let their unfriendly witnesses go. Byrnes and Johnston laid out the choices and urged the studio executives to fire the Ten. A few producers objected, but Johnston pressed them. "I think I used the expression 'they would have to fish or cut bait,'" he recalled. The resisters soon capitulated and the group adopted what later came to be known as the "Waldorf Statement." They announced that they were firing the Ten and pledged not to "knowingly employ a Communist or a member of any party or group which advocated the overthrow of the Government of the United States by force or by illegal or unconstitutional methods."[44]

The unfriendly witnesses had been expecting the blow. But unemployment was only the most immediate of their problems; they were also facing the prospect of prison for contempt of Congress. Like most other communist defendants, they fought their case in the public arena as well as the courts. Under Biberman's leadership, they mobilized the entire left-wing community for a campaign of fund-raising, signature gathering, and protest rallies. For the next few years, the Ten would travel the radical lecture circuit, speaking to union, college, and community groups about their challenge to HUAC. Despite their conviction at the trial stage, the blacklist, and other signs that their outside support was dwindling, they expected to win. The free-speech issues involved in their case would bring it before the Supreme Court, which would, they were confident, exonerate them.[45]

But the Cold War caught up with them — just as it had with Dorothy Bailey, Carl Marzani, and many of the other protagonists in the key political cases of the late 1940s and 1950s. As the Ten's appeal made its way through the judicial system, the issue of domestic Communism became a matter of national security. The appeals court decision indicates the context within which the case had become embedded by 1949. Judge Bennett C. Clark could have supported HUAC by relying on judicial restraint, invoking the principle of separation of powers, and ruling, as other judges did, that courts should not limit Congress's investigative role. Instead, he chose to discuss national security and the "current ideological struggle between communistic-thinking and democratic-thinking peoples of the world" on which the "destiny of all nations hangs." Because motion pictures had such a "critically important role" as "a potent medium of propaganda dissemination," Clark explained, the Ten's refusal to answer the $64 question actually endangered the nation.[46]

The prison terms that the Ten served after the Supreme Court refused to take their case in November 1949 were in many respects less of a punishment than their expulsion from Hollywood. The two types of sanctions reinforced each other; the firings bolstered the criminal prosecution and the prosecution legitimized the blacklist. The Ten and their lawyers recognized these interconnections and they accompanied their legal battle against HUAC with a series of lawsuits against the studios. Though they won a few small victories, especially when they could get their story to a jury, most of the time they lost on appeal or when unfriendly judges refused to allow them to present evidence about the operation of the blacklist.[47]

As their cases wound through the judicial system, the Hollywood Ten tried to salvage their careers. Some were able to get work under the table. They submitted screenplays under false names or else found fronts who would pretend to have written the scripts. But they could no longer command their earlier fees. The blacklist, Dalton Trumbo explained, "simply requires that I work three times as fast for about one-fifth of my former price." Moreover, employing a front created problems, as Lester Cole found out when the screenwriter friend who was pretending to have written his scripts refused to turn over the proceeds and then gave his name to HUAC. Later on, Cole discovered that the FBI knew about his undercover screenwriting and was investigating him for tax fraud.[48]

The blacklist soon spread beyond the initial witnesses. The rest of the Nineteen were among the first victims. So, too, were the other well-known Hollywood radicals. Biberman's wife, the Academy Award–winning actress Gail Sondergaard, got only one role after her husband defied the committee. By the end of 1947, Paul Jarrico "found that I was getting less employment and less from major studios and more from the independents." By the summer of 1950, when the Ten finally began their one-year prison sentences, it was clear that the blacklist would claim almost everyone who had been close to the Hollywood CP.[49]

No one else would go to jail, however. In 1951, when HUAC resumed its interrupted hearings on the film industry, the unfriendly witnesses took the Fifth Amendment, not the First. By this point, both the legal procedures and the economic sanctions had become routinized — and not just in Hollywood. Former Communists in the film industry who wanted to remain employed knew they had to name names. Some had already given them to the FBI, but, because of the studios' sensitivity to publicity, reinstatement usually required a public confession as well. It was a degrading process, as the experience of actor Larry Parks reveals. Parks was on the verge of stardom when he became one of the original Nineteen in 1947. He had never been much of a political activist and when he received a subpoena in 1951, he was ready to cooperate to save his career. He became the first friendly witness in HUAC's second round of Hollywood hearings. But he found it demeaning. The committee, he protested, was "forcing me to really crawl through the mud to be an informer." Though he finally broke down and named names, his obvious reluctance destroyed his career. Future friendly witnesses learned the lesson. They kept their reservations to themselves and stayed off the blacklist. Fifty-eight of the 110 men and women summoned before the committee in the spring of 1951 took that route.[50]

329

The others were uncooperative; they had already been affected by the blacklist and they knew that their refusal to name names would end their Hollywood careers. Dismissal was automatic. When Jarrico was subpoenaed, he released a statement maintaining, "If I have to choose between crawling in the mud with Larry Parks or going to jail like my courageous friends of the Hollywood Ten, I shall certainly choose the latter." He was fired at once, not even allowed onto the studio lot at RKO to pick up his personal belongings. When he went before HUAC a few weeks later, he was, in his words "a most unfriendly witness"; he took the Fifth to everything but his name and address.[51]

The operation of the blacklist is well known. All the unfriendly witnesses were unemployable. So, too, were all the people who had been named as Communists before the committee. They got little outside help. Even the talent unions that they had done so much to build refused to support them. The Screen Actors Guild officially washed its hands of unfriendly witnesses, informing its members that "if any actor by his own actions . . . has so offended American public opinion that he has made himself unsaleable at the box office, the Guild cannot and would not want to force any employer to hire him."[52]

Besides the more or less official blacklist of the two hundred men and women who had refused to cooperate with HUAC between 1951 and 1954, there was an unofficial graylist of some three hundred politically tainted people whose names had been given to the film industry by the American Legion. These were Hollywood's liberals, non-Communists who had supported the Committee for the First Amendment in the innocent days of 1947 or signed the wrong kinds of petitions during and after World War II. The anticommunist network operated the machinery for clearing these people. They had to expiate their sins in letters to their studios, which were then vetted by the likes of columnist George Sokolsky, J. B. Matthews, Benjamin Mandel, and such film industry heavies as Roy Brewer and the Motion Picture Alliance's Ward Bond. If the sinners were not suitably contrite, they might have to revise their confessions several times before being cleared. In 1952, Marlon Brando had to submit three increasingly more detailed drafts of a statement explaining why he had signed the Stockholm Peace Petition.[53]

★

In an industry that by 1952 was so traumatized that it had essentially surrendered control over its hiring practices to the professional anti-Communists, it is easy to see why the efforts of Jarrico and his colleagues to produce a film about the striking Mexican American miners of Local 890 and their wives would become controversial. The makers of *Salt of the Earth* had resolved, in Jarrico's words, to "commit a crime to fit the punishment." Not only would they defy the film industry by using blacklisted actors and technicians, but they would also show that it was possible to make an artistically successful and commercially viable film about the real lives of ordinary American workers. The enormous opposition that the film encountered reveals how powerful the anticommunist crusade was and how strongly it was committed to suppressing unorthodox views.[54]

Work on the picture began as soon as Jarrico returned from New Mexico. He would be its producer and Herbert Biberman would direct it. Jarrico asked his brother-in-law, the Academy Award–winning screenwriter Michael Wilson, to write the script. Wilson, who had taken the Fifth before HUAC the same time Jarrico had, was interested and set off for New Mexico. He spent a month in Silver City, Bayard, and the other mining towns of the area, hanging out with the strikers and their wives on the picket line and working on his script.[55]

By May 1952, Jarrico and his team were ready to start filming. Despite some reservations about taking on new burdens at a time when the union was already beseiged, Mine-Mill's international executive board agreed to coproduce the movie. It could promise no cash but would supply whatever in-kind services it could. The filmmakers wanted to work with a union crew, but they feared that Roy Brewer, the powerful chief of the film technicians' union, would oppose the project. They were right. When Simon Lazarus, the Hollywood businessman who handled most of the project's finances, met with Brewer, the IATSE leader pounded on the table and yelled, "You will never make the picture and if you succeed in making it somewhere else it will never be exhibited in the United States. . . . I will see you and your gang in Hell before you will make any pictures." Brewer's hostility kept most Hollywood technicians off the film. Ultimately, Biberman and Jarrico were able to put together a crew of documentary filmmakers, blacklisted IATSE people, and African Americans ineligible for membership in Brewer's lily-white organization. Jencks's Local 890 gave them all temporary cards so that the production was at least formally unionized.[56]

331

The filmmakers had planned to cast *Salt of the Earth* with blacklisted actors like Biberman's wife, Gale Sondergaard. But they soon realized that it would be subtly discriminatory to have Anglo actors in Mexican American roles. The blacklist, however, limited their options. Though they were able to cast a Mexican actress, Rosaura Revueltas, as the female lead, they could find no Mexican or Mexican American actors willing to defy the boycott and work on the film. Finally, they decided to use the miners and their wives in most of the roles. Local 890 president Juan Chacon was the lead; Jencks and his wife played themselves.

These preproduction problems delayed the start of the filming until January 1953. Despite the inexperience of the technical crews and amateur actors, the shooting went well at first. A local eccentric had let the company erect its sets on his ranch and, at least initially, the leading citizens of Grant County welcomed the filmmakers. Biberman and Jarrico were, after all, spending money and, despite the filmmakers' unpopular politics, they still retained some of their former Hollywood allure.[57]

By early February, however, opposition began to mount. Significantly, it first came from the anticommunist professionals. On February 9, a Hollywood trade paper announced that Walter Pidgeon, Ronald Reagan's successor as president of the Screen Actors Guild, had been tipped off about the "feature-length anti-American racial issue propaganda movie" being shot in Silver City. Three days later, columnist Victor Riesel weighed in. Riesel, who was the main journalistic point man on labor matters for the anticommunist network, may well have been alerted to *Salt* by the FBI. He had been attacking Mine-Mill for years, often on the grounds that the union threatened national security because it controlled the strategic copper industry. His February 12 column reiterated that contention and commended Pidgeon for "discovering how Red is a valley not too far from the Los Alamos atomic proving grounds. . . . Where you try to hide secret weapons . . . you find concentrations of Communists." Riesel also played the race card and claimed that "Tovarish Paul [Jarrico]" had imported two carloads of Negroes and was planning to use them in scenes of mob violence. That same day the Pathé Laboratory canceled its contract to process the company's film. Local businessmen soon followed suit and boycotted the production.[58]

On February 24, HUAC member Donald Jackson denounced *Salt of the Earth* on the floor of the House. After repeating Riesel's allegations about the filmmakers' proximity to Los Alamos and their plans "to inflame racial ha-

332

treds and to depict the United States of America as the enemy of all colored peoples," he promised to "do everything in my power to prevent the showing of this Communist-made film in the theaters of America." The next day, two Immigration and Naturalization Service officials turned up on the set, arrested Revueltas, and hustled her off to El Paso, where she was held without bail pending deportation on the technicality that her passport lacked an entry stamp.[59]

Meanwhile, incited by the local radio station's repeated airing of Congressman Jackson's speech and the *Silver City Daily Press*'s red-baiting articles, the denizens of Grant County turned against *Salt of the Earth*. Anonymous callers threatened the film crew and union officials, and on March 2, as the company prepared to shoot a major scene in the small town of Central, a group of local citizens confronted the filmmakers and threatened to break their cameras. That night five shots were fired into Clinton Jencks's car. The next day when the crew again tried to film the scene, this time in the town of Bayard, another group of vigilantes arrived. "All of you Communists better get out of here," the group's leader yelled, "or you'll go out in black boxes." He then turned on Jencks and began to beat him up. Soon after, Bayard's mayor ordered the filmmakers to leave.

Far from deploring the violence, the local press encouraged it. The *El Paso Herald* congratulated the people of Bayard and Central for "their determination to clear away the pink overcast from their beautiful country." Local businessmen supported the red-baiting; they arranged free showings of patriotic films and set up loudspeakers to play "American" music outside the theaters. Rumors of further violence, including a possible armed attack on the ranch where most of the filming took place, made it clear that additional work on the movie would be impossible. With state troopers standing guard, the film crew rushed through a few last shots and by March 7 it had left the area. The violence continued. Local 890's union hall was set on fire and, after three attempts, arsonists burned down the home of the union's only other Anglo officer.[60]

The filmmakers completed the shooting by taking some scenes in Mexico with Revueltas and a few last shots in Los Angeles. But their struggle was far from over; the battleground now shifted from the mining towns of Grant County to the film laboratories, recording studios, and editing rooms of the motion picture industry. At the request of Congressman Jackson, official Hollywood refused to touch *Salt of the Earth*. Like the lawyers who would not represent communist clients, allegedly liberal laboratory owners would not handle the picture; they did not want to risk the rest of their business by defying IATSE and the big studios. To get their processing done, Biberman and Jarrico went underground, using aliases and sending out separate pieces of the film to different companies. The editing encountered similar problems. The technicians who were willing to work on the film turned out to be inept; and one of the few competent editors the filmmakers located was an FBI informer. Roy Brewer was determined to keep *Salt* from being processed; when he lost its trail, IATSE notified its members to contact union headquarters if they ran across copies of the movie. Despite these obstacles, the film got finished, though the post–production work took a year instead of the normal four to five months.[61]

The boycott extended to *Salt*'s exhibition as well. Because of the major studios' opposition to the film, it turned out to be nearly impossible to book a commercial theater for its release. Even at a time when competition from television darkened almost half the nation's movie screens, theater owners routinely refused to allow *Salt* to be shown. Ultimately, the producers had to agree to exorbitant terms for second- or third-run theaters. Even then, there was no guarantee that the picture would be shown; most projectionists were members of IATSE and were not allowed to run the film. The irony was obvious. A pro-union movie had to be exhibited by nonunion workers.

The film encountered other obstacles as well. In Los Angeles, for example, newspapers and radio stations would not accept advertising for it. In Detroit, the threat of an American Legion protest prevented its showing. Foreign distribution was no more successful. The film industry had a long reach, especially in places like Canada, where American chains owned most of the theaters. As a result, despite some favorable reviews *Salt of the Earth* was a commercial disaster. Though it became something of a cult classic on the left and won prizes in Europe, it never got the general audience that its makers had been trying to reach.[62]

Nonetheless, Jarrico and his partners refused to give up the fight. The tenacity of their struggle — they were deeply in debt and had given more than three years of their lives to the film — attests to their political commitment. In the spring of 1955, after a yearlong battle to get the picture shown, the producers sued IATSE's Chicago projectionists' local on the grounds that its refusal to run *Salt of the Earth* violated the Sherman Anti-Trust Act.

At first, the filmmakers seemed successful. The free-speech issues involved brought the ACLU into the case and Judge Philip C. Sullivan supported the plaintiffs on the grounds that "the public has the same interest in being able to see motion pictures of its choice as it has in being able to read books and newspapers and see plays and attend meetings of its choice." IATSE responded by diverting the case from censorship to Communism. It sent interrogatories to Biberman and the others that were full of questions about their political views and affiliations. Whatever relevance such information may have had, someone like Biberman was not going to answer the same questions he had gone to prison for refusing. IATSE then hired the judge's nephew as its attorney to force Sullivan off the case. The new judge was less sympathetic to the filmmakers and ruled that they had to answer the interrogatories. They dropped the suit instead.[63]

They reopened it the following year, this time on a much broader scale. The suit named every group and individual that had participated in what the filmmakers claimed was a conspiracy to maintain the blacklist and suppress *Salt of the Earth*. The sixty-eight defendants ranged from MGM and IATSE to the film laboratories and sound studios that refused to process the picture. The defense again tried to deflect attention to the filmmakers' politics. One of the defendants' attorneys, Myles Lane, the former lead prosecutor in the Rosenberg trial, enlisted the aid of J. B. Matthews and Benjamin Mandel in preparing his case. He and his colleagues also tried to force Biberman and Jarrico to answer questions about their association with the CP. The legal maneuvers took years and the case did not reach the trial stage until 1963. The jury sided with *Salt*'s producers, but the lack of a smoking gun rendered them unable to rule in the filmmakers' favor. Thus, more than ten years after Biberman and Jarrico had begun their film in Silver City, their effort to bring the struggle of the Empire Zinc miners to the screen had come to an ambiguous end.[64]

What was so striking about the unofficial censorship that Jarrico and his partners encountered was how many different forces were arrayed against the making and showing of their movie. From IATSE to the INS, dozens of public and private institutions took part in the action. Though it required a lot of pressure, the anticommunist network did manage to suppress *Salt of the Earth*. Few people ever got to see a film that looked seriously at racial issues, male chauvinism, and the problems of organized labor.

★

Salt of the Earth was born controversial. Even if Biberman, Wilson, and Jarrico had tried to produce a different movie, they would still have encountered opposition from IATSE and the major studios. They were, after all, defying the Hollywood blacklist and if they could succeed in making a film, any film, they would have, as they well knew, greatly weakened McCarthyism's economic sanctions within the film industry and, given the visibility of Hollywood, the rest of the country as well. Their project's connection to the International Union of Mine, Mill and Smelter Workers made it even more provocative. Already under attack for its party ties, Mine-Mill's association with *Salt of the Earth* increased the pressures that the beleaguered union was facing.

Clinton Jencks was the first target. On April 20, 1953, six weeks after Biberman and his crew packed up their equipment and left Silver City, two FBI agents showed up at Jencks's home and put him under arrest. The charge: perjury. He had, so the government claimed, falsified the noncommunist affidavit that the 1947 Taft-Hartley Act required of all union officials. Since Jencks was a relatively minor functionary, it was clear that the furor about *Salt of the Earth* had prompted his arraignment.

But Jencks was not the only union official to be prosecuted for falsifying his Taft-Hartley affidavits; other labor leaders, including Hugh Bryson, the president of the Marine Cooks and Stewards Union, faced similar charges. Like so many of the loyalty-security programs, these criminal cases were part of the broader assault on the left-wing unions.[65]

By the time Jencks was indicted, the noncommunist affidavits required by Section 9(h) of the Taft-Hartley Act had already done quite a lot of damage. Belatedly tacked on to a measure whose main function was to roll back the gains organized labor had made since the New Deal, the affidavits were designed to weed Communists out of the labor movement. Unions whose officers did not submit the affidavits could not use the services of the National Labor Relations Board. They could not participate in representation elections or be certified as bargaining agents, nor would the NLRB process those unions' complaints about unfair labor practices.[66]

At the time the Taft-Hartley Act was passed, it was by no means clear that its 9(h) affidavits would have much of an impact. Communist labor leaders could presumably retain power by ignoring the law and forgoing the services of the NLRB. In addition, the measure had been so poorly drafted that its implementation threatened to become an administrative nightmare.

The affidavits with their vague language about "belief in" and "support" for Communism cried out for litigation. Important First Amendment issues were at stake and the Supreme Court would clearly have to rule on the measure. Moreover, Truman's opposition to the bill and his electoral victory in 1948 raised the possibility that the law might be repealed. Finally, much of the labor movement was hostile to Taft-Hartley and, at least initially, threatened to nullify its effectiveness. Many noncommunist labor leaders — John L. Lewis and CIO president Philip Murray among them — refused to sign the affidavits. They saw them as both an attack on free speech and a special burden on labor.[67]

For the communist-led unions, Section 9(h) turned out to be an unmitigated disaster. Besides their symbolic importance as an indication that the government wanted to rid the labor movement of reds, the affidavits provided a concrete issue around which the opponents of the left-led unions could mobilize. Now, instead of merely denouncing the Communists who controlled a particular union, they could call for compliance with the new law. The tactic worked beautifully. By the end of 1947, even before it was clear that the NLRB's rigid enforcement of Taft-Hartley would, in fact, cause hardships for a noncomplying union, anticommunist factions within several unions, including the Screen Writers Guild, had used the issue to drive the left from power.[68]

Employers also took advantage of Section 9(h) by refusing to bargain with unions whose officers did not sign the affidavits. Some companies used the ploy to disguise their intransigence over wages and working conditions. They wrapped themselves in the flag and claimed that national security was at stake. "At this time of danger to our country," the president of the American Zinc Company announced in June 1948, when he refused to bargain with a striking Mine-Mill local in Fairmont, Illinois, "we will not deal with men who take orders from, and who are loyal to, the government of communist Russia. Ours is a critical industry for America's defense. We will not endanger it." Unable to rely on the NLRB, the noncomplying unions had to adopt more militant tactics to win contracts and settle grievances. As a result, strikes became both more common and more bitter.[69]

Taft-Hartley also exacerbated the left-wing unions' other problems. Mine-Mill's experiences were typical. Already torn by intense factionalism, its failure to sign the affidavits exposed it to intensified raids from other unions and new threats of secession from disheartened members who wanted to comply with the law. Until its officers signed the affidavits, for example, Mine-Mill could not participate in the representation elections that employers and rival unions forced the NLRB to hold. When those elections took place, workers who wanted to support Mine-Mill or one of the other noncomplying unions could do so only by casting their ballots for "no union." Such an option was hardly satisfactory; the communist-led unions lost many more elections than they won.[70]

What was particularly demoralizing, at least from the perspective of these unions, was the apparent collaboration of the CIO's top brass. Opposition from employers, even from AFL unions, all that was to be expected, but to find the CIO, the organization to which the CP's labor members had devoted so many years of their lives, also turning against them was a major blow. Since the CIO theoretically prohibited internecine raiding, the participation of such important unions as the UAW and the Steelworkers in the attacks on Mine-Mill, UE, and the rest of the labor left indicated that the CIO was willing to purge its communist-led unions.[71]

By the middle of 1949, it was clear that the left-wing unions had too many enemies to enjoy the luxury of opposing Section 9(h). The prospect that the Supreme Court might rule against the affidavits was becoming increasingly less likely. Though the final decision in *American Communications v. Douds,* as the test case was called, did not come down until the following year, there were strong indications by the middle of 1949 that the litigation against Taft-Hartley might fail. Thus, if they were to avoid damaging strikes or win representation elections, the officers of Mine-Mill and the other beleaguered unions had to sign the affidavits. Accordingly, one after another in the summer of 1949, the communist-led unions voted to comply with the Taft-Hartley Act.[72]

The decision brought little respite. By then, the multipronged campaign against these unions was so intense that there was probably no way that they could defuse the hostility they faced. Moreover, signing the affidavits caused problems; many of the left-wing unions' leaders *were* Communists. If they were to avoid perjury charges, they would either have to give up their union positions or else leave the party. Most adopted a "resign and sign" strategy. They submitted formal resignations to the party and some even resigned from the front groups they belonged to. Though most of these resignations were secret, a few of the more conspicuous Communists like Mine-Mill Secretary-Treasurer Maurice Travis publicly announced their departure from the CP. Quitting the party, he explained in an open letter to the union newspaper,

> has not been an easy step for me to take. Membership in the Communist Party has always meant to me . . . that I could be a better trade unionist. . . . I want to make it crystal clear that my belief in Communism is consistent with what I believe to be the best interests of the members of this Union and the American people generally.

Such sentiments in the overheated political atmosphere of August 1949 were hardly designed to alleviate the pressures on his union. And, in fact, despite the official NLRB recognition that Mine-Mill's compliance brought, the raids and secessions did not let up. In addition, the union was about to be expelled from the CIO.[73]

Such a step had been under consideration for years. The turning point came in 1948 after Truman's veto of the Taft-Hartley Act won him trade union support and solidified the conviction of the CIO's top leaders that the well-being of the labor movement required a close alliance with the White House and the Democratic party. The left-wing unions' criticism of the administration's foreign policy and their support for the presidential candidacy of Henry Wallace precipitated the rupture. In January 1948, the CIO's executive board passed a resolution stating its opposition to a third party. Since the CP had forced its labor members to sign on to the Wallace campaign, a split was inevitable.[74]

The denouement occurred at the CIO's annual convention in the fall of 1949 when the delegates voted to expel UE on the spot and to investigate charges of communist domination against ten other left-wing unions.* Each union got a separate hearing before a three-man committee. There was, of course, no question about the outcome. A former CIO staff member recalls writing up the trial committee's recommendations to expel Harry Bridges's ILWU while the hearings were still taking place.[75]

The proceedings against Mine-Mill were the same as those against all

---

*Besides Mine-Mill, they included the American Communications Association; Food, Tobacco, Agricultural and Allied Workers of America; Fur and Leather Workers; International Fishermen's Union; International Longshoremen's and Warehousemen's Union; National Union of Marine Cooks and Stewards; United Office and Professional Workers; United Public Workers; and the United Furniture Workers (the last-named was not expelled, because it changed its leaders).

the other left unions. Significantly, they were also similar to all the other anticommunist trials and loyalty board hearings of the period. The same assumptions ruled and the same kinds of witnesses and texts were produced. The formal charges that were read at the opening of Mine-Mill's hearing on January 18, 1950, mirrored the standard demonization of Communism. They noted the CP's "slavish adherence to the ideology of a foreign country" and included the oft-quoted and presumably damaging passage from Lenin's *Left-Wing Communism, An Infantile Disorder* that exhorted his followers "to resort to all sorts of devices, maneuvers and illegal methods, to evasion and subterfuge, in order to penetrate the trade unions, to remain in them and to carry on Communist work in them at all costs." At CIO headquarters, as in every other anticommunist tribunal of the period, the operating assumption was that all Communists always obeyed the party line.[76]

The literary evidence that the CIO's director of education and research then read into the record was supposed to prove that Mine-Mill had followed the CP's every flip and flop. It consisted of excerpts from party and union publications showing the parallels between Mine-Mill's position and that of the CP on such matters as the Nazi-Soviet pact, the second front, the Marshall Plan, and the Progressive party. Two former union officials then testified about the party connections of Mine-Mill's top leaders and the mechanisms through which the CP allegedly determined the union's policies. The testimony of the former Communist Kenneth Eckert, who had quit the union because of its opposition to the Taft-Hartley affidavits, was particularly damaging. He described Mine-Mill's communist caucus and the secret meetings that he, Travis, and a few other union officials had held with the CP's top leaders. There is no reason to believe that Eckert was lying; certainly the CIO panel assumed that he was telling the truth and promptly recommended Mine-Mill's eviction from the house of labor.[77]

Weakened as Mine-Mill had been by its leaders' refusal to sign the Taft-Hartley affidavits and its expulsion from the CIO, it still retained its core locals in places like Montana's copper belt and Grant County, New Mexico. And its left-wing officials remained in power. For those employers, union rivals, and federal bureaucrats who wanted to drive Mine-Mill and the other left-led unions out of business, the facility with which those unions apparently evaded the intent of the law and retained their supposedly communist leaders, was enormously frustrating. As a result, pressure for other sanctions began to mount.[78]

Criminal charges were an obvious alternative. The NLRB was especially eager to prosecute the allegedly communist officials for perjury. Upset that he could not decertify Mine-Mill and the other left-wing unions once their leaders signed the noncommunist affidavits, Robert Denham, the Republican lawyer whom Truman had appointed as the board's general counsel, announced that he was sending the 9(h) forms of Maurice Travis and other suspected Communists to the Justice Department. Between the middle of 1949 and the beginning of 1952, Denham and his successor forwarded hundreds of affidavits to the Attorney General's office. If the NLRB could not punish them, perhaps the Justice Department would.[79]

But Denham's dilemma could not be so easily resolved. The wording of the affidavits made it extremely difficult for the government to indict the alleged perjurers. Section 9(h) was no $64 question; it pertained only to a union official's present — not past — party membership. Though the Justice Department certainly wanted to prosecute people like Travis and had ordered the FBI to keep an eye on every suspected Communist who filed a Taft-Hartley affidavit, it hesitated to indict them. It had no evidence that these people were still in the party. "Difficulty is experienced," Attorney General J. Howard McGrath admitted in 1951, "because of the necessity of proving that an affiant at the time of the making of his affidavit was a member of the Communist Party or affiliated with the Party."[80]

McGrath was not equivocating. As with its other anticommunist cases, the Department of Justice had trouble developing its Taft-Hartley prosecutions. It was, after all, hard to find evidence of a crime when none had been committed. As a result, surprisingly few 9(h) prosecutions ever reached the trial stage or when they did they often entailed the use of illegitimate tactics. In the case of Clinton Jencks, for example, the government knowingly relied on a perjured witness.

There were, of course, other ways to drum up indictments. Congress could become involved. As was so often the case during the McCarthy era, if one component of the anticommunist crusade could not come into play, another could. And congressional committees could not only hassle the

stigmatized unions, they could also create grounds for criminal proceedings — either for perjury or for contempt of Congress. Both HUAC and the
SISS subpoenaed the left-wing labor leaders and grilled them about their
affidavits. Naturally, they took the Fifth Amendment. The NLRB, which was
eager to see these people prosecuted, sent the committees copies of their
9(h) forms. It also routinely transmitted those witnesses' affidavits to the
Justice Department along with transcripts of their hearings. Nonetheless,
even after the Eisenhower administration came into office and seemed more
willing to prosecute, the Attorney General and his staff still could not find
enough evidence to indict these people for falsifying their noncommunist
affidavits.[81]

Clinton Jencks's was one of the first such cases the new administration
opened. As Jencks's FBI files reveal, the Bureau had been investigating him
under the Taft-Hartley Act since 1950. Harvey Matusow was willing to identify him as a Communist on the basis of his conversations at the San Cristobal Valley Ranch in the summer of 1950. But, he told the Bureau at the end
of 1951,

> I have never attended a meeting of the Communist Party in New Mex-
> ico, and have never been present at a Communist Party meeting where
> Jencks was in attendance. I have never been told by Jencks that he is a
> member of the Communist Party, and I have never seen any direct evi-
> dence to prove that he is a member of the Communist Party. However,
> there is no question in my mind but that Jencks is a member of the
> Communist Party.

None of the Bureau's other informants would make even that equivocal a
statement. "The evidence," even J. Edgar Hoover had to admit, "is not substantial." His agents had interviewed over fifty people but "none [had] evidentiary information" that could link Jencks to the CP after 1949, when he
signed his affidavit. In addition, the Bureau was unhappy about letting its
active informers surface in the case. Many field offices had been loath to
surrender their informants during the far more important Smith Act trial;
they were equally resistant to releasing them for a mere case of perjury. Allowing its best informant to testify openly against Jencks, the Albuquerque
bureau chief argued, would mean "jeopardizing the entire Communist program of the Albuquerque Office."[82]

But the Justice Department was under pressure for a Taft-Hartley prosecution and Jencks's connection to *Salt of the Earth* made him an obvious candidate. In addition, although Jencks's FBI file reveals no connection here, the mining industry was publicly pushing for action. On March 16, barely a month before the indictment, the personnel manager of Empire Zinc's parent company testified before the House Committee on Education and Welfare about the "disruptive, subtle, confusing, mean, tricky, and unfair" New Mexico strike. Moreover, the statute of limitations was running out. And, finally, Jencks had already provided what many people assumed was definitive proof that he was a Communist: he had taken the Fifth before a congressional committee.[83]

He had done so in October 1952 during the Senate Internal Security Subcommittee's hearings on Mine-Mill. The subcommittee's chair, Nevada's Pat McCarran, had been hostile to the union ever since it opposed his reelection in 1944. Nineteen fifty-two was an election year and, though McCarran was not running, his colleague on the committee, Utah's Arthur Watkins, was. A public investigation of the communist infiltration of Mine-Mill would, Don Connors, a former FBI agent on the McCarran committee's staff, noted in July, "lend itself to a particularly good public hearing in a Western city sometime this fall." Accordingly, the SISS scheduled a session for Salt Lake City. Besides getting information from its usual sources in the anticommunist network — HUAC, the FBI, J. B. Matthews, and Jay Lovestone — the committee also seemed to have gotten some help from the mining industry, though it is unclear what that consisted of beyond supplying some names and addresses. In addition, the SISS had access to the material that had been compiled for the CIO's expulsion hearings.[84]

To a large extent the Salt Lake City hearings simply replicated those CIO proceedings. J. B. Matthews led off by identifying the union's alleged Communists and fellow travelers and their incriminating affiliations. Then several former Mine-Mill officials testified about their brushes with the union's Communists. Kenneth Eckert repeated the damaging allegations he had made at the CIO trial about belonging to a four-man communist "steering committee" that ran the union for the party. He also identified about a dozen Mine-Mill officials (including Clinton Jencks) as Communists and noted that others, like the union's president, "were much more valuable to the party . . . than they would be as an official member of the Communist Party."[85]

343

There were unfriendly witnesses as well. The McCarran committee called up eleven Mine-Mill officials and rank-and-file members and asked them the usual questions. They all took the Fifth. Travis, whom the committee considered "the real boss of the union," got the most intensive grilling. Using "a long and detailed run-down sheet" supplied by the FBI, the SISS's interrogators questioned him extensively about his political activities, as well as his visits to the San Cristobal Valley Ranch and his relationship with Craig and Jenny Vincent. Just as HUAC had produced the party cards of the Hollywood Ten to bolster its charges against them, McCarran confronted Travis with photostats of Communist party documents about him that may well have come from the FBI's informers or "black bag" jobs.[86]

The union's general counsel, Nathan Witt, was also put on the stand. Witt had been controversial ever since his tenure as secretary of the National Labor Relations Board in the 1930s. His later identification by Whittaker Chambers as a member of the same underground communist group Alger Hiss belonged to made him even more notorious. Because of Witt's reputation as one of the nation's leading labor lawyers and his crucial position within the union that controlled the copper industry, professional anti-Communists like the SISS's research director, Benjamin Mandel, considered him to be a particularly dangerous member of the communist conspiracy. The SISS plied him with embarrassing questions. "Have you ever been an espionage agent on behalf of Soviet Russia?" "Did you ever give information to Mr. J. David Whittaker Chambers?" Witt's reluctant use of the Fifth Amendment simply reinforced the committee's portrayal of the union as a threat to national security.[87]

On the following day, Harvey Matusow testified about Clinton Jencks. In the year and a half since his expulsion from the Communist party, Matusow had transformed himself into one of the nation's leading professional witnesses. When he left the San Cristobal Valley Ranch, he knocked around the Southwest for a few months and then joined the air force. A few months later he was transferred to the Wright Patterson Air Force Base in Dayton, Ohio. But he soon felt as unappreciated by the military as he had been by the CP. Fearing that his communist background might be creating problems, he tried to clear himself and was told to contact an air force public relations officer named Martha Edmiston. Along with her journalist husband, John, Edmiston had been an undercover informant for the FBI in the early 1940s and had testified before HUAC in 1950. They were willing to help Matusow become a professional witness.[88]

The couple worked up his testimony with him and coached him in the etiquette of testifying, warning him against falsely identifying people as Communists and correcting some of his "crude mannerisms" like his "bad table manners" and "insistence on being the center of attention of all persons present." They also put him in touch with HUAC. After his discharge from the air force, Matusow signed on with the anticommunist network. He peddled his story to the media and proffered himself as an expert on the party. In the beginning of 1952, he spent a month as a research assistant for the Ohio Un-American Actvities Committee, collecting information and preparing for his HUAC debut. Ever eager for the limelight, Matusow decided that he needed a "gimmick" to distinguish him from the other ex-Communists on the circuit. When he realized that he was the youngest of the professional witnesses, he set himself up as a specialist on the party's youth work. His HUAC hearing on February 7 and 8, though a success in establishing him as an expert, was a disappointment. "What a hell of a break for me," Matusow noted in his diary at the time. "The King [of England] had to die on my day of 'triumph.' Pushed me right off the front page."[89]

Still, Matusow had reached the pinnacle of professional anticommunism. The Hearst press published a series of articles about him. He got gigs with the New York City Board of Education, the Subversive Activities Control Board, the Justice Department, and the McCarran committee. For a few months in the spring and summer of 1952, he was on the payroll of *Counterattack,* the anticommunist newsletter that Father Cronin and Alfred Kohlberg had helped a trio of former FBI agents set up. He did fact checking and general research but was soon let go because his employers, so they were later to claim, did not trust him and suspected that he was stealing material from their files. Matusow also made contact with Senator McCarthy and volunteered to campaign for the Republican party. He was, as he put it, in the "Big Leagues."[90]

Because so many anticommunist proceedings used communist literature as evidence, Matusow realized he could capitalize on his experience in the party's bookstores by claiming that CP bigwigs had told him to promote specific titles. This kind of testimony turned out to be a useful way to get particularly damaging information into the record. At the McCarran committee's IPR hearings on the "loss of China," for example, Matusow testified that he was told to sell Owen Lattimore's books; at the second-string Smith Act trial in New York, he introduced particularly lurid passages from Andrei Vishinsky's *The Law of the Soviet State* by maintaining that one of the defendants had ordered him to push it. Matusow was lying. According to an FBI agent who was present during U.S. Attorney Roy Cohn's early interviews with Matusow in preparation for the Smith Act trial, the subject of the Vishinsky book never came up. "Cohn did not attempt to put words in Matusow's mouth, but would ask him what he knew concerning certain matters and would then rephrase the answers and ask Matusow if they were not true."[91]

Matusow had mentioned Clinton Jencks at his HUAC appearance but had not emphasized that part of his story. When he found out that the SISS was going to investigate Mine-Mill, he volunteered to testify. The committee took up the offer and brought him to Salt Lake City. Matusow began his testimony by describing his sojourn at the San Cristobal Valley Ranch. He identified both Craig and Jenny Vincent as party members and implied that their resort "about eighty miles northeast of Los Alamos" had some connection with atomic espionage. He then talked about Jencks, identifying him as a party member and elaborating on a conversation he and Jencks supposedly had about the possibility that the Communists in Mine-Mill might call a strike to "cut down production of copper for the Korean war effort." Matusow ended his testimony by fingering Maurice Travis as a party member and making the irrelevant and gratuitous charge that over a hundred Communists worked for the *New York Times* and seventy-six for *Time*.[92]

Much of this testimony was false. In a memo that the former FBI agent Don Connors prepared for the committee summarizing the information he expected each witness to give, there is no indication whatsoever that Matusow was going to make the sensational allegation that Mine-Mill planned to call a copper strike to sabotage the Korean war effort. Actually, what turned out to be the most damaging aspect of Matusow's testimony was that it supposedly placed Jencks in the Communist party in July 1950, several months *after* he had signed a Taft-Hartley affidavit. The committee expected Jencks to be a hostile witness and planned to cross-examine him about Matusow's testimony. "I think it will be a dramatic ending," Connors predicted, "if we have a confrontation between Matusow and Jencks. We will, of course, have Jenck's [sic] complete Communist Party background on which to question him."[93]

The SISS got its expected confrontation. Jencks proved to be a very hostile witness indeed. Not only did he take the Fifth repeatedly, but he attacked "the intentions and the procedures of this committee" as "arbitrary and tyrannical." After the hearings ended, McCarran submitted a report describing the communist influence within Mine-Mill and calling for legislation that would both bar Communists from union office and let employers discharge people who belonged to organizations on the Attorney General's list. McCarran also recommended that the Justice Department prosecute all the Mine-Mill officials his committee had identified as Communists.[94]

At first, little happened. Clinton Jencks went back to New Mexico to resume his union activities and prepare for the filming of *Salt of the Earth*. Matusow continued his career as a professional witness. J. B. Matthews, whom he met at the SISS hearings, befriended the younger man and drew him into his circle of anticommunist luminaries. For the next few months, Matusow was a frequent chess partner and dinner guest along with the likes of Elizabeth Bentley and columnist George Sokolsky. Matusow also gravitated into the entourage of Joe McCarthy, where he did odd jobs, made speeches, and helped Arvilla Bentley, the wealthy ex-wife of a Michigan congressman, fly to the Bahamas to escape a congressional investigation of her financial dealings with the Wisconsin senator. In March 1953, Arvilla Bentley became Mrs. Harvey Matusow.[95]

A few weeks later, Matusow was in El Paso to repeat his testimony before the federal grand jury that was about to indict Jencks for perjury. The trial began the following January. From the start, Mine-Mill's leaders assumed that the case was part of the larger attack on all the left-led unions and, in the usual traditions of labor defense, they tried to mount a major fund-raising and publicity campaign. They arranged showings of *Salt of the Earth* and sent Jencks on a nation-wide speaking tour, but by 1953 it was not possible to mobilize much support outside of the increasingly beleaguered circle of the left-wing unions and their allies. During the trial, a media boycott, like that which plagued *Salt of the Earth* in Los Angeles, prevented

Mine-Mill from bringing its case to the people of El Paso. Though the union tried to buy time on the city's four main radio stations, none of them would carry the broadcast. Similar attempts to take out ads in the city's two newspapers also failed. The blackout was international; a radio station in Juarez, Mexico, also refused to air Mine-Mill's program.[96]

The trial itself contained few surprises. It was a replay of all the earlier proceedings, including a Texas Industrial Commission hearing into Mine-Mill that had taken place only a few weeks before. Matusow was the star witness. In his testimony, he added new details to the story that he had told the SISS and claimed that Jencks had told him about making arrangements with the Mexican miners union to collaborate in sabotaging the Korean war effort. He also related several conversations in which, he said, Jencks encouraged him to move to New Mexico, because "we can use you out here, we need more active Party members." The government's other witnesses included Kenneth Eckert and several other ex-communist Mine-Mill officials as well as a former Albuquerque minister who had worked undercover for the FBI. They all testified about attending party meetings with Jencks but none of them could place him in the CP after he had signed the Taft-Hartley affidavit. Because Jencks and his lawyers feared that the prosecutors might ask him to identify other people and thus force him to invoke the Fifth Amendment, he did not take the stand in his own defense. The jury deliberated all of twenty-two minutes before delivering its guilty verdict.[97]

Like many McCarthy era defendants, Jencks had treated his case almost as an abstraction. He knew that he had been selected for prosecution because the government was trying to punish his union. Thus, despite the "constant pressure and stress" he felt, he tended to view his activities in drumming up support for his defense as part of his regular political work. When the verdict was announced, however, the reality of what was happening to him sank in. "The judge," Jencks recalled,

> could hardly wait to get me into jail. I was standing there with the marshal holding one of my arms and [attorney] John McTernan holding the other, being pulled by both sides. That brought it really home that *they were talking about my body.*[98]

Sentenced to five years in prison, Jencks appealed his conviction. His attorneys, who had been planning to appeal all along, based part of their case on the assumption that the prosecution's witnesses had lied and they asked to see the original FBI reports that had been filed about Matusow and the other witnesses. Such arguments had become routine defense maneuvers in anticommunist proceedings, though judges usually rejected them on national security grounds. Jencks, however, was fortunate, for Harvey Matusow recanted.[99]

Matusow's instability was hard to conceal. The FBI had doubts about him soon after he publicized his past connection to the Bureau. Informants who craved the limelight embarrassed the FBI but Hoover and his men could do little to control Matusow other than alert their field offices not to recruit anyone with a tendency "to brag or emphasize his own importance." In 1952, the FBI warned the Justice Department that Matusow had been diagnosed by army doctors as having a "psychoneurosis of a mild but acute form," but the department continued to use him as a witness. The federal attorneys who built their cases on the testimony of professional informers like Matusow may have suspected that these people embellished their stories, but it was so hard to find *any* usable evidence against Communists that the prosecutors shut their eyes to the perversions of justice that their reliance on such witnesses entailed.[100]

Even before the Jencks trial, Matusow began to have doubts about his new career as a professional witness. By the summer of 1953, his marriage had fallen apart and he set out for the West, pausing to visit the Edmistons in Ohio, where he asked to be "forgiven" and admitted that he had not always told the truth. In August, he wrote a letter to Senator McCarthy, confessing in his typically grandiose manner to

> twenty-seven years of being a coward and being dishonest. I have gone through life hurting the things I love and believe in. . . . I don't want to go near politics ever again. And I never want to be part of the Communist question, pro or con.

At about the same time, he told an FBI agent in New Mexico that he did not want to be a witness at the forthcoming Jencks trial. Over the next few months, Matusow continued to appear on the anticommmunist circuit, while at the same time expressing a desire for self-abnegation and a need to atone for his dishonesty.[101]

He was also writing a book, or so he said. But money was a problem.

He could not finish the manuscript without it and the publishers to whom he was trying to peddle *Blacklisting Was My Business,* as he was then calling his memoir, would not give him an advance without seeing the finished work. Some of the people who had dealings with him during this period recall that he tried to cadge loans by hinting that he could be paid off to keep their names out of the book. In April 1954, he went to see G. Bromley Oxnam, a Methodist bishop frequently targeted by the anti-Communists. Matusow told Oxnam that he wanted to repent for having lied about so many people and expressed a desire to do something to compensate his victims. He saw Oxnam a second time in May, this time to repeat his confession and borrow money. In the beginning of June, Oxnam made Matusow's recantation public.[102]

Matusow's about-face was political dynamite. Many observers had long suspected that some ex-communist witnesses were lying, but had no definitive proof. Matusow's recantation confirmed their suspicions. Moreover, if Harvey Matusow had perjured himself, it was possible that witnesses like Louis Budenz or Elizabeth Bentley had done the same. And, in fact, the testimony of some informers had begun to unravel even before Matusow recanted. In 1951, the professional ex-Communist Manning Johnson had admitted under cross-examination that he would willingly lie under oath if ordered to do so by the FBI. "If the interests of my government are at stake . . . I will do it a thousand times."[103]

Now Matusow's even more damaging confession might torpedo the entire anticommunist project. Suspicions about the veracity of government witnesses might lead juries to acquit communist defendants and judges to reverse their convictions. More specifically, since Matusow was the only prosecution witness to place Clinton Jencks in the CP after he had signed his Taft-Hartley affidavit, if he retracted his testimony Jencks might win his case.

But Matusow was not easy to pin down. HUAC got to him first; on July 12, 1954, he disavowed his recantation. "I did not say and I do not say now that I ever lied under oath." Then Matusow fled to the Southwest, where he worked at a succession of menial jobs, wrote poetry, converted to Mormonism, and talked about prospecting for uranium. By the time Jencks and his supporters contacted him in October, he had reversed himself yet again.[104]

The Jencks defense team hoped that Matusow would sign an affidavit retracting his original testimony in return for assistance in publishing his book. Albert Kahn, a left-wing writer who had just gone into the publishing business with Angus Cameron, a blacklisted editor from Little, Brown, would edit the manuscript; Mine-Mill would underwrite it, ostensibly as an advance order for several thousand copies. Matusow dictated his story into a tape recorder; and Kahn then turned the transcript into a book. Though there is no reason to doubt the broad outlines of *False Witness,* as the book was called, Matusow was probably as eager to please Kahn as he had been to please Roy Cohn and may well have been willing to take suggestions with regard to the nuances of his account or the spin he put on it. In January 1955, he submitted affidavits withdrawing his testimony against Jencks and two Smith Act defendants. Kahn then arranged for the columnist Stewart Alsop to break the story.[105]

As expected, the furor about *False Witness* was enormous. From the FBI (which had tried to suppress it) to the American Legion, the entire anticommunist network swung into action, denouncing Matusow's revelations as part of a communist plot designed, so SISS research director Benjamin Mandel explained, "to wreck the prosecutory machinery of the Government against the Communist Party." If the campaign against American Communism was to continue, Matusow had to be discredited. The Justice Department mounted two grand jury investigations: one that questioned Matusow and his publishers in New York and a second that grilled a group of Mine-Mill officials in Denver. The SISS also subpoenaed the culprits and held several days of hearings. All these proceedings sought to show that the communist conspiracy had tricked Matusow into writing *False Witness.*[106]

This scenario was easy for SISS staff members and Justice Department attorneys to flesh out. Every principal had the kind of incriminating associations that placed him in or near the CP. Kahn had even been a friend of Gerhart Eisler. And Nathan Witt, Jencks's lawyer, who Mandel believed was the "leading legal mind" behind the whole "Matusow maneuver," was already notorious. Moreover, when called before the SISS and New York grand jury, all the people involved implicated themselves by taking the Fifth. Mandel and his colleagues were ready to believe that Matusow had lied, but that it was Witt and Kahn, not federal prosecutors like Roy Cohn, who had suborned the perjury. In order to show that Matusow's initial testimony was true while his recantation was false, the SISS and Justice Department officials emphasized the discrepancies between his original book outline and tape-recorded recollections and the final texts of his affidavits and *False Witness.* The government also claimed that it had corroborating evidence for almost everybody identified by Matusow as a Communist. And, no doubt, it did — though it may well have been illegally obtained. But nothing that the congressional investigators or the Justice Department could uncover could conceal the damaging fact that the government's campaign against Communism had relied on tainted testimony.[107]

On April 22, 1955, Judge Edward J. Dimock overturned the convictions of the two New York second-string Smith Act defendants who had been found guilty on the basis of Matusow's testimony. His recantation, Judge Dimock observed, was probably no more sincere than his original testimony, but his present lack of credibility did not make his initial statements true. That assessment of Matusow's veracity, though widely shared, was not universal. Unfortunately for Clinton Jencks and Harvey Matusow, one of the places where the anticommunist crusade still retained its power was the El Paso, Texas, courtroom of Judge Robert E. Thomason. Like many other conservatives, Thomason believed that Matusow's about-face was part of a communist plot and he rejected Jencks's plea for a new trial. That decision did not stand. Though the Fifth Circuit Court of Appeals upheld Jencks's conviction, it may well have done so in order to allow the case to reach the Supreme Court, which finally threw it out.[108]

Such mixed signals within the federal judiciary were common. By the mid-1950s, the Supreme Court, as we have already seen, had also begun to turn against the anticommunist furor and was rendering increasingly liberal decisions. Since it did so mainly on procedural grounds, it had little trouble in overturning convictions based on the perjured testimony of prosecution witnesses. It was, therefore, hardly a surprise when on June 3, 1957, the court, by a 7–1 majority, voided Clinton Jencks's conviction. Justice William Brennan's opinion did more than just overturn the lower courts' decisions; it also ruled that the defense should have been allowed to look at the original FBI reports on Matusow. Brennan recognized that the fear of revealing "state secrets and other confidential information" might make prosecutors reluctant to produce such records, but, he insisted, the integrity of the judicial process was just as important. Though the decision actually opened few

Bureau files, it was, nonetheless, a stunning reassertion of the rights of individual defendants in the face of the government's claim that national security would brook no restrictions on the FBI.[109]

Brennan had, however, gone too far. Even though McCarthyism was waning, the Bureau remained sacrosanct. As the language of Justice Tom Clark's indignant dissent reveals, the Court had trod upon forbidden turf. "Unless Congress changes the rule announced by the Court today," he roared,

> those intelligence agencies of our Government engaged in law enforcement may as well close up shop for the Court has opened their files to the criminal and thus afforded him a Roman holiday for rummaging through confidential information as well as vital national secrets.

J. Edgar Hoover was equally apoplectic and went on the offensive at once, mounting an all-out lobbying campaign to reverse Brennan's ruling.[110]

Actually, even before the *Jencks* decision came down, Congress had been considering dozens of proposals to curb the Court and limit its jurisdiction over internal security. Segregationists had been on the offensive since the 1954 *Brown v. Board of Education* decision. Because the Court's other liberal rulings now threatened the anticommunist crusade, the already mobilized Southerners were able to clothe their racial agenda in patriotic prose and enlist new allies in their campaign against Earl Warren and his colleagues. But only Hoover had the clout to reverse a Supreme Court ruling. He and his allies invoked national security and urged immediate action. Otherwise, as President Eisenhower explained, there would be "incalculable damage." Since few lawmakers could or would challenge the FBI's misleading assessment of the dire consequences of the *Jencks* decision, Hoover's measure breezed through Congress with the briefest of hearings, barely any debate, and only two negative votes. The so-called "Jencks Law" essentially nullified Brennan's ruling by exempting most of the Bureau's records from its purview. Actually, since the FBI and the Justice Department had largely stopped using informers as witnesses, the law had more significance as a symbol of Hoover's power and prestige than it did as a forensic tool.[111]

A week after the *Jencks* decision, Harvey Matusow went to prison, a victim of the government's determination to punish him for recanting. The

Justice Department had too many of its key political cases resting on the testimony of ex-communist witnesses for it to overlook Matusow's transgressions. In July 1955, it got a grand jury to indict him for claiming that Roy Cohn had doctored his Smith Act testimony. The trial, which began in September 1956, was a low-keyed affair. Matusow had remarried and was having trouble finding a job. He doubted that an acquittal would make the Justice Department abandon his case and he wanted to end the ordeal even if it meant a prison term. Accordingly, he did not mount a strong defense and merely denied that he had lied about Cohn. Since it was his word against Cohn's, it took the jury less than two hours to find him guilty. He lost his appeal and had to spend over three years in prison.[112]

Though he stayed out of prison, Clinton Jencks did not have an easy life. His legal ordeal had been hard on him and his family. He was rarely home, for he had to put in "thousands of hours" traveling around the country to drum up support for his defense. Even after the Supreme Court overturned his conviction, the threat of a new trial hung over him for a year and a half until the Justice Department officially dropped the case. Mine-Mill took care of his legal bills, but in the middle of 1956, with his appeal still pending, the union's executive board forced him to resign from his position as an organizer. He hadn't wanted to, for he felt that it would just "encourage the witch-hunters." But he was too controversial a figure for the embattled union to retain.[113]

Like so many of the other men and women caught up in the McCarthy era purges, Jencks soon found that his political problems made it hard for him to earn a living. "My name was so well-known," he recalled, "I couldn't get a job anywhere in the Southwest." He moved to the San Francisco Bay area only to discover that the blacklist applied there as well. Though the California economy was booming and his skills as a machinist and millwright were in demand, the FBI, it seems, was on his trail. "I would get a job, join the union, be doing a good job, then all of a sudden I'd be called into the manager's office." This pattern recurred so often that, as Jencks recalled, an official in the state employment office told him, not entirely in jest, "We've got a new classification to cover you, Jencks, you're politically unemployable."[114]

The insecurity took a huge personal toll and Jencks finally decided to return to graduate school and get a Ph.D. in economics. Academia, he hoped, might give him "a little better chance of surviving." But the witch-hunters would not leave him alone. In July 1959, he appeared before HUAC and took the Fifth. He had just won a prestigious Woodrow Wilson Fellowship and the committee was seeking publicity and a way to attack the Ford Foundation, which funded him. Though the Wilson Fellowship's directors were nervous about Jencks, they did not revoke his grant as they might well have done a few years before. Jencks was thus able to pursue his graduate work at Berkeley and, in 1964, get a teaching position at San Diego State College. But his troubles still were not over. A story about his appointment appeared in the local press and he was called into the president's office and asked about his case. But by the mid-1960s, McCarthyism had lost its bite; his fellow faculty members stood up for him and he retained his job.[115]

Clinton Jencks survived the McCarthy period, his former union did not. Jencks's 9(h) prosecution was, it turned out, only the first of the many legal battles that Mine-Mill had to confront as the federal government tried to put it out of business. The tenacity of the official campaign against the union is remarkable. It lasted until the mid-1960s and involved at least half a dozen different actions. Whatever the venue, the same charges, witnesses, and literary exhibits were trotted out. In their basic outlines, if not in their specifics, the multiple proceedings against Mine-Mill resembled all the other official actions against the organizations in the communist world. And the outcome was the same; most of these groups were forced to fold.

Legally, Mine-Mill emerged victorious. It usually appealed the decisions against it and it usually won. The litigation, however, took years and the effort of defending itself against so many different charges sapped the union's vitality as well as its treasury. Moreover, the repeated allegations of communist infiltration that accompanied each proceeding reinforced the demonization of the organization and increased its isolation. When the harassment ended, Mine-Mill was all but defunct.

The NLRB was an early nemesis. From the start, the board was determined to find a way to decertify the left-led unions and deny them the use of its facilities. In 1954, it tried to rule Mine-Mill out of compliance with Taft-Hartley by claiming that the union's secretary-treasurer, Maurice Travis, had falsified his noncommunist affidavits and so had automatically deprived the union of any official status under the law. The board's formal hearing on the matter was a replay of Mine-Mill's CIO trial and SISS hearings. Travis's 1949 open letter about his resignation from the Communist party supposedly proved that he had falsified his affidavit. It was, the NLRB's attorneys claimed, an example of the CP's "Aesopian language" and actually meant the opposite of what it said. The board agreed, though its February 1955 decision to rule Mine-Mill out of compliance did not stand up on appeal. Still, it did drive Travis out of office. He had long been a source of dissension within the union and less than two weeks after the NLRB's decertification order, his colleagues on Mine-Mill's executive board forced him to resign. His ouster might neutralize some of the internal unrest as well as overcome the government's main objections to certification.[116]

But Travis's — and the union's — legal troubles were hardly over, for he was also facing perjury charges. Ever since he published his resignation letter, the Mine-Mill secretary-treasurer had been an obvious target for a 9(h) prosecution. Whenever politicians and businessmen complained about the ineffectiveness of the Taft-Hartley affidavits, they invariably cited Travis as someone especially deserving of indictment. The NLRB and Justice Department also wanted to prosecute. On the day after Travis's resignation statement appeared, the board forwarded his affidavits to the department. The FBI questioned him about them a few months later. What seems surprising was that the indictment did not come down until November 1954.[117]

Travis's December 1955 trial featured all the usual witnesses with all the usual stories about the Mine-Mill leader's dealings with high party officials and the Aesopian nature of his 1949 statement. The government added a new fillip to the proceedings; it had one of the prosecution witnesses offer the theory that "once having joined the Communist Party, you could not leave without being expelled." This "can't resign" theory had become a staple of many anticommunist prosecutions. Since it was hard to prove that someone had been a Communist within three years of his or her indictment as the statute of limitations required, asserting the permanent nature of party membership might serve instead. Convicted and sentenced to an unprecedentedly long eight-year prison term, Travis underwent over five more years of trials, appeals, and reversals before the Supreme Court finally threw out the case early in 1961 on the technical grounds that the government had brought the prosecution in Denver instead of in Washington, D.C.[118]

But the harassment of Mine-Mill did not let up. Travis was facing yet another Taft-Hartley-related prosecution, this time as one of several Mine-

Mill officials accused of conspiring to defraud the government by filing false affidavits. As it did in its Smith Act prosecution of the CP's top leaders, the government found conspiracy a convenient charge in a case where concrete evidence of illegal activity was hard to find. The case, which began in November 1956 with the indictment of fourteen present and former Mine-Mill officials and staff members for plotting with the party to falsify the union's noncommunist affidavits, dragged on for nearly a decade. There was considerable irony in the fact that when the Supreme Court finally threw out the case in June 1966, it invoked the *Jencks* decision, claiming that the defendants had been improperly denied access to the grand jury testimony of several prosecution witnesses.[119]

But the union's troubles continued. It was also fighting an attempt by the Justice Department to make it register with the Subversive Activities Control Board as a "Communist-infiltrated" organization. These proceedings also lasted for years. They began in July 1955 when the Eisenhower administration decided to use the machinery created by the recently enacted Communist Control Act of 1954 to put Mine-Mill out of business by asking the SACB to designate the union as a "communist infiltrated" organization. If the move succeeded, the union would lose all its legal privileges as a labor organization. Of course, the move did not succeed. There were the usual hearings, appeals, and rehearings. The litigation dragged on until the end of 1965, when the U.S. Court of Appeals decided that the evidence was too "stale" and shipped the dispute back to the SACB for a new hearing. At that point, the government dropped the case.[120]

By then, the union was on the rocks. It had been fending off the Justice Department for over thirteen years and its financial situation was so desperate that in 1961 it even signed a mutual assistance pact with Jimmy Hoffa's International Brotherhood of Teamsters in return for a $100,000 loan. The alliance between the nation's largest and most crime-ridden union and one of its reddest drew the attention of Mine-Mill's traditional enemies on Capitol Hill and led to a new set of hearings before the SISS. The committee, eager to find evidence that the left-led unions were funding the CP, spent several years investigating Mine-Mill's finances. But it got nowhere. After a final blast at the "outrageous abuses" of tax-exempt union funds that "virtually encourage litigation by Communists," Mississippi senator James Eastland ended his committee's probe. No one paid any attention.[121]

The harassment of the International Union of Mine, Mill and Smelter

357

Workers finally petered out in the mid-sixties. Unlike most of the other left-led unions and front groups, Mine-Mill did not succumb during the McCarthy period. It survived more than fifteen years of the combined efforts of congressional committees, federal agencies, employers, and rival unions to put it out of business. It had been vindicated by the federal judiciary in almost every proceeding directed against it. It is possible, therefore, to view this outcome, as many observers have, as exemplifying the resiliency of the American legal system. Such a triumph-of-the-law approach, however, seems overly formalistic. To assess the real impact of the concerted campaign against Mine-Mill, one must look beyond the courtroom to the real world of the labor movement. And there, the union did survive, but barely.[122]

Debilitated by its legal battles, Mine-Mill was diverted from its core functions as a labor organization at a moment when the mining industry was itself in decline. As a result, by the mid-sixties, other unions were finally beginning to make serious inroads into Mine-Mill's traditional strongholds. Communism was no longer an issue, for the union had long since sloughed off its allegedly communist leaders and was only trying to preserve its institutional autonomy. But it had become too weak to protect the economic well-being of its members. In August 1966, it signed a no-raiding and mutual assistance pact with its main rival, the Steelworkers. A year later, the two unions merged. Though the anticommunist crusade was by then only a dim, bad dream, Mine-Mill's belated demise may well have been McCarthyism's last victory.[123]

★

CHAPTER 10

"A GOOD DEAL OF TRAUMA"

THE IMPACT OF McCARTHYISM

UNDER NORMAL circumstances, Josephine Black would have gone to her cousin Lucy Durr's wedding in Montgomery, Alabama. But the summer of 1957 was no normal time in the South. The civil rights movement, stimulated by the Supreme Court's *Brown v. Board of Education* decision in 1954 and the Montgomery bus boycott of the following year, was stirring. Segregationists, mobilized to defend their white-supremacist way of life, fought with whatever weapons they could find — red-baiting included. As a result, Josephine's father, Supreme Court justice Hugo Black, a "renegade" Southerner who had joined the unanimous *Brown* decision, felt himself vulnerable to such attacks and worried that something "unpleasant" might happen if it became known that his daughter had been at a wedding at which some of the guests were alleged to be Communists.[1]

Even without their left-wing friends, the bride's parents were controversial enough. Justice Black's sister-in-law Virginia Durr was an outspoken Southern progressive who had already had a brush with the Senate Internal Security Subcommittee; her husband, Clifford Durr, the only Truman administration official to resign in protest against the loyalty-security program in 1947, had once headed the National Lawyers Guild. Worse yet, some of the Durrs' best friends were Communists, including the writer Jessica Mitford, then a Bay Area activist married to Dobby Walker's law partner Robert

Treuhaft. Justice Black, fearing that segregationists might somehow use Mitford's presence at the wedding to attack him and the Court, kept his daughter at home.[2]

Black's caution speaks for itself. Anticommunism, at least as it developed in the Deep South in the late fifties, was so virulent that it interfered with the family life of one of the most powerful and respected public figures in the United States. Obviously, McCarthyism inflicted far more painful sanctions than Josephine Black's disappointment at missing her cousin's wedding. Still, as the incident reveals, the anticommunist furor of the early Cold War had a surprisingly long reach. It frightened liberals as well as radicals.[3]

Fear usually accompanies political repression. It blossomed during the McCarthy years and reverberates to this day — most visibly in the continuing reluctance of so many otherwise politically savvy protagonists to let their full stories go into the historical record. When I tried to get information from these people, some of them, like Judith Coplon, simply refused to talk. Others, like Harry Magdoff, a highly respected Marxist economist named by Elizabeth Bentley, said that they did not want to reopen old wounds. When asked if they had been Communists, both Clinton Jencks and Jenny Wells Vincent gave evasive answers. Some people never told their own children what happened. And those children, meeting at a "red diaper baby" conference in the early 1980s, refused to let their last names be used in the published edition of their discussions.[4]

But McCarthyism bequeathed America much more than an incomplete record. It changed the lives of thousands of people at the same time that it changed the nation's political culture. This chapter will assess that legacy. Not only will it look at the direct effects of the anticommunist crusade on the individuals caught up in it, but it will also explore the other, more subtle — and more important — ways in which the McCarthy era shaped our society. Because the anticommunist crusade was so complex and touched so many areas of American life, I can offer but a preliminary survey. Future explorers will have to provide more detailed maps.

There was, to begin with, a lot of human wreckage. From Hollywood to Harvard, the anticommunist crusade blighted thousands of lives, careers, and marriages. People's experiences varied, as did their reactions to them. Some folks flourished; others were destroyed; most managed to survive. They all experienced stress. How seriously McCarthyism affected someone tended to be more a matter of that person's temperament and the intensity of his or her political commitment than of the severity of the sanctions. Genuine innocents or apolitical individuals blindsided by the inquisition had the worst time. People who could put their experiences into an ideological framework coped most effectively. "So I lost my job," a blacklisted college teacher recalled. "Nothing came as a surprise. A radical, a left-winger who is shocked, surprised, dismayed at the materialization of his own understanding is indeed basically disoriented." Yet even such political sophisticates suffered. If nothing else, as playwright Lillian Hellman noted, "Life had changed."[5]

For some, it ended. There were a handful of suicides. I know of about ten; no doubt there were more that got no attention. Some were prospective witnesses, like the Stanford University biologist William Sherwood, who killed himself on the eve of a HUAC appearance in June 1957, terrified of being, as he explained in his suicide note, "assassinated by publicity." Others, like the blacklisted actor Philip Loeb, were desperate. Unemployed, homeless, losing his eyesight, and distraught about his inability to keep his mentally ill son in a private clinic, Loeb went into a serious depression that finally ended on the Labor Day weekend of 1955 when he checked into a New York City hotel and took an overdose of sleeping pills.[6]

Sometimes the stress of the investigations and blacklists could be fatal. Harry Dexter White was recovering from an earlier heart attack when he faced HUAC in the summer of 1948; his doctor tried to get the committee to ease up on him, but it did not. White died three days later. The blacklisted actor J. Edward Bromberg met a similar fate a few years later, as did the film star John Garfield, whose health was destroyed by his attempt to fend off the inquisition. There were even a few murders, including that of William Remington, brutally beaten by two other inmates at the Lewisburg Federal Penitentiary.[7]

While not normally lethal, incarceration also inflicted suffering. It was part of the legal process, designed along with such demeaning procedures as handcuffs, fingerprints, and mug shots to emphasize the criminal nature of Communists and other political defendants. Accordingly, prosecutors tried to incarcerate these people whenever they could. Bail was hard to get and, for aliens facing deportation, unobtainable. About two hundred political prisoners spent time behind bars or in INS detention centers during the 1940s and 1950s. Though these people's sentences were comparatively short, usually no more than a year or two, prison was no picnic. Remington's was the only murder, but not the only beating. Other people had health problems; the inadequate treatment he received in the racially segregated Terre Haute facility cost the CP's black leader Henry Winston his eyesight.[8]

Nor did the political repression party members experienced in the larger society stop at the jailhouse door. The more prominent Communists were the most harassed, often denied the privileges that ordinary inmates received. They could not work in prison industries, get time off for good behavior or, in some cases, receive the two books a month that other prisoners were entitled to. The prison authorities viewed them as difficult cases. By challenging the racial segregation they encountered, they refused to conform to the unstated mores of the federal correctional system. Worse yet, they were unregenerate. In the eyes of the prison authorities, they did not deserve the "privileges and rewards" accorded to "those who did repent." Even when the prison conditions were relatively benign, incarceration was a demeaning "experience" that, *Salt of the Earth* director Herbert Biberman concluded, had "no positive values."[9]

Extralegal sanctions also caused suffering. People who were identified as Communists were sometimes physically attacked by superpatriots who took the law into their own hands. The worst incident took place at Peekskill, New York, in September 1949 when a mob of stone-throwing vigilantes disrupted a Paul Robeson concert. Though there were no fatalities, nearly a hundred and fifty people were hurt while the state police stood by and watched. Labor struggles precipitated much of the other anticommunist violence. Mine-Mill was particularly embattled. The arson, shootings, and beatings that plagued Clinton Jencks and his colleagues in the early 1950s were not uncommon. Fights broke out during strikes and during bitter NLRB election campaigns.[10]

Crank calls, hate mail, and other forms of harassment also tormented the victims of McCarthyism, especially in those cities where local newspapers printed the names and addresses of subpoenaed witnesses. Sometimes the callers just breathed heavily; sometimes they were more menacing. A New York City teacher remembered how terrified his children were by the telephoned death threats as well as by the letter with a picture of "gibbets and myself hanging from the scaffold." A Southern college teacher active in the Wallace campaign had his home smeared with red paint; a blacklisted writer found a burning cross in his front yard. This kind of harassment was so widespread that almost everybody whose case became public experienced at least one such incident.[11]

People's main problems, however, were economic. The men and women who refused to cooperate with anticommunist investigators or were otherwise identifed as Communists routinely lost their jobs and could rarely find new ones. The body count comes to somewhere between ten and twelve thousand. It may well have been higher, but those casualties, like my sixth-grade teacher, kept their problems to themselves and so escaped the historical scorecard. McCarthyism affected certain groups more than others. Besides government employees, the purges targeted people who worked with ideas or human services or else were clustered within those industries that had been organized by the communist-led unions: few bankers or Wall Street lawyers, but a lot of teachers, writers, and longshoremen.[12]

Losing one's job or being blacklisted was, to put it mildly, economically disastrous. In every field, people's incomes plummeted. Actor Joseph Julian had been making good money in the late 1940s: $18,236 in 1947, $14,453 in 1948, $18,071 in 1949, and $17,394 in 1950, the year he was listed by the professional anticommunists who published *Red Channels*. In 1951, he earned $11,858, in 1952, $6,710, and in 1953, $1,630. Blacklisted screenwriters had the same problems. Though they could sell their work under the table, they could not command their previous fees. At the other end of the economic spectrum, black workers like Lawrence Parker were in desperate straits, since racial as well as political discrimination kept them from making a living. Legal expenses compounded the financial strain. Even when an attorney worked for free or an outside support group covered the costs, fighting back could be a full-time job.[13]

People scraped by as people always have in such circumstances. They sold their homes and rented cheaper ones or moved in with relatives. Their spouses took jobs, though they, too, sometimes encountered the blacklist. Courtney Cazden almost lost the teaching position she found after her husband, Norman, was bounced from his job at the University of Illinois by the FBI's Responsibilities Program. To the extent that its dwindling resources allowed, the communist movement tried to take care of its own. Harry Bridges's ILWU, for example, helped blacklisted Marine Cooks and Stewards members find work on the docks. But most people had to fend for themselves. Like Clinton Jencks, they often landed jobs only to lose them when an FBI agent showed up at the plant or principal's office.[14]

Like many of the other political unemployables, Jencks finally changed careers, though his switch from blue-collar work to academia was unusual. Most of the time people found something that built upon their preexisting skills. When they were screened off their ships, for example, some MC and S people capitalized on their culinary experience and opened restaurants. Harold Christoffel, who had been an electrician before he organized the UAW local at Allis-Chalmers, became an electrical contractor. My sixth-grade teacher operated a private day camp.[15]

Emigration was an option that allowed some scientists and screenwriters to continue working in their fields. By the mid-fifties there were clusters of Hollywood expatriates in Mexico and Europe. After they finished *Salt of the Earth,* both Paul Jarrico and his brother-in-law Michael Wilson moved to France. But political dissenters could not always get passports; and it was not easy to uproot entire families and settle in a new country. With only a few exceptions, these political exiles eventually came home.[16]

In most fields, the blacklisting ended sometime in the mid-sixties. Hollywood's began to ease up in 1959 when Dalton Trumbo, the most marketable of the Ten, revealed that he had won the 1956 Oscar for writing *The Brave One* as "Robert Rich." By 1960 he was working under his own name. Rehabilitation for other blacklisted entertainers usually took longer and, all too often, never occurred at all. In their definitive study of the inquisition in Hollywood, Larry Ceplair and Steven Englund estimate that only 10 percent of the people forced out of the film industry ever returned to work. The ones who did found their careers seriously damaged.[17]

Though most of the fired college professors eventually returned to the classroom, the public school teachers did not. Nor did the victims of the government's loyalty-security program re-enter the civil service. John Stewart Service was an exception; he went back to the State Department after the Supreme Court reinstated him in 1957. But he was still a political liability and quit after a few years of being shunted from one dead-end assignment to another. Judicial reinstatement was even less helpful to workers in declining industries like shipping, where the jobs these people once filled had disappeared along with the ocean liners they used to sail.[18]

Even people who kept their jobs suffered. Owen Lattimore is perhaps the most well known of the McCarthy era victims to have his career destroyed without being fired. The men and women who survived the government's loyalty purges were particularly vulnerable. Though cleared, they remained under a cloud, never knowing when they might again be subject to investigation. Moreover, their political liabilities limited their effectiveness. The State Department's China hands, for example, were no longer allowed to deal with East Asia. As one of them later noted, "There was a good deal of trauma in not being made use of when so much of your life had been devoted to something." Ironically, officials who did want to leave the government were sometimes locked into their jobs; they could not resign without incurring the suspicion that they were security risks or worse.[19]

Much of the damage that McCarthyism imposed was psychological. For an entire generation of law-abiding men and women it was devastating to be suddenly transformed into social and political pariahs. The lawyers who worked with these people invariably talked about their clients' emotional problems. The federal employees whose cases Clifford Durr handled could not deal with "the trauma of having been accused by their own government of being disloyal to their country. They would just go to pieces." Whether or not they lost their jobs, the men and women involved in the witch-hunt had been singled out and censured for activities that they had not considered deviant at the time they engaged in them. The situation was most disorienting for people who had no connection with the left, but even political activists suffered.[20]

People tended to blame themselves for their troubles. Though the radio and TV personality John Henry Faulk certainly knew that his career had flagged for political reasons, he still felt that he might have been inadequate as a performer. Other people internalized the accusations against them. "Even though you know what takes place in that committee," a former witness told an interviewer for a Ford Foundation–funded study in the mid-1950s, "you can't control the fear. An insidious form of self-guilt sets in. You accept the views of the committee in spite of yourself." The China scholars fingered during the hearings on the Institute of Pacific Relations also "absorbed the values of their accusers," Harvard professor John King Fairbank explained. "People who were named began to feel that maybe there was something wrong with them for having made contacts with Communists or something like that."[21]

And then there was the fear, an undercurrent of anxiety that reached from the highest levels of the CP's leadership to the friends and colleagues of blacklisted workers. Obviously, not *everybody* lived in terror of the witch-hunt, but at least in certain sectors of American society — among people on the left and those in vulnerable occupations like teaching and civil service — there was considerable apprehension. In a 1955 survey of 2,451 college professors, nearly half the respondents admitted that they were scared, a figure that reached 75 percent for people who belonged to a controversial group or taught at a school that had experienced some trouble.[22]

Not surprisingly, the people with the most to fear feared the most. That they expected to be persecuted did not diminish the anxiety so many Communists experienced. It was unnerving to receive death threats or see strange cars parked in front of the house. The Rosenberg case intensified the fear. Ross Lomanitz, a former Manhattan Project physicist who had been involved with the FAECT local at the Berkeley Radiation Laboratory during World War II, had been under investigation for years. Called before HUAC in 1949, he was fired, blacklisted, and prosecuted for contempt. But what really frightened him, he later confessed, was the possibility of a "frame-up akin to what I believe was done to Julius and Ethel Rosenberg."[23]

The paranoia was pervasive, but not unrealistic. People who worried about losing their jobs took precautions that in retrospect seem silly. But with loyalty-security panels questioning federal workers about their reading habits, it made a certain kind of sense to purge one's library or buy the *Nation* at a newsstand instead of subscribing. One woman recalls that in her childhood "all the red Lenin books were kept hidden in the basement." Other people burned their copies of Marx or else gave them away. They took false names when they vacationed at left-wing resorts.[24]

Children could not escape the anxieties of their parents or the furtive atmosphere that the CP's clandestine practices imposed. After all, their unguarded chatter might disclose the family's political secrets as readily as a *Daily Worker* on the coffee table. "From the age of five," one red diaper baby recalled, "I was cautioned not to talk to strangers because of the FBI." For the children of underground party leaders like the fugitive *Dennis* defendant Gil Green, the tension was even worse. The FBI was a not so lamb-like presence that followed them to school each day — and to summer camp and everywhere else as well. The execution of the Rosenbergs brought the dangers home. The children of the left identified with the couple's orphaned sons. "If they could be framed," one woman explained, "the same thing could happen to our parents."[25]

These children were lonely as well as scared. After journalist Carl Bernstein's mother appeared before HUAC, his best friends were told not to play with him. His younger sister was expelled from nursery school. His experiences were common. Unless they grew up in one of the left's few small enclaves, "Commie kids" were taunted, beaten up, ostracized — just like their parents. The stigma was so pervasive that even someone as totally guiltless as the daughter of China hand John Carter Vincent found herself red-baited by fellow students at Goucher College. The taint of Communism was like a contagious disease. People shunned the carriers, dropping close friends and colleagues, even cutting family ties. Almost every survivor of the McCarthy years — Communist and political innocent alike — has a story of someone crossing the street to avoid eye contact.[26]

It was hard to have a normal family life when husbands, wives, and parents went to prison or into the underground or, like Clinton Jencks, spent almost every night at meetings or on the road. Intact households suffered from the tensions and uncertainties of litigation and unemployment. The blacklist was especially hard on men whose self-esteem was tied to their identity as breadwinners. After a former colleague of several of the people Elizabeth Bentley had named was forced to resign from the Treasury Department in 1953, he used to put on a suit and tie every morning, take his briefcase, and go to the Library of Congress so that it would look as though he were still at work. Understandably, many marriages did not survive the strain. Even when they did, "tempers were short," the child of a blacklisted screenwriter recalled. His parents "were less patient with me. There was just not a warm, happy feeling." Obviously, the political repression of the McCarthy era didn't create troubled families, but it certainly intensified the problems that the people who experienced it had to face.[27]

It also limited their political effectiveness. The men and women who were blacklisted and called before congressional committees were the most active members of the Popular Front generation. The repression unleashed against them essentially silenced their voices. They became preoccupied with their own defense. Grappling with a loyalty-security case, coping with unemployment, or fighting criminal charges or deportation left little time or energy for other political work. In addition, though these people certainly cared about peace, unionization, and racial equality, they feared that active involvement with such causes might only lead to more harassment.

They also feared that their participation might injure the causes they supported. They were political pariahs, if not openly rebuffed by the groups they wanted to work with, then consciously avoiding contact so as not to spread the infection. Both liberals and radicals pulled in their horns. "I have for years confined my political activities to conversations with individuals," Ross Lomanitz admitted, "and often not a great deal of that — mostly because I didn't want to have anyone or any group smeared with 'guilt by association.'" Other people would not even voice a political opinion. A University of Washington professor who survived a loyalty investigation "felt the need to be evasive with persons who asked his opinion about political or social issues." [28]

Those evasions were widespread. The self-censorship that McCarthyism imposed reached far beyond the actual victims of the witch-hunt. Contemporaries remarked on it at the time, insisting, as Justice Black's colleague William O. Douglas did in a celebrated article in 1951, that the nation had descended into a "Black Silence of Fear." Many people had stopped speaking out. Moreover, when they did take a political stand or gave money to someone's defense, they often sent cash or covered themselves in other ways. As late as 1959, when a group of physicists who were upset by the role of former Atomic Energy Commission chair Lewis Strauss in the Oppenheimer case circulated a petition against his nomination as secretary of commerce, they enclosed a card for their fellow scientists to mail back. "Your response may be either anonymous or signed, as you choose," they explained. "The serial number on the card is not associated with your name, but is a check on the total mailing." [29]

Surprisingly, despite the widespread recognition that the impact of McCarthyism extended far beyond the lives and careers of the men and women directly caught up in it, there has been no systematic attempt to catalogue those effects or assess their long-term influence. Some connections are obvious. Senator McCarran's IPR hearings and the purge of the State Department's China hands crippled America's East Asian policy. Other connections are harder to identify, often because other factors were involved. Thus, for example, Hollywood's reluctance to make films about social problems during the 1950s, while certainly related to the anticommunist blacklist, also reflected the financially battered industry's fear of offending any segment of its dwindling audience. Similarly, the decline in the militancy of organized labor and its failure to expand beyond its traditional constituency certainly owed much to the purge of the CIO's left-led unions, but it was also a consequence of the postwar resurgence of the business community and the overall affluence of American society. Nonetheless, anticommunism was an important thread in these and other phenomena — and one that can be traced.[30]

If nothing else, McCarthyism destroyed the left.

It wiped out the communist movement — the heart of the vibrant left-labor Popular Front that had stimulated so much social and political change in the 1930s and 1940s. Though the party itself survived, all the political organizations, labor unions, and cultural groups that constituted the main institutional and ideological infrastructure of the American left simply disappeared. An entire generation of political activists had been jerked off the stage of history. Though most of the individual victims of the McCarthy era put their lives back together by the mid-1960s, the network of causes and organizations through which they had offered a meaningful alternative to the American mainstream was gone forever. Clinton Jencks became a college professor; the International Union of Mine, Mill and Smelter Workers disappeared.

As we assess the consequences of McCarthyism's assault on the left, we encounter a world of things that did not happen: reforms that were never implemented, unions that were never organized, movements that never started, books that were never published, films that were never produced. And questions that were never asked. We are, in short, looking at "might have beens" and at a wide range of political and cultural possibilities that did not materialize.

We are also looking at a lost moment of opportunity, when in the immediate aftermath of World War II the left-labor coalition that McCarthyism destroyed might have offered an alternative to the rigid pursuit of the Cold War and provided the basis for an expanded welfare state. But such a development never occurred. McCarthyism was only one of many factors that made a new wave of reform unlikely. Still, for a few short years in the late

1940s, the American people had more political options than they would ever have again. McCarthyism destroyed those options, narrowing the range of acceptable activity and debate. From race relations to the mass media, almost every area of American life felt the chill. Understandably, the repercussions were greatest where the Communists had been most active: labor, civil rights, international affairs, and culture.[31]

The federal government, as the chief target of such high-profile red-baiters as HUAC and Joe McCarthy, got hit hard. Because much of that damage was structural, the anticommunist crusade's impact on public policy was not always apparent but, as the early development of the nation's intelligence operations reveals, it could often be profound. When the OSS folded right after World War II, many of its employees, Carl Marzani among them, transferred into the State Department. In 1946, a congressional attack on these former OSS officials and their "strong Soviet leanings" forced the department to disband the intelligence-gathering unit these people staffed. The disappearance of that unit changed the nature of the federal government's intelligence setup, reorienting it from the relatively unbiased collection and assessment of information to a more cloak-and-dagger approach. When the Central Intelligence Agency was established in 1947, it favored covert operations over research — an emphasis that in the long run not only deprived the nation's leaders of accurate information about the world, but also encouraged the CIA's dirty deeds and undemocratic activities.[32]

In the short term, the anticommunist crusade interfered with the ongoing work of the federal agencies that came under attack. Understandably, those divisions that attracted the most attention suffered the most noticeable damage. Thus, for example, by the time Senator McCarthy had finished interrogating the electrical engineers at the Army's Signal Corps Engineering Laboratories at Fort Monmouth, thirty-eight people had been suspended. Not only did their ouster disrupt the facility's ongoing research, but it also undermined the morale of the remaining engineers. Within a year many of Fort Monmouth's top professionals had quit. Replacements were hard to find and a panel of outside scientists investigating the situation in 1955 warned that unless the installation's personnel problems were corrected, its laboratories might actually be "incapable of carrying out their assigned missions." Similar staffing problems surfaced in the government's other laboratories, especially after the Oppenheimer case further alienated the scientific community. By 1957, as a survey of job applicants showed, physicists did not want to work for the government.[33]

The tensions of the McCarthy era undermined morale and affected recruiting in every branch of the civil service, not just in science. Few independent souls wanted to set themselves up for a run-in with the loyalty-security program. There was a real decline in both the quality and the quantity of applicants for government jobs, especially within the more sensitive agencies. In 1950, 14,200 college graduates took the civil service exam for entry-level management positions; in 1954, 4,200 did. Other factors were at work, of course, including the Eisenhower administration's downsizing and the relative attractiveness of the private sector. Still, it was clear that by the mid-fifties the security program had deterred many people from seeking federal jobs.[34]

The State Department's troubles were notorious. Its morale, already weakened by the attacks of McCarthy and his allies, plummeted farther after the Republicans took over and the department's new security chief, former FBI agent Scott McLeod, began a partisan campaign to root out the so-called "Acheson clique." Career diplomats who had already been investigated and cleared several times were interrogated yet again, often in what they considered an extremely insulting manner. Rumors flowered; people worried that their mail was being opened, their telephones tapped. Understandably, recruitment suffered. "I find it almost impossible to interest able seniors in a Foreign Service career," a college professor explained. "They prefer to go to the Central Intelligence Agency . . . because it stood up for its own people." To make matters worse, security procedures had become so lengthy and onerous that it sometimes took years for job candidates to be cleared. Few qualified individuals had the time to wait that long. Between 1952 and 1954 no new foreign service officers were appointed at all.[35]

The politically motivated ouster of the State Department's China hands was particularly demoralizing. The firing of John Paton Davies in November 1953 was the final blow. In January 1954, five impeccably credentialed former ambassadors wrote an open letter to the *New York Times* expressing the fear that the "exaggerated emphasis on security" might "cripple the Foreign Service." Clearly, something had to be done; and it was. The undersecretary of state appointed a high-level study committee, McLeod was shipped off as ambassador to Ireland, and the most egregious abuses came to an end.[36]

By then, however, the lessons of McCarthyism had taken hold. Career officials scrambled to ensure that they would not suffer the fate of the unfortunate East Asia experts and lose their jobs for reporting honestly about unpleasant events. Accordingly, they ducked assignments to parts of the world that might go communist and, of course, stayed away from anything to do with China. The desire to avoid controversy permeated every level of the State Department. It had been eight years, a senior official told a Rutgers social scientist in 1960, since he had seen a chief of mission forward a report from a subordinate with which he disagreed but which he thought the department should get anyhow. Other officials even distorted their dispatches, as one of them explained, "so as *not* to give an accurate picture of conditions, but rather to keep the man writing the report in the clear." No wonder, then, that a foreign service officer could describe his work in 1954 as "an intense effort to fade into the wallpaper."[37]

Such timidity had obvious consequences for the nation's foreign policy. The purges had so thoroughly weeded out the government's China hands that by the mid-fifties no one who knew anything about that part of the world remained in the State Department's Far Eastern division. As a result, a combination of ignorance, fear, and their own conservatism led American policymakers to embrace a hard-line, Manichaean view of East Asia that bore little relation to what was happening there. Federal officials were afraid to take any initiative that might let congressional right-wingers accuse them of condoning the communist regime. China was thoroughly demonized, becoming a noncountry that was, especially after the Korean War, seen as America's bitterest enemy. There was no trade, no diplomatic contact, and so much willful blindness about the regime that for years the CIA hesitated to report on the existence of the Sino-Soviet dispute.[38]

Within a decade, the legacy of denial that McCarthyism bequeathed to the State Department would lead to disaster. As even Robert McNamara, one of the main architects of the Vietnam War, admits, had experienced and knowledgeable China hands like John Stewart Service and John Paton Davies remained in the government, it is possible that the United States might have avoided the conflict. Presumably these officials would have risen far enough within the State Department to have had a voice in making American policy and would have known enough about the area to have advised against intervention. These men were not indispensable; there were plenty of foreign service officers who could also have offered a realistic assessment of what was happening in Southeast Asia. But the residual fears of a repeat of the McCarthy era militated against their being heard. In the late 1950s and early 1960s, for example, when the conflict in Vietnam was just heating up, a few of the younger China specialists who had not been touched by McCarthyism were sent to Saigon. When they began to point out the similarities between the South Vietnamese regime of Ngo Dinh Diem and that of Chiang Kai-shek, their superiors refused to send their reports to Washington.[39]

More than ignorance was at issue here. At the very highest levels of the Eisenhower, Kennedy, and Johnson administrations, the memories of the damage inflicted by McCarthy and his colleagues limited the options that policymakers felt able to exercise. Both Kennedy and Johnson believed that they could not risk a replay of the "loss" of China by abandoning yet another country to Communism. Johnson feared, so he told Doris Kearns in 1970, that a communist takeover in South Vietnam would lead to

> an endless national debate — a mean and destructive debate — that would shatter my Presidency, kill my administration, and damage our democracy. I knew that Harry Truman and Dean Acheson had lost their effectiveness from the day that the Communists took over in China. I believed that the loss of China had played a large role in the rise of Joe McCarthy.

In order to avoid a similar fate, Johnson escalated the war in Vietnam and so shattered *his* presidency. It would, of course, be a mistake to claim that the repercussions of McCarthyism were solely responsible for that debacle. Still, the dishonesty and unrealistic policies that the anticommunist crusade fostered, as well as the fear of a revival, certainly contributed to the tragedy. So, too, did the destruction of those elements within American society that suggested the possibility of a more progressive form of internationalism.[40]

By narrowing the debate on American foreign policy, McCarthyism intensified the Cold War. The anticommunist purges wiped out the means through which it was possible to offer an alternative vision of the world. Expressed in the left-wing organizations that were demolished, that vision was also expressed in a set of ideas, a Popular Front sensibility that created conceptual linkages between race, class, and international affairs. While other groups and individuals also wanted to ban the bomb or support liberation struggles in the Third World, few of these single-interest groups did so within the broader framework that the communist movement encouraged.

Because of the problematic nature of the CP's ties to the Soviet Union, there is a tendency to overlook the more positive elements of its international program. It is, after all, easy to caricature this aspect of American Communism's political culture, to lampoon the impulse that made a union local adopt a resolution about the Spanish Civil War or the Chinese revolution, and to portray those actions as meaningless gestures primarily indicative of Russian control.

But such an interpretation, though partly correct, misses the internationalist sensibility that characterized American Communism. At a time when most of their fellow citizens were ignorant and uninterested, Communists knew about the world and cared about it. They belonged to an international movement that alerted them to what was going on in places like South Africa and Vietnam and helped them do something about it. Though often originating in the Kremlin, many of the causes the CP supported — like the Spanish Republic or the independence of Israel — had value on their own. Its internationalism was, in fact, one of the reasons so many Americans joined the communist movement in the 1930s and 1940s. As the former editor of the CP's West Coast newspaper recalled, participating in that movement let him view such events as

> a mutiny aboard a Dutch cruiser in waters off the Dutch East Indies, a strike of diamond miners in South Africa, peasant uprisings in French Indochina . . . not as a distant observer, but as an allied combatant.[41]

Even after World War II, when the CP's internationalism manifested itself in an often mindless pro-Soviet stance, it also touched on issues that certainly warranted attention — like decolonization or nuclear disarmament. Though other organizations and individuals also addressed these matters, the communist movement was unique in emphasizing their interrelatedness and bringing it to the attention of more mainstream groups. When McCarthyism destroyed that movement, it severed the connections between domestic issues and international ones that Communists and their allies had created.

These connections had been commonplace before the Cold War. In the 1940s, for example, the civil rights movement had a global perspective. Articulated by the most influential black leaders within the party's orbit, this perspective enabled people like W. E. B. Du Bois and Paul Robeson to link their struggle for racial equality to that of the Africans and other colonized peoples for national liberation. American racism, they claimed, was rooted in the same kind of economic exploitation that led to imperialism elsewhere in the world. By the early forties, most African American intellectuals and civil rights leaders subscribed to this interpretation and to the progressive internationalism that undergirded it. World War II reinforced this view of the world. The African American press covered freedom struggles and strikes in Africa and even featured regular columns by Chinese and Indian journalists. Mainstream black leaders, like the NAACP's Walter White, denounced imperialism in the same quasi-Marxist language as Robeson and Du Bois. Even as late as June 1946, the party-linked Council on African Affairs could draw 19,000 people to a rally in New York City.[42]

Within a year, however, White had abandoned his opposition to imperialism and was no longer talking about Africa. The political repression that had narrowed debate in so many other areas of American life vitiated the black community's internationalism and muzzled its main advocates. Red-baiting and blacklisting destroyed Paul Robeson's career, reputation, and health, while the elderly W. E. B. Du Bois was first marginalized and then fired by the NAACP, the organization that he himself had founded. The Council on African Affairs, the main conduit for information on and solidarity with the struggles of Nelson Mandela and other African nationalists, was also silenced — a victim of internal schisms, the Attorney General's list, and a Justice Department attempt to make it register with the Subversive Activities Control Board. By the time the CAA folded in 1955, it had been so totally anathematized that some of its supporters could only give money in secret.[43]

The destruction of the anti-imperialist left changed the way Americans viewed the struggles for independence in Africa and elsewhere. By the late 1940s, the NAACP and the mainstream civil rights groups had made the same kind of implicit deal with the White House that the labor movement had: in return for the Truman administration's support for their domestic agenda, they would back its foreign policy. Because the United States was aligned with the main colonial nations of Western Europe, the NAACP thus had to mute its opposition to imperialism. On those few occasions when the association did refer to Africa, it did so in Cold War terms, calling for independence as "the best answer to Communist intrigue." But since the imperialists claimed that they, too, were fighting Communism, the civil rights movement's repudiation of its earlier policy deprived the African nationalists of their main American ally, thus indirectly strengthening that continent's colonial regimes.[44]

The rest of the black community simply let Africa drop off the map. The *Chicago Defender,* which had run editorials about Africa and colonialism in every single issue until 1946, published four in the first five months of 1950. Moreover, the quality of the little information that did reach African Americans declined precipitously. Gone were the informed analyses of Africa's social and economic conditions that had been common during the early forties. Instead black readers (like white ones) got a condescending portrayal of African society as underdeveloped, exotic, and primitive. By the mid-1950s, few American blacks either knew or cared about Africa; the groups that had once nurtured interest in that part of the world had either folded or become absorbed in the civil rights struggle at home. White ministers, not black intellectuals, dominated the liberal successor organization to the CAA, while the CIA covertly encouraged interest in Africa's culture instead of its politics. As a result, when American blacks finally did reconnect with Africa in the 1960s, they tended to do so in cultural or nationalist terms rather than political or economic ones. That legacy of ignorance persists; Americans, both black and white, know less about Africa today than they did in the 1940s.[45]

Similar disruptions occurred within the Chinese-American community. The devastating impact of McCarthyism on the nation's China experts is well known, but the drive to eliminate support for Mao Zedong and the Chinese Communists also reached those elements of the American population most directly affected by the 1949 revolution — the Chinese Americans. Though Chiang Kai-shek had lost control of China, his supporters in the United States still retained enough power to dominate the nation's Chinatowns and induce the federal government to crack down on anyone who backed the communist regime. As the troubles of the rocket scientist Tsien Hsue-shen revealed, deportations were part of the process. So, too, was the 1954 prosecution of the *China Daily News,* the leading independent Chinese-language newspaper in the United States.[46]

The case grew out of the Treasury Department's ban on all financial transactions with China after Beijing intervened in Korea late in 1950. This embargo meant that Chinese immigrants who sent money back to their relatives in the old country were breaking the law. Many Chinatown residents were unaware of these restrictions, however, and continued their traditional, though now illegal, practice. Obviously, prosecuting the thousands of ordinary Chinese Americans who were technically in violation of the Treasury Department's regulations was out of the question. Instead, the government took on the *China Daily News* and its directors.[47]

The paper's ostensible crime was that it ran ads for the banks that handled these remittances, these ads serving, so the prosecution claimed, as "the instrument used by these defendants . . . to aid and assist Communist China." The paper's real crime had occurred on its editorial pages, where it continued to support the mainland regime and offer Chinese Americans a more nuanced perspective on East Asia than that of Chiang Kai-shek. Prosecuting it for trading with the enemy long after it had halted the illicit advertisements was simply a useful way to silence what the government called "nothing more than a mouthpiece for Communist China in this country." Though an obvious stretch, the Justice Department's technical case was strong enough to support a conviction and muffle the main independent voice within the Chinese-American world.[48]

Ultimately, as the fate of the *China Daily News* reveals, any criticism of American foreign policy that paralleled a communist position could invite prosecution. The Cold War and the GOP's campaign against the Truman administration's alleged softness on Communism had transformed dissent into disloyalty. As a result, even peace became a dangerous issue.[49]

The Korean War intensified the danger, though by then there was little public opposition to Washington's increasingly militarized conduct of foreign affairs. The movement to limit nuclear arms, for example, was an early victim. In the immediate aftermath of Hiroshima and Nagasaki, there had been several sporadic attempts among scientists, churchmen, and advocates of world government to do something about the atomic bomb. The Cold War

377

soon brought those efforts to a halt. Few people were willing to face the federal government's hostility to anything that would interfere with its growing reliance on nuclear weapons. Supporting disarmament might, after all, lead to a subpoena from Congress or the loss of a job. Scientists were particularly vulnerable. Even before Klaus Fuchs was uncovered, HUAC's high-profile search for atomic spies within the Manhattan Project damaged the credibility of the scientific community by portraying it as potentially subversive. Loyalty-security programs sent similar signals. Both the Oppenheimer case and the denials of visas to foreign physicists who criticized the arms race further underlined the consequences of opposing the bomb.[50]

The prosecution of the leaders of the main CP-linked peace group reinforced that message. Communists were not pacifists. Nonetheless, in the beginning of 1950 the party and its allies began a campaign for nuclear disarmament by circulating the so-called Stockholm Peace Petition, which called for the "unconditional prohibition" of atomic weapons and their "strict international control." The petition, though the product of a Soviet-run peace initiative, was so moderately worded that it got two and a half million signatures — or so its sponsors claimed. But even they had few illusions about its effectiveness. Its main impact may well have been to get its signers into trouble later on.[51]

The group that organized the petition drive got into trouble much sooner. In August 1950, the Justice Department dusted off the 1939 Foreign Agents Registration Act and demanded that the Peace Information Center, the ad hoc front group that circulated the petition, register "as an agent of a foreign principal." Instead of complying, the Center went out of business. Even so, the Justice Department continued to pursue it; in February 1951, it indicted the head of the organization, W. E. B. Du Bois, and four of his associates for failing to register. The government's case was rather slight — and not only because it brought the indictment four months after the Peace Information Center folded. It had also never identified the organization's "foreign principal." When pressed for specifics, the head of the Justice Department's Foreign Agents Registration Section "seemed hesitant and unwilling to reveal this," the center's attorney reported. "He preferred the identifying formulation that I must surely be aware that a 'number' of foreign organizations were 'doing the same things.'"[52]

Recognizing the weakness of their position and perhaps embarrassed to be prosecuting the eighty-three-year-old Du Bois, the federal attorneys tried to cut a deal with him before the trial began. Du Bois refused and was vindicated when the judge threw the whole case out after six days. The lack of any concrete evidence for the center's foreign connection was fatal to the prosecution. The Justice Department did not even try to prove that the organization was under Kremlin control. Instead, it based its entire case on the assertion that the center's propaganda followed the Soviet line. The judge, who seemed puzzled by the prosecutors' failure to make a stronger argument, granted the defense's motion for acquittal.[53]

Nonetheless, though the government lost, it also won. Not only had the charges against him destroyed whatever credibility Du Bois had outside the far left, the case also discouraged opposition to the Korean War and forced the noncommunist peace movement to keep a low profile. Though much of that movement shared the agenda of Du Bois and his supporters, it did not want to share their fate.

The timidity of the Women's International League for Peace and Freedom was typical. Though WILPF was emphatically anticommunist, it did not impose a political test on its members. After some of those members and their spouses had run-ins with the anticommunist crusade, and others, including Clinton Jencks's wife, Virginia, were attacked as Communists, conservative factions demanded a purge. WILPF's leaders resisted for a while, but finally compromised and in 1954 issued a set of guidelines to help their chapters identify subversives and stave off "Infiltration and Attack." Other peace groups took similar actions. But they satisfied neither their members nor their enemies. In 1960, the most promising liberal peace initiative since Hiroshima was aborted when SISS red-baited the Committee for a Sane Nuclear Policy. SANE, as the organization was called, responded by purging a key staff member and excluding Communists from its ranks. The internal dissension that followed crippled SANE, diverting the organization from its primary mission and revealing how corrosive anticommunism could be to any movement that shared its goals with those of the American Communist party.[54]

Nowhere was that damage as extensive as in the labor movement, where the political repression of the 1940s and 1950s wiped out an entire generation of activists by driving the Communists and their allies from the mainstream unions and destroying the left-wing ones. Only Harry Bridges and his ILWU survived the onslaught. All the other left-led unions went under. A few disappeared entirely, like the Marine Cooks and Stewards; most of the others, like Clinton Jencks's Mine-Mill, merged with one or another of their noncommunist rivals. Though the once powerful UE remained independent, it retained only a remnant of its former membership and clout.[55]

Among the main victims were the workers the left-led unions had represented. These unions were on the whole well-run, honest, and effective organizations that won economic packages and working conditions that were as good as, and often better than, those of other unions. But the multipronged assault they faced made it hard for them to serve their members as well as they once had done. Weakened by schisms and raiding, they often accepted unfavorable contracts rather than mount strikes they knew would be lost. At the same time, their leaders had to contend with criminal charges and the threat of deportation. Though they often won their cases, the effort took years and seriously drained the already diminished resources of their unions. Ultimately, as one ILWU leader explained, the fight against McCarthyism became "too damn expensive," because it began "to preempt the economic struggle where the guy's bread and butter and paycheck are on the line."[56]

The rest of the labor movement suffered as well. Anticommunism proved to be a costly diversion from other union issues. Though its sponsors had used red-baiting to help get the 1947 Taft-Hartley Act through Congress, the measure attacked all of organized labor, not just its communist elements. Its well-known anticommunist provisions did, of course, facilitate the destruction of the left-wing unions. But its more obscure technical ones, like the exclusion of supervisors from collective bargaining and the prohibition of secondary boycotts, were just as damaging. They rolled back many of the gains that organized labor had made since the 1930s and made it harder for unions to recruit new members or take them out on strike. Nonetheless, instead of mobilizing a coalition to repeal Taft-Hartley, labor squabbled over the measure's noncommunist affidavit. Moreover, by the early 1950s, most of the nation's unions had adjusted to the law and abandoned their struggle against it.[57]

It was a serious mistake. Taft-Hartley created an unfavorable legal environment that forced the entire labor movement onto the defensive. Unable to employ the aggressive organizing tactics that had been successful in the 1930s, unions found it difficult to expand. As a result, by the 1970s, when the postwar boom began to falter and the well-paid blue-collar jobs of its members began to disappear, labor was unable to mobilize either the political or the economic clout to protect its earlier gains. Its numbers dropped and its percentage of the overall workforce declined even more drastically. In 1945, 35 percent of the nation's nonagricultural workers were unionized; by the early 1990s, that figure had fallen below 16 percent (10–11 percent if government workers are excluded).[58]

Debilitating as Taft-Hartley was, it was not solely responsible for labor's disastrous failure to replenish its ranks. Here, again, the anticommunist crusade bears much of the responsibility, for it diverted the mainstream unions from organizing the unorganized. Instead of reaching beyond its traditional white male constituency in the heavy industry and skilled trades of the Northeast, Midwest, and West, the labor movement turned inward and raided its own left wing. Not only did these raids distract the mainstream unions from recruiting new members, but they also disrupted the often left-led organizing drives within those areas of the economy, like the service sector, where the labor movement most needed to grow. The communist-influenced unions had, after all, been wooing white-collar workers and professionals for years. They also appealed to groups, like women and people of color, that the traditional unions largely ignored.[59]

The labor movement's failure to expand in the 1940s and 1950s had serious political consequences. In particular, the absence of strong unions in the South made it all but impossible to challenge the power of the conservative Southern Democrats in Congress. The CIO's one attempt to organize the region, its ill-fated "Operation Dixie" organizing drive in 1946–47, floundered in part because it refused to challenge the region's power structure or dominant values. It focused mainly on white workers and distanced itself from the communist-led unions that had successfully recruited Southern blacks. Whether "Operation Dixie" would have succeeded had it been more militant and less skittish about African Americans and the left is unclear. There was so much opposition to unionization in the South that, moderate as the CIO's venture was, it did not escape either red- or race-baiting and folded within six months. Without a strong labor movement to anchor it, Southern liberalism withered, diminishing the range of political options in that part of the country and strengthening the forces that were pushing the rest of the nation to the right.[60]

Except for supporting the Democratic party in elections, labor did little to combat those forces. Its rupture with the left hastened its transformation from a movement to a bureaucracy. The radical organizers who had built and sustained the CIO were ousted, replaced by less imaginative individuals with neither their predecessors' vision nor their drive. Labor also lost its political independence. It operated as a junior partner within the American system, seeking higher wages and benefits for its members and forgoing any attempt to push for major social and economic change. The domestication of the labor movement was not entirely the result of the anticommunist purges. Business was strong, well organized, and determined to reassert its dominant position within American society. The passage of the Taft-Hartley Act was only part of a larger corporate effort to destroy the legitimacy and power of American unions. Nonetheless, the ouster of its left-wingers weakened the labor movement by limiting its options and depriving it of just those elements that might have offered a stronger defense of collective action.[61]

The Communists and their allies were, after all, labor's most militant voices. Their ideology encouraged them to champion workers against bosses. They understood how capitalism operated and were often willing to challenge management at every level. They were, for example, among the first labor leaders to raise such crucial issues as deindustrialization and runaway plants. In addition, because they recognized the importance of retaining the loyalty of their rank-and-file members, they tried to create a broader community that would keep those members involved with the union. A typical left-wing local, like the one Harold Christoffel organized at Allis-Chalmers, ran dances, held classes, *and* aggressively pursued grievances. Moreover, as long as the CP retained a presence, its opponents also had to work the grass roots.[62]

Once the left-wingers were gone, organized labor lost its dynamism. It became more centralized, corrupt, and distant from its members. Not surprisingly, those members responded in kind. They lost interest in their unions, stopped going to meetings, and no longer viewed belonging to a union as central to their own identity. That apathy forced the labor movement to rely on federal intervention instead of the support of its own members. When the political climate became hostile to organized labor, as it did during the Reagan administration, the AFL-CIO was blindsided.[63]

The labor movement's failure to retain the loyalty of its own members and organize the unorganized may well turn out to be fatal. Whether the more militant and progressive tactics of the communist-led unions could have staved off labor's present decline is hard to say. At the very least, however, at a moment in the late 1940s when the mainstream labor movement might have set itself upon a different trajectory, its collaboration with McCarthyism diverted it from addressing the problems that it would soon need to solve.[64]

The disappearance of the labor left affected more than just the labor movement. Because Communists and their allies had a broader political agenda than most trade union leaders, they used their position within the labor movement to implement that agenda, providing institutional support for a wide range of social reforms from housing to health care. To be sure, other unions as well as other communist and noncommunist organizations pushed for the same measures. But when McCarthyism splintered the labor-left coalition, the drive to obtain the kind of social democratic welfare state that existed in Western Europe sputtered to a halt. Liberals were discouraged from working for measures that Communists supported and the party-linked groups that pressed for them were destroyed. Again, it would be an exaggeration to give the anticommunist crusade full credit for aborting the campaign to expand the welfare state. American politics had been moving to the right since the late 1930s, so it was unlikely that Congress would have implemented any major changes. Nonetheless, in this area as well, the debate was narrowed, the dissenting voices silenced.[65]

In the medical field, as in so many others, the late 1940s saw the prospects for reform expand and then quickly disappear. The Truman administration repeatedly proposed a national health insurance plan, only to see it founder in the face of a well-financed American Medical Association campaign against it. Federal provision of health care was, the AMA insisted, "socialized medicine" and, thus, clearly incompatible with the American system of free enterprise. At the same time, the labor movement, which had long been the main advocate of universal health insurance, abandoned the cause. In 1947, the CIO's largest unions turned inward and began to seek medical benefits for their members through collective bargaining rather than political action. Other groups that might have supported Truman's health plan held back, unwilling to press for a reform that had become increasingly identified with the left. By 1950, the president gave up as well.[66]

Ultimately, it was only the far left and a few special interest groups that continued to call for universal health care, but they had little impact. Projects like the International Workers Order's incipient network of clinics and prepaid health plans disappeared along with the organization that sponsored them. And the Physicians Forum, the main left-liberal group within the medical profession, found itself isolated and under attack. Though the forum continued to campaign for health reform, the presence of party members within its ranks exposed it and its leaders to red-baiting and gave some McCarthy-era plausibility to the AMA's claim that compulsory health insurance was "a foreign ideology." By the mid-1950s, the anticommunist investigations, loyalty programs, and dismissals had taken such a toll on the left wing of the medical community that, one physician activist explained, "One doesn't talk about politics or political trends and even national health insurance is taboo." As a result, health care reform disappeared from the nation's political agenda for a generation, thus ensuring that the United States would be the only major industrial nation that did not provide medical insurance to all its citizens.[67]

While the impact of McCarthyism within the health-care field was to prevent reform, in the area of social welfare it actually rolled it back. That regression occurred when the left-wing unions and their most radical members were ousted from the nation's public and private social service agencies. These unions were unique in that they not only sought higher wages and better working conditions for their members, but they also fought for the rights of their clients. During the 1930s and 1940s, the idealism that had traditionally attracted many social workers to the field, as well as those workers' own economic problems, encouraged them to identify with the people they served, to view them as fellow victims of social injustice instead of, as was later to become the case, individuals with psychological, cultural, and — though it was never explicitly noted — possibly even racial, flaws.[68]

By the late 1940s, however, social workers who sided with their clients became political liabilities. The general shift to the right put pressure on welfare agencies to limit the numbers of people they served. This was especially the case in New York, where conservative politicians, eager to save money, claimed to be ideologically opposed to welfare. Aid to families, Governor Thomas E. Dewey explained, relied on the "Communist concept" that children were "the property of the state." Such a position was, of course, anathema to the radical social workers, who were soon in conflict with their superiors' demands to stiffen eligibility requirements and kick people off the rolls. It is probable that even without the budgetary cutbacks, welfare agencies would still have purged their left-wingers. Both of the unions in the field, the United Public Workers and the United Professional and Office Workers of America, were under attack and would soon be expelled from the CIO. New York City's welfare commissioner Raymond M. Hilliard fought the UPW head on. "We Threw the Commies Out," he told the readers of the *Saturday Evening Post,* by "firing the most blatant ringleaders," shifting "the less important troublemakers to jobs where they could no longer sabotage our programs, and allowing the "[d]opes and dupes who had trustingly followed the party line . . . to pull out of the union and make a new start." Fifty people got the ax; the union disappeared.[69]

Similar purges took place in other cities and states, often as the result of anticommunist loyalty programs or tips from the FBI. In 1948, about fifteen caseworkers lost their jobs in Los Angeles when they refused to sign a noncommunist affidavit and affirm that they did not belong to the CP, the UPW, or 140 other suspect organizations. Private agencies handled the situation more quietly. They did not want to be identified with Communism in any form and their tainted employees did not want any publicity. That secrecy makes it hard to produce definitive figures. But, whether they were in the dozens or the hundreds, the chilling effect of the McCarthy era investigations and dismissals profoundly altered the nature of American social work.[70]

The elimination of the left-led unions and the class-conscious philosophy they espoused increased the gulf between caseworkers and clients. It also created a two-tier system within the world of social work that ranked practitioners according to the status of those clients. But even the welfare investigators at the bottom of the profession no longer thought of themselves as workers. They had become professionals, distancing themselves from the people they served, whose problems they increasingly came to believe stemmed from psychological or cultural handicaps rather than an unjust economic system. In the more prestigious private agencies, social workers adopted a psychiatric perspective; and they, too, stopped treating their clients' problems as social ones. Instead, they dealt with the increasingly middle-class people they saw as neurotics in need of psychotherapy. Social workers at every level had abandoned the reform impulse and active political engagement that had once been such an important component of their profession. As a result, when the issue of welfare returned to the nation's agenda, social workers did not enter the debate on behalf of their clients and counter the hostile stereotyping of welfare recipients. The McCarthy era purges had silenced those voices that might have raised the issues of poverty and unemployment without blaming the victim.[71]

Those voices might also have drawn attention to the special problems of women. Though it would be an exaggeration to credit the anticommunist purges with the decline of women's activism in the 1950s, there was a connection. In the field of social work, for example, where women predominated yet men led the profession, the left-wing unions, though hardly bastions of feminist consciousness, had encouraged some female leadership. When those unions disappeared, women social workers became less active and visible — as they became less active and visible throughout American society. To the extent that the left-wing unions and other organizations within the communist orbit made demands for women or encouraged female leaders, their destruction retarded progress toward the equality of women within the workplace and everywhere else. In another and less obvious way, the McCarthy era purges also changed the nature of American feminism by severing it from the left's peculiar sensibility that had fused a concern about women with opposition to racism and attention to economic issues.[72]

Attention to women's issues was not, it is true, central to the world of American Communism. Nonetheless, by the 1940s the party was relatively more attuned to what would now be considered feminism than any other political organization, even if, as was often the case, its egalitarianism was more rhetorical than real. Still, lip service was preferable to silence; and the discussions about "male chauvinism" in the CP's publications at least acquainted folks with the problem. Moreover, to the extent that the female activists and intellectuals within the communist orbit concerned themselves with what was then called the "woman question," they actually constituted a kind of missing generation within American feminism. They criticized the cultural, as well as economic and political, subjugation of women, exposing sexism within their own movement as well as in the outside world. And they had an impact. Party publications stopped running pictures of bathing beauties; party schools taught women's history; and some party couples even shared the housework. In the 1950s, this was radical indeed. It was, therefore, no coincidence that a number of the New Leftists who shaped the women's liberation movement in the late sixties were red diaper babies from communist homes.[73]

American Communism also empowered women by encouraging them to become politically active. Though the CP's top leadership remained overwhelmingly male, women often had considerable influence at the neighborhood level. Throughout the 1930s and 1940s, for example, they organized consumer boycotts and set up day care centers; in the fifties, they circulated peace petitions and worked for racial integration. There was also a kind of "Popular Front feminism" that expressed itself in support for economic self-reliance as well as in the activities of a strong cohort of talented women in fields like law and labor who, if they were not self-consciously feminist, nonetheless exercised considerable autonomy and provided important role models for younger activists. When the women's movement revived in the 1960s, some of these Popular Front feminists like Betty Friedan, Bella Abzug, and the pioneering women's historian Gerda Lerner were among its first leaders.[74]

Much of the CP's feminism surfaced within the labor movement. To begin with, Communists and their allies organized women. From the tobacco factories of North Carolina to the welfare agencies of New York City, unions within the party's orbit sought out the subjugated, poorly paid, and often nonwhite female workers that the rest of the labor movement had largely overlooked. In addition, the communist-led unions addressed women's issues and allowed strong female leaders to emerge. During and immediately after World War II, the UE, which had more female members than any other major industrial union, was particularly aggressive in fighting for women's rights. Not only did it call for equal pay for equal work, but it also opposed the inequities involved in shunting women off into poorly paid "women's jobs." The anticommunist crusade brought most of these efforts to a halt, not only in the deeply crippled UE, but throughout the labor movement, where the chilling effect of McCarthyism silenced the main advocates for women and shoved gender issues under the rug.[75]

Until it was squelched, Popular Front feminism extended far beyond the workplace. Like the other social movements associated with the communist world, it sought to establish connections between the movement for women's rights and the other struggles of the left — for peace, racial equality, and economic justice. The Congress of American Women, a short-lived women's group of the late 1940s, exemplifies those linkages. Established in 1946 as the American branch of a largely communist-led international women's organization, the CAW initially appealed to a wide spectrum of left and liberal women. Its national program embraced the full range of feminist issues from equal pay and the provision of child care to the elimination of negative images of women in the mainstream media. Its local affiliates offered seminars in women's history, supported striking workers, and campaigned against high prices for meat. It also struggled against racism at every level. Not only did the organization support efforts to eliminate segregation in the larger society, but it also tried to integrate its own membership and worked hard to bring African American women into leadership positions.[76]

McCarthyism destroyed the group. By the time the CAW folded in 1950, it was already on the Attorney General's list and had been the subject of a special HUAC report. Its liberal members had fled; and the organization, now under increasingly obvious party control, concentrated on opposing the Cold War. Since the CP had little interest in keeping alive what was essentially a small, middle-class women's peace group, when the Department of Justice ordered the CAW to register as the agent of a foreign power, the organization disbanded. Though a few pockets of left feminism survived the purges, the nexus between race, class, and gender that a group like the CAW had forged had largely disappeared.[77]

The work of Betty Friedan reveals the consequences of that disappearance. She had been in the Popular Front since the early 1940s, first at Smith College and then at Berkeley, where she dated David Bohm, one of the young Manhattan Project scientists whose involvement with the left brought him a contempt citation from HUAC, blacklisting, and permanent exile after he lost his job at Princeton. From 1946 to 1953, Friedan worked as a reporter for the UE's newspaper. Her 1952 pamphlet "UE Fights for Women Workers" was a classic statement of left-labor feminism, offering a strong argument for equal pay as well as recognizing the "double bars" that African American women faced.[78]

It was also one of the last pieces of overtly class-conscious writing that Friedan ever published. Dismissed from the *UE News* when McCarthyism forced the union to downsize, she spent ten years as a freelance writer before publishing *The Feminine Mystique*. In a recent work on Friedan, cultural historian Daniel Horowitz suggests that her book's main weakness, its single-minded focus on the problems of relatively privileged, middle-class white suburban housewives, is a legacy of the McCarthy era and of her fear that red-baiting might undermine her book's influence. She was not paranoid. Had Friedan been as prominent in the mid-fifties as she was later to become, it is clear that her compromising connections — to Bohm, to the UE, and to the left-wing world she once inhabited — would have exposed her to serious manhandling by the professional anti-Communists, who were no friendlier to feminism than they were to any other progressive cause. Thus, it would not be surprising if she decided that in order to get her message across she had to domesticate it. She had to eliminate all such telltale indications of left-wing influence as references to race or class. Though such a decision might have been an overreaction, still the narrow and essentially psychological focus of what was to become the single most important statement of the revitalized women's movement diverted many members of that movement from recognizing how their own personal problems related to the broader issues of class and race that Betty Friedan and the other labor feminists of the 1930s and 1940s had once explored.[79]

A similar rollback occurred within the civil rights movement, though it is important not to overestimate its impact. Racism was formidable enough in itself. And all of the initiatives that McCarthyism aborted might well have foundered anyhow when confronted by the strong currents of racism in American society. Nonetheless, a case can be made that the anticommunist crusade, besides isolating an important group of activists, deflected the civil rights movement from pressing for economic, as well as legal and political, change. Communists were, of course, deeply involved in the struggle for black equality. The CP, one of its main Southern leaders noted, "really meant business on racism." From Mine-Mill's registration of black voters in Birmingham, Alabama, to the picket lines that local chapters of the Congress of American Women threw up outside segregated swimming pools in the North, the communist movement battled segregation as indefatigably as any civil rights group. For many black Communists, in fact, the party *was* a civil rights group. Marginalizing it and its white and black adherents, thus, changed the struggle against racial discrimination.[80]

Within the South, McCarthyism eliminated options and narrowed the struggle for black equality. Again, it is a question of lost opportunities. For a brief moment in the late forties, there was the possibility that the region's organized black workers and its more liberal whites might have been able to build an interracial civil rights movement with a strong grassroots base in the African American community. Had such a movement existed in the mid-1950s, it might have provided a counterweight to the hardcore segregationists who mobilized against the *Brown* decision. It might, in other words, have influenced the Southern moderates to implement integration rather than resist it. But the anticommunist crusade anathematized the individuals and destroyed the institutions that would have provided both the leadership and the community support for mobilizing a vigorous mass movement. Without that movement, most civil rights groups in the 1950s were conservative, respectable, and small — and posed little challenge to the entrenched Southern way of life.[81]

The left-wing unions were at the heart of the stillborn movement. Many of them had been functioning as quasi–civil rights groups for years. The communist-led Food, Tobacco, and Agricultural Workers Union (FTA) Local 22 in Winston-Salem, North Carolina, exemplifed this type of rights-based unionism. The local represented the thousands of primarily black and female workers who held menial jobs in the R. J. Reynolds Company's huge tobacco plant. Like other left-led unions, Local 22 not only gave its members the usual economic benefits of unionization, but also offered them a vibrant social life with a wide array of classes, clubs, and cultural events. In addition, it gave them a new sense of self-worth, enabling them to challenge the demeaning way in which the company had traditionally treated its powerless black women workers. Because the union recognized the interconnection between its own struggles and those of the larger community, it encouraged its members to vote and join the NAACP — efforts that helped elect an African American to Winston-Salem's board of aldermen and obtain better services for the city's black residents.[82]

But Local 22 could not withstand the anticommunist crusade. R. J. Reynolds had never wanted the union. In 1947, the company's refusal to accede to the demand for a wage hike provoked a bitter strike that attracted HUAC's attention. The hearings highlighted the communist connections of Local 22's leaders and weakened its support within the broader community. Encouraged by the CIO, rival unions took advantage of the FTA's failure to sign the Taft-Hartley affidavits and raided the local. The company damaged the union further by redesigning its manufacturing process to eliminate the jobs of the local's most loyal black members. By the time the CIO expelled the FTA in 1950, Local 22 was no longer functioning. Winston-Salem's civil rights movement foundered as well. The NAACP chapter that had swelled from 11 to 1,991 members between 1942 and 1946 fell below 500 during the 1950s and lost its working-class orientation. Middle-class blacks regained their leadership of the civil rights movement and tried to accommodate themselves to the white power structure.[83]

Similar struggles, with similar outcomes, occurred in Birmingham, Memphis, New Orleans, and elsewhere. The destruction of the progressive unions in the South stilled the voices that sought economic change along with racial equality. The civil rights groups that operated during the 1950s concentrated only on legal and political issues; the South's increasingly beleaguered unions did not challenge Jim Crow.[84]

Middle-class whites who might have worked for integration in the South were also silenced during the McCarthy years. Though some of these people were in or near the party and others were in the left-wing unions, many were New Deal liberals like Clifford and Virginia Durr, who just wanted to democratize their native region. They and the organizations they worked with, like the Southern Conference for Human Welfare or the Highlander Folk School, encountered serious red-baiting. Highlander, which trained union activists and civil rights workers, managed to survive the onslaught. The SCHW, an interracial body that tried to stimulate support for liberal reforms, did not. Internal conflicts and a 1947 HUAC report listing the subversive connections of its leaders did the group in. By the end of the 1940s, only a tiny band of white Southerners, most of them in the SCHW's beleaguered successor, the Southern Conference Educational Fund, would dare to call for integration.[85]

Anticommunism proved invaluable to white supremacists during the 1940s and 1950s. It provided them with a more up-to-date and respectable cover than mere racism and hooked them into a national network of right-wing activists. At the same time it reinforced their traditional contention that outside agitators were behind the move for civil rights. "The attempt to abolish segregation in the South," the Alabama Citizens Councils explained, "is fostered and directed by the Communist party." That allegation increased the South's traditional penalties for whites who opposed Jim

Crow. Not only would these people face the social isolation and economic sanctions that racial dissidents ordinarily incurred, they would also have to contend with McCarthyism.[86]

The experiences of Carl and Anne Braden illustrate how conveniently anticommunism bolstered segregation. The couple had the kinds of connections to the left that would have created problems even in the North. Their active espousal of racial equality in Louisville, Kentucky, simply made the situation worse. Their troubles began in 1954 when they agreed to help Andrew Wade, a black electrical contractor, purchase a home in a white area of town. Local vigilantes harassed the Wades from the start. They burned a cross on the family's front lawn, shot out their windows, and finally blew up the house. Invoking an old statute left over from the post–World War I red scare, the local grand jury that investigated the explosion indicted Carl Braden and six of the Wades' other white supporters for sedition. Braden's was the main case. The prosecutor deployed the standard paraphernalia of anticommunism, importing such big-time professional witnesses as Manning Johnson, Benjamin Gitlow, and Matt Cvetic to identify the subversive literature found in Braden's home and explain how Communists were ordered to incite racial unrest.[87]

Though Braden eventually won on appeal, he spent eight months in jail before he could raise the $40,000 bail that the trial judge had imposed. He lost his job, of course. His employer, the ostensibly liberal publisher of the Louisville *Courier-Journal,* decided that his controversial copy editor did "not possess and cannot exercise the objectivity which must characterize the handling of news." Two years later, Braden, by then a field secretary for the Southern Conference Educational Fund, was again under indictment, this time for contempt of Congress. HUAC had been investigating the civil rights movement and subpoenaed him for its 1958 hearings in Atlanta. Braden took the First instead of the Fifth Amendment in a conscious attempt to test the Supreme Court's willingness to uphold free speech. He lost, primarily because his appeal did not reach the Court until 1961, by which time some of the justices had pulled back from their more liberal position of the late 1950s and so ruled 5–4 against him. "This is a decision," Hugo Black tellingly noted in his dissent, "which may well strip the Negro of the aid of many of the white people who have been willing to speak up in his behalf."[88]

392

Significantly, even before the Kentucky grand jury decided that integrating the Louisville housing market was a seditious activity, the local NAACP had begun to distance itself from Andrew Wade's problems. Its action — or rather its inaction — was in keeping with the cautious policy of its parent organization. In the late 1940s, the NAACP's leaders, anticommunist themselves and worried about the group's vulnerability to charges of communist infiltration, began to purge their ranks. They stopped collaborating with the Popular Front, cracked down on the independence of local branches, and fired the organization's elderly founder, W. E. B. Du Bois. By 1950, when the NAACP's annual convention officially sanctioned its political housecleaning, the group was so edgy about Communism that many local chapters would not accept white members. Such precautions were of little use; the NAACP's prominence as the nation's leading civil rights organization ensured that it would be red-baited anyhow, especially after its attorneys won the *Brown v. Board of Education* case in 1954. Moreover, the purges weakened the organization. It became more moderate, more middle class, and smaller. The Detroit branch, which had had 25,000 members during the war, had dwindled to 5,162 in 1952.[89]

The surge of racism in the South after *Brown* gave the professional anti-Communists a new venue for their activities just as they were losing respectability elsewhere in the nation. Segregationists enlisted their aid to prove that integration was a communist plot. An early target was the *Brown* decision itself and its reliance on the influential work of the Swedish economist Gunnar Myrdal. Within a year, James Eastland of Mississippi, the Senate's leading racist as well as its main anti-Communist, was calling for an investigation of Myrdal and the "alleged 'scholars and experts' assigned him by the Carnegie Corporation of Alger Hiss fame." J. B. Matthews was soon compiling lists of those scholars' incriminating affiliations, as well as those of the NAACP and its board. He became a fixture on the segregation circuit, testifying before investigating committees in Arkansas, Mississippi, and Florida about the CP's inroads into the civil rights movement.[90]

Those committees were the most visible product of the alliance between anti-Communists and white supremacists. As the civil rights movement began to revive in the mid-1950s, Southern politicians responded by adopting the machinery of anticommunism. Almost every state had its own little HUAC clone or registration statute modeled on the 1950 McCarran

Act. Several states even outlawed the NAACP. Long after they had lost their mainstream audiences in the North, professional witnesses like J. B. Matthews and Manning Johnson traveled around Dixie peddling their tales of communist infiltration and incitement. Instead of harassing Communists, however, Southern investigators usually took on civil rights activists. Florida's Legislative Investigating Committee, which also pursued gays and lesbians, launched contempt charges against the president of Miami's NAACP for refusing to turn over its membership lists; Louisiana's Un-American Activities Committee raided the headquarters of SCEF and indicted three of its officers for sedition. There were economic sanctions as well; membership in the NAACP or support for integration was as bad for the career of a state employee or college teacher in the South as taking the Fifth Amendment before HUAC was in the North.[91]

But none of the Florida or Louisiana defendants went to prison. The Supreme Court, though still upholding the convictions of alleged Communists like Carl Braden, did not countenance the political repression of civil rights workers. Its position reveals the ironic fact that anticommunism actually bolstered the struggle for racial equality. The Cold War encouraged the liberal establishment to embrace integration. When the Truman administration formally committed itself to civil rights, it was not only responding to the increased political clout of blacks in the North and the need to win liberals away from Henry Wallace in 1948, but also to the recognition that, as Secretary of State Dean Acheson noted, "The existence of discrimination against minority groups in this country has an adverse effect on our relations with other countries." The United States, in other words, might not be able to win the Cold War until it cleaned up its own act. As long as the civil rights movement was itself suitably anticommunist, the nation's political establishment gave it considerable support. An implicit deal had been made: liberals would sacrifice reds for blacks.[92]

The deal unraveled a bit in the early 1960s, when it became clear that the leaders of the new mass-based movements, like Martin Luther King and the young radicals in the Student Nonviolent Coordinating Committee, did not share the anticommunist instincts of the Cold War liberals. SNCC imposed no political tests and was willing to work with the likes of SCEF, the Bradens, and the National Lawyers Guild, much to the despair of the liberal establishment, which sought unsuccessfully to make the group sever its ties with the NLG attorneys who were helping it in Mississippi.[93]

King, however, capitulated. Two of his top aides had once been in the party; and Hoover, who believed that the civil rights movement was communist-inspired, passed that information to the president, who in turn forced the civil rights leader to break with the men. King's housecleaning did not end the pressure on him, though it shifted from standard red-baiting to a much nastier form of blackmail. The bugs and wiretaps that the FBI had planted to get evidence about the subversive activities of King's entourage discovered the sexual ones instead. Since Hoover was convinced that the SCLC leader was a communist pawn, he had no compunctions about using that information as the basis of a vicious COINTELPRO campaign against King.[94]

To the extent that the smear campaign cut into the SCLC leader's effectiveness — and it certainly did — it damaged the civil rights movement as well. By the mid-sixties, that movement had begun to unravel. Obviously, anticommunism was only one, and hardly the most important, element in that tragic disintegration. The Vietnam War, the movement's own internal conflicts, and the deep-seated racism within American society all played a larger role. Still, McCarthyism did have an impact. From the start, it had narrowed the movement's agenda, separated it from potential allies, and kept it from seriously challenging the poverty that blighted the lives of most African Americans. Even when someone like Martin Luther King, Jr., called for economic as well as racial equality, the McCarthy era had so thoroughly erased class issues from the political agenda that his words did not get heard.

Doors closed in the cultural arena as well. Again, it is a matter of imponderables and missed opportunities. Nonetheless, it is clear that the anticommunist crusade transformed the mental contours of American life, changing the way that millions of ordinary people thought about themselves and their society. Gone was the Popular Front mind-set with its glorification of the little man and its celebration of labor and cultural diversity. Gone, too, was the class consciousness and the emphasis on collective struggle that had pervaded so much of American culture during the 1930s and 1940s.[95]

Even the language through which that view of the world was articulated disappeared. Scholars were particularly sensitive to the transformation. "You'd talk about 'industrialization' instead of 'industrial capitalism,'" an MIT Americanist recalled. Class-laden terminology that was common in the mainstream media during the 1940s was gone by the 1950s. References to "working stiffs" disappeared and the word "boss" lost its pejorative connotations. By 1963, a leading Protestant bishop threatened to quit the March on Washington if the Student Nonviolent Coordinating Committee's chair, John Lewis, used the words "masses" and "revolution" in his speech. A recent study of the topics cited in the *Readers' Guide to Periodical Literature* notes a similar linguistic shift.[96]

At the same time, American culture mellowed, changing its tone as well as its tune. In thousands of subtle ways, the men and women who produced that culture — teachers, writers, artists, and movie directors among others — eliminated its sharp edges. When a group of sociologists interviewed nearly 2,500 academics in 1955, they found that hundreds of them had consciously modulated their voices. Not only had they suppressed their political opinions, but, like the professor who revised an article to read "TV is 97 per cent tinsel" instead of "97 per cent trash," they tried to seem less confrontational. From Harvard to Hollywood, moderation had become the passion of the day.[97]

McCarthyism bore much of the responsibility for that banality. Though self-censorship was common, it rested on a base of overt repression. Even in the publishing industry, where, if anywhere, free expression should have been protected, many were the authors who consigned controversial manuscripts to their desk drawers because they had been told their work could not be published. The evidence here is anecdotal but indicates a fairly widespread pattern of suppression. Communist writers, of course, were completely unacceptable. Marketability was not, as it presumably is today, at issue. In 1951, after serving a prison term for contempt, the bestselling novelist Howard Fast had to publish *Spartacus* on his own. Though it became a movie and sold hundreds of thousands of copies, the FBI had made sure that no major publisher would touch the book. Fast was not the only blacklisted novelist. A former editor at Harper's recalls seeing an enthusiastic reader's report from the mid-fifties that complained about being unable to publish Doris Lessing's second novel. It was wonderful, but the writer was a Communist.[98]

Sometimes the subject matter, not the author, got censored. After all, as writer Tillie Olsen noted, the fifties was a "time when you didn't have books about people who had to work for a living." Nor were there many mainstream trade books published about the witch-hunt. Clifford Durr was in the midst of negotiating the size of his advance for a book about the loyalty program when the Korean War broke out and the publisher backed down. The book, it seemed, was no longer "saleable." Similar market concerns kept other publishers from taking on the casebook about civil liberties that Yale Law School professor Thomas Emerson wrote in the early 1950s. A small house published the book — and did quite well by it. Other writers faced similar difficulties when they wrote about unpopular subjects or individuals. Harper's turned down Eleanor Flexner's classic history of the women's movement because it devoted too much attention to blacks. And before he could publish his *Famous Negro Music Makers,* Langston Hughes had to excise all mention of Paul Robeson; otherwise, he was told, the book would be barred from school libraries. Other writers got the message. They stopped writing about unacceptable topics, turned to genres like science fiction, or else stopped writing. And, significantly, they stopped founding small literary magazines.[99]

Nonetheless, politically incorrect literature didn't completely disappear during the McCarthy era; there were always marginal presses and even desk drawers. Writers could still write, even if they could not reach a large audience. People in other media faced more crippling barriers. Paul Robeson, for example, simply disappeared from public view. Probably no other individual was as heavily censored. By the time he became the first person barred from American television early in 1950, the most charismatic black actor and singer of his generation had already become a nonperson. In 1949, four years after the NAACP had awarded him its prestigious Spingarn medal, it left his name off its list of past winners. By the mid-fifties, hundreds of other men and women in the entertainment industry were experiencing the same treatment. They, too, had been forced out of show business and denied access to an audience. That exclusion profoundly affected the nation's mass media, though it is sometimes hard to separate out the specific effects of the blacklist from the overall conservative backlash of the early Cold War.[100]

Certainly, at the time, observers believed McCarthyism had influenced the content of motion pictures and TV. Such, after all, had been the goal of HUAC, the FBI, and the film industry's right-wingers. They were determined to stamp out the subversive messages that they believed were creeping onto the nation's movie screens; and to a large extent they succeeded. The anticommunist crusade and the blacklist that it imposed ended Hollywood's brief flirtation with the real world and ensured that the fledgling television industry would never even begin one.

In that aborted social democratic moment right after the end of World War II, when a revitalized labor-left liberal coalition might have emerged, the major studios were making films about social problems. Though it is hard today to realize that the 1948 movie *The Boy with Green Hair* was intended to counter racial prejudice, the film and the others of its genre did indicate a new sensibility and raise the possibility of a more engaged and socially conscious American cinema. Antisemitism, alcoholism, lynching, mental illness, even miscegenation, appeared on screen, though often in an oblique manner that perpetrated traditional racial and ethnic stereotypes. Still, real issues were raised. The Academy Award–winning *The Best Years of Our Lives,* for example, not only dealt with unemployment, insensitive bankers, and physical disabilities, but also showed a few black faces in crowd scenes. Communists and their allies were disproportionately involved in making these movies, but the impetus for them came, as it always did within the film industry, from the top. The 1947 HUAC hearings brought this experiment to a halt; "social problem" films decreased from 20.9 percent of the studios' output in 1947 to 9 percent in 1950 and 1951.[101]

Part of the retrenchment was economic. These serious films did not make money. And, during the early Cold War years, the anticommunist crusade was only one of Hollywood's many problems. Not only was it losing its audience to television and suburban life, but it also had to restructure its distribution system after losing a major lawsuit. The film world responded to the crisis by instituting the blacklist and dumbing down. It did not want to put anything on the screen that might offend any segment of its shrinking audience. Musicals, westerns, war films, and technologically innovative blockbusters filled the nation's movie theaters. There was, however, an exception; during the height of the blacklist, about fifty unprofitable but explicitly anticommunist films were made.[102]

McCarthyism did, thus, reach the screen, though the hardcore propaganda of *The Red Menace* or *I Was a Communist for the FBI* won no acclaim. The most effective cinematic artifact of the witch-hunt was *On the Water-*

front, Elia Kazan's 1954 depiction of a longshoreman who testifies against the gangsters in control of his union. Though the film's working-class milieu reflected a Popular Front grittiness, its message was profoundly conservative. Not only did it glorify the role of the informer and thus presumably justify Kazan and his colleagues' own recent collaboration with HUAC, but it also hurt the labor movement by portraying union leaders in a negative way.[103]

Equally conservative, though less obviously political, were the messages that the ordinary genre films of the period purveyed: the good guy/bad guy polarization of the Westerns, the unthinking patriotism of the war movies, the global triumphalism of the Bible epics, and the constricted sexuality of the romantic comedies. Hollywood was selling an escapist oeuvre that indirectly sanctioned the ostensibly homogenized society of Cold War America by keeping blacks, workers, and uppity women off the screen. Never brave to begin with, the film industry's panicky response to the anticommunist crusade had simply intensified its traditional reluctance to challenge conventional mores or question the status quo.[104]

Timid as Hollywood was, the infant television industry was even more so. It was, after all, just beginning to reach a mass audience when McCarthyism hit. As a result, both its structure and its content were profoundly shaped by the blacklist era. The pressures on the industry to behave itself and shed its politically tainted workers were enormous. J. Edgar Hoover forced the FCC to deny licenses to applicants who "have affiliated themselves sympathetically with the activities of the communist movement." The main pressure came from the private sector. The sponsors and their advertising agencies, who in the 1940s and 1950s actually exercised direct control over programs, were terrified of controversy. As producer Mark Goodson noted, the agencies above all wanted to keep out of trouble. "The favorite slogan along Madison Avenue is 'Why buy yourself a headache?'" They thus forced the networks to capitulate to the professional anti-Communists and drop hundreds, perhaps thousands, of actors, writers, and technicians from their payrolls.[105]

A lot of talent was lost. Between April 1955 and March 1956, producer David Susskind could not get clearance for a third of the five thousand names that he submitted for one of his programs. The men and women who did get through were hardly controversial. But, as one CBS executive complained, "The trouble with people who've never joined anything and therefore are 'safe' for us to use is that they usually aren't very good writers or actors or producers or, hell, human beings."[106]

The blacklist was not, of course, entirely responsible for what Susskind deplored as the "steady deterioration" of the industry's offerings. Sponsors censored content as well as personnel, eliminating anything that aroused controversy or detracted from the consumerist message they were trying to convey. Naturally, programs about racial issues or civil liberties were verboten, but so, too, were ones that showed businessmen as villains or featured ordinary people with real-life problems. By the early fifties, the television industry had become so timid that, as one critic noted at the time, "virtually everything from pregnancy to freedom of religion is considered a controversial subject, leaving almost nothing except homicide as a fit topic to enter our houses."[107]

Most of the entertainment that reached the nation's living rooms during the 1950s supported the status quo. Quiz shows celebrated capital accumulation. Westerns and crime stories offered simplistic morality tales that got resolved by violence. Sitcoms reinforced traditional gender roles. And what passed for documentaries were often recyled World War II propaganda films produced by the armed forces. The news was equally oversimplified and militaristic. Except when they handled special events like the Army-McCarthy hearings, networks rarely had the resources to cover stories live. They usually relied on government briefings and official footage, especially when dealing with warfare and foreign policy. Public affairs programming was predictably bland. The networks consciously decided not to run editorials in order to avoid controversy. Though television inherited talk-show panels from radio, it narrowed the range of opinions expressed on them. Moreover, the conviviality that suffused these programs trivialized the issues they dealt with and reinforced the notion that Americans had nothing to disagree about.[108]

Not much has changed. Though the mass media did open up slightly during the 1960s, the patterns of institutional restraint and self-censorship established during the McCarthy era are still around. So, too, are the limitations on the range of issues that receive exposure.

★

High culture as well as low absorbed the impact of the anticommunist crusade, but the response of the nation's artists and intellectuals was more complicated and ambiguous. This was not because McCarthyism exerted less pressure or encountered more resistance. The men and women who ran America's symphony orchestras and universities were just as ready to dismiss and blacklist political undesirables as any movie mogul or advertising executive. And most artists and intellectuals were equally ready to conform their work to the political climate of the era. In the fine arts, for example, serious painters abandoned realism, depoliticized their work, and adopted an "art for art's sake" ideology. The huge canvases of the abstract expressionists, with their obvious lack of content, seemed to reiterate the point: there was no politics in art.

But, of course, there was. The situation was complicated by the fact that the art world both fought against and embraced the anticommunist crusade. Such contradictions plagued Cold War liberals in every field. They were waging a two-front war, defending themselves against the McCarthyist right at their rear while at the same time taking the offensive against the supposedly greater threat from the left. They used the same approach on both fronts, for they believed that a strong attack on the communist menace was the most effective defense against the anticommunist one. Besides eliminating left-wing motifs (usually by avoiding all political content), the liberals who dominated the fine arts during the 1940s and 1950s also accommodated themselves to the political climate of the times by emphasizing themes, like individualism and opposition to regimentation, that could be utilized in the larger Cold War struggle.

Thus, for example, the controversies that swirled around the paintings of Jackson Pollock and his fellow abstract expressionists were the art world's equivalent of the partisan conflict over the "loss" of China. These artists, like the Truman administration, opposed Communism. Their conservative critics, however, subscribed to such a different view of the world that they could only come to terms with the drips and splotches of someone like Pollock by treating them as subversive and insisting that they receive no federal largesse. Thus, in the eyes of a right-wing congressman like Michigan's George Dondero, abstract art was part of a "sinister conspiracy conceived in the black heart of Russia." In the eyes of the more sophisticated Cold War liberals, however, that art was a weapon against Communism, essential, as one critic put it, to the "survival" of "the future course of Western civiliza-tion as a whole."[109]

Actually, it was neither. The relationship between art and politics was hardly so straightforward. Like other intellectuals, artists had been attracted to the communist movement during the 1930s. Most of them took part in a kind of visual Popular Front that sought to democratize American art and make it accessible to ordinary men and women. They created a public art whose quintessential products were the Works Progress Administration murals that adorned federal buildings, celebrating local scenery, brawny workers, and fresh-faced girls in braids. But even before the Cold War, this representational style had fallen out of political as well as aesthetic favor. It was, in the words of the influential New York critic Clement Greenberg, "kitsch," the American equivalent of the Soviet Union's "socialist realism" and, thus, identified with the worst excesses of Stalin's regime.[110]

Because they relied mainly on the patronage of wealthy individuals and elite institutions, visual artists were not as vulnerable to blacklisting as people in other fields. Though hard-core anti-Communists like Congress-man Dondero made some attempts to crack down on left-wing artists and keep their work from reaching the public, overt political repression was not a serious problem for the American art world during the McCarthy years.[111]

A more subtle form of censorship destroyed the artistic vision of the Popular Front, marginalizing entire schools of representation and severing the connection between art and social responsibility. As in the thirties, the fate of Western civilization was still at stake, only now it called for individ-ual creativity, not collective action. The abstract expressionism of Jackson Pollock and his colleagues, with its apparent lack of subject matter, became the main vehicle for this depoliticization. Instead of toeing a party line and trying to reach the masses, these artists turned inward, using their painting in highly individualistic ways to explore the formalistic limits of their me-dium as well as to express their own personal needs and psychic anxieties. Or so the critics said. The abstract expressionists had abandoned politics and were now, it was claimed, producing art for art's sake. "The big moment came," critic Harold Rosenberg explained, "when it was decided to paint . . . just to PAINT. The gesture on the canvas was a gesture of liberation, from Value — political, aesthetic, moral." And, where else but in America could the creative genius of these avant-garde artists have found the freedom for such an intensely individual form of expression?[112]

Actually, the abstract expressionists were not as apolitical as they were being made out to be. Many of them had once been Trotskyists and their evolution away from the organized left resembled that of the New York intellectuals who championed their work. By the late 1940s, Pollock and his colleagues had long since abandoned what they viewed as the inauthenticity of the Popular Front brand of artistic realism, but they were still radical and they had not given up their desire to communicate. They just did not feel that the traditional forms of representation could convey their own deep pessimism about Cold War politics or their anxiety about the atomic bomb. The individualism that suffused their paintings was, therefore, not so much a disengagement from the world as a protest against it.[113]

Though Pollock and his fellow artists insisted that their work dealt with universal human concerns, its inaccessibility helped undermine the earlier populist cultural aspirations of the American left. By insisting that only an enlightened few could appreciate the greatest products of the human spirit, the promoters of this new school of painting sought to sever the ties between high culture and ordinary people that the Popular Front had tried to create. The reactionary assault on abstract art actually reinforced this elitism. Avant-garde artists and their intellectual allies conflated the right with the left and attacked the anti-intellectualism of McCarthyism as an example of the threat that mass politics posed to liberal values. Representational art, embraced by both the CP and the far right, thus got a bad reputation. "Looking around one," the Museum of Modern Art's Alfred Barr noted in 1956, "it is clear that abstract painting is the dominant, characteristic art of the midcentury. (That is, in the free world. Painters controlled by the Communists, however, are enjoined to use a realistic style.)"[114]

Realism was thus banished from the art galleries, as was the political engagement associated with that style of painting. A chill had descended over the American art world during the 1950s. Not only did the avant-garde lose its diversity, but it had become aesthetically incorrect for artists to involve themselves with social or political issues. Though representational art has reemerged, the ideological legacy of the McCarthy era still lingers in the frequent demand that artists should stay in their studios and keep controversy out of their canvases.

★

Political content could not be banished as easily from America's colleges and universities as it was from its art galleries. Nonetheless, a similar kind of transformation occurred; previously accepted modes of analysis were marginalized and whole lines of inquiry simply disappeared. Marxism, of course, was demonized; questions of class and power that previously concerned both Marxist and other scholars were no longer considered fit subjects for academics to explore. At the same time, a sense of elitism suffused many fields, along with a stress on individualism and a related reliance on psychological rather than historical explanation. And, of course, professors, like most other Americans, curtailed their off-campus political activities.[115]

More important, the academy lost its critical edge. College teachers embraced a cautious impartiality that in reality supported the status quo. Professors who took sides in their books or in the classroom, so the accepted wisdom went, were neglecting their scholarly obligation to be balanced, objective, mature. Some teachers finessed the issue by avoiding all controversy, others tried to tame it. In a 1955 survey of social scientists, 68 percent of the respondents were willing to deal with sensitive issues, but only 38 percent would give their own views; on the other hand, 44 percent said they would give all sides impartially. In their more introspective moments, many college professors admitted that their evenhandedness may well have been self-censorship. "When I lecture on Marxism," a young historian confessed at the time, "I probably am led to spend greater time giving my disagreements with it than previously. . . . I'm embarrassed to say so."[116]

In the face of the anticommunist crusade, such caution made considerable sense. Despite the supposed protection afforded by academic freedom, faculty members were almost as vulnerable to the operations of HUAC, McCarthy, and J. Edgar Hoover as any maritime worker or federal bureaucrat. During the late 1940s and 1950s, over a hundred college teachers lost their jobs and were barred from new ones. Most of these people were former party members who had refused to name names or cooperate with anticommunist investigators. The faculty committees and university administrators responsible for their ouster knew that these people were not sabotaging their laboratories or subverting their students. But they had been contaminated by Communism and so had to go. A lot of high-sounding rhetoric about intellectual integrity and the obligations of scholarship accompanied the dismissals, but it did not conceal the academy's collaboration with the witch-hunt.[117]

Besides limiting the political freedom that professors enjoyed, McCarthyism affected their intellectual work. That impact, however, was not always direct, nor did it fall uniformly on every discipline. Scholars in controversial areas like East Asian studies experienced the repercussions of the witch-hunt more heavily than those in technical fields like accounting. Liberals were also disproportionately affected by the chill, which, since at least one study indicates that they were more productive than their conservative colleagues, no doubt amplified the effect of McCarthyism within their disciplines. In assessing the specific ways in which the anticommunist crusade shaped the content of American scholarship during the early Cold War, it is important not to overexaggerate the impact of the actual repression that took place. Other factors, including the appeal of patriotism and the even greater attraction of federal money, were just as influential — as were, of course, internal developments within each field of study.[118]

Nonetheless, the McCarthy era's depoliticizing zeitgeist pervaded even those disciplines like English that attracted little systematic repression or outside funding. A handful of left-wing teachers got the ax; scholarship about the social context of literature receded from sight; and the nation's leading Marxist critic revised his earlier oeuvre by eliminating all its references to Communism. Under the influence of the "New Criticism" that dominated the field, America's English departments disengaged from history and looked only at texts. Literature was put on a pedestal, where it was either treated as a storehouse of abstract ideals or else subjected to psychoanalysis. By embracing "art for art's sake," literary critics, both in the academy and elsewhere, sent the same libertarian, subliminally anticommunist message that the promoters of abstract expressionism had peddled. They also embraced a similar elitism that isolated high culture from ordinary life so as to better defend it from the unwashed masses. The fact that the threat from below could come from either the left or the right simply encouraged the further retreat of literary scholarship from political reality.[119]

Since science was deeply enmeshed in the real world, the anticommunist crusade affected its practitioners on several levels. There was the direct damage caused by the dismissals of unfriendly witnesses, the deportations of foreign-born scientists, and the denials of visas to visitors from abroad. Researchers who were denied security clearances could not work on classified projects or in facilities sponsored by the Defense Department and the AEC. Politically tainted chemists and biologists had trouble attracting graduate students to their laboratories. To the extent that American science was deprived of these people's contributions, the purges exacted a toll.[120]

But the damage may not have been as serious nor as widespread as the highly publicized attacks on people like Oppenheimer and his students might seem to imply. Sometimes the blacklisting could be beneficial. As Nobel laureate Salvador Luria recalled, his exclusion from the federal government's peer review panels was "a delightful thing. . . . I didn't waste time going to Washington." Moreover, since the scientific community had expanded so rapidly during the early years of the Cold War, there were more than enough apolitical younger scientists who had come to intellectual maturity during the McCarthy era to carry out whatever research needed to be done. In addition, it turned out that the defense establishment which funded most of that research was politically less vulnerable than other sectors of American society and, thus, did not feel outside pressures to concern itself about the political ideology of the people whose work it supported. As a result, many scientists whose radical affiliations might have embarrassed them in other venues got admitted to federal installations or received grants from the Office of Naval Research and AEC.[121]

The real impact of McCarthyism on the scientific community occurred at a deeper level. To the extent that it stifled criticism of America's increasingly militarized foreign policy and thus contributed to the growth of the big-spending defense establishment, the anticommunist crusade reoriented priorities within the nation's research laboratories and academic institutions. Scientists went where the money was; and by the time of the Korean War it was clear that fields with military applications were by far the most lucrative. Prestige was also involved; defense-related work conferred status. By the late 1940s, as one engineer recalled, "if the memos and reports you wrote weren't stamped 'secret,' they just weren't important; they didn't involve 'real' science or engineering." Academic administrators pushed departments to specialize in areas that the military would fund. As a result, fields like electronic engineering prospered, while other areas of equally valid work like whole animal biology stagnated.[122]

The social sciences faced similar pressures. Though fewer social scientists than scholars in other disciplines experienced McCarthyism directly, the field itself was subject to more suspicion. Such had always been the case. In the late nineteenth and early twentieth centuries as the first generation of American economists, political scientists, and sociologists sought to define their disciplines, they adopted a posture of scientific objectivity to defend themselves against charges of advocating social reform or, worse yet, Socialism. The Cold War reinforced that tendency. By the 1950s, social science had become even more methodologically rigorous and ostensibly neutral. It embraced survey research and quantitative analysis. Controversial questions about class structure or the allocation of economic resources simply disappeared from the academic mainstream.[123]

As in the hard sciences, it was not so much the stick of overt repression that impelled social scientists to distance themselves from controversial projects as it was the carrot of financial support. The federal government funded some important research in economics and psychology, but most of the patronage came from private foundations like Carnegie, Rockefeller, and Ford. All these funders, public and private, created an intellectual climate that promoted elitism and avoided embarrassing questions. During the height of the McCarthy era, for example, the National Science Foundation not only restricted its grants to research that converged with hard science, but explicitly warned prospective applicants to steer clear of "social reform movements and welfare activities."[124]

Private foundations were no bolder. McCarthyism, it turned out, had influenced the agenda of the nation's main philanthropies. Not only had HUAC and the SISS raised questions about some of their grants, but two Southern congressmen, Eugene Cox and B. Carroll Reece, mounted separate investigations of the big foundations. Rockefeller's support for the Institute of Pacific Relations had triggered the initial inquiries. But other projects, like the Carnegie Corporation's underwriting of Gunnar Myrdal's study of American race relations and the survey of the entertainment industry blacklist that the Ford Foundation's Fund for the Republic sponsored, also came under attack. The foundations' response was predictable. Dependent as they were on the nation's corporate elite, they had never been in the business of funding social change. McCarthyism just made them more timid. Thus, for example, none of the big foundations made any major grants for study or action in the field of race relations between 1950 and 1960. "When I attempted to discuss the matter with friends who are officials of a large foundation," a Rutgers political scientist explained in the mid-sixties, "I was told that it could not be discussed by letter or on the telephone, and it was very plainly hinted that the Reece committee investigations in the early 1950s had put the foundations out of this sort of business." They were also, of course, not in the business of handing out fellowships to politically tainted individuals. As the head of the Guggenheim Foundation imperiously announced, scholars who belong to a "movement, organization, group which does their thinking for them" will "get no help from us." [125]

To the extent that the big foundations shaped the overall parameters of American knowledge by their strategic planning and institution building, they transformed the way social scientists looked at the world. In the 1950s, Ford consciously stimulated the "behavioral sciences" — empirical studies that looked at such things as voting and child-rearing practices in order to understand how individuals adjusted to society. It also encouraged the dissemination of modernization theory, the widely popular notion that all of what were then called underdeveloped nations would eventually follow the same course of economic and political maturation as the United States. Designed to support the status quo both at home and abroad, much of this work was based on ideological assumptions that bore little relation to the historic situation within each country or what was actually going on. It also, of course, limited the intellectually respectable options available for dealing with social change. [126]

Foreign area studies were another priority. Despite the controversial nature of anything that dealt with Communism, the demand for knowledge about the nation's main Cold War adversaries stimulated foundations and the federal government to pour millions of dollars into interdisciplinary studies of strategic regions like East Asia and the Soviet Union. It is unclear what the funders got for their money. The East Asian specialists produced good work, but the legacy of McCarthyism kept their scholarship from influencing American foreign policy. The Sovietologists had more of an impact, but they were so deeply drawn into the anticommunist consensus that their work tended to demonize rather than describe the country they were studying. As a result, because they emphasized the USSR's supposedly timeless and totalitarian nature and ignored what was actually going on, their scholarship gave little guidance when the Soviet Union no longer conformed to their model of Stalinist rigidity. [127]

Scholars who studied the United States saw an equally monolithic reality. Here, they noted, the serenity that pervaded American history came not from repression, but from the nation's genius for solving its problems and unifying its people. The McCarthy years were the highpoint of what has been called "consensus history," an interpretation of the American past that overlooked internal conflicts — as well as all those folks who were not white, elite, upper- and middle-class males of European descent. Though the consensus historians offered differing explanations for the nation's placid trajectory, they generally agreed that it had produced an essentially classless society that had solved what the New York intellectual Daniel Bell called "the great challenge to Western — and now world — society . . . : how, within the framework of freedom, to increase the living standards of the majority of people and at the same time maintain or raise cultural levels." The sweeping ideological formulations associated with Communism, the apostles of consensus explained, were not just wrong or evil; they were irrelevant. The United States had raised pragmatic muddling through to a political art form. Whatever few small problems remained could be fixed by jiggling a little with the controls.[128]

Because McCarthyism challenged their vision of a benign, conflict-free polity, Bell and the other public intellectuals of the 1950s had to make sense of America's present as well as its past. Some of them, it is true, had previous radical connections that invited the attentions of the anticommunist apparatus, but they were not seeking to insinuate themselves into the good graces of HUAC or J. Edgar Hoover. They were on a parallel mission. Their analysis of McCarthyism as a populist aberration was part of the broader exegesis of Communism, anticommunism, and Western society that they had been collectively working up since the late 1930s. The productivity and verbal facility of the New York intellectuals and their academic colleagues like Arthur M. Schlesinger, Jr., as well as their access to such outlets as *Life* magazine and the *New York Times,* gave their work enormous influence, especially since it both reflected and amplified ideas that the nation's political leaders had already embraced.[129]

Their discussion of Communism, though more elegant, was no less oversimplified than that of J. Edgar Hoover and the anticommunist right. They, too, believed that the Soviet Union and the American CP endangered the nation; and they, too, agreed that Communists deserved no civil liberties and could, therefore, be fired. Not only were party members totalitarians (the New York intellectuals had popularized the term), they were also

409

under orders to subvert the U.S. The "totalitarian liberals" were, in the eyes of *Partisan Review,* almost as dangerous, since their willingness to work alongside the CP might blind other Americans to its vicious nature. In short, the New York intellectuals' depiction of Communism differed little in its main outlines from that of Joe McCarthy. "The unpalatable truth we have been discovering," literary critic Leslie Fiedler confessed in 1954, "is that the buffoons and bullies, those who *knew* really nothing about the Soviet Union at all, were right — stupidly right, if you will, accidentally right, right for the wrong reasons, but damnably right."[130]

And yet, the New York intellectuals knew that "the buffoons and bullies" were also wrong about a lot of things. Somehow, these writers had to explain the rise of Joe McCarthy without acknowledging how much their own views about Communism jibed with his. Their solution, promulgated in a 1955 book of essays edited by Daniel Bell, was to ignore Communism altogether. There was, they implied, no political content to McCarthy's crusade. Instead, as Columbia historian Richard Hofstadter explained, it was "a pseudo-conservative revolt," an essentially irrational phenomenon motivated by the status anxieties of downwardly mobile middle-class WASPs and upwardly mobile ethnics. McCarthy himself got a similar depoliticization at the hands of his original biographer, Richard Rovere, who trivialized the Wisconsin senator by portraying him as such a thoroughly aberrant character that his career had no relation to ordinary political events. Psychology, not politics, was thus the key to understanding the anticommunist extremists.[131]

Hofstadter and his colleagues did, however, offer a historical explanation. They viewed McCarthy and his allies as populists, situating them within an anti-intellectual strand of American politics that had traditionally expressed the resentment of the unenlightened little people against the cultivated upper classes. Such an interpretation cloaked considerable hostility to and suspicion of mass political action. It also delegitimized American Communism by indirectly identifying its celebration of the common man with the excesses of the far right. And it strengthened the elitism that was such an important component of the cultural criticism of the 1950s. The New York intellectuals were vociferous in their denunciations of the conformity of American life. McCarthyism, suburbia, television, tailfins, "kitsch," Communism, and nazism — they were all, in one way or another, products of mass society. Far better to leave matters of culture and politics in the hands of the educated elites, who could be counted on to maintain standards and preserve Western civilization from its enemies on both the right and the left. That many of the same themes reverberate in the contemporary assault on multiculturalism and political correctness is no surprise. Some of the same people are involved.[132]

To a large extent, the New York intellectuals and their allies were the literary point men for Cold War liberalism. They defined its mission and established its ideological frontiers. Along with Democratic politicians like Hubert Humphrey, civil libertarians like Morris Ernst, and labor leaders like Walter Reuther, they also ran the main liberal organizations. Though these people had turned against the CP long before McCarthyism heated up, the necessity to defend themselves against the right may have induced the Cold War liberals to pull their political punches. "It is inevitable," the NAACP's Roy Wilkins noted in a 1949 report to the association's head, Walter White, "that the things against which Liberals fight are in many instances the things against which the Comrades fight." And, rather than run into right-wing flak by taking the same stand as the "Comrades," the leaders of the main liberal groups hung back.[133]

Thus it was that the NAACP, the ACLU, the Americans for Democratic Action, the American Association of University Professors, and the American Committee for Cultural Freedom put up little opposition to the Hollywood blacklist, the firing of communist teachers, the Smith Act's incursions against the First Amendment, or any of the other big and little violations of civil liberties and political freedom during the early Cold War. Often, it is true, the inaction of these groups was the product of serious internal splits. Liberals who tried to stand up against McCarthyism were stymied by their more timid colleagues. When the attorney Joseph Rauh wanted the ADA to issue a public statement denouncing the *Dennis* decision, Schlesinger and a majority of the organization's board of directors "strongly" opposed its release. It would do "infinite harm," the group's chair, former Attorney General Francis Biddle, explained, "and would cause a great many resignations to no purpose." Within the ACLU, to take another example, the turmoil caused by the board's refusal to abide by its own bylaws and accept the membership's rejection of an anticommunist resolution so drained the organization's energy that it was unable to protect civil liberties during the height of McCarthyism in 1953 and 1954.[134]

The overall legacy of the liberals' failure to stand up against the anticommunist crusade was to let the nation's political culture veer to the right. Movements and ideas that had once been acceptable were now beyond the pale. Though Communists and their allies were the direct victims, the mainstream liberals and former New Dealers within the Democratic party were the indirect ones. Condoning the campaign against Communism did not protect them from being denounced for "losing" China or, like Supreme Court Justice Black, for supporting desegregation in the South. Moreover, because the left had been destroyed, when liberals came under attack they had to defend themselves from a more politically exposed position than they would otherwise have occupied. This may seem obvious, but it is a point that needs to be stressed. The disappearance of the communist movement weakened American liberalism. Because its adherents were now on the left of the political spectrum, instead of at its center, they had less room within which to maneuver.[135]

It would, of course, be incorrect to give the anticommunist repression of the McCarthy period too much credit for the attenuation of American political culture. Radicalism had never really taken hold in the United States. Communism, which dominated the American left in the 1930s and 1940s, had its own internal problems and, in any event, never had as much influence as either its enemies feared or its supporters believed. Even without McCarthyism, it might well have disintegrated, but it might also have left a more lasting legacy. The repression that it faced destroyed the possibility that it might have evolved into a more authentic American radicalism.

The rupture, however, was complete. When the left revived under the stimulus of the civil rights movement, it did so in a historical vacuum. Though many ex-Communists — both capital letter *C* and lowercase — took part as individuals in the movements of the 1960s, they could not replace what the New Left leader Todd Gitlin called "the missing radical generation." McCarthyism did not so much destroy this cohort of left-wing activists as prevent it from coming into existence. The men and women who came of age at the height of the anticommunist crusade and who might have participated in an ongoing radical movement like the Communist party had to duck and cover instead. They had little useful political experience to pass on to the next generation of radicals. The New Left that had to craft itself almost from scratch was a fractured, deracinated movement that could never reconstruct the ideological and cultural unity of its predecessor or overcome its own divisions. Even today, what passes for the left, the identity politics that all too often segregates rather than unifies its adherents, lacks the sense of interconnectedness that disappeared with the lost world of American Communism.[136]

But while McCarthyism wiped out the institutional and ideological infrastructure of the old left, it created a legacy of a different sort. It showed how effectively political repression could operate within a democratic society. Because such mainstream institutions as the Supreme Court collaborated with the anticommunist crusade, the Constitution offered few barriers to the ability of a group of dedicated and well-connected militants to use the machinery of government to demonize and then destroy an unpopular political movement. Moreover, the willingness of so many American politicians and community leaders to subscribe to that demonized view of the world and limit political debate in the name of national security set unfortunate precedents.

So, too, did the illegal behavior and injustice that suffused so much of what happened. The process of destroying Communism seriously deformed American politics. Countersubversion was not good for democracy. The basic illegitimacy of the project tainted everything it touched. From the FBI's illegal break-ins to the secrecy of the entertainment industry's blacklists to the ACLU board's refusal to accept its members' rejection of an anticommunist referendum, every public and private institution that fought Communism resorted to lies and dirty tricks. The hypocrisy was corrosive, laying the foundation for the widespread cynicism and apathy that suffuses contemporary political life.[137]

Nor has the blatant disregard for the rights of individuals that characterized the anticommunist crusade necessarily vanished from the scene. It may in fact have intensified. Certainly during the 1960s, the brutal repression practiced against such dissenting organizations as the Black Panthers built upon the foundations laid during the McCarthy era. And it remains unclear, for example, whether the police state apparatus that J. Edgar Hoover and his allies tried to put into place has been entirely dismantled. During the 1980s, the Bureau was still engaging in COINTELPRO-type operations against opponents of the Reagan administration's foreign policy in Central America. National security, now as then, still cloaks this kind of illegitimate activity. It offers those who would unjustly turn the power of the state against its own citizens a rationalization that can still resist challenge.[138]

The contempt for constitutional limitations that McCarthyism bred among its perpetrators has also continued to fester within the American polity. It was, after all, HUAC's most famous alumnus, Richard Nixon, who mounted a COINTELPRO-type of offensive against the very structure of the American government during the Watergate years. Nixon owed his career to the anticommunist crusade. He won elections by red-baiting and gained a national reputation by pursuing Alger Hiss. His political success conveyed respectability on the illicit practices he and his allies employed. By the time he reached the White House, the secrecy and deceit that had marked his early triumphs had become routine. He snooped on aides and rivals, authorized dirty tricks against domestic opponents, and illegally bombed a country (Cambodia) with which the United States was not at war. These crimes were far more serious than the offense artifacts that someone like Clinton Jencks was charged with during the McCarthy era.[139]

Nixon's subversive activities were not merely the excesses of an out-of-control politician. They had been nurtured in a system that, from the 1940s on, had justified the illegitimate use of state power against the supposed enemies of the state. Nixon simply identified himself with the state and carried on business as usual. Watergate was, thus, the logical result of the tendency to insulate affairs of state from the Constitution. During the McCarthy era, that tendency nullified the First Amendment; during Watergate it overrode much of the rest of the Constitution. Though Nixon was forced from office, there was no repudiation of the mentality that tempted him to break the law in the name of some greater national purpose.

The equally illegal Iran-Contra operation reveals how deeply engrained that propensity for criminal behavior had become. Ronald Reagan's top advisers — and possibly the president himself — knowingly contravened Congress's express prohibition on supplying arms to the Nicaraguan Contras and funded the operation by an illegal deal to trade arms for hostages in the Middle East. Like Nixon, they tried to cover it up. And, like the protagonists of the McCarthy era, they tried to justify it in terms of national security. To the extent, then, that the secret and illegal use of state power for illegitimate purposes became routinized during the McCarthy era, it is clear that the anticommunist crusade contributed to the undermining of respect for lawful procedures at the very highest levels of government. Ultimately, it may well be that the sleaziness McCarthyism introduced to American politics constitutes its main legacy.[140]

Can it happen again? Certainly not in the same way. The Cold War is over and there are no more Communists to chase. HUAC has disappeared and it is hard to conceive of a successor. But American politics has never lacked for supposed enemies within; and, when the anticommunist crusade petered out, no barriers were erected to prevent its recurrence. Though the specific historical circumstances of the early Cold War produced both its content and its institutional structure, the *process* through which McCarthyism came to dominate American politics is infinitely replicable. The demonization of politically marginalized groups and the use of state power to repress them goes on all the time, as does the willingness of so many important individuals and institutions to collaborate with the process. Only now, under the impact of a globalized, yet atomized, capitalist system, political repression may have become so diffuse that we do not recognize it when it occurs.

★

ACKNOWLEDGEMENTS

THIS BOOK began more than twenty years ago. I had been teaching a freshman composition class on the 1950s and could find no general book about McCarthyism that would explain it to my students. Having no other project at the time, I decided to write such a book. In 1977–78 a fellowship at the Bunting Institute of Radcliffe College gave me the time and confidence to begin what I soon realized was an impossible task. I temporarily opted for a narrower study of the academic community, but I never abandoned the larger project. That earlier work, *No Ivory Tower: McCarthyism and the Universities* (1986), as well as the introductory essay in *The Age of McCarthyism: A Short History with Documents* (1993), helped me conceptualize the present book.

I could not, however, have written it without the generous cooperation of the many scholars, writers, attorneys, and others who sent me materials, offered bibliographical advice, and let me see the FBI files, private papers, and other documents in their possession. Among them are Barton Bernstein, Don Carleton, Norah Chase, Amy Chen, Vern Countryman, Sigmund Diamond, Ben Fordham, Marge Frantz, Dorothy Gallagher, Ann Fagin Ginger, Michael Goldfield, Ed Greer, Daniel Horowitz, Michael Krinsky, Dan Leab, Steven I. Levine, Wilbur Miller, Frank Murphy, Victor Navasky, Francis V. O'Connor, Marshall Perlin, Joan Pinkham, Gerda Ray, Steve Rosswurm,

ACKNOWLEDGMENTS

Annette Rubinstein, Nora Sayre, Walter and Miriam Schneir, Martin Sherwin, Amy Srebnick, Patricia Sullivan, Penny von Eschen, Alan Wald, Doris Brin Walker, Daniel Walkowitz, Jerry Zahavi, Maurice Zeitlin, and Ross Zucker. I am especially indebted to my attorney James Lesar for expediting my FOIA request and obtaining thousands of pages of FBI files.

This book also benefited from the expertise and kindness of the professional staffs at the archives I visited. Whitney Bagnall of the Columbia University Law School Library, Deborah Barnhart and Peter Filardo of the Tamiment Institute Library and Wagner Labor Archives, Rodney A. Ross of the National Archives, Dennis Bolger of the Harry S. Truman Library, David Rosenberg of the Archives of Industrial Society at the University of Pittsburgh, David Wigdor of the Library of Congress, and Ann Fagin Ginger of the Meiklejohn Institute of Civil Liberties were especially helpful.

I am also grateful for the comments of the people who read pieces of this book in manuscript and helped me make it both more accurate and more readable. My largest debt is to Steve Rosswurm. But Adam Fairclough, Robert Ferguson, Erica Harth, Daniel Horowitz, Mary and Howard Hurtig, David Konstan, Nelson Lichtenstein, Alan Nadel, Fraser Ottanelli, Susan Rosenfeld, Carole Silver, Thomas Sugrue, Lise Vogel, Luise White, and William Wiecek also helped me here. In the final stages of the manuscript, Josh Breitbart proved to be an ideal research assistant.

Assistance from the Harry S. Truman Library, the Lyndon Baines Johnson Library, the Princeton University Research Fund, and Yeshiva University facilitated my archival research. A fellowship at the National Humanities Center during 1994–95 made it possible for me to write up much of the manuscript under what are, for scholars, nothing less than ideal conditions.

Ronald Goldfarb has been everything a literary agent should be and then some — cheerleader, goad, and a tough, perceptive reader. More than anything else, I am grateful that he brought me together with my editor at Little, Brown, Fredrica Friedman, whose brilliant editing and high standards pushed me to revise the manuscript in ways that have improved it more than I ever believed possible. Thanks also to my copyeditor, Betty Power. My main support, as always, has come from Marv Gettleman. Both husband and colleague, he took on far more than his share of housekeeping while reading countless drafts of chapters and listening to hours of monologues about McCarthyism. Both this book and my life have been immeasurably enriched by his love and loyalty, even if I didn't always appreciate his cooking.

418

★

ABBREVIATIONS

ABA	American Bar Association
ACA	American Communications Association
ACPFB	American Committee for Protection of Foreign Born
ACLU	American Civil Liberties Union
ACTU	Association of Catholic Trade Unionists
ADA	Americans for Democratic Action
AEC	Atomic Energy Commission
AFL	American Federation of Labor
ALP	American Labor Party
AMA	American Medical Association
CIO	Congress of Industrial Organizations (initially Committee for Industrial Organization)
COINTELPRO	Counterintelligence Program
Comintern	Communist International
CP	Communist Party
CRC	Civil Rights Congress
FAECT	Federation of Architects, Engineers, Chemists and Technicians
FBI	Federal Bureau of Investigation

FOIA	Freedom of Information Act
FTA	Food, Tobacco, Agricultural and Allied Workers
HUAC	House Committee on Un-American Activities
IATSE	International Alliance of Theatrical Stage Employees
ILWU	International Longshoremen's and Warehousemen's Union
INS	Immigration and Naturalization Service
IRS	Internal Revenue Service
IWO	International Workers Order
IWW	Industrial Workers of the World
JAFRC	Joint Anti-Fascist Refugee Committee
KMT	Kuomintang
MC & S	National Union of Marine Cooks and Stewards
Mine-Mill	International Union of Mine, Mill and Smelter Workers
NAACP	National Association for the Advancement of Colored People
NLG	National Lawyers Guild
NLRB	National Labor Relations Board
PP	Progressive Party
SACB	Subversive Activities Control Board
SISS	Senate Internal Security Subcommittee (of the Senate Judiciary Committee)
SP	Socialist Party
SWP	Socialist Workers Party (Trotskyists)
TWU	Transport Workers Union
UAW	United Automobile Workers of America
UE	United Electrical, Radio and Machine Workers of America
UOPWA	United Office and Professional Workers of America

★

SOURCES

A NOTE ON SOURCES

Having spent over twenty years studying McCarthyism and its impact, I visited many archives and talked with many people. In some cases, it was not until I encountered the same document for the third or fourth time in someone's papers or a set of union records that I realized its significance and Xeroxed it. The citations in the notes that follow are, thus, skewed in that they tend to be representative of the materials that I saw later in my research. I could have referred to several archival sources or FBI files for almost every piece of evidence I used. Accordingly, the notes are more a guide to the kinds of materials I have worked with than an attempt to account for every document I read or interview I held.

Many of these materials came from the FBI, though not directly. It is difficult to obtain Bureau files through the Freedom of Information Act. It took six years and the services of an attorney before I got the materials I had requested. I did, however, look at files that had been released to other people, many of which (like the Rosenberg case files) are also available at the FBI's headquarters in Washington. Of particular value were the FBI records that Sigmund Diamond collected and donated to the Columbia Law School Library and the labor-related files that Marshall Perlin graciously let me use in his law office. There are also some FBI files on microfilm.

The notes contain references to most of the printed sources that I used. Accordingly, I am only going to list the interviews, archives, and FBI files that I consulted. For a more extended discussion of the archival resources for the study of the

McCarthy era, see my essay "Archival Sources for the Study of McCarthyism," *Journal of American History* 75 (June 1988): 197–208.

INTERVIEWS

Unless otherwise indicated, the interviews are with the author. I deposited most of the tapes of the interviews that I conducted in the 1970s and early 1980s with the Oral History Project of Columbia University (hereafter COHP).

José Alvarez, Mar. 15, 1983, by Paul Buhle, in Oral History of the American Left, Tamiment Institute Library and Wagner Labor Archives, Elmer Holmes Bobst Library, New York University (hereafter OHAL)

Walter Barry, Oct. 21, 1980, by Ruth Prago, OHAL

Bertha Bazell, Mar. 10, 1981, by Bill Schecter, OHAL

Robert Bellah, Aug. 25, 1977

Bonnie Bird, Apr. 15, 1982

Dorothy Borg, Apr. 4, 1977

Herbert Brownell, Feb. 24, 1977, Dwight D. Eisenhower Library (hereafter DDEL)

Hugh M. Burns, 1978, Regional Oral History Office, Bancroft Library, University of California, Berkeley

Angus Cameron, Dec. 30, 1976; Apr. 5, 1977

Francis Carpenter, Apr. 6, 1978

Courtney Cazden, May 1, 1981

Norman Cazden, June 9, 1978

Tom C. Clark, Oct. 17, 1972, Harry S. Truman Library (hereafter HSTL), Independence, Mo.

Martin M. Cooper, Dec. 30, 1985; Jan. 7, 1986, by Rachel Bernstein (courtesy of Amy Srebnick)

Joseph Curran, transcript of interview, 1964, Columbia Oral History Project, Rare Book and Manuscript Library, Butler Library, Columbia University (hereafter COHP)

Pauline Dougherty, Jan. 1982, by Simon Singer, OHAL

Benjamin Dreyfus, oral history, Dec. 28, 1978, Bancroft Library

Barrows Dunham, interview by Fred R. Zimring, in Barrows Dunham/Fred Zimring Oral History Collection, Conwellana-Templana Collection, Paley Library, Temple University, Philadelphia

Clifford J. Durr, 1974, COHP

Thomas I. Emerson, 1953–55, COHP

Julius Emspak, 1960, COHP

John King Fairbank, Mar. 10, 1977

Elmer Felhaber, Feb. 5, 1981, by Bill Schecter, OHAL

Abram Flaxer, Apr. 23, 1981, by Debra E. Barnhart, Tamiment

Joseph Forer, Mar. 31, 1978

Marge Frantz, Apr. 17, 1991

David Friedman, transcript of interview for "Seeing Reds," Oct. 23, 1979, OHAL

Sender Garlin, Mar. 15, 1991

Madeline Lee Gilford, Jan. 17, 1990

Beryl Gilman, Oct. 6, 1993

Richard Gladstein, Aug. 19, 1978, by Stanley I. Kutler, Bancroft Library

Louis Goldblatt, 1978–79, by Estolv Ethan Ward, Regional Oral History Office, Bancroft Library

Gil Green, Dec. 29, 1976

Harry Grundfest, Oct. 20, 1978

Michael Hanusiak, Mar. 30, 1983, by Paul Buhle, OHAL

Clarence Hiskey, July 27, 1980

Jane Hodes, Apr. 5, 1980

Robert H. Jackson, 1952, COHP

Paul Jarrico, by telephone, Jan. 6, 1990

Clinton Jencks, Apr. 14, 1993; by telephone, Apr. 23, 1997

Claude Lightfoot, transcript of interview for "Seeing Reds," OHAL

David Lubell, Nov. 8, 1977

Salvador Luria, Apr. 9, 1981

Vito Magli, Mar. 15, 1983, OHAL

Leo Marx, Apr. 11, 1978

Carl Marzani, Sept. 16, 1992

Frances McCullough, July 1, 1976

Belle Meyers, Feb. 4, 1989

Charles S. Murphy, July 15, 1969, HSTL

Steve Nelson, June 17, 1981

Warren Olney III, Mar. 25, 1974, Earl Warren Oral History Project, Bancroft Library

William Pearlman, July 11, 1978

Frances Perkins, 1955, COHP

Rose Podmaka, transcript of interview for "Seeing Reds," Oct. 27, 1979, OHAL

Robert V. Pound, Jan. 26, 1978

Don K. Price, Sept. 21, 1979

Maxwell M. Rabb, May 13, 1975, DDEL

Victor Rabinowitz, Apr. 10, 1990; 1979, COHP

David Rein, Mar. 31, 1978

Annette Rubinstein, July 7, 1993

Junius Scales, Apr. 11, 1991

Morris U. Schappes, Mar. 7, 1983

Richard Schlatter, Oct. 21, 1981

Henry Schmidt, Regional Oral History Office, Bancroft Library

Irving Seid, July 4, 1976, by Daniel Czitrom, OHAL

Tauhma Seid, July 4, 1976, by Daniel Czitrom, OHAL

John Stewart Service, Aug. 25, 1977

SOURCES

Oscar Shaftel, Apr. 13, 1978
Bernard M. Shanley, May 16, 1975, DDEL
Conrad E. Snow, July 2, 1973, HSTL
Stephen J. Spingarn, Mar. 20–29, 1967, HSTL
Clarence Stoecker, transcript of interview for "Seeing Reds," Oct. 20, 1978, OHAL
Joseph Swing, June 21, 1967, by Ed Edwin, COHP
Jenny Wells Vincent, Nov. 6, 1994, by telephone
Doris Brin Walker, June 19, 1995
Samuel Wallach, Nov. 20, 1993
Don Watson, June 19, 1995
Michael Wilson, transcript of oral history, 1975, Bancroft Library
Nathan Witt, 1969, COHP
Ruth Watt Young, transcript of oral history, Lyndon B. Johnson Library, Austin, Tex.

FBI FILES

Unless otherwise indicated, all the files mentioned in the notes and in the attached list of sources are headquarters files.

Louis Budenz (headquarters and New York files), Reading Room, FBI Headquarters, Washington, D.C. (hereafter FBI HQ)
Harold Christoffel, Columbia University Law School Library, Sigmund Diamond Papers (hereafter Diamond Papers)
COINTELPRO, C.P.U.S.A., FBI HQ
Confidential Plant Informants, Diamond Papers
Dissemination of Information Policy, in "McCarthy Era Blacklisting of School Teachers, College Professors, and Other Public Employees: The FBI Responsibilities Program File and the Dissemination of Information Policy File," microfilm, ed. Kenneth O'Reilly (Bethesda, Md.: University Publications of America, 1989)
Gerhart Eisler, in the author's possession
Weldon Bruce Dayton, in Rosenberg case FBI files, Columbia University Law School Library
Federation of Architects, Engineers, Chemists, and Technicians (FAECT), Diamond Papers
J. Edgar Hoover Official and Confidential, FBI HQ
Everest Melvin Hupman, in the possession of Marshall Perlin (hereafter Perlin Papers)
Institute of Pacific Relations, FBI HQ
Clinton Jencks, Headquarters, Albuquerque, and El Paso files in the author's possession
Lenin School, Diamond Papers
Benjamin Mandel, in the possession of Steve Rosswurm
Clement Markert, in the possession of Clement Markert

Carl Marzani, Perlin Papers

George Mink, in the possession of Dorothy Gallagher

Motion picture industry, communist infiltration of, "Communist Infiltration of the Motion Picture Industry," Federal Bureau of Investigation, Confidential Files, Communist Activity in the Entertainment Industry, FBI Surveillance Files on Hollywood, 1942–1958, ed. Daniel J. Leab (Bethesda, Md.: University Publications of America, 1991)

National Defense Informants, Diamond Papers

National Security Informants, Diamond Papers

Elba Chase Nelson, in the possession of Norah Chase

Louis B. Nichols, Official and Confidential Files, FBI HQ

J. Robert Oppenheimer, FBI HQ

Responsibilities Program, in "McCarthy Era Blacklisting of School Teachers, College Professors, and Other Public Employees: The FBI Responsibilities Program File and the Dissemination of Information Policy File," ed. Kenneth O'Reilly (Bethesda, Md.: University Publications of America, 1989)

Muriel Rukeyser, in Rukeyser Papers, Library of Congress

N. Gregory Silvermaster, Columbia University Law School Library (these files are also available at FBI HQ)

Smith Act, FBI HQ

United Automobile Workers–CIO, Communist Infiltration of, Diamond Papers

United Electrical, Machine, and Radio Workers of America, Perlin Papers

Doris Brin Walker, in the possession of Doris Brin Walker

Harry Dexter White, in the possession of Joan Pinkham

ARCHIVES

Bancroft Library, University of California, Berkeley

Carpenters and Joiners of America, Bay Counties District Council of Carpenters, Report

Gladstein, Leonard, Patsey, and Anderson Papers

John Francis Neylan Papers

Karl G. Yoneda Papers

Bentley Historical Library, Michigan Historical Collections, University of Michigan, Ann Arbor

American Legion, Michigan, Papers

Homer Ferguson Papers

Clare Hoffman Papers

University of Colorado, Historical Collections, Boulder

Archives of the Western Federation of Miners & Mine-Mill

SOURCES

Columbia University, Rare Book and Manuscript Library

Bill of Rights Fund Papers
Emergency Civil Liberties Committee Papers
Frances Perkins Papers

Library of Congress, Washington, D.C.

Hannah Arendt Papers
Hugo L. Black Papers
Harold Hitz Burton Papers
Emanuel Celler Papers
William O. Douglas Papers
Philip Caryl Jessup Papers
James P. McGranery Papers
Joseph L. Rauh, Jr., Papers
Robert A. Taft Papers

Duke University, Special Collections Department, William R. Perkins Library, Durham, N.C.

J. B. Matthews Papers

Dwight D. Eisenhower Library, Abilene, Kan.

Dwight D. Eisenhower Papers (Ann Whitman File)
C. D. Jackson Papers
Gerald D. Morgan Papers
William P. Rogers Papers
Louis S. Rothschild Papers, Records of the Commission on Government Security
Fred A. Seaton Papers
Bernard Shanley Papers
White House Central Files
Official Files

Emory University, Special Collections, Robert W. Woodruff Library, Atlanta, Ga.

Theodore Draper Papers

Hagley Museum and Library, Wilmington, Del.

Jasper Crane Papers
National Association of Manufacturers Papers
J. Howard Pew Papers

Harvard University, Houghton Library, Cambridge, Mass.

Ruth Fischer Papers

Hoover Institution on War, Revolution and Peace, Stanford University, Stanford, Calif.

Karl Baarslag Papers
Paul Crouch Papers
Benjamin Gitlow Papers
Sidney Hook Papers
Alfred Kohlberg Papers
Hede Massing Papers
Lee Robert Pennington Papers
National Republic Papers
Herbert Solow Papers
Freda Utley Papers
Bertram David Wolfe Papers

Lyndon B. Johnson Library, Austin, Tex.

Lyndon Baines Johnson Senate Papers

Labadie Collection, University of Michigan Library, Department of Rare Books and Special Collections, Harlan Hatcher Graduate Library, Ann Arbor

American Committee for Protection of Foreign Born Papers

Meiklejohn Civil Liberties Institute, Berkeley, Calif.

Human Rights Casefinder Collection
National Lawyers Guild Papers

Karl E. Mundt Library, Dakota State College, Madison, S.D.

Karl E. Mundt Papers (microfilmed by library)

National Archives, Washington, D.C. (now in College Park, Md.)

Joint Committee on Labor-Management Relations, 80th Congress, Record Group 128
National Labor Relations Board, Record Group 25
U.S. Senate, Committee on the Judiciary, Subcommittee on Internal Security, Records, Record Group 46
Subversive Activities Control Board, Record Group 220

Nevada Historical Society, University of Nevada, Special Collections Department, Reno

Eva B. Adams Papers
Patrick A. McCarran Papers

New York State Archives, Albany

New York State Police, Bureau of Criminal Investigations, Non-Criminal Investigations Files

SOURCES

University of Pittsburgh, Archives of Industrial Society, UE/Labor Archives, Hillman Library, Pittsburgh

Thomas J. Quinn Papers
Charles Owen Rice Papers
Hymen Schlesinger Papers
M. Y. Steinberg Papers
UE Local 601 Papers

Princeton University, Seeley G. Mudd Manuscript Library, Princeton

American Civil Liberties Union Papers
John Foster Dulles Papers
James V. Forrestal Papers
Paul Tillett Papers

Archives of Labor History and Urban Affairs, Walter P. Reuther Library, Wayne State University, Detroit, Mich.

CIO Secretary-Treasurer's Office
Nat Ganley Papers
Walter P. Reuther Papers

Franklin D. Roosevelt Library, Hyde Park, N.Y.

Francis Biddle Papers
Official Files
President's Secretary's Files
James Rowe Papers

Rutgers University, Special Collections and Archives, New Brunswick, N.J.

International Union of Electrical, Radio and Machine Workers Papers

Syracuse University Library, George Arents Research Library for Special Collections, Syracuse, N.Y.

Fulton Lewis, Jr., Papers
Norman Vincent Peale Papers

Tamiment Institute Library and Robert F. Wagner Labor Archives, Elmer Holmes Bobst Library, New York University, New York

American Committee for Cultural Freedom Papers
Samuel Adams Darcy Papers
District 65–UAW Records
Marine Workers Historical Collection
Retail, Wholesale, and Department Store Workers Union, Local 1S

National Council of American-Soviet Friendship Papers
Charlotte Todes Stern Papers

University of Texas at Austin

Tom C. Clark Papers, Tarleton Law Library, University of Texas School of Law
Morris L. Ernst Papers, Harry Ransom Humanities Research Center
John Henry Faulk Papers, Center for American History

Harry S. Truman Library, Independence, Mo.

Eben Ayers Papers
Eleanor Bontecou Papers
Tom C. Clark Papers
Clark Clifford Papers
George M. Elsey Papers
John F. X. McGohey Papers
J. Howard McGrath Papers
Sherman Minton Papers
Charles S. Murphy Papers
Richard E. Neustadt Papers
Official Files
J. Anthony Panuch Papers
Post-Presidential Files
Records of the President's Commission on Immigration and Naturalization
Records of the President's Commission on Internal Security and Individual Rights
President's Secretary's Files
Stephen J. Spingarn Papers
A. Devitt Vanech Papers
White House Central Files, Confidential File

State Historical Society of Wisconsin, Madison

American Communications Association Records
Herbert Biberman–Gale Sondergaard Papers
Carl and Anne Braden Papers
Committee to Secure Justice for Morton Sobell Papers
William T. Evjue Papers
Betty Gannett Papers
Highlander Research and Education Center Papers
United Packinghouse Workers Union Papers
Richard Rovere Papers
Alexander Trachtenberg Papers
Dalton Trumbo Papers
Alexander Wiley Papers

★

NOTES

/

INTRODUCTION

1. Judd Conway, telephone interview with the author, Dec. 7, 1996.

2. Historians are in general agreement that it was "the worst Red Scare in the history of the United States." Harriet Hyman Alonso, "Mayhem and Moderation: Women Peace Activists during the McCarthy Era," in Joanne Meyerowitz, ed., *Not June Cleaver: Women and Gender in Postwar America* (Philadelphia: Temple University Press, 1994), 129.

3. The classic version of this "McCarthyism-as-populism" thesis is Daniel Bell, ed., *The New American Right* (New York: Criterion, 1955). Most of the contributors argued, in the words of historian Richard Hofstadter, that McCarthyism was a "pseudo-Conservative revolt," representing an essentially irrational phenomenon motivated in large part by the status anxieties of downwardly mobile WASPs and upwardly mobile ethnics. A recent restatement of this view, albeit in a considerably modified form, can be found in Michael Kazin, *The Populist Persuasion: An American History* (New York: Basic Books, 1995), 165–93.

4. There is no definitive accounting of the victims of McCarthyism, especially since so many people, like my sixth-grade teacher, kept their cases secret. Though incomplete, the most useful tally is in Ralph S. Brown, Jr., *Loyalty and Security: Employment Tests in the United States* (New Haven: Yale University Press, 1958), 176–82.

Robert H. March, tape-recorded reminiscences, spring 1978, in the possession of the author.

431

5. For a useful comparison, see Joan Mahoney, "Civil Liberties in Britain during the Cold War: The Role of the Central Government," *American Journal of Legal History* 33 (Jan. 1989): 53–100.

6. David Caute, *The Great Fear: The Anti-Communist Purge under Truman and Eisenhower* (New York: Simon and Schuster, 1978). A more recent, shorter narrative is Richard Fried, *Nightmare in Red: The McCarthy Era in Perspective* (New York: Oxford University Press, 1990).

7. There are several good books on the entertainment industry, especially Larry Ceplair and Steven Englund, *The Inquisition in Hollywood: Politics in the Film Community, 1930–1960* (Garden City, N.Y.: Anchor Press/Doubleday, 1980) and Victor S. Navasky, *Naming Names* (New York: Viking, 1980). On the academic world, see Ellen W. Schrecker, *No Ivory Tower: McCarthyism and the Universities* (New York: Oxford University Press, 1986).

8. See the "Note on Sources" for a list of the FBI files that I used. For some background on the Venona translations see Robert Louis Benson and Michael Warner, eds., *Venona: Soviet Espionage and the American Response, 1939–1957* (Washington, D.C.: National Security Agency, Central Intelligence Agency, 1996) and National Security Agency, Center for Cryptologic History, "Introduction: History of VENONA and Guide to the Translations" (Fort George G. Meade, Md.: National Security Agency, 1995).

1: "WE WERE SITTING DUCKS": THE WORLD OF AMERICAN COMMUNISM

1. Steve Nelson, James R. Barrett, and Rob Ruck, *Steve Nelson, American Radical* (Pittsburgh: University of Pittsburgh Press, 1981), 17–20.

2. For a good discussion of the historiography of the American left, see Michael Kazin, "The Agony and Romance of the American Left," *American Historical Review* 100 (Dec. 1995): 1488–1512; Hayden White, "The Value of Narrativity in the Representation of Reality," in White, *The Content of the Form: Narrative Discourse and Historical Representation* (Baltimore: Johns Hopkins University Press, 1987), 21–25.

3. A good portrayal of the world of the "small *c*" Communists can be found in Carl Bernstein's *Loyalties: A Son's Memoir* (New York: Simon and Schuster, 1989).

4. V. I. Lenin, *What Is To Be Done?* (New York: International Publishers, 1929), 94–143.

5. Earl Ofari Hutchinson, *Blacks and Reds: Race and Class in Conflict, 1919–1990* (East Lansing: Michigan State University Press, 1995), 29–40.

6. Most of the serious analyses of American Communism deal with the problem of reform versus revolution in some detail. See, for example, Joseph R. Starobin, *American Communism in Crisis, 1943–1957* (Cambridge: Harvard University Press, 1972), 26–27.

7. The best book about the activities of rank-and-file party members is Paul Ly-

ons, *Philadelphia Communists, 1936–1956* (Philadelphia: Temple University Press, 1982). See also Harvey Klehr, *The Heyday of American Communism: The Depression Decade* (New York: Basic Books, 1984), 153–66; Jessica Mitford, *A Fine Old Conflict* (New York: Knopf, 1977); Sidney Eisenberger, "Political Memoirs of Sidney Eisenberger," unpublished ms., 1979, in the author's possession, 7; David Friedman, transcript of interview for "Seeing Red," Oct. 23, 1979, in Oral History of the American Left, Tamiment Institute Library and Wagner Labor Archives, Elmer Holmes Bobst Library, New York University, New York City (hereafter OHAL).

8. Bernstein, *Loyalties,* passim; Lyons, *Philadelphia Communists,* 134–35; Ellen W. Schrecker, *No Ivory Tower: McCarthyism and the Universities* (New York: Oxford University Press, 1986), 58–61; Carl Marzani, interview with the author, Sept. 16, 1992; Annette Rubinstein, interview with the author, July 7, 1993.

9. Nathan Glazer, *The Social Basis of American Communism* (New York: Harcourt, Brace and World, 1961), 219.

10. Most of this discussion of the origins of American Communism comes from Theodore Draper's definitive *The Roots of American Communism* (New York: Viking, 1957), 11–196.

11. Harvey Klehr, *Communist Cadre: The Social Background of the American Communist Party Elite* (Stanford: Hoover Institution Press, 1978), 117; Klehr, John Earl Haynes, and Fridrikh Igorevich Firsov, *The Secret World of American Communism* (New Haven: Yale University Press, 1995), 20–31.

12. Draper, *The Roots of American Communism,* 353–75.

13. Harvey Klehr, "U.S.: The Bridgman Delegates," *Survey* 99 (Spring 1976): 87–94.

14. Draper, *The Roots of American Communism,* 197–280, 303–95.

15. Theodore Draper, *American Communism and Soviet Russia* (New York: Viking, 1960) is the most comprehensive discussion of the CP in the 1920s. See also Edward P. Johanningsmeier, *Forging American Communism: The Life of William Z. Foster* (Princeton: Princeton University Press, 1994), 151–248.

16. Glazer, *The Social Basis of American Communism,* 38–89.

17. Klehr, *The Heyday of American Communism,* 28–68; Fraser M. Ottanelli, *The Communist Party of the United States: From the Depression to World War II* (New Brunswick, N.J.: Rutgers University Press, 1991), 17–48; Robin D. G. Kelley, *Hammer and Hoe: Alabama Communists during the Great Depression* (Chapel Hill: University of North Carolina Press, 1990), 13–91. There is a lot of information about the CP's activities during this period in the memoirs of former Communists. See, for example, George Charney, *A Long Journey* (Chicago: Quadrangle, 1968); John Gates, *The Story of an American Communist* (New York: Thomas Nelson and Sons, 1958); Dorothy Healey and Maurice Isserman, *Dorothy Healey Remembers* (New York: Oxford University Press, 1990); Nelson, Barrett, and Ruck, *Steve Nelson.*

18. Klehr, *The Heyday of American Communism,* 21–25, 87–88; Maurice Isserman, *Which Side Were You On? The American Communist Party During the Second*

World War (Middletown, Conn.: Wesleyan University Press, 1982), 16, 23; Peggy Dennis, *The Autobiography of an American Communist: A Personal View of a Political Life, 1925–1975* (Berkeley, Calif.: Lawrence Hill, Creative Arts Book Co., 1977), 34.

19. Ottanelli, *The Communist Party of the United States*, 49–80; Browder, quoted in Klehr, *The Heyday of American Communism*, 94.

20. Fernando Claudin, *The Communist Movement: From Comintern to Cominform* (New York: Monthly Review Press, 1975), 171–207; Klehr, *The Heyday of American Communism*, 170–85.

21. On Jews in the Communist party, see Lyons, *Philadelphia Communists*, 71–76; Glazer, *The Social Basis of American Communism*, 130–68.

On Spain and the Lincoln Brigade, see Peter N. Carroll, *The Odyssey of the Abraham Lincoln Brigade: Americans in the Spanish Civil War* (Stanford: Stanford University Press, 1994); Robert A. Rosenstone, *Crusade of the Left: The Lincoln Battalion in the Spanish Civil War* (Lanham, Md.: University Press of America, 1980); Nelson, Barrett, and Ruck, *Steve Nelson*, 183–239; Gates, *The Story of an American Communist*, 42–67.

22. Klehr, *The Heyday of American Communism*, 367.

23. Starobin, *American Communism in Crisis*, 24–25; Browder quoted in Klehr, *The Heyday of American Communism*, 279, 222.

24. Isserman, *Which Side Were You On?*, 32–43; Klehr, *The Heyday of American Communism*, 388–95; Roy A. Medvedev, *Let History Judge* (New York: Knopf, 1971, Vintage ed., 1973), 442–43; Milton Wolff, speech, May 1941, quoted in Klehr, Haynes, and Firsov, *The Secret World of American Communism*, 268–69.

25. Charney, *A Long Journey;* Dennis, *Autobiography*, 133, 136; Al Richmond, *A Long View from the Left* (Boston: Houghton Mifflin, 1973), 283; A. T., interview with the author, March 16, 1979; Richard Schlatter, interview with the author, October 21, 1981; Gates, *The Story of an American Communist*, 74; Healey and Isserman, *Dorothy Healey Remembers*, 82.

26. Abner Berry, quoted in Mark Naison, *Communists in Harlem during the Depression* (Urbana: University of Illinois Press, 1983), 291; Claude Lightfoot, transcript of interview for "Seeing Red," OHAL; Nelson, Barrett, Ruck, *Steve Nelson*, 248–49.

27. Kelley, *Hammer and Hoe*, 122, 176, 190; Naison, *Communists in Harlem*, 256–57, 272, 287–94; Joshua B. Freeman, *In Transit: The Transport Workers Union in New York City, 1933–1966* (New York: Oxford University Press, 1989), 194; Joseph Curran, transcript of interview, 1964, Columbia Oral History Project, Rare Book and Manuscript Library, Butler Library, Columbia University (hereafter COHP), 75–76, 150–51. According to Ronald L. Filippelli, surveys of the labor press at the end of 1940 revealed near unanimity in opposition to entering the war. "The United Electrical, Radio and Machine Workers of America, 1933–1949: The Struggle for Control" (Ph.D. diss., Pennsylvania State University, 1970), 67.

28. Nelson, Barrett, and Ruck, *Steve Nelson*, 249–50; Schrecker, *No Ivory Tower*, 54–57; Barrows Dunham, interview with Fred R. Zimring, in Barrows Dunham/Fred

Zimring Oral History Collection, Conwellana-Templana Collection, Paley Library, Temple University, Philadelphia, Pennsylvania, 91–92.

29. Richmond, *A Long View from the Left,* 285; Ronald D. Cohen and Dave Samuelson, "Protest Music and the American Left, 1926–1953: The Recorded Legacy," unpublished ms. in the author's possession; Starobin, *American Communism in Crisis,* 34; Isserman, *Which Side Were You On?,* 144–48, 178–80.

30. Isserman, *Which Side Were You On?,* 206–8; Starobin, *American Communism in Crisis,* 57–58; Johanningsmeier, *Forging American Communism,* 293–301.

31. According to James R. Prickett, calling the article a "letter" implies that it was a direct communication from Moscow to the American CP, "New Perspectives on American Communism and the Labor Movement," in Maurice Zeitlin and Howard Kimeldorf, eds., *Political Power and Social Theory,* vol. 4 (Greenwich, Conn.: JAI Press, 1984), 5. The Duclos article may, in fact, have had little to do with the American CP. Isserman notes that Duclos later remarked that he had been misinterpreted. Joseph Starobin, transcript of interview with Theodore Draper, Dec. 20, 1956, Box 16, Draper Papers, Special Collections, Robert W. Woodruff Library, Emory University, Atlanta, Ga.; Isserman, *Which Side Were You On?,* 214–43; Starobin, *American Communism in Crisis,* 71–106.

32. Starobin, *American Communism in Crisis,* 19, 117; Dennis, *Autobiography,* 174; Johanningsmeier, *Forging American Communism,* 304–309. For examples of CP rigidity, see Freeman, *In Transit,* 300; Charney, *A Long Journey,* 136–42.

33. Starobin, *American Communism in Crisis,* 108–14; David A. Shannon, *The Decline of American Communism* (New York: Harcourt Brace, 1959), 92–97.

34. According to Joseph Starobin, the former foreign editor of the *Daily Worker,* the Soviet leaders disagreed with Foster's dire picture of the international scene in 1951. See *American Communism in Crisis,* 170–77, 216–19.

35. Starobin, *American Communism in Crisis,* 195–205; Charney, *A Long Journey,* 206–208; John D'Emilio, *Sexual Politics, Sexual Communities: The Making of a Homosexual Minority in the United States, 1940–1970* (Chicago: University of Chicago Press, 1983), 40–91; D'Emilio and Estelle B. Freedman, *Intimate Matters: A History of Sexuality in America* (New York: Harper and Row, 1988), 292–95; Junius Scales, *Cause at Heart* (Athens: University of Georgia Press, 1987), 223–24; Healey and Isserman, *Dorothy Healey Remembers,* 125–32; Griffin Fariello, *Red Scare: Memories of the American Inquisition* (New York: W. W. Norton, 1995), 236–37; Hutchinson, *Blacks and Reds,* 223–38; Rubinstein, interview with the author.

36. The best study of the CP's 1956–57 crisis is Maurice Isserman, *If I Had a Hammer: The Death of the Old Left and the Birth of the New Left* (New York: Basic Books, 1987), 3–34; Charney, *A Long Journey,* 195, 207; Gates, *The Story of an American Communist,* 157–91; Nelson, Barrett, and Ruck, *Steve Nelson,* 380–98.

37. On the purges, see Robert Conquest, *The Great Terror: A Reassessment* (New York: Oxford University Press, 1990) and Medvedev, *Let History Judge.*

38. Frank A. Warren III, *Liberals and Communism* (Bloomington: Indiana Univer-

sity Press, 1966), 163–91; Alan M. Wald, *The New York Intellectuals: The Rise and Decline of the Anti-Stalinist Left from the 1930s to the 1980s* (Chapel Hill: University of North Carolina Press, 1987), 128–29; Gates, *The Story of an American Communist*, 54–55; Dennis, *Autobiography*, 118; Schrecker, *No Ivory Tower*, 37; Lyons, *Philadelphia Communists*, 139–41.

39. Alexander Bittelman, quoted in Isserman, *Which Side Were You On?*, 15; Charney, *A Long Journey*, 116–17; Scales, *Cause at Heart*, 225–26.

40. Charney, *A Long Journey*, 116–17; Healey and Isserman, *Dorothy Healey Remembers*, 57–58; Sender Garlin, interview with the author, Mar. 15, 1991; Lyons, *Philadelphia Communists*, 139–41; Pauline Dougherty, interview with Simon Singer, Jan. 1982, OHAL; Nelson, Barrett, and Ruck, *Steve Nelson*, 287–92, 386–93; Marge Frantz, interview with the author, Apr. 17, 1991.

41. Kelley, *Hammer and Hoe*, xiv. The North Carolina Communist Junius Scales agreed that much of what came from headquarters was irrelevant to Southern Communists, Scales, interview with the author, Apr. 11, 1991; Rose Podmaka, transcript of interview for "Seeing Red," Oct. 27, 1979, OHAL. The CP on the West Coast seemed to have more autonomy than elsewhere; see Richmond, *A Long View from the Left*, 367; Healey and Isserman, *Dorothy Healey Remembers*, 125, 142–51.

42. Starobin, *American Communism in Crisis*, 39; Lyons, *Philadelphia Communists*, 135; Naison, *Communists in Harlem during the Depression*, 185–87.

43. Jessica Mitford, *A Fine Old Conflict* (New York: Knopf, 1977), 268–72; Tauhma Seid, interview with Daniel Czitrom, July 4, 1976, OHAL; Lyons, *Philadelphia Communists*, 120, 132; Dougherty, OHAL.

44. Klehr, *The Heyday of American Communism*, 159–60; Dennis, *Autobiography*, 51; Kelley, *Hammer and Hoe*, xii; Podmaka, OHAL; José Alvarez, interview with Paul Buhle, Mar. 15, 1983, OHAL.

45. The undercover apparatus is the main focus of the documents in Klehr, Haynes, and Firsov, *The Secret World of American Communism*, 42–70, 205–258, 292–321. For a discussion of the recently released texts of the so-called Venona decrypts of the KGB's wartime telegrams, see National Security Agency, Center for Cryptologic History, "Introduction: History of VENONA and Guide to the Translations" (Fort George G. Meade, Md.: National Security Agency, 1995). For some first-person accounts of Comintern operations, see Dennis, *Autobiography*, 47–86; Nelson, Barrett, and Ruck, *Steve Nelson*, 137–52.

46. Isserman, *Which Side Were You On?*, 51; Dennis, *Autobiography*, 137–38; Nelson, Barrett, and Ruck, *Steve Nelson*, 250–51.

47. Starobin, *American Communism in Crisis*, 219–23; Gil Green, *Cold War Fugitive* (New York: International Publishers, 1985). For the story of a CP family that fled to Czechoslovakia, see Ann Kimmage, *An Un-American Childhood* (Athens: University of Georgia Press, 1996).

48. Charney, *A Long Journey*, 208; Starobin, *American Communism in Crisis*, 214–23; Scales, *Cause at Heart*, 231–52; Healey and Isserman, *Dorothy Healey Remembers*, 119–25; Fariello, *Red Scare*, 236–54.

49. Freeman, *In Transit,* 74, 236; Roy Hudson, quoted in Klehr, *The Heyday of American Communism,* 239; John J. Abt with Michael Myerson, *Advocate and Activist: Memoirs of an American Communist Lawyer* (Urbana: University of Illinois Press, 1993), 136–38; Starobin, *American Communism in Crisis,* 40; Charney, *A Long Journey,* 80; Lester Cole, *Hollywood Red: The Autobiography of Lester Cole* (Palo Alto: Ramparts Press, 1981), 201. Sometimes the party ordered people who wanted to be open to conceal their membership, as it did with one of its most important Southern cadres; see Kelley, *Hammer and Hoe,* 130.

50. Schrecker, *No Ivory Tower,* 40–42; Tauhma Seid, OHAL; Morris U. Schappes, interview with the author, Mar. 7, 1983.

51. Starobin, *American Communism in Crisis,* 95–97; Clarence Stoecker, transcript of interview for "Seeing Red," Oct. 20, 1978, OHAL; Podmaka, OHAL; Charney, *A Long Journey,* 79–80; Walter Barry, interview with Ruth Prago, Oct. 21, 1980, OHAL; Elmer Felhaber, interview with Bill Schechter, Feb. 5, 1981, OHAL.

52. Barry, OHAL; "Lew" (probably Lewis Merrill), quoted in Starobin, *American Communism in Crisis,* 97; Stoecker, OHAL.

53. Stoecker, OHAL.

54. References to the duck test were especially common among congressional investigators. See George Taylor, testimony, U.S. Senate, Committee on the Judiciary, Subcommittee on Internal Security, "Hearings on the Institute of Pacific Relations," Aug. 7, 1951, 82nd Cong., 2d sess., 346. But I have encountered this formulation in many other places as well. See, for example, its use by a judge who sentenced five people to jail for scrawling "PEACE" on a Brooklyn wall, cited in David M. Oshinsky, *A Conspiracy So Immense: The World of Joe McCarthy* (New York: Free Press, 1983), 173.

55. Ronald L. Filippelli and Mark McColloch, *Cold War in the Working Class: The Rise and Decline of the United Electrical Workers* (Albany: State University of New York Press, 1995), 63; Kelley, *Hammer and Hoe,* 147; Johanningsmeier, *Forging American Communism,* 151–213; Draper, *Roots of American Communism,* 311–21; Draper, *American Communism and Soviet Russia,* 69–71, 215–33, 282–97; Bert Cochran, *Labor and Communism: The Conflict That Shaped American Unions* (Princeton: Princeton University Press, 1977), 20–44; Klehr, *The Heyday of American Communism,* 29–30; Roger Keeran, *The Communist Party and the Auto Workers Unions* (Bloomington: Indiana University Press, 1980), 28–120.

56. Bruce Nelson, *Workers on the Waterfront: Seamen, Longshoremen, and Unionism in the 1930s* (Urbana: University of Illinois Press, 1988), 76–155. For an overview of the labor struggles of the 1930s see Irving Bernstein, *The Turbulent Years* (Boston: Houghton Mifflin, 1969).

57. For the best general overviews of the CP's role in the CIO, see Cochran, *Labor and Communism* and Harvey A. Levenstein, *Communism, Anticommunism, and the CIO* (Westport, Conn.: Greenwood Press, 1981). See also Steve Rosswurm, "Introduction: An Overview and Preliminary Assessment of the CIO's Expelled Unions," in

Rosswurm, ed., *The CIO's Left-Led Unions* (New Brunswick, N.J.: Rutgers University Press, 1992), 1–16.

58. Labor historians have written a lot about the UAW and its Communists. Besides Cochran, Keeran, and Levenstein, see Nelson Lichtenstein, *The Most Dangerous Man in Detroit* (New York: Basic Books, 1995) and Martin Halpern, *UAW Politics in the Cold War Era* (Albany: State University of New York Press, 1988).

59. There are several excellent studies of Bridges and his union, including Nelson, *Workers on the Waterfront;* Howard Kimeldorf, *Reds or Rackets? The Making of Radical and Conservative Unions on the Waterfront* (Berkeley and Los Angeles: University of California Press, 1988); Charles Larrowe, *Harry Bridges* (Westport, Conn.: Lawrence Hill, 1972); Sanford Zalburg, *The Spark Is Struck! Jack Hall and the ILWU in Hawaii* (Honolulu: University Press of Hawaii, 1979). On Bridges's membership in the CP, see Harvey Klehr and John E. Haynes, "Communists and the CIO: From the Soviet Archives," *Labor History* 35 (Summer 1994): 444–46.

60. On the UE, see Filippelli and McColloch, *Cold War in the Working Class;* Ronald Schatz, *The Electrical Workers: A History of Labor at General Electric and Westinghouse, 1923–60* (Urbana: University of Illinois Press, 1983); Filippelli, "The United Electrical, Radio and Machine Workers of America."

61. Besides the references to Mine-Mill in Cochran and Levenstein, see Vernon H. Jensen, *Nonferrous Metals Industry Unionism, 1932–1954* (Ithaca, N.Y.: Cornell University Press, 1954); Horace Huntley, "Iron Ore Miners and Mine Mill in Alabama: 1933–1952" (Ph.D. diss., University of Pittsburgh, 1977).

62. Kelley, *Hammer and Hoe,* 35–77; Healey and Isserman, *Dorothy Healey Remembers,* 42–58; Cletus E. Daniel, *Bitter Harvest: A History of California Farmworkers, 1870–1941* (Ithaca, N.Y.: Cornell University Press, 1981), 105–257.

63. There is no overall study of the white-collar and professional unions. There is, as usual, a little bit of information in Cochran, *Labor and Communism,* Levenstein, *Communism, Anticommunism, and the CIO,* and Rosswurm, ed., *The CIO's Left-Led Unions.* For information on individual unions, see Mark McColloch, *White Collar Workers in Transition* (Westport, Conn.: Greenwood Press, 1983); Sharon Hartman Strom, "'We're no Kitty Foyles': Organizing Office Workers for the Congress of Industrial Organizations, 1937–50," in Ruth Milkman, ed., *Women, Work, and Protest: A Century of U.S. Women's Labor History* (Boston: Routledge and Kegan Paul, 1985), 206–34; Robert Iversen, *The Communists and the Schools* (New York: Harcourt, Brace, 1959); Daniel J. Leab, *A Union of Individuals: The Formation of the American Newspaper Guild, 1933–1936* (New York: Columbia University Press, 1970), 282; Larry Ceplair and Steven Englund, *The Inquisition in Hollywood: Politics and the Film Community, 1930–1960* (Garden City, N.Y.: Anchor Press/Doubleday, 1980), 16–46; Bernstein, *Loyalties;* Victor Rabinowitz, *Unrepentant Leftist: A Lawyer's Memoir* (Urbana: University of Illinois Press, 1996); Felhaber, OHAL.

64. Robert H. Zieger, *The CIO, 1935–1955* (Chapel Hill: University of North Carolina Press, 1995), 253–73; Rosswurm, "Introduction."

65. Rosswurm, "Introduction"; Rosemary Feurer, "William Senter, the UE, and Civil Unionism in St. Louis," in Rosswurm, ed., *The CIO's Left-Led Unions,* 103; Zieger, *The CIO,* 255; Freeman, *In Transit,* 156–60; George Lipsitz, *Class and Culture in Cold War America* (South Hadley, Mass.: J. F. Bergin, 1981), 147–50.

66. Feurer, "William Sentner, the UE, and Civic Unionism in St. Louis," 95–117.

67. Kimeldorf, *Reds or Rackets?,* 117–18; Lyons, *Philadelphia Communists,* 126.

68. Charney, *A Long Journey,* 167–75; Dougherty, OHAL; Barry, OHAL.

69. Naison, *Communists in Harlem during the Depression,* 106, 266–67, 307–8; Zieger, *The CIO,* 233–34, 239–40; Freeman, *In Transit,* 151–56; Levenstein, *Communism and Anticommunism in the CIO,* 174; Schatz, *The Electrical Workers,* 129–32; Kimeldorf, *Reds or Rackets?,* 145–68; Dougherty, OHAL; Louis Goldblatt, oral history interview with Estolv Ethan Ward, 1978, 422, copy in COHP.

70. Kimeldorf, *Reds or Rackets?,* 168; Michael K. Honey, *Southern Labor and Black Civil Rights: Organizing Memphis Workers* (Urbana: University of Illinois Press, 1993), passim; Honey, "Labor, the Left, and Civil Rights in the South: Memphis during the CIO Era, 1937–1955," in Judith Joel and Gerald M. Erickson, eds., *Anti-Communism: The Politics of Manipulation* (Minneapolis, Minn.: Marxist Educational Press, 1987), 57–85; Barbara S. Griffith, *The Crisis of American Labor: Operation Dixie and the Defeat of the CIO* (Philadelphia: Temple University Press, 1988), 64–87; Robert Korstad and Nelson Lichtenstein, "Opportunities Found and Lost: Labor Radicals, and the Early Civil Rights Movement," *Journal of American History* 75 (1988): 786–811; Huntley, "Iron Ore Miners and Mine Mill in Alabama"; Mario T. Garcia, "Border Proletarians: Mexican-Americans and the International Union of Mine, Mill, and Smelter Workers, 1939–1946," in Robert Asher and Charles Stephenson, eds., *Labor Divided: Race and Ethnicity in United States Labor Struggles, 1835–1960* (Albany: State University of New York Press, 1990), 85–103.

71. See Draper, *American Communism and Soviet Russia,* 315–56, for the traditional interpretation of the "Black Belt" strategy as a ridiculous gesture. Earl Ofari Hutchinson, *Blacks and Reds,* 48–81, locates the issue within the context of black nationalism and Garveyism during the 1920s. Robin D. G. Kelley in *Hammer and Hoe,* 13, and Mark Naison, *Communists in Harlem during the Depression,* 16–19, make a convincing case for the value of the policy in bringing the issue of race to the party's attention.

72. Naison, *Communists in Harlem during the Depression,* 35–42, 58–88, 132–33, 156–57, 195–97, 293–99; James E. Goodman, *Stories of Scottsboro* (New York: Pantheon, 1994); Richmond, *A Long View from the Left,* 99–100; Lightfoot, OHAL; Kelley, *Hammer and Hoe,* 15, 79–91. On the CRC, see Gerald Horne, *Communist Front? The Civil Rights Congress, 1946–1956* (Rutherford, N.J.: Fairleigh Dickinson University Press, 1988).

73. Because the best work on race and Communism deals with the 1930s and later studies of the CP deal primarily with its response to war and Cold War, there is little scholarship on the CP's civil rights activities in the 1940s and 1950s. For some evi-

dence about this increasingly important aspect of the communist movement, see Gerald Horne, *Black Liberation/Red Scare: Ben Davis and the Communist Party* (Newark: University of Delaware Press, 1994), 63, 125–28, 154–66; Jules Tygiel, *Baseball's Great Experiment: Jackie Robinson and His Legacy* (New York: Oxford University Press, 1983, Vintage ed., 1984), 36–37, 40, 225; Bernstein, *Loyalties,* 95–98; Mitford, *A Fine Old Conflict,* 118–38; Lyons, *Philadelphia Communists,* 76–85; Rabinowitz, *Unrepentant Leftist,* 91; Amy Swerdlow, "The Congress of American Women: Left-Feminist Peace Politics in the Cold War," in Linda K. Kerber, Alice Kessler-Harris, and Kathryn Kish Sklar, *U.S. History as Women's History: New Feminist Essays* (Chapel Hill: University of North Carolina Press, 1995), 306–308; William Pearlman, interview with the author, July 11, 1978.

74. Hutchinson, *Blacks and Reds,* 61–68, 223–38; Healey and Isserman, *Dorothy Healey Remembers,* 125–29; Scales, *Cause at Heart,* 210–11.

75. Klehr, *Communist Cadre,* 53–60; Nelson, Barrett, and Ruck, *Steve Nelson,* 125–26; Lightfoot, OHAL.

76. New York City eliminated its system of proportional representation in order to oust Davis. Horne, *Black Liberation/Red Scare,* 97–191; Isserman, *Which Side Were You On?,* 215.

77. Steve Nelson, quoted in Isserman, *Which Side Were You On?,* 198; Klehr, *The Heyday of American Communism,* 88.

78. Isserman, *Which Side Were You On?,* 208–13; John Earl Haynes, *Dubious Alliance: The Making of Minnesota's DFL Party* (Minneapolis: University of Minnesota Press, 1984), 19–20, 100–102, 109–19; Starobin, *American Communism in Crisis,* 98.

79. Klehr, *The Heyday of American Communism,* 252–80, offers a convenient overview of the party's participation in political coalitions during the 1930s.

80. Starobin, *American Communism in Crisis,* 162–94, is scathing about the impact of the Wallace campaign on the CP. For other views, see Norman Markowitz, *The Rise and Fall of the People's Century: Henry A. Wallace and American Liberalism, 1941–1948* (New York: Free Press, 1973); Curtis D. MacDougall, *Gideon's Army* (New York: Marzani and Munsell, 1965); Patricia Sullivan, *Days of Hope: Race and Democracy in the New Deal Era* (Chapel Hill: University of North Carolina Press, 1996).

81. Starobin, *American Communism in Crisis,* 175.

82. Starobin, *American Communism in Crisis,* 186–90; Abt, *Advocate and Activist,* 140–68; Scales, *Cause at Heart,* 192–201; Lyons, *Philadelphia Communists,* 148–153.

83. All the CP memoirs describe the cultural world of American Communism. See also Michael Denning, *The Cultural Front* (London: Verso, 1996); Vivian Gornick, *The Romance of American Communism* (New York: Basic Books, 1977); Robbie Lieberman, *"My Song Is My Weapon": People's Songs, American Communism and the Politics of Culture 1930–1950* (Urbana: University of Illinois Press, 1989), 14–19; Lyons, *Philadelphia Communists,* 49–69.

84. There is no good general survey of the front groups, though most of the schol-

arship about the American CP discusses them in passing. For the CP and some individual groups, see Horne, *Communist Front?,* 25; Lowell Dyson, *Red Harvest: The Communist Party and American Farmers* (Lincoln: University of Nebraska Press, 1982), 60.

85. Dyson, *Red Harvest,* 80–81; *Partisan Review,* quoted in Alexander Bloom, *Prodigal Sons: The New York Intellectuals and Their World* (New York: Oxford University Press, 1986), 60.

86. Arthur J. Sabin, *Red Scare in Court: New York versus the International Workers Order* (Philadelphia: University of Pennsylvania Press, 1993), 12–19; Thomas Joseph Edward Walker, "The International Workers Order" (Ph.D. diss., University of Chicago, 1982), 23–27.

87. Edward I. Aronow to J. Howard McGrath, Aug. 3, 1950, J. Howard McGrath Papers, Box 99, Harry S. Truman Library, Independence, Mo. (hereafter HSTL); Klehr, *The Heyday of American Communism,* 385; Walker, "The International Workers Organization," 43–46, 93; Sabin, *Red Scare in Court,* 15.

88. Michael Hanusiak, interview with Paul Buhle, March 30, 1983, OHAL.

89. Roger Keeran, "The International Workers Order and the Origins of the CIO," *Labor History* 30 (Summer 1989): 385–408.

90. Walker, "The International Workers Order," 53–58, 63–64, 104, 161, 201; Sabin, *Red Scare in Court,* 20–22.

91. For information about a similar group within the medical profession, see Jane Pacht Brickman, "'Medical McCarthyism': The Physicians Forum and the Cold War," *Journal of the History of Medicine and Allied Sciences* 49 (July 1994): 380–418.

92. Jerold S. Auerbach, *Unequal Justice: Lawyers and Social Change in Modern America* (New York: Oxford University Press, 1976), 198–99; Ann Fagin Ginger and Eugene M. Tobin, eds., *The National Lawyers Guild: From Roosevelt to Reagan* (Philadelphia: Temple University Press, 1988), 3–10.

93. Ginger and Tobin, *The National Lawyers Guild,* 7–21.

2: "RED-BAITERS, INC.": THE ANTICOMMUNIST NETWORK

1. E. A. Tamm, memorandum to Director, Sept. 11, 1947, Smith Act, #973; J. Patrick Coyne, memorandum to D. M. Ladd, Dec. 10, 1947, ibid., #1214.

2. Report [name deleted], Washington, D.C., Feb. 10, 1953, Benjamin Mandel, #15; report [name deleted], Washington, D.C., Feb. 27, 1953, ibid., #35.

3. Karl Baarslag, "Autobiographical Manuscript," Box 3, Karl Baarslag Papers, Hoover Institution on War, Revolution and Peace, Stanford University, Stanford, Calif. (hereafter Hoover Institution). Besides information from the usual published sources, Steele also got information from at least one local red squad, see Detective C. E. Neuser (Seattle Police Department) to Walter Steele, Feb. 7, 1946, National Republic Papers, Hoover Institution.

4. Baarslag, "Autobiographical Manuscript"; Benjamin Mandel to J. B. Matthews,

July 13, 1946, in J. B. Matthews Papers, Box 692, Special Collections Department, William R. Perkins Library, Duke University.

5. Murray Kempton, *Part of Our Time: Some Ruins and Monuments of the Thirties* (New York: Simon and Schuster, 1955), 151–79; Harvey Matusow, *False Witness* (New York: Cameron and Kahn, 1955), 175–77.

6. There is extensive correspondence with Mandel in the papers of both J. B. Matthews and Alfred Kohlberg, whose papers are at the Hoover Institution. For an uncritical biography of Kohlberg, see Joseph Keeley, *The China Lobby Man* (New Rochelle, N.Y.: Arlington House, 1969). On the China lobby, see Ross Y. Koen, *The China Lobby in American Politics* (New York: Macmillan, 1960).

7. Undated list, in "Autobiographical Manuscript," Baarslag Papers; Baarslag to Matthews, Feb. 3, 1955, Box 692, Matthews Papers; seating list, Robert Morris Reception and Dinner, Jan. 28, 1954, Box 674, ibid.

8. For a suggestive analysis of the way in which experts shape public opinion, see John R. Zaller, *The Nature and Origins of Mass Opinion* (New York: Cambridge University Press, 1992).

9. For a sophisticated analysis of the process through which left-wing anti-Stalinists became conservative, see Alan M. Wald, *The New York Intellectuals: The Rise and Decline of the Anti-Stalinist Left from the 1930s to the 1980s* (Chapel Hill: University of North Carolina Press, 1987).

10. The classic attempt to define McCarthyism in psychological terms is Richard Hofstadter, *The Paranoid Style in American Politics and Other Essays* (New York: Knopf, 1965). For a more recent dip into the rhetoric of medicalization, see Joel Kovel, *Red-Hunting in the Promised Land: Anticommunism and the Making of America* (New York: Basic Books, 1994).

11. Michael Paul Rogin, *"Ronald Reagan," The Movie and Other Episodes in Political Demonology* (Berkeley and Los Angeles: University of California Press, 1987), 290.

12. For a classic statement about countersubversion as the belief that "some influence originating abroad threatened the very life of the nation from within," see John Higham, *Strangers in the Land: Patterns of American Nativism* (New York: Atheneum, 1981 ed.), 4.

13. Rogin offers the most persuasive presentation of this argument with regard to American anticommunism in *"Ronald Reagan," the Movie.* There is a vast and growing scholarly literature about the way in which the construction of the identity of the "other" has enabled Western ruling classes to expand into and take over so much of the rest of the world. See, for example, Edward W. Said, *Orientalism* (New York: Pantheon, 1978).

14. Rogin, *"Ronald Reagan," the Movie,* 134–68; Higham, *Strangers in the Land,* 55; Robert J. Goldstein, *Political Repression in Modern America from 1870 to the Present* (Cambridge, Mass.: Schenkman, 1978), 41. I deal with the representations of American Communism in chapter 4. See also Kovel, *Red Hunting in the Promised*

Land, 141, and Nora Sayre, *Running Time: Films of the Cold War* (New York: Dial Press, 1982), 13.

15. Winthrop D. Jordan, *White Over Black* (Baltimore: Penguin, 1969 ed.), 114, 121; Samuel F. B. Morse quoted in David H. Bennett, *The Party of Fear: From Nativist Movements to the New Right in American History* (New York: Vintage ed., 1990), 40–41; Higham, *Strangers in the Land,* 55; Robert K. Murray, *Red Scare: A Study in National Hysteria, 1919–1920* (Minneapolis: University of Minnesota Press, 1955), 150; "A Brief Study Concerning the Internal Security of the United States," NSC-17, June 28, 1948, President's Secretary's Files, Harry S. Truman Library, Independence, Mo. (hereafter HSTL-PSF).

16. The most useful overviews of American anticommunism are M. J. Heale, *American Anticommunism: Combating the Enemy Within, 1830–1970* (Baltimore: Johns Hopkins University Press, 1990) and Goldstein, *Political Repression in Modern America.*

17. Heale, *American Anticommunism,* 23–29; Goldstein, *Political Repression in Modern America,* 23–34; Higham, *Strangers in the Land,* 30–31.

18. Paul Avrich, *The Haymarket Tragedy* (Princeton: Princeton University Press, 1984), 215–39; Frank Donner, *Protectors of Privilege: Red Squads and Police Repression in Urban America* (Berkeley and Los Angeles: University of California Press, 1990), 7–21; Higham, *Strangers in the Land,* 53–55; Goldstein, *Political Repression in Modern America,* 34–44, 54–58; Bruce C. Nelson, *Beyond the Martyrs: A Social History of Chicago's Anarchists* (New Brunswick, N.J.: Rutgers University Press, 1988), 177–242; Leon Fink, *Workingmen's Democracy: The Knights of Labor and American Politics* (Urbana: University of Illinois Press, 1983).

19. Jerold S. Auerbach, *Labor and Liberty: The La Follette Committee and the New Deal* (Indianapolis, Ind.: Bobbs-Merrill, 1966), 134–35; Goldstein. *Political Repression in Modern America,* 3–19, 79, 94.

20. Donner, *Protectors of Privilege,* 7–43; Gerda W. Ray, "Contested Legitimacy: Creation of the State Police in New York, 1890–1930" (Ph.D. diss., University of California, Berkeley, 1990).

21. For an insider's assessment of a big-city red squad, see Anthony Bouza, "The Operations of a Police Intelligence Unit" (M.A. thesis, John Jay College of Criminal Justice, City University of New York, 1968). See also Donner, *Protectors of Privilege,* 44–59; Alan Wolfe, *The Seamy Side of Democracy: Repression in America* (New York: David McKay, 1973), 106.

Though the literature on the culture of American police does not directly address the political content of that culture, it is suggestive. See especially William A. Westley, *Violence and the Police* (Cambridge, Mass.: MIT, 1970); Robert Fogelson, *Big City Police* (Cambridge: Harvard University Press, 1977); Arthur Niederhoffer, *Behind the Shield: The Police in Urban Society* (Garden City, N.Y.: Doubleday, 1967); and Samuel Walker, *A Critical History of Police Reform* (Lexington, Mass.: D. C. Heath, 1977).

22. Richard Gid Powers, *Secrecy and Power: The Life of J. Edgar Hoover* (New

York: Free Press, 1987), 6–43, has a good discussion of Hoover's cultural background and values. Athan Theoharis views Hoover in psychological terms as an extraordinarily repressed, authoritarian personality. Theoharis and John Stuart Cox, *The Boss: J. Edgar Hoover and the Great American Inquisition* (Philadelphia: Temple University Press, 1988), 16–41. See also Curt Gentry, *J. Edgar Hoover: The Man and the Secrets* (New York: W. W. Norton, 1991).

23. The source of the gamiest allegations about Hoover is Anthony Summers, *Official and Confidential: The Secret Life of J. Edgar Hoover* (New York: G. P. Putnam's Sons, 1993). But all Hoover's biographers note the decidedly weird quality of his personal life.

24. Michal R. Belknap, *Cold War Political Justice: The Smith Act, the Communist Party, and American Civil Liberties* (Westport, Conn.: Greenwood Press, 1988), 17–19; Donner, *Protectors of Privilege*, 56, 307; Goldstein, *Political Repression in Modern America*, 110; Karl Baarslag, "Office of Naval Intelligence," unpublished ms., Baarslag Papers.

25. Melvin Dubofsky, *We Shall Be All: A History of the Industrial Workers of the World* (Chicago: University of Chicago Press, 1969), 349–422; William Preston, Jr., *Aliens and Dissenters: Federal Suppression of Radicals, 1903–1933* (Cambridge: Harvard University Press, 1963), 92–110.

26. For an argument that the administration's fear of the antiwar movement was realistic, see Goldstein, *Political Repression in Modern America*, 105–107.

27. David M. Kennedy, *Over Here: The First World War and American Society* (New York: Oxford University Press, 1980), 45–92; Goldstein, *Political Repression in Modern America*, 125–31; Heale, *American Anticommunism*, 52; Carol S. Gruber, *Mars and Minerva: World War I and the Uses of the Higher Learning in America* (Baton Rouge: Louisiana State University Press, 1975); Sherry Gorelick, *City College and the Jewish Poor* (New Brunswick, N.J.: Rutgers University Press, 1981), 97.

28. Kennedy, *Over Here*, 80–81; Goldstein, *Political Repression in Modern America*, 109, 114, 119–21; James Weinstein, *The Decline of Socialism in America, 1912–1925* (New York: Vintage, 1969 ed.), 156; Daniel Aaron, *Writers on the Left* (New York: Harcourt, Brace and World, 1961), 36–45.

29. Preston, *Aliens and Dissenters*, 118–51; Dubofsky, *We Shall Be All*, 423–44; Weinstein, *The Decline of Socialism*, 161; Neil A. Wynn, *From Progressivism to Prosperity: World War I and American Society* (New York: Holmes and Meier, 1986), 56.

30. On one of the key free speech cases of this period, see Richard Polenberg, *Fighting Faiths: The Abrams Case, the Supreme Court, and Free Speech* (New York: Viking, 1987). See also Goldstein, *Political Repression in Modern America*, 118; Weinstein, *The Decline of Socialism*, 172; Dubofsky, *We Shall Be All*, 445–68; Preston, *Aliens and Dissenters*, 118–51.

31. Dubofsky, *We Shall Be All*, 463; Murray, *Red Scare*, 34, 36–39, 52; Stanley Coben, "A Study in Nativism: The American Red Scare of 1919–20," *Political Science Quarterly* 79 (March 1964): 64.

32. Murray, *Red Scare*, 94–97.

33. David Brody, *Labor in Crisis: The Steel Strike of 1919* (Philadelphia: Lippincott, 1965), 133–45; Edward P. Johanningsmeier, *Forging American Communism: The Life of William Z. Foster* (Princeton: Princeton University Press, 1994), 111–49; Murray, *Red Scare,* 129; Coben, "Nativism," 67.

34. Murray, *Red Scare,* 58–79; Coben, "Nativism," 64; Stanley Coben, *A. Mitchell Palmer: Politician* (New York: Columbia University Press, 1963). Leo P. Ribuffo, *The Old Christian Right: The Protestant Far Right from the Great Depression to the Cold War* (Philadelphia: Temple University Press, 1983), xii–xv, 5–7, shows that much of the ideology peddled by the right-wing extremists of the 1930s and 1940s had respectable establishment roots.

35. Milton R. Konvitz, *Civil Rights in Immigration* (Ithaca, N.Y.: Cornell University Press, 1953). On the political culture of the Immigration and Naturalization Service, see Preston, *Aliens and Dissenters,* passim, and Stanley I. Kutler, *The American Inquisition: Justice and Injustice in the Cold War* (New York: Hill and Wang, 1982), 118–51; Joseph Swing, interview by Ed Edwin, June 21, 1967, Columbia Oral History Project, Rare Book and Manuscript Library, Butler Library, Columbia University (hereafter COHP).

36. Powers, *Secrecy and Power,* 70; Brody, *Labor in Crisis,* 132–49.

37. Goldstein, *Political Repression in Modern America,* 154.

38. Powers, *Secrecy and Power,* 56–74; Theoharis and Cox, *The Boss,* 51–70.

39. Murray, *Red Scare,* 51; Powers, *Secrecy and Power,* 96–101.

40. Theoharis and Cox, *The Boss,* 57; Coben, *A. Mitchell Palmer,* 217–18; Preston, *Aliens and Dissenters,* 180–207. Michael Heale makes the interesting geographical observation that much of the pre–Cold War anticommunist repression spread from the West to the East, *American Anticommunism,* 42–78.

41. Preston, *Aliens and Dissenters,* 181–207.

42. Coben, *A. Mitchell Palmer,* 219–22; Theoharis and Cox, *The Boss,* 62–63.

43. Coben, *A. Mitchell Palmer,* 223–30; Goldstein, *Political Repression in Modern America,* 157; Preston, *Aliens and Dissenters,* 209–37; Murray, *Red Scare,* 210–22.

44. Coben, *A. Mitchell Palmer,* 230–45; Murray, *Red Scare,* 239–62.

45. On New York's Lusk Committee, see Lawrence H. Chamberlain, *Loyalty and Legislative Action* (Ithaca, N.Y.: Cornell University Press, 1951), 12–51; Murray, *Red Scare,* 230–38.

On the thirties, see Auerbach, *Labor and Liberty,* 119, 183. The most notorious prosecutions of the 1950s under these laws were those of Communist party leader Steve Nelson in Pennsylvania, MIT mathematics professor Dirk Struik in Massachusets, and civil rights activist Carl Braden in Kentucky.

46. *Schenck v. United States,* 249 U.S. 47; *Abrams v. United States,* 250 U.S. 616; *Gitlow v. New York,* 268 U.S. 652. There is, to put it mildly, a massive literature on these cases and the development of First Amendment law. The classic analysis is Zechariah Chafee, *Free Speech in the United States* (Cambridge: Harvard University Press, 1941). For an elegant historical (rather than jurisprudential) treatment of the *Abrams* case, see Polenberg, *Fighting Faiths.*

47. Most of the scholarship on the American right deals with individuals or ideas; its institutional structure has been pretty much ignored. For the American Legion, see Rodney S. Minott, *Peerless Patriots: Organized Veterans and the Spirit of Americanism* (Washington, D.C.: Public Affairs Press, 1962) and William Pencak, *For God and Country: The American Legion, 1919–1941* (Boston: Northeastern University Press, 1989). For the Legion during the Cold War, see the unpublished memoir by Karl Baarslag, "What Has Really Happened to the American Legion?" Box 3, Baarslag Papers.

48. Minott, *Peerless Patriots,* 29–41; Pencak, *For God and Country,* 48–105.

49. Minott, *Peerless Patriots,* 31–41, 55–56; Ribuffo, *The Old Christian Right,* 5; Pencak, *For God and Country,* 279–80.

50. Pencak, *For God and Country,* 10, 144–57; Minott, *Peerless Patriots,* 58; Murray, *Red Scare,* 181–85.

51. Minott, *Peerless Patriots,* 85; Pencak, *For God and Country,* 265–76.

52. For a more detailed treatment of some of these people, see Richard Gid Powers, *Not Without Honor: The History of American Anticommunism* (New York: Free Press, 1995), 43–91.

53. Elizabeth Dilling, *The Red Network: A "Who's Who" and Handbook of Radicalism for Patriots* (Kenilworth, Ill.: Elizabeth Dilling, 1934), 111; Pencak, *For God and Country,* 8–9, 160–64, 304; Minott, *Peerless Patriots,* 46–49, 99, 136.

54. For the CP's revival in the 1930s, see Harvey Klehr, *The Heyday of American Communism: The Depression Decade* (New York: Basic Books, 1984), 34; Irving Bernstein, *The Lean Years: A History of the American Worker, 1920–1933* (Boston: Houghton Mifflin, 1960), 426–35; Bert Cochran, *Labor and Communism: The Conflict That Shaped American Unions* (Princeton: Princeton University Press, 1977), 43–81; Robin D. G. Kelley, *Hammer and Hoe: Alabama Communists during the Great Depression* (Chapel Hill: University of North Carolina Press, 1990), 71–91.

55. Both the autobiographical and the secondary literature on the CP in the 1930s is replete with instances of repression. For a few examples, see Kelley, *Hammer and Hoe,* 33, 71–74, 121–30; Klehr, *The Heyday of American Communism,* 34, 59; Steve Nelson, James R. Barrett, and Rob Ruck, *Steve Nelson, American Radical* (Pittsburgh, Pa.: University of Pittsburgh Press, 1981), 101; James Wechsler, *Revolt on the Campus* (New York: Covici-Friede, 1935), 152–64, 305–309, 331–32, 340–41; Goldstein, *Political Repression in Modern America,* 201–206; José Alvarez, interview by Paul Buhle, Mar. 15, 1983, in Oral History of the American Left, Tamiment Institute Library and Wagner Labor Archives, Elmer Holmes Bobst Library, New York University, New York City (hereafter OHAL); Peggy Dennis, *The Autobiography of an American Communist: A Personal View of a Political Life, 1925–1975* (Westport, Conn., and Berkeley, Calif.: Lawrence Hill, Creative Arts Book Co., 1977), 40–54; John Gates, *The Story of an American Communist* (New York: Thomas Nelson and Sons, 1958), 30–33; Irving Seid, interview by Daniel Czitrom, July 4, 1976, OHAL; Tauhma Seid, interview by Czitrom, July 4, 1976, OHAL.

56. Belknap, *Cold War Political Justice,* 11–12; Goldstein, *Political Repression in Modern America,* 218; Cletus E. Daniel, *Bitter Harvest: A History of California Farmworkers 1870–1941* (Ithaca, N.Y.: Cornell University Press, 1981), 119–26, 252–54; Dorothy Healey and Maurice Isserman, *Dorothy Healey Remembers: A Life in the American Communist Party* (New York: Oxford University Press, 1990), 37, 40, 42–56; Julius Emspak, interview, 1959–1960, COHP, 224–25; Ronald L. Filippelli, "The United Electrical, Radio and Machine Workers of America, 1933–1949: The Struggle for Control" (Ph.D. diss., Pennsylvania State University, 1970), 61–62; Auerbach, *Labor and Liberty,* 119.

57. Kelley, *Hammer and Hoe,* shows how effective the violent repression was in the South. See also Auerbach, *Labor and Liberty,* 33–47, 94–96, and Michael K. Honey, *Southern Labor and Black Civil Rights: Organizing Memphis Workers* (Urbana: University of Illinois Press, 1993), 1–5, 44–92.

58. Anthony C. Troncone, "Hamilton Fish, Sr., and the Politics of American Nationalism" (Ph.D. diss., Rutgers University, 1993); August Raymond Ogden, *The Dies Committee* (Westport, Conn.: Greenwood Press, 1984, orig. ed. 1945), 20–31; Powers, *Not Without Honor,* 87–91; Louise Pettibone Smith, *The Torch of Liberty* (New York: Dwight-King, 1959), 35–42.

For a good example of the kinds of evidence the Fish Committee gathered, see the testimony of the former New York City Police Commissioner Grover Whalen and that of John A. Lyons, head of the NYPD's red squad, "Investigation of Communist Propaganda," Hearings Before a Special Committee to Investigate Communist Activities in the United States, House of Representatives, 71st Cong., 2d sess., July 18, 19, 1930 (hereafter Fish Committee). Frank Donner notes the importance of this testimony in revealing the extent of Red Squad surveillance, *Protectors of Privilege,* 44, 47–50, 53–54, 59.

59. Ellen W. Schrecker, *No Ivory Tower: McCarthyism and the Universities* (New York: Oxford University Press, 1986), 68–71; Chamberlain, *Loyalty and Legislative Action,* 53–64; Robert W. Iversen, *The Communists and the Schools* (New York: Harcourt, Brace, 1959), 178–92.

60. The role of the press in American anticommunism has not received anywhere near the scholarly attention it deserves; yet, just about every treatment of countersubversion does mention it, even if only in passing, e.g., Heale, *American Anticommunism,* 110–13.

On the Hearst chain and the role of Richard Berlin, see Lindsay Chaney and Michael Cieply, *The Hearsts: Family and Empire — The Later Years* (New York: Simon and Schuster, 1981), 103–50. See also Jim Tuck, *McCarthyism and New York's Hearst Press: A Study of Roles in the Witch Hunt* (Lanham, Md.: University Press of America, 1995). FBI files and private papers reveal something of Berlin's views and activities, e.g., the correspondence between Berlin and J. B. Matthews in Box 652, Matthews Papers.

61. Pencak, *For God and Country,* 224; Kelley, *Hammer and Hoe,* 140–41.

62. Lowell Dyson, *Red Harvest: The Communist Party and American Farmers* (Lincoln: University of Nebraska Press, 1982), 83–92; Healey and Isserman, *Dorothy Healey Remembers,* 42–52; Auerbach, *Labor and Liberty,* 177–96; Pencak, *For God and Country,* 222, 250; Donner, *Protectors of Privilege,* 32; Daniels, *Bitter Harvest,* 141–257; Howard Kimeldorf, *Reds or Rackets? The Making of Radical and Conservative Unions on the Waterfront* (Berkeley and Los Angeles: University of California Press, 1988), 53–61; Bruce Nelson, *Workers on the Waterfront: Seamen, Longshoremen, and Unionism in the 1930s* (Urbana: University of Illinois Press, 1988), 71; Larry Ceplair and Steven Englund, *The Inquisition in Hollywood: Politics in the Film Community, 1930–1960* (Garden City, N.Y.: Anchor Press/Doubleday, 1980), 35–37.

63. Nelson, *Workers on the Waterfront,* 127–55; Kimeldorf, *Reds or Rackets?,* 101–10; Charles Larrowe, *Harry Bridges* (Westport, Conn.: Lawrence Hill, 1972), 32–61.

64. Kutler, *The American Inquisition,* 118–51; Larrowe, *Harry Bridges,* 138–248; Kimeldorf, *Reds or Rackets,* 61.

65. Irving Bernstein, *Turbulent Years* (Boston: Houghton Mifflin, 1969), 499–571; Cochran, *Labor and Communism,* 103–26; Roger Keeran, *The Communist Party and the Auto Workers Unions* (Bloomington: Indiana University Press, 1980), 148–85; Barbara S. Griffith, *The Crisis of American Labor: Operation Dixie and the Defeat of the CIO* (Philadelphia: Temple University Press, 1988), 8–11; Donner, *Protectors of Privilege,* 52–55; Pencak, *For God and Country,* 208–37; Auerbach, *Labor and Liberty,* 97–113, 131–50; Glen Jeansonne, *Gerald L. K. Smith: Minister of Hate* (New Haven: Yale University Press, 1988), 64–79.

66. "To become respectable," Daniel Bell notes, "was Gompers' and labor's main aim." See Bell, "The Problem of Ideological Rigidity," in John H. M. Laslett and Seymour Martin Lipset, *Failure of a Dream? Essays in the History of American Socialism* (New York: Doubleday, 1974), 95. On AFL anticommunism see Murray, *Red Scare,* 106–109, 268–69; Heale, *American Anticommunism,* 92; Pencak, *For God and Country,* 209, 215–16; Cochran, *Labor and Communism,* 39–41; Ellis Searles, testimony, Sept. 26, 1930, Fish Committee, 16–17.

67. For some examples of AFL red-baiting, see Nelson, *Workers on the Waterfront,* 118–26, 143; Mario T. Garcia, "Border Proletarians: Mexican-Americans and the International Union of Mine, Mill, and Smelter Workers, 1939," in Robert Asher and Charles Stephenson, eds., *Labor Divided: Race and Ethnicity in United States Labor Struggles, 1835–1960* (Albany: State University of New York Press, 1990), 91; Cochran, *Labor and Communism,* 67–68; Keeran, *The Communist Party and the Auto Workers Unions,* 97–117; Harvey A. Levenstein, *Communism, Anticommunism, and the CIO* (Westport, Conn.: Greenwood Press, 1981), 23–31, 104–109; Troncone, "Hamilton Fish, Sr., and the Politics of American Nationalism," 128–47; Matthew Woll, testimony, June 17, 1930, Fish Committee, 1–760.

68. The best general surveys of the labor movement's internal conflicts are Cochran, *Labor and Communism* and Levenstein, *Communism, Anticommunism, and the*

CIO. Useful on individual unions are Keeran, *The Communist Party and the Auto Workers Unions;* Ronald L. Filippelli and Mark McColloch, *Cold War in the Working Class: The Rise and Decline of the United Electrical Workers* (Albany: State University of New York Press, 1995); Joshua B. Freeman, *In Transit: The Transport Workers Union in New York City, 1933–1960* (New York: Oxford University Press, 1989); Vernon H. Jensen, *Nonferrous Metals Industry Unionism, 1932–1954* (Ithaca, N.Y.: Cornell University Press, 1954).

69. Iversen, *The Communists and the Schools,* 20–23, 33–58, 99–118; Marjorie Murphy, *Blackboard Unions: The AFT and the NEA, 1900–1980* (Ithaca, N.Y.: Cornell University Press, 1990), 150–74; David A. Shannon, *The Socialist Party of America* (Chicago: Quadrangle ed., 1967, orig. ed. 1955), 165.

70. On the factionalism within the UAW, see Nelson Lichtenstein, *The Most Dangerous Man in Detroit: Walter Reuther and the Fate of American Labor* (New York: Basic Books, 1995), 47–153; Bernstein, *Turbulent Years,* 554–71; Cochran, *Labor and Communism,* 127–38; Keeran, *The Communists and the Auto Workers Unions,* 186–207; Levenstein, *Communism, Anticommunism, and the CIO,* 52–56; Martin Halpern, *UAW Politics in the Cold War Era* (Albany: State University of New York Press, 1988), 13–26.

71. Lichtenstein, *The Most Dangerous Man in Detroit,* 122–28.

72. Filippelli and McColloch, *Cold War in the Working Class,* is the most recent treatment of the UE's internal politics. For the TWU, see Freeman, *In Transit.*

73. Jensen, *Nonferrous Metals Industry Unionism,* 49–138; Huntley, "Iron Ore Miners and Mine Mill in Alabama: 1933–1952," 95–109; Huntley, "The Red Scare and Black Workers in Alabama: The International Union of Mine, Mill, and Smelter Workers, 1945–1953," in Asher and Stephenson, *Labor Divided,* 134–36.

74. Donald F. Crosby, S.J., "The Politics of Religion: American Catholics and the Anti-Communist Impulse," in Robert Griffith and Athan Theoharis, eds., *The Specter* (New York: Franklin Watts, 1974), 20–38.

75. On Father Walsh, see Louis J. Gallagher, S.J., *Edmund A. Walsh, S.J.* (New York: 1962). On the relationship between Catholics, labor, and the left, see Steve Rosswurm, "The Catholic Church and the Left-Led Unions: Labor Priests, Labor Schools, and the ACTU," in Rosswurm, ed., *The CIO's Left-Led Unions* (New Brunswick, N.J.: Rutgers University Press, 1992), 119–37; David J. O'Brien, *American Catholics and Social Reform: The New Deal Years* (New York: Oxford University Press, 1968), 70–96; Marc Karson, "Catholic Anti-Socialism," in Laslett and Lipset, eds., *Failure of a Dream?,* 165–80.

76. Donald F. Crosby, S. J., "Boston's Catholics and the Spanish Civil War: 1936–1939," *New England Quarterly* 44 (March 1971): 82–100.

77. For an insightful discussion of Catholics and labor, see Joshua B. Freeman and Steve Rosswurm, "The Education of an Anti-Communist: Father John F. Cronin and the Baltimore Labor Movement," *Labor History* 33 (Spring 1992): 217–47; see also Rosswurm, "The Catholic Church and the Left-Led Unions," 119–37; O'Brien,

American Catholics and Social Reform, 97–119; Neil Betten, *American Catholicism and the Industrial Worker* (Gainesville: University Presses of Florida, 1976), passim; Gary Gerstle, "Catholic Corporatism, French-Canadian Workers, and Industrial Unionism in Rhode Island, 1938–1956," in Asher and Stephenson, eds., *Labor Divided,* 213–23; Patrick J. McGeever, *Rev. Charles Owen Rice: Apostle of Contradiction* (Pittsburgh, Pa.: Duquesne University Press, 1989); Freeman, *In Transit,* 104–107.

78. Rosswurm, "The Catholic Church and the Left-Led Unions"; Betten, *American Catholicism and the Industrial Worker,* 124–50; Freeman, *In Transit,* 137–51.

79. In addition to the works cited in 77 supra, see Douglas P. Seaton, *Catholics and Radicals: The Association of Catholic Trade Unionists and the American Labor Movement from Depression to Cold War* (Lewisburg, Pa.: Bucknell University Press, 1981).

80. Louis Francis Budenz, *This Is My Story* (New York: McGraw-Hill, 1947); Bella Dodd, *School of Darkness* (New York: Kenedy, 1954), 231–37, 244–45; L. L. Laughlin to Director, Dec. 8, 1958, Louis Budenz, no serial #; R.U.C. [name deleted], report, Nov. 20, 1953, Harry Dexter White, no serial #.

81. Francis Cardinal Spellman, "Do We Want a Soviet Peace?" *Cosmopolitan,* Nov. 1946, 27; George Sirgiovanni, *An Undercurrent of Suspicion* (New Brunswick, N.J.: Transaction, 1990), 27; Gerstle, "Catholic Corporatism, French-Canadian Workers, and Industrial Unionism in Rhode Island, 1938–1956," 222–23; O'Brien, *American Catholics and Social Reform,* 95–96; Freeman and Rosswurm, "The Education of an Anti-Communist." On the Knights of Columbus, see Christopher J. Kauffman, *Faith and Fraternalism: The History of the Knights of Columbus 1882–1982* (New York: Harper and Row, 1982).

82. Monsignor Charles Owen Rice, "Confessions of an Anti-Communist," *Labor History* 30 (Summer 1989), 453–54.

83. Frank Donner, "The Informers," *The Nation,* April 10, 1954; Herbert L. Packer, *Ex-Communist Witnesses* (Stanford: Stanford University Press, 1962), passim; Robert Morris, *No Wonder We Are Losing* (New York: Bookmailer, 1958), 121.

84. On the Socialist party, see W. A. Swanberg, *Norman Thomas: The Last Idealist* (New York: Scribner's, 1976) and Shannon, *The Socialist Party of America.* Much of the scholarship on the SP in the 1920s and 1930s looks at why the party declined. See, for example, the essays in Laslett and Lipset, eds., *Failure of a Dream?.* An informed critique of the most common view that Norman Thomas's "ideological rigidity," to use Daniel Bell's influential formulation, torpedoed the SP can be found in Frank A. Warren, *An Alternative Vision: The Socialist Party in the 1930's* (Bloomington: Indiana University Press, 1974).

85. Shannon, *The Socialist Party of America,* 210–17, 235–48; Swanberg, *Norman Thomas,* 166–73, 188–213.

86. Norman Thomas, "Your World and Mine," Socialist *Call,* Dec. 16, 1939, quoted in Corliss Lamont, ed., *The Trial of Elizabeth Gurley Flynn by the American Civil Liberties Union* (New York: Horizon Press, 1968), 147–48.

On the SFTU debacle, see Anthony Dunbar, *Against the Grain: Southern Radicals and Prophets, 1929–59* (Charlottesville: University of Virginia Press, 1981), 164–85; Dyson, *Red Harvest*, 150–67.

87. Steven M. Gillon, *Politics and Vision: The ADA and American Liberalism, 1947–1985* (New York: Oxford University Press, 1987), 9–11; Shannon, *The Socialist Party of America*, 241–48.

88. On the various anti-Stalinist sects, see Myers, *The Prophet's Army; Trotskyists in America, 1928–1941* (Westport, Conn.: Greenwood Press, 1977); Wald, *The New York Intellectuals;* Robert J. Alexander, *The Right Opposition: The Lovestoneites and the International Communist Opposition of the 1930s* (Westport, Conn.: Greenwood Press, 1981), 42–75; Jo Ann Ooiman Robinson, *Abraham Went Out: A Biography of A. J. Muste* (Philadelphia: Temple University Press, 1981); A. J. Muste, "My Experience in the Labor and Radical Struggles of the Thirties," in Rita James Simon, ed., *As We Saw the Thirties* (Urbana: University of Illinois Press, 1967), 125–50. On the 1934 strikes, see Bernstein, *Turbulent Years*, 218–52. On Mandel's earlier career in the Teachers Union, see Iversen, *The Communists and the Schools*, 21–22. On Gitlow, see his autobiography, Benjamin Gitlow, *I Confess: The Truth about American Communism* (New York: E. P. Dutton, 1940), as well as the many references to his CP career in Theodore Draper's *The Roots of American Communism* (New York: Viking, 1957) and *American Communism and Soviet Russia* (New York: Viking, 1960). On Budenz, see his autobiography, *This Is My Story*.

89. Myers, *The Prophet's Army*, 82–141; Alexander, *The Right Opposition*, 92–111.

90. Among the most important New York intellectuals were the following: Lionel Abel, James Burnham, F. W. Dupee, James T. Farrell, Sidney Hook, Mary McCarthy, Dwight Macdonald, William Phillips, Philip Rahv, Meyer Schapiro, Delmore Schwartz, Diana Trilling, Lionel Trilling, and Edmund Wilson. There was also a slightly younger generation of New York intellectuals like Leslie Fiedler, Irving Howe, Alfred Kazin, Irving Kristol, Seymour Martin Lipset, and Norman Podhoretz, who did not have quite the same experiences with the American CP.

The scholarship about the New York intellectuals is generally excellent, although almost as contradictory as its protagonists. In constructing what of necessity has had to be a grossly oversimplified account of their ideas and activities, I have relied upon the following works: Aaron, *Writers on the Left;* Alexander Bloom, *Prodigal Sons: The New York Intellectuals and Their World* (New York: Oxford University Press, 1986); Terry A. Cooney, *The Rise of the New York Intellectuals: Partisan Review and Its Circle* (Madison: University of Wisconsin Press, 1986); Arthur A. Ekirch, Jr., *Ideologies and Utopias: The Impact of the New Deal on American Thought* (Chicago: Quadrangle, 1969); James Burkhart Gilbert, *Writers and Partisans: A History of Literary Radicalism in America* (New York: John Wiley and Sons, 1968); Richard H. Pells, *Radical Visions and American Dreams: Culture and Social Thought in the Depression Years* (New York: Harper, 1973); and Wald, *The New York Intellectuals*.

91. Bloom, *Prodigal Sons,* 98–120; Cooney, *Rise of the New York Intellectuals,* 67–119; Wald, *The New York Intellectuals,* 101–27; John P. Diggins, *Up From Communism: Conservative Odysseys in American Intellectual History* (New York: Harper and Row, 1975), 160–98.

92. Bloom, *Prodigal Sons,* 109–119; Cooney, *The Rise of the New York Intellectuals,* 120–45; Wald, *The New York Intellectuals,* 128–63.

93. Max Shachtman, "Radicalism in the Thirties: The Trotskyist View," in Simon, ed., *As We Saw the Thirties,* 42.

94. Cooney, *The Rise of the New York Intellectuals,* 68, 87, 92, 95–119, 125, 136–39. See also Abbott Gleason, *Totalitarianism: The Inner History of the Cold War* (New York: Oxford University Press, 1995), 72–88.

95. Bloom, *Prodigal Sons,* 98–120; Myers, *The Prophet's Army,* 170–71.

96. For examples of Morris Ernst's correspondence, see Ernst to Franklin D. Roosevelt, Dec. 11, 1939, Mar. 4, 1940, Jan. 21, Feb. 21, Oct. 17, 1941, Roosevelt to Ernst, Mar. 6, 1940, Folder #96; Ernst to Roosevelt, Jan. 2, April 8, 28, Sept. 25, Dec. 28, 1942, April 1, 1943, Mar. 2, 1944, Roosevelt to Ernst, April 7, 1943, Folder #97; Ernst to Truman, Sept. 13, Nov. 14, 1945, Folder #181; Ernst to Hubert H. Humphrey, Aug. 7, 1949, Folder #138; Ernst to Dwight D. Eisenhower, May 2, 1952, Folder #220, all in Morris L. Ernst Papers, Harry Ransom Humanities Research Center, University of Texas at Austin. See also Harrison E. Salisbury, "The Strange Correspondence of Morris Ernst and John Edgar Hoover, 1939–1964," *The Nation* (Dec. 1, 1984): 575–89.

97. Neil Brant to Ernst, Jan. 7, 1938, Ken Crawford to Ernst, Jan. 24, 1940, Folder #175; Ernst to Roy Howard, Oct. 20, 24, 1945, Folder #163, Ernst Papers. For examples of Ernst's campaign for disclosure, see Ernst to Roosevelt, Dec. 11, 1939, Jan. 21, 31, 1941, to Marguerite LeHand, Feb. 7, 1941, LeHand to Ernst, Feb. 10, 1941, Folder #96; Nathaniel Goodrich to Ernst, Jan. 20, 1940, Folder #175; Harold Ickes to Ernst, Nov. 15, 1939, Folder #171; Ernst to Tom Clark, Oct. 9, 1946, Folder #181; John Haynes Holmes to Ernst, Jan. 27, 1949, Folder #146; Marquis Childs to Ernst, March 15, 1944, Folder #138; Ernst to Richard Nixon, Jan. 26, Feb. 25, 1948, Feb. 15, 1949, Folder #55, Ernst Papers.

98. W. H. Holly to Ernst, Oct. 15, 1937, Ernst to John P. Devaney, Oct. 19, 1937, M. L. Severn to Ernst, Nov. 19, 1937, Philip Nichols, Jr., to Osmund K. Fraenkel, Dec. 9, 1937, Ernst to Nichols, Dec. 23, 1937, to Mortimer Riemer, Dec. 30, 1937, to Felix Cohen, Jan. 10, 1938, to Thurmond Arnold, Feb. 17, 1938, Folder #334; "Criticism of the Report of the Committee on International Law of the National Lawyers Guild with respect to the relations between the United States and Spain," mimeo, Dec. 30, 1937, Folder #335, Ernst Papers.

99. Ann Fagan Ginger, "The Third Annual Convention: 1939 in Chicago," in Ginger and Eugene M. Tobin, eds., *The National Lawyers Guild: From Roosevelt through Reagan* (Philadelphia: Temple University Press, 1988), 32–34; Minutes of the Meeting, Feb. 10, 1939, National Lawyers Guild Records, Meiklejohn Civil Liberties Institute, Berkeley, Calif. (hereafter NLG Records).

On the situation within labor see Cochran, *Labor and Communism,* 143–55. On the similar conflicts within the Hollywood left-liberal community, see Ceplair and Englund, *The Inquisition in Hollywood,* 134–53.

100. Martin Popper, "Resignations from the National Lawyers Guild," in Ginger and Tobin, eds., *The National Lawyers Guild,* 34–36; Press Release, Feb. 24, 1939, NLG Records; Report of the Secretary of the National Lawyers Guild for the Period April 1–September 30, 1939, mimeo, Folder #335, Ernst Papers.

101. Lucille Milner, *Education of an American Liberal* (New York: Horizon Press, 1954), 263–65; Lamont, ed., *The Trial of Elizabeth Gurley Flynn,* 12–20; Samuel Walker, *In Defense of American Liberties: A History of the ACLU* (New York: Oxford University Press, 1990), 127–33.

102. Lamont, ed., *The Trial of Elizabeth Gurley Flynn,* 97–176.

103. Eugene Lyons to J. B. Matthews, Nov. 18, 1948, Matthews Papers, Box 672; Joseph Kornfeder to "Dear Friend," n. d., ibid., Box 668; "Certification of Incorporation of the Federation of Former Communists, Inc." Paul Crouch Papers, Box 2, Hoover Institution.

3: "IN THE INTEREST OF NATIONAL SECURITY": THE ROOSEVELT ADMINISTRATION

1. A recent example of such left-wing revisionism occurs in Ann Fagan Ginger's biography of the civil liberties lawyer Carol Weiss King, in which Ginger claims incorrectly that Roosevelt vetoed the 1940 Smith Act. Ginger, *Carol Weiss King: Human Rights Lawyer, 1895–1952* (Niwot, Colo.: University Press of Colorado, 1993), 320.

2. Frances Perkins, oral history interview, VII, 238, Columbia Oral History Project, Rare Book and Manuscript Library, Butler Library, Columbia University (hereafter COHP); Henry A. Wallace, *The Price of Vision: The Diary of Henry Wallace,* ed. John Blum (Boston: Houghton Mifflin, 1973), 131.

3. Franklin D. Roosevelt, memoranda, to Frances Perkins, Aug. 29, Sept. 18, 1935, in Official File (hereafter FDR-OF) 1750, Franklin D. Roosevelt Library, Hyde Park, N.Y. (hereafter FDRL). See also Roosevelt, *The Public Papers and Addresses of Franklin D. Roosevelt,* 1940 vol., Samuel I. Rosenman, ed. (New York: Macmillan, 1941), 35–36; 92–93; Robert Cohen, *When the Old Left Was Young: Student Radicals and America's First Mass Student Movement, 1929–1941* (New York: Oxford University Press, 1993), 299–300.

For Roosevelt's views about deporting Harry Bridges, see Roosevelt to Francis Biddle, May 4, 1942, Box 2, Francis Biddle Papers, FDRL; Roosevelt to Biddle, Jan. 14, 1944, President's Secretary's File (hereafter FDR-PSF), FDRL; Francis Biddle, *In Brief Authority* (Garden City, N.Y.: Doubleday, 1962), 238.

4. Richard Gid Powers, *G-Men: Hoover's FBI in American Popular Culture* (Carbondale: Southern Illinois University Press, 1983). On Roosevelt's relations with Hoover, see Powers, *Secrecy and Power: The Life of J. Edgar Hoover* (New York: Free Press, 1987), 179–274; Athan G. Theoharis and John Stuart Cox, *The Boss: J. Edgar*

Hoover and the Great American Inquisition (Philadelphia: Temple University Press, 1988), 133–56; Biddle, *In Brief Authority,* 166.

5. For the text of Hoover's Aug. 24, 1936, memorandum about his meeting with Roosevelt see Athan Theoharis, ed., *From the Secret Files of J. Edgar Hoover* (Chicago: Ivan R. Dee, 1991), 180–81. The existence of this memo was revealed in the mid-1970s by the Senate's post-Watergate investigations of the FBI and CIA. See U. S. Congress, Senate, Select Committee to Study Governmental Operations with Respect to Intelligence Activities, *Final Report,* Book III, "Supplementary Detailed Staff Reports on Intelligence Activities and the Rights of Americans," 94th Cong., 2d sess., Apr. 23, 1976, 392–405 (hereafter SDSRIARA); Kenneth O'Reilly, *Hoover and the Un-Americans: The FBI, HUAC, and the Red Menace* (Philadelphia: Temple University Press, 1983), 22; Athan Theoharis, *Spying on Americans: Political Surveillance from Hoover to the Huston Plan* (Philadelphia: Temple University Press, 1978), 65–70; Frank J. Donner, *The Age of Surveillance: The Aims and Methods of America's Political Intelligence System* (New York: Knopf, 1980), 52–56.

6. Theoharis, *From the Secret Files of J. Edgar Hoover,* 180–81.

7. George Wolfskill, *The Revolt of the Conservatives: A History of the American Liberty League, 1934–1940* (Boston: Houghton Mifflin, 1962); M. J. Heale, *American Anticommunism: Combating the Enemy Within, 1830–1970* (Baltimore: Johns Hopkins University Press, 1990), 116; Harvey Klehr, *The Heyday of American Communism: The Depression Decade* (New York: Basic Books, 1984), 194; Robert J. Goldstein, *Political Repression in Modern America from 1870 to the Present* (Cambridge, Mass.: Schenkman, 1978), 217.

8. On the congressional opposition to the New Deal, see James T. Patterson, *Congressional Conservatism and the New Deal: The Growth of the Conservative Coalition in Congress, 1933–1939* (Lexington: University of Kentucky Press, 1967).

9. Alan Brinkley, *The End of Reform: New Deal Liberalism in Recession and War* (New York: Knopf, 1995), 15–30.

10. August Raymond Ogden, *The Dies Committee* (Westport, Conn.: Greenwood Press ed., 1984, orig. ed. 1945), 30–46; Walter Goodman, *The Committee: The Extraordinary Career of the House Committee on Un-American Activities* (New York: Farrar, Straus, and Giroux, 1968), 3–23.

11. Representative Herman Eberharter, quoted in Goodman, *The Committee,* 87–88.

12. Robert E. Stripling, *The Red Plot Against America,* ed. Bob Considine (Drexel Hill, Pa.: Bell Publishing, 1949), 31, 38; Ogden, *The Dies Committee,* 57–62; O'Reilly, *Hoover and the Un-Americans,* 38–60; Theoharis and Cox, *The Boss,* 155–56; William Pencak, *For God and Country: The American Legion, 1919–1941* (Boston: Northeastern University Press, 1989), 249–50; Rodney G. Minott, *Peerless Patriots: Organized Veterans and the Spirit of Americanism* (Washington, D.C.: Public Affairs Press, 1962), 98.

The papers of J. B. Matthews in the Special Collections Department, William R. Perkins Library, Duke University, contain interesting correspondence from Benjamin Mandel about the committee's operations from the late 1930s and early 1940s.

13. Roosevelt, press release, Oct. 25, 1938, in FDR-OF 320; Harold Ickes, *The Secret Diary of Harold Ickes,* vol. 2 (New York: Simon and Schuster, 1954), 455, 506–507, 528–29, 547–49, 574; Norman Markowitz, *The Rise and Fall of the People's Century: Henry A. Wallace and American Liberalism, 1941–1948* (New York: Free Press, 1973), 127–28.

14. O'Reilly, *Hoover and the Un-Americans,* 57–60; *The Secret Diary of Harold Ickes,* vol. 2, 641–42; "K," memorandum for (Stephen) Early, Jan. 9, 1940, FDR-OF 320.

15. Perkins, COHP, VII, 176; Robert H. Jackson, oral history interview, COHP, 939–40. The fullest accounts of the NLRB's troubles during this period are in James A. Gross, *The Reshaping of the National Labor Relations Board* (Albany: State University of New York Press, 1981) and Frances Perkins's oral history.

16. Gross, *The Reshaping of the National Labor Relations Board,* passim; James H. Rowe, Jr., memoranda to Roosevelt, Aug. 31, Sept. 7, 1940, FDR-OF 716.

17. On the Bridges case, see Stanley I. Kutler, *The American Inquisition: Justice and Injustice in the Cold War* (New York: Hill and Wang, 1982), 118–51, and Charles P. Larrowe, *Harry Bridges* (Westport, Conn.: Lawrence Hill, 1972). I have also relied on Frances Perkins's oral history and the biography of Bridges's attorney, Ginger, *Carol Weiss King.*

18. Perkins, COHP, VII, 472; Martin Dies to Robert Jackson, Oct. 29, 1938, FDR-OF 320.

19. Perkins, COHP, VII, 475, 500–521; George Martin, *Madame Secretary: Frances Perkins* (Boston: Houghton Mifflin, 1976), 413–16; *The Secret Diary of Harold Ickes,* vol. 2, 550; James Farley to the president, July 26, 1939, FDR-OF 1750.

20. Landis, quoted in Ginger, *Carol Weiss King,* 275, 277; Larrowe, *Harry Bridges,* 176–215; Kutler, *The American Inquisition,* 131–33.

21. Michal R. Belknap, *Cold War Political Justice: The Smith Act, the Communist Party, and American Civil Liberties* (Westport, Conn.: Greenwood Press, 1977), 22; Jackson, COHP, 879.

22. The most useful overview of Roosevelt's foreign policy during this period is in Robert Dallek, *Franklin D. Roosevelt and American Foreign Policy, 1932–1945* (New York: Oxford University Press, 1979).

23. James G. Ryan, *Earl Browder: The Public Life of an American Communist* (Tuscaloosa: University of Alabama Press, 1997), 172–83.

24. Mimeo, n. d., "We Fight for Freedom," in Samuel Adams Darcy Papers, Tamiment Institute Library and Wagner Labor Archives, Elmer Holmes Bobst Library, New York University; *The Secret Diary of Harold Ickes,* vol. 3, 97.

25. Ogden, *The Dies Committee,* 142, 196–98; Frank Donner, *Protectors of Privilege: Red Squads and Police Repression in Urban America* (Berkeley and Los Ange-

les: University of California Press, 1990), 52–53, 56–57; O'Reilly, *Hoover and the Un-Americans,* 44–46.

26. O'Reilly, *Hoover and the Un-Americans,* 44–46; Powers, *Secrecy and Power,* 235; Peter N. Carroll, *The Odyssey of the Abraham Lincoln Brigade: Americans in the Spanish Civil War* (Stanford: Stanford University Press, 1994), 230–31.

27. Mimeo, "People's Rights Reporter," Sept. 26, 1940; typed newsletter, Dec. 23, 1940; Southern California branch of the American Civil Liberties Union, *The Open Forums,* Aug. 16, 1941, all in Darcy Papers; Maurice Isserman, *Which Side Were You On? The American Communist Party during the Second World War* (Middletown, Conn.: Wesleyan University Press, 1982), 67–71.

28. Thomas Joseph Edward Walker, "The International Workers Order" (Ph.D. diss., University of Chicago, 1982), 55. On the Rapp-Coudert investigations, see Ellen W. Schrecker, *No Ivory Tower: McCarthyism and the Universities* (New York: Oxford University Press, 1986), 63–83; Lawrence H. Chamberlain, *Loyalty and Legislative Action: A Survey of Activity by the New York State Legislature, 1919–1949* (Ithaca, N.Y.: Cornell University Press, 1951). For other state investigations during the late 1930s and early 1940s, see Edward L. Barrett, Jr., *The Tenney Committee: Legislative Investigation of Subversive Activities in California* (Ithaca, N.Y.: Cornell University Press, 1951); Michael Heale, "Patriots All," unpublished ms. in the author's possession; memorandum, SAC, Philadelphia, to Director, Mar. 14, 1951, Responsibilities Program, #119, reel 1, "McCarthy Era Blacklisting of School Teachers, College Professors, and Other Public Employees: The FBI Responsibilities Program File and the Dissemination of Information Policy File," ed. Kenneth O'Reilly (Bethesda, Md.: University Publications of America, 1989) (hereafter Responsibilities Program).

29. Kutler, *The American Inquisition,* 134–35; Monsignor John A. Ryan to Roosevelt, Jan. 19, 1940, FDR-OF 133-A; unsigned, undated memorandum, on H.R. 6724, in FDR-OF 5708; Civil Service Commission, Departmental Circular, No. 222, June 20, 1940, Box 41, James Rowe Papers, FDRL; Belknap, *Cold War Political Justice,* 25–26; James H. Rowe, Jr., memorandum, n. d., Harold Smith to Steve Early, June 27, 1940, Robert Jackson to Harold Smith, June 25, 1940, all in FDR-OF 5708.

The communist attorney John Abt recalls that at the time Jackson took over the Justice Department, he told Abt, "Well, John, while I'm attorney general at least, the Roosevelt years won't end like the second Wilson administration with the Palmer Raids." John J. Abt with Michael Myerson, *Advocate and Activist: Memoirs of an American Communist Lawyer* (Urbana: University of Illinois Press, 1993), 73.

30. Congressman Hobbs, quoted in Larrowe, *Harry Bridges,* 222.

31. Congressman Albert Gore to Roosevelt, Feb. 6, 1940, Robert Jackson to Roosevelt, Feb. 9, 1940, Jackson to Sumner Welles, May 15, 1940, Welles to Roosevelt, May 18, 1940, press release, May 22, 1940, all in FDR-OF 15-D; Robert H. Jackson, COHP, 998–1000, 1030–34.

32. Dallek, *Franklin D. Roosevelt and American Foreign Policy,* 171–217.

33. On the CP's antiwar activities, see Isserman, *Which Side Were You On?*, 55–102; Hoover, memorandum, Nov. 15, 1939, in Hoover to Watson, Nov. 15, 1939; Hoover to Watson, July 13, 1940, both in FDR-OF 10-B. See also Summary of File references, Mar. 13, 1950, George Mink, #258; Jackson, COHP, 1040; Perkins, COHP, VII, 279–80.

34. Bruce Nelson, *Workers on the Waterfront: Seamen, Longshoremen, and Unionism in the 1930s* (Urbana: University of Illinois Press, 1988), 262.

35. Nelson Lichtenstein, *Labor's War at Home: The CIO in World War II* (New York: Cambridge University Press, 1982), 45–46; Bert Cochran, *Labor and Communism: The Conflict That Shaped American Unions* (Princeton: Princeton University Press, 1977), 64, 156–64; Isserman, *Which Side Were You On?*, 94; Ronald L. Filippelli, "The United Electrical, Radio and Machine Workers of America, 1933–1949: The Struggle for Control" (Ph.D. diss., Pennsylvania State University, 1970), 91.

36. Cochran, *Labor and Communism*, 156–63; *The Secret Diary of Harold Ickes*, vol. 3, 190; J. Parnell Thomas, telegram to Roosevelt, May 5, 1941, FDR-OF 263.

37. Jackson, COHP, 948.

38. J. Parnell Thomas, telegram to Roosevelt, May 13, 1941, OF 263, FDRL; Cochran, *Labor and Communism*, 163.

39. Lichtenstein, *Labor's War at Home*, 56–63; Roger Keeran, *The Communist Party and the Auto Workers Unions* (Bloomington: Indiana University Press, 1980), 216–18; Jackson, COHP, 947–52; Isserman, *Which Side Were You On?*, 87–100.

40. The most useful source for the labor troubles at Allis-Chalmers is Steven Meyer, *"Stalin Over Wisconsin," The Making and Unmaking of Militant Unionism, 1900–1950* (New Brunswick, N.J.: Rutgers University Press, 1992).

41. Hoover to Watson, May 24, June 14, 1940, FDR-OF 10-B; Robert Patterson, memorandum to the president, April 2, 1941, and Henry Stimson to FDR, April 5, 1941, both in FDR-PSF; Perkins, COHP, VII, 903–907; *The Secret Diary of Harold Ickes*, vol. 3, 455.

42. James H. Rowe, Jr., memorandum to Attorney General, April 9, 1942, Box 42, Rowe Papers, FDRL.

43. Ibid.; Isserman, *Which Side Were You On?*, 130–32.

44. Morris Ernst to Roosevelt, April 8, 1942, Morris L. Ernst Papers, Harry Ransom Humanities Research Center, University of Texas at Austin. See also Wallace, *The Price of Vision*, 121–22, 130–31, 158; Isserman, *Which Side Were You On?*, 130; Ickes, *The Secret Diary of Harold Ickes*, vol. 3, 135; George Sirgiovanni, *An Undercurrent of Suspicion: Anti-Communism in America during World War II* (New Brunswick, N.J.: Transaction Publishers, 1990). Teamster president Dan Tobin also wanted the Soviet Union to clamp down on the party. Tobin, telegram to FDR, Sept. 25, 1941, FDR-OF 263; "We Proudly Present: The Story of the National Council of American-Soviet Friendship, 1943–1953," pamphlet, Box 1, National Council of American-Soviet Friendship Papers, Tamiment.

45. Ryan, *Earl Browder*, 204–5; for examples of elite efforts to obtain Browder's

release, see Edwin Borchard, Zechariah Chafee, Jr., et al. to Dear Friend, Mar. 5, 1942, Elbert Thomas to Roosevelt, Feb. 9, 1942, Ickes to Roosevelt, April 1, 1942, press release, May 16, 1942, all in FDR-OF 3997; Charles Burlingham to Francis Biddle, Dec. 5, 1951, Biddle, memorandum of luncheon with Roosevelt, May 4, 1942, Box 2, Biddle Papers; Ryan, Browder ms., 359–61. On the campaign to deport Raïssa Browder, see Grace Hutchins to Molly Dewson, Dec. 19, 1943, Dewson to Eleanor Roosevelt, Dec. 21, 1941, Biddle, memorandum for the president, Jan. 6, 1944, Roosevelt to Biddle, Jan. 14, 1944, all in FDR-PSF.

46. Biddle, *In Brief Authority*, 297–305; Biddle, memorandum of luncheon with FDR, May 4, 1942, Box 2, Biddle Papers. For a sample of the correspondence urging FDR to drop the Bridges case, see Sheridan Downey to Roosevelt, Dec. 23, 1941, Philip E. Murray to Roosevelt, Feb. 7, 1945, Mon C. Wallgren to Roosevelt, Feb. 28, 1945, J. F. Byrnes, memorandum to Roosevelt, Mar. 14, 1945, all in FDR-OF 1750.

47. Ginger, *Carol Weiss King*, 363–80, 398–411; *Schneiderman v. United States*, 320 U. S. 118 (1943); *Bridges v. Wixon*, 326 U.S. 135 (1945).

48. Isserman, *Which Side Were You On?*, 143–45; Karl G. Yoneda, "Manzanar Diary," Mar. 23, 1942, in Yoneda Papers, Bancroft Library, University of California, Berkeley. This acceptance of Japanese relocation was so widespread that even CIO unions with large numbers of Japanese members did not protest. See Chris Friday, *Organizing Asian American Labor: The Pacific Coast Canned-Salmon Industry, 1870–1942* (Philadelphia: Temple University Press, 1994), 187. On the civil liberties issues involved in the Japanese internment, see Peter Irons, *Justice at War: The Story of the Japanese American Internment Cases* (New York: Oxford University Press, 1983).

49. There is little scholarship on the Trotskyist Smith Act case. While recognizing its implications for the later Smith Act cases, most writers tend to dismiss it in a sentence or two. Belknap, *Cold War Political Justice*, 39; Robert McCloskey, *The Modern Supreme Court* (Cambridge: Harvard University Press, 1972), 49; Isserman, *Which Side Were You On?*, 123–24.

50. Trial transcript in *Vincent Raymond Dunne et al. v. United States*, U.S. Circuit Court of Appeals, 8th Circuit, filed April 1, 1943, reel 35, microfilm ed., filmed for the Fund for the Republic, Inc., New York; Biddle, *In Brief Authority*, 151–52; Constance Ashton Myers, *The Prophet's Army: Trotskyists in America, 1928–1941* (Westport, Conn.: Greenwood Press, 1977), 177–85.

51. S.T.E. [Early] memorandum for the president, Mar. 20, 1942, FDR-PSF; Biddle, *In Brief Authority*, 237–48; Belknap, *Cold War Political Justice*, 40; Leo P. Ribuffo, *The Old Christian Right: The Protestant Far Right from the Great Depression to the Cold War* (Philadelphia: Temple University Press, 1983), 178–224.

52. On the persistence of anticommunism during the war, see Sirgiovanni, *An Undercurrent of Suspicion* and Les K. Adler, *The Red Image: American Attitudes toward Communism in the Cold War Era* (New York: Garland, 1991).

53. Robert A. Rosenstone, *Crusade of the Left: The Lincoln Battalion in the Span-*

ish Civil War (Lanham, Md.: University Press of America, 1980), 346–50; Carroll, *The Odyssey of the Abraham Lincoln Brigade,* 244–49, 252–64, 269–75; Harvey Klehr, John Earl Haynes, and Fridrikh Igorevich Firsov, *The Secret World of American Communism* (New Haven: Yale University Press, 1995), 259–86; Isserman, *Which Side Were You On?,* 182–83; Earl Browder to Roosevelt, Oct. 22, 1942, FDR-OF 3997; Jack Bjoze (executive secretary, Veterans of the Abraham Lincoln Brigade) to Roosevelt, Jan. 15, 1943, FDR-OF 5308; Bjoze to Eleanor Roosevelt, Mar. 12, 1943, FDR-OF 320; Elmer Fehlhaber, interview with Bill Schechter, Feb. 5, 1981, Oral History of the American Left, Tamiment Institute Library and Wagner Labor Archives, Elmer Holmes Bobst Library, New York University, New York City; Saul Wellman, unpublished autobiography, Box 15, Nat Ganley Papers, Archives of Labor and Urban Affairs, Walter P. Reuther Library, Wayne State University, Detroit, Mich.; Robert G. Colodny, "An American Dark Age: Echoes and Memories," *Pittsburgh History* (Summer 1990): 83–85.

54. Roosevelt, confidential memorandum to secretaries of State, Treasury, War, Navy, Commerce, Postmaster General, and Attorney General, June 26, 1939, FDR-OF 1661; Hoover to Watson, July 6, 1940, FDR-OF 10-B; Biddle, memorandum to Roosevelt, Oct. 8, 1941, FDR-PSF; Belknap, *Cold War Political Justice,* 36; Donner, *The Age of Surveillance,* 56–60.

55. Roosevelt, memorandum to Attorney General Jackson, May 21, 1940, FDR-PSF. For a useful discussion of the FBI's wiretapping operations, see Athan Theoharis, "FBI Wiretapping: A Case Study of Bureaucratic Autonomy," *Political Science Quarterly* 107 (1992): 101–22.

56. Michael Krinsky, Jonathan Moore, and Ann Mari Buitrago, "FBI Operations, 1940–1941," in Ann Fagan Ginger and Eugene M. Tobin, eds., *The National Lawyers Guild: From Roosevelt through Reagan* (Philadelphia: Temple University Press, 1988), 36–37; Biddle to Assistant Attorney General Cox and Hoover, July 16, 1943, SDSRIARA, 420–21. For more on the custodial detention program see ibid., 413–20 and Theoharis, *Spying on Americans,* 40–44.

57. Jackson, COHP, 974–81; Perkins, COHP, VII, 290; memorandum, D. M. Ladd to Director, April 12, 1944, Confidential Plant Informants, #231; memorandum, Ladd to Director, Oct. 10, 1944, ibid., serial # illegible; memorandum, Executives Conference to Director, July 14, 1950, ibid., #26[4?]; Joan Jensen, *Army Surveillance in America, 1775–1980* (New Haven: Yale University Press, 1991), 211–29.

58. Lieutenant Colonel G. E. Strong, enclosure in Browder to Roosevelt, Oct. 22, 1942, FDR-OF 3997; Rowe, memorandum for the president, June 26, 1941, FDR-PSF; Rowe, memorandum to Attorney General, April 9, 1942, Box 42, Rowe Papers; Hugh De Lacy to Biddle, Mar. 12, 1945, FDR-OF 133-A.

James Carey, the ousted president of the UE, told the FBI that he feared the union might be a security danger if Russia made a separate peace. Guy Hottel to Director, July 3, 1943, United Electrical, Machine, and Radio Workers of America, #316 (hereafter UE).

59. There is almost no scholarship on FAECT apart from Bernard Palmer, "The Heritage of Architects, Engineers, Chemists and Technicians (FAECT-CIO)," in Ann Fagan Ginger and David Christiano, eds., *The Cold War Against Labor* (Berkeley, Calif.: Meiklejohn Civil Liberties Institute, 1987), 378–84. I have also relied on two interviews, one with Martin Cooper that Rachel Bernstein conducted in December 1985 (transcript in the author's possession) and one I did with Beryl Gilman in November 1993.

For some representative FBI responses to the union, see S. V. Constant to Assistant Chief of Staff, G-2, May 20, 1941, in Sherman Miles to Director, June 4, 1941, FAECT #25; [name deleted], report, San Francisco, Jan. 7, 1943, ibid., #140; R. A. Guerin to Director, May 1, 1945, ibid., #295; [name deleted], report, Norfolk, Va., May 29, 1945, ibid., #302; memorandum, SAC, San Francisco to Director, Jan. 18, 1946, ibid., #317.

While they were on the HUAC staff in the early 1940s, both Benjamin Mandel and J. B. Matthews were interested in FAECT and its leaders. See Mandel to Matthews, Apr. 18, 19, 23, 29, 30, May 23, 1940, Box 692, Matthews Papers.

60. Henry Stimson, memorandum for the president, Sept. 9, 1943, File W3, Map Room, 171, FDRL (document courtesy of Barton Bernstein).

61. Jackson, COHP, 1039–40; Perkins, COHP, VII, 279–80; E. E. Conroy, report, Jan. 1, 1943, UE, #193; SAC, New Haven, report, Jan. 27, 1943, ibid., #213; SAC, St. Louis, report, Feb. 18, 1943, ibid., #228; Conroy, telegram to Director, Apr. 1, 1943, ibid., #260.

62. Memorandum, A. H. Belmont to Ladd, July 28, 1950, Confidential Plant Informants, #263; memorandum, Lawrence M. C. Smith to Director, May 2, 1942, UE, #22; Smith to Director, April 22, 1942, FAECT, serial # illegible; report [name deleted], Newark, Nov. 21, 1944, ibid., #266; Ickes, *The Secret Diary of Harold Ickes,* vol. 3, 461; Jackson, COHP, 976–79; John M. Coffee to Roosevelt, May 31, 1943, FDR-OF 10B,; report [name deleted], New York, Mar. 23, 1945, FAECT, #289; Jensen, *Army Surveillance in America,* 220–21, 226; Perkins, COHP, VII, 906.

63. Jane DeHart Mathews, *The Federal Theatre, 1935–1939, Plays, Relief, and Politics* (Princeton: Princeton University Press, 1967), 199–234; Ogden, *The Dies Committee,* 48–63, 70, 88–96, 142–45; Goodman, *The Committee,* 59–166.

64. Ogden, *The Dies Committee,* 48–63, 70, 88–96, 142–45; O'Reilly, *Hoover and the Un-Americans,* 37–74; Robert E. Cushman, "The Purge of Federal Employees Accused of Disloyalty," *Public Administration Review* 3 (Autumn 1943): 297–316; Ladd to Director, Nov. 27, 1953, Harry Dexter White, no serial number.

65. Martin Dies to Attorney General, Oct. 17, 1941, quoted in Edwin D. Dickinson, memorandum to Fahy, Rowe, Carusi, Aug. 26, 1942, Box 42, Rowe Papers; Ogden, *The Dies Committee,* 244–48, 260–63, 274–76; Goodman, *The Committee,* 131–33; Markowitz, *The Rise and Fall of the People's Century,* 67–73; Milo Perkins, memorandum for the vice president, Mar. 30, 1942, FDR-OF 320.

66. Text of Public Law No. 135, 77th Cong., in letter from Attorney General, Sept. 1,

1942, House of Representatives, 77th Cong., 2d sess., Document No. 833; Biddle to Roosevelt, Oct. 26, 1942, FDR-OF 10-L.

67. Allen Weinstein, *Perjury: The Hiss-Chambers Case* (New York: Knopf, 1978), 346, 351; S. B. McKee to Hoover, Jan. 5, 1942, White, #1; Ladd to E. A. Tamm, March 30, 1942, ibid., #3; report, April 8, 1942, ibid., #4.

68. Nathan Witt to Rowe, Dec. 22, 1941, Rowe to Witt, Dec. 24, 1941, Edward H. Hickey to Rowe, Jan. 6, 1942, all in Box 43, Rowe Papers; Witt to Rowe, Jan. 26, 1942, Box 41, ibid.; "Federal Bureau of Investigation Report," August 22, 1942, in Attorney General Letter to Congress, Sept. 1, 1942, 16–17; Interdepartmental Committee on Employee Investigations, draft "Outline of Policy and Procedure," n. d., Box 2, Biddle Papers; Goodman, *The Committee*, 139–52.

69. Cushman, "The Purge of Federal Employees Accused of Disloyalty"; Rowe, memoranda to Attorney General, Feb. 13, 14, March 23, 1942, Box 42, Rowe Papers.

70. Rowe, memoranda for Attorney General, Feb. 13, 14, 1942, June 23, 1943, Box 42, Rowe Papers; Rowe, memorandum for Attorney General, July 1, 1942, Box 2, Biddle Papers; Ickes to Roosevelt, May 15, June 3, 1943, Biddle to Roosevelt, May 27, June 10, 1943, Roosevelt to Ickes, June 15, 1943, all in FDR-OF 1661-A; Ickes to Roosevelt, Aug. 11, 1943, FDR-OF 10-L.

71. Biddle, memorandum to the president, Oct. 8, 1941, FDR-PSF; Director to Karl E. Mundt, Jan. 28, 1947, Carl Marzani, #26x.

72. Letter from Attorney General, Sept. 1, 1942, House Doc., No. 833; Director, memorandum for Attorney General, Mar. 18, 1942, Box 42, Rowe Papers; Ladd to Director, Nov. 27, 1953, White, no serial number; Ladd to Director, Nov. 10, 1953, ibid., #59; E. A. Tamm to Director, Dec. 8, 1947 in Belmont to Ladd, Nov. 11, 1953, ibid., #75; Louis B. Nichols to Clyde Tolson, Nov. 20, 1953, ibid., no serial number; Ladd, memorandum, to Director, Jan. 21, 1947, Marzani, #70.

73. Director to Col. William J. Donovan, Aug. 20, 1942, Marzani, #9; Director, memorandum to the Interdepartmental Committee on Employee Investigation, June [date unclear] 1943, ibid., #14; Lt. W. H. Miley to Lt. Col. O. C. Doering, Oct. 7, 1944, ibid., no serial number; Stephen J. Spingarn, "Memorandum on the Report of the Investigation of Thomas I. Emerson, Dated October 31, 1941," Jan. 16, 1942; Spingarn to T. F. Wilson, April 7, 8, 1942; draft letter from administrative assistant to secretary [of the Treasury] to Hoover, April 7, 1942, Box 38, Stephen J. Spingarn Papers, Harry S. Truman Library, Independence, Missouri (hereafter HSTL).

74. Director, memorandum for Attorney General, Mar. 18, 1942, Box 42, Rowe Papers.

75. Rowe, memorandum for Attorney General, April 9, 1942, Box 42, Rowe Papers; Spingarn to T. F. Wilson and Jordan, May 4, 1942, Box 38, Spingarn Papers.

76. Director to Roosevelt, June 2, 1942, FDR-OF 10-B.

77. Director to Roosevelt, June 2, 1942, FDR-OF 10-B; Herbert Mitgang, *Dangerous Dossiers: Exposing the Secret War against America's Greatest Writers* (New York: Ballantine, 1989), 124–27; Natalie Robins, *Alien Ink: The FBI's War on Freedom of Ex-*

pression (New York: William Morrow, 1992), 218–29; Wallace, *The Price of Vision,* 72, 332; XXX, "Washington Gestapo," *The Nation,* July 17, 24, 1943.

78. Carl Marzani, interview with the author, Sept. 16, 1992; Gary May, *Un-American Activities: The Trials of William Remington* (New York: Oxford University Press, 1994), 62–67.

79. Eleanor Bontecou, *The Federal Loyalty-Security Program* (Ithaca, N.Y.: Cornell University Press, 1953), 15.

4: "THEY ARE EVERYWHERE": THE COMMUNIST IMAGE

1. Report [name deleted], Washington, D.C., July 31, 1942, in Carl Marzani, #9; Marzani, interview with the author, Sept. 16, 1992.

2. Robert J. Lamphere and Tom Schachtman, *The FBI–KGB War* (New York: Random House, 1986), 64–65. On the "image-creating" capacity of the criminal justice system, see Otto Kirchheimer, *Political Justice: The Use of Legal Procedure for Political Ends* (Princeton: Princeton University Press, 1961), 4–20; Lawrence M. Friedman, *Crime and Punishment in American History* (New York: Basic Books, 1993), 3–15; and Michal R. Belknap, *Cold War Political Justice: The Smith Act, the Communist Party, and American Civil Liberties* (Westport, Conn.: Greenwood Press, 1977), 174.

3. D. M. Ladd, memorandum to Director, Jan. 22, 1948, cited in U. S. Congress, Senate, Select Committee to Study Governmental Operations with Respect to Intelligence Activities, Final Report, Book III, "Supplementary Detailed Staff Reports on Intelligence Activities and the Rights of Americans," 94th Cong., 2d sess., April 23, 1976, 439 (hereafter SDSRIARA); Director, memorandum to E. A. Tamm, Ladd, Clyde Tolson, Oct. 30, 1947, Smith Act, #1123.

4. Belknap, *Cold War Political Justice,* 101; John M. Kelley, Jr., statement, May 12, 1947, in *U. S. v. Carl Aldo Marzani,* District Court of United States for District of Columbia, transcript of the trial, reel 39 (microfilm ed., Fund for the Republic, New York) (hereafter Marzani trial), 76–78.

Even as late as 1955, government witnesses in communist cases were still inserting general information about CP practices in their testimony. See "Information Bulletin No. 1 on Trial of Maurice E. Travis," Dec. 2, 1955, in American Communications Association Records (hereafter ACA Records), State Historical Society of Wisconsin, Madison (hereafter SHSW).

5. *I Was a Communist for the FBI,* produced by Brian Foy, screenplay by Crane Wilburn, directed by Gordon Douglas, 1951. See also Daniel J. Leab, "Anti-Communism, the FBI, and Matt Cvetic: The Ups and Downs of a Professional Informer," *Pennsylvania Magazine of History and Biography,* 115 (Oct. 1991): 558–68 and Nora Sayre, *Running Time: Films of the Cold War* (New York: Dial Press, 1982), 79–91.

6. Leab, "Anti-Communism, the FBI, and Matt Cvetic," 570–80; Stephen J. Whit-

field, *The Culture of the Cold War* (Baltimore: Johns Hopkins University Press, 1991), 134–36.

7. The demonization of Gerhart Eisler was so successful that even contemporary scholars refer to him as a Soviet espionage agent. See David Oshinsky, *A Conspiracy So Immense: The World of Joe McCarthy* (New York: Free Press, 1983), 109n.

8. On the relationship between aliens and political repression before the New Deal, see William Preston, Jr., *Aliens and Dissenters: Federal Suppression of Radicals, 1903–1933* (Cambridge: Harvard University Press, 1963). For a discussion of the role of immigration proceedings during the McCarthy period, see Ellen Schrecker, "Immigration and Internal Security: Deportations during the McCarthy Era," *Science & Society* 60 (Winter 1996–97): 393–426.

9. Earl Browder to Georgi Dimitroff, Sept. 2, 1935, in Harvey Klehr, John Earl Haynes, and Fridrikh Igorevich Firsov, *The Secret World of American Communism* (New Haven: Yale University Press, 1995), 62; Gerald Horne, *Black Liberation/Red Scare: Ben Davis and the Communist Party* (Newark: University of Delaware Press, 1994), 68; Browder, "In the Matter of Louis F. Budenz," March 5, 1956, Theodore Draper Research Files, Special Collections, Robert W. Woodruff Library, Emory University, Atlanta, Ga.; summary, Gerhart Eisler testimony before Alien Hearing Board, March 31, 1947, in Robert J. Lamphere, report, May 12, 1947, Eisler #452x; Lamphere, report, May 20, 1946, ibid., #210.

10. E. E. Conroy, report, Sept. 24, 1943, Eisler, #18; [name deleted], report, Oct. 2, 1945, Eisler, #99x.

11. Eisler's FBI files reveal considerable evidence of the Bureau's various dirty tricks. See, for example, report [name deleted], New York, Apr. 11, 1944, Eisler NY, #33; memorandum, SAC, NY to Director, Feb. 12, 1945, ibid., #67; memorandum [name deleted], June 2, 1945, ibid., #106; memorandum [name deleted], July 23, 1945, ibid., #126; memorandum [name deleted], Nov. 26, 1945, ibid., #170; memorandum, n.d. [name deleted], Conroy, report, Oct. 10, 1945, Eisler, #99.

12. E. E. Conroy to Director, Apr. 9, 1945, Eisler, #60.

13. Eisler's own account of his activities is contained in two FBI reports, one recounting an interview with him by Robert J. Lamphere of the FBI, July 19, 1946, and the other his hearing before the Alien Hearing Board, March 31, 1947. Conroy, report, Aug. 6, 1946, Eisler #120; Lamphere, report, May 12, 1947, Eisler, #452x. On the "Eisman" money and Eisler's connection to the Joint Anti-Fascist Refugee Committee, see Minutes, National Executive Board, JAFRC, Nov. 21, 1946, in Charlotte Todes Stern Papers, Tamiment Institute Library and Wagner Labor Archives, Elmer Holmes Bobst Library, New York University, New York City.

14. Joseph R. Starobin, *American Communism in Crisis, 1943–1957* (Cambridge: Harvard University Press, 1972), 304n; Joseph Starobin, interview with Theodore Draper, Dec. 20, 1956, Box 16, Draper Papers, Special Collections, Robert W. Woodruff Library, Emory University, Atlanta, Ga.; Al Richmond, *A Long View from the Left* (Boston: Houghton, Mifflin, 1973), 261; Browder, "In the Matter of Louis F. Budenz";

Sender Garlin, interview with the author, Mar. 15, 1991; Robert Bellah, interview with the author, Aug. 25, 1977.

15. Director, teletype to SAC, New York, July 18, 1946, Eisler NY, #222; Director to Edward Scheidt, Feb. 12, 1947, ibid., #427; list of questions submitted to Louis Budenz by the FBI in J. C. Strickland to Ladd, Dec. 3, 1945, Budenz, #149x; Scheidt, telegram to Bureau, Apr. 21, 1950, Budenz NY, #200; Theron L. Caudle to Director, Oct. 15, 16, 1946, Budenz, #174, #175; Scheidt to Director, Nov. 15, 1946, ibid., #185; Scheidt to Director, Nov. 26, 1946, ibid., #186; Winterrowd to Strickland, Feb. 7, 1947, ibid., #211; SAC, New York, to Director, Aug. 3, 1948, ibid., #288; Scheidt to Director, May 1, 1950, Budenz NY, #210. Budenz, quoted in Walter Goodman, *The Committee: The Extraordinary Career of the House Committee on Un-American Activities* (New York: Farrar, Straus, and Giroux, 1968), 184.

16. Ladd to Tamm, Dec. 7, 1945, Budenz, #139; J. Patrick Coyne to Tamm, Sept. 30, 1946, ibid., #192; Strickland to Ladd, Dec. 3, 1945, ibid., #149x; Caudle to Director, Oct. 15, 16, 1946, ibid., #174, #175; Scheidt to Director, Nov. 15, 1946, ibid., #185; Scheidt to Director, Nov. 26, 1946, ibid., #186; Winterrowd to Strickland, Feb. 7, 1947, ibid., #211; J. K. Mumford to Ladd, Oct. 22, 1946, Eisler HQ, #141; Tamm, memorandum for Director, Oct. 30, 1946, ibid., #208; Ladd to Director, Nov. 15, 1946, ibid., #203; Strickland to Ladd, Oct. 16, 1946, ibid., #140; Director to Attorney General, Oct. 24, 1946, ibid., #141; Coyne to Tamm, Oct. 15, 1946, ibid., #142; Carol King to Tom C. Clark, Oct. 31, 1946, ibid., #189; Ladd to Director, Nov. 15, 1946, ibid., #203; Director to Attorney General, Jan. 13, 1947, ibid., #207.

17. Lamphere, *FBI–KGB War,* 64–65; Conroy to Director, April 9, 1945, Eisler, #60; Conroy to Director, July 3, 1946, ibid., #116; Ladd to Director, Feb. 7, 1947, ibid., #236.

18. Tom C. Clark, testimony, U.S. Congress, House Un-American Activities Committee (hereafter HUAC), "Hearings on Proposed Legislation to Curb or Control the Communist Party of the United States," Feb. 5, 1948, 80th Cong., 2d sess., 21; Kirchheimer, *Political Justice,* 52; Steve Nelson, James R. Barrett, and Rob Ruck, *Steve Nelson, American Radical* (Pittsburgh, Pa.: University of Pittsburgh Press, 1981), 298–379.

19. Strickland to Ladd, Dec. 3, 1945, Budenz, 149x; Scheidt, telegram to Bureau, April 21, 1950, Budenz NY, #200; Caudle to Director, Oct. 15, 16, 1946, Budenz, #174, #175; Scheidt to Director, Nov. 15, 1946, ibid., #185; Scheidt to Director, Nov. 26, 1946, ibid., #186; Winterrowd to Strickland, Feb. 7, 1947, ibid., #211; Scheidt, telegram, to Director, Dec. 22, 1946, Eisler, #200; SAC, New York, to Director, Jan. 3, 1947, ibid., #203; [name deleted], to Ladd, Feb. 5, 1947, ibid., #254; Director to Commissioner, INS, Oct. 16, 1946, ibid., #140; Director to Honorable Joseph D. Nunan, Jr., Commissioner of Internal Revenue, Oct. 26, 1946, ibid., #140; Director to Attorney General, Oct. 24, 1946, ibid., #141.

20. Eisler, testimony, Feb. 6, 1947, "Hearings on Gerhart Eisler," HUAC, 80th Cong., 1st sess., 2–3; Goodman, *The Committee,* 191; Carl Beck, *Contempt of Congress* (New Orleans, La.: Hauser Press, 1959), 44.

21. Ladd to Director, Feb. 6, 1947, Eisler, #233; Robert E. Stripling, *The Red Plot Against America,* ed. Bob Considine (Drexel Hill, Pa.: Bell Publishing, 1949), 58–69.

22. Conroy to Director, Apr. 9, 1945, Eisler, #60; Conroy to Director, July 3, 1946, ibid., #116; Ladd to Director, Feb. 7, 1946, ibid., #236; Mr. Elliff to Mr. Caudle, Oct. 31, 1946, Gerhart Eisler File, Criminal Division, Department of Justice (hereafter Eisler DOJ); Virginia Gabriel to Mr. [William E.] Foley, March 24, 1948, unsigned memorandum, Apr. 20, 1948, Alexander M. Campbell to George Morris Fay, Nov. 9, 1948, Eisler DOJ; memorandum, "Summary of Decisions on Eisler's Contempt Case," Nov. 20, 1948, reel 4, in Black Studies Research Sources, General Editors: August Meier and John H. Bracey, Jr., Manuscript Collections from the Schomburg Center for Research in Black Culture, Papers of the Civil Rights Congress (Frederick, Md.: University Publications of America, 1988) (hereafter CRC); Joseph Forer and the editors, "Who Won the Cold War," in Ann Fagan Ginger and Eugene M. Tobin, eds., *The National Lawyers Guild: From Roosevelt through Reagan* (Philadelphia: Temple University Press, 1988), 175.

23. John B. Hogan to Foley, Feb. 4, 1948, Eisler to Attorney General, Feb. 3, 1948, Eisler DOJ; "Five Men on a Hunger Strike," pamphlet, n. d. [March 1948], in American Civil Liberties Union Papers, General Correspondence 1948, vol. 2, Seeley G. Mudd Manuscript Library, Princeton University (hereafter ACLU).

24. Memorandum, SAC, New York, to Director, June 14, 1947, Eisler NY, #605; teletype, Scheidt to Director, Apr. 6, 1949, ibid., #814; memorandum, name deleted, Jan. 7, 1947, Eisler NY, #188.

25. Memorandum, sender unknown, New York, Apr. 25, 1949, Eisler NY, #818.

26. Report [name deleted], New York, Nov. 25, 1947, Eisler NY, #703; memorandum, SAC, Boston, to Director, Jan. 27, 1948, ibid., #710; report [name deleted], New York, date illegible, ibid., serial # illegible; report [name deleted], New York, Feb. 23, 1949, ibid., #806; report [name deleted], New York, May 19, 1949, ibid., #867; Eisler to David Rein, Aug. 19, 1948, CRC, reel 4; Ellen W. Schrecker, *No Ivory Tower: McCarthyism and the Universities* (New York: Oxford University Press, 1986), 89–90; *Harvard Crimson,* April 27, 1948.

27. Isaiah Matlack to Campbell, June 8, 1949, and enclosures, Eisler DOJ, contains affidavits from crew members on the *Batory* about Eisler's escape. Francis X. Walker to Ford, Jan. 18, 1950, Eisler DOJ; Joan Mahoney, "Civil Liberties in Britain during the Cold War: The Role of the Central Government," *American Journal of Legal History* 33 (Jan. 1989): 80; Eisler, "My Return Home to Germany," translation from *The German American,* July 1949, in Eisler NY, #964; HICOP, Berlin, to Secretary of State, Aug. 5, 1950, in Eisler, #916.

28. Teletype, Scheidt, to Director, May 11, 1949, Eisler NY, #822; memorandum, Belmont, May 11, 1949, ibid., #825; memorandum, SAC, New York, to Director, May 17, 1949, ibid., #851; memorandum, Belmont, June 3, 1949, ibid., #903.

29. For an academic reference to Eisler, see Gabriel A. Almond, *The Appeals of Communism,* with Herbert E. Krugman, Elsbeth Lewin, Howard Wriggins (Princeton: Princeton University Press, 1954), 143; Director to SAC, New York, Mar. 4, 1946,

Smith Act, #41; SAC, New York, to Director, Nov. 25, 1947, ibid., #1219 ; SAC, Boston, to Director, FBI, Dec. 22, 1948, ibid., #2430; Scheidt, teletype to Director, n. d., ibid., #2531; Budenz, testimony, Mar. 24, 1949, in *United States of America, appellee, vs. Eugene Dennis et al., defendants-appellants.* United States Court of Appeals for the Second Circuit, 1950, transcript of the trial, microfilm ed. (New York: Fund for the Republic) (hereafter Dennis trial), 3559; testimony of Nathan Gregory Silvermaster, Aug. 4, 1948, 593, Victor Perlo, Aug. 9, 1948, 683, John Abt, Aug. 20, 1948, 1021, Nathan Witt, Aug. 20, 1948, 1032, all in HUAC, "Hearings Regarding Communist Espionage in the United States Government," 80th Cong., 2d sess.; John S. Wood to Dear Colleague, Oct. 6, 1949, in Emanuel Celler Papers, Library of Congress.

Eisler had been in China for the Comintern in the early 1930s and the FBI was tracking down rumors that he had been associated with members of a famous Soviet spy ring in Japan. Memorandum, SAC, New York, to Director, May 25, 1951, Eisler NY, serial # illegible; memorandum, Director to SAC, New York, May 28, 1951, ibid., #1053.

30. William Tanner, "The Passage of the Internal Security Act of 1950," (Ph.D. diss., University of Kansas, 1971), 117–22, 278–81; Joseph Zack Kornfeder, testimony, May 22–June 5, 1951, Manning Johnson, testimony, Oct. 10, 12, 1951, both in Research Collections in American Radicalism, General Editors: Mark Naison and Maurice Isserman, Records of the Subversive Activities Control Board, 1951–1972 (Frederick, Md.: University Publications of America, 1989) (hereafter SACB Records), Part I, reel 1; Howard C. Wood, memorandum to SACB, Oct. 4, 1951, SACB Records, Part I, reel 4.

31. Lamphere, *The FBI–KGB War,* 64–65; Cvetic, "I Posed as a Communist for the FBI," *Saturday Evening Post,* July 15, 1950, 18, July 22, 1950, 53; Kim Sigler, testimony, HUAC, "Investigation of Un-American Propaganda Activities in the United States," Mar. 28, 1947, 80th Cong., 1st sess., 310; Ronald L. Filippelli, "The United Electrical, Radio and Machine Workers of America, 1933–1949: The Struggle for Control" (Ph.D. diss., Pennsylvania State University, 1970), 163; Robert Stripling, July 23, 1947, HUAC, "Hearings Regarding Communism in Labor Unions in the United States," 80th Cong., 1st sess., 109.

32. Memorandum [name deleted], May 15, 1949, in Eisler NY, #845A; Fulton Lewis, Jr., column, May 10, 1951, enclosure in Director to SAC, New York, May 31, 1951, ibid., #1055; "Report of the Committee on Un-American Activities to the United States House of Representatives, 80th Congress," 80th Cong., 2d sess., Dec. 31, 1948 (Washington, D.C.: U.S. Government Printing Office, 1949).

33. For an important compendium of all these traits, see Title I, Internal Security Act of 1950, 64 Stat. 987 (1950). For an example of a vivid statement of the prevailing wisdom, see Justice Robert Jackson, concurring opinion, *American Communications Association v. Douds,* 70 S. Ct. 674 (1950), 701.

34. "Brief to Establish the Illegal Status of the Communist Party of the United States of America," Feb. 3, 1948, Smith Act, #1269 (hereafter FBI brief). See also, "A

Brief Study Concerning the Internal Security of the United States," NSC-17, June 28, 1948, in President's Secretary's File, Harry S. Truman Library, Independence, Mo. (hereafter HST-PSF).

35. For the FBI, see report, "Communist Infiltration of and Agitation in the Armed Forces," enclosure in Director to Harry Vaughan, Feb. 6, 1946, HST-PSF.

Citations of the Duclos article were common during the 1949 Smith Act trial. Budenz, for example, refers to it at length in his testimony, Mar. 24–25, 1949, Dennis trial, 3521–3559. See also Angela Calomiris, *Red Masquerade: Undercover for the F.B.I.* (Philadelphia: Lippincott, 1950), 149–56; HUAC, Cumulative Index to Publications, 1938–1954 (Washington, D.C.: U.S. Government Printing Office, 1962); A. R. Hilen to Benjamin Gitlow, Oct. 27, 1948, Box 8, Gitlow Papers, Hoover Institution on War, Revolution and Peace, Stanford University, Stanford, California (hereafter Hoover Institution); Ruth Fischer, "The Comintern in Hollywood," *New York Journal American,* Nov. 23, 1946, cited in report [name deleted], New York, Dec. 19, 1946, Eisler, #211.

36. For references to the oaths, see FBI brief, 137–138; Hilen to Gitlow, Oct. 27, 1948, Gitlow Papers; Jackson, opinion, in *American Communications Association v. Douds,* 701.

On J. Peters and his oath, see Gitlow, speech, American Legion Conference on Subversive Activities, Feb. 12–13, 1949, Box 5, Gitlow Papers; Calomaris, *Red Masquerade,* 270–73. For evidence that the FBI knew that oaths were not standard party practice, see Scheidt to Director, Nov. 2, 1948, Smith Act, #2086.

On the demonization of J. Peters, see Whittaker Chambers, *Witness* (Random House: New York, 1952); Budenz, testimony, Mar. 24, Apr. 1, 1949, Dennis trial; Louis F. Budenz, *This Is My Story* (New York: McGraw-Hill, 1947), 139; "Report of the Committee on Un-American Activities to the United States House of Representatives, 80th Congress." A more recent assessment of Peters's activities can be found in Harvey Klehr, John Earl Haynes, and Fridrikh Igorevich Firsov, *The Secret World of American Communism* (New Haven: Yale University Press, 1995), 71–83.

37. Budenz, quoted in *Washington Daily News,* Oct. 13, 1945, clipping in reel 122, Karl E. Mundt Papers, Karl E. Mundt Library, Dakota State College, Madison, S.D.; see also Hoover, statement, May 2, 1950, in *New York Times,* May 8, 1950; Elizabeth Bentley, *Out of Bondage* (New York: Devin-Adair, 1951), 281; J. P. Matthews, speech, to American Legion Conference on Subversive Activities, Feb. 12–13, 1949, Box 5, Gitlow Papers.

38. Richard Wright, in Richard Crossman, ed., *The God That Failed* (New York: Bantam, 1959, orig. ed. 1950), 134; Bentley, *Out of Bondage,* 89; Sidney Hook to unnamed correspondent, Mar. 7, 1949, Box 121, Hook Papers, Hoover Institution; Almond, *The Appeals of Communism,* 332–69, 390.

39. Mr. Amen, in Transcript of Proceedings, Fourteenth Meeting of the Loyalty Review Board, Feb. 13–14, 1951, Official File, 2-E, HSTL (hereafter HST-OF); airtel, Foster to Director, July 21, 1953, Everest Melvin Hupman, Labor Management Re-

lations Act (hereafter LMRA), #36; testimony of Kenneth Eckert cited in *Travis v. United States,* opinion, *Labor Relations Reporter,* 44 LRRM, 2714 (this an enclosure in Box 695, National Labor Relations Board Records, Record Group 25, National Archives, Washington, D.C. (hereafter NLRB Records); Judge David Bazelon, opinion, *Gold v. United States,* U.S. Court of Appeals, District of Columbia Circuit, Apr. 19, 1956, enclosure in Box 317, Western Federation of Miners/Mine Mill and Smelter Workers Papers, University of Colorado, Boulder (hereafter Mine-Mill Papers).

40. J. Edgar Hoover, *Masters of Deceit* (New York: Holt, 1958, Cardinal paperback ed. 1961), 119–120; Bentley, *Out of Bondage,* 285; Bella Dodd, *School of Darkness* (New York: Kenedy, 1954), 207–223; Congressman Jackson, quoted in Frank J. Donner, *The Un-Americans* (New York: Ballantine, 1961), 128; Bazelon, opinion, *Gold v. U.S.;* Nichols to Morris L. Ernst, Jan. 8, 1951, Ernst Papers, Harry Ransom Humanities Research Center, University of Texas at Austin.

41. Jessica Mitford, *A Fine Old Conflict* (New York: Knopf, 1977), 323–33; Chambers, *Witness,* 204; Cvetic, "I Posed as a Communist for the FBI," 34; Arthur Koestler, in Crossman, ed., *The God that Failed,* 41; Bella Dodd, quoted in Harry and Bonaro Overstreet, *What We Must Know about Communism* (New York: W. W. Norton, 1958), 299.

42. Abbott Gleason, *Totalitarianism: The Inner History of the Cold War* (New York: Oxford University Press, 1995), 89–107; Edward Hunter, *Brain-Washing in Red China: The Calculated Destruction of Men's Minds* (New York: Vanguard Press, 1953); Eugene Kinkead, *In Every War But One* (New York: W. W. Norton, 1959); Robert J. Lifton, *Thought Reform and the Psychology of Totalism: A Study of "Brainwashing"* (New York: W. W. Norton, 1961).

43. Hubert Kay, "The Career of Gerhart Eisler as a Comintern Agent," *Life,* Feb. 17, 1947, 99; Sayre, *Running Time,* 191–214; Michael Paul Rogin, *"Ronald Reagan," the Movie and Other Episodes in Political Demonology* (Berkeley and Los Angeles: University of California Press, 1987), 264. On the way the Japanese were viewed during World War II, see John W. Dower, *War Without Mercy* (New York: Pantheon, 1986).

44. Hubert Humphrey to Richard F. Cornwell, Sept. 13, 1954, in William W. Keller, *The Liberals and J. Edgar Hoover: Rise and Fall of a Domestic Intelligence State* (Princeton: Princeton University Press, 1989), 67; Cvetic, "I Posed as a Communist for the FBI," 103; Jackson, opinion, *American Communications Association v. Douds.*

45. Klehr, Haynes, and Firsov, *The Secret World of American Communism,* 202–4; Ladd to Director, Mar. 29, 1947, Lenin School, serial # illegible; memorandum, E. G. Fitch to Ladd, May 27, 1947, ibid., #8; George Hewitt, testimony, May 14, 1947, in Marzani trial; William Odell Nowell, testimony, July 9, 1951, hearings before the Subversive Activities Control Board, Part I, reel 1, SACB Records; FBI report, "Present International Situation and the Role of American Communists in the Event of War," Aug. 24, 1950, HST-PSF; Hoover to SAC, New York, July 10, 1953, George Mink, no serial #; Arthur J. Sabin, *Red Scare in Court: New York versus the International Workers Order* (Philadelphia: University of Pennsylvania Press, 1993), 146–

47, 156; clipping, *El Paso Herald Post,* Jan. 18, 1954, Clinton Jencks, El Paso, #333; Cvetic, "I Posed as a Communist for the FBI," 50; Hoover, *Masters of Deceit,* 60; Herbert Philbrick, *I Led Three Lives* (Washington, D.C.: Capitol Hill Press, 1972, orig. ed. 1953), 110; John F. X. McGohey, statement, Dennis trial, 3220; Bentley, *Out of Bondage,* 71.

46. Kenneth Eckert, testimony, Oct. 7, 1952, "Communist Domination of Union Officials in Vital Defense Industry — International Union of Mine, Mill, and Smelter Workers," Hearings before the Subcommittee to Investigate the Administration of the Internal Security Act and other Internal Security Laws of the Committee on the Judiciary, U.S. Senate, 82nd Congress, 2d session, 67 (hereafter SISS Mine-Mill); Louis Wyman, quoted in Gregory Scott Clayton, "Red Probe: The Wyman Investigation of Subversive Activities in New Hampshire," undergraduate thesis, Dartmouth College, 1979 (copy in the author's possession, courtesy of Norah Chase), 158; Robert H. Jackson, concurring opinion, *Dennis v. United States* 341 U.S. 494 (1951); Almond, *The Appeals of Communism,* 378; J. Howard McGrath, speech to Advertising Club of New York, Apr. 19, 1950, in Emanuel Celler Papers, Library of Congress; report [name deleted], San Francisco, May 17, 1950, Mink, #269; comment by N. D. Dixon, head of Texas Department of Public Safety subversive intelligence division, 1951, cited in Don E. Carleton, *Red Scare! Right-Wing Hysteria, Fifties Fanaticism, and Their Legacy in Texas* (Austin: Texas Monthly Press, 1985), 99; Bernard Shanley diaries, June 1953, 940–42, Shanley Papers, Dwight D. Eisenhower Library, Abilene, Kan. (hereafter DDEL).

47. Sayre, *Running Time,* 83; Calomaris, *Red Masquerade,* 226; Cvetic, "I Posed as a Communist for the FBI," 34. On the unsolved killing or suicide of the former KGB agent Walter Krivitsky, see Allen Weinstein, *Perjury: The Hiss-Chambers Case* (New York: Knopf, 1978), 331; Sam Tanenhaus, *Whittaker Chambers: A Biography* (New York: Random House, 1997), 157–70.

48. Chambers, *Witness,* 36; Weinstein, *Perjury,* 310–11; Gitlow, unpublished manuscript about Soviet espionage, Box 5, Gitlow Papers; Paul Crouch, unpublished manuscript, Box 1, Crouch Papers, Hoover Institution; Ruth Fischer, "You Can't Retire from the N.K.V.D.," *New York Journal American,* Nov. 20, 1946.

49. Report [name deleted], New York, Jan. 17, 1936, Mink, #17; undated document [no date or title page], ibid., probably #20 or #21; document [cover page withheld], May 15, 1941, ibid., #41; report [name deleted], New York, Dec. 26, 1942, ibid., #65; memorandum, Nov. 15, 1945, ibid., #148.

50. Crouch, unpublished manuscript; Bruce Nelson, *Workers on the Waterfront: Seamen, Longshoremen, and Unionism in the 1930s* (Urbana: University of Illinois Press, 1988), 91–93; Chambers, *Witness,* 302–3; Stephen Koch, *Secret Lives* (New York: Free Press, 1994), 290; Victor Riesel, "Red Trouble-Maker Hopes to Stop Coast Shipping," *Oakland Tribune,* Apr. 5, 1950, clipping, Box 16, Crouch Papers; Lamphere, report, May 12, 1947, Eisler, #452x; Herbert Solow, undated memorandum, Box 11, Solow Papers, Hoover Institution; "Summary of File References," Mar. 13,

1950, Mink, #258; report [name deleted], June 27, 1941, ibid., #47; report [name deleted], New York, Dec. 26, 1942, ibid., #65; report [name deleted], New York, Sept. 18, 1945, ibid., #144; John N. Speakes, Mexico City, to Director, Jan. 9, 1947, ibid., #210; SAC, Baltimore, to Director, Jan. 6, 1948, ibid., #240; Director to SAC, Seattle, Oct. 3, 1950, ibid., #276; report [name deleted], New York, Feb. 29, 1952, ibid., #291; [name deleted] to Director, Oct. 29, 1952, ibid., #292.

51. Report [name deleted], New York, Nov. 14, 1945, Mink, #155; memorandum, SAC, New York, to Director, June 19, 1946, ibid., #199; memorandum, SAC, New York, to Director, Oct. 11, 1946, ibid., #206; memorandum, Ladd to Director, Apr. 26, 1950, ibid., no serial #; teletype, Director to SAC, San Francisco, Los Angeles, Portland, New York, Apr. 5, 1950, ibid., #262; teletype, Kimball, San Francisco, Apr. 7, 1950, ibid., #263; memorandum, Nichols to Tolson, Apr. 19, 1950, ibid., #268; report [name deleted], Los Angeles, June 5, 1950, ibid., #273; telegram, Director to SAC, New York, July 27, 1953, ibid., #293; SAC, New York, to Director, Apr. 26, 1954, ibid., #300.

52. FBI, report, "Present International Situation and the Role of American Communists in the Event of War," Aug. 24, 1950, in HST-PSF; A. Warren Littman, memorandum to Joseph Alderman, June 28, 1955, Box 135, U.S. Senate, Committee on the Judiciary, Subcommittee on Internal Security, Records, Record Group 46, National Archives (hereafter SISS Records); NSC-17.

53. Clark, quoted in Peter Steinberg, *The Great "Red Menace": United States Prosecution of American Communists, 1947–1952* (Westport, Conn.: Greenwood, 1984), 42; see also the similar statement by the U.S. solicitor general Philip B. Perlman in the government's oral argument in support of the Smith Act conviction of the CP's leaders, cited in Michal Belknap, *Cold War Political Justice,* 136; Frank Ober, quoted in William Tanner, "The Passage of the Internal Security Act of 1950" (Ph.D. diss., University of Kansas, 1971), 241; Schrecker, *No Ivory Tower,* 105–12; Norman Thomas, cited in Corliss Lamont, ed., *The Trial of Elizabeth Gurley Flynn by the American Civil Liberties Union* (New York: Horizon, 1968), 150; Robert Jackson, *American Communications Association v. Douds.*

54. Memorandum, Ladd to Director, Mar. 26, 1946, Smith Act, #124; Hoover, testimony, Mar. 26, 1947, HUAC, "Hearings on H.R. 1884 and H.R. 2122," 80th Cong., 1st sess.; Hoover, *Masters of Deceit,* 201; NSC-17; Loyd Wright, statement before House Committee on Post Office and Civil Service, Apr. 30, 1959, in Official File, 104-J, DDEL (hereafter DDE-OF); Sidney Hook, "Heresy, Yes — But Conspiracy, No," *New York Times Magazine,* July 9, 1950, 38; Harry and Bonaro Overstreet, *What We Must Know about Communism,* 68; Joseph and Stewart Alsop, "Will the CIO Shake the Communists Loose?" *Saturday Evening Post,* Feb. 22, 1947; Jacob Potofsky, Emil Mazey, and Joseph Curran, "Report of the Committee to Investigate Charges Against the Food, Tobacco, Agricultural and Allied Workers of America," Box 109, CIO Secretary-Treasurer's Office Papers, Archives of Labor History and Urban Affairs, Walter P. Reuther Library, Wayne State University, Detroit, Mich. (hereafter ALHUA); David McDonald, Joseph Froesch, and Harry Sayre, "Report of Executive Board Com-

mittee Appointed by President Murray to Investigate Charges against the American Communications Association," Box 108, ibid.

55. Morris L. Ernst and David Loth, *Report on the American Communist* (New York: Henry Holt, 1952, Capricorn Books ed. 1962), 185; Lloyd Stryker, quoted in Weinstein, *Perjury,* 414. In his dissenting opinion in *Dennis v. U.S.,* Justice William O. Douglas notes the CP's "deceit and cunning" even as he decries its prosecution under the Smith Act; Eisenhower to Brownell, Nov. 4, 1953, in Robert Newman, *Owen Lattimore and the "Loss" of China* (Berkeley and Los Angeles: University of California Press, 1992), 449; Brownell to Eisenhower, Mar. 22, 1954, Box 8, DDE (Ann Whitman) Administration File, DDEL.

56. Budenz, *This Is My Story,* 129, 135–39; Philbrick, *I Led Three Lives,* 110; Bentley, *Out of Bondage,* 71; excerpts from an article by Dorothy Thompson, *New York Post,* Oct. 29, 1946, in report [name deleted], New York, Dec. 19, Eisler, #211; A. R. Hilen to Benj. Gitlow, Oct. 27, 1948, Gitlow Papers; John M. Kelley, May 12, 1947, Marzani trial, 69, George Hewitt, testimony, May 19, 1947, ibid., 404–6, Louis O. Harper, testimony, May 14, 1947, ibid., 439.

57. For some representative pronouncements, see Hoover's testimony before HUAC, Mar. 26, 1947; Hoover, "Could Your Child Become a Red?" *Parade,* May 11, 1952; Philbrick, *I Led Three Lives,* 131–32, 136, 177–90; Budenz, *This Is My Story,* 132–33.

58. Hoover, testimony to HUAC, Mar. 26, 1947; Morris Ernst to Franklin D. Roosevelt, Dec. 11, 1939, to Henry Morgenthau, Feb. 20, 1940, to Tom Clark, Oct. 9, 1946, to Fred Vinson, Nov. 17, 1945, to John Haynes Holmes, Jan. 26, 1949, to Richard Nixon, Jan. 19, 1948, Feb. 15, 1949, Ernst Papers; HUAC, "Hearings on Proposed Legislation to Curb or Control the Communist Party of the United States," Feb. 5, 6, 9, 10, 11, 19, and 20, 1948, 80th Cong., 2d sess. (especially testimony of Tom C. Clark, Feb. 5 and Morris Ernst, Feb. 11, 1948); William Tanner, "The Passage of the Internal Security Act of 1950"; Ellen Schrecker, "Introduction" to *Records of the Subversive Activities Control Board, 1950–1972* (Frederick, Md.: University Publications of America, 1989), v–xvi.

59. Herbert Brownell, Jr., "The Public Security and Wiretapping," *Cornell Law Quarterly* 39 (1954): 195, cited in SDSIARA, 284; J. Howard McGrath, remarks to Advertising Club of New York, Apr. 19, 1950, Celler Papers; Philbrick, *I Led Three Lives,* 235; Samuel A. Stouffer, *Communism, Conformity, and Civil Liberties* (Garden City, N.Y.: Doubleday, 1955), 176–77.

60. Frances Perkins, oral history transcript, VII, 265, 253, Columbia Oral History Project, Rare Book and Manuscript Library, Butler Library, Columbia University (hereafter COHP); Tom C. Clark, "Civil Rights: The Boundless Responsibility of Lawyers," *American Bar Association Journal* 32 (1946): 457; Kay, "The Career of Gerhart Eisler as a Comintern Agent," 102, 108; Sayre, *Running Time,* 98, 193, 198; Jack Anderson and Ronald W. May, *McCarthy, the Man, the Senator, the "Ism"* (Boston: Beacon Press, 1952), 181; Hoover, *Masters of Deceit,* 104.

For an important contemporary discussion of the relationship between anticommunism and anti-intellectualism, see Richard Hofstadter, *Anti-intellectualism in American Life* (New York: Knopf, 1963), 3–51.

61. Alsop and Alsop, "Will the CIO Shake the Communists Loose?"; Stripling, *The Red Plot Against America,* 14; Hoover, speech to American Legion convention, Sept. 30, 1946, cited in Tanner, "The Passage of the Internal Security Act of 1950," 117; Hoover, testimony, HUAC, Mar. 26, 1947; Hoover, speech to the Grand Lodge of Masons, May 2, 1950, cited in *New York Times,* May 8, 1950.

62. Editorial, *Saturday Evening Post,* Jan. 18, 1947, 132; Clark, "Civil Rights: The Boundless Responsibility of Lawyers," 456; Homer Ferguson, press release, Dec. 31, 1953, Ferguson Papers, Michigan Historical Collections, Bentley Library, Ann Arbor; Cvetic, "I Posed as a Communist for the FBI," 50; J. C. Rich, "How the Garment Workers Licked the Communists," *Saturday Evening Post,* Aug. 9, 1947, 83; Charles Owen Rice, "How to De-Control Your Union of Communists," Box 6, UE Local 601 Papers, Archives of Industrial Society, University of Pittsburgh (this pamphlet was widely distributed).

63. Harvey Matusow, *False Witness* (New York: Cameron and Kahn, 1955), 97–99; Hoover, *Masters of Deceit,* 199–226, 297–308.

64. Homer Chaillaux, quoted in William Pencak, *For God and Country: The American Legion, 1919–1941* (Boston: Northeastern University Press, 1989), 13; Hoover, testimony to HUAC, Mar. 26, 1947; John F. X. McGohey, statement, Dennis trial, 3222; Judge Edward Dimock, quoted in Marc Rohr, "Communists and the First Amendment: The Shaping of Freedom of Advocacy in the Cold War Era," *San Diego Law Review* 28 (1991): 61–62; Archer Drew, testimony, May 15, 1947, Marzani trial, 567–68.

Many contemporary discussions of the CP include the observation about the small size of Lenin's party. See, for example, Ernst and Loth, *Report on the American Communist,* 183.

65. Hoover, speech to American Legion, Sept. 30, 1946; Hoover, testimony to HUAC, Mar. 26, 1947; Hoover, speech to the Grand Lodge of Masons, May 2, 1950; Brownell, speech, Mar. 21, 1955, in *U.S. News and World Report,* Apr. 1, 1955; memorandum, Belmont to L. V. Boardman, Aug. 28, 1956, in Athan Theoharis, *Spying on Americans: Political Surveillance from Hoover to the Huston Plan* (Philadelphia: Temple University Press, 1978), 176; Francis Walters, statement, June 29, 1958, in Proceedings Against Frank Wilkinson, House of Representatives, Report No. 2583, 85th Cong., 2d. sess.

66. NSC-17; McGrath, speech, Apr. 19, 1950; a California judge, quoted in Hugo Black's dissent, *Carlson v. Landon* 342 U.S., 524 (1952), 550; Hoover, testimony, HUAC, Mar. 26, 1947; Hubert H. Humphrey statement, Mar. 17, 1952, "Hearings before a Subcommittee on Labor of the Committee on Labor and Public Welfare on Communist Domination of Unions and National Security," 82nd Cong., 2d sess., 57; Stevenson, quoted in Sayre, *Running Time,* 201.

67. Hoover, cited in Richard Gid Powers, *Secrecy and Power: The Life of J. Ed-*

gar Hoover (New York: Free Press, 1987), 311; report, SAC [name deleted], St. Paul, Aug. 1, 1946, Smith Act, #228; Stouffer, Communism, Conformity, and Civil Liberties, 166–69.

The Knights of Columbus, for example, were especially worried about Communism's contribution to the decline of moral fiber and the disintegration of family life. Christopher J. Kauffman, Faith and Fraternalism: The History of the Knights of Columbus 1882–1982 (New York: Harper and Row, 1982), 360–68, 385; Whitfield, The Culture of the Cold War, 77–100.

68. Daniel Bell, The End of Ideology: On the Exhaustion of Political Ideas in the Fifties (New York: Collier Books, 1962), 400; Richard Crossman, "Introduction," in Crossman, ed., The God That Failed, 6; Learned Hand, opinion in U.S. v. Dennis, 183 F. 2d 201, 210 (C.A. 2); Ernst and Loth, Report on the American Communist, 118–19; Alsop and Alsop, "Will the CIO Shake the Communists Loose?" 106; Max Ascoli, The Power of Freedom (New York: Farrar, Straus, 1949), 3.

69. Alsop and Alsop, "Will the CIO Shake the Communists Loose?"; Ernst and Loth, Report on the American Communist, 112. For a good discussion of the extremism of the centrists during the Cold War, see Leo P. Ribuffo, The Old Christian Right: The Protestant Far Right from the Great Depression to the Cold War (Philadelphia: Temple University Press, 1983), 224–57. For an informed view of the medicalization and psychologizing of political and sexual issues during the 1950s, see Robert J. Corber, In the Name of National Security: Hitchcock, Homophobia, and the Political Construction of Gender in Postwar America (Durham, N.C.: Duke University Press, 1993), 1–55.

70. Ernst and Loth, Report on the American Communist, 127.

71. Hoover, "Could Your Child Become a Red?" Parade, May 11, 1952. For a discussion of the mixed messages about gender roles that were common in the 1950s, see Wini Breines, Young, White, and Miserable: Growing Up Female in the Fifties (Boston: Beacon Press, 1992) and Joanne Meyerowitz, ed., Not June Cleaver: Women and Gender in Postwar America (Philadelphia: Temple University Press, 1994).

72. Kay, "The Career of Gerhart Eisler as a Comintern Agent"; Hunter, Brain-Washing in Red China, 51–57; Almond, The Appeals of Communism, 40, 120, 143, 154–59; Bentley, Out of Bondage, 101. The notion of the CP as stunting its members' personal lives pervades Vivian Gornick's semifictionalized account of CP life in The Romance of American Communism (New York: Basic Books, 1977).

73. Marge Frantz, interview with the author, April 17, 1991; Clinton Jencks, interview with the author, April 23, 1997; Peggy Dennis, The Autobiography of an American Communist: A Personal View of a Political Life, 1925–1975 (Berkeley, Calif.: and Westport, Conn.: Creative Arts Book Company and Lawrence Hill, 1977), 88–87, 112–25, 144–53; Dorothy Healey and Maurice Isserman, Dorothy Healey Remembers: A Life in the American Communist Party (New York: Oxford University Press, 1990), 38, 89, 123; Robin D. G. Kelley, Hammer and Hoe: Alabama Communists during the Great Depression (Chapel Hill: University of North Carolina Press,

1990), 26. Paul Lyons, *Philadelphia Communists 1936–1956* (Philadelphia: Temple University Press, 1982), 87–108, is good on the personal lives of rank-and-file party members. A friend, who will remain anonymous, has told me that when she was a baby, her parents went into the underground and left her with her grandmother for a year.

74. Ronald Radosh and Joyce Milton, *The Rosenberg File: The Search for the Truth* (New York: Holt, 1983), 376; Virginia Carmichael, *Framing History: The Rosenberg Story and the Cold War* (Minneapolis: University of Minnesota Press, 1993), 96–103; Ilene Philipson, *Ethel Rosenberg: Beyond the Myths* (New York: Franklin Watts, 1988), 243–356; Victor Navasky, *Naming Names* (New York: Viking, 1980), 225–32; "In the matter of Mollie Portnoy, memorandum of case," Feb. 2, 1951, and Bennett D. Brown to Civil Rights Congress, Feb. 14, 1951, reel 4, CRC Papers. After his wife sued him for divorce, a former FBI informer retaliated by claiming that since she was still in the CP, she couldn't raise the children "properly." *Time,* Jan. 31, 1955, clipping in Doris Brin Walker Papers in the possession of Doris Brin Walker.

75. Ernst and Loth, *Report on the American Communist,* 180; Bentley, *Out of Bondage,* 185; Isaac Don Levine, "The Mystery of Mrs. Earl Browder," *Plain Talk* 3 (Dec. 1948): 19; Karl Baarslag, "Our Unknown Anti-Communist Dead," unpublished manuscript, Box 3, Baarslag Papers, Hoover Institution; Paul Crouch to Alfred Kohlberg, "Memorandum regarding Kitty Harris," n. d., Box 45, Kohlberg Papers, Hoover Institution. For a more recent discussion of Raïssa Browder, see Klehr, Haynes, and Firsov, *The Secret World of American Communism,* 243–48.

76. Radosh and Milton, *The Rosenberg File,* 358; Eisenhower to "Johnnie," June 16, 1953, Dwight D. Eisenhower diary, Eisenhower Papers, DDEL. For evidence that FBI officials believed Priscilla Hiss was dominating Alger, see Curt Gentry, *J. Edgar Hoover: The Man and the Secrets* (New York: Penguin, 1991), 366.

77. Telegram, "Anton" [Leonid Romanovich Kvasnikov] to "Viktor" [Lt. Gen. P. M. Fitin], Nov. 27, 1944, in Part I, "Venona Translations," Center for Cryptologic History, National Security Agency, Fort George G. Meade, Md.; Carmichael, *Framing History,* 101; Radosh and Milton, *The Rosenberg File,* 417.

78. Kate Weigand, "The Red Menace, the Feminine Mystique, and the Ohio Un-American Activities Commission: Gender and Anti-Communism in Ohio, 1951–1954," *Journal of Women's History* 3 (Winter 1992): 70–94.

79. Van Gosse, " 'To Organize in Every Neighborhood, in Every Home': The Gender Politics of American Communists between the Wars," *Radical History Review* 50 (1991): 109–141; Lyons, *Philadelphia Communists,* 87–108; Robert K. Murray, *Red Scare: A Study in National Hysteria, 1919–1920* (Minneapolis: University of Minnesota Press, 1955), 94–98; Almond, *The Appeals of Communism,* 40; Ernst and Loth, *Report on the American Communist,* 162.

80. Oshinsky, *A Conspiracy So Immense,* 157, 196; Warren I. Cohen, *The Chinese Connection: Roger S. Greene, Thomas W. Lamont, George E. Sokolsky and American-East Asian Relations* (New York: Columbia University Press, 1978), 270–71; John

D'Emilio and Estelle B. Freedman, *Intimate Matters: A History of Sexuality in America* (New York: Harper and Row, 1988), 292–95; Corber, *In the Name of National Security,* 19–23. There is a fairly homophobic message in the most important of the explicitly anticommunist films of the 1950s, Leo McCarey's 1952 *My Son John,* in which the subversive character camps it up a bit with his pathetic, yet religious, mother, see Sayre, *Running Time,* 94–99, 145.

When the civil rights movement began in Florida in the mid-50s, segregationists called it a communist plot and decided to investigate. Finding no evidence that the NAACP was a party front, the legislators harassed gays instead. Before the inquisition ended, the University of Florida had dropped fifty students and twenty staff members for their alleged sexual misdeeds. See James A. Schnur, "Academic Freedom and Intellectual Inquiry in Florida's Public Universities, 1956–1964," unpublished paper in the author's possession; Schnur, "Cold Warriors in the Hot Sunshine: The Johns Committee's Assault on Civil Liberties in Florida, 1956–1965," unpublished ms.

81. Almond, *The Appeals of Communism,* 153; Calomiris, *Red Masquerade,* 128–30; Sayre, *Running Time,* 81; John Huber, testimony before McCarran Immigration and Naturalization Subcommittee, clipping from *Chicago Daily Tribune,* Dec. 21, 1949, reel 124, Mundt Papers; Bentley, *Out of Bondage,* 128; Hoover, *Masters of Deceit,* 65–66; Philbrick, *I Led Three Lives,* 90.

82. Walter Reuther, quoted in Ronald Edsforth, "Affluence, Anti-Communism, and the Transformation of Industrial Unionism Among Automobile Workers, 1933–1973," in Edsforth and Larry Bennett, eds., *Popular Culture and Political Change in Modern America* (Albany: State University of New York Press, 1991), 122–23; Norman Thomas, introduction to Sidney Lens, "The Mine Mill Conspiracy Case," pamphlet, n. d., Mine-Mill Records, Box 801; Emil Rieve, quoted in Steven M. Gillon, *Politics and Vision: The ADA and American Liberalism, 1947–1985* (New York: Oxford University Press, 1987), 64.

83. Almond, *The Appeals of Communism,* 210–215.

84. Gerald Horne, *Communist Front? The Civil Rights Congress, 1946–1956* (Rutherford, N.J.: Fairleigh Dickinson University Press, 1988), 334; James Goodman, *Stories of Scottsboro* (New York: Pantheon, 1994), 32–38; Mary L. Dudziak, "Desegregation as a Cold War Imperative," *Stanford Law Review* 41 (Nov. 1988): 61–120; Hubert H. Humphrey to Herbert H. Lehman, Oct. 30, 1952, Lehman Papers, School of International Affairs, Columbia University.

85. Hoover, quoted in Powers, *Secrecy and Power,* 127; Philbrick, *I Was a Communist for the FBI;* for the best treatment of the FBI and racial issues, see Kenneth O'Reilly, *"Racial Matters": The FBI's Secret File on Black America, 1960–1972* (New York: Free Press, 1989), 9–47; Gerald Horne, *Communist Front?,* 334; Cvetic, testimony, at Carl Braden trial, clipping from *Louisville Courier,* Dec. 5, 1954, Box 3, Gitlow Papers; Wilson Record, *Race and Radicalism: The NAACP and the Communist Party in Conflict* (Ithaca, N.Y.: Cornell University Press, 1964), 140; Hoover to Harry Vaughan, Feb. 6, 1946, "Re: Communist Infiltration of and Agitation in the Armed

Forces," HST-PSF; Sylvia Crouch, testimony before the Johns Committee, Florida, Jan. 7, 1958, Box 1, Crouch Papers.

86. NSC-17; Hoover, testimony, HUAC, Mar. 26, 1947; Hoover, "Could Your Child Become a Red?"; Stephen J. Spingarn, memorandum for the files, Jan. 20, 1947, Spingarn Papers; Arthur M. Schlesinger, Jr., *The Vital Center* (Boston: Houghton Mifflin, 1949), 35–50; Granville Hicks, *Where We Came Out* (New York: Viking, 1954), 164–74; Cvetic, "I Posed as a Communist for the FBI," 50, 52; Joseph and Stewart Alsop, "Will the CIO Shake the Communists Loose?"

87. Questionnaire answer cited in Milnor Alexander, "The Right to Counsel for the Politically Unpopular," *Law in Transition* 22 (1962): 40; Dee Garrison, "'Our Skirts Gave Them Courage,' The Civil Defense Protest Movement in New York City, 1955–1961," in Joanne Meyerowitz, ed., *Not June Cleaver: Women and Gender in Postwar America*, 1994), 207; Benjamin Harris, "The Red Deb, Her Black Lover, and the Politics of Mental Illness," paper presented to the Ninth Berkshire Conference on the History of Women, June 11, 1993, Vassar College, Poughkeepsie, N.Y.

88. Schlesinger, *The Vital Center*, 104; Ernst and Loth, *Report on the American Communist*, 5, 128–30; Almond, *The Appeals of Communism*, 103–105, 230–57, 291, 307; Hoover, *Masters of Deceit*, 103–106; Calomiris, *Red Masquerade*, 78; Cvetic, "I Posed as a Communist for the FBI," 99.

89. Oshinsky, *A Conspiracy So Immense*, 113; Dean Deborah Bacon, quoted in Schrecker, *No Ivory Tower*, 88–89; Dean Wilbur Bender, speech to Cincinnati, Ohio, Harvard Club, Feb. 1949, in Sigmund Diamond, *Compromised Campus* (New York: Oxford University Press, 1992), 19; Alsop and Alsop, "Will the CIO Shake the Communists Loose?" 105; Almond, *The Appeals of Communism*, xiv, 216, 243–94; Ernst and Loth, *Report on the American Communist*, 78–92, 127–41; Hoover, *Masters of Deceit*, 104; Robert Lindner, *The Fifty Minute Hour* (New York: Bantam, 1956, orig. ed. 1955), 48–78.

5: "A GREAT AND TOTAL DANGER": THE COMMUNIST THREAT

1. Thomas Emerson, David Haber, and Norman Dorsen, *Political and Civil Rights in the United States*, vol. 1 (Boston: Little, Brown, 1967), 269.

2. Frank Kofsky, *Harry S. Truman and the War Scare of 1948: A Successful Campaign to Deceive the Nation* (New York: St. Martin's Press, 1993), 136; James Forrestal, *The Forrestal Diaries*, ed. Walter Millis (New York: Viking, 1951), 72, 182. See also Melvyn P. Leffler, "The American Conception of National Security and the Beginnings of the Cold War, 1945–48," *American Historical Review* 89 (April 1984): 346–81.

3. For background on the early stages of the Cold War, see Melvyn P. Leffler, *A Preponderance of Power: National Security, the Truman Administration and the Cold War* (Stanford: Stanford University Press, 1992); Deborah Welch Larson, *Ori-*

gins of Containment: A Psychological Explanation (Princeton: Princeton University Press, 1985); Robert L. Messer, *The End of Alliance: James F. Byrnes, Roosevelt, Truman, and the Origins of the Cold War* (Chapel Hill: University of North Carolina Press, 1982); Daniel Yergin, *Shattered Peace: The Origins of the Cold War* (Boston: Houghton Mifflin, 1977).

4. On the controversy over the bomb and the atomic diplomacy of the early Cold War, see Gar Alperovitz, *Atomic Diplomacy: Hiroshima and Potsdam* (New York: Simon and Schuster, 1965; rev. ed. 1994); Gregg Herken, *The Winning Weapon: The Atomic Bomb in the Cold War, 1945–1950* (New York: Knopf, 1980); Martin J. Sherwin, *A World Destroyed: Hiroshima and the Origins of the Arms Race* (New York: Knopf, 1975); David Holloway, *Stalin and the Bomb: The Soviet Union and Atomic Energy, 1939–1956* (New Haven: Yale University Press, 1994).

5. NSC-68, April 7, 1950, *Foreign Relations of the United States 1950,* vol. 1 (Washington, D.C.: U.S. Government Printing Office, 1977).

6. On the Korean War, see Bruce Cumings, *The Origins of the Korean War,* vol. 2, *The Roaring of the Cataract, 1947–1950* (Princeton: Princeton University Press, 1990).

7. NSC-68, 263, 288.

8. Daniel J. Leab, "The Red Menace and Justice in the Pacific Northwest: The 1946 Trial of the Soviet Naval Lieutenant Nikolai Gregorevitch Redin," *Pacific Northwest Quarterly* 87 (Spring 1996): 83; Clark Clifford, "American Relations with the Soviet Union" (Sept. 1946), Box 63, George M. Elsey Papers, Harry S. Truman Library, Independence, Mo. (hereafter HSTL); "A Brief Study Concerning the Internal Security of the United States," NSC-17, June 28, 1948, in President's Secretary's File, HSTL (hereafter HST-PSF); FBI report, "Soviet Government Purchasing Commission," Mar. 29, 1946, encl. in T. C. C. [Clark] to Matt [Connelly], Apr. 4, 1946, HST-PSF; J. Edgar Hoover to Harry Hawkins Vaughan, Jan. 17, 1948, ibid.; Hoover to Hugh B. Cox, Sept. 8, 1944, to Attorney General, July 30, 1946, both in D. M. Ladd to Director, Nov. 24, 1953, Harry Dexter White, #813; "Soviet Activities in the United States," FBI report, July 25, 1946, Box 15, Clark M. Clifford Papers, HSTL; Hoover to Vaughan, May 23, 1947, HST-PSF; Karl E. Mundt, speech to the Export Advertising Club, Mar. 17, 1948, in Karl E. Mundt Papers, reel 124, Karl E. Mundt Library, Dakota State College, Madison, S.D.; Mundt to L. W. Robinson, Mar. 17, 1949, reel 123, ibid.; Morse Salisbury (director, Information Services, AEC) to Alexander Wiley, Apr. 21, 1953; Wiley to Guy Gillette, Homer Ferguson, Jan. 16, 1954, all in Box 74, Alexander Wiley Papers, State Historical Society of Wisconsin (hereafter SHSW).

9. On the Gouzenko case and its connection to the U.S., see Reg Whitaker and Gary Marcuse, *Cold War Canada: The Making of a National Insecurity State, 1945–1957* (Toronto: University of Toronto Press, 1994), 27–110; Merrily Weisbord, *The Strangest Dream: Canadian Communists, the Spy Trials, and the Cold War* (Toronto: Lester and Orpen Dennys Ltd., 1983), 141–42; Royal Commission to Investigate the Facts . . . , *The Report of the Royal Commission* (Ottawa: June 27, 1946); Robert Both-

well and J. L. Granatstein, eds., *The Gouzenko Transcripts* (Ottawa: Deneau Publishers, n. d. [prob. 1983]), 9–10, 136; Hoover to Matthew Connelly, Sept. 12, 1945, HST-PSF; James Barros, "Alger Hiss and Harry Dexter White: The Canadian Connection," *Orbis* 21 (Fall 1977): 593–605.

E. E. Conroy to Director, Nov. 21, 1945, Bentley-Silvermaster, #56; Ladd to Director, Nov. 26, 1945, ibid, #108x12; Elizabeth Bentley, *Out of Bondage* (New York: Devin-Adair, 1951); Whittaker Chambers, *Witness* (New York: Random House, 1952), 405–46; Robert Chadwell Williams, *Klaus Fuchs, Atom Spy* (Cambridge: Harvard University Press, 1987), 70–74, 167, 195–202; Robert J. Lamphere and Tom Schachtman, *The FBI–KGB War: A Special Agent's Story* (New York: Random House, 1986), 28–31, 101–14; National Security Agency, Center for Cryptologic History, "Introduction: History of VENONA and Guide to the Translations," (Fort George G. Meade, Md.: National Security Agency, 1995).

10. Lamphere, *The FBI–KGB War,* 101–14.

11. Clifford, "American Relations with the Soviet Union"; William Remington, statement to the FBI, quoted in Gary May, *Un-American Activities: The Trials of William Remington* (New York: Oxford University Press, 1994), 91.

12. For a discussion of the ideological component in early perceptions of the Soviet danger, see Leffler, "The American Conception of National Security and the Beginnings of the Cold War, 1945–48."

13. Joint Chiefs of Staff, memo to the president, July 26, 1946, Box 14, Clifford Papers; Clifford, "American Relations with the Soviet Union"; Hoover to George E. Allen, Sept. 25, 1946, HST-PSF; Stephen J. Spingarn, notes on meeting, Jan. 24, 1947, Box 7, Stephen J. Spingarn Papers, HSTL: "Communist Infiltration of and Agitation in the Armed Forces," in Hoover to Vaughan, Feb. 6, 1946, HST-PSF.

14. Archer Drew, testimony, May 15, 1947, in *U. S. v. Carl Aldo Marzani,* District Court of United States for District of Columbia, transcript of the trial, reel 39 (microfilm ed., Fund for the Republic, New York) (hereafter Marzani trial); Herbert Philbrick, testimony, April 8, 1949, *United States of America, appellee, vs. Eugene Dennis et al.,* defendants-appellants. United States Court of Appeals for the Second Circuit, 1950, transcript of the trial, microfilm ed. (New York: Fund for the Republic) (hereafter Dennis trial), 4282; Louis Budenz, testimony, March 29–30, 1949, ibid., 3653, 3740–41.

15. Larson, *Origins of Containment,* 240.

On the servicemen's pressure for demobilization, see R. Alton Lee, "The Army 'Mutiny' of 1946," *Journal of American History* 53 (Dec. 1966): 555–571; "Communist Infiltration of and Agitation in the Armed Services," Feb. 6, 1946; see also Hoover to Vaughan, Jan. 9, Jan. 11, 1946, HST-PSF.

16. Statement of charges, Marzani trial, 76; Martin Bauml Duberman, *Paul Robeson* (New York: Knopf, 1988), 336–62; Mary L. Dudziak, "Desegregation as a Cold War Imperative," *Stanford Law Review* 41 (November 1988): 61–120.

17. *The Forrestal Diaries,* 243–44; NSC-68, 240; S. J. Chamberlin [director of intelligence, War Department] to A. Devitt Vanech, Feb. 11, 1947, and Thomas B. Inglis

[naval intelligence] to Vanech, Jan. 8, 1947, in Official File, 252-I, HSTL (hereafter HST-OF).

18. For a recent, but not particularly convincing, restatement of such allegations, see Harvey Klehr, John Earl Haynes, and Fridrikh Igorevich Firsov, eds., *The Secret World of American Communism* (New Haven: Yale University Press, 1995), 118. For Hoover's view, see Hoover to George E. Allen, May 29, 1946, HST-PSF.

19. Allen Weinstein, *Perjury: The Hiss-Chambers Case* (New York: Knopf, 1978), 58–59, 366; Ladd to A. H. Belmont, Nov. 23, 1953, in Harry Dexter White, #1157. For the text of the long statement Chambers made to the FBI in the spring of 1949, see *In Re Alger Hiss,* ed. Edith Tiger (New York: Hill and Wang, 1979), 198.

20. For a discussion of the partisan allegations about Hiss at Yalta, see Athan G. Theoharis, *The Yalta Myths* (Columbia: University of Missouri Press, 1970); "Report on Harry Dexter White," Feb. 1, 1946, in Truman to Fred M. Vinson, Feb. 6, 1946, HST-PSF; Director to Attorney General, Feb. 4, 1946, White, #8; Guy Hottel, report, Nov. 16, 1950, ibid., #21; Elizabeth Bentley, signed confession, Nov. 30, 1945, in Thomas G. Spencer, Summary Report, Dec. 5, 1945, Bentley-Silvermaster, #220; Louis B. Nichols to Clyde Tolson, Apr. 2, 1955, ibid., #1311; W. A. Branigan to Belmont, June 27, 1955, ibid., #1338.

21. For the most important airing of these allegations, see U.S. Senate, Committee on the Judiciary, Subcommittee on Internal Security, "Hearings on the Institute of Pacific Relations," 82nd Cong., 2d sess., 1951–1952. See also John N. Thomas, *The Institute of Pacific Relations* (Seattle: University of Washington Press, 1974); Ross Y. Koen, *The China Lobby in American Politics* (New York: Macmillan, 1960).

22. The best single book on Oppenheimer and his case is still Philip M. Stern, *The Oppenheimer Case: Security on Trial* (New York: Harper and Row, 1969). See also Barton J. Bernstein, "The Oppenheimer Loyalty-Security Case Reconsidered," *Stanford Law Review* 42 (July 1990): 1383–1484 and the transcript of Oppenheimer's 1954 case itself, United States Atomic Energy Commission, *In the Matter of J. Robert Oppenheimer: Transcript of Hearing before Personnel Security Board and Texts of Principal Documents and Letters* (Cambridge, Mass.: MIT Press, 1970, reprint of 1954 ed.).

23. Custodial detention memo, May 27, 1941, in J. Robert Oppenheimer, San Francisco, #1; Hoover to Byrnes, Nov. 15, 1945, Hoover to Vaughan, Nov. 15, 1945, Oppenheimer, #20; Hoover to Vaughan, Feb. 28, 1947, HST-PSF; William L. Borden to J. Edgar Hoover, Nov. 7, 1953, in *In the Matter of J. Robert Oppenheimer,* 837–38.

For a discussion of the policy issues involved in the Oppenheimer case, see Martin J. Sherwin, "J. Robert Oppenheimer: Enemies in High Places," paper delivered at the American Historical Association meeting, Dec. 29, 1990; Herbert F. York, *The Advisors: Oppenheimer, Teller and the Superbomb* (Stanford: Stanford University Press, 1988 ed.); and Bernstein, "The Oppenheimer Loyalty-Security Case Reconsidered."

24. Clifford, "American Relations with the Soviet Union"; Herken, *The Winning Weapon,* 116.

25. National Security Agency, "Introduction: History of VENONA," 7–9.

26. N. J. L. Pieper to Director, Nov. 26, 1943, FAECT, #172; Henry Stimson, memorandum for the president, Sept. 9, 1943, in File W3, Map Room, 171, Franklin D. Roosevelt Library, Hyde Park, New York (document courtesy of Barton Bernstein).

27. FBI, report, March 5, 1946, "U.S. [sic] Infiltration of the Radiation Laboratory, University of California, Berkeley, California," cited in J. Patrick Coyne to E. A. Tamm, July 24, 1946, in Belmont to Ladd, Nov. 9, 1953, White, #1261; Hoover to Harry Hopkins, May 7, 1943, in Robert Louis Benson and Michael Warner, eds., *Venona: Soviet Espionage and the American Response* (Washington, D.C.: National Security Agency, Central Intelligence Agency, 1996), 49–50. See also Ellen W. Schrecker, *No Ivory Tower: McCarthyism and the Universities* (New York: Oxford University Press, 1986), 126–42. Though I have seen sections of the FBI's FAECT file, the documents that come from the San Francisco field office that would have discussed the Berkeley Radiation Lab are all completely blacked out.

28. Schrecker, *No Ivory Tower*, 130–38; Warren Olney III, oral history interview, 351–54, Bancroft Library, University of California, Berkeley.

29. Herken, *The Winning Weapon*, contains a good discussion of the fallacy of the "secret" of the bomb.

30. For a discussion of the scientists' campaign against military control of atomic energy, see Alice Kimball Smith, *A Peril and a Hope* (Chicago: University of Chicago Press, 1965). See also Hoover to Allen, Nov. 6, 1945, Hoover to Vaughan, Dec. 7, 1945, both in HST-PSF. On the related case of E. U. Condon, see Jessica Wang, "Science, Security, and the Cold War: The Case of E. U. Condon," *Isis* 83 (June 1992): 238–69.

31. For these hearings, see House Un-American Activities Committee (hereafter HUAC), "Excerpts from hearings regarding investigation of Communist activities in connection with the atom bomb," September 9, 14, 16, 1948, 80th Cong., 2d sess.; "Hearings regarding Communist infiltration of radiation laboratory and atomic bomb project at the University of California, Berkeley, Calif., vol. 1, April 22, 26, May 25, June 10, 14, 1949, vol. 2 (identification of Scientist X), Aug. 26, 1949, July 1, Sept. 10, 1948, Aug. 14, Sept. 14, 27, 1949, 81st Cong., 1st sess., vol. 3, Dec. 20–22, 1950, 81st Cong., 2d sess.; Rep. Burr Harrison, remarks, HUAC, ibid., Dec. 20, 1950, 3422.

32. Kenneth O'Reilly, *Hoover and the Un-Americans: The FBI, HUAC, and the Red Menace* (Philadelphia: Temple University Press, 1983); HUAC, "Report on Soviet Espionage Activities in Connection with the Atom Bomb," Sept. 27, 1948, in *New York Times*, Sept. 28, 1948; Herken, *The Winning Weapon*, 115–36, 272–75.

33. Schrecker, *No Ivory Tower*, 139–48.

34. On the Gouzenko case, see the works cited in 9 *supra*.

35. Whitaker and Marcuse, *Cold War Canada*, 27–55.

36. For some differing theories about the source of the leak to Pearson, see Herken, *The Winning Weapon*, 114–36, 362–63; Weisbord, *The Strangest Dream*, 144; Whitaker and Marcuse, *Cold War Canada*, 27–57; Bothwell and Granatstein, *The Gouzenko Transcripts*, 10–12, 18; O'Reilly, *Hoover and the Un-Americans*, 80.

37. Bothwell and Granatstein, *The Gouzenko Transcripts*, 11–12, 14, 16–17;

Weisbord, *The Strangest Dream*, 141; Whitaker and Marcuse, *Cold War Canada*, 78–100. According to Gregg Herken, the Canadian government did not try all the suspected Soviet agents because Leslie Groves did not want a public discussion about controlling uranium supplies, see Herken, *The Winning Weapon*, 131, 363.

38. Royal Commission, *Report*, 44, 167, 188, 222, 230–37, 311–12, 361–65, 397, 435, 507–14, 624.

39. Harvey Klehr and Ronald Radosh, *The Amerasia Spy Case: Prelude to McCarthyism* (Chapel Hill: University of North Carolina Press, 1996); Athan Theoharis and John Stuart Cox, *The Boss: J. Edgar Hoover and the Great American Inquisition* (Philadelphia: Temple University Press, 1988), 239–48; Curt Gentry, *J. Edgar Hoover, The Man and the Secrets* (New York: Penguin, 1992, W. W. Norton, 1991), 338–40; Director to Connelly, Sept. 12, 1945, HST-PSF; Truman, handwritten note on "smg" to Connelly, July 5, 1950, HST-PSF; Bothwell and Granatstein, *The Gouzenko Transcripts*, 10, 136; Barros, "Alger Hiss and Harry Dexter White: The Canadian Connection," 595; Whitaker and Marcuse, *Cold War Canada*, 40–50; FBI Report, "Soviet Activities in the United States," July 25, 1946, Box 15, Clifford Papers; George M. Elsey, handwritten memo to Clifford, July 22, 1946, Box 63, Elsey Papers; Frances Perkins to William D. Hassett, Nov. 25, 1947, HST-OF, 2-E.

40. Bentley's initial story is contained in her signed statement to the FBI, Nov. 8, 1945, in E. E. Conroy to Director, Nov. 13, 1945, Bentley-Silvermaster, #581.

41. Conroy, teletype to Director, Nov. 8, 1945, Silvermaster-Bentley, #1; Thomas G. Spencer, Summary Report, Dec. 5, 1945, contains Bentley's long signed statement of November 30, 1945, ibid., #220; teletype (signature page omitted, but probably SAC, New York) to Director, Jan. 30, 1946, ibid., #485; Edward W. Dooley, Summary Report, Feb. 11, 1946, ibid., #762; SAC [name deleted], New Orleans, report, Nov. 20, 1953, Harry Dexter White, no serial number.

42. May, *Un-American Activities*, 87–88, 138, 143, 167, 203, 226–30, 279–85; Lini de Vries, *Up from the Cellar* (Minneapolis: Vanilla Press, 1979), 156–59; Conroy to Director, May 8, 1946, Silvermaster-Bentley, #1048; Director to Communications Section, October 26, 1953, White, #33; Herbert L. Packer, *Ex-Communist Witnesses* (Stanford: Stanford University Press, 1962), 59–119; Murray Kempton, *Part of Our Time* (New York: Simon and Schuster, 1955), 217–22.

43. Director to Vaughan, Nov. 8, 1945, HST-PSF; teletype, SAC, New York, to Director, Nov. 8, 1945, Silvermaster-Bentley, #1; Ladd to Director, Nov. 26, 1945, ibid., #108x12; Spencer, Summary Report, December 5, 1945, ibid., #220; Harold V. Kennedy, Summary Report, Dec. 7, 1945, Silvermaster-Bentley, New York #248; Kennedy, Summary Report, Dec. 21, 1945, ibid., #249; C. W. Evans to G. C. Callan, Nov. 26, 1945, Silvermaster-Bentley, #75; Ladd to Tamm, Nov. 19, 1945, ibid., #37; R. C. Hendon to Tolson, Nov. 19, 1945, ibid., #38; H. B. Fletcher to Ladd, Feb. 2, 1950, White, no serial number; Guy Hottel, Summary Report, Nov. 16, 1950, ibid., #21; "Budget Estimates, Federal Bureau of Investigation, Nov. 30, 1945," HST-PSF.

44. Ladd to Director, Nov. 14, 1953, White, #62; Ladd to Tamm, Nov. 26, 1945,

Silvermaster-Bentley, #76. In a 1970 request to destroy the transcripts of the telephone taps in the case, the agent in charge of the FBI's Washington office ruefully admitted, "All efforts have failed to break the apparent conspiracy of silence." SAC, Washington, to Director, Mar. 6, 1970, White, no serial number.

45. Klehr, Haynes, and Firsov, *The Secret World of American Communism,* 309–16; John J. Abt with Michael Myerson, *Advocate and Activist: Memoirs of an American Communist Lawyer* (Urbana: University of Illinois Press, 1993), 40–42, 76–77; May, *Un-American Activities,* 306.

46. Klehr, Haynes, and Firsov, *The Secret World of American Communism,* 96–118, 295, 309–17; New York to Moscow, #586, April 29, 1944, *Third VENONA Release* (Fort George G. Meade, Md.: National Security Agency, Central Security Service, Mar. 1996) (hereafter VENONA, III).

47. The most important book on the Hiss case is Weinstein, *Perjury,* but because it relies mainly on Chambers's testimony and FBI reports that rely on Chambers's testimony, it does not definitively prove that Hiss was a spy. See also Tanenhaus, *Whittaker Chambers;* Conroy, telex, Nov. 10, 1946, Silvermaster-Bentley, #13; Conroy, telex, Nov. 16, 1945, ibid., #26; Conroy to Director, Dec. 3, 1945, Silvermaster-Bentley, New York, #421; *In Re Alger Hiss,* 253–57.

48. Belmont to Ladd, Dec. 22, 1953, White, no serial number; Weinstein, *Perjury,* 360–68.

49. Frank G. Johnstone, Summary Report, Dec. 4, 1948, reproduced in *In Re Alger Hiss,* 267–73. The film is described in ibid., 6; Belmont to Ladd, Dec. 22, 1953, White, no serial number; Weinstein, *Perjury,* 169–78; Chambers, *Witness,* 40–41, 445.

50. Washington to Moscow, #1822, Mar. 30, 1945, VENONA, III. Hiss's *Recollections of a Life* (New York: Seaver Books/Henry Holt, 1988) is completely evasive. For evidence on Chambers's contradictions, see *In Re Alger Hiss,* 53–64, 183–288, 273, and Weinstein, *Perjury,* 333–46. On the significance of the typewriter, see *In Re Alger Hiss,* 65–100, and Weinstein, *Perjury,* 386–97.

51. There is little scholarship on the Coplon case. Coplon herself is alive and well and living in Brooklyn but will not talk about the case. I could not obtain her FBI file. The main source for the case, therefore, is the trial transcript, *United States of America v. Judith Coplon, defendant.* Washington, D.C. District Court, 1949 (microfilm ed., Fund for the Republic, New York) (hereafter Coplon trial). See also Lamphere, *The FBI–KGB War,* 99–125.

52. Coplon trial, passim; New York to Moscow, #1014, July 20, 1944, #1587, Nov. 12, 1944, #1714, Dec. 5, 1944, #1845, Dec. 31, 1944, #25, Jan. 8, 1945, #992, June 26, 1945, #268, Mar. 24, 1945, VENONA, III.

53. New York to Moscow, #911, June 27, 1944, #1053, July 26, 1944, #1491, Oct. 22, 1944, #1600, Nov. 14, 1944, #1657, Nov. 27, 1944, #1715, Dec. 5, 1944, #1773, Dec. 16, 1945, #28, Jan. 8, 1945, #200, Mar. 6, 1945, VENONA, I.

54. Report [name deleted], New York, Mar. 23, 1945, FAECT, #289; Lamphere, *The FBI–KGB War,* 90–98, 178–207; Williams, *Klaus Fuchs, Atom Spy,* 1–8, 116–35.

55. The key scholarly indictment of the Rosenbergs is Ronald Radosh and Joyce

Milton, *The Rosenberg File: A Search for the Truth* (New York: Holt, Rinehart and Winston, 1983). The main defense is in Walter and Miriam Schneir, *Invitation to an Inquest* (New York: Pantheon, 1983) and Robert and Michael Meeropol, *We Are Your Sons,* 2d ed. (Urbana: University of Illinois Press, 1986). The Venona transcripts led the Schneirs to revise their assessments.

56. Radosh and Milton, *The Rosenberg File,* 146–47, 417. There is a Venona document that implies that Ethel Rosenberg knew about her husband's espionage activities, though probably did not participate in them. See New York to Moscow, #1657, Nov. 27, 1944, VENONA, I.

57. Radosh and Milton, *The Rosenberg File,* 275–90; Nicholas von Hoffman, *Citizen Cohn: The Life and Times of Roy Cohn* (New York: Doubleday, 1988), 101–104.

58. On Fuchs and other Soviet spies, see Williams, *Klaus Fuchs, Atom Spy;* Vladimir Chikov, "How the Soviet intelligence service 'split' the American atom," *New Times* 16 (April 23, 1991): 37–40; ibid., 17 (April 30, 1991), 36–39; Joseph Albright and Marcia Kunstel, "The Boy Who Gave Away the Bomb," *New York Times Magazine,* Sept. 14, 1997, 70–73; New York to Moscow, #972, 979, 983, June 22–23, 1943; ibid., #212, Feb. 11, 1944; ibid., #1585, Nov. 12, 1944; ibid., #1773, Dec. 16, 1944; ibid., #298, Mar. 31, 1945, VENONA, I.

On the Soviet bomb, see Holloway, *Stalin and the Bomb.* See also Yuli Khariton and Yuli Smirnov, "The Khariton Version," *Bulletin of Atomic Scientists* 49 (May 1993): 20–31; Roald Sagdeev, "Russian Scientists Save American Secrets," ibid., 32–36; Sergei Leskov, "Dividing the Glory of the Fathers," ibid., 37–39.

On the type of information that reached the Soviet Union, see New York to Moscow, #1053, July 26, 1944, VENONA, I; New York to Moscow, #732, May 20, 1944, ibid., #928, June 28, 1944, Moscow to New York, #1048, July 25, 1944, New York to Moscow, #211, 212, Feb. 10, 1945, Moscow to New York, #154, Feb. 16, 1945; ibid., #305, Apr. 1, 1945, all in VENONA, II; May, *Un-American Activities,* 305; Whitaker and Marcuse, *Cold War Canada,* 72–75, 92; Royal Commission, *Report,* 89–169, 304–5, 379–406, 455, 617–24; Weinstein, *Perjury,* 236–37; Herken, *The Winning Weapon,* 131; Merrily Weisbord, *The Strangest Dream,* 128–34.

59. New York to Moscow, #590, April 29, 1944, ibid., #598–599, May 2, 1944, ibid., #900, June 24, 1944, ibid., #1119–21, Aug. 4–5, 1944, ibid., #1234, Aug. 29, 1944, ibid., #1469, Oct. 17, 1944, ibid., #55, Jan. 15, 1945, ibid., #83, Jan. 18, 1945, Moscow to New York, #192, Mar. 3, 1945, ibid., #195, May 3, 1945, ibid., #220, Mar. 11, 1945, Washington to Moscow, #3598, June 21, 1945, ibid., #3655, June 25, 1945, ibid., #3640, June 23, 1945, ibid., #3688, June 28, 1945, VENONA, II; Weinstein, *Perjury,* 235–55; Klehr, Haynes, and Firsov, *The Secret World of American Communism,* 110–18, 143–51.

60. John Stewart Service, *The Amerasia Papers* (Berkeley: University of California Press, 1971), 30.

61. New York to Moscow, #83, Jan. 18, 1945, VENONA, III. Sections II and III of the VENONA documents are full of such information. See also Klehr, Haynes, and Firsov, *The Secret World of American Communism,* 118, 143–51.

62. Abt, *Advocate and Activist,* 40–42, 76–77.

63. New York to Moscow, #687, May 13, 1944, ibid., #1313, Sept. 13, 1944, ibid., #1433–35, Oct. 10, 1944, Moscow to New York, #1065, July 28, 1944, ibid., #284, 286, Mar. 28, 1945, VENONA, III.

This phrase comes from the response to a Comintern questionnaire by the acknowledged Soviet agent Morris Cohen. Klehr, Haynes, and Firsov, *The Secret World of American Communism,* 218–20.

64. Weisbord, *The Strangest Dream,* 130; May, *Un-American Activities,* 129, 165; teletype, New York to Director, Nov. 30, 1945, Bentley-Silvermaster, New York, #432.

65. May, *Un-American Activities,* 290.

66. William L. Ryan and Sam Summerlin, *The China Cloud: America's Tragic Blunder and China's Rise to Nuclear Power* (Boston: Little, Brown, 1968), 134–38, 142–45.

67. Iris Chang, *Thread of the Silkworm* (New York: Basic Books, 1995), 68–171.

68. Chang, *Thread of the Silkworm,* 172–98; Ryan and Summerlin, *The China Cloud,* 81–184; John Wilson Lewis and Xue Litai, *China Builds the Bomb* (Stanford: Stanford University Press, 1988), 50, 147.

69. SANACC [State-Army-Navy-Air Force Coordinating Committee], ad hoc committee report, Nov. 4, 1948, NSC meeting, #36, HST-PSF; report [name deleted], Washington, D.C., Nov. 22, 1946, Smith Act, #357.

70. Clifford, "American Relations with the Soviet Union"; Hoover, memo, cited in Sigmund Diamond, "Labor History vs. Labor Historiography: The FBI, James B. Carey, and the Association of Catholic Trade Unionists," in *Religion, Ideology and Nationalism in Europe and America: Essays Presented in Honor of Yehoshua Arieli* (Jerusalem: Historical Society of Israel and Zalman Shazar Center for Jewish History, 1986), 308; Steve Rosswurm, "Introduction: An Overview and Preliminary Assessment of the CIO's Expelled Unions," in Rosswurm, ed., *The CIO's Left-Led Unions* (New Brunswick, N.J.: Rutgers, 1992), 1–16.

71. On the business community's attitudes toward labor in the immediate postwar years, see Howell John Harris, *The Right to Manage: Industrial Relations Policies of American Business in the 1940s* (Madison: University of Wisconsin Press, 1982); Elizabeth Fones-Wolf, *Selling Free Enterprise: The Business Assault on Labor and Liberalism, 1945–1960* (Urbana: University of Illinois Press, 1994); and Peter H. Irons, "American Business and the Origins of McCarthyism," in Robert Griffith and Athan Theoharis, eds., *The Specter* (New York: Franklin Watts, 1974), 74–89.

On the strike wave and the origins of Taft-Hartley, see Harry A. Millis and Emily Clark Brown, *From the Wagner Act to Taft-Hartley* (Chicago: University of Chicago Press, 1950), 286–318; R. Alton Lee, *Truman and Taft-Hartley* (Lexington: University Press of Kentucky, 1966), 18, 52; George Lipsitz, *Class and Culture in Cold War America* (South Hadley, Mass.: J. F. Bergin, 1981), 37–84; Martin Halpern, *UAW Politics in the Cold War Era* (Albany: State University of New York Press, 1988), 39.

72. Truman, quoted in Harvey A. Levenstein, *Communism, Anticommunism, and the CIO* (Westport, Conn.: Greenwood Press, 1981), 242; Nelson Lichtenstein,

Labor's War at Home: The CIO in World War II (New York: Cambridge University Press, 1982), 203–32; report, "Communist Influence in Present Labor Disturbances," Oct. 31, 1945, in Director, FBI, to Vaughan, Oct. 31, 1945; see also Director to Vaughan, Nov. 29, 1945, Jan. 5, 9, 11, Feb. 5, May 29, 1946, Aug. 6, 1947, Director to Allen, June 5, 7, 1946, all in HST-PSF.

73. Halpern, *UAW Politics in the Cold War Era,* 173–83; Roger Keeran, *The Communist Party and the Auto Workers Unions* (Bloomington: Indiana University Press, 1980), 266–78; Irving Richter, *Labor's Struggles, 1945–1949: A Participant's View* (New York: Cambridge University Press, 1994), 55–95; Hugh Swofford, "Account of the Christoffel Case," Jan. 1950, Nat Ganley Papers, Archives of Labor History and Urban Affairs, Walter P. Reuther Library, Wayne State University, Detroit, Mich. (document courtesy of Steven Rosswurm).

74. Louis Budenz, testimony, March 13, 1947, House of Representatives, Committee on Education and Labor, "Hearings, Amendments to the National Labor Relations Act," 80th Cong., 1st sess., 3609–13 (hereafter HCEL). See also the testimony of Robert Buse and Harold Christoffel, Mar. 1, 1947, ibid., 1974–2134; Budenz, testimony, Mar. 30, 1949, Dennis trial, 3748–49.

On the questionable nature of Budenz's testimony, see Packer, *Ex-Communist Witnesses,* 121–77; SAC, New York, to Director, Oct. 23, 1951, Budenz, New York, #404; list of questions drawn up for Budenz in J. C. Strickland to Ladd, Dec. 3, 1945, Budenz, HQ, #149x; summary of interviews with Budenz in Winterrowd to Strickland, Feb. 7, 1947, ibid., #211.

75. John F. Kennedy, March 13, 1947, HCEL, 3616; Swofford, "Account of the Christoffel Case"; Stephen Meyer, *"Stalin Over Wisconsin" The Making and Unmaking of Militant Unionism, 1900–1950* (New Brunswick, N.J.: Rutgers University Press, 1992), 227; "The Case of Harold Christoffel," pamphlet, n. d.; "The Case of Harold Christoffel, II," pamphlet, n. d., both in reel 20, Black Studies Research Sources, August Meier and John H. Bracey, Jr., general editors; Manuscript Collections from the Schomburg Center for Research in Black Culture, Papers of the Civil Rights Congress (Frederick, Md.: University Publications of America, 1988) (hereafter CRC); press release, Sept. 19, 1952, reel 3, CRC.

76. Meyer, *"Stalin Over Wisconsin,"* 198–210; H. K. Johnson to Director, Feb. 27, 1947, Communist Infiltration, UAW-CIO, #948; Director to T. Lamar Caudle, Aug. 21, 1946, ibid., #907; Nichols to Tolson, memorandum, March 11, 1947, ibid., #954x; Johnson to Director, March 21, 1947, Harold Christoffel, #145; Ladd to Director, memorandum, June 17, 1947, ibid., #177; statement by Charles Kersten, in clipping from *Milwaukee Journal,* March 7, 1948, Christoffel, #261.

77. David Lilienthal, quoted in "Specifications for a Sound National Labor Policy," mimeographed statement in H[arold] W. Story to Clare E. Hoffman, Mar. 21, 1949, Clare Hoffman Papers, Michigan Historical Collections, Bentley Historical Library, University of Michigan, Ann Arbor; *American Communications Association v. Douds,* 339 U.S. 382 (1950).

78. Floyd D. Lucia, testimony, Feb. 27, 1947, "Hearings Regarding Communism in Labor Unions in the United States," HUAC, 80th Cong., 1st sess., 5.

79. Ronald Filippelli, "The United Electrical, Radio and Machine Workers of America, 1933–1949: The Struggle for Control" (Ph.D. diss., Pennsylvania State University, 1970), 91; Senator John Marshall Butler, press release, n. d. [Aug. 1954], in Series II, Hymen Schlesinger Papers, Archives of Industrial Society, University of Pittsburgh; R. N. Denham to Board, Nov. 25, 1949, and "NLRB Summary of Section 9(h) Problems," undated memorandum, Box 692, National Labor Relations Board Records, Record Group 25, National Archives (hereafter NLRB Records); Christopher John Gerard, " 'A Program of Cooperation': The FBI, the Senate Internal Security Subcommittee, and the Communist Issue, 1950–1956" (Ph.D. diss., Marquette University, 1993), 230; Howard B. Gliedman, affidavit, Sept. 27, 1956, in Ray Klausner to Joseph Selley, Nov. 8, 1956, Box 10, American Communications Association Papers, SHSW; Levenstein, *Communism, Anticommunism, and the CIO,* 310; Lilienthal to Charles E. Wilson, Sept 27, 1948, Gordon Dean to Hubert H. Humphrey, Dec. 14, 1951, both in "Communist Domination of Certain Unions," Part 2, U.S. Senate, Report of the Subcommittee on Labor of the Committee on Labor and Public Welfare, 82nd Cong., 2d sess., 1952, 3, 13–14.

80. Senator John Marshall Butler, press release, n. d. [Aug. 1954], in Schlesinger Papers; Butler, quoted in *Washington Post,* Sept. 2, 1953; Victor Rabinowitz, interview with the author, Apr. 10, 1990.

81. Victor Riesel, speech, Nov. 28, 1951, published in *Management Record,* Apr. 1951; Harvey Matusow, testimony, Oct. 8, 1952, "Communist Domination of Union Officials in Vital Defense Industry — International Union of Mine, Mill, and Smelter Workers," Hearings before the Subcommittee to Investigate the Administration of the Internal Security Act and other Internal Security Laws of the Committee on the Judiciary, U.S. Senate, 82nd Cong., 2d sess. (hereafter SISS), 153; Vernon H. Jensen, *Nonferrous Metals Industry Unionism 1932–1954* (Ithaca, N.Y.: Cornell University Press, 1954), xiii.

82. On the politicization of waterfront workers, see Bruce Nelson, *Workers on the Waterfront* (Urbana: University of Illinois Press, 1988) and Howard Kimeldorf, *Reds or Rackets? The Making of Radical and Conservative Unions on the Waterfront* (Berkeley and Los Angeles: University of California Press, 1988). On maritime workers during the Cold War, see Charles P. Larrowe, *Harry Bridges* (Westport, Conn.: Lawrence Hill, 1972); Levenstein, *Communism, Anticommunism, and the CIO,* 145–48, 235; and Ralph S. Brown, Jr., and John D. Fassett, "Security Tests for Maritime Workers: Due Process under the Port Security Program," *Yale Law Journal* 62 (July 1953): 1163–1208.

83. Bruno Stein, "Loyalty and Security Cases in Arbitration," *Industrial and Labor Relations Review* 17 (Oct. 1963); Mark McColloch, *White Collar Workers in Transition, The Boom Years, 1940–1970* (Westport, Conn.: Greenwood Press, 1983), 72; Carl Bernstein, *Loyalties: A Son's Memoir* (New York: Simon and Schuster, 1989),

173–258; James J. Matles and James Higgins, *Them and Us* (Englewood Cliffs, N.J.: Prentice-Hall, 1974), 174–80.

84. Report of the Broyles committee, quoted in E. Houston Harsha, "Illinois," in Walter Gellhorn, ed., *The States and Subversion* (Ithaca, N.Y.: Cornell University Press, 1952), 83–84; Benjamin Gitlow, manuscript article on espionage, n. d., Gitlow Papers, Hoover Institution on War, Revolution and Peace, Stanford University (hereafter Hoover Institution).

85. American Business Consultants, *Red Channels* (New York: American Business Consultants, 1950), 5; Robert Denham to John M. Houston, July 5, 1950, Box 696, NLRB Records; Herbert Mitgang, *Dangerous Dossiers* (New York: Ballantine, 1989); Natalie Robins, *Alien Ink: The FBI's War on Freedom of Expression* (New York: William Morrow, 1992); Stein, "Loyalty and Security Cases in Arbitration," 107.

86. Director to SAC, New York, July 7, 1945, Smith Act #x; Director, memorandum to Clark, Jan. 27, 1948, cited in U. S. Congress, Senate Select Committee to Study Governmental Operations with Respect to Intelligence Activities, *Final Report,* Book III, "Supplementary Detailed Staff Reports on Intelligence Activities and the Rights of Americans," 94th Cong., 2d sess., Apr. 23, 1976, 392–405 (hereafter SDSRIARA), 439; Director to SAC, New York, Mar. 4, 1946, Smith Act, #41; memo, J. P. Coyne to Ladd, Aug. 14, 1947, ibid., #855.

87. Ladd, memorandum to Director, Jan. 22, 1948, SDSRIARA, 439; Director, memorandum to Tamm, Ladd, Tolson, Oct. 30, 1947, Smith Act, #1123.

88. Michal R. Belknap, *Cold War Political Justice: The Smith Act, the Communist Party, and American Civil Liberties* (Westport, Conn.: Greenwood Press, 1977), 45–47; Peter Steinberg, *The Great "Red Menace": United States Prosecution of American Communists, 1947–1952* (Westport, Conn.: Greenwood Press, 1984), 80, 105; memorandum, Tamm to Director, Apr. 3, 1947, Smith Act #813; memorandum, Director to T. Vincent Quinn, Oct. 22, 1947, ibid., #1103; Director, memorandum to Tolson, Tamm, Ladd, Nichols, Jan. 13, 1948, ibid., #1222; handwritten memorandum, Director, Feb. 9, 1948, ibid., #1265; memorandum, Director to Quinn, Feb. 17, 1948, ibid., #1286; "Brief to Establish the Illegal Status of the Communist Party of the United States of America," Feb. 3, 1948, enclosure in Director to Attorney General, Feb. 5, 1948, ibid., #1269; John F. X. McGohey, handwritten memorandum of preparations for the Smith Act prosecution, Box 1, John F. X. McGohey papers, HSTL; memorandum, Ladd to Director, July 19, 1948, Smith Act, #1539; memorandum, executives conference to Director, Apr. 6, 1948, Smith Act, #1370; memorandum, Ladd to Director, Apr. 30, 1948, ibid., #1384; memorandum, Fletcher to Ladd, June 12, 1948, ibid., #1466; memorandum, Ladd to Tamm, June 22, 1948, ibid., #1488; memorandum, Ladd to Director, June 19, 1948, ibid., #1522.

89. Memorandum, Ladd to Director, July 19, 1948, Smith Act, #1539; George F. Kniep, memorandum, "The Communist Party of the United States of America," n. d., Box 1, McGohey Papers.

90. Hoover, handwritten comments on memorandum, Ladd to Director, June 22,

1948, Smith Act, #1511; memorandum, Fletcher to Ladd, June 12, 1948, ibid., #1466; Kniep, memorandum, "The Communist Party of the United States of America"; memorandum, Ladd to Director, Dec. 12, 1946, Smith Act, #378x; Justice Frank Murphy, opinion, in *Schneiderman v. United States,* 320 U.S. 118, 155, 157; memorandum, J. A. Carlson to H. H. Clegg, May 17, 1947, Smith Act, #814.

91. Memorandum, Director to SAC, New York, Dec. 31, 1946, Smith Act, #385; memorandum, Ladd to Tamm, Jan. 20, 1948, ibid., #1275; teletype, Edward Scheidt to Director, Jan. 7, 1949, ibid., #2685.

92. Summary of brief in Ladd to Director, Feb. 7, 1948, Smith Act, #1340; Director to SAC, New York, and other field offices, July 16, 1946, ibid., #218; report [name deleted], Seattle, Nov. 8, 1946, ibid., #345; memorandum, Fletcher to Ladd, June 16, 1948, ibid., #1477; Scheidt to Director, Oct. 26, 1948, ibid., #2097; McGohey, "Opening Statement on Behalf of the Government," March 21, 1949, in Dennis trial, 3208–9.

93. Belknap, *Cold War Political Justice,* 109–10; teletype, Scheidt to Director, Nov. 1, 1948, Smith Act, #2224; memo, SAC, New York, to Director, Nov. 26, 1948, ibid., #2291; M. B. Rhodes, SAC, St. Paul, to Director, Mar. 22, 1946, ibid., #47; report [name deleted], Chicago, Dec. 5, 1946, ibid., #377; Scheidt to Director, Mar. 22, 1949, ibid., #3086; memorandum, SAC, Philadelphia, to Director, Mar. 7, 1949, ibid., #3200.

94. Conroy to Director, Aug. 1, 1946, Smith Act, #227; report [name deleted], Washington, D.C., Nov. 11, 1946, ibid., #357; Scheidt to Director, Oct. 26, 1948, ibid., #2097; Budenz, testimony, March 24, 29, 30, 1949, Dennis trial, 3559–62, 3627–28, 3664–71, 3747–50; report on Gus Hall, June 29, 1948, in "Appendix of Exhibits for Individual Brief Summaries Concerning National Leaders and Officers of Communist Party," Smith Act, no serial #.

95. Memorandum, Ladd to Director, Dec. 12, 1946, Smith Act, #378x1; memorandum, Director to SAC, New York, Dec. 31, 1946, ibid., #385.

96. Memorandum, SAC, Detroit, to Director, Mar. 22, 1947, Smith Act, #679; A. C. Cornelius, SAC, Albany, to Director, Mar. 21, 1947, ibid., #678; memorandum, SAC, Seattle, to Director, Mar. 20, 1947, ibid., #680; memorandum, SAC, Philadelphia, to Director, Mar. 29, 1947, ibid., #681; Harry M. Kimball, SAC, San Francisco, to Director, Mar. 27, 1947, ibid., #682; G. R. McSwain, SAC, Chicago, to Director, Mar. 22, 1947, ibid., #683; memorandum, SAC, Buffalo, to Director, Mar. 17, 1947, ibid., #685; memorandum, SAC, Boston, to Director, Mar. 24, 1947, ibid., #687; SAC, St. Louis, to Director, Mar. 31, 1947, ibid., #702; Guy Hottel to Director, Mar. 17, 1947, ibid., #704; memorandum, SAC, Newark, to Director, Mar. 14, 1947, ibid., #507; Scheidt to Director, Sept. 20, 1947, ibid., #970; Budenz, testimony, March 29, 30, 1949, Dennis trial, 36 [last 2 digits illegible], 3707.

For the use of Aesopian language in other prosecutions, see George A. Downing, Order, June 7, 1954, IUMMSW Compliance, Box 317, Archives Western Federation of Miners & Mine-Mill, Historical Collections, University of Colorado, Boulder (hereafter Mine-Mill Records); David Bazelon, opinion, *Gold v. United States,* April 19, 1956, ibid.

97. On the use of literature in earlier political trials, see William Preston, Jr., *Aliens and Dissenters: Federal Suppression of Radicals, 1903–1933* (Cambridge: Harvard University Press, 1963), 118–30, 146–51; Leo P. Ribuffo, *The Old Christian Right: The Protestant Far Right from the Great Depression to the Cold War* (Philadelphia: Temple University Press, 1983), 201–203.

Memorandum, Ladd to Tamm, Jan. 20, 1948, Smith Act, #1275; memorandum, Ladd to Director, Feb. 7, 1948, ibid., #1340; teletype, Scheidt to Washington, Baltimore, Los Angeles field offices, Jan. 18, 1949, ibid., #2639; Budenz, testimony, Mar. 30, 31, 1949, Dennis trial, 3740–41, 3764, 3780–82. On the FBI's collection of party literature, see memorandum, Director to SAC, New York, Dec. 20, 1946, Smith Act, #386; memorandum, Director to SAC, New York, Sept. 24, 1947, ibid., #1013; memorandum, SAC, New York, to Director, Jan. 7, 1947, ibid., #387.

98. Memorandum, Ladd to Tamm, Jan. 20, 1948, Smith Act, #1275; report [name deleted], Cleveland, Aug. 29, 1947, ibid., #888; memorandum, Whitson to Coyne, Aug. 8, 1947, ibid., #947; Scheidt to Director, Sept. 20, 1947, ibid., #970; Kniep, memorandum, "The Communist Party of the United States of America."

99. Memorandum, Fletcher to Director, Sept. 30, 1948, Smith Act, #1816; memorandum, Director to SAC, San Francisco, Oct. 4, 1948, ibid., #1839; memorandum, Fletcher to Director, Oct. 1, 1948, ibid., #1881; memorandum, Fletcher to Director, Oct. 4, 1948, ibid., #1902; Director to Communications Section, teletype to SAC, St. Louis, n. d., ibid., #1916; memorandum, Fletcher to Director, Oct. 14, 1948, ibid., #1926; teletype, Norris to Director, n. d., ibid., #1933; memorandum, Fletcher to Ladd, Oct. 26, 1948, ibid., #2048; A. E. Ostholthoff, SAC, Cincinnati, to Director, Nov. 24, 1948, ibid., #2425; H. G. Maynor, SAC, Buffalo, to Director, Apr. 12, 1949, ibid., #3244.

100. SAC Letter, No. 11, Series 1949, Jan. 28, 1949, Smith Act, no serial #; memorandum, Fletcher to Ladd, Sept. 28, 1948, ibid., #1814; memorandum [name deleted], New York, Oct. 12, 1948, ibid., #1893; Scheidt to Director, Oct. 20, 1948, ibid., #1995; Scheidt to Director, Nov. 10, 1948, ibid., #2303; memorandum, Fletcher to Ladd, Oct. 25, 1948, ibid., #2052; memorandum, Fletcher to Ladd, Oct. 26, 1948, ibid., #2037; teletype, D. K. Brown, El Paso, to Director, Feb. 1, 1948, ibid., #2723; Brown to Director, Feb. 2, 1949, ibid., #2753; teletype, Scheidt to Director, n. d. [Oct. 1948], ibid., #1962; Scheidt to Director, Nov. 2, 1948, ibid., #2086; memorandum, SAC, New York, to Director, Dec. 9, 1948, ibid., #2455; memorandum, Ladd to Director, Oct. 17, 1948, ibid., #2117; memorandum, SAC, Detroit, to Director, Nov. 3, 1948, ibid., #2124; memorandum, SAC, New York, to Director, Nov. 3, 1948, ibid., #2153; J. B. Wilcox, SAC, Seattle, to Director, Nov. 2, 1948, ibid., #2200; R. J. Abbaticchio, Jr., SAC, Cleveland, Dec. 2, 1948, ibid., #2468; Wilcox to Director, Dec. 9, 1948, ibid., #2379; teletype, Scheidt to Director, Dec. 8, 1948, ibid., #2401; memorandum, Fletcher to Director, Oct. 15, 1948, ibid., no serial #; teletype, Scheidt to Director, April 7, 1949, ibid., #3317.

101. Richard Gladstein, oral history interview, Bancroft Library, University of California, Berkeley, 5, 8–14; Stanley I. Kutler, *The American Inquisition: Justice*

and Injustice in the Cold War (New York: Hill and Wang, 1982), 156; Belknap, *Cold War Political Justice,* 5–117; George Charney, *A Long Journey* (Chicago: Quadrangle, 1968), 202; memorandum, Fletcher to Ladd, Jan. 14, 1949, Smith Act, #2663.

102. John Gates, *The Story of an American Communist* (New York: Thomas Nelson and Sons, 1958), 126–27; Gladstein, oral history, 6–12; Kutler, *The American Inquisition,* 156–57.

103. Kniep, memorandum, "The Communist Party of the United States of America"; McGohey, memorandum, Sept. 30, 1948, Box 1, McGohey Papers; memorandum, Coyne to Tamm, Nov. 25, 1946, Budenz, #190; memorandum, Coyne to Tamm, Sept. 30, 1946, ibid., #192; Scheidt to Director, Oct. 27, 1948, Smith Act, #2074; summary of interviews with Budenz, Dec. 1945 and April 1945, in Winterrowd to Strickland, Feb. 7, 1947, Budenz, #211; Budenz, testimony, Mar. 25, 1949, Dennis trial, 3559–62.

104. Herbert Philbrick, testimony, April 6, 7, 8, 1949, Dennis trial, 4153–4251, 4282.

105. Abraham Isserman, remarks, Mar. 30, 31, 1949, Dennis trial, 3689, 3729, 3799; Judge Harold Medina, remarks, Mar. 30, 1949, Dennis trial, 3761.

106. Kutler, *The American Inquisition,* 155; Steinberg, *The Great "Red Menace,"* 156–77; memorandum, Fletcher to Ladd, Feb. 15, 1949, Smith Act, #283; Medina, remarks, Mar. 21, 24, 1949, Dennis trial, 3238, 3231, 3469.

107. Memorandum, Fletcher to Ladd, Feb. 4, 1949, Smith Act, #2913; memorandum, Baumgardner to Ladd, Mar. 18, 1949, ibid., #3098; teletype, Scheidt to Director, Mar. 18, 1949, ibid., serial # illegible; memorandum, Director to Assistant Attorney General Alexander Campbell, Mar. 31, 1949, ibid., #3213. On Medina's behavior, see Belknap, *Cold War Political Justice,* 76–112; Kutler, *The American Inquisition,* 157–59; Steinberg, *The Great "Red Menace,"* 156–77; Gladstein, oral history, 16.

108. Belknap, *Cold War Political Justice,* 113; conference notes, Dec. 9, 1950, Box 206, No. 336 (d), *Dennis v. U.S.* Cert: Conf. and Misc. Memoranda, William O. Douglas Papers, Library of Congress, Washington, D.C.

109. Opinion of Vinson, C. J., in *Dennis et al. v. United States,* 341 U.S., 510–11.

110. *Dennis v. U.S.,* 498. There is a useful discussion of this opinion in Marc Rohr, "Communists and the First Amendment: The Shaping of Freedom of Advocacy in the Cold War Era," *San Diego Law Review* 28 (1991), 42–43.

111. Belknap, *Cold War Political Justice,* 144; Al Richmond, *A Long View from the Left* (Boston: Houghton Mifflin, 1973), 298; Charney, *A Long Journey,* 206–208.

6: "A JOB FOR PROFESSIONALS": THE FBI AND ANTICOMMUNISM

1. Memorandum, D. M. Ladd to Director, Feb. 27, 1946, U. S. Congress, Senate Select Committee to Study Governmental Operations with Respect to Intelligence Activities, *Final Report,* Book III, "Supplementary Detailed Staff Reports on Intelli-

gence Activities and the Rights of Americans," 94th Cong., 2d sess., April 23, 1976 (hereafter SDSRIARA), 429–30; Kenneth O'Reilly, *Hoover and the Un-Americans: The FBI, HUAC, and the Red Menace* (Philadelphia: Temple University Press, 1983), 76–79; "Budget Estimates," Federal Bureau of Investigation, Nov. 30, 1945, in Harry S. Truman, President's Secretary's File (hereafter HST-PSF), Harry S. Truman Library (hereafter HSTL).

2. William W. Keller, *The Liberals and J. Edgar Hoover: Rise and Fall of a Domestic Intelligence State* (Princeton: Princeton University Press, 1989), 3–27.

3. McCarthy, quoted in David Oshinsky, *A Conspiracy So Immense: The World of Joe McCarthy* (New York: Free Press, 1983), 257. On the FBI's internal culture, see Curt Gentry, *J. Edgar Hoover: The Man and the Secrets* (New York: W. W. Norton, 1991); Richard Gid Powers, *Secrecy and Power: The Life of J. Edgar Hoover* (New York: Free Press, 1987); and Athan G. Theoharis and John Stuart Cox, *The Boss: J. Edgar Hoover and the Great American Inquisition* (Philadelphia: Temple University Press, 1988); M. Wesley Swearingen, *FBI Secrets: An Agent's Exposé* (Boston: South End Press, 1995).

4. Memorandum, Ladd to Director, Feb. 27, 1946, SDSRIARA, 430; on the FBI's public relations operations, see Richard Gid Powers, *G-Men: Hoover's FBI in American Popular Culture* (Carbondale: Southern Illinois University Press, 1983) and O'Reilly, *Hoover and the Un-Americans,* 75–100.

5. SDSRIARA, 399–404; Gentry, *J. Edgar Hoover,* 391–92, 417–18; Theoharis and Cox, *The Boss,* 189–91, 200; Powers, *Secrecy and Power,* 271–74; William C. Sullivan with Bill Brown, *The Bureau: My Thirty Years in Hoover's FBI* (New York: W. W. Norton, 1979), 40–41, 62–63, 70–71, 84, 183; V. P. Keay to A. H. Belmont, Nov. 18, 1953, Harry Dexter White, no serial #. The information about Venona came in a statement by Robert Louis Benson of the National Security Agency, Oct. 3, 1996, Venona Conference, Washington, D.C.

6. Memorandum, C. W. Stein to Hoover, July 7, 1954, Confidential Plant Informants, no serial #; Athan Theoharis, *Spying on Americans: Political Surveillance from Hoover to the Huston Plan* (Philadelphia: Temple University Press, 1978), 76–78; W. J. McNeil (special assistant to the secretary of defense) to Donald S. Dawson (administrative assistant to the president), July 8, 1948, Harry S. Truman Official File, 252-K, HSTL (hereafter HST-OF); memorandum, Attorney General to Director, FBI, Jan. 7, 1948, unsigned memorandum to Director, Jan. 14, 1948, both in Box 1, A. Devitt Vanech Papers, HSTL; Director to SAC, San Francisco, May 14, 1951, Confidential Plant Informants File, no serial #; memorandum, Ladd to Director, May 24, 1951, ibid., #362; Harry N. Rosenfield, memorandum for the files, Oct. 30, 1952, Records of the President's Commission on Immigration and Naturalization, HSTL.

7. The presidential libraries at Hyde Park, New York, Independence, Misssouri, and Abilene, Kansas, contain boxes full of these documents.

8. Tom C. Clark, oral history, Oct. 17, 1972, 119, HSTL; memorandum, n. d., and Pat McCarran to Director, FBI, Oct. 11, 1952, both in U.S. Senate, Committee on the

Judiciary, Subcommittee on Internal Security, Records, Record Group 46, National Archives (hereafter SISS Records); Gentry, *J. Edgar Hoover,* 407–8; Theoharis and Cox, *The Boss,* 212–14; Richard D. Auerbach, memorandum, July 25, 1944, in Louis B. Nichols, Official and Confidential Files, "Bridges, Styles."

9. For examples of the kinds of information the Bureau gathered on individual congressmen, see Athan Theoharis, ed., *From the Secret Files of J. Edgar Hoover* (Chicago: Ivan R. Dee, 1991), 66–84; Theoharis and Cox, *The Boss,* 308–12; Cartha DeLoach, quoted in Gentry, *J. Edgar Hoover,* 376.

10. Gentry, *J. Edgar Hoover,* 407–8; Anthony Marro, "FBI Break-in Policy," in Athan G. Theoharis, ed., *Beyond the Hiss Case: The FBI, Congress, and the Cold War* (Philadelphia: Temple University Press, 1982), 107.

11. Theoharis, *Spying on Americans,* 66–84; Theoharis, ed., *From the Secret Files,* 179–84.

12. Richard Neustadt to Stephen J. Spingarn, June 29, 1950, Stephen J. Spingarn Papers, HSTL.

13. Memorandum, Ladd to Director, Feb. 27, 1946, SDSRIARA, 429.

14. Susan Rosenfeld, letter to the author, Oct. 26, 1996; Francis Biddle to Assistant Attorney General Cox and Director, FBI, July 16, 1943, SDSRIARA, 413–21; Theoharis, *Spying on Americans,* 40–44; memorandum, Nichols to Clyde Tolson, Feb. 12, 1951, "McCarthy Era Blacklisting of School Teachers, College Professors, and Other Public Employees: The FBI Responsibilities Program File and the Dissemination of Information Policy File," ed. Kenneth O'Reilly (Bethesda, Md.: University Publications of America, 1989) (hereafter Responsibilities Program), #4.

15. SDSRIARA, 413–20, 443–47, 451; SAC Letter, Hoover to Field Offices, Sept. 22, 1948, Everest Melvin Hupman, no serial #; Theoharis, *Spying on Americans,* 40–44.

16. Warren Olney III, oral history, 344, Bancroft Library, University of California, Berkeley; memorandum, Joseph E. Thornton to [name deleted], April 21, 1951, Elba Chase Nelson, Boston, #528; memorandum, Thornton to [name deleted], June 1, 1951, ibid., #551.

17. Memorandum, Ladd to Director, Oct. 10, 1944, Confidential Plant Informants, serial # illegible; memorandum, Executives Conference to Director, July 14, 1950, ibid., #26(4?); memorandum, F. H. McIntire to H. H. Clegg, Jan. 15, 1951, ibid., #322; memorandum, A. H. Belmont to Ladd, July 28, 1950, ibid., #263; SAC Letter, No. 62, Series 1950, Aug. 31, 1950, ibid., serial # illegible; memorandum, Belmont to Ladd, Oct. 31, 1950, ibid., #283; memorandum, SAC, Newark, to Director, Nov. 18, 1950, ibid., #289; Director to SAC, Baltimore, May 31, 1951, ibid., serial # illegible; memorandum, Ladd to Director, Apr. 11, 1951, ibid., #347; memorandum, Ladd to Director, July 18, 1951, ibid., #374; memorandum, Ladd to Director, Oct. 29, 1951, ibid., serial # illegible; memorandum, Ladd to Director, Jan. 29, 1952, ibid., #392; memorandum, Ladd to Director, April 28, 1952, ibid., serial # illegible; memorandum, Ladd to Director, July 29, 1952, ibid., #407; memorandum, Lester V. Boardman to Director,

Apr. 16, 1954, ibid., #1431; memorandum, Ladd to Director, July 14, 1953, ibid., serial # illegible; memorandum, Stein to Director, July 27, 1954, ibid., no serial #.

18. Keller, *J. Edgar Hoover and the Liberals,* 28–71.

19. Alan Harper, *The Politics of Loyalty: The White House and the Communist Issue* (Westport, Conn.: Greenwood Press, 1969), 24; William R. Corson, *The Armies of Ignorance: The Rise of the American Intelligence Empire* (New York: Dial Press, 1977), 271–73; *Report on H. R. 66,* House of Representatives, Committee on Post Office and Civil Service, 80th Cong., 1st sess., July 20, 1946.

20. Memorandum, Hoover to Tom C. Clark, July 25, 1946, in A. Devitt Vanech Papers, Box 1, HSTL.

21. Vanech to Hoover, Nov. 25, 1946, Vanech Papers.

22. Spingarn, memorandum for the file, Jan. 14, 1947, notes on meeting of Temporary Commission on Jan. 17, 1947, memorandum to Foley, Jan. 19, 1947, notes on Commission meeting of Feb. 14, 1947, all in Spingarn Papers, Box 7.

23. Memoranda, Director to Attorney General, Jan. 29, Mar. 28, 1947, Vanech Papers, Box 1; Spingarn, memoranda for the file, Jan. 14, 15, 1947, notes on subcommittee meeting of Jan. 31, 1947, all in Spingarn Papers, Box 7.

24. Memoranda, Director to Attorney General, Jan. 29, Mar. 19, 28, 1947, Vanech Papers, Box 1; Eleanor Bontecou, *The Federal Loyalty-Security Program* (Ithaca, N.Y.: Cornell University Press, 1953), 34, 76; [Clark Clifford], unsigned memorandum, May 2, 1947, Clifford, memoranda for the president, May 7, 23, 1947, George M. Elsey Papers, Box 69, HSTL; Spingarn to Foley, Apr. 4, 1947, Spingarn Papers, Box 7; Harry B. Mitchell and Frances Perkins to the president, April 25, 1947, Tom Clark, memorandum for the president, May 1, 1947, Donald S. Dawson, memorandum for the president, Oct. 24, 1947, all in HST-OF, 252K.

25. Bontecou, *The Federal Loyalty-Security Program,* 34, 74, 82, 149; Theoharis and Cox, *The Boss,* 7; Spingarn, memorandum for the file, Jan. 14, 1947, notes on meeting of Temporary Commission on Jan. 17, 1947, memorandum to Foley, Jan. 19, 1947, all in Spingarn Papers, Box 7.

26. For examples of apparent FBI pressure on employers, see Bill Bailey, *The Kid from Hoboken;* Ellen W. Schrecker, *No Ivory Tower: McCarthyism and the Universities* (New York: Oxford University Press), 258–60; typewritten list of political activities, n. d., private papers of Norman Cazden, copy in author's possession; Cazden, questionnaire response, Paul Tillett Papers, Seeley G. Mudd Manuscript Library, Princeton University; Cazden, interview with the author, June 9, 1978.

27. Memorandum, Boardman to Director, Oct. 28, 1954, Responsibilities Program, serial # illegible; Director to SAC, New York, Dec. 2, 1954, ibid., #2524; report, SAC, Detroit, Mar. 5, 1954, Clement Markert, no serial #.

28. Anthony Bouza, quoted in Frank Donner, *Protectors of Privilege: Red Squads and Police Repression in Urban America* (Berkeley and Los Angeles: University of California Press, 1990), 49; SAC Letter No. 96, Series 1948, June 22, 1948, Dissemination of Information Policy, #787; memorandum, Ladd to Director, June 11, 1948,

ibid., #167; O'Connor [SAC, Detroit], teletype to Director, Feb. 10, 1951, Responsibilities Program, #10; memorandum, Belmont to Ladd, Feb. 2, 1951, ibid., #96; memorandum, Belmont to Ladd, May 7, 1951, ibid., #229; SAC, New York to Director, Oct. 26, 1954, ibid., no serial #; telegram, SAC, Chicago, to Director, Nov. 19, 1947, United Electrical, Radio, and Machine Workers of America, #1049 (hereafter UE); SAC Letter No. 27, Series 1952, Mar. 15, 1952, Confidential Plant Informants, no serial #; Director, memorandum to Tolson, Ladd, Nichols, Feb. 6, 1951, Responsibilities Program, #6; Arthur Cornelius, teletype to Director, Feb. 3, 1951, ibid., #2; memorandum, Belmont to Ladd, Feb. 5, 1951, ibid., #7; memorandum, SAC, Philadelphia, to Director, Jan. 29, 1951, ibid., #2.

29. Memorandum, Ladd to Director, May 17, 1947, Carl Marzani, #132; memorandum, E. A. Tamm to Director, May 22, 1947, ibid., #133; memorandum, Director to Tamm, Ladd, Tolson, May 20, 1947, ibid., serial # illegible; Director, handwritten note on clipping from *Washington Post,* May 23, 1947, ibid., #117.

30. Powers, *Secrecy and Power,* 300; Robert P. Newman, *Owen Lattimore and the "Loss" of China* (Berkeley and Los Angeles: University of California Press, 1992), 274.

31. Director, FBI, to Col. Church, Rear Admiral Walter S. Anderson, Apr. 26, 1940, UE, #x; R. C. Suran to Director, Dec. 2, 1942, ibid., #168; report, S. J. Dayton (SAC, Chicago), Jan. 13, 1943, ibid., #195; Director to General Hayes A. Kroner, Oct. 17, 1942, FAECT, #109; H. K. Johnson (SAC, Milwaukee) to Director, Feb. 27, 1947, Communist Infiltration of UAW-CIO (hereafter UAW), #948; Director to SAC, Buffalo, Jan. 14, 1948, UE, #1087; Joan M. Jensen, *Army Surveillance in America, 1775–1980* (New Haven: Yale University Press, 1991), 211–47; Director to agents in the field, Feb. 6, 1941, Confidential Plant Informants, #31; SAC Letter, No. 62, Series 1950, Aug. 31, 1950, ibid., #362; V. P. Keay to Belmont, Nov. 18, 1953, White, no serial #; memorandum, E. G. Fitch to Ladd, May 27, 1947, Lenin School, #8.

32. All the books on Hoover and the FBI deal with the Bureau's relationship with the congressional investigators; see, especially, O'Reilly, *Hoover and the Un-Americans.*

33. Athan G. Theoharis, "In-House Cover-up: Researching FBI Files," in Theoharis, ed., *Beyond the Hiss Case,* 55–58; Theoharis and Cox, *The Boss,* 251–52; Allen Weinstein, *Perjury: The Hiss-Chambers Case* (New York: Knopf, 1978), 357–66.

34. Theoharis, *Spying on Americans,* 134, 164; O'Reilly, *Hoover and the Un-Americans,* 92–94; memorandum, Nichols to Tolson, Aug. 21, 1947, "Communist Infiltration of the Motion Picture Industry," Federal Bureau of Investigation, Confidential Files, Communist Activity in the Entertainment Industry, FBI Surveillance Files on Hollywood, 1942–1958, microfilm ed. by Daniel J. Leab (Bethesda, Md.: University Publications of America, 1991) (hereafter Hollywood), serial # illegible; J. P. Coyne to Ladd, Sept. 6, 1947, ibid., serial # illegible; R. B. Hood to Director, Sept. 13, 17, 1947, ibid., serial #s illegible; J. C. Strickland to Ladd, Nov. 8, 1946, Gerhart Eisler, #176; memorandum, Ladd to Director, June 17, 1947, Harold Christoffel, #177; Hoo-

ver, handwritten note, in Ladd, memorandum to Director, Apr. 26, 1950, National Defense Informants, no serial #; memorandum, Nichols to Tolson, Sept. 10, 1947, Hollywood, serial # illegible; Hood to Director, Sept. 20, 1947, ibid., serial # illegible.

35. Christopher John Gerard, "'A Program of Cooperation': The FBI, the Senate Internal Security Subcommittee, and the Communist Issue, 1950–54" (Ph.D. diss., Marquette University, 1993), 47–52, 61–62, 83–84, 157, 285–86; Nichols to Tolson, Nov. 11, 1953, White, #424; Nichols to Tolson, Nov. 24, 1953, ibid., no serial #; Nichols to Tolson, Mar. 22, 1954, ibid., #1241.

36. Theoharis and Cox, *The Boss,* 283–96.

37. Report [name deleted], Newark, June 3, 1946, in FAECT, #328; memorandum, SAC, San Francisco, to Director, Jan. 18, 1946, ibid., #317; report [name deleted], Indianapolis, Aug. 15, 1951, William Sentner, #130; memorandum, Belmont to Ladd, July 28, 1950, Confidential Plant Informants, #263; SAC Letter, No. 62, Series 1950, Aug. 21, 1950, ibid., serial # illegible; memorandum, SAC, Butte to Hoover, Feb. 19, 1951, Responsibilities Program, no serial #.

38. Memorandum, Nichols to Tolson, Nov. 19, 1953, White, #433. On the Bureau's relations with writers, see Natalie Robins, *Alien Ink: The FBI's War on Freedom of Expression* (New York: William Morrow, 1992), 112–42; O'Reilly, *Hoover and the Un-Americans,* 80; Warren I. Cohen, *The Chinese Connection: Roger S. Greene, Thomas W. Lamont, George E. Sokolsky and American–East Asian Relations* (New York: Columbia University Press, 1978), 243.

39. Hoover to SAC, New York, May 25, 1943, Communist Infiltration of Labor Organizations, #5; Ladd to Belmont, Nov. 23, 1953, White, #1157.

40. Athan Theoharis, "The FBI and the American Legion Contact Program, 1940–1966," *Political Science Quarterly* 100 (Summer 1985): 271–86; Theoharis and Cox, *The Boss,* 193–98; memorandum, F. H. McIntire to Clegg, Confidential Plant Informants, #322; SAC Letter, No. 54-36, July 13, 1954, ibid., no serial #; O'Reilly, *Hoover and the Un-Americans,* 88–90.

41. Peter L. Steinberg, *The Great "Red Menace": United States Prosecution of American Communists, 1947–1952* (Westport, Conn.: Greenwood Press, 1984), 101; statement of Loyd Wright, April 30, 1959, Dwight D. Eisenhower, Official Files (hereafter DDE-OF), 104-J, Dwight D. Eisenhower Library (hereafter DDEL); SDSRIARA, 443; Olney, oral history, 336; Newman, *Owen Lattimore and the "Loss" of China,* 401; Gary May, *Un-American Activities: The Trials of William Remington* (New York: Oxford University Press, 1994), 87–94, 159–80; Ralph Brown, Jr., *Loyalty and Security: Employment Tests in the United States* (New Haven: Yale University Press, 1958), 28; Charlotte Knight, "What Price Security?" *Collier's* (July 9, 1954), 61–64; Powers, *Secrecy and Power,* 318; Theoharis and Cox, *The Boss,* 212–13, 283–96; memorandum, SAC, Milwaukee, to Director, Mar. 10, 1947, Communist Infiltration of the CIO, #952; Donner, *Protectors of Privilege,* 58; memorandum, SAC, Cincinnati, to Director, Mar. 17, 1953, Ohio Un-American Activities Commission, #50; SAC, New York, to Director, Oct. 26, 1954, Responsibilities Program, no serial #; Gerda W. Ray,

"Informal Cooperation and Formal Coordination: The Role of the New York State Police in Political Surveillance," paper presented to the Annual Meeting of the Organization of American Historians, Louisville, Ky., April 1991.

42. Theoharis, ed., *From the Secret Files of J. Edgar Hoover,* 362; Program, Fifth Industrial Security Conference, Jan. 8, 1954, in Benjamin Gitlow Papers, Hoover Institution; memorandum, H. K. Johnson to Director, Feb. 27, 1947, UAW, #948; memorandum, Johnson to Hoover, Mar. 7, 1947, ibid., #947; Richard Nixon to Bill Rogers, Jan. 19, 1954, William P. Rogers Papers, Box 50, DDEL.

43. Memorandum, Ladd to Tamm, June 16, 1947, UAW, #970x; Merle Miller, *The Judges and the Judged* (Garden City, N.Y.: Doubleday, 1952), 63–94; *Red Channels* (New York: American Business Consultants, 1950); Alfred Kohlberg to Father John F. Cronin, Dec. 19, 1946, Cronin to Kohlberg, Dec. 31, 1946, both in Kohlberg Papers, Hoover Institution.

44. Memorandum, Attorney General to Director, Oct. 25, 1954, Responsibilities Program, #2501.

45. Weinstein, *Perjury,* 295.

46. Director to Morris Ernst, Oct. 22, 1939, Morris L. Ernst Papers, Harry Ransom Humanities Research Center, University of Texas at Austin; F. C. Holloman, memorandum to Tamm, Feb. 3, 1941, Confidential Plant Informants, #35.

47. Memorandum, Director to Attorney General, Feb. 3, 1951, Responsibilities Program, #1; Ernst to Hoover, Oct. 14, 1941, to Freda Kirchwey, Aug. 26, 1943, Hoover to Ernst, Oct. 17, 1941, Aug. 3, 4, 30, 1943, Ernst to Hoover, Jan. 20, Mar. 12, Nov. 29, 1948, Hoover to Ernst, Jan. 19, Nov. 28, 1948, Dec. 1, 9, 1949, James Fly to Ernst, Nov. 10, 15, 1949, Nichols to Ernst, Jan. 5, 23, 1950, Ernst to Alice Hamilton, Jan. 9, 1950, Hoover to Ernst, June 23, 1950, Ernst to Bruce Bliven, Sept. 24, 1941, to Clifford Forster, Oct. 31, 1941, all in Ernst Papers; Salisbury, "The Strange Correspondence of Morris Ernst and John Edgar Hoover, 1939–1964," *The Nation* (Dec. 1, 1984): 575–89.

48. FBI, press release, Jan. 4, 1949, in Eleanor Bontecou Papers, HSTL; Bontecou, *The Federal Loyalty-Security Program,* 314.

49. Director to Attorney General, Jan. 6, 1942, CIO, serial # illegible; memorandum, J. K. Mumford to Ladd, June 24, 1942, UE, #41; memorandum, Belmont to Ladd, July 28, 1950, Confidential Plant Informants, #263; Section 87, "Security Investigations," Manual of Rules and Regulations, August 1, 1952, Sigmund Diamond FBI records, Box 10, Columbia University Law School Library; memorandum, Director to SAC, Albany, and other offices, April 13, 1953, National Security Informants, #766; teletype, Director to SAC, St. Louis, n. d., Sentner, #176; Bontecou, report on interview with D. M. Ladd, Oct. 18, 1948, Bontecou Papers.

50. Hoover to Ernst, Nov. 4, 1941, in Ernst Papers; teletype, SAC O'Connor (Detroit) to Director, Feb. 10, 1951, Responsibilities Program, #10; Nichols to Tolson, Nov. 4, 1954, ibid., no serial #; Clark, statement, Sept. 29, 1948, SDSRIARA, 461; Clark, speech to Des Moines Trades and Labor Assembly, Sept. 6, 1948, Box 30, Spingarn Papers.

51. Memorandum, Director to Tolson, Boardman, Belmont, Nichols, Nov. 9, 1954, Responsibilities Program, serial # illegible; Kenneth O'Reilly, "Adlai E. Stevenson, McCarthyism, and the FBI," *Illinois Historical Journal* (Spring 1988): 45–60; Keller, *The Liberals and J. Edgar Hoover,* 28–71; memorandum, Nichols to Tolson, Jan. 17, 1955, Responsibilities Program, #2641; Belmont to Boardman, May 31, 1955, ibid., no serial #.

52. Section 87, "Security Investigations"; memorandum, Belmont to Ladd, Mar. 4, 1953, Responsibilities Program, #1161; Mumford to Ladd, Oct. 22, 1946, Eisler, #141; memorandum, Tamm to Director, Oct. 30, 1946, ibid., #208; Carol King [Eisler's attorney] to Attorney General, Oct. 31, 1946, ibid., #189; memorandum, Fletcher to Ladd, Oct. 18, 1947, Hollywood, no serial #; Charles Larrowe, *Harry Bridges* (Westport, Conn.: Lawrence Hill, 1972), 282.

53. Memorandum, Director to Tolson, Ladd, Nichols, Belmont, Nov. 9, 1953, White, #43; Hoover to Ernst, Nov. 23, 1953, Ernst to Hoover, Dec. 21, 1953, Ernst Papers; Attorney General to Director, Oct. 19, 1951, Smith Act, #9243; memorandum, E. G. Fitch to Ladd, May 29, 1946, in Belmont to Ladd, Nov. 9, 1953, White, #1261; memorandum, Tamm to Director, Apr. 14, 1947, UE, #887; Hoover to SAC, San Francisco, Jan. 31, 1952, Responsibilities Program, no serial #.

54. Director to Rear Admiral Thomas R. Inglis, July 15, 1948, UE, # 1180; memorandum, Keay to Ladd, July 14, 1948, ibid., #1182; memorandum, Ladd to Director, July 14, 1948, ibid., #1198; Ladd to Tamm, June 18, 1947, Communist Infiltration of the CIO, #974; memorandum, Belmont to Boardman, Nov. 10, 1954, Responsibilities Program, #2532; memorandum, Belmont to Boardman, May 31, 1955, ibid., no serial #; Robins, *Alien Ink,* 112–15.

55. Memorandum, Director to Attorney General, Feb. 3, 1951, Responsibilities Program, #1; Hoover, quoted in Theoharis and Cox, *The Boss,* 257, 266; memorandum, Director to Tolson, Ladd, Nichols, Belmont, Nov. 9, 1953, White, #43.

56. Theoharis and Cox, *The Boss,* 256–61.

57. The data slips are reproduced in the microfilmed transcripts of the Coplon trial that were reproduced by the Fund for the Republic in the 1950s; see *United States of America v. Judith Coplon, defendant,* Washington, D.C., District Court, 1949 (microfilm ed., Fund for the Republic, New York).

58. Theoharis, "In-House Cover-up," 21–28, 42–46, 58–59; Anthony Marro, "FBI Break-in Policy," in Theoharis, ed., *Beyond the Hiss Case,* 84–86; Theoharis and Cox, *The Boss,* 258; O'Reilly, *Hoover and the Un-Americans,* 126–27; Attorney General to Director, Oct. 19, 1951, Smith Act, #9243.

59. Robins, *Alien Ink,* 143–84; memorandum, Director to Tolson, Nichols, Ladd, Belmont, Feb. 10, 1954, White, no serial #.

60. Percival R. Baily, "The Case of the National Lawyers Guild, 1939–1958," in Theoharis, ed., *Beyond the Hiss Case,* 129–75; O'Reilly, *Hoover and the Un-Americans,* 130–40; Clifford Durr to Truman, June 20, 1949, Jan. 19, 1950, in HST-OF, 10-B.

61. *National Lawyers Guild v. Attorney General, et al.,* Plaintiff's Principal Factual Papers in Opposition to the Motion of the United States of America for Partial Summary Judgment Dismissing the Damage Claims arising from the FBI's Conduct and in Support of Plaintiff's Cross-Motion for Partial Summary Judgment, Sept. 26, 1984 (hereafter NLG motion), 45–46.

62. Baily, "The Case of the National Lawyers Guild," 134–43; NLG motion, 3–75.

63. For examples of the FBI's use of published sources, see Hood to Director, Sept. 26, 1941, FAECT, #41; Director to SAC, Chicago, May 17, 1941, UE, #1; report, SAC, New Haven, to Director, Jan. 27, 1943, ibid., #213; report, SAC, Boston, Dec. 4, 1943, ibid., #394; Garrow, *The FBI and Martin Luther King, Jr.,* 23; Steven Rosswurm and Toni Gilpin, "The FBI and the Farm Equipment Workers: FBI Surveillance Records as a Source for CIO Union History," *Labor History* 27 (Fall 1986): 485–505.

64. Memorandum, Tolson to Director, Oct. 1939, in SDSRIARA, 413; Kohlberg to Patrick McCarran, Nov. 21, 1950, Kohlberg Papers.

65. SDSRIARA, 280.

66. Marro, "FBI Break-in Policy," 78–128; Griffin Fariello, *Red Scare: Memories of the American Inquisition* (New York: W. W. Norton, 1995), 84–97; Swearingen, *FBI Secrets,* 23–37; SDSRIARA, 360; Robins, *Alien Ink,* 146; Theoharis, *From the Secret Files of J. Edgar Hoover,* 128; Gerard, "A Program of Cooperation," 198; NLG motion, 33, 37; memorandum, Coyne to Ladd, July 9, 1947, Hollywood, #251; G. B. Norris to Director, Mar. 21, 1946, Smith Act, #89; R. E. Fogarty, report, Mar. 22, 1949, New York State Police, Bureau of Criminal Investigations, Non-Criminal Investigations Files Collection, New York State Archives, Albany, Box 7, Case 192 (hereafter NYSP).

67. SDSRIARA, 279–85, 300–310, 316–17; Athan Theoharis, "FBI Wiretapping: A Case Study of Bureaucratic Autonomy," *Political Science Quarterly* 107 (1992): 101–22.

68. For evidence of the Bureau's heavy use of bugs and wiretaps, see memorandum, Director to Attorney General, Sept. 24, 1947, UE, #984; memorandum, Director to Attorney General, Nov. 24, 1947, ibid., #1046; memoranda, SAC, Albany, to Director, Jan. 3, 1948, ibid., #1076, Jan. 5, 1948, ibid., #1077, Jan. 9, 1948, ibid., #1081, Feb. 13, 1948, ibid., #1114; teletype, Director to SAC, Philadelphia, Feb. 17, 1947, ibid., #849; memorandum, Fletcher to Ladd, Apr. 9, 1948, ibid., #1148; memorandum, SAC, St. Louis, to Director, Apr. 20, 1951, Sentner, #122; report, SAC, Cleveland, Aug. 5, 1946, Smith Act, #232; SAC, New York, to Director, Apr. 3, 1947, ibid., #756; SAC, Los Angeles, to Director, Mar. 17, 1949, ibid., #3093; memoranda, Hottel to Director, Dec. 8, 1947, Hollywood, #364, Dec. 11, 1947, ibid., #373; NLG motion, 51–52; Robins, *Alien Ink,* 140; Garrow, *The FBI and Martin Luther King, Jr.,* 41; memorandum, Ladd to Director, Apr. 26, 1946, Robert J. Oppenheimer, serial # unknown.

69. Marro, "FBI Break-in Policy," 101–3; Garrow, *The FBI and Martin Luther King, Jr.,* 58–59; memoranda, SAC, Albany, to Director, Jan. 3, 1948, UE, #1076, Jan. 5, 1948, ibid., #1077, Jan. 9, 1948, ibid., #1081, Feb. 13, 1948, ibid., #1114.

70. NLG motion, 40–41, 51–52; memorandum, Hottel to Director, Dec. 8, 1947, Hollywood, #364; memorandum, Director to Assistant Attorney General T. Vincent Quinn, Dec. 11, 1948, ibid., #364; memorandum, Director to Assistant Attorney General Alexander Campbell, Mar. 31, 1949, Smith Act, #3213.

71. Theoharis, *Spying on Americans,* 133–40; O'Reilly, *Hoover and the Un-Americans,* 198–207; Frank J. Donner, *The Age of Surveillance: The Aims and Methods of America's Political Intelligence System* (New York: Knopf, 1980, Vintage ed. 1981), 178–94; NLG motion, 257–64.

72. Memorandum, Coyne to Ladd, July 9, 1947, Hollywood, #251; SAC Letter, No. 52–17, Mar. 3, 1953, in memorandum, Baumgardner to Belmont, June 18, 1952, National Defense Informants, #684; memorandum, Belmont to Ladd, Mar. 14, 1950, ibid., #480; memorandum, Director to Tolson, Ladd, Nichols, et al., Mar. 20, 1952, ibid., no serial #; SAC Letter, No. 32, Series 1952, Apr. 1, 1952, ibid., no serial #; memorandum, Belmont to Ladd, Apr. 14, 1952, ibid., #652; memorandum, Baumgardner to Belmont, Oct. 23, 1952, ibid., #729; memorandum, Belmont to Ladd, July 2, 1953, ibid., #786.

73. Susan Rosenfeld, letter to the author, Oct. 28, 1996; memorandum, Tamm to Director, Feb. 11, 1941, Confidential Plant Informants, no serial #; Sigmund Diamond, *Compromised Campus: The Collaboration of Universities with the Intelligence Community, 1945–55* (New York: Oxford University Press, 1992), 34–35; Diamond, "Labor History vs. Labor Historiography: The FBI, James B. Carey, and the Association of Catholic Trade Unionists," in *Religion, Ideology and Nationalism in Europe and America: Essays Presented in Honor of Yehoshua Arieli* (Jerusalem: Historical Society of Israel and the Zalman Shazar Center for Jewish History, 1986), 299–328; Theoharis, ed., *From the Secret Files of J. Edgar Hoover,* 115; report [name deleted], Los Angeles, Apr. 20, 1944, Hollywood, #26; report [name deleted], Los Angeles, Oct. 12, 1944, ibid., #54; report [name deleted], Los Angeles, Sept. 12, 1947, ibid., serial # illegible; Hood to Director, Sept. 12, 1947, ibid., serial # illegible; memorandum, F. J. Baumgardner to Belmont, Apr. 16, 1953, National Security Informants, #775.

74. Memorandum, F. J. Baumgardner to Belmont, Apr. 16, 1953, National Security Informants, #775; memorandum, Executives Conference to Director, Sept. 22, 1950, Confidential Plant Informants, #270; memorandum, Executives Conference to Director, Sept. 6, 1950, ibid., #275; memorandum, Ladd to Director, Oct. 25, 1950, National Defense Informants, #539; memorandum, Nichols to Tolson, Jan. 5, 1954, National Security Informants, no serial #; memorandum, Belmont to Ladd, Jan. 14, 1954, ibid., no serial #; Edward Scheidt, teletype to Director, n. d. (Oct. 1948), Smith Act, #1962; letter, Scheidt to Director, Apr. 4, 1949, ibid., #3263; Director to Assistant Attorney General Warren Olney III, Oct. 22, 1953, Clinton Jencks LMRA, #142; Subversive Activities Control Board, recommended decision in case of Marvin Joel Markman, recommended decision in case of Ralph Nelson, Part I, reel 7, Records of the Subversive Activities Control Board, 1950–1972, microfilm edition (Frederick, Md.: University

Publications of America, 1988) (hereafter SACB Records); SAC, Baltimore, to Director, Feb. 5, 1953, Responsibilities Program, no serial #; memorandum, SAC, Minneapolis, to Director, Oct. 20, 1953, National Security Informants, #815; Ellen W. Schrecker, *No Ivory Tower: McCarthyism and the Universities* (New York: Oxford University Press, 1986), 259–64.

75. Section 87, "Security Investigations"; SAC Letter, No. 32, Series 1952, Apr. 1, 1952, National Defense Informants, no serial #; SAC Letter, No. 39, Apr. 22, 1952, ibid., no serial #; memorandum, SAC, Los Angeles, to Director, June 18, 1951, ibid.; Ladd to Director, Sept. 15, 1952, National Security Informants, no serial #; SAC Letter, No. 53–48, July 14, 1953, ibid., no serial #; memorandum, SAC, San Francisco, to Director, Sept. 25, 1952, ibid., #711; memorandum, Director to SAC, Albany, Oct. 13, 1952, ibid., #719; memorandum, Director to SAC, Albany, Oct. 14, 1952, ibid., #720; Director to SAC, Albany, Dec. 18, 1952, ibid., #734; memorandum, Baumgardner to Belmont, Apr. 8, 1953, ibid., #766; Director to SAC, Chicago, Apr. 8, 1953, ibid., #771; memorandum, Belmont to Ladd, Apr. 15, 1953, ibid., #772; Director to SAC, Chicago, July 15, 1953, ibid., #791; memorandum, SAC, Minneapolis, to Director, Aug. 20, 1953, ibid., #800; Baumgardner to Belmont, Dec. 14, 1956, COINTELPRO, C.P.U.S.A., # 116; NLG motion, 389–90, 414–34; Garrow, *The FBI and Martin Luther King, Jr.,* 35–42; memorandum, Baumgardner to Belmont, Aug. 15, 1950, National Security Informants, #497; memorandum, Baumgardner to Belmont, June 18, 1952, ibid., #684; memorandum, Baumgardner to Belmont, Oct. 14, 1952, ibid., #724; memorandum, Baumgardner to Belmont, Oct. 23, 1952, ibid., #729; memorandum, Belmont to Ladd, July 20, 1953, ibid., #786; memorandum [name deleted], to Director, Feb. 2, 1953, ibid., no serial #; letter, Norris to Director, Oct. 13, 1948, Smith Act, #1934; memorandum, Belmont to Ladd, July 28, 1950, Confidential Plant Informants, #263; J. A. Sizoo to Tolson, Oct. 23, 1950, National Defense Informants, #538; SAC Letter, No. 39, Apr. 22, 1952, ibid., no serial #; memorandum, Belmont to Ladd, Oct. 1, 1952, ibid., #715; memorandum, Ladd to Director, Feb. 26, 1952, ibid., #643; Subversive Activities Control Board, recommended decision in case of Albert Jason Lima, Dec. 31, 1962, recommended decision in case of Burt Gale Nelson, Jan. 21, 1963, recommended decision in case of Claude Mack Lightfoot, Mar. 5, 1963, all in Part I, reel 6, SACB Records; witness reports, National Council for American-Soviet Friendship, Part II, reel 2, ibid.

76. Memorandum, Executives Conference to Director, Jan. 11, 1949, Smith Act, #2612; memorandum, Director to SAC, New York, Mar. 17, 1949, ibid., #3260; memorandum, Executives Conference to Director, Oct. 4, 1950, National Defense Informants, #525; memorandum, Ladd to Director, Jan. 31, 1951, ibid., #553; memorandum, Executives Conference to Director, Sept. 6, 1951, ibid., #599; Ladd to Director, Sept. 22, 1953, National Security Informants, no serial #.

77. Ladd to Director, Sept. 22, 1953, National Security Informants, no serial #; Wood to Director, Dec. 4, 1947, Hollywood, #358; memorandum, Ladd to Director, Oct. 22, 1947, ibid., #270; memorandum, SAC, Memphis, to Director, May 19, 1952,

National Defense Informants, #662; clipping, *Washington Post,* Sept. 4, 1953, in Hupman, serial # illegible; memorandum, SAC, New York, to Director, July 5, 1951, Budenz, #425; Nichols to Tolson, July 7, 1951, ibid., #427; Ernst to Nichols, Jan. 4, 1951, Nichols to Ernst, Jan. 8, 1951, Ernst Papers; memorandum, Ladd to Director, Apr. 26, 1950, National Defense Informants, no serial #; SAC Letter, #88, Sept. 1, 1955, ibid., no serial #; memorandum, Baumgardner to Belmont, Sept. 5, 1950, ibid., serial # illegible; memorandum, Executives Conference to Director, Sept. 20, 1950, ibid., serial # illegible; memorandum, Executives Conference to Director, Oct. 4, 1950, ibid., #525; Director to Assistant Attorney General James McInerney, Nov. 1, 1950, ibid., #525; memorandum, Baumgardner to Belmont, Nov. 30, 1951, ibid., #624; SAC Letter, No. 7, Series 1952, Jan. 18, 1952, ibid., no serial #; memorandum, Ladd to Director, May 17, 1950, ibid., #484; memorandum, Director to Tolson, Ladd, Belmont, Rosen, July 11, 1950, ibid., #491.

78. Memorandum, Belmont to Ladd, May 20, 1953, National Security Informants, #781; memorandum, Baumgardner to Belmont, Feb. 27, 1952, National Defense Informants, #645.

79. Memorandum, Ladd to Director, Jan. 31, 1950, National Defense Informants, #464; memorandum, Ladd to Director, Mar. 14, 1950, ibid., #480; memorandum, Ladd to Director, May 17, 1950, ibid., #484; unidentified document (probably SAC Letter), n. d. (probably Jan. 1950), ibid., no serial #; memorandum, Baumgardner to Belmont, Oct. 6, 1950, ibid., #535; J. A. Sizoo to Tolson, Oct. 23, 1950, ibid., #538; memorandum, Baumgardner to Belmont, Feb. 27, 1952, ibid., #645; SAC Letter, No. 29, Series 1952, March 22, 1952, ibid., no serial #; memorandum, Belmont to Ladd, Oct. 1, 1952, National Security Informants, #715; memorandum, Belmont to Ladd, May 20, 1953, ibid., #781; Ladd to Director, Sept. 22, 1953, ibid., no serial #.

80. SAC Letter, No. 15, Series 1951, National Defense Informants, no serial #; Scheidt to Director, Nov. 12, 1948, Smith Act, #2216.

81. Ladd to Director, Sept. 22, 1953, National Security Informants, no serial #; memorandum, Baumgardner to Belmont, Dec. 1, 1953, ibid., serial # illegible; Belmont to Ladd, Oct. 24, 1953, White, #73; Director to Communications Section, Oct. 26, 1953, ibid., #33; Ladd to Director, Dec. 30, 1953, ibid., no serial #; memorandum, Ladd to Director, May 15, 1948, Budenz, #282; memorandum, L. L. Laughlin to Ladd, Sept. 25, 1951, ibid., #431; memorandum, Belmont to Boardman, May 29, 1955, ibid., #513; SAC, New York, to Director, Aug. 5, 1955, Budenz, NY, #246; May, *Un-American Activities,* 279–83.

82. Ruth Greenglass, quoted in Ronald Radosh and Joyce Milton, *The Rosenberg File: A Search for the Truth* (New York: Holt, Rinehart and Winston, 1983), 165; SAC, New York, to Director, July 14, 1950, Budenz, #351; memorandum, Strickland to Ladd, Dec. 3, 1945, Budenz, #149x; Scheidt to Director, July 25, 1947, Budenz NY, #86; Ladd to Belmont, Nov. 23, 1953, White, #1157.

83. Memorandum, Coyne to Tamm, Sept. 30, 1946, Budenz, #192.

84. Marro, "FBI Break-in Policy," 109; memorandum, Director, FBI, to SAC, Phila-

delphia, Aug. 29, 1947, UE, #963; memorandum, SAC, New York, to Director, May 16, 1951, Hollywood, #813; memorandum, SAC, St. Louis, to Director, Sept. 23, 1952, National Security Informants, #712; SAC Letter, No. 27, Series 1952, Mar. 15, 1952, Confidential Plant Informants, no serial #; memorandum, SAC, St. Louis, to Director, July 5, 1951, Sentner, #123; Director to Attorney General, Apr. 5, 1947, Vanech Papers, Box 1; report [name deleted], St. Louis, Aug. 26, 1958, Senter, #234; Bethuel M. Webster to Eisenhower, July 17, 1953, White House Central Files, Confidential File-Subject Series, Box 66, "Security Program (1)," DDEL.

85. Truman to George H. Earle, Feb. 28, 1947, HST-OF, 263; Truman, handwritten note on memorandum, Clifford to Truman, May 23, 1947, Box 69, Elsey Papers; memorandum (Clifford?), May 2, 1947, ibid.; memorandum, Elsey to Truman, Feb. 2, 1950, Box 31, Spingarn Papers; Spingarn to Truman, Oct. 15, 1948, Box 32, ibid.; SDSRIARA, 463; Powers, *Secrecy and Power*, 305–11; Theoharis and Cox, *The Boss*, 261–65.

86. Memorandum, Spingarn to Director, Aug. 22, 1950, Box 33, Spingarn Papers; Gentry, *J. Edgar Hoover*, 401–2.

87. Powers, *Secrecy and Power*, 280–91.

88. Director to Karl E. Mundt, Jan. 28, 1947, Marzani, #26x; Ladd to Director, Jan. 21, 1947, ibid., #70; Ladd to Director, Jan. 3, 1947, ibid., #22; memorandum, Director to Tolson, Feb. 24, 1947, memorandum, Tamm to Director, Dec. 8, 1947, both in Belmont to Ladd, Nov. 11, 1953, White, #75; Director to Tolson, Tamm, Ladd, Feb. 21, 1946, ibid., #100; Director to Attorney General, Jan. 17, 1949, in Nichols to Tolson, Nov. 14, 1953, ibid., #825.

89. Tom C. Clark, oral history, Oct. 17, 1972, 108, 193, in HSTL.

90. Memorandum, Director to Attorney General, Jan. 27, 1947, Marzani, #59; Director to Attorney General, Jan. 17, 1947, ibid., #38; memorandum, Director to Tolson, Tamm, Ladd, Feb. 25, 1946, in Nichols to Tolson, Nov. 14, 1953, White, #825; Tolson, memorandum, Jan. 20, 1947, in memorandum, Ladd to Director, Nov. 14, 1953, ibid., #1215; Director, memorandum, Jan. 22, 1947, Marzani, #37; Director, handwritten comment on memorandum, Mumford to Ladd, Jan. 21, 1947, ibid., #49x; memorandum, Director to Attorney General, Feb. 7, 1947, Eisler, #226.

91. Theoharis, "In-House Cover-up," 32; SDSRIARA, 443.

92. Theoharis, "In-House Cover-up," 48–49; NLG motion, 42–46; memorandum, Tamm to Director, May 12, 1947, Smith Act, #791; Daniel Patrick Moynihan, speech, Venona Conference, Washington, D.C., Oct. 3, 1996.

93. NLG motion, 143–44; memorandum, Quinn to Director, May 19, 1948, UE, #1175; Director, handwritten notation on Ladd to Director, Apr. 21, 1948, ibid., #1156; SDSRIARA, 438; William R. Tanner, "The Passage of the Internal Security Act of 1950" (Ph.D. diss., University of Kansas, 1970), 181–82, 200; Truman comment on memorandum, Clifford to Truman, May 23, 1947, Box 69, Elsey Papers; Director to Attorney General, Jan. 17, 1948, in Nichols to Tolson, Nov. 14, 1953, White, #825.

94. Director to Attorney General, Jan. 13, 1947, Eisler, #207; Director to Attorney General, Oct. 24, 1946, ibid., #141; Mumford to Ladd, Oct. 22, 1946, ibid., #141;

Tamm to Director, Jan. 31, 1947, ibid., #223; Ladd to Hoover, Feb. 3, 1947, ibid., #220; memorandum, Ladd to Director, Nov. 6, 1947, J. Robert Oppenheimer, #312.

95. For a thorough study of the case from the FBI's perspective, see Harvey Klehr and Ronald Radosh, *The Amerasia Spy Case: Prelude to McCarthyism* (Chapel Hill: University of North Carolina Press, 1996). See also Theoharis and Cox, *The Boss,* 239–48.

96. Klehr and Radosh, *The Amerasia Spy Case,* 81–135.

97. Klehr and Radosh, *The Amerasia Spy Case,* 128, 132; Nichols to Director, Feb. 24, 1955, quoted in Powers, *Secrecy and Power,* 553; Theoharis and Cox, *The Boss,* 244–46.

98. Klehr and Radosh, *The Amerasia Spy Case,* 136–202.

99. Memoranda, Tamm to Director, Nov. 24, 1946, Director to Attorney General, Dec. 10, 1946, Jan. 27, 1947, all in Summary Brief, in Boardman to Director, Aug. 26, 1954, White, #1245; memorandum of meeting, Jan. 22, 1947, in Ladd to Director, Nov. 12, 1953, ibid., #59; Director to Tolson, Feb. 19, 1947, in Belmont to Ladd, Nov. 11, 1953, ibid., #75; Belmont to Ladd, Nov. 10. 1953, ibid., #48; memoranda, Ladd to Tamm, March 26, 1948, Director to Tolson, Feb. 19, 1947, April 1, 1948, all in Belmont to Ladd, Nov. 11, 1953, ibid., #75.

100. Hoover to Ernst, Nov. 23, 1953, Ernst Papers; memorandum, Director to Tolson, Ladd, Nichols, Belmont, Nov. 9, 1953, White, #43.

101. Olney, oral history, 373–74; memorandum, Director to Tolson, Ladd, Nichols, June 3, 1953, White, #28; memorandum, Director to Olney, June 3, 1953, ibid., #29.

102. Memorandum, Director to Tolson, Nichols, Ladd, Nov. 14, 1953, White, #60 or 61; James Byrnes to Director, Feb. 6, 1946, in Ladd to Director, Nov. 15, 1953, ibid., #742; memorandum, Director to Tolson, Tamm, Ladd, Feb. 25, 1946, in Nichols to Tolson, Nov. 14, 1953, ibid., #825.

103. Hoover, Statement before the Subcommittee to Investigate the Administration of the Internal Security Act and Other Internal Security Laws, Nov. 17, 1953.

104. M. A. Jones to Nichols, Dec. 4, 1953, White, #918.

7: "IN THE GUTTER": THE ANTICOMMUNISM OF JOE McCARTHY

1. The most useful biographies of McCarthy are David M. Oshinsky, *A Conspiracy So Immense: The World of Joe McCarthy* (New York: Free Press, 1983), 348–53; Thomas C. Reeves, *The Life and Times of Joe McCarthy: A Biography* (New York: Stein and Day, 1982), 529–31; see also Robert Griffith, *The Politics of Fear: Joseph McCarthy and the Senate* (Lexington: University Press of Kentucky, 1970), and Richard M. Fried, *Men Against McCarthy* (New York: Columbia University Press, 1976).

2. The most influential rendition of the McCarthy-as-aberration thesis is Richard H. Rovere, *Senator Joe McCarthy* (New York: Harper, 1959). On the anticommunist network, see J. B. Matthews, telegram to George Sokolsky, Feb. 13, 1962, Box 681, J. B. Matthews Papers, Duke University.

3. Griffith, *The Politics of Fear,* 11, notes that McCarthy did not stress Commu-

nism in his senatorial campaign. Oshinsky, *A Conspiracy So Immense*, 81, thinks that he did.

4. Oshinsky, *A Conspiracy So Immense*, 103–14; Reeves, *The Life and Times of Joe McCarthy*, 222–33; Fried, *Men Against McCarthy*, 44–48.

5. Reeves, *The Life and Times of Joe McCarthy*, 202, and Oshinsky, *A Conspiracy So Immense*, 506.

6. Jack Anderson and Ronald W. May, *McCarthy: The Man, the Senator, the "Ism"* (Boston: Beacon Press, 1952), 207, 243; Oshinsky, *A Conspiracy So Immense*, 233.

7. Willard Edwards, quoted in Oshinsky, *A Conspiracy So Immense*, 118.

8. Edwin R. Bayley, *Joe McCarthy and the Press* (Madison: University of Wisconsin Press, 1981), 51, 140; Jim Tuck, *McCarthyism and New York's Hearst Press: A Study of Roles in the Witch Hunt* (Lanham, Md.: University Press of America, 1995), passim; Oshinsky, *A Conspiracy So Immense*, 170; Anderson and May, *McCarthy: The Man, the Senator, the "Ism,"* 268.

9. Oshinsky, *A Conspiracy So Immense*, 108–12; Griffith, *The Politics of Fear*, 48–51. There is a vast literature on Service, since he was implicated in the *Amerasia* case; see Harvey Klehr and Ronald Radosh, *The Amerasia Spy Case: Prelude to McCarthyism* (Chapel Hill: University of North Carolina Press, 1996), and E. J. Kahn, Jr., *The China Hands: America's Foreign Service Officers and What Befell Them* (New York: Viking, 1975). On Duran, see David Caute, *The Great Fear: The Anti-Communist Purge Under Truman and Eisenhower* (New York: Simon and Schuster, 1978), 331–38.

10. Oshinsky, *A Conspiracy So Immense*, 133.

11. Oshinsky, *A Conspiracy So Immense*, 257–58; Athan G. Theoharis and John Stuart Cox, *The Boss: J. Edgar Hoover and the Great American Inquisition* (Philadelphia: Temple University Press, 1988), 280, 283–91; Lindsay Chaney and Michael Cieply, *The Hearsts: Family and Empire — The Later Years* (New York: Simon and Schuster, 1981), 103–34; Griffith, *The Politics of Fear*, 63.

12. Alfred Kohlberg to Freda Utley, Feb. 28, 1945, Freda Utley Papers, Hoover Institution on War, Revolution and Peace, Stanford University; Benjamin Mandel to Kohlberg, Apr. 10, Aug. 8, Oct. 7, Dec. 10, 1945, Mar. 7, Nov. 4, 1946, Sept. 22, 1948, Sept. 16, 1949, Kohlberg to Mandel, Mar. 7, 1946, Feb. 24, Aug. 22, 1947, Sept. 29, 1948, Dec. 7, 1949, Richard Nixon to Kohlberg, Mar. 3, 12, 1949, Kohlberg to Nixon, Mar. 8, 1949, Kohlberg to Styles Bridges, Jan. 14, 1947, n. d., Kohlberg to Patrick McCarran, Aug. 15, 22, 1949, all in Kohlberg Papers, Hoover Institution; Joseph Keeley, *The China Lobby Man* (New Rochelle, N.Y.: Arlington House, 1969), 76–92; Ross Koen, *The China Lobby in American Politics* (New York: Macmillan, 1960), 155–56.

13. Lewis McCarroll Purifoy, *Harry Truman's China Policy: McCarthyism and the Diplomacy of Hysteria, 1947–1951* (New York: New Viewpoints, 1976).

14. Michael Schaller, *The United States and China in the Twentieth Century* (New York: Oxford University Press, 2d ed., 1990).

15. Michael Schaller, *The U.S. Crusade in China, 1938–1945* (New York: Columbia University Press, 1979).

16. Warren I. Cohen, *America's Response to China: An Interpretative History of Sino-American Relations* (New York: John Wiley and Sons, 1971), 183–202.

17. Schaller, *The United States and China in the Twentieth Century,* 122; Nancy Bernkopf Tucker, *Patterns in the Dust: Chinese-American Relations and the Recognition Controversy, 1949–1950* (New York: Columbia University Press, 1983).

18. Koen, *The China Lobby in American Politics,* 90–94.

19. Griffith, *The Politics of Fear,* 75; Mandel to Kohlberg, Mar. 1, 1950, Kohlberg Papers.

20. Mandel to Kohlberg, Aug. 8, 1945, Nov. 4, 1946, Kohlberg to Styles Bridges, Jan. 14, 1947, Kohlberg to Karl Baarslag, Nov. 7, 1949, Kohlberg Papers; for an exhaustively detailed account of the Lattimore case, see Robert P. Newman, *Owen Lattimore and the "Loss" of China* (Berkeley and Los Angeles: University of California Press, 1992).

21. Stanley I. Kutler, *The American Inquisition: Justice and Injustice in the Cold War* (New York: Hill and Wang, 1982), 210; Newman, *Owen Lattimore and the "Loss" of China,* 216.

22. Newman, *Owen Lattimore and the "Loss" of China,* 215–24.

23. Newman, *Owen Lattimore and the "Loss" of China,* 265–86; Robert Morris, *No Wonder We Are Losing* (New York: Bookmailer, 1958), 104.

24. Griffith, *The Politics of Fear,* 101–9; Fried, *Men Against McCarthy,* 81–92.

25. Kenneth O'Reilly, *Hoover and the Un-Americans: The FBI, HUAC, and the Red Menace* (Philadelphia: Temple University Press, 1983), 171–72; Alonso Hamby, *Beyond the New Deal: Harry S. Truman and American Liberalism* (New York: Columbia University Press, 1973), 398; William R. Tanner and Robert Griffith, "Legislative Politics and 'McCarthyism': The Internal Security Act of 1950," in Griffith and Athan Theoharis, eds., *The Specter* (New York: New Viewpoints, 1974), 174–89.

26. Griffith, *The Politics of Fear,* 127–31; Fried, *Men Against McCarthy,* 124–39; Oshinsky, *A Conspiracy So Immense,* 175–78.

27. Oshinsky, *A Conspiracy So Immense,* 395.

28. For information on the McCarran Committee's IPR hearings, see John N. Thomas, *The Institute of Pacific Relations* (Seattle: University of Washington Press, 1974); Koen, *The China Lobby in American Politics,* passim; Morris, *No Wonder We Are Losing,* 116–33; Christopher John Gerard, "'A Program of Cooperation': The FBI, the Senate Internal Security Subcommittee, and the Communist Issue, 1950–54," (Ph.D. diss., Marquette University, 1993), 68–123; Kohlberg to Mandel, Mar. 12, 14, 26, May 8, 11, 1951, Kohlberg to Morris, April 18, 30, May 23, Sept. 21, 25, Nov. 19, Dec. 13, 1951, Matthews to Mandel, Feb. 26, 1951, Mandel to Kohlberg, May 10, 1951, Kohlberg Papers; Freda Utley to Morris and Mandel, June 21, 1951, Utley Papers; Mandel to Matthews, Feb. 25, 1951, Matthews Papers.

29. Newman, *Owen Lattimore and the "Loss" of China,* 314–57; Thomas, *The Institute of Pacific Relations,* 17, 23, 55–65.

30. Frederick Vanderbilt Field, *From Right to Left: An Autobiography* (Westport, Conn.: Lawrence Hill, 1983), 116–33, 165–85.

31. Hede Massing, testimony, Aug. 2, 1951, U.S. Senate, Committee on the Judiciary, Subcommittee on Internal Security, "Hearings on the Institute of Pacific Relations," 82nd Cong., 2d sess., 1951–1952, 224 (hereafter IPR hearings).

32. Kutler, *The American Inquisition,* 183–203; Newman, *Owen Lattimore and the "Loss" of China,* 396–403.

33. Kutler, *The American Inquisition,* 204–11. According to Nicholas von Hoffman, George Sokolsky was also involved in getting McGranery to put Cohn on the case, *Citizen Cohn* (New York: Doubleday, 1988), 110, 134–5.

34. Newman, *Owen Lattimore and the "Loss" of China,* 396–403, 435–84.

35. Harvey Matusow, *False Witness* (New York: Cameron and Kahn, 1955), 102–107; Newman, *Owen Lattimore and the "Loss" of China,* 449.

36. Newman, *Owen Lattimore and the "Loss" of China,* 437–43, 457; Koen, *The China Lobby,* 151; Dorothy Borg, interview with the author, April 4, 1977; Klehr and Radosh, *The Amerasia Spy Case,* 39, 168–72.

37. Anderson and May, *McCarthy: The Man, the Senator, the "Ism,"* 223–33; Oshinsky, *A Conspiracy So Immense,* 209–213.

38. Emmet John Hughes, *The Ordeal of Power: A Political Memoir of the Eisenhower Years* (New York: Atheneum, 1963), 63; Griffith, *The Politics of Fear,* 190–204. On the splits within the Republican Party, see Ronald J. Caridi, *The Korean War and American Politics: The Republican Party as a Case Study* (Philadelphia: University of Pennsylvania Press, 1968). For a sophisticated discussion of the political and economic forces that underlay the differing positions on foreign policy, see Bruce Cumings, *The Origins of the Korean War,* vol. 2, *The Roaring of the Cataract, 1947–1950* (Princeton: Princeton University Press, 1990), 79–121.

39. Oshinsky, *A Conspiracy So Immense,* 244–45; Griffith, *The Politics of Fear,* 194–95; Fried, *Men Against McCarthy,* 247–53.

40. Oshinsky, *A Conspiracy So Immense,* 200.

41. Hughes, *The Ordeal of Power,* 42–44; Griffith, *The Politics of Fear,* 189–94.

42. Reeves, *The Life and Times of Joe McCarthy,* 204, 462–66; Oshinsky, *A Conspiracy So Immense,* 252–55; von Hoffman, *Citizen Cohn,* 138–45.

43. Martin Merson, *The Private Diary of a Public Servant* (New York: Macmillan, 1955); Oshinsky, *A Conspiracy So Immense,* 266–76.

44. Merson, *The Private Diary of a Public Servant,* 11–19; Oshinsky, *A Conspiracy So Immense,* 277–78.

45. Charlotte Knight, "What Price Security?" *Collier's,* July 9, 1954; Hughes, *The Ordeal of Power,* 84–85, 93; Oshinsky, *A Conspiracy So Immense,* 262–63; Fred I. Greenstein, *The Hidden Hand Presidency: Eisenhower as Leader* (New York: Basic Books, 1982), 166.

46. Gary May, *China Scapegoat: The Diplomatic Ordeal of John Carter Vincent* (Washington, D.C.: New Republic Books, 1979); Kahn, *The China Hands,* 247–62.

47. Greenstein, *The Hidden Hand Presidency,* 167–68; Oshinsky, *A Conspiracy So Immense,* 286–300.

48. The White House diaries of Eisenhower's counsel Bernard Shanley are just

one of many sources that reveal the pressures on Eisenhower to condemn McCarthy. Bernard Shanley Diaries, March 1953, 733, 737, 743, June 1953, 2, 942, Shanley Papers, Dwight D. Eisenhower Library, Abilene, Kansas (hereafter DDEL); C. D. Jackson, Log, Dec. 2, 1953, C. D. Jackson Papers, DDEL; Hughes, *The Ordeal of Power*, 90–92; Greenstein, *The Hidden Hand Presidency*, 155–227; Griffith, *The Politics of Fear*, 196–207.

49. Oshinsky, *A Conspiracy So Immense*, 299, 309; von Hoffman, *Citizen Cohn*, 144–70.

50. For an influential contemporary statement of the argument that McCarthy hurt the anticommunist cause, see the American Committee for Cultural Freedom–sponsored volume by James Rorty and Moshe Decter, *McCarthy and the Communists* (Boston: Beacon Press, 1954); Chambers, cited in Oshinsky, *A Conspiracy So Immense*, 309; Sam Tanenhaus, *Whittaker Chambers: A Biography* (New York: Random House, 1997), 475–83.

51. Griffith, *The Politics of Fear*, 224–32; Oshinsky, *A Conspiracy So Immense*, 318–21; Shanley Diary, July 1953, 1015, Shanley Papers.

52. Theoharis and Cox, *The Boss*, 295–99; Curt Gentry, *J. Edgar Hoover: The Man and the Secrets* (New York: W. W. Norton, 1991), 379–80, 431–36.

53. John G. Adams, *Without Precedent: The Story of the Death of McCarthyism* (New York: W. W. Norton, 1983), 71–91; von Hoffman, *Citizen Cohn*, 193; Oshinsky, *A Conspiracy So Immense*, 330–44.

54. Oshinsky, *A Conspiracy So Immense*, 349–53; Reeves, *The Life and Times of Joe McCarthy*, 530–31.

55. Herbert Brownell, oral history interview, Feb. 24, 1977, DDEL. For an insider's account of the army's maneuvering in response to McCarthy, see Adams, *Without Precedent;* Greenstein, *The Hidden Hand Presidency*, 183–84.

56. Oshinsky, *A Conspiracy So Immense*, 172–78; Reeves, *The Life and Times of Joe McCarthy*, 537–59.

57. On the rumors of homosexuality surrounding Cohn, Schine, and McCarthy, see von Hoffman, *Citizen Cohn*, 183–90.

58. Adams, *Without Precedent*, 117–18, 140–43; Greenstein, *The Hidden Hand President*, 212; W. H. Godel to Fred A. Seaton, Mar. 4, 1954, Fred A. Seaton Papers, Box 4, DDEL.

59. Griffith, *The Politics of Fear*, 260n; Oshinsky, *A Conspiracy So Immense*, 458–59.

60. Erik Barnouw, *Tube of Plenty: The Evolution of American Television* (New York: Oxford University Press, rev. ed. 1982), 172–84; Oshinsky, *A Conspiracy So Immense*, 410–11, 465; Bayley, *Joe McCarthy and the Press*, 174–213.

61. Oshinsky, *A Conspiracy So Immense*, 472–92; Reeves, *The Life and Times of Joe McCarthy*, 639–64; Griffith, *The Politics of Fear*, 270–317; Fried, *Men Against McCarthy*, 291–313.

62. Oshinsky, *A Conspiracy So Immense*, 492.

8: "A BADGE OF INFAMY": ANTICOMMUNIST ECONOMIC SANCTIONS AND POLITICAL DISMISSALS

1. Transcript of Security Appeal Hearing, Lawrence E. Parker, Mar. 30, 1951, in Box 30, Gladstein, Leonard, Patsey, and Anderson Papers, Bancroft Library, University of California, Berkeley (hereafter, Gladstein Papers); on the port security program, see Ralph S. Brown and John D. Fassett, "Security Tests for Maritime Workers: Due Process under the Port Security Program," *Yale Law Journal* 62 (July 1953): 1163–1208; David Caute, *The Great Fear: The Anti-Communist Purge Under Truman and Eisenhower* (New York: Simon and Schuster, 1978), 392–400.

2. Parker, transcript; "Case No. _____," draft ms., probably from Adam Yarmolinsky, Gladstein Papers, Box 29.

3. Merlin O'Neill (commandant, U.S. Coast Guard), affidavit, May 16, 1951, Gladstein Papers, Box 30.

4. Brown and Fassett, "Security Tests for Maritime Workers," 1187; O'Neill, affidavit; *Report of the Commission on Government Security,* pursuant to Public Law 304, 84th Cong., as amended, June 21, 1957 (hereafter Wright Report), 333.

5. Excerpt from Transcript of Meeting of Joint Labor-Management Group on the Maritime Industry, Jan. 16, 1951, Washington, D.C., in Box 31, Gladstein Papers; Wright report, 335; Hugh Bryson to Richard Gladstein, Oct. 4, 1950, Box 29, Gladstein Papers; Statement of National Union of Marine Cooks and Stewards before the Subcommittee of the Senate Committee on Interstate and Foreign Commerce, Oct. 23, 1953, Box 30, ibid.; minutes, Northwest Conference on Blacklisting, Mar. 18, 1951, enclosure in Bill Gettings to Participating Unions, Mar. 22, 1951, Box 29, ibid.; George R. Andersen to Ralph S. Brown, Jr., Aug. 22, 1952, Box 30, ibid.

6. Parker, transcript; handwritten memorandum, n. d. (probably early 1951), Box 30, Gladstein Papers; memorandum, "Case no. 1, Theodore Allen," Box 29, ibid.

7. Parker, transcript; Howard Kimeldorf, *Reds or Rackets? The Making of Radical and Conservative Unions on the Waterfront* (Berkeley and Los Angeles: University of California Press, 1988), 150; J. Keene, "The Story of Screening," pamphlet published by the Marine Cooks and Stewards Union, n. d., and Bryson to Gladstein, Oct. 4, 1950, Box 29, Gladstein Papers.

8. *Parker v. Lester,* 227 F.2d 708 (9th Cir. 1955).

9. Richard Gladstein, Norman Leonard, statement, n. d., Box 31, Gladstein Papers.

10. Gladstein to "those checked on pink list, lawyers," Nov. 26, 1956, John Caughlan to Leonard, Jan. 31, 1957, Leonard to friends, Mar. 20, 1957, Victor Rabinowitz to Leonard, Apr. 10, 1957, Box 31, Gladstein Papers; J. R. Stewart to Albert Johnson, Sept. 5, 1957, W. L. Maloney to Clarence Roland Carlson, Jan. 20, 1959, Box 29, ibid.

11. Gladstein to "those checked on pink list, lawyers," Nov. 26, 1956, Rabinowitz to Leonard, Dec. 19, 1957, Mar. 12, 1958, "The Lookout," Mar. 1958, Rabinowitz to Leonard, May 28, 1959, Walter Stich to Sir and Brother, Jan. 7, 1960, Gladstein Papers, Box 31.

12. Samuel G. Whitney to President Harry S. Truman, Nov. 25, 1947, in National Association for the Advancement of Colored People, Papers of the NAACP (microform) Part 13, Series C, reel 4 (Bethesda, Md.: University Publications of America [1982] –) (hereafter NAACP Papers).

13. *Wieman v. Updegraff,* 433 U.S. 183, 190–91; Eleanor Bontecou, *The Federal Loyalty-Security Program* (Ithaca, N.Y.: Cornell University Press, 1953), 65. For a similar statement by Judge Henry W. Edgerton in the main test case of the loyalty-security program, see *Bailey v. Richardson,* 182 F.2d., 46, 70. See also Solicitor General Philip Perlman, testimony, June 9, 1955, in "Administration of the Federal Employees' Security Program," Hearings before a Subcommittee of the Committee on Post Office and Civil Service, U.S. Senate, 84th Cong., 1st sess., May 26, June 2, 9, 14, 22, 28, Aug. 29, 30, 31, Sept. 26, 27, and 28, 1955, Part I (hereafter Johnston hearings), 112.

14. The most extensive treatment of the political tests for employment is in Caute, *The Great Fear.*

15. On the most well known passport denial, see Martin Bauml Duberman, *Paul Robeson* (New York: Knopf, 1988), 381–445; Roland Watts, *The Draftee and Internal Security* (New York: Workers Defense League, 1955), 7; Walter Gellhorn, *Security, Loyalty, and Science* (Ithaca, N.Y.: Cornell University Press, 1950).

16. On the academic community, see Ellen W. Schrecker, *No Ivory Tower: McCarthyism and the Universities* (New York: Oxford University Press, 1986); on the entertainment industry, see Larry Ceplair and Steven Englund, *The Inquisition in Hollywood: Politics in the Film Community, 1930–1960* (Garden City, N.Y.: Anchor Press/Doubleday, 1980); John Cogley, *Report on Blacklisting,* 2 vols. (New York: Fund for the Republic, 1956); Merle Miller, *The Judges and the Judged* (Garden City, N.Y.: Doubleday, 1952).

17. Adam Yarmolinsky, ed., *Case Studies in Personnel Security* (Washington, D.C.: Bureau of National Affairs, 1955); Watts, *The Draftee and Internal Security,* 56–58; Schrecker, *No Ivory Tower,* 224–32; for samples of Hollywood questions, see J. B. Matthews Papers, Box 695.

18. Schrecker, *No Ivory Tower,* 161–93; G. Clark Thompson, in *Industrial Security: I. Combating Subversion and Sabotage* (New York: National Industrial Conference Board, 1952), 5.

19. Bruno Stein, "Loyalty and Security Cases in Arbitration," *Industrial and Labor Relations Review* 17 (Oct. 1963): 98; Helen Epstein, *Joe Papp: An American Life* (Boston: Little, Brown, 1994), 129–30; memorandum, SAC, Kansas City, to Director, Feb. 8, 1952, "McCarthy Era Blacklisting of School Teachers, College Professors, and Other Public Employees: The FBI Responsibilities Program File and the Dissemination of Information Policy File," ed. Kenneth O'Reilly (Bethesda, Md.: University Publications of America, 1989) (hereafter Responsibilities Program), #775.

20. Carl Bernstein, *Loyalties: A Son's Memoir* (New York: Simon and Schuster, 1989), 176; Abram Flaxer, oral history interview by Debra E. Barnhart, April 23,

1981, in Robert E. Wagner Labor Archives, New York University; Bontecou, *The Loyalty-Security Program,* 119, 132; Michael C. Slotnick, "The Anathema of the Security Risk: Arbitrary Dismissals of Federal Government Civilian Employees and Civilian Employees of Private Contractors Doing Business with the Federal Government," *University of Miami Law Review* 17 (1962): 10–50; Thurman Arnold, *Fair Fights and Foul: A Dissenting Lawyer's Life* (New York: Harcourt, Brace and World, 1965), 206–207.

21. John Henry Faulk, *Fear on Trial* (New York: Simon and Schuster, 1964); J. Howard Pew to J. B. Matthews, June 23, 1958, Box 676, Matthews Papers; Robert Donner to Matthews, Feb. 24, 1949, Box 658, ibid.

22. Wright Report, 357; Gellhorn, *Security, Loyalty, and Science,* 222; Faulk, *Fear on Trial,* 252; David Oshinsky, *A Conspiracy So Immense: The World of Joe McCarthy* (New York: Free Press, 1983), 204–205.

23. Stephen J. Spingarn, memorandum for the files, Jan. 20, 1947, Box 7, Stephen J. Spingarn Papers, Harry S. Truman Library, Independence, Mo. (hereafter HSTL).

24. Testimony of James B. Carey, Sept. 2, 1948, before special subcommittee of House Education and Labor Committee, 80th Cong., 2d sess., 57.

25. Executive Order 9835, 12 Fed. Reg. 1935 (1947), Mar. 21, 1947.

26. *Cole v. Young,* 351 U.S. 536 (1956); Yarmolinsky, *Case Studies in Personnel Security,* 32; Watts, *The Draftee and Internal Security.*

27. Bontecou, *The Federal Loyalty-Security Program,* 110; memorandum for the file re: Richard Raymond Parker, n. d. [probably Feb. 1951], Box 69, Gladstein Papers.

28. Yarmolinsky, *Case Studies in Personnel Security,* 297–98; Fred W. Friendly, *Due to Circumstances Beyond Our Control . . .* (New York: Random House, 1967), 4–20; Thomas Rosteck, *"See It Now" Confronts McCarthyism: Television Documentary and the Politics of Representation* (Tuscaloosa: University of Alabama Press, 1994), 55–84.

29. Francis Carpenter, interview with the author, April 6, 1978; Harry Read, memorandum to James Carey, Aug. 29, 1951, Box A.108, International Union of Electrical, Radio and Machine Workers Papers, Special Collections and Archives, Rutgers University, New Brunswick, N.J. (hereafter IUE Papers); memorandum, n. d., Dwight D. Eisenhower Official Files 50 (hereafter DDE-OF), Dwight D. Eisenhower Library, Abilene, Kansas (hereafter DDEL).

30. Transcript of Security Appeal Hearing of Royal L. Lundgren, Mar. 30, 1951, Box 69, Gladstein Papers; Arnold, *Fair Fights and Foul,* 206–207.

31. Daniel H. Pollitt, testimony, Aug. 29, 1955, "Administration of the Federal Employees' Security Program," Hearings before a Subcommittee of the Committee on Post Office and Civil Service, U.S. Senate, 84th Cong., 1st sess., May 26, June 2, 9, 14, 22, 28, Aug. 29, 30, 31, Sept. 26, 27, and 28, 1955 (Washington, D.C.: Government Printing Office, 1956) (hereafter Johnston Hearings), 488.

32. Statement of James H. Smith, Jr., Aug. 31, 1955, Johnston Hearings, 618–21; Scientists' Committee on Loyalty and Security, "Fort Monmouth One Year Later,"

Bulletin of the Atomic Scientists 11 (April 1955): 149; Arnold, *Fair Fights and Foul,* 210–13.

33. Watts, *The Draftee and Internal Security,* 12–61.

34. Lloyd McMurray to A. Harry Levitan, June 30, 1951, Jeff Kibre to McMurray, Oct. 23, 1953, both in Box 30, Gladstein Papers; memorandum for file, hearing, Feb. 5, 1951, Richard Raymond Parker, Box 69, ibid.; Report to the National Security Council by the Interdepartmental Committee on Internal Security on Government Employee Security Program, May 2, 1952, NSC-113/1, Harry S. Truman, President's Secretary's Files (hereafter HST-PSF), Harry S. Truman Library (hereafter HSTL).

On the case of two Army employees who were cleared once a federal court of appeals required that they be given a bill of particulars, see Bontecou, *The Federal Loyalty-Security Program,* 125, 226.

35. Arnold, *Fair Fights and Foul,* 206; Yarmolinsky, *Case Studies in Personnel Security,* 164–68.

36. Transcript of Proceedings, Fourteenth Meeting of the Loyalty Review Board, Feb. 13–14, 1951, Harry S. Truman, Official Files (hereafter HST-OF), 2-E, HSTL; Bontecou, *The Federal Loyalty-Security Program,* 84–89; Gellhorn, *Security, Loyalty, and Science,* 209–21.

37. Gellhorn, *Security, Loyalty, and Science,* 221; Bontecoe, *The Federal Loyalty-Security Program,* 125–31; Norman A. Stoll to Mastin G. White, Feb. 28, 1950, Box 35, Spingarn Papers.

38. Seth W. Richardson, mimeographed statement, Dec. 23, 1947, Frances Perkins Papers, Box 84, Rare Book and Manuscript Library, Columbia University; Richardson, "The Federal Employee Loyalty Program," *Columbia Law Review* 51 (1951): 549; *Industrial Personnel Security Review Program, First Annual Report,* Director, Office of Personnel Security Policy, Office of Assistant Secretary of Defense, 1956 (hereafter *First Annual Report*), 6–7; J. Edgar Hoover, testimony, Mar. 27, 1950, Subcommittee of the Committee on Foreign Relations, "State Department Loyalty Investigation, Hearings," 81st Cong., 2d sess.

39. *Friedman v. Schwellenbach,* 159 F.2d 22 (D.C. Cir. 1946); Theron L. Caudle to Tom Clark, Apr. 18, 1947, Box 1, L. Devitt Vanech Papers, HSTL; Robert J. Morgan, "Federal Loyalty Security Removals, 1946–1956," *Nebraska Law Review* 36 (1957): 416–17.

40. Bontecou, *The Loyalty-Security Program,* 119; Arnold, *Fair Fights and Foul,* 207; Transcript of Proceedings, Fourteenth Meeting of the Loyalty Review Board, Feb. 13–14, 1951, HST-OF, 2-E.

41. *Bailey v. Richardson* 182 F.2d 42; Morgan, "Federal Loyalty Security Removals," 412–22; Slotnick, "The Anathema of the Security Risk," 28–40.

42. Bernard Schwartz, *Superchief: Earl Warren and His Supreme Court, A Judicial Biography* (New York: New York University Press, 1983), 5–59; "JGB," memorandum, *Bailey v. Richardson,* Oct. 14, 1950, 1950 term, no. 49; handwritten notes on the conference, Oct. 14, 1950, both in Box 198, William O. Douglas papers, Library

of Congress, Washington, D.C.; Felix Frankfurter, memorandum for the Conference, Apr. 27, 1951, Box 201, ibid.

43. In his dissent in *Bailey v. Richardson*, appeals court judge Henry Edgerton refers to the question about segregated blood, see *Bailey v. Richardson* 182 F.2d 46, 73. The question was referred to in almost every liberal attack on the loyalty program. See, for example, Michael Straight et al. to Truman, Apr. 19, 1950, HST-OF, 2-E; notes on the conference, Oct. 14, 1950, Douglas Papers.

44. Harry W. Blair, cited in Bontecou, *The Federal Loyalty-Security Program,* 139–40n; Gellhorn, *Security, Loyalty, and Science,* 156.

45. The best overall description of the kinds of inquiries that federal loyalty-security panels conducted can be found in Bontecou, *The Federal Loyalty-Security Program,* 73–156. For other examples of these questions, see Yarmolinsky, *Case Studies in Personnel Security,* passim; Watts, *The Draftee and Internal Security,* passim; Keene, "The Story of Screening," Box 69, Gladstein Papers; memorandum, L. M. [Lloyd McMurray] to file, Sept. 7, 1951, ibid.; Charlotte Gourdine, affidavit, Dec. 1952, Edward B. Barlow, statement, n. d., both in Box 10, ibid.; transcript, In the matter of *Gunnar Benonys et al. v. Allen Johnson,* Aug. 8, 14, Sept. 4, 1951, Trial Committee, Bay Counties District Council of Carpenters, Bancroft Library; Schrecker, *No Ivory Tower,* 225.

46. Carpenter, interview with the author; Transcript of Proceedings, Fourteenth Meeting of the Loyalty Review Board.

47. Frances Perkins, memorandum, June 12, 1951, to Robert Sproul, May 23, 1951, memorandum, Feb. 5, 1953, all in Box 84, Perkins Papers; Charlie Willis to Sherman Adams, Feb. 5, 1953, DDE-OF, 53-B; Wright Report, 298, 356–8; *First Annual Report,* 4–16; Bontecou, *The Federal Loyalty-Security Program,* 35–48, 76–82; Felix Rackow, "The Federal Loyalty Program: Politics and Civil Liberty," *Western Reserve Law Review* 12 (September 1961): 711; Ralph S. Brown, Jr., *Loyalty and Security: Employment Tests in the United States* (New Haven: Yale University Press, 1958), 28, 290. For additional, albeit anecdotal, information about security officials, see Johnston Hearings, 145–96, 289–363, 389–90.

48. *First Annual Report,* 44, 59–60, 83–84, 136–37; Herbert Brownell, Jr., memorandum, Mar. 22, 1954, Dwight D. Eisenhower Papers (Ann Whitman), Administration File, Box 8, DDEL.

49. Brown, *Loyalty and Security,* 49–50; Joseph Rauh to Harold A. Cranefield, Nov. 15, 1952, Box 96, Rauh Papers, Library of Congress; *First Annual Report,* 44, 59–60, 83–84, 136–37; Bernstein, *Loyalties,* 215.

50. Unsigned memorandum, Oct. 19, 1950, Box 29, Gladstein Papers.

51. Schrecker, *No Ivory Tower,* 161–240, 260–63. For information about some New York City school teachers who had been in the CP and had to name names to keep their jobs, see Victor Rabinowitz, *Unrepentant Leftist: A Lawyer's Memoir* (Urbana: University of Illinois Press, 1996), 149.

52. Yarmolinsky, *Case Studies in Personnel Security,* passim; *First Annual Report,*

passim; Transcript of Proceedings, Fourteenth Meeting of the Loyalty Review Board; Barton J. Bernstein, "The Oppenheimer Loyalty-Security Case Reconsidered," *Stanford Law Review* 42 (July 1990): 1383–1484. Abraham Chasanow, a civilian employee in the Navy Department's Hydrographic Office, took his case to the press and received so much publicity that he was reinstated. See Chasanow, testimony, Aug. 31, 1955, Johnston hearings.

53. Oshinsky, *A Conspiracy So Immense,* 323–35.

54. Bontecou, *The Federal Loyalty-Security Program,* 69–72; Brown, *Loyalty and Security,* 50; Henry Mayer, "How the Loyalty-Security Program Affects Private Employment," *Lawyers Guild Review* 15 (Winter 1955–56): 126.

55. Bontecou, *The Federal Loyalty-Security Program,* 69–72; Brown, *Loyalty and Security,* 50; George Moore to Philip Young, Dec. 8, 1954, DDE-OF, 104-J.

56. David Fellman, "The Loyalty Defendants," *Wisconsin Law Review* (1957): 29; Parker, transcript; Yarmolinsky, *Case Studies in Personnel Security,* passim.

57. Clark Clifford, quoted in Bernstein, *Loyalties,* 197–98; J. Anthony Panuch, testimony, May 13, 1947, in *U. S. v. Carl Aldo Marzani,* District Court of United States for District of Columbia, transcript of the trial, reel 39 (microfilm ed., Fund for the Republic, New York) (hereafter Marzani trial), 271–82; memorandum, D. M. Ladd to Director, FBI, Nov. 12, 1953, Harry Dexter White, #59; memorandum, A. H. Belmont to Ladd, Nov. 11, 1953, ibid., #75; Robert P. Patterson to Truman, July 27, 1946, in Box 63, George M. Elsey Papers, HSTL; memorandum, Clark M. Clifford to Truman, Aug. 4, 1948, Edward H. Foley to Clifford, Aug. 5, 1948, Foley to William P. Rogers, Aug. 5, 1948, Rogers to Foley, Aug. 3, 1948, all in Box 68, ibid.; "Investigation of Federal Employees Loyalty Program," Interim Report of the Investigations Subcommittee of the Committee on Expenditures in the Executive Departments, Sept. 4, 1948, Senate Report No. 1775, 80th Cong., 2d sess. (Washington, D.C.: Government Printing Office, 1948); memorandum, "Appropriations Committee Investigations of State Department," n. d., Box 2, Homer Ferguson Papers, Michigan Historical Collections, Bentley Historical Library, University of Michigan; Wright Report, 16–17.

58. Clark Clifford, quoted in Bernstein, *Loyalties,* 197–200; Elsey, handwritten memorandum, Aug. 26, 1948, Elsey Papers; Elsey to Clifford, Sept. 19, 1949, Box 69, ibid.; Spingarn, memorandum to Donald Dawson, June 17, 1949, Box 35, Spingarn Papers; Mangum Fox to John R. Steelman, filed June 9, 1950, HST-OF, 252-K; Alfred N. Richard to Truman, Feb. 11, 1949, ibid.

59. Memorandum, Charles Murphy and Stephen Spingarn to Truman, May 24, 1950, Box 31, Spingarn Papers; memorandum, Spingarn to Murphy, Apr. 27, 1950, Box 35, ibid.; Seth Richardson to Donald S. Dawson, June 15, 1950, Dawson, memorandum for Murphy, June 8, 1950, HST-OF, 2-E.

60. Public Law 733, 81st Cong., 2d sess., 64 Stat. 476 (1950).

61. There are varying estimates of the percentages of dismissals that were reversed. For some estimates, see Fellman, "The Loyalty Defendants," 33; Spingarn, memorandum, Apr. 30, 1953, Box 38, Spingarn Papers; Frances Perkins, memoran-

dum on conversation with Meloy, May 2, 1951, Box 84, Perkins Papers; memo, n. d., Nos. 8, 7, 71 JAFRC v. McGrath, Cert. Conf. and Misc. memos, Box 201, Douglas Papers; Francis Biddle to Truman, with enclosure, May 22, 1951, HST-OF 2750; Transcript of Proceedings, Fourteenth Meeting of the Loyalty Review Board; Hiram Bingham to John A. Danaher, Feb. 19, 1951 with enclosure, Box 2, Records of the President's Commission on Internal Security and Individual Rights, HSTL; Alonzo L. Hamby, *Beyond the New Deal: Harry Truman and American Liberalism* (New York: Columbia University Press, 1973), 387–89.

62. Alan D. Harper, *The Politics of Loyalty: The White House and the Communist Issue, 1946–1952* (Westport, Conn.: Greenwood Press, 1969), 164–85. For evidence about the Nimitz panel's conservatism, see, for example, R. C. Leffingwell to John A. Danaher, Mar. 6, 1951, Leffingwell to Nimitz, Mar. 20, 1951, Box 3, Records of the President's Commission on Internal Security and Individual Rights, HSTL.

63. Richardson, "The Federal Employee Loyalty Program," 555; Donald A. Hansen, memorandum, "Federal Employees Loyalty Program," Jan. 3, 1952, Box 36, Spingarn Papers; Transcript of Proceedings, Fourteenth Meeting of the Loyalty Review Board; Executive Order 10241, 16 Fed. Reg. 3690 (1953), Apr. 21, 1951.

64. E. J. Kahn, Jr., *The China Hands: America's Foreign Service Officers and What Befell Them* (New York: Viking, 1975), 223–39; Ross Y. Koen, *The China Lobby in American Politics* (New York: Macmillan, 1960), 199–202.

65. Report to the National Security Council by the Interdepartmental Committee on Internal Security on Government Employee Security Program, May 2, 1952; memorandum for the president, May 29, 1952, HST-PSF, NSC Meetings; Brownell, memorandum, Mar. 22, 1954 (Ann Whitman), Administration File, Box 8, DDEL.

66. Jeff Broadwater, *Eisenhower and the Anti-Communist Crusade* (Chapel Hill: University of North Carolina Press, 1992), 85–91; Rackow, "The Federal Loyalty Program," 716; memorandum, Special Committee to Eisenhower, Dec. 21, 1952, DDE-OF, 104-J.

67. Memorandum, J. Lee Rankin to Bernard Shanley, Feb. 18, 1953, DDE-OF, 104-J; Executive Order 10450, 18 Fed. Reg. 2489 (1953), April 27, 1953.

68. Rackow, "The Federal Loyalty Program," 718–22; Thomas C. Reeves, *The Life and Times of Joe McCarthy: A Biography* (New York: Stein and Day, 1982), 545.

69. Friendly, *Due to Circumstances Beyond Our Control . . .*, 4–20; Thomas Rosteck, *"See It Now" Confronts McCarthyism*, 55–84.

70. Abraham Chasanow, testimony, Aug. 31, 1955, Johnston hearings, 621–30.

71. The most useful sources on the Oppenheimer case are Bernstein, "The Oppenheimer Loyalty-Security Case Reconsidered"; Atomic Energy Commission, *In the Matter of J. Robert Oppenheimer: Transcript of Hearing Before Personnel Security Board and Texts of Principal Documents and Letters* (Cambridge, Mass.: MIT Press, 1971, reprint of 1954 ed.); Philip M. Stern, *The Oppenheimer Case: Security on Trial* (New York: Harper and Row, 1969); Martin J. Sherwin, "J. Robert Oppenheimer: Enemies in High Places," paper delivered at the American Historical Association meeting, Dec. 29, 1990 (copy in the author's possession); and Herbert F. York, *The*

Advisors: Oppenheimer, Teller and the Superbomb (Stanford: Stanford University Press, 1988 ed.). The text of the letter by William Borden is in *In the Matter of J. Robert Oppenheimer,* 837–38.

72. Sherwin, "Robert J. Oppenheimer: Enemies in High Places"; Bernstein, "The Oppenheimer Loyalty-Security Case Reconsidered"; Broadwater, *Eisenhower and the Anti-Communist Crusade,* 99–104; Shanley Diary, July 16, 1954, Box 2, Shanley Papers; Paul T. Carroll, memorandum, July 9, 1954, C. F. Security Program, no #, DDEL; Gordon Gray to Robert Cutler, Jan. 10, 24, 1955, Cutler, memorandum to Sherman Adams, Jan. 13, 1955, in White House Central Files, Confidential Files Subject Series, Box 66, DDEL.

On the growing criticism of the loyalty-security program, both within and outside the administration, see William P. Rogers, memorandum for Attorney General, Aug. 4, 1954, Box 15, Rogers Papers, DDEL; Harry Cain, "The Individual Is of Supreme Importance," speech, May 5, 1956, in DDE-OF 50-SACB; Minutes of Meeting, Democratic Policy Committee, Feb. 16, 1954, Lyndon B. Johnson, Senate, Box 374, Lyndon B. Johnson Library, Austin, Texas (hereafter LBJL).

73. R. L. Farrington to Brownell, Jan. 13, 1955, Hubert H. Humphrey to Eisenhower, Jan. 13, 1955, both in DDE-OF, 104-J.

74. Philip Young to Adams, Jan. 13, 1955, DDE-OF, 104-J; Percival Brundage, memorandum for Adams, Jan. 29, 1955, White House Central Files, Confidential File, Subject Files, Box 66, Security Programs (4), DDEL; Brownell to Eisenhower, Mar. 4, 1955, DDE (Ann Whitman) Administration File, Box 8, DDEL; Karl Baarslag to Matthews, Feb. 3, 1955, Box 650, Matthews Papers.

75. Wayne [no last name] to Adams, Oct. 5, 1955, DDE-OF, 104-J-1.

76. Michal R. Belknap, *Cold War Political Justice: The Smith Act, the Communist Party, and American Civil Liberties* (Westport, Conn.: Greenwood Press, 1977), 236–51.

Communist defendants and their attorneys tried to keep their cases in the courts as long as they could; see Al Richmond, *A Long View from the Left* (Boston: Houghton Mifflin, 1973), 356–62.

77. The four key decisions of the 1955–56 term were *Communist Party v. Subversive Activities Control Board,* 351 U.S. 115; *Pennsylvania v. Nelson,* 350 U.S. 497; *Cole v. Young,* 351 U.S. 536; and *Slochower v. Board of Higher Education of New York City,* 350 U.S. 551. On the Court's overall performance during the late 1950s, see Robert G. McCloskey, *The Modern Supreme Court* (Cambridge: Harvard University Press, 1972), and Walter F. Murphy, *Congress and the Court: A Case Study in the American Political Process* (Chicago: University of Chicago Press, 1962).

78. Jane Pacht Brickman, "'Medical McCarthyism': The Physicians Forum and the Cold War," *Journal of the History of Medicine and Allied Sciences* 49 (July 1994): 398–99; *Peters v. Hobby,* 349 U.S. 331 (June 6, 1955).

79. Arnold, *Fair Fights and Foul,* 207–10; Arnold, testimony, July 21, 1955, Johnston hearings, 365–71.

80. Jeri Jan Baldwin, "COLE vs YOUNG: Loyalty vs. Security: The Cole Case of

1956," undated student paper in possession of Annette Rubinstein. I also used a collection of clippings on *Cole v. Young* in Rubinstein's possession that included the following: *New York Times,* July 29, Nov. 22, 1955, Mar. 4, 1956; *New York Post,* Mar. 16, 1955, June 12, 13, 1956; *Newsday,* June 14, 1956; *Washington Post,* Oct. 23, 1954.

81. *Cole v. Young,* 351 U.S. 536 (1956).

82. John W. Macy, Jr., Departmental Circular, No. 859, June 14, 1956, DDE-OF, 104-J; Harris Ellsworth to Tom Murray, July 2, 1958, ibid.

83. *Cole v. Young.*

84. Murphy, *Congress and the Court,* 87, 174–82; C. Herman Pritchett, *Congress versus the Supreme Court, 1957–1960* (Minneapolis: University of Minnesota Press, 1961), 96–106; William P. Rogers to Eisenhower, Mar. 26, 1959, Eisenhower to Rogers, Apr. 1, 1959, Roger W. Jones to Attorney General et al., Mar. 19, 1959, DDE-OF, 104-J.

85. "Department of the Interior Security Program," Jan. 3, 1963, Senate Interior Department, Box 249, U.S. Senate, Committee on the Judiciary, Subcommittee on Internal Security, Records, Record Group 46, National Archives (hereafter SISS Records); H. B. Montague to Samuel J. Scott, Oct. 5, 1962, Post Office Department, ibid.; Paul Tillett, "The Social Costs of the Loyalty Programs: A Preliminary Draft" (unpublished ms., n. d., copy in possession of the author).

86. Clarence Mitchell to Roy Wilkins, Nov. 18, 1948, NAACP Papers, Part 13, Series C, reel 5; Spingarn, memorandum, Apr. 30, 1953, Box 38, Spingarn Papers; Kimbell Johnson to Mr. Irons, Mar. 26, 1959, DDE-OF, 104-J.

87. Philip Young, statement to Subcommittee on Government Employment Security Program of the Senate Post Office and Civil Service Committee, Sept. 26, 1955, DDE-OF, 104-J. On the impact of the loyalty program on federal employment, see Tillett, "The Social Costs of the Loyalty Programs"; National Lawyers Guild vs. Attorney General, et al., Plaintiff's Principal Factual Papers in Opposition to the Motion of the United States of America for Partial Summary Judgment Dismissing the Damage Claims arising from the FBI's Conduct and in Support of Plaintiff's Cross-Motion for Partial Summary Judgment, Sept. 26, 1984 (hereafter NLG motion), 216–17.

88. Doris Brin Walker, interview with the author, June 19, 1995; Barry Winograd, "An Interview with Doris Brin Walker," *California Labor and Employment Law Quarterly* 9 (Summer 1994): 14–18. Several memoirs discuss Walker, among them Bernstein, *Loyalties,* 70–76, and Jessica Mitford, *A Fine Old Conflict* (New York: Knopf, 1977), 47–75.

89. Bernard Young to Lewis Alan Berne, Aug. 29, 1947, in Doris Brin Walker Papers, in personal possession of Walker.

90. Fred A. Cutter to Benjamin Mandel, Oct. 5, 1956, Box 35, SISS Records; report, Perry W. Moothart, San Francisco, Jan. 31, 1949, Doris Brin Walker FBI file, no serial number; telegram, Whelan to Director, Apr. 30, 1955, ibid., no serial number; Correlation Summary, Jan. 30, 1959, ibid., #45; text of company letter in *Black v. Cutter Laboratories,* 351 U.S. 292 (1956).

91. *Black v. Cutter Laboratories.*

92. *Black v. Cutter Laboratories,* 300–391; "Brief of the National Association of Manufacturers of the United States of America, as Amicus Curiae, in Support of Respondent," in the Supreme Court of the United States, October term, 1955, *Mabel Black and T. Y. Wulff v. Cutter Laboratories,* enclosure in Cutter to Mandel, Oct. 5, 1956.

93. Walker, interview; Stanley I. Kutler, *The American Inquisition: Justice and Injustice in the Cold War* (New York: Hill and Wang, 1982), 215–42; Winograd, "An Interview with Doris Brin Walker."

94. Except for some law review articles, there is surprisingly little scholarship on the legal profession's response to McCarthyism. The most useful sources have been Eugene M. Tobin, "The Legal Defense of Hated People: Lawyers and Loyalty-Security Litigation," paper presented at the American Historical Association Annual Meeting, Washington, D.C., 1987 (in author's possession); Jerold S. Auerbach, *Unequal Justice: Lawyers and Social Change in Modern America* (New York: Oxford University Press, 1976), 231–62; and Kutler, *The American Inquisition.*
Tom C. Clark, "Civil Rights: The Boundless Responsibility of Lawyers," *American Bar Association Journal* 32 (August 1946): 453–57.

95. Memorandum, SAC, Seattle, to Director, Mar. 2, 1953, Responsibilities Program, #1194; memorandum, Belmont to Ladd, Mar. 26, 1953, ibid., #1199; NLG motion, 114–15, 189–91, 220–21, 316; Athan Theoharis and John Stuart Cox, *The Boss: J. Edgar Hoover and the Great American Inquisition* (Philadelphia: Temple University Press, 1988), 218–29.

96. John Porter to Doris Brin Walker, Nov. 23, 1956; Vincent J. Mullins to Walker, Nov. 9, 1956; transcript of Walker hearing, undated; memorandum of James Purcell regarding proceedings before committee, Dec. 14, 1956; Walker to A. L. Wirin, Nov. 30, 1956; Jack E. Frankel to Walker, Sept. 24, 1957; Richard Gladstein to Walker, Oct. 7, 1957, all in Walker Papers.

97. Memorandum, Executive Conference to Director, Oct. 14, 1953, Responsibilities Program, #1710; Kutler, *The American Inquisition,* 165–81; Tobin, "The Legal Defense of Hated People"; Auerbach, *Unequal Justice,* 241–52. The key cases with regard to admission to the bar are *Schware v. Board of Bar Examiners of New Mexico,* 353 U.S. 232 (1957), *Konigsberg v. State Bar of California,* 353 U.S. 252 (1957), *Konigsberg v. State Bar of California,* 366 U.S. 36 (1961), and *In re Anastaplo,* 366 U.S. 82 (1961). On the *Schware* case, see Murphy, *Congress and the Court,* 111. For an important expression of the fear that radical defendants could not find lawyers, see William O. Douglas, "The Black Silence of Fear," *New York Times Magazine,* Jan. 13, 1952.

98. Milnor Alexander, "The Right to Counsel for the Politically Unpopular," *Law in Transition* 22 (1962): 19–45; Fortas, quoted in Clifford Durr, oral history transcript, Columbia Oral History Project, Rare Book and Manuscript Library, Columbia University (hereafter COHP), 220.

99. Samuel Walker, *In Defense of American Liberties: A History of the ACLU* (New

York: Oxford University Press, 1990), 173–236; Mary Sperling McAuliffe, *Crisis on the Left: Cold War Politics and American Liberals* (Amherst: University of Massachusetts Press, 1978), 89–107.

100. Auerbach, *Unequal Justice,* 247; Vern Countryman and Ted Finman, *The Lawyer in Modern Society* (Boston: Little, Brown, 1966), 578; Belknap, *Cold War Political Justice,* 219–34; Steve Nelson, James R. Barrett, Rob Ruck, *Steve Nelson, American Radical* (Pittsburgh, Pa.: University of Pittsburgh Press, 1981), 325–40; Robert Treuhaft, testimony, Dec. 3, 1953, House Committee on Un-American Activities, "Investigation of Communist Activities in the San Francisco Area," Part 3, 83rd Cong., 1st sess.

101. Auerbach, *Unequal Justice,* 254–58; Joseph Forer, interview with the author, Mar. 31, 1978; David Rein, interview with the author, Mar. 31, 1978; Alexander, "The Right to Counsel," 32–36; Durr, COHP.

102. Vern Countryman and Ted Finman, *The Lawyer in Modern Society,* 578–86.

103. Victor Rabinowitz, COHP, 1978; Rabinowitz, *Unrepentant Leftist,* 137, 163–64.

9: "HOW RED IS A VALLEY": CLINTON JENCKS AND HIS UNION

1. Correlation Summary, Jan. 1, 1959, Doris Brin Walker, #45; report [name deleted], Albuquerque, Oct. 27, 1950, Clinton Jencks, #9; memorandum, SAC, San Francisco, to Director, Feb. 17, 1955, Walker, no serial number.

2. Jenny Wells Vincent, telephone interview by the author, November 6, 1994.

3. Vincent, interview; Mr. and Mrs. Craig S. Vincent to Harry Deckerhoff, Dec. 1, 1953, Box 302, Archives Western Federation of Miners and Mine-Mill, Historical Collections, University of Colorado, Boulder (hereafter Mine-Mill Records).

The New York State Police files show that checking out the license plate numbers at left-wing resorts was a standard procedure during the late 1940s and 1950s. See Case 75, New York State Police, Bureau of Criminal Investigations, Non-Criminal Investigations Files Collection, New York State Archives, Albany.

4. On the world of left-wing folk music, see Robbie Lieberman, *"My Song Is My Weapon": People's Songs, American Communism and the Politics of Culture 1930–1950* (Urbana: University of Illinois Press, 1989); David King Dunaway, *How Can I Keep from Singing: Pete Seeger* (New York: McGraw-Hill, 1981); "Jenny Vincent," in Jim Sagel, *Dancing to Pay the Light Bill* (Santa Fe: Red Crane Books, 1992); Vincent, interview.

5. Harvey Matusow, *False Witness* (New York: Cameron and Kahn, 1955), 24; Matusow, typewritten statement, Oct. 19, 1951, in Box 231, U.S. Senate, Committee on the Judiciary, Subcommittee on Internal Security, Records, Record Group 46, National Archives, Washington, D.C. (hereafter SISS Records).

6. Labor Research Association, memorandum, "Notes on Harvey M. Matusow (based on reports to attorneys, 1952)" in Box 302, Mine-Mill Records; Vincent, interview; Paul Jarrico, telephone interview with the author, January 6, 1990; Clinton Jencks, interview with the author, April 14, 1993; Dunaway, *How Can I Keep from*

Singing, 129–30; Ronald D. Cohen and Dave Samuelson, "Protest Music and the American Left, 1926–1953," unpublished ms. in the author's possession.

7. Matusow, *False Witness,* 27–32; "Notes on Harvey Matusow," Mine-Mill Records; Vincent, interview; Matusow, testimony, Oct. 8, 1952, "Communist Domination of Union Officials in Vital Defense Industry — International Union of Mine, Mill, and Smelter Workers," hearings before the Subcommittee to Investigate the Administration of the Internal Security Act and other Internal Security Laws of the Committee on the Judiciary, U.S. Senate, 82nd Cong., 2d sess. (hereafter SISS Mine-Mill), 151.

8. Matusow statement, Dec. 29, 1951, in report [name deleted], Cincinnati, Jan. 9, 1952, Jencks #24; Jencks, interview; Deborah Silverton Rosenfelt, *Salt of the Earth* (New York: Feminist Press, 1978), 115; Jack Cargill, "Empire and Opposition: The 'Salt of the Earth Strike,'" in Robert Kern, ed., *Labor in New Mexico: Unions, Strikes, and Social History since 1881* (Albuquerque: University of New Mexico Press, 1983), 255.

9. Rosenfelt, *Salt of the Earth,* 109–113; Cargill, "Empire and Opposition," 195.

10. Mario T. Garcia, "Border Proletarians: Mexican-Americans and the International Union of Mine, Mill and Smelter Workers, 1939–1946," in Robert Asher and Charles Stephenson, eds., *Labor Divided: Race and Ethnicity in United States Labor Struggles, 1935–1960* (Albany: State University of New York Press, 1990); Horace Huntley, "Iron Ore Miners and Mine Mill in Alabama: 1933–1952" (Ph.D. diss., University of Pittsburgh, 1977); pamphlet, "The Company says:" n. d. [probably 1953], Box 301, Mine-Mill Records; memorandum, M. E. Travis to Executive Board, Mar. 31, 1954, Box 63, ibid.; draft speech for Clinton Jencks, n. d., Box 302, ibid.; John Clark, Action Memorandum, n. d. [probably 1953], ibid.

11. On the anti-union drive by employers after World War II, see Howell John Harris, *The Right to Manage: Industrial Relations Policies of American Business in the 1940s* (Madison: University of Wisconsin Press, 1982), and Elizabeth Fones-Wolf, *Selling Free Enterprise: The Business Assault on Labor and Liberalism, 1945–1960* (Urbana: University of Illinois Press, 1994). On the postwar labor struggles, see George Lipsitz, *Class and Culture in Cold War America* (South Hadley, Mass.: J. F. Bergin, 1981), 113–32, 163–68; Harry A. Millis and Emily Clark Brown, *From the Wagner Act to Taft-Hartley* (Chicago: University of Chicago Press, 1950), 286–95, 533–630, and Vernon H. Jensen, *Nonferrous Metals Industry Unionism, 1932–1954* (Ithaca, N.Y.: Cornell University Press, 1954), 210–50.

12. The best account of the Empire Zinc strike is Cargill, "Empire and Opposition." See also Rosenfelt, *Salt of the Earth,* 117–26, and Clark, Action Memorandum.

13. Memorandum, SAC, Albuquerque, to Director [date illegible, probably Apr. 1950], Jencks, #13; report [name deleted], El Paso, June 30, 1948, Jencks, #39; Rosenfelt, *Salt of the Earth,* 122.

14. Robert S. Keitel, "The Merger of the International Union of Mine, Mill and Smelter Workers into the United Steelworkers of America," *Labor History* 15 (Winter 1974): 37.

15. Clark, Action Memorandum; Vincent, interview.

16. Jarrico, interview; Herbert Biberman, *Salt of the Earth: The Story of a Film* (Boston: Beacon Press, 1965), 31–37; Rosenfelt, *Salt of the Earth,* 108.

17. The most useful treatment of the Hollywood left and its activities is in Larry Ceplair and Steven Englund, *The Inquisition in Hollywood: Politics in the Film Community, 1930–1960* (Garden City, N.Y.: Anchor Press/Doubleday, 1980), 47–128.

18. Dalton Trumbo, *Additional Dialogue: Letters of Dalton Trumbo, 1942–1962,* ed. Helen Manfull (New York: M. Evans and Co., 1970), 21; Ceplair and Englund, *The Inquisition in Hollywood,* 104–28, 186–99. On the Actors' Laboratory Workshop, one of the main institutions of the Hollywood left in the 1940s, see Helen Epstein, *Joe Papp: An American Life* (Boston: Little, Brown, 1994), 57–71.

19. On the political content of the Hollywood left's films, see Ceplair and Englund, *The Inquisition in Hollywood,* 299–324; Dorothy B. Jones, "Communism and the Movies: A Study of Film Content," in John Cogley, *Report on Blacklisting, I: Movies* (New York: Fund for the Republic, 1956), 196–233; Lester Cole, *Hollywood Red: The Autobiography of Lester Cole* (Palo Alto, Calif.: Ramparts Press, 1981), 143–49, 158–59, 189–97, 202; Alvah Bessie, *Inquisition in Eden* (Dresden: Seven Seas Books, 1967, 1st ed., 1965, Macmillan, New York), 80–81.

20. Ceplair and Englund, *The Inquisition in Hollywood,* 129–223; memorandum, J. Patrick Coyne to D. M. Ladd, Sept. 6, 1947, Communist Infiltration of the Motion Picture Industry, #236, Federal Bureau of Investigation, "Confidential Files, Communist Activity in the Entertainment Industry, FBI Surveillance Files on Hollywood, 1942–1958," microfilm, ed. Daniel J. Leab (Bethesda, Md.: University Publications of America, 1991) (hereafter Hollywood); Bessie, *Inquisition in Eden,* 157–58; on the similar struggles of cartoonists, see Michael Denning, *The Cultural Front* (New York: Verso, 1996), 403–22.

21. Bessie, *Inquisition in Eden,* 223; Ceplair and Englund, *The Inquisition in Hollywood,* 209–11; Cogley, *Report on Blacklisting, I: Movies,* 62–73, 80–83.

22. Walter Goodman, *The Committee: The Extraordinary Career of the House Committee on Un-American Activities* (New York: Farrar, Straus, and Giroux, 1968), 101–3; Edward L. Barrett, *The Tenney Committee* (Ithaca, N.Y.: Cornell University Press, 1951).

23. August Raymond Ogden, *The Dies Committee* (Westport, Conn.: Greenwood Press, 1984, orig. ed. 1945), 211–13; Edward L. Barrett, "California," in Walter Gellhorn, ed., *The States and Subversion* (Ithaca, N.Y.: Cornell University Press, 1952), 1–27; Kenneth O'Reilly, *Hoover and the Un-Americans: The FBI, HUAC, and the Red Menace* (Philadelphia: Temple University Press, 1983), 90–91; Ceplair and Englund, *The Inquisition in Hollywood,* 154–58, 208, 255–61; memorandum, R. B. Hood to Director, July 25, 1947, Hollywood, #228.

24. Ceplair and Englund, *The Inquisition in Hollywood,* 257–61; report [name deleted], Los Angeles, Aug. 7, 1947, Hollywood, serial # illegible; memo, Executive Conference to Director, Sept. 11, 1947, ibid., serial # illegible.

25. Report [name deleted], Los Angeles, July 10, 1943, Hollywood, #9; report

[name deleted], Los Angeles, Apr. 20, 1944, ibid., #26; Director to SAC, Los Angeles, Apr. 29, 1944, ibid., no serial #; memorandum, Director to Attorney General, Oct. 31, 1944, ibid., #59; report [name deleted], Los Angeles, Aug. 7, 1947, ibid., serial # illegible; report [name deleted], Los Angeles, Sept. 12, 1947, ibid., serial # illegible; memorandum, Executive Conference to Director, Sept. 11, 1947, ibid., serial # illegible; report [name deleted], Los Angeles, Oct. 20, 1947, ibid., #273; Cogley, *Report on Blacklisting, I: Movies,* 11.

On the public relations campaign of the business community, see Fones-Wolf, *Selling Free Enterprise,* passim.

26. O'Reilly, *Hoover and the Un-Americans,* 91–94; memorandum, Louis B. Nichols to Clyde Tolson, Sept. 2, 1947, Hollywood, serial # illegible; memorandum, Nichols to Tolson, Aug. 21, 1947, ibid., serial # illegible; Hood to Director, Aug. 22, 1947, ibid., serial # illegible; memorandum, Coyne to Ladd, Sept. 6, 1947, ibid., serial # illegible; memorandum, Ladd to Hoover, Sept. 4, 1947, ibid., serial # illegible; Hood to Director, Sept. 13, 17, 20, 1947, ibid., all serial #'s illegible; memorandum, Coyne to Ladd, July 9, 1947, ibid., #251; Hood to Director, Oct. 7, 1947, ibid., serial # illegible; memorandum, Harold B. Fletcher to Ladd, Oct. 18, 1947, ibid., no serial #.

27. O'Reilly, *Hoover and the Un-Americans,* 92; Ceplair and Englund, *The Inquisition in Hollywood,* 262, 439–40; memorandum, Nichols to Tolson, Aug. 21, 1947, Hollywood, serial # illegible; Hood to Director, Sept. 20, 1947, ibid., serial # illegible; memorandum, SAC, Los Angeles, to Director, Oct. 20, 1947, ibid., #343; Cole, *Hollywood Red,* 267; Jarrico, interview.

28. Victor S. Navasky, *Naming Names* (New York: Viking, 1980), 393; Cole, *Hollywood Red,* 266–67.

29. Bessie, *Inquisition in Eden,* 210–11; Cole, *Hollywood Red,* 201.

30. For evidence that the FBI had tapped the phones of at least two of the Hollywood Ten's lawyers and transmitted some of the information it received to the Department of Justice, see letter [name illegible, probably SAC, Washington, D.C.] to Director, Oct. 9, 1947, Hollywood, serial # illegible; memorandum, Fletcher to Ladd, Oct. 18, 1947, ibid., no serial #; memorandum, Guy Hottel to Director, Nov. 1, 1947, ibid., no serial #; memorandum, SAC, San Francisco, to Director, Sept. 24, 1947, ibid., #332; memorandum, SAC, San Francisco, to Director, Nov. 26, 1947, ibid., #355; memorandum, Hottel to Director, Dec. 8, 1947, ibid., #364; memorandum, Hottel to Director, Dec. 11, 1947, ibid., #373; memorandum, Hottel to Director, Dec. 23, 1947, ibid., #376.

31. Carl Beck, *Contempt of Congress* (New Orleans: Houser Press, 1959), 24–41; Ceplair and Englund, *The Inquisition in Hollywood,* 347–49.

32. Biberman, *Salt of the Earth,* 9–10; Ceplair and Englund, *The Inquisition in Hollywood,* 264–70.

33. Beck, *Contempt of Congress,* 65–91.

34. Charles Katz, quoted in Ceplair and Englund, *The Inquisition in Hollywood,* 267–68; Cole, *Hollywood Red,* 267–68.

35. Hood, letter, to Director, Oct. 7, 1947, Hollywood, serial # illegible; memorandum, Ladd to Director, Oct. 22, 1947, ibid., #270; memorandum, Hottel to Director, Nov. 1, 1947, ibid., serial # illegible; letter, Hood to Director, Oct. 25, 1947, ibid., #331; memorandum, SAC, Los Angeles, to Director, Oct. 20, 1947, ibid., #343.

36. Biberman, *Salt of the Earth,* 10.

37. Bessie, *Inquisition in Eden,* 211; Cogley, *Report on Blacklisting, I: Movies,* 3–5; Wyler, quoted in Ceplair and Englund, *The Inquisition in Hollywood,* 276–77.

38. Cole, *Hollywood Red,* 269, 272–73; Ceplair and Englund, *The Inquisition in Hollywood,* 260.

39. Ceplair and Englund, *The Inquisition in Hollywood,* 270; Navasky, *Naming Names,* 270, 418.

40. Schary, quoted in Navasky, *Naming Names,* 84, 98–99; Cogley, *Report on Blacklisting, I: Movies,* 8; memorandum, SAC, San Francisco, to Director, Sept.(?) 24, 1947, Hollywood, #332; memorandum, SAC, San Francisco, to Director, Nov. 26, 1947, ibid., #355.

41. Memorandum, Nichols to Tolson, Oct. 28, 1947, Hollywood, #286; letter, Hood to Director, Oct. 25, 1947, ibid., #331; letter, Hood to Director, Oct. 28, 1947, ibid., #334.

42. Ceplair and Englund, *The Inquisition in Hollywood,* 285–92; Cogley, *Report on Blacklisting, I: Movies,* 4–8; Navasky, *Naming Names,* 153.

43. Letter, Hood to Director, Nov. 20, 1947, Hollywood, #344.

44. Evidence about the Waldorf meeting and the inauguration of the blacklist came out during the Hollywood Ten's lawsuit against the blacklist, *Cole v. Loew's.* The records of the plaintiffs and their lawyers are at the State Historical Society of Wisconsin, Madison (hereafter SHSW). See also Ceplair and Englund, *The Inquisition in Hollywood,* 328–31, 445; Biberman, *Salt of the Earth,* 248–9.

45. Bessie, *Inquisition in Eden,* 252–56; Ceplair and Englund, *The Inquisition in Hollywood,* 350–54; Cole, *Hollywood Red,* 219; Navasky, *Naming Names,* 182; Trumbo, *Additional Dialogue,* 93, 103, 133–34.

46. Judge Bennett C. Clark, opinion, quoted in Ceplair and Englund, *The Inquisition in Hollywood,* 348.

47. Cole, *Hollywood Red,* 298–301; Trumbo, *Additional Dialogue,* 120; Navasky, *Naming Names,* 182.

48. Bessie, *Inquisition in Eden,* 252–56; Ceplair and Englund, *The Inquisition in Hollywood,* 350–54; Cole, *Hollywood Red,* 219, 296–97, 311–21; Navasky, *Naming Names,* 182; Trumbo, *Additional Dialogue,* 102–105, 137; Bruce Cook, *Dalton Trumbo* (New York: Scribner's, 1977), 190–207.

49. Cogley, *Report on Blacklisting, I: Movies,* 77–80; Jarrico, interview; Navasky, *Naming Names,* 225.

50. On talking with the FBI, see Navasky, *Naming Names,* 231, 246–47. These figures come from Ceplair and Englund, *The Inquisition in Hollywood,* 361–97.

51. Ceplair and Englund, *The Inquisition in Hollywood,* 368; Cogley, *Report on Blacklisting, I: Movies,* 108.

52. Ceplair and Englund, *The Inquisition in Hollywood*, 368; Cogley, *Report on Blacklisting, I: Movies*, 108; Lary May, "Movie Star Politics: The Screen Actors' Guild, Cultural Conversion, and the Hollywood Red Scare," in May, ed., *Recasting America: Culture and Politics in the Age of Cold War* (Chicago: University of Chicago Press, 1989).

53. On the clearance process, see Cogley, *Report on Blacklisting, I: Movies*, 118–60; Navasky, *Naming Names*, 90–96; Ceplair and Englund, *The Inquisition in Hollywood*, 387–97.

Both J. B. Matthews's papers and the files of the Senate Internal Security Subcommittee contain dozens of copies of the clearance letters that Hollywood figures sent to their studios. For the Brando letters, see Marlon Brando to Jay Kanter, May 9, June 3, 1952, to Nicholas Schenck, July 8, 1952; Frank Freeman to James O'Neil, May 27, 1952, all in Box 114, SISS Records.

54. Paul Jarrico and Herbert Biberman, "Breaking Ground," in Deborah Silverton Rosenfelt, *Salt of the Earth* (New York: Feminist Press, 1978), 171; Biberman, "Memorandum (III) on the Making of a Motion Picture," in *IPC v. Loew's et al.*, exhibits, papers, relevant 1954, 1956, Box 38, Herbert Biberman-Gale Sondergaard Papers, SHSW.

55. Rosenfelt, *Salt of the Earth*, 126–27; Biberman, *Salt of the Earth*, 38–41.

56. M. E. Travis to International Executive Board, June 23, Oct. 2, 1952, to all Officers, et al., Mar. 2, 1953, Ernest S. Velasquez and Clinton E. Jencks to Travis, Jan. 2, 1953, Box 119, Mine-Mill Records; Simon Lazarus, recollection of meeting in memorandum, n. d., Box 38, Biberman-Sondergaard Papers; Biberman, *Salt of the Earth*, 31–36, 43–60.

57. Biberman, *Salt of the Earth*, 82–83.

58. Rosenfelt, *Salt of the Earth*, 131; Steven Rosswurm, "The FBI and the CIO from 1940 to 1955," paper presented to the Organization of American Historians, Philadelphia, Pa., April 1987.

59. Elizabeth Kerby, "Violence in Silver City: Who Caused the Trouble?" *Frontier*, May 1953, 7–8; Rosenfelt, *Salt of the Earth*, 132; Rosaura Revueltas, "Reflections on a Journey," in Rosenfelt, *Salt of the Earth*, 174–76.

60. Kerby, "Violence in Silver City," 9–10.

61. Howard Hughes to Donald Jackson, Mar. 18, 1953, Roy Brewer to Jackson, Mar. 18, 1953, both in Biberman, *Salt of the Earth*, 123–25, 132–56, 283; Independent Productions Corporation, A Report on "Salt of the Earth," July 16, 1954, Box 119, Mine-Mill Records.

62. Biberman, *Salt of the Earth*, 169–202. The refusal of newspapers to run ads for communist-linked events or causes was common. See Michal R. Belknap, *Cold War Political Justice: The Smith Act, the Communist Party, and American Civil Liberties* (Westport, Conn.: Greenwood Press, 1977), 136.

63. Biberman, *Salt of the Earth*, 203–12; ACLU, Weekly Bulletin, July 25, 1955, Box 119, Mine-Mill Records.

64. Myles J. Lane to Benjamin Mandel, May 9, 1955, Box 138, SISS Records; Biberman, *Salt of the Earth,* 227–312.

65. Clark, Action Memorandum; Jencks to Nathan Witt, Apr. 29, 1953, Box 302, Mine-Mill Records; memorandum, Alan H. Belmont to Ladd, Mar. 5, 1953, Jencks, #38; teletype, Ellsworth to Director, Apr. 20, 1953, ibid., #71.

66. On the origins of the Taft-Hartley Act, see Millis and Brown, *From the Wagner Act to Taft-Hartley;* R. Alton Lee, *Truman and Taft-Hartley, A Question of Mandate* (Lexington: University Press of Kentucky, 1966); Susan M. Hartmann, *Truman and the 80th Congress* (Columbia: University of Missouri Press, 1971); Fred A. Hartley, Jr., *Our New National Labor Policy* (New York: Funk and Wagnalls, 1948); James T. Patterson, *Mr. Republican: A Biography of Robert Taft* (Boston: Houghton Mifflin, 1972); Gerard D. Reilly, "The Legislative History of the Taft-Hartley Act," *George Washington Law Review* 29 (Dec. 1960): 285–300.

67. Lee, *Truman and Taft-Hartley,* 161–64; Lipsitz, *Class and Culture in Cold War America,* 135; Millis and Brown, *From the Wagner Act to Taft-Hartley,* 540–48.

68. Millis and Brown, *From the Wagner Act to Taft-Hartley,* 630; Martin Halpern, "Taft-Hartley and the Defeat of the Progressive Alternative in the United Auto Workers," *Labor History* 27 (Spring 1986): 204–26; Ceplair and Englund, *The Inquisition in Hollywood,* 292–96.

69. Report [name deleted], El Paso, Dec. 2, 1948, Jencks, #27; Howard I. Young, quoted in Lipsitz, *Class and Culture,* 155–59, 165; Jensen, *Nonferrous Metals Industry Unionism,* 210–30; Charles P. Larrowe, *Harry Bridges* (Westport, Conn.: Lawrence Hill, 1972), 294–95; Millis and Brown, *From the Wagner Act to Taft-Hartley,* 555–91, 640–43.

70. For the most complete account of the in-fighting within Mine-Mill, see Jensen, *Nonferrous Metals Industry Unionism.* On conflicts in other unions, see Ronald L. Filippelli, "The United Electrical, Radio and Machine Workers of America, 1933–1949: The Struggle for Control," (Ph.D. diss., Pennsylvania State University, 1970), 138–72; Millis and Brown, *From the Wagner Act to Taft-Hartley,* 533; Ronald Filippelli and Mark McColloch, *Cold War in the Working Class: The Rise and Decline of the United Electrical Workers* (Albany: State University of New York Press, 1995), 89–112; Harvey A. Levenstein, *Communism, Anticommunism, and the CIO* (Westport, Conn.: Greenwood Press, 1981), 269–278; Bert Cochran, *Labor and Communism: The Conflict that Shaped American Unions* (Princeton: Princeton University Press, 1977), 127–55, 272–96.

71. Minutes, Executive Board Meeting, Aug. 20–24, 1947, in Box 294, Mine-Mill Records; Executive Board, Resolution, May 31, 1949, Box 62, Walter Reuther Papers, UAW President's Office, Archives of Labor History and Urban Affairs, Wayne State University, Detroit (hereafter ALHUA). For an interesting discussion of the forces involved in a local Pittsburgh battle within UE, see James T. Fitzpatrick, memorandum to James Carey, n. d., Les Finnegan files, Box A2.05, International Union of Electrical, Radio and Machine Workers Papers, Special Collections and Archives, Rutgers University, New Brunswick, N.J.

72. Victor Rabinowitz, *Unrepentant Leftist: A Lawyer's Memoir* (Urbana: University of Illinois Press, 1996), 49–56; Filippelli, "The United Electrical, Radio and Machine Workers of America," 209–213; Larrowe, *Harry Bridges,* 295; Executive Board Statement on Taft-Hartley Affidavits, July 20, 1949, Box 65, Mine-Mill Records.

73. Travis's statement received wide publicity. There were similar statements by other union officials, including the Fur Workers president Ben Gold, Max Perlow, the Secretary-Treasurer of the Furniture Workers International Union, and Talmadge Raley, a low-level UE official in Ohio. "NLRB Summary of Section 9(h) Problems," undated memorandum, Box 694, National Labor Relations Board Records, Record Group 25, National Archives (hereafter NLRB Records); John A. Hull, Jr., to William O. Murdock, Feb. 19, 1954, in Box 693, NLRB Records; Jensen, *Nonferrous Metals Industry Unionism,* 248–50; Levenstein, *Communism, Anticommunism, and the CIO,* 208–17.

74. Frank Emspak, "The Breakup of the CIO," in Maurice Zeitlin and Howard Kimeldorf, eds., *Political Power and Social Theory,* vol. 4 (Greenwich, Conn.: JAI Press, 1984); Filippelli, "The United Electrical, Radio, and Machine Workers," 149–81; Levenstein, *Communism, Anticommunism, and the CIO,* 219–29.

75. Filippelli, "The United Electrical, Radio and Machine Workers of America," 216–23; Larrowe, *Harry Bridges,* 325; Levenstein, *Communism, Anticommunism, and the CIO,* 298–306; Cochran, *Labor and Communism,* 297–312.

76. "Resolution and Report Expelling the International Union of Mine, Mill & Smelter Workers from the Congress of Industrial Organizations," Feb. 15, 1950 (hereafter "Resolution and Report"). This report received wide circulation; the copy I used was printed by the United Steelworkers of America and came from Box 1, Mine-Mill Records.

77. "Resolution and Report"; "W.P.R. Notes," n. d., in Walter Reuther, Box 88, UAW Presidential Papers, ALHUA.

78. Jensen, *Nonferrous Metals Industry Unionism,* 269–92.

79. Robert Denham, press release, June 14, 1949, in "The Function of the NLRB with Respect to Section 9(h) Affidavits," unsigned memorandum, n. d., Box 694, NLRB Records; list (names of union officials whose 9(h) forms were sent to the Justice Department between June 1949 and Jan. 1952), n. d., Box 693, ibid.; "NLRB Summary of Section 9(h) Problems," n. d., Box 694, ibid.; Denham to James M. McInerney, Mar. 24, 1950, Box 696, ibid.; George Murdock to all Regional Directors, Nov. 28, 1951, Box 692, ibid.; Ellen W. Schrecker, "McCarthyism and the Labor Movement," in Steve Rosswurm, ed., *The CIO's Left-Led Unions* (New Brunswick, N.J.: Rutgers University Press, 1992), 151–54; Levenstein, *Communism, Anticommunism, and the CIO,* 291.

80. Report [name deleted], June 15, 1950, Director to McInerney, June 27, 150, both in Everest Melvin Hupman Labor-Management Relations Act, #4 (hereafter LMRA); McInerney to George J. Bott, Oct. 17, 1950, Box 693, NLRB Records; unsigned memorandum to McInerney, June 20, 1950, Clinton Jencks, LMRA, #4; John A. Morgan, Jr., "The Supreme Court and the Non-Communist Affidavit," *Labor Law*

Journal 10 (Jan. 1959), 43; statements by Andrew S. Oehmann, A. Devitt Vanech, and Warren Olney III, cited in *Clinton E. Jencks v. U.S.,* Appellants Opening Brief, U.S. Court of Appeals, 5th District, in Box 317, Mine-Mill Records.

81. Senator Pat McCarran to J. Howard McGrath, Nov. 5, 1951, Box 150, SISS Records; J. Walter Yeagley to Senator James Eastland, April 24, 1958, Box 130, ibid.; Ellery Stone to Charles B. Murray, Oct. 3, 1952, Bott to Senator William Jenner, July 17, 1953, both in Box 693, NRLB Records; unsigned memoranda listing Fifth Amendment witnesses, n. d. [1953], Harold A. Boire to Ellison D. Smith, Jr., Feb. 19, 1953, unsigned handwritten memorandum, Sept. 5, 1956, Kenneth C. McGuiness to Bernard L. Alpert, Feb. 21, 1958, all in Box 694, ibid.

Even as late as 1956, the board's attorneys were still urging their colleagues to report back on "subversive forces" in the labor movement. McGuiness to All Regional Directors and Officers in Charge, Jan. 9, 1956, Box 692, ibid.; Olney, testimony, April 9, 1953, Senate Committee on Labor and Public Welfare, cited in *Clinton E. Jencks v. United States,* Appellants Opening Brief, U.S. Court of Appeals, Fifth District, Box 317, Mine-Mill Records.

82. Report [name deleted], Cincinnati, Jan. 9, 1952, Jencks LMRA, #6; Memorandum, W. V. Cleveland to Alan H. Belmont, Jan. 8, 1952, Jencks, ibid., #25; report [name deleted], Apr. 10, 1952, ibid., #30; report [name deleted], Albuquerque, Oct. 17, 1952, ibid., #35; Director to Olney, Oct. 22, 1953, ibid., #142; memorandum, SAC, Albuquerque, to Director [date illegible, c. April 1950], ibid., #10; memorandum, SAC, Albuquerque, to Director, Apr. 5, 1950, ibid., #2; memorandum, SAC, Albuquerque, to Director, June 5, 1950, ibid., #5; memorandum, SAC, Albuquerque, to Director, Nov. 22, 1950, ibid., #10; memorandum, SAC, Cincinnati, to Director, Oct. 23, 1952, Hupman, LMRA, no serial #; telegram, Director to SAC, Cincinnati, Sept. 24, 1952, ibid., no serial #; report [name deleted], Cincinnati, Oct. 20, 1952, ibid., #23; Paul Herzog, testimony, "Hearings before a Subcommittee on Labor of the Committee on Labor and Public Welfare on Communist Domination of Unions and National Security," 82nd Cong., 2d sess., 1952.

83. Robert A. Taft to Herbert Brownell, Feb. 11, 1953, Olney to Brownell, Feb. 12, 17, 1953, Brownell to Taft, Feb. 27, 1953, all in Box 821, Robert A. Taft Papers, Manuscript Division, Library of Congress, Washington, D.C.; Director to SAC, Albuquerque, Feb. 27, 1950, Jencks, no serial #; report [name deleted], Albuquerque, May 16, 1953, ibid., #72; Richard Berresford, testimony, March 16, 1953, House Committee on Education and Labor, copy in Box 302, Mine-Mill Records.

84. "Information from the Files of the Committee on Un-American Activities, U.S. House of Representatives," mimeo, 1950, Victor Riesel to Mandel, Sept. 10, 1951, both in Box 137, SISS Records; memorandum, "J." [Sourwine?] to "Mitch," Mar. 5, 1952, memorandum, Donald D. Connors, Jr., July 15, 1952, memorandum, Connors to Ken Earl, July 31, 1952, memorandum, "Ken" [Earl] to "Don" [Connors], Sept. 3, 1952, Mandel to Connors, Sept. 5, 1952, memorandum, Connors to McCarran and Watkins, Sept. 18, 1952, all in Box 138, ibid.; Christopher John Gerard, "'A Program

of Cooperation': The FBI, the Senate Internal Security Subcommmittee, and the Communist Issue, 1950–1956" (Ph.D. diss., Marquette University, 1993), 231–38; Jerome E. Edwards, *Pat McCarran: Political Boss of Nevada* (Reno: University of Nevada Press, 1982), 166–69.

85. Testimony of J. B. Matthews, Stanley Ruttenberg, and Kenneth Eckert, October 7, 1952, SISS Mine-Mill, Oct. 6, 7, 8, and 9, 1952, 8, 26–27, 53, 56, 68.

86. Connors to McCarran and Watson, Sept. 18, 1952, Box 138, SISS Records; Travis, testimony, Oct. 7, 1952, SISS Mine-Mill, 68–112.

87. Riesel to Mandel, Sept. 10, 1951, Box 137, SISS Records; Witt, testimony, Oct. 7, 1952, SISS Mine-Mill, 112–21.

88. Martha N. Edmiston and John J. Edmiston, Affidavit, Feb. 15, 1955, Box 231, SISS Records; Matusow, *False Witness,* 33–38.

89. Sidney Isaacs to Mandel, Feb. 7, 1955, Box 230, SISS Records; Edmiston, Affidavit; Matusow, *False Witness,* 36–81.

90. Francis J. McNamara to Mandel, Feb. 17, 1955, Box 231, SISS Records; Matusow, *False Witness,* 81–122, 136–44; John Henry Faulk, *Fear on Trial* (New York: Simon and Schuster, 1964), 265.

91. Matusow, *False Witness,* 47–129; Nicholas von Hoffman, *Citizen Cohn* (New York: Doubleday, 1988), 89.

92. Matusow, testimony, Oct. 8, 1952, SISS Mine-Mill, 150–56, 161–63.

93. Memorandum, Connors to McCarran and Watkins, Sept. 18, 1952, Box 138, SISS Records.

94. Jencks, testimony, Oct. 8, 1952, SISS Mine-Mill, passim: "Report from the Subcommittee Investigating Communist Domination of Union Officials in Vital Defense Industry — International Union of Mine, Mill, and Smelter Workers," in ibid., ix–xiii.

95. Memorandum, Sourwine to Frank Schroeder, Feb. 25, 1955, Box 230, SISS Records; J. B. Matthews, handwritten memorandum [list of social engagements with Matusow], n. d., Box 673, Matthews Papers; Matusow, *False Witness,* 172–83.

96. Memo, Jencks Defense Commmittee, July 30, 1953, David Jenkins to Rod Holmgren, Oct. 14, 1953, Holmgren to Clark et al., Dec. 23, 1953, Holmgren to John T. McTernan, Dec. 30, 1953, Clark to C. D. Smotherman, Oct. 1, 1953, Jencks to Herbert Lerner et al., Oct. 8, 1953, all in Box 301, Mine-Mill Records; memorandum, Travis to Executive Board, Mar. 31, 1954, ibid., Box 317; Defense Committee Report, Oct. 15, 1954, Travis to Michael Wilson, June 11, 1954, Box 63, ibid.

97. On the Texas proceedings, see James N. Castleberry, Jr. to Edward Duffy, Dec. 18, 1953, and Industrial Commission of Texas, "Preliminary Report to Governor Allan Shivers," Dec. 7, 1953, Box 137, SISS Records; Holmgren, "Memo on the 'Investigation' of Mine-Mill, DPOWA and Fur & Leather By the Texas State Industrial Commission," Box 302, Mine-Mill Records; telegram, Chiles to Director, Dec. 2, 1953, Budenz, serial # illegible.

On Jencks's trial, see Matusow, quoted in *Clinton E. Jencks v. U.S.,* Brief for the

Petitioner, in the Supreme Court of the United States, Oct. term, 1956, 12; memorandum, Travis to Executive Board, Mar. 31, 1954, Box 63, Mine-Mill Records; mimeo, "Jencks Trial Bulletin" No. 1, Jan. 11, 1954, No. 2, Jan. 13, 1954, No. 3, Jan. 14, 1954, No. 4, Jan. 15, 1954, No. 5, Jan. 18, 1954, No. 6, Jan. 20, 1954, No. 7, Jan. 22, 1954, "Mine-Mill Defense Bulletin," June 30, 1954, Box 302, ibid.

98. Jencks, telephone interview, Apr. 23, 1997.

99. Memorandum, Belmont to Ladd, July 31, 1952, National Defense Informants, #701.

100. SAC, New York, to SAC, Salt Lake City, Aug. 10, 1953, Jencks, #104; memorandum, F. J. Baumgardner to Belmont, Feb. 27, 1952, National Defense Informants, #645; SAC Letter No. 29, Series 1952, Mar. 22, 1952, ibid., no serial #; memo, Belmont to Ladd, May 20, 1953, ibid., #781; Ladd to Director, Sept. 22, 1953, ibid., no serial #; Appendix II, "Summary of Evidence Adduced at Hearing on Motion for New Trial, Arranged in Chronological Order," Plaintiff's Brief, to Supreme Court, *Jencks v. U.S.,* in Box 317, Mine-Mill Records (hereafter Appendix II, Plaintiff's Brief); Albert E. Kahn, *The Matusow Affair: Memoir of a National Scandal* (Mt. Kisco, N.Y.: Moyer Bell, 1987), 224–35.

101. Appendix II, Petitioner's Brief; Edmistons, affidavit; Matusow to Martha and Ed (Edmiston), Feb. 11, 1954, in Box 231, SISS Records; Matusow, *False Witness,* 224.

102. On an attempt by Matusow to interest Edward R. Murrow in his story, see Fred W. Friendly, *Due To Circumstances Beyond Our Control . . .* (New York: Random House, 1967), 44–45. On other attempts to peddle his book, see memorandum, Schroeder to Sourwine, Feb. 28, 1955, Box 230, SISS Records; handwritten memorandum (about conversation with Murray Kempton), n. d., memorandum, Lou Colombo to Sourwine, Feb. 10, 1955, Box 231, ibid.; Matthews to Senator Herman Welker, April 8, 1955, Box 685, Matthews Papers.

103. Frank J. Donner, "The Informer," *The Nation,* April 10, 1954; Navasky, *Naming Names,* 14–15; William P. Rogers to Brownell, Sept. 1, 1954, in Box 16, Rogers Papers, DDEL.

104. Clipping, *El Paso Herald Post,* Oct. 8, 1954, in Jencks, El Paso, #458; Appendix II, Plaintiff's Brief; J. C. Phillips to Lyndon Johnson, Mar. 1, 1955, with clipping that shows Matusow in Dallas, Aug. 8, 1954, interested in giving speeches on Communism, in LBJA, Box 115G, Lyndon B. Johnson Library, Austin, Texas.

105. Holmgren to G. Bromley Oxnam, Aug. 25, 1954, Box 302, Mine-Mill Records; Kahn, *The Matusow Affair,* 12–32, 47–96; Matusow, testimony, Feb. 21, 1955, "Strategy and Tactics of World Communism: The Significance of the Matusow Case," hearing before the Subcommittee to Investigate the Administration of the Internal Security Act and other Internal Security Laws of the Committee on the Judiciary, United States Senate, 84th Cong., 1st sess., 77 (hereafter SISS Matusow).

106. "Firing Line," Mar. 1, 1955, Frank McNamara, untitled article, Feb. 28, 1955, in Veterans of Foreign Wars, *Guardpost for Freedom,* in Box 231, SISS Records; memo, Mandel to Sourwine, n. d., SISS, press release, Mar. 19, 1955, Thomas Hen-

nings to Eastland, July 27, 1955, Box 230, ibid.; Kahn, *The Matusow Affair,* 107–70; subpoena, Feb. 28, 1955, Box 63, Mine-Mill Records.

107. Memorandum, Mandel to Sourwine, Mar. 9, 1955, Box 230, SISS Records; SISS, press release, Mar. 16, 1955, memorandum, Robert McManus to Sourwine et al., Mar. 28, 1955, Box 231, ibid.

108. E. J. Dimock, opinion, *U.S. v. Elizabeth Gurley Flynn, et al.,* April 22, 1955, U.S. District Court, Southern District of New York; Witt to Sam Feldman, Feb. 4, 1956, Mine-Mill, press release, Mar. 15, 1955, Box 317, Mine-Mill Records; Kahn, *The Matusow Affair,* 249; Robert E. Thomason, D. J., opinion, quoted in Herbert Brownell, speech, Mar. 21, 1955, in *U.S. News & World Report,* April 1, 1955.

109. Walter F. Murphy, *Congress and the Court: A Case Study in the American Political Process* (Chicago: University of Chicago Press, 1962), 84, 99; Hugo Black to Felix Frankfurter, Apr. 4, 1956, Frankfurter to William O. Douglas, May 1, 1956, Frankfurter to Brethren, April 2, 1956, John Harlan, memorandum for the conference, Mar. 7, 1956, Tom Clark, memorandum for the conference, Feb. 24, 1956, Frankfurter, notes on conference, Mar. 8(?), 1956, conference remarks, Nov. 18, 1955, Box 84, Frankfurter Papers, Harvard University Law School Library. (I saw these papers in manuscript; they are also on microfilm, Frankfurter Papers, Part II, reels 15–16); Clark, memorandum to the conference, April 17, 1956, Clark, handwritten memorandum, n. d., Box A43, Tom C. Clark Papers, Tarleton Law Library, University of Texas, School of Law, Austin, Texas; *Jencks v. United States,* 353 U.S. 657 (1957).

110. *Jencks v. United States,* 353 U.S. 657 (1957).

111. On the attempts to limit the Court's jurisdiction, see Senator William Jenner, statement, Aug. 7, 1957, in Box 666, Matthews Papers; Murphy, *Congress and the Court;* C. Herman Pritchett, *Congress versus the Supreme Court, 1957–1960* (Minneapolis: University of Minnesota Press, 1961); Robert G. McCloskey, *The Modern Supreme Court* (Cambridge: Harvard University Press, 1972), 221–32; Curt Gentry, *J. Edgar Hoover: The Man and the Secrets* (New York: W. W. Norton, 1991), 449–50; Director, FBI, to Lyndon B. Johnson, Aug. 12, 1957, Box 5, LBJA, Johnson to A. M. Willis, Nov. 18, 1958, Box 116, ibid., LBJ Papers; clipping, *New York Times,* Aug. 30, 1957, Drew Pearson, column, *The Denver Post,* July 5, 1957, both in Box 204, Mine-Mill Records; Richard Gid Powers, *Secrecy and Power: The Life of J. Edgar Hoover* (New York: Free Press, 1987), 337–42; Athan Theoharis and John Stuart Cox, *The Boss: J. Edgar Hoover and the Great American Inquisition* (Philadelphia: Temple University Press, 1988), 312.

112. Kahn, *The Matusow Affair,* 240–65.

113. John Clark to All Local Unions and Delegates, Mar. 30, 1956, Box 317, Mine-Mill Records; Jencks, interviews; Griffin Fariello, *Red Scare: Memories of the American Inquisition* (New York: W. W. Norton, 1995), 387–90.

114. Clippings, *New York Times,* Jan. 1, 2, 1958, in Box 317, Mine-Mill Records; clipping, *Rocky Mountain News,* July 23, 1959, clipping, *El Paso Herald,* July 24, 1959, Box 120, ibid.; Jencks, interviews.

115. Jencks interviews.

116. John Eugene E. Dixon, Intermediate Report and Recommended Order, Oct. 23, 1953, NLRB, Determination and Order, May 28, 1954, Box 692, NLRB Records; Olney to Bott, date unintelligible, NLRB Brief, *Guy Farmer et al. v. International Fur and Leather Workers Union,* May 24, 1953, NLRB Press Release, Oct. 23, 1953, Box 693, ibid.; memo, Charles T. Douds to W. O. Murdock, Nov. 28, 1952, "Presentment," Nov. 25, 1952, in Edward Weinfeld to Paul N. Herzog, Nov. 26, 1952, Order, Richmond B. Keech, Nov. 23, 1953, Box 694, ibid.; NLRB, Order Directing Administrative Investigation and Hearing, Feb. 4, 1954, George A. Downing, Report of Hearing Officer, September 11, 1954, Box 695, ibid.; memorandum, David P. Findling to Board, Mar.1, 1955, Box 696, ibid.; George E. Bader to Joseph McCarthy, May 2, 1953, David H. Armstrong to Schroeder, Aug. 10, 1953, Box 138, SISS Records; memorandum, Connors to Richard Arens, Feb. 11, 1953, Box 141, ibid.; Witt to Travis, May 3, 1954, Travis to NLRB, May 7, 1954, Brief for Appellant, *International Union of Mine, Mill and Smelter Workers v. Guy Farmer et al.,* in the United States Court of Appeals for the District of Columbia, Box 317, Mine-Mill Records; Linus Wampler to Clark, Aug. 17, 1949, Box 109, ibid.; Clark to all local unions, Feb. 24, 1955, Albert Pezzati to all local unions, Feb. 24, 1955, Box 63, ibid.; *Leedom et al. v. International Union of Mine, Mill and Smelter Workers,* 352 U.S. 145 (1956); Morgan, "The Supreme Court and the Non-Communist Affidavit," 40; Francis A. Cherry, "Recommended Decision," Dec. 26, 1961, Subversive Activities Control Board, Docket No. 116–56, Robert F. Kennedy v. IUMMSW, in Box 537, Mine-Mill Records (hereafter Cherry, "Recommended Decision").

117. Memoranda, Travis, Dec. 1, 1949, Jan. 26, 1950, Box 109, Mine-Mill Records; undated list of names sent to Justice Department, Box 693, NLRB. For an example of the kinds of calls for Travis's indictment, see the Statement of Charles R. Kuzell and Denison Kitchel on behalf of the American Mining Congress, before the Senate Committee on Labor and Public Welfare, 83rd Cong., 1st sess., March 1953, in Box 59, Mine-Mill Records.

118. David Bazelon, dissent in *Ben Gold v. U.S.,* April 19, 1956, in Box 317, Mine-Mill Records; Jeff Kibre to National Officers, April 7, 1954, Clark to "Dear Friend," Mar.15, 1956, Box 63, ibid.; *Travis v. U.S.,* U.S. Circuit Court of Appeals, Tenth Circuit, Decision, Aug. 3, 1959, 44 LRRM 2709, in Box 695, NLRB; *Travis v. U.S.* 364 U.S. 631 (1961).

119. Department of Justice, press release, Nov. 16, 1956, Al Skinner et al. to Joseph Selly, June 23, 1966, in Box 10, American Communications Association Records, SHSW; Sidney Lens, "The Mine Mill Conspiracy Case," pamphlet in Box 801, Mine-Mill Records; Skinner to [Telford] Taylor [?], Francis, and Witt, Sept. 15, 1963, Box 303, ibid.

120. William P. Rogers, "Report . . . with Respect to the Subversive Activities Control Board," June 1, 1959, Lawrence Walsh [acting Attorney General] to Eisenhower, June 1, 1960, DDE-OF, 133-E-10; Herbert Brownell, Jr., v. International Union of

Mine, Mill and Smelter Workers, Petition to the Subversive Activities Control Board, Department of Justice, Petition to SACB, Witt to Harold Sanderson, Dec. 7, 1960, to IEB, Feb. 3, 1961, to Harold, Feb. 4, 1961, Box 537, Mine-Mill Records; Witt to Stuart Rothman, May 26, 1962, misc. clippings (publication not indicated), Feb. 20, 21, 1963, Box 538, ibid.; memorandum, "A Brief History of the Twelve-Year Conspiracy to Destroy Mine-Mill," n. d., Box 1, ibid.; Cherry, "Recommended Decision,"; Ann Fagan Ginger and David Christiano, eds., *The Cold War Against Labor* (Berkeley: Meiklejohn Civil Liberties Institute, 1987), 611–12; Robert S. Keitel, "The Merger of the International Union of Mine, Mill and Smelter Workers into the United Steelworkers of America," *Labor History* 15 (Winter 1974): 40–41.

121. James R. Hoffa to John Clark, Jan. 6, 1960, Mine-Mill press release, Oct. 11, 1961, misc. material used in SISS hearing, clipping, *Denver Post,* Sept. 16, 1964, James O. Eastland, subpoena, Sept. 6, 1962, Witt to Senator John L. McClellan, Aug. 25, 1962, to Officers, Sept. 8, 1962, Box 538, Mine-Mill Records; F. S. O'Brien, "The 'Communist-dominated' Unions in the United States since 1950," *Labor History* 9 (Spring 1968): 200–201; Schroeder to Sourwine, Apr. 22, May 26, 1955, Box 64, SISS Records; Rogers to Director, 1957, Box 16, Rogers Papers.

122. For a representative statement of the "triumph-of-the-law" thesis, see Stanley I. Kutler, *The American Inquisition: Justice and Injustice in the Cold War* (New York: Hill and Wang, 1982).

123. Keitel, "The Merger of the International Union of Mine, Mill and Smelter Workers," 36–43. Most of the other left-led unions that were expelled from the CIO also folded or merged into another union; see O'Brien, "The 'Communist-dominated' Unions," 200; Levenstein, *Communists, Anticommunists, and the CIO,* 318–19; Cochran, *Labor and Communism,* 315–31.

10: "A GOOD DEAL OF TRAUMA": THE IMPACT OF McCARTHYISM

1. Virginia Durr to Hugo Black. June, 5, 1957, and undated; Black to Durr, July 3, 1957, Box 7, Hugo L. Black papers, Library of Congress, Washington, D.C.; Roger K. Newman, *Hugo Black: A Biography* (New York: Pantheon, 1994), 440–44.

2. Virginia Foster Durr, *Outside the Magic Circle,* ed. Hollinger F. Barnard (Tuscaloosa: University of Alabama Press, 1985), 162–63, 307–8; Linda Reed, *Simple Decency and Common Sense: The Southern Conference Movement, 1938–1963* (Bloomington: Indiana University Press, 1991), 170–71.

3. William O. Douglas, "The Black Silence of Fear," *New York Times Magazine,* Jan. 13, 1952.

4. In her memoir about her family's flight and exile in Czechoslovakia and China during the McCarthy years, Ann Kimmage notes that her parents never told her why they left the country. See Kimmage, *An Un-American Childhood* (Athens: University of Georgia Press, 1996). On the red diaper babies, see the edited transcripts of con-

ferences held at World Fellowship Center, Conway, N.H., July 31–August 1, 1982, July 9–10, 1983, *Red Diaper Babies: Children of the Left,* Judy Kaplan and Linn Shapiro, eds. (Washington, D.C.: Judy Kaplan and Linn Shapiro, 1985). Daniel J. Walkowitz encountered the same anxiety among the radical social workers he interviewed for his forthcoming book, *The Muddle of the Middle Class: Social Workers and Metropolitan Culture in Twentieth-Century America,* unpublished ms. in the author's possession, 375.

5. Frank Donner, interview with Paul Tillett, June 18, 1962, Tillett Papers, Seeley G. Mudd Manuscript Library, Princeton University; David Rein, interview with the author, March 31, 1978; on the personal experiences of blacklisted professors, see Ellen W. Schrecker, *No Ivory Tower: McCarthyism and the Universities* (New York: Oxford University Press, 1986), 283–307; Oscar Shaftel, interview with the author, April 13, 1978; Helen Epstein, *Joe Papp: An American Life* (Boston: Little, Brown, 1994), 122; Lillian Hellman, *Scoundrel Time* (Boston: Little, Brown, 1976), 113.

6. Frank Donner, *The Un-Americans* (New York: Ballantine, 1961), 175; Sam Tanenhaus, *Whittaker Chambers: A Biography* (New York: Random House, 1997), 284; Kate Mostel and Madeline Gilford, *170 Years of Show Business* (New York: Random House, 1978), 117; Gilford, interview with the author, Jan. 17, 1990. The other suicides that I know of, besides those of Loeb and Sherwood, were Lawrence Duggan, Minnie Gutride, Raymond Kaplan, F. O. Matthiesen, Herbert Norman, Marvin Smith, and someone whose name I cannot reveal.

7. Charlotte Knight, "What Price Security?" *Collier's,* July 9, 1954, 60; Mostel and Gilford, *170 Years of Show Business,* 139; Robert Vaughan, *Only Victims* (New York: G. P. Putnam's Sons, 1972), 141–47; Epstein, *Joe Papp,* 123; Martin Bauml Duberman, *Paul Robeson* (New York: Knopf, 1988), 429–45; Patricia Lynden, "Red Diaper Baby," *New York Woman,* Aug. 1988, 72–73; Carl Bernstein, *Loyalties: A Son's Memoir* (New York: Simon and Schuster, 1989), 236; Gary May, *Un-American Activities: The Trials of William Remington* (New York: Oxford University Press, 1994), 3–9. Another murder was that of the chair of the Henry Wallace campaign in South Carolina; see Curtis D. MacDougall, *Gideon's Army* (New York: Marzani and Munsell, 1965), 407–8.

8. Though hundreds of men and women were indicted and convicted, many of them never actually served their sentences. I've counted about 160 but am by no means certain that this figure is complete. The memoirs of most of the people who went to prison usually discuss their incarceration, an indication of how traumatic it was felt to be. See, for example, Dorothy Healey and Maurice Isserman, *Dorothy Healey Remembers: A Life in the American Communist Party* (New York: Oxford University Press, 1990), 133–39; Al Richmond, *A Long View from the Left: Memoirs of an American Revolutionary* (Boston: Houghton Mifflin, 1973), 295–330; Louise Gilbert, to "Fellow Social Workers," May 18, 1955, Carl and Anne Braden Papers, Box 9, State Historical Society of Wisconsin, Madison (hereafter SHSW).

9. On the prison experiences of American Communists, see George Charney, *A*

Long Journey (Chicago: Quadrangle, 1968), 233; Elizabeth Gurley Flynn, *The Alderson Story: My Life as a Political Prisoner* (New York: International Publishers, 1963); John Gates, *The Story of an American Communist* (New York: Thomas Nelson and Sons, 1958), 139–48; Lester Cole, *Hollywood Red: The Autobiography of Lester Cole* (Palo Alto, Calif.: Ramparts Press, 1981), 321; Richmond, *A Long View from the Left,* 346–49; John Williamson, *Dangerous Scot: The Life and Work of an American "Undesirable"* (New York: International Publishers, 1969), 183–95; Larry Ceplair and Steven Englund, *The Inquisition in Hollywood: Politics in the Film Community, 1930–1960* (Garden City, N.Y.: Anchor Press/Doubleday, 1980), 355–57; Dalton Trumbo, *Additional Dialogue: Letters of Dalton Trumbo, 1942–1962,* ed. Helen Manfull (New York: M. Evans, 1970), 157; Howard Fast, *Being Red: A Memoir* (New York: Dell, 1990), 246–68; Junius Irving Scales and Richard Nickson, *Cause at Heart: A Former Communist Remembers* (Athens: University of Georgia Press, 1987), 345–415. Stanley I. Kutler, *The American Inquisition: Justice and Injustice in the Cold War* (New York: Hill and Wang, 1982), 164; Carl Marzani, interview with the author, Sept. 16, 1992; Mary M. Kaufman to Warden Nina Kinsella, Nov. 28, 1955, to James Bennett, Nov. 29, 1955, Betty Gannett to Mary Kaufman, Dec. 11, 1955, Judge Francis L. Van Dusen to Betty Gannett, May 7, 1957, James Bennett to Mary M. Kaufman, Mar. 12, 1956, all in Box 10, Betty Gannett Papers, SHSW; Albert Wahl, Presentence Report, June 13, 1955, in Box 39, Gladstein, Leonard, Patsey, and Anderson Papers, Bancroft Library, University of California, Berkeley (hereafter Gladstein Papers).

10. Howard Fast, *Peekskill: USA* (New York: Civil Rights Congress, 1951); Donner, *The Un-Americans,* 41; George Lipsitz, *Class and Culture in Cold War America* (South Hadley, Mass.: J. F. Bergin, 1981), 160–67; Jurisdictional Statement, Appendix 4, Plaintiff's Brief, in *Jeremiah Stamler, M.D., Yolanda F. Hall, and Milton M. Cohen v. Edwin E. Willis et al.,* 1968 (hereafter Stamler brief), 70–71, in author's possession.

11. Paul Lazarsfeld and Wagner Thielens, Jr., *The Academic Mind* (Glencoe, Ill.: Free Press, 1958), 59; Vaughan, *Only Victims,* 260; Jonah Raskin, *Out of the Whale* (New York: Links Books, 1974), 17; Bonnie Bird, interview with the author, Apr. 15, 1982; Marge Frantz, interview with the author, Apr. 17, 1991; David Friedman, transcript of interview for "Seeing Reds," Oct. 23, 1979, in Oral History of the American Left, Tamiment Institute Library and Wagner Labor Archives, Elmer Holmes Bobst Library, New York University (hereafter OHAL); Clarence Hiskey, interview with the author, July 27, 1980; David Lubell, interview with the author, Nov. 8, 1977.

12. Daniel H. Pollitt, "The Fifth Amendment Plea before Congressional Committees Investigating Subversion, Motives and Justifiable Presumptions — A Survey of 120 Witnesses," *University of Pennsylvania Law Review* 106 (1958): 1118; Paul Tillett, "The Social Costs of the Loyalty Programs: A Preliminary Draft," unpublished ms., n. d., in the author's possession, 7.

13. Paul Lyons, *Philadelphia Communists 1936–1956* (Philadelphia: Temple University Press, 1982), 159; Mostel and Gilford, *170 Years of Show Business,* 124–38;

Karen Sue Byers Cailteux, "The Political Blacklist in the Broadcast Industry: The Decade of the 1950s" (Ph.D. diss., Ohio State University, 1972); Merle Miller, *The Judges and the Judged* (Garden City, N.Y.: Doubleday, 1952), 50; Lipsitz, *Class and Culture in Cold War America,* 161; Carl Marzani, *The Education of a Reluctant Radical: From Pentagon to Penitentiary* (New York: Topical Books, 1995), 237.

14. Jack Mathews, "Children of the Blacklist," *Los Angeles Times Magazine* 42 (Oct. 15, 1989); Bill Bailey, *The Kid from Hoboken: An Autobiography* (San Francisco: Circus Lithographic Prepress, 1993), 398–99, 415; Griffin Fariello, *Red Scare: Memories of the American Inquisition* (New York: W. W. Norton, 1995), 360–61; Lini de Vries, *Up from the Cellar* (Minneapolis, Minn.: Vanilla Press, 1979), 282–83, 300–303; Courtney Cazden, interview with the author, May 1, 1981; Clinton Jencks, interview with the author, Apr. 14, 1993; Don Watson, interview with the author, June 19, 1995; Shaftel, interview; Emil Felhaber, interview with Bill Schechter, Feb. 5, 1981, OHAL.

15. Watson, interview; Stephen Meyer, *"Stalin Over Wisconsin": The Making and Unmaking of Militant Unionism, 1900–1950* (New Brunswick, N.J.: Rutgers University Press, 1992), 227–28; Friedman, OHAL.

16. Ceplair and Englund, *The Inquisition in Hollywood,* 399; Mathews, "Children of the Blacklist"; de Vries, *Up from the Cellar;* Diana Anhalt, "Mexico for the Political Expatriate: Haven or Last Resort," *Voices of Mexico* (Jan.–Mar., 1994): 16–23; Schrecker, *No Ivory Tower,* 291–97; Nora Sayre, *Previous Convictions: A Journey through the 1950s* (New Brunswick, N.J.: Rutgers University Press, 1995), 302–47.

17. Ceplair and Englund, *The Inquisition in Hollywood,* 418–22; Gilford, interview; Howard Suber, "The Anti-Communist Blacklist in the Hollywood Motion Picture Industry" (Ph.D. diss., University of California at Los Angeles, 1968), 127–57.

18. Schrecker, *No Ivory Tower,* 297–98; Samuel Wallach, interview with the author, Nov. 20, 1993; David Caute, *The Great Fear: The Anti-Communist Purge under Truman and Eisenhower* (New York: Simon and Schuster, 1978), 441–42.

19. E. J. Kahn, Jr., *The China Hands: America's Foreign Service Officers and What Befell Them* (New York: Viking, 1975), 164n; Charlotte Knight, "What Price Security?" *Collier's,* July 9, 1954, 61.

20. Clifford Durr, oral history transcript, Columbia Oral History Project, Rare Book and Manuscript Library, Columbia University (hereafter COHP), 223; Rein, interview; Paul Chodoff, "Loyalty Programs and Mental Health in the Washington Area," *Psychiatry: Journal for the Study of Interpersonal Processes* 16: 4 (Nov. 1953): 399–400; Charlotte A. Kaufman and Herbert Kaufman, "Some Problems of Treatment Arising from the Federal Loyalty and Security Program," *American Journal of Orthopsychiatry: A Journal of Human Behavior* 25: 4 (October 1955): 813–25; Lillian Hellman, lecture, Harvard University, Oct. 25, 1977.

21. Frank Donner, *The Un-Americans,* 69; John King Fairbank, interview with the author, Mar. 10, 1977; John Henry Faulk, *Fear on Trial* (New York: Simon and Schuster, 1964), 78.

22. On the apprehensiveness among college teachers, see Lazarsfeld and Thelens, *The Academic Mind.*

23. Pauline Dougherty, interview with Simon Singer, Jan. 1982, OHAL; Giovanni Rossi Lomanitz, questionnaire response, Tillett Papers.

24. Selma R. Williams, *Red-Listed: Haunted by the Washington Witch Hunt* (Reading, Mass.: Addison-Wesley, 1993), 79; Paul Lyons, *Philadelphia Communists 1936–1956* (Philadelphia: Temple University Press, 1982), 155; Marie Jahoda and Stuart W. Cook, "Security Measures and Freedom of Thought: An Exploratory Study of the Impact of Loyalty and Security Programs," *Yale Law Journal* 61: 3 (March 1952), 308; Kaplan and Shapiro, *Red Diaper Babies,* 14; Deborah Millan, "The Impact of the Anti-Communist Crusade on Red Diaper Babies," unpublished ms. in the author's possession; Jonah Raskin, *Out of the Whale,* 1.

25. Deborah A. Gerson, " 'Is Family Devotion Now Subversive?': Familialism against McCarthyism," in Joanne Meyerowitz, ed., *Not June Cleaver: Women and Gender in Postwar America* (Philadelphia: Temple University Press, 1994): 151–76; Kim Chernin, *In My Mother's House* (Boston: Ticknor and Fields, 1983), 213–25; Gil Green, interview with the author, Dec. 29, 1976; Kaplan and Shapiro, *Red Diaper Babies,* 15, 17, 24; Lynden, "Red Diaper Baby"; Bernstein, *Loyalties,* 102; Millan, "The Impact of the Anti-Communist Crusade on Red Diaper Babies"; Mathews, "Children of the Blacklist."

26. Bernstein, *Loyalties,* 115–22; Kaplan and Shapiro, *Red Diaper Babies,* 11, 18; Mathews, "Children of the Blacklist," 13; Kahn, *The China Hands,* 264; Chernin, *In My Mother's House,* 225; Kaplan and Shapiro, *Red Diaper Babies,* 11, 18; Fariello, *Red Scare,* 168; Donner, *The Un-Americans,* 97; Abraham Chasanow, interview with Paul Tillett, 1962, cited in Tillett, "The Social Costs of the Loyalty Programs."

27. Tauhma Seid, interview with Daniel Czitrom, July 4, 1978, OHAL; Annette Rubinstein, interview with the author, July 7, 1993; Kaplan and Shapiro, *Red Diaper Babies,* 30; Williams, *Red-Listed,* 86–100; Mathews, "Children of the Blacklist," 13; Marge Frantz, interview with the author, Apr. 17, 1991; Chernin, *In My Mother's House,* passim; Jencks, interview with the author, Apr. 23, 1997.

28. Kahn, *The China Hands,* 268; Dan Gillmor, *Fear, the Accuser* (New York: Abelard-Schuman, 1954), 62–66; Donner, *The Un-Americans,* 97; Chasanow, quoted in Tillett, "The Social Costs of the Loyalty Program," 10; Lomanitz, questionnaire response, Tillett Papers; Jane Sanders, *Cold War on the Campus: Academic Freedom at the University of Washington, 1946–1964* (Seattle: University of Washington Press, 1979), 96.

29. Ceplair and Englund, *The Inquisition in Hollywood,* 345; Kahn, *The China Hands,* 236; Robert V. Pound, interview with the author, Jan. 26, 1978; John W. DeWire et al. (Last Strauss Committee) to Dear Fellow Members, April 17, 1959, in Fulton Lewis, Jr., Papers, George Arents Research Library for Special Collections, Syracuse University.

30. I am well aware that the following analysis may put too much stress on the

importance of McCarthyism. In the interest of clarity and length, I have omitted many of the qualifications that a more academic treatise might contain.

31. On the existence of a major turning point in the late 1940s (or what Michael Denning, in his survey of Popular Front culture, calls "the shakedown of 1947–48"), see Denning, *The Cultural Front: The Laboring of American Culture in the Twentieth Century* (London: Verso, 1996), 464; Nelson Lichtenstein, "From Corporatism to Collective Bargaining: Organized Labor and the Eclipse of Social Democracy in the Postwar Era," and Ira Katznelson, "Was the Great Society a Lost Opportunity?" in Steve Fraser and Gary Gerstle, eds., *The Rise and Fall of the New Deal Order, 1930–1980* (Princeton: Princeton University Press, 1989); Michael Goldfield, "The Failure of Operation Dixie: A Critical Turning Point in American Political Development?" in Gary M. Fink and Merl E. Reed, *Race, Class, and Community in Southern Labor History* (Tuscaloosa: University of Alabama Press, 1994); Irving Richter, *Labor's Struggles, 1945–1949, A Participant's View* (New York: Cambridge University Press, 1994), 2; Studs Terkel, "The End and The Beginning," *The Nation* (May 15, 1995), 670–72. On the influence of the right, see James T. Patterson, *Congressional Conservatism and the New Deal: The Growth of the Conservative Coalition in Congress, 1933–1939* (Lexington: University of Kentucky Press, 1967) and Elizabeth Fones-Wolf, *Selling Free Enterprise: The Business Assault on Labor and Liberalism, 1945–1960* (Urbana: University of Illinois Press, 1994). For an interpretation that stresses the attractions of affluence, see Ronald Edsforth, "Affluence, Anti-Communism, and the Transformation of Industrial Unionism Among Automobile Workers, 1933–1973," in Edsforth and Larry Bennett, eds., *Popular Culture and Political Change in Modern America* (Albany: State University of New York Press, 1991), 107–25.

32. William R. Corson, *The Armies of Ignorance: The Rise of the American Intelligence Empire* (New York: Dial Press, 1977), 271–349.

33. Scientists' Committee on Loyalty and Security, "Fort Monmouth One Year Later," *Bulletin of the Atomic Scientists* 11 (Apr. 1955): 150; Paul Forman, "Beyond Quantum Electronics: National Security as Basis for Physical Research in the United States, 1940–1960," *Historical Studies in the Physical and Biological Sciences* 18 (1987), 205–6; James Rorty and Moshe Decter, *McCarthy and the Communists* (Boston: Beacon Press, 1954), 87–90; Robert R. Wilson, "The Conscience of a Physicist," in Richard S. Lewis and Jane Wilson, *Alamogordo Plus Twenty-Five Years* (New York: Viking, 1971), 74; Tillett, "The Social Costs of the Loyalty Programs," 60.

34. Marie Jahoda, "Morale in the Federal Civil Service," *Annals of the American Academy of Political and Social Science* 300 (July 1955): 110–13; Tillett, "The Social Costs of the Loyalty Programs," 26–33.

35. Gillmor, *Fear, the Accuser,* 288–90; Knight, "What Price Security?" 64–66; Tillett, "The Social Costs of the Loyalty Programs," 35–68.

36. Kahn, *The China Hands,* 305.

37. Knight, "What Price Security?" 64–65; Tillett, "The Social Costs of the Loyalty Programs," 9; Michael Schaller, *The United States and China in the Twentieth Century* (New York: Oxford University Press, 2d ed., 1990), 134.

38. Bruce Cumings, *The Origins of the Korean War*, vol. 2, *The Roaring of the Cataract* (Princeton: Princeton University Press, 1990), 107ff; Schaller, *The United States and China in the Twentieth Century*, 134–36; Lewis McCarroll Purifoy, *Harry Truman's China Policy: McCarthyism and the Diplomacy of Hysteria, 1947–1951* (New York: New Viewpoints, 1976), 267–306; Nancy Bernkopf Tucker, *Patterns in the Dust: Chinese-American Relations and the Recognition Controversy, 1949–50* (New York: Columbia University Press, 1983); Corson, *The Armies of Ignorance,* 379; John Stewart Service, interview with the author, Aug. 25, 1977.

39. Robert S. McNamara, *In Retrospect: The Tragedy and Lessons of Vietnam* (New York: Times Books, 1995), 33; John King Fairbank, *Chinabound: A Fifty-Year Memoir* (New York: Harper and Row, 1982), 349–50; Kahn, *The China Hands,* 8; David Halberstam, *The Best and the Brightest* (New York: Random House, 1972), 462–78 and passim.

40. Doris Kearns, *Lyndon Johnson and the American Dream* (New York: Harper and Row, 1976), 252; James C. Thomson, Jr., "How Could Vietnam Happen?" *Atlantic Monthly* 221 (April 1968): 47–53.

41. Richmond, *A Long View from the Left,* 126–27.

42. The most useful discussion of the relationship between African Americans and the anti-imperialist struggle is in Penny M. von Eschen, "African Americans and Anti-Colonialism, 1937–1957: The Rise and Fall of the Politics of the African Diaspora" (Ph.D. diss., Columbia University, 1994), subsequently published as *Race Against Empire: Black Americans and Anticolonialism, 1937–1957* (Ithaca, N.Y.: Cornell University Press, 1996). See also Gerald Horne, *Black and Red: W. E. B. Du Bois and the Afro-American Response to the Cold War, 1944–1963* (Albany, State University of New York Press, 1986), 20–23; Wilson Record, *Race and Radicalism: The NAACP and the Communist Party in Conflict* (Ithaca, N.Y.: Cornell University Press, 1964), 15, 112; David W. Southern, *Gunnar Myrdal and Black-White Relations: The Use and Abuse of "An American Dilemma," 1944–1969* (Baton Rouge: Louisiana State University Press, 1987), 67.

43. Duberman, *Paul Robeson,* 316–445; Horne, *Black and Red,* 97–124, 183–91.

44. Brenda Gayle Plummer, *Rising Wind: Black Americans and U.S. Foreign Affairs, 1935–1960* (Chapel Hill: University of North Carolina Press, 1996), 186–88, 212–13; von Eschen, "African Americans and Anti-Colonialism," 194–240. By the end of 1947, the NAACP was officially supporting the Marshall Plan. See Minutes, Board of Directors Meeting, Nov. 10, 1947, Jan. 5, 1948, Apr. 11, 1949, reel 3, NAACP Papers, Part 1: Records of Meetings of Board of Directors (Frederick, Md.: University Publications of America, 1982).

45. Von Eschen, "African Americans and Anti-Colonialism," 290–338.

46. On the *China Daily News* case and its meaning within the Chinese American community, see Renqiu Yu, *To Save China, To Save Ourselves: The Chinese Hand Laundry Alliance of New York* (Philadelphia, Pa.: Temple University Press, 1992), 179–91; *United States v. China Daily News, Inc., Eugene Moy, Albert Wong, Chin*

You Gong, Tom Sung, and Chin Hong Ming, trial transcript, April 6, 20, 30, 1953, April 19, 1954, June 7, 8, 9, 10, 11, 15, 17, 1954 (in the possession of Amy Chen).

47. On the possibility that political heavyweights like Nevada's Senator Pat Mc-Carran may have been interested in cracking down on the publication, see W. C. Gilbert to Pat McCarran, Feb. 25, 1952, Box 41, U.S. Senate, Committee on the Judiciary, Subcommittee on Internal Security, Records, Record Group 46, National Archives, Washington, D.C. (hereafter SISS Records).

48. *U.S. v. China Daily News,* trial transcript, 242, 262, 476, 577–78, 589, 608.

49. Maurice Isserman, *If I Had a Hammer . . . The Death of the Old Left and the Birth of the New Left* (New York: Basic Books, 1987), 138–40.

50. On the early response to the bomb and the scientists' movement that sought to put it under international control, see Paul Boyer, *By the Bomb's Early Light* (New York: Pantheon, 1985); Alice Kimball Smith, *A Peril and a Hope: The Scientists' Movement in America, 1945–1947* (Chicago: University of Chicago Press, 1965); Spencer R. Weart, *Nuclear Fear: A History of Images* (Cambridge: Harvard University Press, 1988), 111–51; Lawrence S. Wittner, *One World or None: A History of the World Nuclear Disarmament Movement Through 1953* (Stanford: Stanford University Press, 1993), 175–209, 267.

51. Harriet Hyman Alonso, *Peace as a Women's Issue: A History of the U.S. Movement for World Peace and Women's Rights* (Syracuse, N.Y.: Syracuse University Press, 1993), 157–92; Wittner, *One World or None,* 83, 203; Horne, *Black and Red,* 125–36.

52. Horne, *Black and Red,* 126–36, 151–53; Manning Marable, *W. E. B. Du Bois: Black Radical Democrat* (Boston: Twayne, 1986), 179–84; W. E. B. Du Bois, *In Battle for Peace* (Millwood, N.Y.: Kraus-Thomson Organization Limited, 1976, reprint of 1951 edition), 34–42, 51–61.

53. Du Bois, *In Battle for Peace,* 119–159; Horne, *Black and Red,* 154–181; Marable, *W. E. B. Du Bois,* 182–87.

54. Wittner, *One World or None,* 175–209; Alonso, *Peace as a Women's Issue,* 157–92; Amy Swerdlow, *Women Strike for Peace: Traditional Motherhood and Radical Politics in the 1960s* (Chicago: University of Chicago Press, 1993); Charles DeBenedetti with Charles Chatfield, *An American Ordeal: The Antiwar Movement of the Vietnam Era* (Syracuse, N.Y.: Syracuse University Press, 1990), 34.

55. David Brody, *The Butcher Workmen* (Cambridge: Harvard University Press, 1964), 259–62; Ronald L. Filippelli, "The United Electrical, Radio and Machine Workers of America, 1933–1949: The Struggle for Control" (Ph.D. diss., Pennsylvania State University, 1970), 231; Louis Goldblatt, oral history interview with Estolv Ethan Ward, 1978–79, Regional Oral History Office, Bancroft Library, University of California, Berkeley, copy in COHP, 618–19; F. S. O'Brien, "The 'Communist-dominated' Unions in the United States since 1950," *Labor History* 9 (Spring 1968): 184–205; Jane Cassels Record, "The Rise and Fall of a Maritime Union," *Industrial and Labor Relations Review* 10 (Oct. 1956): 81–92.

56. On the economic practices of the left-led unions, see Mark McColloch, "The Shop-Floor Dimension of Union Rivalry: The Case of Westinghouse in the 1950s," in Steve Rosswurm, ed., *The CIO's Left-Led Unions* (New Brunswick, N.J.: Rutgers University Press, 1992), 183–200; Judith Stepan-Norris and Maurice Zeitlin, "'Red' Unions and 'Bourgeois' contracts," *American Journal of Sociology* 96 (March 1991): 1151–1200; O'Brien, "The 'Communist-dominated' Unions in the United States since 1950," 184–205; Louis Goldblatt, COHP, 605.

57. Robert H. Zieger, *The CIO, 1935–1955* (Chapel Hill: University of North Carolina Press, 1995), 248–51; Irving Richter, *Labor's Struggles, 1945–1949, A Participant's View* (New York: Cambridge University Press, 1994), 47–95; Harry A. Millis and Emily Clark Brown, *From the Wagner Act to Taft-Hartley* (Chicago: University of Chicago Press, 1950); Melvyn Dubofsky, *The State and Labor in Modern America* (Chapel Hill: University of North Carolina Press, 1994), 199–217.

58. Labor historians are still arguing about why the labor movement lost its militance. For some representative views, see Goldfield, "The Failure of Operation Dixie," 167–88; David Brody, *Workers in Industrial America: Essays on the Twentieth Century Struggle*, 2d ed. (New York: Oxford University Press, 1993), 155–95; Steve Rosswurm, "Introduction: An Overview and Preliminary Assessment of the CIO's Expelled Unions," in Rosswurm, ed., *The CIO's Left-Led Unions*, 1–17; Gerald Zahavi, "Fighting Left-wing Unionism: Voices from the Opposition to the IFLWU in Fulton County, New York," in Rosswurm, *The CIO's Left-Led Unions*, 180–81; Sharon Hartman Strom, "'We're no Kitty Foyles': Organizing Office Workers for the Congress of Industrial Organizations, 1937–50," in Ruth Milkman, ed., *Women, Work, and Protest: A Century of US Women's Labor History* (Boston: Routledge and Kegan Paul, 1985), 227–28; Barbara Griffith, *The Crisis of American Labor: Operation Dixie and the Defeat of the CIO* (Philadelphia: Temple University Press, 1988); Lichtenstein, "From Corporatism to Collective Bargaining"; Michael K. Honey, *Southern Labor and Black Civil Rights: Organizing Memphis Workers* (Urbana: University of Illinois Press, 1993), 215–77; Michael Goldfield, *The Decline of Organized Labor in the United States* (Chicago: University of Chicago Press, 1987).

59. Harvey A. Levenstein, *Communism, Anti-Communism, and the CIO* (Westport, Conn.: Greenwood Press, 1981), 330–31; Goldblatt, COHP, 457; Mark McColloch, *White Collar Workers in Transition: The Boom Years, 1940–1970* (Westport, Conn: Greenwood Press, 1983); Strom, "'We're no Kitty Foyles,'" 227–28; Walkowitz, "The Muddle of the Middle Class," 359; Richter, *Labor's Struggles*, 69; Rosswurm, "Introduction," 1–16; Millis and Brown, *From the Wagner Act to Taft-Hartley*, 554–55, 643–47.

60. Honey, *Southern Labor and Black Civil Rights*, 214–37; Zieger, *The CIO*, 227–41; Griffith, *The Crisis of American Labor;* Goldfield, "The Failure of Operation Dixie."

61. Zieger, *The CIO*, 241; Ann Fagan Ginger and David Christiano, eds., *The Cold War Against Labor* (Berkeley: Meiklejohn Civil Liberties Institute, 1987), 617; Fones-

Wolf, *Selling Free Enterprise;* Howell John Harris, *The Right to Manage: Industrial Relations Policies of American Business in the 1940s* (Madison: University of Wisconsin Press, 1982); Kim McQuaid, *Big Business and Presidential Power from FDR to Reagan* (New York: Morrow, 1982), 122–49; Brody, *Workers in Industrial America,* 199–239; Levenstein, *Communism, Anticommunism, and the CIO,* 331.

62. Stepan-Norris and Zeitlin, "'Red' Unions and 'Bourgeois' Contracts?"; Thomas J. Sugrue, "'Forget about Your Inalienable Right to Work': Deindustrialization and Its Discontents at Ford, 1950–1953," *International Labor and Working-Class History* 48 (Fall 1995): 112–30; Rosswurm, "Introduction," 13–15; Meyer, *Stalin Over Wisconsin,* 68–70; Roger Keeran, *The Communist Party and the Auto Workers Unions* (Bloomington: Indiana University Press, 1980), 275.

63. Lipsitz, *Class and Culture in Cold War America,* 170.

64. On the business community's attempt to roll back unions, see Harris, *The Right to Manage;* McQuaid, *Big Business and Presidential Power,* 122–49; and Fones-Wolf, *Selling Free Enterprise,* passim. Nelson Lichtenstein argues that Walter Reuther's failure to restructure the UAW's relationship with General Motors during the 1945–46 strike limited and ultimately weakened the overall power of the labor movement. Lichtenstein, *The Most Dangerous Man in Detroit: Walter Reuther and the Fate of American Labor* (New York: Basic Books, 1995).

65. On the communist movement's activities in housing, see Henry Kraus, "In the City Was a Garden," in Ginger and Christiano, *The Cold War against Labor,* 514–22; Joel Schwartz, "Tenant Power in the Liberal City, 1943–1971" in Ronald Lawson, ed., *The Tenant Movement in New York City, 1904–1984* (New Brunswick, N.J.: Rutgers, 1986), 143–59; Beryl Gilman, interview with the author, Oct. 6, 1993.

66. Monte M. Poen, *Harry S. Truman Versus the Medical Lobby: The Genesis of Medicare* (Columbia: University of Missouri Press, 1979); Stephen Fritchman, "A Community Medical Center for Workers," in Ginger and Christiano, eds., *The Cold War against Labor,* 528–32; Paul Starr, *The Social Transformation of American Medicine* (New York: Basic, 1982), 272–320.

67. On health care, and especially on the New York–based Physicians Forum that fought for national health insurance in the 1940s and 1950s, see Jane Pacht Brickman, "'Medical McCarthyism': The Physicians Forum and the Cold War," *Journal of the History of Medicine and Allied Sciences* 49 (July 1994): 380–418; Walter J. Lear, "A Sampler of the Past," *Health and Medicine* 4 (Spring 1987): 4; Fitzhugh Mullan, *Plagues and Politics: The Story of the United States Public Health Service* (New York: Basic Books, 1989), 131. See also Vito Magli, interview, Mar. 15, 1983, OHAL; Harry Grundfest, interview with the author, Oct. 20, 1978.

68. This section relies mainly on Walkowitz's forthcoming *The Muddle of the Middle Class.* See also Yvonne Taylor Cullen, "An Alternative Tradition in Social Work: Bertha Capen Reynolds, 1885–1978," *Catalyst* 15 (1983): 55–73.

69. McColloch, *White Collar Workers in Transition,* 74–77; Raymond M. Hilliard, "We Threw the Commies Out," *Saturday Evening Post,* June 30, 1951; Walkowitz, *The Muddle of the Middle Class,* chapters 6 and 7.

70. *June Hirschman et al. v. County of Los Angeles,* Notice of Application for Peremptory Writ of Mandate, June 27, 1949, and attached, Gladstein Papers, Box 70; memo, Loyalty Check Committee to Count Employees, n. d., in NAACP Papers, Part 13, Series C, reel 5; memo, SAC, Milwaukee, to Director, Apr. 10, 1951, Responsibilities Program, #100; *Globe and Nelson v. Los Angeles County,* discussed in Meiklejohn Civil Liberties Index 342.10, Meiklejohn Civil Liberties Institute, Berkeley, Calif.; Walkowitz, *The Muddle of the Middle Class,* chapter 7.

71. Walkowitz, *The Muddle of the Middle Class,* chapter 7; Cullen, "An Alternative Tradition in Social Work," 59–64; Paul Lyons, "Philadelphia Jews and Radicalism: The American Jewish Congress Cleans House," in Murray Friedman, ed., *Philadelphia Jewish Life 1940–1985* (Ardmore, Pa.: Seth Press, 1986).

72. Walkowitz, *The Muddle of the Middle Class,* chapter 7.

73. On the relationship between women and the Communist party, see Elsa Jane Dixler, "The Woman Question: Women and the American Communist Party, 1929–1941" (Ph.D. diss., Yale University, 1974); Kathleen Anne Weigand, "Vanguards of Women's Liberation: The Old Left and the Continuity of the Women's Movement in the United States, 1945–1970s" (Ph.D. diss., Ohio State University, 1995); Van Gosse, "'To Organize in Every Neighborhood, in Every Home': The Gender Politics of American Communists between the Wars," *Radical History Review* 50 (Spring 1991): 109–41; Robert Schaffer, "Women and the Communist Party, USA, 1930–1940," *Socialist Review* 45 (May–June 1979): 73–118; Rosalyn Baxandall, "The Question Seldom Asked: Women and the CPUSA," in Michael E. Brown, Randy Martin, Frank Rosengarten, and George Snedeker, *New Studies in the Politics and Culture of U.S. Communism* (New York: Monthly Review Press, 1993), 141–61; Amy Swerdlow, "The Congress of American Women: Left-Feminist Peace Politics in the Cold War," in Linda K. Kerber, Alice Kessler-Harris, and Kathryn Kish Sklar, *U.S. History as Women's History: New Feminist Essays* (Chapel Hill: University of North Carolina Press, 1995); Lyons, *Philadelphia Communists,* 87–108; Sherna Gluck, "Socialist Feminism between the Two World Wars: Insights from Oral History," in Lois Scharf and Joan M. Jensen, eds., *Decades of Discontent: The Women's Movement, 1920–1940* (Westport, Conn.: Greenwood Press, 1983), 279–95.

The cohort of women lawyers within the CP's orbit was particularly striking. See, for example, Ann Fagan Ginger, *Carol Weiss King: Human Rights Lawyer, 1895–1952* (Niwot, Colo.: University Press of Colorado, 1993); Doris Brin Walker, interview with the author, June 19, 1995.

On the red diaper babies in the early women's liberation movement, see Sara Evans, *Personal Politics: The Roots of Women's Liberation in the Civil Rights Movement and the New Left* (New York: Knopf, 1979), 116–25.

74. Joyce Antler, "Between Culture and Politics: The Emma Lazarus Federation of the Jewish Women's Clubs and the Promulgation of Women's History, 1944–1989," and Swerdlow, "The Congress of American Women," in Kerber, Kessler-Harris, and Sklar, *U.S. History as Women's History;* Weigand, "Vanguards of Women's Liberation," passim; Horne, *Black and Red,* 142; Denning, *The Cultural Front,* 136–51.

On Friedan, see Daniel Horowitz, "Rethinking Betty Friedan and *The Feminine Mystique:* Labor Union Radicalism and Feminism in Cold War America," *American Quarterly* 48 (March 1996): 1–42; Horowitz, "The Making of *The Feminine Mystique:* Betty Friedan, 1921–63: The American Left, the Cold War, and Modern Feminism," unpublished ms. in the author's possession. Abzug worked with the Civil Rights Congress and was active in some of its most important civil rights cases. On Lerner, see Swerdlow, "The Congress of American Women," 306, and Ellen C. DuBois, "Eleanor Flexner and the History of American Feminism," *Gender and History* 3 (Spring 1991): 81–90.

75. Lisa Kannenberg, "The Impact of the Cold War on Women's Trade Union Activism: The UE Experience," *Labor History* 34 (Spring–Summer 1993): 309–23; Gerald Zahavi, "Passionate Commitments: Race, Sex, and Communism at Schenectady General Electric, 1932–1954," *The Journal of American History* 83 (Sept. 1996): 526–32; Ruth Milkman, *Gender and Work: The Dynamics of Job Segregation by Sex during World War II* (Urbana: University of Illinois Press, 1987); Rosswurm, "Introduction," 4–5, 14; Denning, *The Cultural Front,* 149; Karl Korstad, "Black and White Together: Organizing in the South with the Food, Tobacco, Agricultural and Allied Workers Union (FTA-CIO), 1946–1952," in Rosswurm, ed., *The CIO's Left-Led Unions,* 86–93.

76. Swerdlow, "The Congress of American Women"; Alonso, *Peace as a Women's Issue,* 185–92; Weigand, "Vanguards of Women's Liberation," 72–117.

77. Swerdlow, "The Congress of American Women."

78. Horowitz, "Rethinking Betty Friedan"; Horowitz, "The Making of *The Feminine Mystique*," chapter 7; Kannenberg, "The Impact of the Cold War on Women's Trade Union Activism," 318.

79. Horowitz, "Rethinking Betty Friedan"; Horowitz, "The Making of *The Feminine Mystique*," chapter 7; Susan M. Hartmann, "Women's Employment and the Domestic Ideal in the Early Cold War Years," in Meyerowitz, ed., *Not June Cleaver,* 96.

80. Robert J. Norrell, "Caste in Steel: Jim Crow Careers in Birmingham, Alabama," *Journal of American History* 73 (Dec. 1986): 669–94; Rick Halpern, "Interracial Unionism in the Southwest: Fort Worth's Packinghouse Workers, 1937–1954," in Robert H. Zieger, ed., *Organized Labor in the Twentieth-Century South* (Knoxville: University of Tennessee Press, 1991): 158–82; Norrell, "Labor Trouble: George Wallace and Union Politics in Alabama," in Zieger, ed., *Organized Labor in the Twentieth-Century South,* 250–72; Robin D. G. Kelley, *Hammer and Hoe: Alabama Communists during the Great Depression* (Chapel Hill: University of North Carolina Press, 1990), 145–51; Horace Huntley, "Iron Ore Miners and Mine Mill in Alabama: 1933–1952" (Ph.D. diss., University of Pittsburgh, 1977); Swerdlow, "The Congress of American Women," 306–7; Robert Korstad and Nelson Lichtenstein, "Opportunities Found and Lost: Labor Radicals, and the Early Civil Rights Movement," *Journal of American History* 75 (1988): 791, 796.

81. Adam Fairclough, *Race and Democracy: The Civil Rights Struggle in Louisi-*

ana, 1915–1972 (Athens: University of Georgia Press, 1995), 135–47; Reed, *Simple Decency and Common Sense;* Patricia Sullivan, *Days of Hope: Race and Democracy in the New Deal Era* (Chapel Hill: University of North Carolina Press, 1996).

82. Korstadt and Lichtenstein, "Opportunities Found and Lost," passim, as well as Larry J. Griffin and Robert R. Korstad, "Class as Race and Gender: Making and Breaking a Labor Union in the Jim Crow South," *Social Science History* 19 (Winter 1995): 425–54; Karl Korstad, "Black and White Together"; Honey, *Southern Labor and Black Civil Rights,* passim.

83. HUAC, "Hearings Regarding Communism in Labor Unions in the United States," 80th Cong., 1st sess., July 23, 1947; Korstad and Lichtenstein, "Opportunities Found and Lost," 801–806; Griffin and Korstad, "Class as Race and Gender," 425–54.

84. Huntley, "Iron Ore Miners and Mine Mill in Alabama: 1933–1952"; Huntley, "The Red Scare and Black Workers in Alabama: The International Union of Mine, Mill, and Smelter Workers, 1945–1953," in Robert Asher and Charles Stephenson, *Labor Divided: Race and Ethnicity in United States Labor Struggles, 1835–1960* (Albany, N.Y.: State University of New York Press, 1990); Honey, *Southern Labor and Black Civil Rights,* 269–91.

85. Sullivan, *A Time of Hope;* John M. Glen, *Highlander: No Ordinary School, 1932–1962* (Lexington: University Press of Kentucky, 1988), 172–209; Reed, *Simple Decency and Common Sense.*

86. Numan V. Bartley, *The Rise of Massive Resistance: Race and Politics in the South During the 1950's* (Baton Rouge: Louisiana State University Press, 1969), 108–25, 189, 211–36; James Graham Cook, *The Segregationists* (New York: Appleton-Century-Crofts, 1962), 16–29, 250–66.

87. Anne Braden, *The Wall Between* (New York: Monthly Review Press, 1958); Summary of Conference at Louisville, Kentucky, March 2, 1955, Braden Papers, Box 2; Louise Gilbert to Fellow Social Workers, May 18, 1955, ibid., Box 9.

88. Press release, Nov. 20, 1956, Barry Bingham to Carl Braden, June 26, 1956, Braden to Bingham, July 4, 1956, all in Braden Papers, Box 9; *Braden v. United States,* 365 U.S. 431.

89. George T. Cordery, Jr., to Wade Defense Committee, July 13, 1954, Braden Papers, Box 9; Wilson Record, *Race and Radicalism: The NAACP and the Communist Party in Conflict* (Ithaca, N.Y.: Cornell University Press, 1964); Horne, *Black and Red,* 20–23, 36, 49, 58–64; Korstad and Lichtenstein, "Opportunities Found and Lost," 797–98; Minutes, Board of Directors, Feb. 11, 1946, Sept. 13, 1948, NAACP Papers, Part 1, reel 3; District 65 to NAACP, Dec. 12, 1949, Herbert Hill to Thomas Squiers, April 20, 1949, Hill to Selly, Apr. 11, 1949, in NAACP Papers, Part 13, Series A, reel 4; John Haynes Holmes to Walter White, Nov. 18, 1946, Feb. 25, 1947, NAACP Papers, Part 16, Series B, reel 8; minutes, meeting of the Committee on Administration, Feb. 24, Apr. 28, Oct. 27, Dec. 22, 1947, NAACP Papers, Part 16, Series B, reel 5; Roy Wilkins, Statement to Board of Directors, Feb. 14, 1950, NAACP Papers, Part 17,

reel 29; Kenneth O'Reilly, *Black Americans: The FBI Files*, ed. David Gallen (New York: Carroll and Graf, 1994), 20–23; Thomas J. Sugrue, *The Origins of the Urban Crisis: Race and Inequality in Postwar Detroit* (Princeton: Princeton University Press, 1996), 170–77; Tillett, "The Social Costs of the Loyalty Programs," 85.

90. David W. Southern, *Gunnar Myrdal and Black-White Relations: The Use and Abuse of "An American Dilemma," 1944–1969* (Baton Rouge: Louisiana State University Press, 1987); Bartley, *The Rise of Massive Resistance,* 108–25; Wayne Addison Clark, "An Analysis of the Relationship between Anti-Communism and Segregationist Thought in the Deep South, 1948–1964" (Ph.D. diss., University of North Carolina, 1976).

91. Fairclough, *Race and Democracy,* 323–25; Reed, *Simple Decency and Common Sense,* 174–75; James Anthony Schnur, "Cold Warriors in the Hot Sunshine: The Johns Committee's Assault on Civil Liberties in Florida, 1956–1965," unpublished ms. in the author's possession.

92. Mary L. Dudziak, "Desegregation as a Cold War Imperative," *Stanford Law Review* 41 (Nov. 1988): 61–120; Taylor Branch, *Parting the Waters: America in the King Years, 1954–63* (New York: Simon and Schuster, 1988), 566; Donald R. McCoy and Richard T. Ruetten, *Quest and Response: Minority Rights and the Truman Administration* (Lawrence: University Press of Kansas, 1973), 66, 96–118, 162, 342; Arthur M. Schlesinger, Jr., *The Vital Center: The Politics of Freedom* (Boston: Houghton Mifflin, 1949), 235.

93. Clayborne Carson, *In Struggle: SNCC and the Black Awakening of the 1960s* (Cambridge: Harvard University Press, 1981), 105–7, 136–37, 180–83, 245–46, 261–63; James Forman, *The Making of Black Revolutionaries* (New York: Macmillan, 1972), 380–82; John Dittmer, *Local People: The Struggle for Civil Rights in Mississippi* (Urbana: University of Illinois Press, 1994), 231–33, 316, 340–41; Adam Fairclough, *To Redeem the Soul of America: The Southern Christian Leadership Conference and Martin Luther King, Jr.* (Athens: University of Georgia Press, 1987), 68–69, 263.

94. Fairclough, *To Redeem the Soul of America,* 41; Branch, *Parting the Waters,* 562–600, 833–41; David J. Garrow, *The FBI and Martin Luther King, Jr. from "Solo" to Memphis* (New York: W. W. Norton, 1981), 101–72; O'Reilly, *Black Americans: The FBI Files,* 29, 40–41.

95. For a thorough discussion of the Popular Front culture that the Cold War destroyed, see Denning, *The Cultural Front;* Kevin Boyle, *The UAW and the Heyday of American Liberalism, 1945–1968* (Ithaca, N.Y.: Cornell University Press, 1995), 80.

96. Leo Marx, interview with the author, April 11, 1978; Margo Anderson, "The Language of Class in Twentieth-Century America," *Social Science History* 12 (Dec. 1988): 349–75; Forman, *The Making of Black Revolutionaries,* 334, 449; Honey, *Southern Labor and Black Civil Rights,* 273–74.

97. Lazarsfeld and Thielens, *The Academic Mind,* 218; Robert Sklar, *Movie-Made America, A Social History of American Movies* (New York: Random House, 1975), 267–68, 283; Ceplair and Englund, *The Inquisition in Hollywood,* 299–324.

98. Fast, *Being Red,* 286–95; Merle Miller, *The Judges and the Judged* (Garden City, N.Y.: Doubleday, 1952), 70–71; Natalie Robins, *Alien Ink: The FBI's War on Freedom of Expression* (New York: William Morrow, 1992), 233–37; Frances Mc-Cullough, interview with the author, July 1, 1976; Angus Cameron, interviews with the author, Dec. 30, 1976, Apr. 5, 1977.

99. Tillie Olsen, quoted in Constance Coiner, *Better Red: The Writing and Resistance of Tillie Olsen and Meridel Le Sueur* (New York: Oxford University Press, 1995), 193; Durr, COHP, 207; Thomas Emerson, COHP, 2260–66; Tom McGrath, questionnaire response, Tillett Papers; Ellen Fitzpatrick, "Foreword," in Eleanor Flexner and Ellen Fitzpatrick, *Century of Struggle: The Woman's Rights Movement in the United States* (Cambridge: Harvard University Press, 1996), xxi; DuBois, "Eleanor Flexner and the History of American Feminism," 68; Horne, *Black and Red,* 208; Tillett, "The Social Costs of the Loyalty Programs," 73; John W. Caughey, *In Clear and Present Danger* (Chicago: University of Chicago Press, 1958), 168.

100. On the destruction of Robeson's career, see Duberman, *Paul Robeson,* 296–428.

101. Dorothy B. Jones, "Communism and the Movies: A Study of Film Content," in John Cogley, *Report on Blacklisting, I: Movies* (New York: Fund for the Republic, 1956), 219, 231; McCoy and Ruetten, *Quest and Response,* 165–70; Nora Sayre, *Running Time: Films of the Cold War* (New York: Dial Press, 1982), 31–56; Denning, *The Cultural Front,* 47; Ceplair and Englund, *Inquisition in Hollywood,* 299–324, 422.

102. Sklar, *Movie-Made America,* 269–85; Ceplair and Englund, *Inquisition in Hollywood,* 340; Sayre, *Running Time,* 79–99; Daniel J. Leab, "Hollywood and the Cold War, 1945–1961," in Robert Brent Toplin, ed., *Hollywood as Mirror: Changing Views of "Outsiders" and "Enemies" in American Movies* (Westport, Conn.: Greenwood Press, 1993), 123–31.

103. Sayre, *Running Time,* 79–99, 151–72; Michael Paul Rogin, *"Ronald Reagan," the Movie and Other Episodes in Political Demonology* (Berkeley and Los Angeles: University of California Press, 1987), 236–71; Navasky, *Naming Names,* 199–222; Fones-Wolf, *Selling Free Enterprise,* 267.

104. Sklar, *Movie-Made America,* 267–68; Sayre, *Running Time,* passim; Alan Nadel, *Containment Culture: American Narratives, Postmodernism, and the Atomic Age* (Durham, N.C.: Duke University Press, 1995), 90–154.

105. Barnouw, Eric, *Tube of Plenty: The Evolution of American Television* (New York: Oxford University Press, 1975, rev. ed. 1982), 117–30; Mark Goodson, quoted in Faulk, *Fear on Trial,* 239.

106. Faulk, *Fear on Trial,* 173–79; Merle Miller, *The Judges and the Judged* (Garden City, N.Y.: Doubleday, 1952), 149; Cogley, *Report on Blacklisting, II: Broadcasting.*

107. Merle Miller, *The Judges and the Judged,* 217; Cogley, *Report on Blacklisting, II: Broadcasting;* Erik Barnouw, *Tube of Plenty,* 130, 154–56; J. Fred MacDonald, *Television and the Red Menace: The Video Road to Vietnam* (New York: Praeger, 1985).

108. MacDonald, *Television and the Red Menace,* passim; Barnouw, *Tube of Plenty,* 130–218.

109. Jane de Hart Matthews, "Art and Politics in Cold War America," *American Historical Review* 81 (October 1976): 773; Erika Doss, *Benton, Pollock and the Politics of Modernism: From Regionalism to Abstract Expressionism* (Chicago: University of Chicago Press, 1991), 392.

110. For background on the CP-led artists group during the Popular Front period, see Matthew Baigell and Julia Williams, eds., *Artists Against War and Fascism: Papers of the First American Artists' Congress* (New Brunswick, N.J.: Rutgers University Press, 1986). See also Doss, *Benton, Pollock and the Politics of Modernism,* chapters 1–3; Doss, "The Art of Cultural Politics: From Regionalism to Abstract Expressionism," in Lary May, ed., *Recasting America: Culture and Politics in the Age of Cold War* (Chicago: University of Chicago Press, 1989); Denning, *The Cultural Front,* 73–80.

111. Matthews, "Art and Politics in Cold War America," 763–72.

112. Harold Rosenberg, "The American Action Painters," in Rosenberg, *The Tradition of the New* (New York: Horizon Press, 1959), 30. Serge Guilbaut, *How New York Stole the Idea of Modern Art: Abstract Expressionism, Freedom, and the Cold War* (Chicago: University of Chicago Press, 1983), offers the most controversial statement of the thesis that abstract expressionism constituted a deliberate depoliticization of modern art. For a more nuanced corroboration of Guilbaut's thesis, see Doss, *Benton, Pollock and the Politics of Modernism,* 363–416.

113. Doss, *Benton, Pollock and the Politics of Modernism,* 332–57; Guilbaut, *How New York Stole the Idea of Modern Art,* 196–200.

114. Alfred Barr, quoted in Doss, *Benton, Pollock and the Politics of Modernism,* 392.

115. Reeve Vanneman and Lynn Weber Cannon, *The American Perception of Class* (Philadelphia: Temple University Press, 1987).

116. Lazarsfeld and Thielens, *The Academic Mind,* 101, 135, 198–200. For a good discussion of the demands for "objectivity" within the historical profession, see Peter Novick, *That Noble Dream: The "Objectivity Question" and the American Historical Profession* (New York: Cambridge University Press, 1988), 281–411.

117. For a full discussion of the impact of McCarthyism on the academic world, see Schrecker, *No Ivory Tower.*

118. Lazarsfeld and Thielens, *The Academic Mind,* 152–55.

119. Denning, *The Cultural Front,* 437–38; Gene H. Bell-Villada, *Art for Art's Sake and Literary Life: How Politics and Markets Helped Shape the Ideology and Culture of Aestheticism, 1790–1990* (Lincoln: University of Nebraska Press, 1996), 188–280; Donald E. Pease, *Visionary Compacts: American Renaissance Writings in Cultural Context* (Madison: University of Wisconsin Press, 1987), 3–49, 244–46, 256–59; Richard Ohmann, "English and the Cold War," in Noam Chomsky, Ira Katznelson, R. C. Lewontin, David Montgomery, Laura Nader, Richard Ohmann, Ray Siever, Im-

manuel Wallerstein, and Howard Zinn, *The Cold War and the University: Toward an Intellectual History of the Postwar Years* (New York: New Press, 1997), 73–87; Robert J. Corber, *In the Name of National Security: Hitchcock, Homophobia, and the Political Construction of Gender in Postwar America* (Durham, N.C.: Duke University Press, 1993), 54, 89.

120. Forman, "Beyond Quantum Electronics," 174, 205–8; Harry Grundfest, interview with the author, Oct. 20, 1978; Clarence Hiskey, interview with the author, July 27, 1980.

121. Salvador Luria, interview with the author, April 9, 1981; Don K. Price, interview with the author, Sept. 21, 1979; R. C. Lewontin, "The Cold War and the Transformation of the Academy," in Noam Chomsky, Ira Katznelson, R. C. Lewontin, David Montgomery, Laura Nader, Richard Ohmann, Ray Siever, Immanuel Wallerstein, and Howard Zinn, *The Cold War and the University: Toward an Intellectual History of the Postwar Years,* 134; Forman, "Beyond Quantum Electronics," 229; Jane Hodes, interview with the author, April 5, 1980.

122. Rebecca Lowen, *Creating the Cold War University: The Transformation of Stanford* (Berkeley and Los Angeles: University of California Press, 1997), 92–190; Forman, "Beyond Quantum Electronics," 213–24; Dan Kevles, "Cold War and Hot Physics: Science, Security, and the American State, 1945–56," *Historical Studies in the Physical and Biological Sciences* 20:2 (1989): 239–264; Stuart W. Leslie, *The Cold War and American Science* (New York: Columbia University Press, 1993).

123. Mary O. Furner, *Advocacy and Objectivity: A Crisis in the Professionalization of American Social Science* (Lexington: University Press of Kentucky, 1975); Dorothy Ross, "Socialism and American Liberalism: Academic Social Thought in the 1880's," *Perspectives in American History* 11 (1977–78); Price, interview; Vanneman and Cannon, *The American Perception of Class,* 49; Sumner Rosen, "Keynes without Gadflies," in Theodore Roszak, ed., *The Dissenting Academy* (New York: Pantheon, 1968), 80–88; Robert Engler, "Social Science and Social Consciousness," in Roszak, ed., *The Dissenting Academy,* 198.

124. Lowen, *Creating the Cold War University,* 191–223; Daniel Lee Kleinman and Mark Solovey, "Hot Science/Cold War: The National Science Foundation After World War II," *Radical History Review* 63 (1995): 121; Michael A. Bernstein, "American Economics and the National Security State, 1941–1953," ibid., 8–26; Ellen Herman, "The Career of Cold War Psychology," ibid., 52–85; Waldemar A. Nielsen, *The Big Foundations* (New York: Columbia University Press, 1972), 39–40, 65, 90, 344, 353–54; Dennis C. Buss, "The Ford Foundation in Public Education: Emergent Patterns," in Robert F. Arnove, ed., *Philanthropy and Cultural Imperialism: The Foundations at Home and Abroad* (Bloomington: Indiana University Press, 1980), 351–57; Peter J. Seybold, "The Ford Foundation and the Triumph of Behavioralism in American Political Science," in Arnove, *Philanthropy and Cultural Imperialism,* 274–98.

125. Nielsen, *The Big Foundations,* 82–86; John N. Thomas, *The Institute of Pa-*

cific Relations (Seattle, Wash.: University of Washington Press, 1974), 110–13; Ellen Condliffe Lagemann, *The Politics of Knowledge: The Carnegie Corporation, Philanthropy, and Public Policy* (Middletown, Conn.: Wesleyan University Press, 1989), 185; *Gunnar Myrdal and Black-White Relations,* 174; Tillett, "The Social Costs of the Loyalty Programs," 89–92; Henry Allen Moe, quoted in Richard Ohmann, "English and the Cold War," in Chomsky et al., *The Cold War and the University,* 75, 104; Sigmund Diamond, *Compromised Campus: The Collaboration of Universities with the Intelligence Community, 1945–1955* (New York: Oxford University Press, 1992), 72–82.

126. Peter J. Seybold, "The Ford Foundation and the Triumph of Behavioralism in American Political Science," in Arnove, ed., *Philanthropy and Cultural Imperialism,* 269–303; David Montgomery, "Introduction," in Chomsky et al., *The Cold War and the University,* xxvi–xxix. The crucial text in modernization theory was W. W. Rostow's explicitly anticommunist *The Stages of Economic Growth: A Non-Communist Manifesto* (New York: Cambridge University Press, 1960).

127. Lagemann, *The Politics of Knowledge,* 172–75; Immanuel Wallerstein, "The Unintended Consequences of Cold War Area Studies," in Chomsky et al., *The Cold War and the University,* 195–210; Diamond, *Compromised Campus,* 50–110; Fairbank, *Chinabound,* 355–65; Stephen F. Cohen, *Rethinking the Soviet Experience: Politics and History Since 1917* (New York: Oxford University Press, 1985), 3–37.

128. Daniel Bell, *The End of Ideology* (New York: Free Press, 1960), 36. Bell's is, of course, one of the classic texts of the consensus school. An equally important one is Daniel Boorstin, *The Genius of American Politics* (Chicago: University of Chicago Press, 1953). Other important texts that in some, though not all respects, bolstered the consensus interpretation were David M. Potter, *People of Plenty* (Chicago: University of Chicago Press, 1954) and Louis Hartz, *The Liberal Tradition in America* (New York: Harcourt, Brace and World, 1955).

129. On the New York intellectuals and their associates, see (in addition to their own writings) Alexander Bloom, *Prodigal Sons: The New York Intellectuals and their World* (New York: Oxford University Press, 1986); Terry A. Cooney, *The Rise of the New York Intellectuals: Partisan Review and Its Circle* (Madison: University of Wisconsin Press, 1986); John P. Diggins, *Up From Communism: Conservative Odysseys in American Intellectual History* (New York: Harper and Row, 1975); James Burkhart Gilbert, *Writers and Partisans: A History of Literary Radicalism in America* (New York: John Wiley and Sons, 1968); Richard H. Pells, *The Liberal Mind in a Conservative Age: American Intellectuals in the 1940s and 1950s* (New York: Harper and Row, 1985); Alan M. Wald, *The New York Intellectuals: The Rise and Decline of the Anti-Stalinist Left from the 1930s to the 1980s* (Chapel Hill, N.C.: University of North Carolina Press, 1987).

130. On the dissemination of the notion of totalitarianism, see Abbott Gleason, *Totalitarianism: The Inner History of the Cold War* (New York: Oxford University

Press, 1995), 74. For some representative examples of the anticommunist rhetoric of the New York intellectuals, see Leslie Fiedler, *An End to Innocence* (Boston: Beacon Press, 1955), 70; Irving Kristol, "Civil Liberties, 1952 — A Study in Confusion," *Commentary* 13 (Mar. 1953): 228–36; Sidney Hook, *Heresy, Yes — Conspiracy, No* (New York: John Day, 1953); Gilbert, *Writers and Partisans*, 257–58.

131. Richard Hofstadter, "The Pseudo-Conservative Revolt," in Daniel Bell, ed., *The New American Right* (New York: Criterion, 1955); Richard Rovere, *Senator Joe McCarthy* (New York: Harcourt, Brace, 1959).

132. Richard Hofstadter, *Anti-Intellectualism in American Life* (New York: Knopf, 1963); Hofstadter, *The Paranoid Style in American Politics and Other Essays* (New York: Knopf, 1966); Schlesinger, *The Vital Center*, 11–34. The notion that the American people can't be trusted with foreign policy or civil liberties appears, for example, in such important books as Gabriel Almond's *The American People and Foreign Policy* (New York: Frederick A. Praeger, 1960) and Samuel A. Stouffer, *Communism, Conformity, and Civil Liberties* (Garden City, N.J.: Doubleday, 1955).

Arthur M. Schlesinger, Jr., *The Disuniting of America: Reflections on a Multicultural Society* (New York: W. W. Norton, 1992); Irving Howe, "The Value of the Canon," in Paul Berman, ed., *Debating P.C.: The Controversy over Political Correctness on College Campuses* (New York: Dell, 1992), 153–71.

133. Wilkins to White, Aug. 12, 1949, in NAACP Records, Part 17, reel 26.

134. The most useful survey of the reluctance of American liberals to challenge McCarthyism is Mary Sperling McAuliffe, *Crisis on the Left: Cold War Politics and American Liberals* (Amherst, Mass.: University of Massachusetts Press, 1978). For an examination of some specific organizations, see Samuel Walker, *In Defense of American Liberties: A History of the ACLU* (New York: Oxford University Press, 1990), 173–236; Steven M. Gillon, *Politics and Vision: The ADA and American Liberalism, 1947–1985* (New York: Oxford University Press, 1987), 57–82, 104–30; Schrecker, *No Ivory Tower*, 308–37.

135. Gillon, *Politics and Vision*, 57–103. For an interesting discussion of the erosion of liberalism with regard to foreign policy, see Cumings, *The Origins of the Korean War*, vol. 2, 79–121.

136. Todd Gitlin, *The Sixties* (New York: Bantam, 1987), 109–26; Isserman, *"If I Had a Hammer,"* 173–219.

137. For information about the expansion of the FBI's illegal activities, see William W. Keller, Jr., *J. Edgar Hoover and the Liberals: Rise and Fall of a Domestic Intelligence State* (Princeton: Princeton University Press, 1989); Athan Theoharis, *Spying on Americans: Political Surveillance from Hoover to the Huston Plan* (Philadelphia: Temple University Press, 1978); and Frank Donner, *The Age of Surveillance: The Aims and Methods of America's Political Intelligence System* (New York: Knopf, 1981).

138. Frank J. Donner, *The Age of Surveillance: The Aims and Methods of Amer-*

ica's Political Intelligence System; Donner, *Protectors of Privilege: Red Squads and Police Repression in Urban America* (Berkeley and Los Angeles: University of California Press, 1990); David Burnham, "The FBI," *The Nation,* Aug. 11/18, 1997.

139. On Nixon's early career, see Roger Morris, *Richard Milhous Nixon: The Rise of an American Politician* (New York: Henry Holt, 1990). On Nixon's later illegal acts, see Stanley I. Kutler, *The Wars of Watergate* (New York: W. W. Norton, 1990); Jonathan Schell, *The Time of Illusion* (New York: Knopf, 1976); Seymour M. Hersh, *The Price of Power: Kissinger in the Nixon White House* (New York: Simon and Schuster, 1983).

140. On Reagan and the FBI, see Athan Theoharis, ed., *From the Secret Files of J. Edgar Hoover* (Chicago: Ivan R. Dee, 1991), 115–17. On Iran-Contra, see Jonathan Marshall, Peter Dale Scott, and Jane Hunter, *The Iran-Contra Connection: Secret Teams and Covert Operations in the Reagan Era* (Boston: South End Press, 1987).

INDEX